The Cricketers' Who's Who 2022

Foreword by
TIM MURTAGH

Editor
BENJ MOOREHEAD

Design
ROB WHITEHOUSE

The
Cricketers'
Who's Who
2022

This edition first published in the UK by Fairfield Books

© Fairfield Books 2022

ISBN: 978-1-915237-12-5

Published by Fairfield Books

Editor: *Benj Moorehead*; Research and editorial: *Jo Harman, Phil Walker*
Design: *Rob Whitehouse Joe Provis*; Images: *Getty Images unless stated*;
Print: *CPI Antony Rowe*

MIX
Paper from
responsible sources
FSC® C013604

Acknowledgements
The publishers would like to thank the county clubs and the players for their assistance in helping to put together this book. We are grateful to John Mallett/JRM Photos for providing images of Tom Hinley and several Leicestershire players. Additional information has been gathered from espncricinfo.com and cricketarchive.com.

CONTENTS

The
Cricketers'
Who's Who
2022

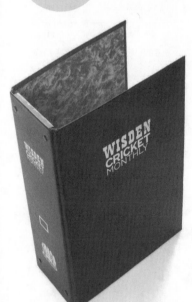

Openers

FOREWORD

By Tim Murtagh

When I first went into a professional dressing room there was always a *Cricketers' Who's Who* in someone's locker. There's a lot of time to talk during matches, and we'd often play 'guess the cricketer': "This guy's 40 years old, he averages 24 with the ball, his highest score is 74 not out and his lookalike is Frank Lampard. Who is he?" (Answer on page 360.) Or we'd open it just to see who's had the dodgiest haircut or to read out some of the amusing comments. It still has a place in the Middlesex dressing room today.

I've been filling out the *Who's Who* questionnaire for some 20 years now! My Championship debut was in May 2001. At the time I was at St Mary's University in Twickenham and had a summer contract at Surrey. On the morning of the match against Leicestershire I got a call saying they needed me at The Oval because Alex Tudor had an injury concern. I'd just had a massive night out at the student's union in Twickenham! I got myself out of bed and tried to sober up. I was still thinking that Tudes would be fine, that I wouldn't have to go out there and play. But when I arrived at the ground Keith Medlycott, then Surrey coach, told me: "You're in for your debut." Panic. I wondered whether I should tell them I wasn't quite right, but you can't do that on your Championship debut. Luckily I didn't have to do too much in the match and ended up taking my first Championship wicket – Dan Marsh, caught behind.

Lots has happened since then. To play for Ireland later in my career – and to play Test cricket as well – was brilliant and unexpected. But winning the Championship with Middlesex in 2016 sits top of my career achievements, because it was the culmination of something that had been building at the club over a few years.

* * *

It's been a hard winter for English cricket. Azeem Rafiq's revelations about racism in the game have been a real wake-up call for everyone, and it was overdue. The biggest thing we can take away from it as individuals is to have a look at ourselves, how we treat people, the language we use, how we have done things in the past and what we can change. Hard though it's been, this must be seen as something positive for the future.

I wasn't surprised that the county game took some blame for England's defeat in Australia. You hear the same thing every time an Ashes series is lost: "Everything has to change." I don't agree with that.

For me, the quality of the players is the big thing. At the start of my career every team would have a high-class overseas player who would generally be there for the whole season, rather than for a month here or there. You'd play against them week in, week out. The end of Kolpaks hasn't helped, because it's meant we've lost a lot of high-quality international players.

Priorities have changed too. I look around the game now and I ask myself: who is actually going to bat for a whole day against us? Who's going to get through the tricky periods? There aren't that many younger players who can do that. When I started playing it was tougher to get people out. Now I feel that if I challenge the batter for long enough, he's going to crack first.

I don't want to sound like a dinosaur. If I was a young player and would get paid much more by playing franchise cricket around the world or white-ball cricket in England then I don't think I'd be that fussed about the longer format. But I do feel there needs to be some redressing of the balance.

We have had a few difficult seasons at Middlesex, but we're excited about this summer. The club have signed the most exciting cricketer in the world in Shaheen Afridi, the 2021 ICC Player of the Year. We've got a new coach in Richard Johnson, who is returning to the club and knows the players. We've also got Mark Ramprakash as batting coach, and I can't think of anyone else a batter would rather work with than Ramps.

I've been happy with my own form over the last few years. Having kids has given me a different perspective and I think it has helped my cricket. Focusing on the four-day game has allowed me some downtime during the T20 Blast, so that I can refresh myself physically and mentally before the big finish at the end of the season. And I do love bowling at Lord's.

Good luck to everyone competing this summer.

Tim Murtagh
March 2022

By Benj Moorehead

Welcome to the 2022 edition of *The Cricketers' Who's Who*.

Every year, when April at last comes round, the image of last summer's flannelled figures casting lean shadows on green fields is sepia-tinted, quite possibly a myth, like recollecting the previous night on Sunday morning. October to April: six long months for everyone, but especially for us. Even so, English cricket hasn't had many winters as long as the one just gone.

Azeem Rafiq's emotional testimony last November painfully exposed racial prejudice at the heart of England's most famous cricketing county. Rafiq's allegations surfaced in August 2020; it took more than a year for Yorkshire to publish the damning results of an independent investigation and, even then, an intervention by the Government was needed to persuade the club to acknowledge its guilt. But what we can all agree on surely, despite the public shaming of institutions and individuals, not all of them relating to Yorkshire, is that this is about every one of us. Pointing a finger at a few rotten apples is an easy way of discharging responsibility. We know that these attitudes trickle right through the game, from professional to club to school, in dressing rooms, offices and stands. The time has come to change, and it begins now.

There wasn't much solace to be found Down Under, where England's men and women were fried like shrimps under the Australian sun. There followed the inevitable inquest into the state of the county game – the quality of the County Championship, the nature of our pitches, the dominance of the short formats, the type of ball we use, the overcrowded schedule, the number of first-class counties, and all the rest of it. Three county stalwarts consider some of these questions in our Comment piece on page 10.

And then, on March 4, quite possibly the greatest cricketer of them all passed away at the age of 52.

It is, then, with some relief that we fall into the lap of the new season. Nothing like the summer game to soothe the soul. And the good news is that the County Championship looks like its old self again; after two years of Covid cricket, we're back to two divisions (see page 17 for details). To some degree the pleas for more four-day cricket in the warmer months have been answered – nearly a third of this summer's Championship fixtures are in June and July.

Intriguing subplots abound. What happens when one of the international game's most fashionable coaches meets one of English cricket's least fashionable counties (Mickey Arthur at Derbyshire)? Will Sussex's bold youth policy pay off? Will the spirit of Warne drive Hampshire to their first Championship title since 1973? What impact will the racism scandal have on Yorkshire's cricket? And what happens when, ahem, England rejects James Anderson and Stuart Broad are unleashed on county batters with a point to prove?

It wasn't long ago that Jeetan Patel, the long-serving Warwickshire spinner, was an exception to the rule that overseas players come and go in the blink of an eye. But the trend has been bucked: you could almost field two XIs of foreign players who will be present throughout the summer.

While the domestic schedule has a more familiar look – albeit with The Hundred smack in the middle of it – England's summer programme still bears the mark of the pandemic. A one-day tour of the Netherlands, postponed last summer, overlaps with the home Test series against New Zealand in June, followed by the rescheduled fifth Test against India, called off last September amid fears of a Covid outbreak with the tourists 2-1 up. South Africa land in July but will play only three Tests, meaning that we won't have the treat of a four- or five-match Test series at home for the first time in 10 years (excluding the Covid-hit 2020 season).

England's women have an unusual schedule too (see page 516), with series against South Africa and India sandwiching a T20 tournament making its debut at this summer's Commonwealth Games in Birmingham. The multi-format series against South Africa is notable in that it begins with a Test match at Taunton. Until recently women's red-ball cricket seemed like a dead duck (there have been 10 Tests since 2011), but the Ashes nail-biter at Canberra earlier this year has whetted the appetite. Asked what they would change about the domestic calendar, many of the women's players in this book – up to 67 this year after the ECB funded a sixth professional contract for each of the eight regional teams – told us would like to see a multi-day format.

This summer the women's schedule has the added allure of an end-of-season 50-over final on a Saturday at Lord's, which also stages the Hundred finals. With squads for The Hundred unconfirmed before the *Who's Who* went to press, we do not cover the competition in these pages. In any case, this book has its heart in the county game.

We'd like to thank Tim Murtagh for his foreword – perfect, of course, in line and length – and, because he was too modest to mention it, point out his extraordinary first-class record over the past four seasons: 196 wickets at 16.03. Not bad for a 40-year-old seamer.

The talking is done; let the games begin!

Benj Moorehead
March 2022

THE POST-ASHES INQUEST

Following last winter's drubbing Down Under, we asked three figures from the heart of the county game about the shortcomings of the County Championship and to consider what can be done to rectify them

THE PANEL

Daryl Mitchell Director of cricket operations for the Professional Cricket Association (PCA) and former Worcestershire opener	Ian Salisbury Sussex head coach and former England leg-spinner	Andy Hurry Somerset director of cricket

To what extent is county cricket to blame for England's performances in the Ashes?

Andy Hurry: I think it's too simplistic to blame county cricket. Historically the domestic game always comes under scrutiny following a series in Australia or the subcontinent and it's really important that we don't have a knee-jerk reaction and that we actually take the time to take the emotion out of things and review how we're operating. It's healthy that domestic cricket is reviewed consistently and we make sure that it's as effective as it possibly can be.

Ian Salisbury: First and foremost, I think the team [were] unlucky in the preparation they had for this trip. History suggests Australia is a really difficult place to go, and that's not just for England. The combination of Covid and then the warm-up games being washed out was really unlucky.

Daryl Mitchell: County cricket has played a part in England's successes and failures over the years, but it's not the sole reason. I think you've got to try and understand what the purpose of county cricket is, and producing cricketers for England is certainly one of those purposes, but you've also got 18 individual businesses that are trying to win trophies. And you've got broadcasters which ultimately finance pretty much everything in the English game. There are so many different stakeholders and it's about trying to come up with a schedule to appease all of them, which is obviously a very difficult thing to do.

The Incora County Ground, Derby
Photo by Gareth Copley

Has the quality of the County Championship decreased in recent years?

Mitchell: I wouldn't argue with that. I think a lot of that is probably down to the mindset of players. Going back to when I started, there wasn't the T20 circuit as there is now, and Championship cricket was your bread and butter. When you were coming through the ranks you built your game around that, you got yourself in the right place to get into the Championship team, and then tried to broaden out from there. I don't think we've got as many players who are prepared to bat for a day for a hundred and grind out innings. The way one-day cricket has evolved and the focus on T20 cricket has taken a little bit away from batting technique and mindset. I also think the bowling has become more difficult to face. As a top-order batter, the wobble-seam delivery was a game-changer. When I first started, every opening bowler tried to swing the ball away and nick you off and you could leave probably the first 60, 70, 80 per cent of your deliveries, and get yourself in that way. Now bowlers will bowl wobble-seam down that fourth- or fifth-stump line and it makes life a lot more difficult at the top of the order.

Hurry: I'm a big advocate of best versus best in domestic cricket and I'm really pleased we've gone back to two divisions, with promotion and relegation. Over the last 24 months some really good plans have been put in place in response to Covid but there have been occasions where the best teams haven't been playing against the best teams as often as they can.

Is 18 first-class counties too many?

Mitchell: I'm a massive fan of 18 counties. Look at the history, and from a PCA perspective you've got members who are contracted for two, three, four years at all these clubs. We've got to do all we can to try and maintain the 18 counties. An important part of that is they're in charge of the governance of the domestic structure. We saw that last year when the ECB wanted to go with a conference-based Championship structure and they needed 12 counties to vote for it and they didn't get that. Ultimately the counties govern what domestic cricket looks like. And I think The Hundred has to remain. It was obviously a huge success and I think the £1.3m on the bottom of each county's balance sheet is vitally important, particularly coming out of a pandemic. I don't think all the counties would survive if that revenue was lost. And on the same basis, the T20 Blast is invaluable to the counties due to the revenue it generates.

Notwithstanding the addition of three rounds of games in July from this summer, the majority of the Championship season is still played in April, May and September, leaving space for the more lucrative white-ball competitions in mid-summer. How big a problem is that for red-ball cricket in this country?

Hurry: We've got to try and get to a point where we play more Championship cricket in the heart of the summer. I think that's really, really important. It gives you a better chance of producing better pitches and more people will want to come and watch the longer format of the game. But I do understand the challenges the administrators have in trying to factor in as much cricket as we've got.

Mitchell: Getting more Championship cricket in the heart of summer has come up a lot and I would agree we need to do that. There's a little bit more this year which I think is important and it will be interesting to see how that pans out. I also think we need to get back to a more meaningful 50-over competition. It's obviously been a poor Ashes series and there's no getting away from that, but if England's form drops in ODI cricket in a couple of years' time then I think we'll be having the same conversations about 50-over cricket.

Over a hundred of our best players are not playing any 50-over cricket domestically. Long term I think that needs to be addressed.

Salisbury: Ultimately we have to bring fans into the game and we need TV money for us all to survive. I don't think realistically we can afford to change when we play Championship games. Whether I believe it is the right thing or not is completely different, I'm just looking at the financial and commercial situation. If there was a masterplan then I think somebody would have come up with it already.

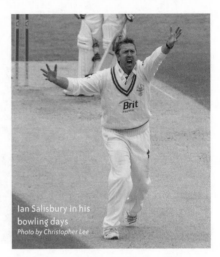

Ian Salisbury in his bowling days
Photo by Christopher Lee

Should the number of Championship fixtures be cut back?

Mitchell: I do think there is an element of quantity over quality at the minute. There are going to have to be compromises somewhere along the line and reducing the number of Championship games might be the way forward. I also think that from the players' point of view they've probably got to accept that we can't have everything in blocks, allowing them to prepare for one format at a time. There's going to have to be some chopping and changing of formats if you want to play Championship cricket in the middle of summer, probably alongside the Blast.

Hurry: Cutting back the fixtures wouldn't be my preference but I understand that to make it work that might have to happen. We all have a view but we don't all understand the whole context of why things are done the way they're done. It might be because we're playing too much cricket, or because we have too many competitions, and we haven't got enough of a window to be able to play everything at the appropriate time, so something might have to give. That might be the number of games that we play, or that might be the number of competitions.

Somerset's Andy Hurry
Photo by Harry Trump

Salisbury: In Australia they have almost a week off between every game to prepare, so that gives you time to work on technique, fitness, and you're peaking for games. But there are 18 counties that vote and they're probably not going to vote for less cricket.

Does the general standard of pitches need to improve?

Mitchell: It's about trying to bridge the gap between Championship cricket and Test match cricket and I do think better wickets would help, trying to replicate Test conditions as best we can, although that's not straightforward. Playing more matches in the middle of summer would help.

Salisbury: At Sussex I've got a bunch of young cricketers and I want them to get better, and I want them to get better to play Test match cricket, four-day cricket, so I instruct our groundsman to give us the best pitch possible, as if we were preparing to play a Test match. If I want Tom Haines to get better, I want him to know how to score hundreds and to trust his technique, and that's by playing on the best wickets possible. If we look at spin, for Jack Carson to get better he has to bowl lots of overs, so I always play a spinner, if I can I'll play two, and I want to play on the flattest wickets I can that could turn towards the end. If I want Ollie Robinson or our young seamers to get better, I want them to bowl on the flattest wickets possible. We could easily play on pitches with grass on and that would bring our young seamers and other, more experienced bowlers closer, but that won't help them in the long run. Ultimately in Test cricket, where are we coming unstuck? We're not scoring enough runs and we haven't produced many spinners. It's the quality of pitches. We need to improve them.

What practical measures could be taken to make that happen?

Salisbury: Either you leave it to the counties to improve pitches and give more power to match referees [to issue penalties], or you could centrally contract the groundsmen. The ECB money which goes to clubs ends up paying the groundsmen anyway, so you'd essentially be cutting out the middleman and then you could control the pitches.

What else could be done to help prepare county players for the challenges of Test cricket?

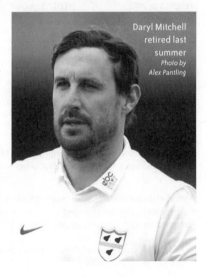

Daryl Mitchell
retired last
summer
*Photo by
Alex Pantling*

Mitchell: I know people have talked about using the Kookaburra ball, whether that would help I don't know. And perhaps there's scope to have North versus South in red-ball cricket, or Lions A versus Lions B, something that can help bridge the gap a little bit more.

Salisbury: You could potentially have more bonus points for 400 runs scored, or 450. So instead of five points, could you have eight? If both teams end up scoring 400-plus runs in a game and it ends up a draw, is that a bad thing for English cricket? Scoring 400 in your first innings should become a habit, but you have to play on good wickets, then you can start talking about technique.

FIXTURES

ECB

CAPTAIN: Joe Root (Test),
Eoin Morgan (ODI/T20I)
COACH: TBC*

ENGLAND'S HOME
FIXTURES IN 2022

June 2
England vs New Zealand
1st Test, Lord's

June 10
England vs New Zealand
2nd Test, Trent Bridge

June 23
England vs New Zealand
3rd Test, Headingley

July 1
England vs India
5th Test, Edgbaston**

July 7
England vs India
1st T20I, Southampton

July 9
England vs India
2nd T20I, Edgbaston

July 10
England vs India
3rd T20I, Trent Bridge

July 12
England vs India
1st ODI, The Oval

July 14
England vs India
2nd ODI, Lord's

July 17
England vs India
3rd ODI, Old Trafford

July 19
England vs South Africa
1st ODI, Chester-le-Street

July 22
England vs South Africa
2nd ODI, Old Trafford

July 24
England vs South Africa
3rd ODI, Headingley

July 27
England vs South Africa
1st T20I, Bristol

July 28
England vs South Africa
2nd T20I, Cardiff

July 31
England vs South Africa
3rd T20I, Southampton

August 17
England vs South Africa
1st Test, Lord's

August 25
England vs South Africa
2nd Test, Old Trafford

September 8
England vs South Africa
3rd Test, The Oval

England play a rescheduled three-match ODI series in the Netherlands in June, with matches overlapping the home Test series against New Zealand. The Netherlands tour was postponed last summer due to the pandemic.

* Paul Collingwood replaced Chris Silverwood as interim head coach for the Test series against West Indies in March.

** Rescheduled after last summer's final Test was postponed due to Covid-19.

The County Championship returns to its pre-Covid structure this year following two seasons in which it was reorganised to cope with the pandemic. Counties will compete in Division One or Division Two according to their finishing positions at the end of the 2019 season. The Bob Willis Trophy has been scrapped.

Division One: Essex, Gloucestershire, Hampshire, Kent, Lancashire, Northamptonshire, Somerset, Surrey, Warwickshire, Yorkshire

Division Two: Derbyshire, Durham, Glamorgan, Leicestershire, Middlesex, Nottinghamshire, Sussex, Worcestershire

April 7-May 19	First seven rounds of the County Championship
May 25-July 9	T20 Blast group stage and quarter-finals
June 12-July 26	Middle five rounds of the County Championship
July 16	T20 Blast Finals Day, Edgbaston
August 2-23	One-Day Cup group stage
August 3-September 3	The Hundred (final at Lord's on September 3)
August 26-30	One-Day Cup quarter- and semi-finals
September 5-26	Final four rounds of the County Championship
September 17	One-Day Cup final, Trent Bridge

UMPIRES

The ECB has re-organised its first-class umpires into a 'Professional Umpires' Team' consisting of 34 officials who will share duties for domestic cricket in 2022.

Hassan Adnan (Derbyshire, 2003-2007)

Naeem Ashraf (Pakistan, 1995)

Rob Bailey (England, Northamptonshire, Derbyshire, 1982-2001)

Neil Bainton

Paul Baldwin

Ian Blackwell (England, Derbyshire, Somerset, Durham, Warwickshire, 1997-2012)

Mike Burns (Warwickshire, Somerset, 1991-2005)

Nick Cook (England, Leicestershire, Northamptonshire, 1978-1994)

Ben Debenham

Michael Gough (Durham, 1998-2003)

Anthony Harris

Peter Hartley (Warwickshire, Yorkshire, Hampshire, 1982-2000)

Richard Illingworth (England, Worcestershire, Derbyshire, 1982-2001)

Richard Kettleborough (Yorkshire, Middlesex, 1994-1999)

Nigel Llong (Kent, 1989-1999)

Graham Lloyd (England, Lancashire, 1988-2002)

Tom Lungley (Derbyshire, Lancashire, 2000-2010)

Neil Mallender (England, Northamptonshire, Somerset, 1980-1994)

James Middlebrook (Yorkshire, Essex, Northamptonshire, 1998-2015)

David Millns (Nottinghamshire, Leicestershire, 1988-2001)

Mark Newell (Sussex, Derbyshire, 1996-1999)

Steve O'Shaughnessy (Lancashire, Worcestershire, 1980-1989)

Paul Pollard (Nottinghamshire, Worcestershire, 1987-2001)

Sue Redfern (England, Derbyshire, Staffordshire, 1995-2008)

Tim Robinson (England, Nottinghamshire, 1978-1999)

Neil Pratt

Martin Saggers (England, Durham, Kent, Essex, 1996-2009)

Jack Shantry (Worcestershire, 2009-2017)

Surendiran Shanmugam

Billy Taylor (Sussex, Hampshire, 1999-2009)

Russell Warren (Northamptonshire, Nottinghamshire, 1992-2006)

Chris Watts

Alex Wharf (England, Yorkshire, Nottinghamshire, Glamorgan, 1994-2009)

Rob White (Northamptonshire, 2000-2012)

Tom Lungley signals a wide
Photo by Ross Kinnaird

THE PLAYERS

LHB – Left-hand batter
LB – Leg-break bowler
LF – Left-arm fast bowler
LFM – Left-arm fast-medium bowler
LM – Left-arm medium bowler
LMF – Left-arm medium-fast bowler
MCCU – Marylebone Cricket Club University
MVP – Denotes a player's presence in the top 50 places of the 2021 PCA County and Domestic Women's MVP Rankings (the number next to 'MVP' denotes the player's specific placing)
OB – Off-break bowler
R – 1,000 or more first-class runs in an English season (the number next to 'R' denotes how many times the player has achieved this feat)
RF – Right-arm fast bowler
RFM – Right-arm fast-medium bowler
RHB – Right-hand batter
RM – Right-arm medium bowler
RMF – Right-arm medium-fast bowler
SLA – Slow left-arm orthodox bowler
SLW – Slow left-arm wrist-spin bowler
UCCE – University Centre of Cricketing Excellence
W – 50 or more first-class wickets in an English season (the number next to 'W' denotes how many times the player has achieved this feat)
WK – Wicketkeeper
* – Not-out innings (e.g. 137*)

THE TEAMS

(s) – A competition has been shared between two or more winners
BWT – Bob Willis Trophy (English domestic first-class competition, 2020-2021)
C&G – Cheltenham & Gloucester Trophy (English domestic 50-over competition, 2001-2006)
CB40 – Clydesdale Bank 40 (English domestic 40-over competition, 2010-2012)
CC1/CC2/CC3 – County Championship Division One/Division Two/Division Three
FP Trophy – Friends Provident Trophy (English domestic 50-over competition, 2007-2009)
Gillette – Gillette Cup (English domestic limited-overs competition, 1963-1980)
NatWest – NatWest Trophy (English domestic limited-overs competition, 1981-2000)
Pro40 – NatWest Pro40 (English domestic 40-over competition, 2005-2009)
REL – A player has been released by the relevant county
RET – A player has retired
RL50 – Royal London One-Day Cup (English domestic 50-over competition, 2014-)
T20 Cup – English domestic T20 competition (2003-)
YB40 – Yorkshire Bank 40 (English domestic 40-over competition, 2013)

NOTES: In the men's section, the statistics given for a player's best batting and best bowling performance are for first-class cricket, except where indicated. In the women's section, these statistics are for List-A cricket, except where indicated. A field within a player's career statistics which is marked with a '-' indicates that a particular statistic is inapplicable – such as a player who has never bowled a ball in first-class cricket – or unavailable. All stats correct as of March 4, 2022.

The
Teams

TEAM PROFILE

FORMED: 1870
HOME GROUND: The Incora County Ground, Derby
ONE-DAY NAME: Derbyshire Falcons
CAPTAIN: Billy Godleman (CC/RL50), TBC (T20)
2021 RESULTS: CC3: 5/6; RL50 9/9 Group B; T20: 8/9 North Group
HONOURS: Championship: 1936; Gillette/NatWest/C&G/FP Trophy: 1981; Benson & Hedges Cup: 1993; Sunday League: 1990

THE LOWDOWN

The arrival of Mickey Arthur at Derby provides one of the intriguing subplots of the summer. Can a man who has coached at the top level all over the world turn an unfancied county from also-rans to contenders? Last year was a case in point: second from bottom in the Championship and the Blast, bottom of their RL50 group. Derbyshire have lost Matt Critchley, who moved to Essex following an impressive season with bat and ball, and keeper Harvey Hosein, sadly forced to retire aged 25 after a series of concussions. But Arthur has already made his presence felt by recruiting two of his former pupils: Pakistan opener Shan Masood and veteran Sri Lanka seamer Suranga Lakmal, both of whom are available for all formats. Lakmal has signed to play until the end of 2023 and will be a valuable asset to a promising young seam attack. A frontline spinner would be handy to replace Critchley, but the key for Derbyshire, as ever, will be runs. Masood, Billy Godleman and Wayne Madsen should be bankers, but Luis Reece and Leus du Plooy will hope to bounce back from stinkers in 2021.

IN: Alex Thomson (War), Suranga Lakmal (SL), Shan Masood (Pak), Mark Watt (Sco, T20)
OUT: Matt Critchley (Ess), Fynn Hudson-Prentice (Sus), Nils Priestley (REL), Harvey Hosein (RET)

HEAD OF CRICKET: MICKEY ARTHUR

Arthur was appointed last November following the resignation of David Houghton. The 53-year-old scored well over 6,000 first-class runs in South African domestic cricket between 1986-2001 before moving into coaching, since when he has had spells as head coach with South Africa (2005-10), Australia (2011-13), Pakistan (2016-19) and Sri Lanka (2020-21). At domestic level Arthur has coached in his native South Africa and Australia, and more recently has taken charge of T20 franchises Karachi Kings and Dhaka Dynamites.

Batting

	Mat	Inns	NO	Runs	HS	Ave	SR	100	50	4s	6s
MJJ Critchley	14	26	3	1000	109	43.47	57.07	1	8	124	7
HR Hosein	8	14	5	371	83*	41.22	46.54	0	4	37	0
WL Madsen	11	20	0	675	111	33.75	52.77	1	4	78	4
BA Godleman	10	18	2	530	100*	33.12	48.26	1	3	75	0
AK Dal	8	13	2	333	106	30.27	50.22	1	1	40	1
BD Guest	12	20	1	489	116	25.73	43.08	1	1	64	1
MH McKiernan	1	1	0	23	23	23.00	47.91	0	0	3	0
JL du Plooy	13	24	1	428	98	18.60	43.40	0	2	51	1
FJ Hudson-Prentice	9	15	2	209	31*	16.07	48.71	0	0	30	0
HRC Came	3	5	0	68	45	13.60	60.17	0	0	10	0
LM Reece	9	17	0	231	63	13.58	34.84	0	1	35	0
BW Aitchison	13	20	4	200	50	12.50	47.05	0	1	15	6
BR McDermott	2	4	0	49	25	12.25	44.54	0	0	7	0
AT Thomson	4	6	0	65	18	10.83	35.91	0	0	9	0
AL Hughes	5	9	1	84	25	10.50	31.11	0	0	9	1
TA Wood	7	13	0	129	31	9.92	38.97	0	0	16	0
EHT Moulton	2	2	1	9	6*	9.00	19.56	0	0	0	0
S Conners	10	16	3	114	39	8.76	41.60	0	0	14	2
DR Melton	5	8	3	39	15	7.80	70.90	0	0	4	1
MA Cohen	5	8	1	41	11	5.85	26.62	0	0	6	0
B Stanlake	1	2	0	8	8	4.00	30.76	0	0	1	0
GLS Scrimshaw	3	5	3	5	5*	2.50	19.23	0	0	1	0

Bowling

	Overs	Mdns	Runs	Wkts	BBI	BBM	Ave	Econ	SR	5w	10w
BW Aitchison	275.4	50	792	34	6/28	6/28	23.29	2.87	48.6	1	0
FJ Hudson-Prentice	182.0	47	548	23	5/68	8/76	23.82	3.01	47.4	1	0
MA Cohen	99.5	19	280	11	5/43	7/87	25.45	2.80	54.4	1	0
AT Thomson	53.2	6	186	7	3/71	4/84	26.57	3.48	45.7	0	0
S Conners	225.5	44	750	26	5/83	7/87	28.84	3.32	52.1	1	0
WL Madsen	43.5	8	130	4	2/8	2/8	32.50	2.96	65.7	0	0
AK Dal	110.0	18	298	9	2/17	4/74	33.11	2.70	73.3	0	0
MJJ Critchley	343.3	42	1230	32	5/67	8/143	38.43	3.58	64.4	1	0
DR Melton	93.0	15	390	9	5/97	5/97	43.33	4.19	62.0	0	0
B Stanlake	17.0	2	91	2	2/91	2/91	45.50	5.35	51.0	0	0
LM Reece	183.3	46	555	12	2/25	3/50	46.25	3.02	91.7	0	0
GLS Scrimshaw	35.0	6	154	3	2/40	2/65	51.33	4.40	70.0	0	0
EHT Moulton	40.0	8	159	3	2/24	2/74	53.00	3.97	80.0	0	0
AL Hughes	31.0	8	83	1	1/9	1/11	83.00	2.67	186.0	0	0
MH McKiernan	4.0	0	16	0	-	-	-	4.00	-	0	0
JL du Plooy	8.0	1	21	0	-	-	-	2.62	-	0	0

Catches/Stumpings:
29 Guest (inc 3st), 20 Madsen, 12 Aitchison, 11 Hosein, 8 Critchley, 6 Dal, Wood, 5 du Plooy, Godleman, 3 Reece, 2 Hudson-Prentice, Melton, 1 Came, Cohen, Conners, Hughes, McDermott, McKiernan, Scrimshaw, Thomson

Batting

	Mat	Inns	NO	Runs	HS	Ave	SR	100	50	4s	6s
FJ Hudson-Prentice	7	6	2	261	93	65.25	118.09	0	3	24	9
BA Godleman	2	2	0	128	116	64.00	92.08	1	0	12	2
NO Priestley	4	3	2	50	25*	50.00	81.96	0	0	3	0
HR Hosein	1	1	0	38	38	38.00	77.55	0	0	3	0
TA Wood	7	6	0	191	109	31.83	115.06	1	0	27	3
BD Guest	7	6	0	170	74	28.33	77.98	0	1	12	1
D Smit	1	1	0	25	25	25.00	67.56	0	0	2	0
HRC Came	7	6	0	141	57	23.50	85.45	0	1	14	4
MH McKiernan	7	6	1	113	38	22.60	129.88	0	0	11	3
MD Wagstaff	5	4	0	74	36	18.50	86.04	0	0	8	1
BW Aitchison	6	4	2	31	19	15.50	93.93	0	0	3	0
AT Thomson	6	3	0	43	24	14.33	76.78	0	0	5	0
CR Marshall	5	5	1	55	19	13.75	63.95	0	0	2	0
R Rampaul	7	3	1	25	25*	12.50	156.25	0	0	0	3
AL Hughes	6	5	0	42	25	8.40	93.33	0	0	5	0
AK Dal	7	6	1	31	9	6.20	86.11	0	0	2	0
GLS Scrimshaw	3	1	1	13	13*	-	52.00	0	0	2	0

Bowling

	Overs	Mdns	Runs	Wkts	BBI	Ave	Econ	SR	4w	5w
TA Wood	17.0	0	93	3	1/13	31.00	5.47	34.0	0	0
R Rampaul	43.0	1	258	3	1/15	86.00	6.00	86.0	0	0
CR Marshall	19.0	0	114	0	-	-	6.00	-	0	0
FJ Hudson-Prentice	37.1	3	227	6	3/37	37.83	6.10	37.1	0	0
AT Thomson	28.0	0	176	5	2/37	35.20	6.28	33.6	0	0
MH McKiernan	29.0	0	200	3	1/26	66.66	6.89	58.0	0	0
BW Aitchison	29.3	0	205	2	2/51	102.50	6.94	88.5	0	0
AK Dal	13.0	0	95	0	-	-	7.30	-	0	0
NO Priestley	6.0	0	46	0	-	-	7.66	-	0	0
GLS Scrimshaw	10.0	0	86	3	2/41	28.66	8.60	20.0	0	0

Catches/Stumpings:
5 Guest (inc 1st), 4 McKiernan, 3 Dal, Hughes, 2 Hudson-Prentice, 1 Aitchison, Rampaul, Wagstaff

VITALITY BLAST AVERAGES 2021

Cricket
DERBYSHIRE

	Mat	Inns	NO	Runs	HS	Ave	SR	100	50	4s	6s
TA Wood	4	4	1	142	63*	47.33	125.66	0	1	16	2
JL du Plooy	12	12	2	395	92	39.50	131.22	0	3	26	14
AL Hughes	2	2	0	66	38	33.00	165.00	0	0	9	0
LM Reece	12	12	0	351	59	29.25	171.21	0	4	37	18
MJJ Critchley	12	12	3	252	80*	28.00	117.75	0	1	12	8
BD Guest	12	12	6	137	34*	22.83	134.31	0	0	5	4
HRC Came	11	11	0	207	56	18.81	119.65	0	1	26	2
AT Thomson	8	4	1	49	28	16.33	188.46	0	0	5	3
FJ Hudson-Prentice	12	11	1	134	41	13.40	131.37	0	0	10	3
BA Godleman	8	8	0	47	15	5.87	79.66	0	0	4	1
LV van Beek	12	5	2	14	5*	4.66	93.33	0	0	1	0
C McKerr	7	3	1	8	7*	4.00	88.88	0	0	1	0
GLS Scrimshaw	10	3	2	4	3*	4.00	57.14	0	0	0	0
MH McKiernan	4	3	0	7	5	2.33	77.77	0	0	1	0
WL Madsen	1	1	1	12	12*	-	133.33	0	0	1	0
MA Cohen	3	1	1	7	7*	-	233.33	0	0	0	1
JW Dernbach	2	1	1	7	7*	-	233.33	0	0	0	1

Batting

	Overs	Mdns	Runs	Wkts	BBI	Ave	Econ	SR	4w	5w
MJJ Critchley	46.0	0	311	12	2/20	25.91	6.76	23.0	0	0
JW Dernbach	8.0	0	57	5	3/23	11.40	7.12	9.6	0	0
MH McKiernan	8.0	0	59	4	3/9	14.75	7.37	12.0	0	0
GLS Scrimshaw	31.0	0	236	14	3/23	16.85	7.61	13.2	0	0
AT Thomson	17.0	0	139	4	3/23	34.75	8.17	25.5	0	0
C McKerr	21.0	0	191	5	2/23	38.20	9.09	25.2	0	0
LM Reece	15.0	0	137	5	2/24	27.40	9.13	18.0	0	0
MA Cohen	6.0	0	55	2	1/6	27.50	9.16	18.0	0	0
FJ Hudson-Prentice	34.0	0	325	16	3/36	20.31	9.55	12.7	0	0
LV van Beek	36.5	0	361	16	3/22	22.56	9.80	13.8	0	0
AL Hughes	7.0	0	70	1	1/42	70.00	10.00	42.0	0	0
JL du Plooy	1.0	0	18	0	-	-	18.00	-	0	0

Bowling

Catches/Stumpings:
11 Guest (inc 1st), 9 Critchley, 8 du Plooy, 7 Reece, 6 van Beek, 5 Came, Godleman, 4 Hudson-Prentice, 3 Wood, 2 McKerr, McKiernan, Scrimshaw, Thomson, 1 Dernbach, Hughes

DURHAM

FORMED: 1882
HOME GROUND: Emirates Riverside
CAPTAIN: Scott Borthwick (CC/RL50),
TBC (T20)
2021 RESULTS: CC2: 3/6; RL50:
Runners-up; T20: 7/9 North Group
HONOURS: Championship: (3) 2008,
2009, 2013; Gillette/NatWest/C&G/FP
Trophy: 2007; Pro40/National League/
CB40/YB40/RL50: 2014

THE LOWDOWN

Durham appear to be inching up the greasy pole they shot down so spectacularly in 2016 when they were demoted to Division Two after an ECB bailout and their ground lost Test status. Their four Championship wins last summer included a thumping of eventual champions Warwickshire, and a third one-day trophy was within their grasp until coming unstuck against Glamorgan in the RL50 final. The batting was propelled by David Bedingham and Alex Lees – the latter called up by England post-Ashes – while Graham Clark topped the RL50 batting charts (646 runs in nine innings, three centuries). The club will hope for more from captain Scott Borthwick, who led the side well but struggled for red-ball runs in his first season back at his home county. Test batter Keegan Petersen will add some quality in the early season before joining up with the touring South Africans in June. The seaming ranks are strong even when deprived of Mark Wood, with Ben Raine and Brydon Carse supporting the phenomenal Chris Rushworth, who last year became the club's all-time leading first-class wicket-taker on the way to a haul of 59 at 18. Unearthing a reliable spinner could be the key to Championship promotion.

IN: George Drissell (unattached), Keegan Petersen (SA, CC)
OUT: Cameron Steel (Sur), Stuart Poynter (REL)

HEAD COACH: JAMES FRANKLIN

Franklin succeeded Jon Lewis in January 2019 as part of a structural overhaul which saw Marcus North become the director of cricket. A former New Zealand allrounder who played in 31 Tests and 110 ODIs, Franklin had four seasons at Middlesex and captained the club to the Championship title in 2016. He also had brief spells with Notts and Essex. North played 21 Tests for Australia as well as scoring over 4,000 first-class runs for six different counties, including a successful season for Durham in 2004.

COUNTY CHAMPIONSHIP AVERAGES 2021

Batting

	Mat	Inns	NO	Runs	HS	Ave	SR	100	50	4s	6s
L Trevaskis	3	4	2	135	77*	67.50	62.21	0	2	16	0
DG Bedingham	13	20	3	1029	257	60.52	59.89	3	3	124	8
WA Young	4	7	0	278	124	39.71	40.11	2	0	33	1
AZ Lees	11	17	1	625	129	39.06	43.10	1	5	72	2
EJH Eckersley	13	18	1	520	113*	30.58	61.83	1	3	60	7
MJ Potts	7	9	2	206	81	29.42	49.63	0	1	27	4
MA Jones	8	13	1	337	81	28.08	44.40	0	2	51	0
G Clark	3	4	1	83	42	27.66	31.67	0	0	8	1
JTA Burnham	10	15	2	357	102*	27.46	48.43	1	1	44	3
SR Dickson	3	4	1	79	46	26.33	42.02	0	0	8	2
CT Bancroft	5	8	1	183	46*	26.14	38.93	0	0	24	1
BA Raine	13	15	3	308	74	25.66	52.47	0	2	36	2
SG Borthwick	13	20	0	474	100	23.70	44.97	1	1	62	0
BA Carse	8	9	2	161	40*	23.00	47.21	0	0	17	2
P Coughlin	4	5	0	89	48	17.80	40.27	0	0	11	0
MET Salisbury	4	5	0	75	41	15.00	38.46	0	0	9	0
SW Poynter	6	8	2	85	52*	14.16	40.28	0	1	8	0
C Rushworth	13	13	6	91	31	13.00	61.07	0	0	15	0
MA Wood	3	3	0	30	17	10.00	44.77	0	0	4	0
BA Stokes	1	-	-	-	-	-	-	-	-	-	-

Bowling

	Overs	Mdns	Runs	Wkts	BBI	BBM	Ave	Econ	SR	5w	10w
C Rushworth	435.3	125	1073	59	6/49	9/108	18.18	2.46	44.2	3	0
BA Stokes	17.0	1	55	3	3/55	3/55	18.33	3.23	34.0	0	0
L Trevaskis	81.4	27	176	9	5/78	6/101	19.55	2.15	54.4	1	0
BA Carse	203.2	26	724	34	5/49	8/119	21.29	3.56	35.8	2	0
BA Raine	406.1	128	968	43	5/9	9/109	22.51	2.38	56.6	2	0
P Coughlin	88.4	22	279	12	5/64	9/75	23.25	3.14	44.3	1	0
MA Wood	79.0	19	233	10	3/28	4/55	23.30	2.94	47.4	0	0
MJ Potts	204.3	51	613	23	4/32	8/98	26.65	2.99	53.3	0	0
MET Salisbury	142.4	38	440	16	4/74	6/136	27.50	3.08	53.5	0	0
SG Borthwick	130.5	22	455	12	4/32	4/61	37.91	3.47	65.4	0	0
EJH Eckersley	4.0	1	7	0	-	-	-	1.75	-	0	0

Catches/Stumpings:
29 Eckersley (inc 1st), 22 Poynter, 14 Borthwick, 11 Bedingham, 6 Lees, 4 Bancroft, 3 Burnham, Coughlin, Potts, Raine, Rushworth, 2 Carse, Jones, Trevaskis, 1 Stokes, Young

Batting

	Mat	Inns	NO	Runs	HS	Ave	SR	100	50	4s	6s
G Clark	9	9	1	646	141*	80.75	98.92	3	1	96	5
AZ Lees	9	9	1	562	126*	70.25	86.99	2	4	53	5
SR Dickson	9	8	3	293	103*	58.60	113.12	1	1	23	9
EJH Eckersley	2	2	1	50	36	50.00	151.51	0	0	2	4
SG Borthwick	9	7	1	260	76	43.33	79.02	0	3	26	1
DG Bedingham	8	7	0	292	67	41.71	140.38	0	4	26	14
L Doneathy	9	5	1	152	69*	38.00	116.03	0	2	10	6
CT Bancroft	9	8	2	189	60*	31.50	105.00	0	2	17	3
L Trevaskis	9	8	2	79	23	13.16	90.80	0	0	5	1
BA Raine	1	1	0	10	10	10.00	52.63	0	0	0	0
PA van Meekeren	7	2	1	5	4*	5.00	27.77	0	0	0	0
MJ Potts	1	1	0	0	0	0.00	0.00	0	0	0	0
C Rushworth	8	3	2	0	0*	0.00	0.00	0	0	0	0
MET Salisbury	4	1	1	2	2*	-	66.66	0	0	0	0
JOI Campbell	5	-	-	-	-	-	-	-	-	-	-

Bowling

	Overs	Mdns	Runs	Wkts	BBI	Ave	Econ	SR	4w	5w
C Rushworth	71.4	6	328	17	4/37	19.29	4.57	25.2	1	0
SG Borthwick	81.1	0	423	10	2/44	42.30	5.21	48.7	0	0
L Trevaskis	76.0	0	401	7	3/38	57.28	5.27	65.1	0	0
MET Salisbury	30.1	0	160	3	2/19	53.33	5.30	60.3	0	0
MJ Potts	10.0	2	55	3	3/55	18.33	5.50	20.0	0	0
PA van Meekeren	56.0	2	310	14	3/33	22.14	5.53	24.0	0	0
BA Raine	10.0	0	58	3	3/58	19.33	5.80	20.0	0	0
G Clark	5.0	0	32	1	1/8	32.00	6.40	30.0	0	0
JOI Campbell	35.0	0	226	6	3/58	37.66	6.45	35.0	0	0
L Doneathy	45.2	0	300	8	4/36	37.50	6.61	34.0	1	0

Catches/Stumpings:
10 Bancroft (inc 1st), Borthwick, 6 van Meekeren, 5 Doneathy, 4 Clark, Lees, 3 Bedingham, Trevaskis, 2 Dickson, 1 Campbell, Eckersley, Potts, Rushworth, Salisbury

	Mat	Inns	NO	Runs	HS	Ave	SR	100	50	4s	6s	
L Trevaskis	10	6	4	85	30*	42.50	177.08	0	0	7	5	
MJ Potts	13	5	3	79	40*	39.50	154.90	0	0	5	4	
BA Carse	11	8	4	150	51	37.50	148.51	0	1	8	3	
SR Dickson	11	11	2	318	53	35.33	128.22	0	2	23	7	
CT Bancroft	13	13	2	283	76*	25.72	119.91	0	2	23	3	
EJH Eckersley	12	10	4	146	50*	24.33	130.35	0	1	12	2	
DG Bedingham	13	13	0	298	65	22.92	152.82	0	3	23	15	Batting
G Clark	13	13	0	272	40	20.92	147.02	0	0	32	8	
SG Borthwick	12	5	0	89	33	17.80	145.90	0	0	7	3	
BA Stokes	6	6	0	103	35	17.16	117.04	0	0	10	5	
P Coughlin	4	3	0	44	21	14.66	125.71	0	0	3	0	
BA Raine	13	11	1	116	32	11.60	112.62	0	0	10	3	
L Doneathy	2	2	1	10	5*	10.00	125.00	0	0	1	0	
JOI Campbell	2	1	0	6	6	6.00	75.00	0	0	1	0	
HM Crawshaw	3	2	0	9	5	4.50	128.57	0	0	2	0	
JTA Burnham	2	2	0	5	3	2.50	55.55	0	0	0	0	
AZ Lees	1	1	0	0	0	0.00	0.00	0	0	0	0	
PA van Meekeren	3	1	1	9	9*	-	300.00	0	0	2	0	

	Overs	Mdns	Runs	Wkts	BBI	Ave	Econ	SR	4w	5w	
L Trevaskis	39.0	0	297	7	1/19	42.42	7.61	33.4	0	0	
SG Borthwick	38.0	0	299	7	2/30	42.71	7.86	32.5	0	0	
BA Raine	38.2	0	326	10	3/19	32.60	8.50	23.0	0	0	
BA Carse	30.3	0	261	6	3/30	43.50	8.55	30.5	0	0	
BA Stokes	19.0	0	169	8	4/27	21.12	8.89	14.2	1	0	
MJ Potts	46.2	0	424	16	3/27	26.50	9.15	17.3	0	0	Bowling
HM Crawshaw	5.0	0	46	0	-	-	9.20	-	0	0	
L Doneathy	2.0	0	19	1	1/19	19.00	9.50	12.0	0	0	
P Coughlin	13.0	0	132	3	2/42	44.00	10.15	26.0	0	0	
JOI Campbell	2.0	0	21	1	1/21	21.00	10.50	12.0	0	0	
PA van Meekeren	9.0	0	96	4	2/31	24.00	10.66	13.5	0	0	
G Clark	2.0	0	37	0	-	-	18.50	-	0	0	

Catches/Stumpings:
6 Bancroft, Borthwick, 5 Dickson, Eckersley, 4 Carse, Potts, Stokes, Trevaskis, 3 Raine, 2 Clark, 1 Bedingham, Coughlin, Lees, van Meekeren

FORMED: 1876

HOME GROUND: The Cloud County Ground, Chelmsford

ONE-DAY NAME: Essex Eagles

CAPTAIN: Tom Westley (CC/RL50), Simon Harmer (T20)

2021 RESULTS: CC2: Winners; RL50: Semi-finalists; T20: 7/9 South Group

HONOURS: Championship: (8) 1979, 1983, 1984, 1986, 1991, 1992, 2017, 2019; Bob Willis Trophy: 2020; Gillette/NatWest/C&G/FP Trophy: (3) 1985, 1997, 2008; B&H Cup: (2) 1979, 1998; Pro40/ National League/CB40/ YB40/RL50: (2) 2005, 2006; Sunday League: (3) 1981, 1984, 1985; T20 Cup: 2019

THE LOWDOWN

Having been the dominant force in county cricket for several years, a shadow fell across Essex last November when three former players made allegations of racism. Chairman John Faragher resigned after being accused of using racist language at a board meeting in 2017, while one of Essex's main sponsors severed ties. This followed a strange summer in which the club were condemned to Division Two after the group phase of the Championship. But they were soon back to their blistering best, topping the division by winning three of their four matches by an innings. The bowling attack remains among the best in the country, with Sam Cook (58 wickets at 14 last summer) in the form of his life. Aussie pacer Mark Steketee has signed up for the first six Championship matches. Essex will be fretting about the availability of their champion spinner after Simon Harmer was recalled by South Africa a month after signing a new four-year deal, although the arrival of Matt Critchley provides some insurance. Tom Westley forms the nucleus of the batting alongside Alastair Cook and Dan Lawrence. Essex are without Ryan ten Doeschate for the first time in two decades.

IN: Matt Critchley (Der), Mark Steketee (Aus, CC)
OUT: Matt Quinn (Ken), Varun Chopra, Ryan ten Doeschate (both RET)

HEAD COACH: ANTHONY MCGRATH

McGrath scored more than 23,000 runs and took 240 wickets for Yorkshire, appearing in four Tests and 14 ODIs. After retiring in 2013, he was assistant coach to Chris Silverwood when Essex were county champions in 2017 and has since won four trophies as head coach including a Championship-T20 double in 2019. Andre Nel has left after three seasons as assistant coach, with former Australian seamer Mick Lewis arriving to oversee the bowlers.

COUNTY CHAMPIONSHIP AVERAGES 2021

	Mat	Inns	NO	Runs	HS	Ave	SR	100	50	4s	6s
DW Lawrence	10	13	1	640	152*	53.33	59.98	1	4	76	8
T Westley	13	18	1	631	213	37.11	44.81	3	1	90	2
PI Walter	13	16	1	544	96	36.26	44.26	0	4	71	3
AN Cook	14	19	0	611	165	32.15	50.74	2	2	87	1
NLJ Browne	14	19	2	524	102	30.82	39.63	1	4	73	0
MS Pepper	6	7	0	204	92	29.14	52.84	0	2	31	1
AJA Wheater	14	16	0	434	87	27.12	53.44	0	2	51	1
SR Harmer	14	16	4	317	82*	26.41	39.18	0	2	31	4
RN ten Doeschate	10	12	0	314	56	26.16	57.82	0	3	42	1
BMJ Allison	2	3	0	69	52	23.00	33.82	0	1	6	0
S Snater	9	8	2	99	48	16.50	48.29	0	0	13	2
JA Porter	12	13	7	73	30	12.16	35.09	0	0	9	1
SJ Cook	13	13	2	126	37	11.45	42.71	0	0	12	0
PM Siddle	6	9	2	70	20	10.00	63.06	0	0	9	1
JS Rymell	3	3	0	23	14	7.66	38.98	0	0	3	0
ASS Nijjar	1	1	0	2	2	2.00	16.66	0	0	0	0
JDS Neesham	1	1	1	10	10*	-	34.48	0	0	1	0

Batting

	Overs	Mdns	Runs	Wkts	BBI	BBM	Ave	Econ	SR	5w	10w
JDS Neesham	4.1	0	15	2	2/15	2/15	7.50	3.60	12.5	0	0
SJ Cook	382.2	128	837	58	5/20	10/41	14.43	2.18	39.5	3	1
S Snater	168.5	42	511	31	7/98	7/56	16.48	3.02	32.6	2	0
SR Harmer	558.4	182	1233	53	9/80	12/202	23.26	2.20	63.2	3	2
PM Siddle	176.2	37	488	20	6/38	6/62	24.40	2.76	52.9	1	0
JA Porter	299.4	73	842	34	4/31	7/58	24.76	2.80	52.8	0	0
DW Lawrence	49.1	7	155	5	2/28	2/35	31.00	3.15	59.0	0	0
RN ten Doeschate	9.0	0	35	1	1/10	1/10	35.00	3.88	54.0	0	0
PI Walter	34.0	4	120	2	2/18	2/18	60.00	3.52	102.0	0	0
BMJ Allison	36.0	7	94	1	1/67	1/67	94.00	2.61	216.0	0	0
AN Cook	1.0	0	5	0	-	-	-	5.00	-	0	0
T Westley	10.0	1	12	0	-	-	-	1.20	-	0	0
ASS Nijjar	13.0	5	21	0	-	-	-	1.61	-	0	0

Bowling

Catches/Stumpings:
27 Wheater (inc 4st), 16 A Cook, 14 Harmer, 9 ten Doeschate, 8 Lawrence, 6 Browne, 5 Walter, Westley, 3 Pepper, 2 Rymell, 1 Allison, S Cook, Porter, Snater

Batting

	Mat	Inns	NO	Runs	HS	Ave	SR	100	50	4s	6s
AN Cook	10	10	2	455	110	56.87	87.66	1	3	57	0
JS Rymell	7	6	0	331	121	55.16	71.95	1	1	31	3
T Westley	10	10	2	415	87*	51.87	85.56	0	4	53	0
FIN Khushi	5	5	0	234	109	46.80	86.98	1	1	17	3
ASS Nijjar	10	8	5	115	32*	38.33	127.77	0	0	7	6
S Snater	6	2	1	36	21*	36.00	97.29	0	0	2	0
SR Harmer	10	8	4	134	32*	33.50	112.60	0	0	10	6
PI Walter	6	5	0	157	50	31.40	98.74	0	1	16	3
AJA Wheater	9	7	0	211	77	30.14	119.88	0	2	21	6
RN ten Doeschate	10	8	0	113	45	14.12	79.02	0	0	9	1
MS Pepper	5	3	0	40	34	13.33	67.79	0	0	5	2
JH Plom	5	4	3	11	9*	11.00	78.57	0	0	2	0
WEL Buttleman	5	5	0	48	23	9.60	51.06	0	0	6	0
BMJ Allison	8	2	1	4	3	4.00	30.76	0	0	0	0
NLJ Browne	1	1	0	3	3	3.00	16.66	0	0	0	0
LM Benkenstein	1	-	-	-	-	-	-	-	-	-	-
JA Porter	2	-	-	-	-	-	-	-	-	-	-

Bowling

	Overs	Mdns	Runs	Wkts	BBI	Ave	Econ	SR	4w	5w
JA Porter	19.2	2	64	2	1/31	32.00	3.31	58.0	0	0
SR Harmer	97.0	9	352	18	3/42	19.55	3.62	32.3	0	0
T Westley	46.0	0	204	8	3/33	25.50	4.43	34.5	0	0
RN ten Doeschate	59.2	0	294	15	4/34	19.60	4.95	23.7	1	0
ASS Nijjar	87.1	2	451	12	2/26	37.58	5.17	43.5	0	0
S Snater	52.4	3	282	13	4/48	21.69	5.35	24.3	1	0
BMJ Allison	57.1	1	351	7	2/33	50.14	6.13	49.0	0	0
JH Plom	36.4	3	243	6	3/34	40.50	6.62	36.6	0	0
LM Benkenstein	4.0	0	30	1	1/30	30.00	7.50	24.0	0	0
PI Walter	6.4	0	59	1	1/13	59.00	8.85	40.0	0	0

Catches/Stumpings:
12 Wheater (inc 2st), 8 Harmer, 5 A Cook, 4 Allison, Rymell, ten Doeschate, Westley, 3 Buttleman, Nijjar, Plom, Walter, 2 Browne (inc 1st), Khushi, 1 Snater

www.essexcricket.org.uk / tel: 01245 252420

VITALITY BLAST AVERAGES 2021

	Mat	Inns	NO	Runs	HS	Ave	SR	100	50	4s	6s
DW Lawrence	8	8	2	252	60	42.00	145.66	0	3	22	8
T Westley	7	7	0	198	53	28.28	124.52	0	1	19	4
MS Pepper	13	13	3	260	55*	26.00	131.31	0	1	19	11
JS Rymell	1	1	0	21	21	21.00	123.52	0	0	4	0
AJA Wheater	10	10	0	209	49	20.90	133.12	0	0	22	1
WEL Buttleman	9	9	1	158	56*	19.75	119.69	0	1	21	4
SR Harmer	13	9	3	109	31	18.16	129.76	0	0	8	4
JDS Neesham	13	11	0	189	53	17.18	135.00	0	1	17	6
PI Walter	13	9	0	120	45	13.33	115.38	0	0	11	3
ASS Nijjar	13	8	3	66	27*	13.20	132.00	0	0	5	3
S Snater	3	2	1	12	7*	12.00	133.33	0	0	2	0
RN ten Doeschate	11	9	2	73	26	10.42	97.33	0	0	4	2
JH Plom	8	6	3	31	12	10.33	106.89	0	0	1	2
FIN Khushi	2	2	0	19	17	9.50	111.76	0	0	1	1
SJ Cook	13	7	4	27	18	9.00	112.50	0	0	1	1
JA Porter	6	1	1	0	0*	-	-	0	0	0	0

	Overs	Mdns	Runs	Wkts	BBI	Ave	Econ	SR	4w	5w
ASS Nijjar	50.3	0	347	13	2/19	26.69	6.87	23.3	0	0
SR Harmer	47.0	0	348	19	4/24	18.31	7.40	14.8	2	0
SJ Cook	46.4	0	365	20	4/15	18.25	7.82	14.0	1	0
JDS Neesham	28.0	0	238	5	2/11	47.60	8.50	33.6	0	0
DW Lawrence	13.0	0	117	5	2/15	23.40	9.00	15.6	0	0
PI Walter	9.0	0	82	1	1/21	82.00	9.11	54.0	0	0
JA Porter	16.0	0	160	2	1/19	80.00	10.00	48.0	0	0
S Snater	11.0	0	116	2	1/36	58.00	10.54	33.0	0	0
JH Plom	24.0	1	262	9	3/31	29.11	10.91	16.0	0	0

Catches/Stumpings:
12 Wheater (inc 5st), 7 Neesham, Nijjar, Pepper, 6 Harmer, 5 Walter, 4 Lawrence, 3 Buttleman (inc 1st), Plom, ten Doeschate, 2 S Cook, 1 Porter, Rymell

TEAM PROFILE

GLAMORGAN

FORMED: 1888
HOME GROUND: Sophia Gardens, Cardiff
CAPTAIN: David Lloyd (CC/T20), Kiran Carlson (RL50)
2021 RESULTS: CC2: 6/6; RL50: Winners; T20: 9/9 South Group
HONOURS: Championship: (3) 1948, 1969, 1997; Pro40/National League/CB40/YB40/RL50: (3) 2002, 2004, 2021; Sunday League: 1993

THE LOWDOWN

The daffodil is blooming in Wales after Glamorgan secured their first one-day knockout trophy in last summer's RL50. The competition may be diminished by The Hundred, which runs concurrently, but it allows young talent to shine. Joe Cooke was one such player to emerge, the 24-year-old allrounder taking 21 wickets at 15 and producing a match-winning performance against Essex in the semi-final (5-61 and 66 not out). The team were led by Kiran Carlson, a 23-year-old local boy who enjoyed a wonder season to reward the faith of the club. Carlson will lead again in this summer's RL50 – unless involved in The Hundred – while David Lloyd has replaced Chris Cooke as captain in four-day and T20 cricket. A reminder of the club's red-ball shortcomings were the three crushing defeats last September which left Glamorgan bottom of Division Two. The batting has beefed up with the arrivals of Sam Northeast and Eddie Byrom, with Marnus Labuschagne returning to complete his contract. Michael Neser has signed on until the end of 2023, no bad thing with fellow Aussie seamer Michael Hogan retiring at the end of the summer after a decade at the club.

IN: Eddie Byrom (Som), James Harris (Mid), Sam Northeast (Ham)
OUT: Roman Walker (Lei), Nick Selman (REL)

HEAD COACH: MATTHEW MAYNARD

Maynard replaced Robert Croft ahead of the 2019 season, stepping up from his previous role as a batting consultant, and last summer delivered the county's first silverware since 2004. He previously coached Glamorgan between 2008 and 2010 and later served as Somerset's director of cricket. A dashing batter for Glamorgan for 20 years, Maynard made a club-record 54 first-class centuries and helped the Welsh county win the Championship in 1997. He played four Tests and 14 ODIs.

Batting

	Mat	Inns	NO	Runs	HS	Ave	SR	100	50	4s	6s
CB Cooke	14	21	7	816	205*	58.28	54.18	4	1	75	6
KS Carlson	14	23	4	928	170*	48.84	66.47	3	5	120	0
HD Rutherford	4	7	0	260	71	37.14	54.16	0	2	38	0
CZ Taylor	6	8	2	215	84	35.83	38.94	0	2	23	1
JAR Harris	2	2	1	35	18*	35.00	32.11	0	0	4	0
DL Lloyd	14	25	1	828	121	34.50	63.59	1	5	116	3
M Labuschagne	6	9	2	228	77	32.57	65.51	0	2	32	0
DA Douthwaite	13	16	1	482	96	32.13	46.88	0	4	63	6
AG Salter	10	11	4	221	90	31.57	34.69	0	1	34	0
EJ Byrom	3	5	0	151	78	30.20	38.03	0	1	22	0
MG Neser	5	3	1	58	24	29.00	53.70	0	0	9	0
WT Root	11	18	2	442	110*	27.62	45.61	1	1	51	3
JM Cooke	8	13	2	203	68	18.45	35.48	0	1	28	1
T van der Gugten	11	13	2	194	85*	17.63	53.29	0	1	24	5
CA Ingram	1	2	0	34	27	17.00	65.38	0	0	4	1
LJ Carey	3	5	0	78	29	15.60	97.50	0	0	12	3
MG Hogan	13	14	6	113	54	14.12	77.39	0	1	17	1
NJ Selman	5	10	0	121	69	12.10	35.38	0	1	15	0
WJ Weighell	4	5	0	52	21	10.40	82.53	0	0	5	3
A Balbirnie	3	6	0	57	29	9.50	41.00	0	0	8	0
SJ Reingold	1	2	0	13	9	6.50	27.65	0	0	2	0
RAJ Smith	1	2	0	12	8	6.00	75.00	0	0	2	0
JP McIlroy	2	1	0	0	0	0.00	0.00	0	0	0	0

Bowling

	Overs	Mdns	Runs	Wkts	BBI	BBM	Ave	Econ	SR	5w	10w
SJ Reingold	6.0	1	15	3	3/15	3/15	5.00	2.50	12.0	0	0
MG Neser	127.0	29	386	23	5/39	7/99	16.78	3.03	33.1	1	0
MG Hogan	332.5	78	874	34	5/28	7/61	25.70	2.62	58.7	1	0
HD Rutherford	8.0	1	26	1	1/26	1/26	26.00	3.25	48.0	0	0
DL Lloyd	170.3	24	558	21	4/11	6/32	26.57	3.27	48.7	0	0
T van der Gugten	274.3	54	823	27	4/34	6/139	30.48	2.99	61.0	0	0
EJ Byrom	16.0	0	64	2	2/64	2/64	32.00	4.00	48.0	0	0
JAR Harris	44.5	3	159	4	2/5	2/21	39.75	3.54	67.2	0	0
KS Carlson	14.3	4	43	1	1/37	1/37	43.00	2.96	87.0	0	0
LJ Carey	54.0	9	179	4	3/56	3/56	44.75	3.31	81.0	0	0
AG Salter	218.5	41	687	15	4/18	4/58	45.80	3.13	87.5	0	0
DA Douthwaite	181.1	18	781	17	2/16	4/48	45.94	4.31	63.9	0	0
WJ Weighell	80.1	9	359	7	2/46	3/69	51.28	4.47	68.7	0	0
M Labuschagne	32.2	3	127	2	2/27	2/27	63.50	3.92	97.0	0	0
RAJ Smith	22.0	3	84	1	1/84	1/84	84.00	3.81	132.0	0	0
CZ Taylor	146.2	16	484	5	2/16	2/78	96.80	3.30	175.6	0	0
JP McIlroy	38.0	10	131	1	1/12	1/38	131.00	3.44	228.0	0	0
WT Root	13.0	0	64	0	-	-	-	4.92	-	0	0

Catches/Stumpings:
41 C Cooke (inc 1st), 7 J Cooke, Lloyd, 5 van der Gugten, 4 Root, 3 Balbirnie, Carlson, Douthwaite, Neser, Salter, Selman, 2 Hogan, Taylor, Weighell, 1 Byrom, Harris, Labuschagne, Reingold

GLAMORGAN

Batting

	Mat	Inns	NO	Runs	HS	Ave	SR	100	50	4s	6s
NJ Selman	10	9	1	421	140	52.62	73.60	1	2	34	1
LJ Carey	10	5	4	51	19*	51.00	121.42	0	0	7	0
AG Salter	7	3	2	42	33	42.00	150.00	0	0	3	1
TN Cullen	10	8	3	175	58*	35.00	79.18	0	1	14	1
JM Cooke	10	8	3	174	66*	34.80	119.17	0	1	20	3
HD Rutherford	10	9	0	308	86	34.22	93.61	0	4	36	7
KS Carlson	10	9	1	232	82	29.00	98.72	0	2	27	4
WT Root	10	8	0	191	67	23.87	77.01	0	2	14	1
SJ Reingold	10	9	0	187	40	20.77	59.74	0	0	22	1
CZ Taylor	3	3	0	53	36	17.66	82.81	0	0	3	1
WJ Weighell	5	3	0	15	15	5.00	107.14	0	0	0	1
MG Hogan	10	2	2	16	12*	-	84.21	0	0	1	1
RI Walker	1	1	1	15	15*	-	68.18	0	0	0	1
AW Gorvin	4	1	1	12	12*	-	66.66	0	0	1	0

Bowling

	Overs	Mdns	Runs	Wkts	BBI	Ave	Econ	SR	4w	5w
MG Hogan	67.1	7	201	16	4/33	12.56	2.99	25.1	1	0
AG Salter	44.0	2	164	9	3/37	18.22	3.72	29.3	0	0
AW Gorvin	18.0	0	74	1	1/11	74.00	4.11	108.0	0	0
JM Cooke	62.5	2	286	20	5/61	14.30	4.55	18.8	0	1
CZ Taylor	18.0	0	91	3	1/6	30.33	5.05	36.0	0	0
LJ Carey	63.2	2	352	12	2/24	29.33	5.55	31.6	0	0
WJ Weighell	30.1	0	169	8	3/7	21.12	5.60	22.6	0	0
RI Walker	9.2	0	53	1	1/53	53.00	5.67	56.0	0	0
SJ Reingold	27.0	0	163	5	1/16	32.60	6.03	32.4	0	0

Catches/Stumpings:
19 Cullen (inc 1st), 9 Selman, 8 Reingold, 5 Carlson, 4 J Cooke, 3 Hogan, Weighell, 2 Root, Salter, 1 Carey, Gorvin, Rutherford, Walker

www.glamorgancricket.com / tel: 02920 409380

GLAMORGAN

	Mat	Inns	NO	Runs	HS	Ave	SR	100	50	4s	6s
M Labuschagne	8	8	1	390	93*	55.71	140.79	0	4	35	11
DL Lloyd	12	12	0	302	52	25.16	147.31	0	2	31	15
WT Root	6	5	1	88	41*	22.00	110.00	0	0	5	5
NJ Selman	6	6	0	130	65	21.66	126.21	0	1	12	5
DA Douthwaite	12	11	1	203	53	20.30	153.78	0	1	7	18
CA Ingram	12	12	1	174	75	15.81	104.19	0	1	18	4
WJ Weighell	7	7	0	96	51	13.71	135.21	0	1	8	6
CB Cooke	11	11	2	122	26	13.55	103.38	0	0	11	1
T van der Gugten	9	5	3	26	18*	13.00	113.04	0	0	1	1
KS Carlson	12	11	0	141	32	12.81	127.02	0	0	12	4
P Sisodiya	8	3	2	10	6*	10.00	250.00	0	0	1	1
CZ Taylor	5	5	1	39	16	9.75	88.63	0	0	2	1
SJ Pearce	4	3	1	11	5	5.50	84.61	0	0	1	0
TN Cullen	1	1	0	5	5	5.00	55.55	0	0	0	0
AG Salter	8	6	2	10	4	2.50	58.82	0	0	0	0
RAJ Smith	5	4	2	2	2*	1.00	50.00	0	0	0	0
RI Walker	6	3	1	2	2	1.00	33.33	0	0	0	0

Batting

	Overs	Mdns	Runs	Wkts	BBI	Ave	Econ	SR	4w	5w
RI Walker	18.0	0	128	8	3/15	16.00	7.11	13.5	0	0
RAJ Smith	19.0	0	138	4	2/13	34.50	7.26	28.5	0	0
P Sisodiya	31.0	0	256	7	2/22	36.57	8.25	26.5	0	0
DA Douthwaite	34.4	0	294	15	3/28	19.60	8.48	13.8	0	0
CZ Taylor	4.0	0	34	2	1/13	17.00	8.50	12.0	0	0
M Labuschagne	22.0	0	193	9	2/22	21.44	8.77	14.6	0	0
DL Lloyd	8.0	0	71	1	1/18	71.00	8.87	48.0	0	0
AG Salter	26.0	0	243	7	2/31	34.71	9.34	22.2	0	0
T van der Gugten	30.2	1	292	7	3/16	41.71	9.62	26.0	0	0
SJ Pearce	11.2	0	117	0	-	-	10.32	-	0	0
WJ Weighell	17.0	0	195	3	1/22	65.00	11.47	34.0	0	0

Bowling

Catches/Stumpings:
10 C Cooke (inc 1st), 5 Labuschagne, Selman, 4 Ingram, van der Gugten, 3 Carlson, Root, 2 Douthwaite, Lloyd, Smith, Weighell, 1 Cullen, Pearce, Salter, Sisodiya, Walker

TEAM PROFILE

FORMED: 1871
HOME GROUND: Seat Unique Stadium, Bristol
CAPTAIN: Graeme van Buuren (CC/RL50), Jack Taylor (T20)
2021 RESULTS: CC2: 2/6; RL50: Quarter-finalists; T20: 6/9 South Group
HONOURS: Gillette/NatWest/C&G/FP Trophy: (5) 1973, 1999, 2000, 2003, 2004; Benson & Hedges Cup: (3) 1977, 1999, 2000; Pro40/National League/CB40/YB40/RL50: (2) 2000, 2015

THE LOWDOWN

Gloucestershire will hope to regain some stability under a new head coach (Dale Benkenstein) and captain (Graeme van Buuren) following a period of flux initiated by ex-coach Richard Dawson leaving the club just before last season, with Chris Dent stepping down as skipper in September. Under interim coach Ian Harvey, Gloucestershire were unusually flat in the shorter formats in 2021, but their red-ball form was encouraging, only narrowly failing to qualify for Division One and winning eight of 14 Championship matches. They play in Division One this summer, belated reward for the promotion they earned in 2019 which was delayed by the pandemic. An impressive seam attack led by Ryan Higgins and David Payne has lost the dependable Dan Worrall but gained Pakistan quick Naseem Shah, who will be available until early July. Shah's compatriot, left-arm spinner Zafar Gohar, has been re-signed for the whole summer after taking 20 wickets in four Championship matches last season. But with runs the gold standard, the key arrival is Australia opener Marcus Harris, who has signed a two-year contract.

IN: Ajeet Dale (Ham), Paul van Meekeren (unattached), Marcus Harris (Aus), Zafar Gohar (Pak), Naseem Shah (Pak, CC/T20)
OUT: George Hankins, Harry Hankins (both REL)

HEAD COACH: DALE BENKENSTEIN

Benkenstein was appointed in November as Richard Dawson's permanent replacement after assistant coach Ian Harvey filled the vacancy on a temporary basis last summer. The 47-year-old South African coached Hampshire between 2014-16 and had a brief spell as Lancashire's batting coach last summer. A prolific batter across his 20-year career, Benkenstein missed out on Test honours but made 23 ODI appearances for South Africa and enjoyed a long career at Durham, winning three Championships.

Batting

	Mat	Inns	NO	Runs	HS	Ave	SR	100	50	4s	6s
JA Tattersall	2	4	1	162	86*	54.00	56.44	0	2	21	2
GL van Buuren	6	9	2	354	110*	50.57	69.96	1	4	49	4
BJJ Wells	1	1	0	40	40	40.00	42.55	0	0	7	0
JR Bracey	11	21	2	715	118	37.63	49.86	1	6	89	2
MAH Hammond	9	17	2	547	94	36.46	46.67	0	4	68	5
TJ Price	6	9	4	177	71	35.40	37.50	0	1	22	0
IA Cockbain	6	11	1	302	117	30.20	44.74	1	2	33	4
KC Brathwaite	6	11	1	295	60	26.81	43.38	0	1	30	0
CDJ Dent	12	23	2	560	91*	26.66	54.00	0	5	73	3
JMR Taylor	3	5	0	133	40	26.60	49.44	0	0	16	2
J Shaw	4	6	2	105	41*	26.25	59.32	0	0	12	2
TC Lace	14	26	4	573	118	26.04	43.67	1	3	74	2
BG Charlesworth	3	5	0	112	49	22.40	43.41	0	0	15	0
RF Higgins	13	19	1	376	73	20.88	53.40	0	1	39	5
GT Hankins	5	7	1	120	37	20.00	44.94	0	0	18	0
JD Warner	2	2	1	20	10*	20.00	14.81	0	0	0	0
MD Taylor	9	12	3	166	56	18.44	31.98	0	1	17	1
GD Phillips	3	6	0	109	47	18.16	39.92	0	0	13	2
OJ Price	4	7	0	110	33	15.71	42.63	0	0	15	0
GFB Scott	5	7	0	100	31	14.28	27.62	0	0	12	1
Zafar Gohar	4	6	0	78	30	13.00	48.44	0	0	11	0
DA Payne	10	12	3	102	34	11.33	39.23	0	0	16	1
TMJ Smith	5	8	1	76	47	10.85	32.47	0	0	10	0
DC Goodman	4	5	3	20	9*	10.00	17.24	0	0	3	0
DJ Worrall	8	12	3	75	24	8.33	56.81	0	0	10	1

Bowling

	Overs	Mdns	Runs	Wkts	BBI	BBM	Ave	Econ	SR	5w	10w
Zafar Gohar	117.3	32	287	20	6/43	11/101	14.35	2.44	35.2	3	1
GL van Buuren	48.4	11	119	7	3/28	5/34	17.00	2.44	41.7	0	0
DA Payne	258.2	59	719	34	6/56	11/87	21.14	2.78	45.5	2	1
RF Higgins	443.0	118	1143	51	7/46	7/87	22.41	2.58	52.1	2	0
DJ Worrall	249.5	80	621	27	5/54	7/80	23.00	2.48	55.5	2	0
TJ Price	128.0	37	368	15	4/72	7/111	24.53	2.87	51.2	0	0
MAH Hammond	19.0	2	85	3	2/37	2/37	28.33	4.47	38.0	0	0
JD Warner	37.3	7	118	4	2/54	3/78	29.50	3.14	56.2	0	0
MD Taylor	266.1	67	818	27	5/40	9/59	30.29	3.07	59.1	1	0
J Shaw	86.0	10	333	9	4/48	4/51	37.00	3.87	57.3	0	0
GD Phillips	40.0	3	159	4	2/67	2/67	39.75	3.97	60.0	0	0
DC Goodman	104.0	25	252	5	2/19	3/55	50.40	2.42	124.8	0	0
GFB Scott	51.0	13	149	2	1/22	1/22	74.50	2.92	153.0	0	0
TMJ Smith	104.0	8	303	4	1/21	1/21	75.75	2.91	156.0	0	0
OJ Price	33.0	5	100	0	-	-	-	3.03	-	0	0

Catches/Stumpings:

33 Bracey, 11 Hammond, 9 Lace, 6 Brathwaite, G Hankins, Payne, 5 Dent, Phillips, 4 O Price, 3 Higgins, Scott, van Buuren, 2 Smith, Tattersall, Wells, 1 Cockbain, T Price, J Taylor, Shaw, Warner

GLOUCESTERSHIRE COUNTY CRICKET CLUB

Batting

	Mat	Inns	NO	Runs	HS	Ave	SR	100	50	4s	6s
TMJ Smith	8	5	4	62	51*	62.00	69.66	0	1	5	0
GFB Scott	8	6	2	238	66*	59.50	84.39	0	2	14	6
BG Charlesworth	6	6	1	260	99*	52.00	82.27	0	2	31	1
JMR Taylor	8	7	2	257	67*	51.40	93.11	0	3	21	5
GL van Buuren	8	8	2	202	51*	33.66	83.12	0	1	22	4
JR Bracey	5	5	0	161	90	32.20	90.96	0	1	13	2
MD Taylor	7	3	1	64	51*	32.00	82.05	0	1	3	4
CDJ Dent	7	7	1	190	112*	31.66	96.93	1	0	22	0
OJ Price	2	2	0	43	24	21.50	52.43	0	0	5	0
TC Lace	6	6	0	90	38	15.00	59.21	0	0	8	0
BJJ Wells	4	2	0	9	7	4.50	25.71	0	0	1	0
J Shaw	6	2	0	2	2	1.00	22.22	0	0	0	0
TJ Price	1	1	0	1	1	1.00	50.00	0	0	0	0
DJ Worrall	5	1	0	1	1	1.00	33.33	0	0	0	0
GT Hankins	1	1	0	0	0	0.00	0.00	0	0	0	0
JD Warner	6	1	0	0	0	0.00	0.00	0	0	0	0

Bowling

	Overs	Mdns	Runs	Wkts	BBI	Ave	Econ	SR	4w	5w
TMJ Smith	71.3	1	305	9	3/28	33.88	4.26	47.6	0	0
GL van Buuren	67.0	0	309	11	3/32	28.09	4.61	36.5	0	0
MD Taylor	50.0	3	231	7	2/22	33.00	4.62	42.8	0	0
JD Warner	46.0	2	246	6	3/42	41.00	5.34	46.0	0	0
DJ Worrall	41.5	1	230	7	4/58	32.85	5.49	35.8	1	0
TJ Price	7.0	0	39	0	-	-	5.57	-	0	0
J Shaw	50.0	0	282	8	4/36	35.25	5.64	37.5	1	0
GFB Scott	12.0	0	78	0	-	-	6.50	-	0	0
BG Charlesworth	2.0	0	13	0	-	-	6.50	-	0	0
JMR Taylor	3.2	0	22	0	-	-	6.60	-	0	0
OJ Price	4.0	0	30	1	1/9	30.00	7.50	24.0	0	0

Catches/Stumpings:
9 Bracey (inc 1st), 3 Dent, Scott, Smith, J Taylor, 2 van Buuren, Warner, Wells, 1
Charlesworth, Lace, Worrall

www.gloscricket.co.uk / tel: 0117 910 8000

GLOUCESTERSHIRE
COUNTY CRICKET CLUB

	Mat	Inns	NO	Runs	HS	Ave	SR	100	50	4s	6s	
GD Phillips	12	12	3	500	94*	55.55	163.39	0	3	30	36	
IA Cockbain	8	8	2	244	72	40.66	135.55	0	2	25	7	
RF Higgins	9	7	4	113	43	37.66	143.03	0	0	8	4	
GL van Buuren	4	4	1	82	28	27.33	160.78	0	0	4	6	
CDJ Dent	9	9	0	241	42	26.77	150.62	0	0	25	10	
BAC Howell	12	11	1	246	53*	24.60	142.19	0	2	21	9	Batting
JMR Taylor	12	11	1	227	38	22.70	119.47	0	0	24	2	
MAH Hammond	12	12	0	222	44	18.50	130.58	0	0	26	9	
JR Bracey	6	5	1	55	33	13.75	119.56	0	0	6	1	
GFB Scott	3	2	1	11	7	11.00	84.61	0	0	1	0	
TMJ Smith	12	4	2	12	7	6.00	109.09	0	0	1	0	
MD Taylor	4	3	2	6	6*	6.00	60.00	0	0	0	0	
DJ Worrall	8	3	3	8	6*	-	114.28	0	0	1	0	
J Shaw	12	1	1	1	1*	-	100.00	0	0	0	0	
DA Payne	9	-	-	-	-	-	-	-	-	-	-	

	Overs	Mdns	Runs	Wkts	BBI	Ave	Econ	SR	4w	5w	
TMJ Smith	41.0	1	294	10	2/17	29.40	7.17	24.6	0	0	
BAC Howell	43.2	0	351	15	4/15	23.40	8.10	17.3	1	0	
J Shaw	34.0	0	278	13	3/32	21.38	8.17	15.6	0	0	
DA Payne	36.0	1	318	12	3/30	26.50	8.83	18.0	0	0	
DJ Worrall	31.0	0	275	3	2/33	91.66	8.87	62.0	0	0	Bowling
GD Phillips	4.0	0	36	2	1/3	18.00	9.00	12.0	0	0	
MD Taylor	11.0	0	107	2	1/30	53.50	9.72	33.0	0	0	
RF Higgins	27.1	0	265	11	3/18	24.09	9.75	14.8	0	0	
GL van Buuren	7.0	0	70	2	1/15	35.00	10.00	21.0	0	0	
GFB Scott	0.2	0	5	0	-	-	15.00	-	0	0	

Catches/Stumpings:
8 Phillips (inc 1st), 6 Hammond, J Taylor, 4 Dent, 3 Bracey (inc 2st), Payne, 2 Higgins, Howell, Shaw, Smith, Worrall, 1 Cockbain, Scott, M Taylor

TEAM PROFILE

FORMED: 1863
HOME GROUND: The Ageas Bowl, Southampton
CAPTAIN: James Vince
2021 RESULTS: CC1: 4/6; RL50 6/9 Group A; T20: Semi-finalist
HONOURS: Championship: (2) 1961, 1973; Gillette/NatWest/C&G/FP Trophy: (3) 1991, 2005, 2009; Benson & Hedges Cup: (2) 1988, 1992; Pro40/National League/CB40/YB40/RL50: (2) 2012, 2018; Sunday League: (3) 1975, 1978, 1986; T20 Cup: (2) 2010, 2012

THE LOWDOWN

Could *this* be Hampshire's year? Such is the talent on the south coast that it's become a routine question before each summer. Victory against Lancashire at Aigburth last September would have secured their first Championship crown since 1973; they lost by one wicket. Defeat in the T20 semi-final only compounded the sense of a near miss. Once again, opposition batters will have to contend with Kyle Abbott and Mohammad Abbas taking the new ball, the latter available for at least the first two months of the season. Keith Barker – 41 wickets at 18 last summer – lies in wait as first change, with the ever-improving Brad Wheal completing the seam attack. Mason Crane and Liam Dawson offer versatile spin options. Recognising some holes in the batting, the club have let go of the inconsistent Sam Northeast and signed a pair of experienced run-getters in Nick Gubbins and Ben Brown. If they can support James Vince, if allrounder Ian Holland can continue to fire at the top of the order, well then who knows…

IN: Ben Brown (Sus), Nick Gubbins (Mid), Ross Whiteley (Wor), Mohammad Abbas (Pak, CC), Ben McDermott (Aus, T20)
OUT: Ajeet Dale (Glo), Sam Northeast (Gla), Tom Scriven (Lei), Ryan Stevenson, Brad Taylor (both RET)

FIRST-TEAM MANAGER: ADRIAN BIRRELL

The vastly experienced Birrell took over from Craig White in December 2018 and led Hampshire to the 50-over final in his first season. A former Eastern Province allrounder, Birrell made his name as coach of the Ireland team which had a famous victory over Pakistan in the 2007 World Cup. In 2010 he was put in charge of England U19 before beginning a four-year stint as South Africa's assistant coach. Ex-Warwickshire seamer Graeme Welch has replaced Alfonso Thomas as bowling coach.

Batting

	Mat	Inns	NO	Runs	HS	Ave	SR	100	50	4s	6s
C de Grandhomme	2	3	2	186	174*	186.00	82.30	1	0	19	3
JM Vince	13	20	0	816	231	40.80	58.87	1	4	126	5
IG Holland	14	24	1	766	146*	33.30	49.83	2	4	106	1
SA Northeast	8	13	2	358	118	32.54	50.35	1	2	44	0
NRT Gubbins	6	11	2	255	137*	28.33	50.79	1	1	33	1
KHD Barker	10	15	1	379	84	27.07	48.52	0	3	44	5
LD McManus	11	14	2	320	91	26.66	41.83	0	2	41	1
TP Alsop	14	24	2	564	149	25.63	40.57	2	0	80	0
LA Dawson	12	20	2	449	152*	24.94	56.76	1	1	50	8
FS Organ	6	10	0	213	67	21.30	38.24	0	1	23	3
JJ Weatherley	13	22	0	406	78	18.45	50.31	0	1	54	0
BTJ Wheal	13	16	6	181	46*	18.10	29.19	0	0	22	0
TJ Prest	2	1	0	18	18	18.00	28.57	0	0	3	0
KJ Abbott	11	12	3	148	58	16.44	35.15	0	1	20	0
MS Crane	6	7	1	92	28	15.33	23.52	0	0	9	0
CT Steel	1	2	0	29	15	14.50	40.27	0	0	4	0
JK Fuller	2	4	0	34	21	8.50	43.58	0	0	4	0
Mohammad Abbas	10	14	7	28	6	4.00	21.53	0	0	3	0
SW Currie	1	2	0	5	4	2.50	27.77	0	0	0	0

Bowling

	Overs	Mdns	Runs	Wkts	BBI	BBM	Ave	Econ	SR	5w	10w
C de Grandhomme	37.0	20	68	6	4/31	5/62	11.33	1.83	37.0	0	0
JK Fuller	17.0	4	37	3	2/22	2/22	12.33	2.17	34.0	0	0
Mohammad Abbas	309.5	113	651	41	6/11	9/39	15.87	2.10	45.3	3	0
KHD Barker	310.0	88	755	41	7/46	7/33	18.41	2.43	45.3	3	0
KJ Abbott	329.3	87	996	46	6/44	11/85	21.65	3.02	42.9	3	1
JJ Weatherley	9.0	2	22	1	1/22	1/22	22.00	2.44	54.0	0	0
MS Crane	195.5	39	587	23	5/41	6/151	25.52	2.99	51.0	1	0
FS Organ	73.0	20	205	8	3/22	3/23	25.62	2.80	54.7	0	0
BTJ Wheal	298.5	62	882	34	4/59	4/63	25.94	2.95	52.7	0	0
SW Currie	27.5	2	109	4	4/109	4/109	27.25	3.91	41.7	0	0
LA Dawson	257.0	55	624	18	5/45	5/53	34.66	2.42	85.6	1	0
IG Holland	147.1	35	433	6	3/19	3/23	72.16	2.94	147.1	0	0
JM Vince	13.0	1	85	1	1/55	1/55	85.00	6.53	78.0	0	0
TJ Prest	1.0	0	5	0	-	-	-	5.00	-	0	0

Catches/Stumpings:
29 McManus (inc 1st), 21 Weatherley, 17 Dawson, 14 Alsop, 13 Vince, 8 Holland, 6 Gubbins, Organ, 2 Abbas, Crane, de Grandhomme, Wheal, 1 Abbott, Barker, Currie, Prest

Hampshire
Cricket

		Mat	Inns	NO	Runs	HS	Ave	SR	100	50	4s	6s
Batting	NRT Gubbins	7	7	1	318	131*	53.00	99.06	1	2	26	7
	TP Alsop	6	6	0	238	68	39.66	78.54	0	3	24	0
	LD McManus	5	5	1	133	50	33.25	96.37	0	1	13	3
	TAR Scriven	5	3	1	63	42	31.50	77.77	0	0	1	1
	JK Fuller	7	6	1	125	54	25.00	113.63	0	1	9	7
	FS Organ	7	5	0	120	79	24.00	71.85	0	1	7	5
	JJ Weatherley	7	7	0	155	54	22.14	67.09	0	1	9	1
	FS Middleton	1	1	0	16	16	16.00	53.33	0	0	2	0
	TJ Prest	7	7	0	108	41	15.42	71.52	0	0	9	1
	KJ Abbott	7	4	2	29	9*	14.50	49.15	0	0	1	0
	IG Holland	7	7	2	65	30*	13.00	76.47	0	0	6	1
	SW Currie	5	4	2	17	8	8.50	65.38	0	0	1	0
	JA Turner	6	2	2	11	6*	-	39.28	0	0	1	0

		Overs	Mdns	Runs	Wkts	BBI	Ave	Econ	SR	4w	5w
Bowling	IG Holland	43.0	1	190	8	4/12	23.75	4.41	32.2	1	0
	TJ Prest	8.0	0	39	2	2/28	19.50	4.87	24.0	0	0
	FS Organ	37.2	1	186	3	2/43	62.00	4.98	74.6	0	0
	KJ Abbott	51.5	6	261	7	5/43	37.28	5.03	44.4	0	1
	NRT Gubbins	15.0	0	81	4	4/38	20.25	5.40	22.5	1	0
	JA Turner	36.0	2	195	7	3/44	27.85	5.41	30.8	0	0
	JK Fuller	32.0	0	188	4	1/25	47.00	5.87	48.0	0	0
	TAR Scriven	7.4	0	46	1	1/6	46.00	6.00	46.0	0	0
	SW Currie	18.3	0	132	6	3/58	22.00	7.13	18.5	0	0

Catches/Stumpings:
5 Currie, Weatherley, 3 McManus, Organ, 2 Alsop, Fuller, Holland, 1 Abbott, Gubbins, Prest, Turner

Batting

	Mat	Inns	NO	Runs	HS	Ave	SR	100	50	4s	6s
JJ Weatherley	13	13	2	410	71	37.27	141.86	0	2	23	20
JM Vince	12	12	0	373	102	31.08	135.63	1	1	50	6
DJM Short	12	12	0	316	69	26.33	138.59	0	1	38	12
TJ Prest	7	7	1	135	59*	22.50	115.38	0	1	11	3
C de Grandhomme	7	7	0	150	66	21.42	153.06	0	1	15	6
LD McManus	13	13	3	199	60*	19.90	140.14	0	1	11	9
JK Fuller	13	12	2	194	38	19.40	135.66	0	0	11	9
CP Wood	11	9	3	72	18	12.00	153.19	0	0	5	3
LA Dawson	9	7	0	83	23	11.85	112.16	0	0	5	3
TP Alsop	3	3	1	21	18	10.50	84.00	0	0	2	0
TE Albert	2	2	0	18	13	9.00	81.81	0	0	3	0
IG Holland	3	3	1	18	10	9.00	78.26	0	0	0	0
SA Northeast	1	1	0	6	6	6.00	50.00	0	0	0	0
BTJ Wheal	13	3	2	5	5*	5.00	125.00	0	0	1	0
SW Currie	9	5	3	5	3	2.50	45.45	0	0	0	0
MS Crane	13	5	5	14	6*	-	116.66	0	0	0	0
RA Stevenson	1	1	1	8	8*	-	400.00	0	0	0	1
KJ Abbott	1	-	-	-	-	-	-	-	-	-	-

Bowling

	Overs	Mdns	Runs	Wkts	BBI	Ave	Econ	SR	4w	5w
KJ Abbott	4.0	0	27	2	2/27	13.50	6.75	12.0	0	0
LA Dawson	35.0	0	249	10	3/24	24.90	7.11	21.0	0	0
MS Crane	49.0	0	382	16	3/23	23.87	7.79	18.3	0	0
BTJ Wheal	45.0	0	354	17	3/39	20.82	7.86	15.8	0	0
SW Currie	31.0	0	244	19	4/24	12.84	7.87	9.7	2	0
CP Wood	41.0	0	325	13	2/26	25.00	7.92	18.9	0	0
DJM Short	26.0	0	228	6	2/25	38.00	8.76	26.0	0	0
IG Holland	4.0	0	41	1	1/14	41.00	10.25	24.0	0	0
C de Grandhomme	10.0	0	106	2	2/41	53.00	10.60	30.0	0	0
RA Stevenson	3.0	0	35	0	-	-	11.66	-	0	0
JK Fuller	2.0	0	31	0	-	-	15.50	-	0	0

Catches/Stumpings:
18 McManus (inc 6st), 11 Vince, 9 Fuller, 5 Short, Wheal, 4 Prest, 3 Currie, de Grandhomme, 2 Crane, Holland, Stevenson, Weatherley, Wood, 1 Albert, Dawson

TEAM PROFILE

FORMED: 1870
HOME GROUND: The Spitfire Ground, St Lawrence, Canterbury
ONE-DAY NAME: Kent Spitfires
CAPTAIN: Sam Billings
2021 RESULTS: CC3: Winners; RL50: 9/9 Group A; T20: Winners
HONOURS: Championship: (7) 1906, 1909, 1910, 1913, 1970, 1977(s), 1978; Gillette/NatWest/C&G/FP Trophy: (2) 1967, 1974; Pro40/National League/CB40/RL50: 2001; Benson & Hedges Cup: (3) 1973, 1976, 1978; Sunday League: (4) 1972, 1973, 1976, 1995; T20 Cup (2): 2007, 2021

THE LOWDOWN

Kent lost seven and won none of their opening 10 Championship matches last summer… before surging to 12 wins in 17 matches across formats to take their second T20 title. Not content with another stunning season with the red ball (three hundreds plus 39 wickets at 18), 45-year-old Darren Stevens broke back into the T20 side for the first time in four years and played a winning hand on Finals Day. (Fear not, he has signed *another* one-year contract.) Buoyed by the T20 tonic, Kent then showed their four-day pedigree by storming to the Championship's Division Three title. It could not mask the shortage of runs in early season, despite the efforts of Jack Leaning and Ollie Robinson. The seamers fared better, Matt Milnes clocking up 100 wickets in three seasons since joining from Notts. Veteran Aussie pacer Jackson Bird is available for the first six Championship games before New Zealand's Matt Henry – 75 wickets in 11 matches for Kent in 2018 – takes over in July. South Africa allrounder George Linde, signed on a two-year deal, should address the lack of a red-ball spinner.

IN: Ben Compton (Not), Matt Quinn (Ess), George Linde (SA), Jackson Bird (Aus, CC), Matt Henry (NZ, CC/RL50), Qais Ahmad (Afg, T20)
OUT: Heino Kuhn (REL)

HEAD COACH: MATT WALKER

Walker scored nearly 20,000 runs for Kent and Essex between 1992 and 2011. He was assistant to Jimmy Adams before his promotion to head coach ahead of the 2017 season, having previously worked with Essex and England Lions. In 2018 Walker led Kent to Championship promotion and a Lord's one-day final before last summer's crowning glory in the T20 Blast. Former England wicketkeeper Paul Downton was appointed director of cricket in 2018. The retired Ryan ten Doeschate replaces Michael Yardy as batting coach.

Batting

	Mat	Inns	NO	Runs	HS	Ave	SR	100	50	4s	6s
HZ Finch	1	2	0	139	115	69.50	52.45	1	0	15	0
JA Leaning	13	21	5	745	127*	46.56	41.92	1	6	81	1
DI Stevens	12	18	3	650	190	43.33	80.84	3	2	75	25
OG Robinson	13	21	1	725	120	36.25	58.42	2	3	93	5
TS Muyeye	4	6	2	142	89	35.50	50.53	0	1	18	0
Hamidullah Qadri	1	2	1	34	30*	34.00	38.20	0	0	3	0
Z Crawley	12	21	2	637	90	33.52	55.48	0	6	93	0
SW Billings	4	5	0	149	72	29.80	64.78	0	1	25	1
JM Cox	13	23	2	579	90	27.57	46.02	0	4	69	3
DJ Bell-Drummond	10	17	1	419	114	26.18	56.54	1	2	56	3
ME Milnes	8	14	4	244	78	24.40	42.80	0	1	30	1
HW Podmore	5	6	1	107	37	21.40	49.76	0	0	10	2
DJ Lincoln	1	2	0	41	41	20.50	37.61	0	0	5	1
MK O'Riordan	7	7	0	140	47	20.00	46.51	0	0	22	0
G Stewart	6	9	2	134	40	19.14	49.08	0	0	18	1
JL Denly	9	14	0	246	63	17.57	50.82	0	1	26	1
MR Quinn	6	5	3	32	13*	16.00	58.18	0	0	1	2
ML Cummins	8	10	2	108	28*	13.50	45.76	0	0	15	3
HG Kuhn	4	8	0	108	32	13.50	40.90	0	0	11	1
JEG Logan	4	6	1	51	21	10.20	28.33	0	0	7	0
NN Gilchrist	9	8	1	52	13	7.42	30.23	0	0	6	0
HF Houillon	1	2	0	9	9	4.50	39.13	0	0	1	0
JA Gordon	1	2	0	8	8	4.00	40.00	0	0	1	0
FJ Klaassen	2	4	1	8	5	2.66	12.90	0	0	1	0
Jaskaran Singh	2	2	0	2	2	1.00	28.57	0	0	0	0
BJ Wightman	1	2	1	0	0*	0.00	0.00	0	0	0	0

Bowling

	Overs	Mdns	Runs	Wkts	BBI	BBM	Ave	Econ	SR	5w	10w
JEG Logan	47.1	11	119	8	3/8	5/47	14.87	2.52	35.3	0	0
DI Stevens	284.0	93	725	39	5/53	7/115	18.58	2.55	43.6	2	0
Jaskaran Singh	40.0	5	140	7	4/51	5/83	20.00	3.50	34.2	0	0
NN Gilchrist	160.1	26	620	30	5/38	8/74	20.66	3.87	32.0	1	0
ME Milnes	205.3	42	687	32	6/53	9/77	21.46	3.34	38.5	2	0
G Stewart	120.0	31	384	17	5/23	7/68	22.58	3.20	42.3	1	0
MR Quinn	149.3	34	413	18	4/54	4/54	22.94	2.76	49.8	0	0
DJ Bell-Drummond	19.0	3	70	3	3/47	3/47	23.33	3.68	38.0	0	0
HW Podmore	114.3	16	419	12	4/77	4/77	34.91	3.65	57.2	0	0
Hamidullah Qadri	17.0	2	44	1	1/20	1/44	44.00	2.58	102.0	0	0
FJ Klaassen	42.5	3	172	3	2/110	2/110	57.33	4.01	85.6	0	0
JA Leaning	103.5	12	356	6	2/101	2/101	59.33	3.42	103.8	0	0
JL Denly	89.2	12	274	4	2/61	2/88	68.50	3.06	134.0	0	0
MK O'Riordan	50.0	9	145	2	1/14	2/58	72.50	2.90	150.0	0	0
ML Cummins	162.2	19	622	6	2/100	2/100	103.66	3.83	162.3	0	0
JM Cox	1.0	0	3	0	-	-	-	3.00	-	0	0
BJ Wightman	12.0	4	23	0	-	-	-	1.91	-	0	0

Catches/Stumpings:
39 Robinson (inc 1st), 11 Leaning, 10 Cox, 9 Crawley, 6 Billings, 4 Kuhn, O'Riordan, Stevens, 3 Houillon, 2 Bell-Drummond, Gilchrist, Milnes, 1 Cummins, Lincoln, Logan, Singh

Batting

	Mat	Inns	NO	Runs	HS	Ave	SR	100	50	4s	6s
Hamidullah Qadri	5	4	3	103	42*	103.00	85.83	0	0	9	0
HG Munsey	7	5	0	302	108	60.40	95.87	1	2	41	4
MK O'Riordan	5	4	1	119	60	39.66	85.61	0	1	10	1
HZ Finch	8	7	1	152	84	25.33	77.55	0	2	15	1
ME Milnes	4	2	1	24	14*	24.00	68.57	0	0	1	0
TS Muyeye	8	7	1	140	30	23.33	99.29	0	0	19	3
JEG Logan	6	4	2	46	17*	23.00	69.69	0	0	3	0
OG Robinson	8	7	0	155	75	22.14	74.51	0	1	14	0
JA Leaning	4	3	0	62	35	20.66	86.11	0	0	5	1
DI Stevens	7	5	0	80	40	16.00	78.43	0	0	9	1
HG Kuhn	4	2	0	25	19	12.50	96.15	0	0	5	0
HW Podmore	3	3	0	29	19	9.66	80.55	0	0	2	0
JA Gordon	1	1	0	9	9	9.00	47.36	0	0	0	0
G Stewart	7	5	0	35	9	7.00	52.23	0	0	1	1
NN Gilchrist	6	4	1	19	8	6.33	86.36	0	0	3	0
MR Quinn	5	3	2	4	3*	4.00	36.36	0	0	0	0

Bowling

	Overs	Mdns	Runs	Wkts	BBI	Ave	Econ	SR	4w	5w
TS Muyeye	6.0	0	16	0	-	-	2.66	-	0	0
DI Stevens	37.0	1	173	2	1/29	86.50	4.67	111.0	0	0
JA Leaning	7.0	0	41	1	1/41	41.00	5.85	42.0	0	0
G Stewart	34.5	1	210	3	1/26	70.00	6.02	69.6	0	0
JEG Logan	33.0	0	207	3	2/45	69.00	6.27	66.0	0	0
Hamidullah Qadri	24.0	0	152	4	3/47	38.00	6.33	36.0	0	0
ME Milnes	24.0	0	153	3	1/29	51.00	6.37	48.0	0	0
MR Quinn	35.0	1	246	6	2/28	41.00	7.02	35.0	0	0
NN Gilchrist	25.3	0	181	8	5/45	22.62	7.09	19.1	0	1
MK O'Riordan	21.0	0	157	1	1/77	157.00	7.47	126.0	0	0
HW Podmore	15.2	0	120	2	2/26	60.00	7.82	46.0	0	0

Catches/Stumpings:
4 Robinson, 3 Quinn, 2 Finch, Leaning, O'Riordan, Stevens, 1 Kuhn, Milnes, Munsey, Muyeye, Qadri, Stewart

www.kentcricket.co.uk / tel: 01227 456 886

VITALITY BLAST AVERAGES 2021

	Mat	Inns	NO	Runs	HS	Ave	SR	100	50	4s	6s
JM Cox	14	12	5	367	64	52.42	142.24	0	3	25	10
HZ Finch	2	2	0	77	47	38.50	116.66	0	0	10	0
DJ Bell-Drummond	14	14	1	492	88	37.84	155.69	0	6	38	20
OG Robinson	4	4	1	103	48	34.33	139.18	0	0	13	1
Z Crawley	12	12	0	380	69	31.66	150.79	0	1	39	14
JA Leaning	14	13	2	321	81*	29.18	131.02	0	3	20	13
SW Billings	5	5	0	116	56	23.20	114.85	0	1	11	3
HG Kuhn	2	2	0	46	42	23.00	109.52	0	0	4	0
DI Stevens	13	10	3	153	47*	21.85	142.99	0	0	16	5
CS MacLeod	2	2	0	38	31	19.00	115.15	0	0	3	1
JL Denly	14	14	0	213	44	15.21	118.33	0	0	19	7
MK O'Riordan	2	2	1	15	13*	15.00	93.75	0	0	1	0
HG Munsey	2	2	0	21	11	10.50	140.00	0	0	3	1
AJ Blake	10	9	2	72	19	10.28	112.50	0	0	7	2
AF Milne	4	2	1	9	8*	9.00	180.00	0	0	0	1
ME Milnes	14	5	3	17	13*	8.50	212.50	0	0	2	1
G Stewart	10	8	3	35	15	7.00	112.90	0	0	4	0
FJ Klaassen	14	1	0	6	6	6.00	100.00	0	0	0	0
Qais Ahmad	12	8	4	22	7	5.50	95.65	0	0	1	0

	Overs	Mdns	Runs	Wkts	BBI	Ave	Econ	SR	4w	5w
JEG Logan	4.0	0	18	2	1/4	9.00	4.50	12.0	0	0
SM Sharif	5.1	0	26	2	2/10	13.00	5.03	15.5	0	0
MK O'Riordan	8.0	0	42	3	2/24	14.00	5.25	16.0	0	0
EO Hooper	8.0	0	47	4	3/24	11.75	5.87	12.0	0	0
Qais Ahmad	43.0	0	286	10	2/13	28.60	6.65	25.8	0	0
JA Leaning	12.0	0	80	7	3/15	11.42	6.66	10.2	0	0
HW Podmore	7.0	0	47	5	3/35	9.40	6.71	8.4	0	0
JL Denly	32.4	0	239	11	3/31	21.72	7.31	17.8	0	0
AF Milne	15.0	0	116	7	4/38	16.57	7.73	12.8	1	0
MR Quinn	5.3	0	44	2	2/13	22.00	8.00	16.5	0	0
ME Milnes	42.2	0	339	22	5/22	15.40	8.00	11.5	1	1
FJ Klaassen	43.1	0	373	19	4/17	19.63	8.64	13.6	2	0
DI Stevens	32.0	0	288	11	3/32	26.18	9.00	17.4	0	0
G Stewart	25.2	0	248	9	3/33	27.55	9.78	16.8	0	0

Catches/Stumpings:
12 Blake, Leaning, 10 Cox, 8 Denly, 6 Bell-Drummond, Milnes, 5 Billings (inc 2st), Cox (inc 2st), Klaassen, 4 Crawley, 3 Ahmad, Robinson 2 Finch, Kuhn, Munsey, 1 Logan, MacLeod, O'Riordan, Quinn, Stewart

Lancashire County Cricket Club

FORMED: 1864
HOME GROUND: Emirates Old Trafford, Manchester
ONE-DAY NAME: Lancashire Lightning
CAPTAIN: Dane Vilas
2021 RESULTS: CC1: Runners-up; RL50: 4/9
Group A; T20: Quarter-finalists
HONOURS: Championship: (9) 1897, 1904, 1926, 1927, 1928, 1930, 1934, 1950(s), 2011; Gillette/NatWest/C&G/FP Trophy: (7) 1970, 1971, 1972, 1985, 1990, 1996, 1998; Benson & Hedges Cup: (4) 1984, 1990, 1995, 1996; Pro40/National League/CB40/YB40/RL50: 1999; Sunday League: (4) 1969, 1970, 1989, 1998; T20 Cup: 2015

THE LOWDOWN

On September 23 there was euphoria at Aigburth after a one-wicket victory against Hampshire put Lancashire top of Division One; less than 24 hours later Warwickshire motored to victory to steal the title. When they had dusted off their disappointment, the club could reflect on a fine season in which they also made the T20 quarter-finals. Seven batters made Championship hundreds, easing the burden on captain Dane Vilas, with Josh Bohannon a model of consistency. The seam attack was carried by the underrated Tom Bailey (50 wickets at 16) and looked short of depth when Saqib Mahmood was on international duty. Pakistan seamer Hassan Ali has signed up for the first six matches of 2022, and county batters will be quaking in their boots if England don't recall James Anderson. Lancashire's trump card is their match-winning spinner, Matt Parkinson, although he too may be needed by England. Phil Salt has arrived from Sussex as a direct replacement for Alex Davies. Known as a big hitter, Salt did not see a red ball last summer but says he wants to show his first-class credentials. Singapore allrounder Tim David has signed for the T20 campaign after impressing at Surrey in 2021.

IN: Phil Salt (Sus), Hassan Ali (Pak, CC), Tim David (Singapore, T20)
OUT: Alex Davies (War), George Burrows, Ed Moulton, Owais Shah (all REL)

HEAD COACH: GLEN CHAPPLE

Chapple took 1,373 wickets in 664 appearances during a 23-year career at Old Trafford and captained the side to the Championship title in 2011. The former seamer took over from Ashley Giles in January 2017, leading the club to a runners-up spot in his first season in charge and coming within a whisker of the title last summer. Ex-captain Mark Chilton has replaced Paul Allott as director of cricket, with former Leicestershire spinner Carl Crowe becoming assistant coach. Crowe has coached in the IPL and Australia's Big Bash.

	Mat	Inns	NO	Runs	HS	Ave	SR	100	50	4s	6s
JJ Bohannon	14	18	2	853	170	53.31	47.65	2	5	101	7
KK Jennings	10	13	1	577	132	48.08	42.89	2	3	57	1
LWP Wells	12	16	2	572	103	40.85	45.57	1	3	87	3
AL Davies	13	19	2	652	84	38.35	58.63	0	6	82	5
DJ Vilas	14	16	1	559	189	37.26	62.80	1	2	56	4
L Wood	9	11	1	357	119	35.70	53.84	1	1	41	2
SJ Croft	10	12	2	327	103*	32.70	49.84	1	1	34	2
MW Parkinson	11	10	8	59	21*	29.50	52.67	0	0	7	0
DJ Lamb	11	14	1	365	125	28.07	42.05	1	2	40	1
GP Balderson	5	7	1	145	77	24.16	33.95	0	1	24	0
TE Bailey	12	14	0	306	63	21.85	57.30	0	2	38	3
TW Hartley	3	4	1	61	25	20.33	33.88	0	0	3	0
RP Jones	8	9	0	180	58	20.00	45.11	0	1	21	0
GID Lavelle	2	3	0	36	32	12.00	69.23	0	0	6	0
LS Livingstone	6	7	0	77	25	11.00	58.33	0	0	9	2
S Mahmood	8	11	4	73	20	10.42	32.15	0	0	8	0
JM Blatherwick	3	3	0	6	4	2.00	10.52	0	0	0	0
JM Anderson	4	2	2	13	8*	-	59.09	0	0	2	0

Batting

	Overs	Mdns	Runs	Wkts	BBI	BBM	Ave	Econ	SR	5w	10w
RP Jones	3.0	0	7	1	1/4	1/4	7.00	2.33	18.0	0	0
JM Anderson	46.0	19	83	11	7/19	8/43	7.54	1.80	25.0	1	0
LWP Wells	46.0	10	109	7	3/8	3/8	15.57	2.36	39.4	0	0
TE Bailey	340.0	108	843	50	7/37	9/61	16.86	2.47	40.8	1	0
MW Parkinson	321.2	87	740	36	7/126	9/164	20.55	2.30	53.5	1	0
S Mahmood	233.1	52	669	28	5/47	6/96	23.89	2.86	49.9	1	0
JM Blatherwick	40.1	8	156	6	4/28	6/95	26.00	3.88	40.1	0	0
GP Balderson	128.5	28	344	12	3/21	5/70	28.66	2.67	64.4	0	0
JJ Bohannon	31.1	5	94	3	1/11	2/38	31.33	3.01	62.3	0	0
L Wood	189.0	30	596	18	3/31	4/73	33.11	3.15	63.0	0	0
DJ Lamb	280.5	67	780	23	4/60	5/98	33.91	2.77	73.2	0	0
TW Hartley	83.0	32	143	4	4/42	4/42	35.75	1.72	124.5	0	0
LS Livingstone	91.0	17	248	4	2/34	3/97	62.00	2.72	136.5	0	0
DJ Vilas	1.0	0	6	0	-	-	-	6.00	-	0	0
SJ Croft	22.0	3	77	0	-	-	-	3.50	-	0	0

Bowling

Catches/Stumpings:
20 Davies (inc 3st), 16 Vilas, Wells, 11 Jones, 8 Croft, Jennings, 7 Bohannon, 5 Lamb, Lavelle, Livingstone, 4 Vilas, 3 Wood, 2 Hartley, Mahmood, 1 Anderson, Bailey, Blatherwick, Parkinson

Batting

	Mat	Inns	NO	Runs	HS	Ave	SR	100	50	4s	6s
DJ Lamb	7	4	1	147	86*	49.00	133.63	0	1	10	8
SJ Croft	7	5	1	183	93	45.75	73.79	0	1	10	4
KK Jennings	5	5	2	133	47	44.33	57.57	0	0	12	0
RP Jones	7	6	1	220	72	44.00	67.48	0	2	17	2
LWP Wells	7	6	1	158	66*	31.60	77.07	0	1	25	0
DJ Vilas	1	1	0	31	31	31.00	114.81	0	0	4	0
JJ Bohannon	7	7	1	163	52	27.16	69.65	0	1	16	3
GID Lavelle	7	4	0	100	52	25.00	96.15	0	1	5	6
GP Balderson	6	4	2	46	19	23.00	71.87	0	0	2	2
TE Bailey	7	3	0	61	45	20.33	88.40	0	0	2	3
LJ Hurt	7	3	1	15	14*	7.50	100.00	0	0	1	0
JP Morley	7	2	1	6	6	6.00	54.54	0	0	1	0
TR Cornall	2	2	2	30	23*	-	130.43	0	0	1	2

Bowling

	Overs	Mdns	Runs	Wkts	BBI	Ave	Econ	SR	4w	5w
KK Jennings	16.0	0	56	0	-	-	3.50	-	0	0
TE Bailey	56.0	6	207	10	3/23	20.70	3.69	33.6	0	0
JP Morley	56.0	2	224	9	2/22	24.88	4.00	37.3	0	0
GP Balderson	27.0	0	136	5	3/25	27.20	5.03	32.4	0	0
LWP Wells	25.0	0	132	4	2/33	33.00	5.28	37.5	0	0
DJ Lamb	52.4	3	298	10	5/30	29.80	5.65	31.6	0	1
LJ Hurt	45.0	0	268	8	3/55	33.50	5.95	33.7	0	0
SJ Croft	13.0	0	81	2	2/57	40.50	6.23	39.0	0	0

Catches/Stumpings:
7 Lavelle (inc 1st), 6 Croft, 5 Lamb, 3 Hurt, Wells, 2 Cornall, Morley, Vilas, 1 Balderson, Bohannon, Jones

VITALITY BLAST AVERAGES 2021

	Mat	Inns	NO	Runs	HS	Ave	SR	100	50	4s	6s
LS Livingstone	6	6	1	279	94*	55.80	147.61	0	2	24	13
RP Jones	9	7	4	161	61*	53.66	127.77	0	1	12	3
KK Jennings	8	8	1	298	88	42.57	126.80	0	2	23	8
JJ Bohannon	1	1	0	35	35	35.00	175.00	0	0	6	0
SJ Croft	14	12	5	240	41	34.28	120.00	0	0	14	6
FH Allen	13	13	1	399	73*	33.25	159.60	0	4	43	15
JC Buttler	5	5	0	127	55	25.40	123.30	0	1	9	4
DJ Vilas	14	14	3	221	42	20.09	122.77	0	0	12	6
AL Davies	14	14	1	260	83*	20.00	128.71	0	2	23	10
L Wood	13	6	3	49	33*	16.33	111.36	0	0	3	1
LWP Wells	7	5	1	48	30	12.00	94.11	0	0	2	1
DJ Lamb	12	6	2	47	20	11.75	162.06	0	0	6	1
TW Hartley	14	5	3	16	7*	8.00	106.66	0	0	1	0
TE Bailey	5	2	0	3	3	1.50	50.00	0	0	0	0
RJ Gleeson	2	1	1	0	0*	-	0.00	0	0	0	0
LJ Hurt	3	-	-	-	-	-	-	-	-	-	-
S Mahmood	4	-	-	-	-	-	-	-	-	-	-
MW Parkinson	10	-	-	-	-	-	-	-	-	-	-

	Overs	Mdns	Runs	Wkts	BBI	Ave	Econ	SR	4w	5w
TW Hartley	51.0	0	338	12	4/16	28.16	6.62	25.5	1	0
SJ Croft	21.0	0	149	5	1/7	29.80	7.09	25.2	0	0
LWP Wells	16.0	0	118	3	1/15	39.33	7.37	32.0	0	0
LS Livingstone	23.0	0	174	3	1/22	58.00	7.56	46.0	0	0
L Wood	44.0	0	365	13	4/20	28.07	8.29	20.3	1	0
LJ Hurt	9.0	0	75	4	3/22	18.75	8.33	13.5	0	0
MW Parkinson	36.0	0	303	13	3/28	23.30	8.41	16.6	0	0
S Mahmood	14.5	1	126	8	4/25	15.75	8.49	11.1	1	0
DJ Lamb	39.0	0	333	11	3/23	30.27	8.53	21.2	0	0
RP Jones	1.0	0	10	0	-	-	10.00	-	0	0
TE Bailey	11.0	0	128	4	3/34	32.00	11.63	16.5	0	0
RJ Gleeson	4.1	0	58	0	-	-	13.92	-	0	0

Catches/Stumpings:
9 Croft, 6 Davies, 5 Hartley, Vilas (inc 1st), Wood, 4 Allen, Jennings, Wells, 2 Buttler (inc 1st), Jones, Lamb, Livingstone, 1 Bailey, Gleeson, Hurt, Mahmood, Parkinson

LEICESTERSHIRE

TEAM PROFILE

LEICESTERSHIRE COUNTY CRICKET CLUB
ESTABLISHED 1879

FORMED: 1879
HOME GROUND: Uptonsteel County Ground, Leicester
ONE-DAY NAME: Leicestershire Foxes
CAPTAIN: Colin Ackermann
2021 RESULTS: CC3: 4/6; RL50: 4/9 Group B; T20: 6/9 North Group
HONOURS: Championship: (3) 1975, 1996, 1998; Benson & Hedges Cup: (3) 1972, 1975, 1985; Sunday League: (2) 1974, 1977; T20 Cup: (3) 2004, 2006, 2011

THE LOWDOWN

Last summer was another tough one for the Foxes but the team is beginning to have a settled look as Paul Nixon enters his fifth year as head coach. Lewis Hill and Harry Swindells, both Academy graduates, averaged over 40 in first-class cricket for the first time, while the seam/spin duo of Chris Wright and Callum Parkinson shared 99 Championship wickets. Wright aside, the rest of the pace attack often struggled, hence the winter signings of South African Test pace pair Wiaan Mulder and Beuran Hendricks. Mulder, an allrounder whose deal to play for the Foxes last summer was binned because of international duties, will be available in the four-day and 50-over formats. Hendricks, a left-armer who has played one Test, is due to appear in all competitions. The club were sorry to lose Aussie opener Marcus Harris, who turned down a new deal and signed for Gloucestershire. But their T20 campaign will be spiced up by the return of Afghan quick Naveen-ul-Haq – leading wicket-taker in the Blast last summer – and the arrival of his big-hitting compatriot Rahmanullah Gurbaz.

IN: Tom Scriven (Ham), Roman Walker (Gla), Beuran Hendricks (SA), Wiaan Mulder (SA, CC/RL50), Rahmanullah Gurbaz, Naveen-ul-Haq (both Afg, T20)
OUT: Harry Dearden, Dieter Klein (both REL)

HEAD COACH: PAUL NIXON

Nixon was appointed in October 2017 to replace Pierre de Bruyn, who had resigned after less than a season as head coach. A former England wicketkeeper who won two Championship titles with the club, Nixon retired in 2011 after inspiring Leicestershire to a stunning T20 triumph at the age of 40. He won the Caribbean Premier League twice as coach of Jamaica Tallawahs and has also worked in the Bangladesh Premier League. Former South Africa and Leicestershire spinner Claude Henderson has become the club's first director of cricket.

	Mat	Inns	NO	Runs	HS	Ave	SR	100	50	4s	6s
MS Harris	8	13	1	655	185	54.58	53.95	3	1	85	1
GH Rhodes	3	4	0	208	90	52.00	44.82	0	2	30	1
LJ Hill	14	22	1	944	145	44.95	59.48	3	5	117	5
HJ Swindells	13	19	3	693	171*	43.31	54.65	2	3	89	3
JP Inglis	2	3	0	128	52	42.66	52.89	0	1	16	0
CN Ackermann	10	15	1	485	126*	34.64	41.52	1	3	63	1
ST Evans	11	18	0	591	138	32.83	38.27	3	1	71	0
E Barnes	10	12	4	259	83*	32.37	55.46	0	2	39	1
LPJ Kimber	4	6	1	151	71	30.20	59.68	0	2	19	3
Hassan Azad	12	20	2	518	152	28.77	41.87	2	1	63	0
BWM Mike	13	19	1	495	74	27.50	52.16	0	4	64	6
HE Dearden	3	6	0	126	62	21.00	54.78	0	1	21	0
RK Patel	5	7	0	143	44	20.42	53.15	0	0	24	1
CJC Wright	12	16	2	257	87	18.35	53.76	0	1	35	3
CF Parkinson	13	18	2	253	41	15.81	34.32	0	0	24	0
GT Griffiths	5	6	3	44	16	14.66	44.44	0	0	7	0
WS Davis	6	7	3	54	42	13.50	65.06	0	0	8	1
A Sakande	3	4	2	23	9	11.50	65.71	0	0	3	0
HA Evans	4	6	2	29	12	7.25	40.27	0	0	3	0
D Klein	3	4	0	12	12	3.00	41.37	0	0	1	0
SD Bates	1	2	0	6	6	3.00	25.00	0	0	1	0

Batting

	Overs	Mdns	Runs	Wkts	BBI	BBM	Ave	Econ	SR	5w	10w
CJC Wright	351.0	74	1116	49	7/53	7/117	22.77	3.17	42.9	4	0
WS Davis	157.4	32	416	15	5/66	8/87	27.73	2.63	63.0	1	0
CF Parkinson	479.4	122	1452	50	5/45	10/108	29.04	3.02	57.5	3	1
CN Ackermann	96.0	22	324	9	3/44	6/99	36.00	3.37	64.0	0	0
E Barnes	204.2	30	724	18	4/61	4/61	40.22	3.54	68.1	0	0
BWM Mike	256.0	40	1002	23	4/34	5/89	43.56	3.91	66.7	0	0
A Sakande	89.2	14	309	7	3/66	3/66	44.14	3.45	76.5	0	0
GT Griffiths	92.0	8	388	7	3/93	3/93	55.42	4.21	78.8	0	0
D Klein	53.5	5	254	4	2/74	2/92	63.50	4.71	80.7	0	0
HA Evans	79.0	8	297	4	2/50	2/50	74.25	3.75	118.5	0	0
HE Dearden	0.5	0	8	0	-	-	-	9.60	-	0	0
LPJ Kimber	3.0	1	15	0	-	-	-	5.00	-	0	0
LJ Hill	4.0	0	22	0	-	-	-	5.50	-	0	0
GH Rhodes	32.0	2	97	0	-	-	-	3.03	-	0	0

Bowling

Catches/Stumpings:
28 Swindells (inc 1st), 20 Ackermann, 7 Harris, 6 Kimber, 4 Azad, Barnes, Inglis, Patel, 3 Bates (inc 1st), Davis, Evans, Hill, 2 Mike, Parkinson, Rhodes, Sakande, Wright, 1 Dearden

Batting

	Mat	Inns	NO	Runs	HS	Ave	SR	100	50	4s	6s
MS Harris	4	4	0	232	127	58.00	86.56	1	1	24	2
LJ Hill	8	7	0	322	108	46.00	94.42	2	1	29	3
RK Patel	8	8	1	319	118	45.57	95.50	1	1	38	4
Rehan Ahmed	7	6	4	89	40*	44.50	66.41	0	0	4	1
HJ Swindells	6	6	1	179	75	35.80	82.11	0	2	18	1
LPJ Kimber	8	6	0	197	85	32.83	104.78	0	2	12	7
NR Welch	1	1	0	32	32	32.00	74.41	0	0	4	0
WS Davis	4	2	1	30	15*	30.00	81.08	0	0	1	0
AM Lilley	8	7	1	162	46	27.00	137.28	0	0	19	5
E Barnes	8	4	2	53	33*	26.50	74.64	0	0	0	1
BWM Mike	6	5	1	79	34	19.75	58.95	0	0	3	2
D Klein	3	2	1	17	12	17.00	141.66	0	0	2	0
GH Rhodes	8	7	1	78	39*	13.00	79.59	0	0	8	1
CJC Wright	4	2	1	8	6*	8.00	80.00	0	0	0	0
GT Griffiths	4	2	0	10	8	5.00	55.55	0	0	1	0
ST Evans	1	-	-	-	-	-	-	-	-	-	-

Bowling

	Overs	Mdns	Runs	Wkts	BBi	Ave	Econ	SR	4w	5w
GH Rhodes	50.0	0	247	7	3/44	35.28	4.94	42.8	0	0
AM Lilley	34.0	0	185	4	3/49	46.25	5.44	51.0	0	0
Rehan Ahmed	55.2	2	318	5	2/25	63.60	5.74	66.4	0	0
E Barnes	59.5	1	346	9	2/34	38.44	5.78	39.8	0	0
GT Griffiths	33.0	0	197	4	2/34	49.25	5.96	49.5	0	0
D Klein	30.0	0	184	4	2/62	46.00	6.13	45.0	0	0
WS Davis	29.0	2	183	6	2/40	30.50	6.31	29.0	0	0
BWM Mike	34.5	1	231	9	3/34	25.66	6.63	23.2	0	0
CJC Wright	29.0	2	207	2	1/45	103.50	7.13	87.0	0	0

Catches/Stumpings:
10 Swindells (inc 2st), 8 Rhodes, 5 Patel, 4 Lilley, 3 Hill, 1 Barnes, Harris, Kimber, Klein, Mike, Welch

VITALITY BLAST AVERAGES 2021

	Mat	Inns	NO	Runs	HS	Ave	SR	100	50	4s	6s	
JP Inglis	14	14	3	531	118*	48.27	175.82	2	1	63	24	
HJ Swindells	5	4	1	95	36	31.66	121.79	0	0	3	3	
S Steel	12	12	1	304	54*	27.63	108.96	0	2	22	7	
AM Lilley	14	14	1	351	99*	27.00	148.72	0	1	32	18	
CN Ackermann	14	13	2	263	40	23.90	139.89	0	0	25	6	
BWM Mike	14	10	4	130	31	21.66	147.72	0	0	9	5	Batting
LJ Hill	14	11	1	191	59	19.10	129.05	0	1	15	7	
LPJ Kimber	9	6	0	102	53	17.00	137.83	0	1	5	5	
RK Patel	14	12	1	175	35	15.90	127.73	0	0	14	7	
CF Parkinson	14	8	3	40	14*	8.00	129.03	0	0	4	0	
GT Griffiths	13	5	3	15	12	7.50	136.36	0	0	1	1	
E Barnes	1	1	0	7	7	7.00	116.66	0	0	1	0	
Naveen-ul-Haq	14	7	3	23	8*	5.75	153.33	0	0	3	1	
WS Davis	2	1	0	0	0	0.00	0.00	0	0	0	0	

	Overs	Mdns	Runs	Wkts	BBI	Ave	Econ	SR	4w	5w	
S Steel	25.2	0	167	5	2/17	33.40	6.59	30.4	0	0	
CF Parkinson	56.0	1	421	18	4/35	23.38	7.51	18.6	1	0	
AM Lilley	25.0	0	205	6	3/26	34.16	8.20	25.0	0	0	Bowling
CN Ackermann	47.5	0	399	12	3/35	33.25	8.34	23.9	0	0	
Naveen-ul-Haq	52.4	0	457	26	3/26	17.57	8.67	12.1	0	0	
GT Griffiths	38.4	1	406	14	4/24	29.00	10.50	16.5	1	0	
E Barnes	3.0	0	34	0	-	-	11.33	-	0	0	
WS Davis	4.0	0	46	0	-	-	11.50	-	0	0	
BWM Mike	14.5	0	186	7	4/22	26.57	12.53	12.7	1	0	

Catches/Stumpings:
13 Lilley, 8 Inglis (inc 2st), 7 Ackermann, Mike, Patel, 6 Hill, Kimber, 4 Parkinson, 3 Griffiths,
Naveen-ul-Haq, 1 Barnes, Davis

MIDDLESEX CRICKET

FORMED: 1864
HOME GROUND: Lord's Cricket Ground, London
CAPTAIN: Peter Handscomb (CC/RL50), Eoin Morgan (T20)
2021 RESULTS: CC3: 2/6; RL50: 8/9 Group A; T20: 8/9 South Group
HONOURS: Championship: (13) 1903, 1920, 1921, 1947, 1949(s), 1976, 1977(s), 1980, 1982, 1985, 1990, 1993, 2016; Gillette/NatWest/C&G/FP Trophy: (4) 1977, 1980, 1984, 1998; Benson & Hedges Cup: (2) 1983, 1986; Sunday League: 1992; T20 Cup: 2008

THE LOWDOWN

Middlesex have gone back to the future by appointing their former seamer and bowling guru Richard Johnson as head coach and club legend Mark Ramprakash as consultant batting coach. Stuart Law's three-year reign was brought to an end last October after another underwhelming season across all formats. It's never easy when the captain comes and goes, thus Tim Murtagh has been made 'club captain' for 2022 and will stand in for Peter Handscomb when needed. Despite the gloomy results there were plenty of bright spots: Sam Robson looks to have recovered the form which brought him seven Test caps in 2014, there was a late-summer cameo by Mark Stoneman, poached from Surrey last August, and young leg-spinning allrounder Luke Hollman took a 10-wicket match haul in his fourth Championship game. The 40-year-old Murtagh marches on (196 wickets at 16.03 since 2018), the 23-year-old Ethan Bamber continues to rise (52 scalps at 21 last summer), and Pakistan left-armer Shaheen Shah Afridi – the 2021 ICC Player of the Year – has been signed until mid-July. If they can keep Toby Roland-Jones fit – an almighty 'if' – Middlesex will be strong contenders for Championship promotion.

IN: Mark Stoneman (Sur), Shaheen Shah Afridi (Pak, CC/T20), Mujeeb Ur Rahman (Afg, T20)
OUT: Steven Finn (Sus), Nick Gubbins (Ham), James Harris (Gla)

FIRST-TEAM COACH: RICHARD JOHNSON

Appointed to replace Stuart Law in January, Johnson returns to the county he has been connected with from the age of 10. The ex-seamer, who played three Tests and 10 ODIs, represented the club between 1992 and 2000 before finishing his career at Somerset. He was Middlesex bowling coach for seven years from 2011, part of the backroom staff that helped the club win the Championship in 2016. Johnson briefly took charge after the departure of Richard Scott in 2018 before working as Surrey's assistant coach for the past three seasons.

	Mat	Inns	NO	Runs	HS	Ave	SR	100	50	4s	6s
MD Stoneman	4	7	0	354	174	50.57	57.46	2	1	47	2
SD Robson	14	27	1	1047	253	40.26	52.74	3	2	139	1
RG White	14	26	4	765	120	34.77	43.09	2	4	87	0
NRT Gubbins	8	15	0	514	124	34.26	52.77	1	4	62	3
DJ Mitchell	2	4	0	134	73	33.50	34.27	0	1	11	2
SS Eskinazi	9	17	2	453	102	30.20	37.81	1	2	61	1
JA Simpson	13	22	2	535	95*	26.75	47.51	0	3	73	1
LBK Hollman	6	9	1	176	46	22.00	39.19	0	0	24	2
MK Andersson	13	24	0	439	88	18.29	60.05	0	2	58	4
MDE Holden	10	19	1	325	52	18.05	45.71	0	1	42	1
TN Walallawita	4	6	3	54	20*	18.00	93.10	0	0	7	2
PSP Handscomb	7	13	0	227	70	17.46	44.77	0	1	32	0
TS Roland-Jones	6	11	2	138	46*	15.33	47.58	0	0	18	1
BC Cullen	4	5	0	55	27	11.00	34.37	0	0	4	0
JB Cracknell	1	2	0	20	13	10.00	40.81	0	0	2	0
NA Sowter	3	6	1	46	24*	9.20	42.20	0	0	5	0
JAR Harris	3	6	0	55	26	9.16	31.42	0	0	9	0
JLB Davies	2	4	0	35	24	8.75	29.66	0	0	4	0
ER Bamber	12	22	4	151	25	8.38	40.37	0	0	21	0
TG Helm	4	8	2	49	17	8.16	35.50	0	0	7	0
JM De Caires	2	4	0	28	17	7.00	26.66	0	0	1	0
TJ Murtagh	12	20	7	88	31	6.76	60.27	0	0	13	0
ST Finn	2	4	1	17	13*	5.66	22.66	0	0	1	0

Batting

	Overs	Mdns	Runs	Wkts	BBI	BBM	Ave	Econ	SR	5w	10w
DJ Mitchell	44.0	8	142	9	4/42	6/74	15.77	3.22	29.3	0	0
TS Roland-Jones	167.4	38	460	25	5/36	7/70	18.40	2.74	40.2	1	0
TJ Murtagh	402.4	113	1079	58	5/64	7/85	18.60	2.67	41.6	1	0
ER Bamber	407.0	111	1084	52	5/41	7/80	20.84	2.66	46.9	1	0
ST Finn	68.2	4	266	12	5/77	6/123	22.16	3.89	34.1	1	0
JAR Harris	65.3	3	230	10	3/50	5/100	23.00	3.51	39.3	0	0
LBK Hollman	105.4	16	363	13	5/65	10/155	27.92	3.43	48.7	2	1
MK Andersson	250.1	41	916	29	4/27	5/130	31.58	3.66	51.7	0	0
SD Robson	17.0	0	72	2	1/8	2/27	36.00	4.23	51.0	0	0
BC Cullen	109.2	19	393	10	3/30	4/114	39.30	3.59	65.6	0	0
TG Helm	131.1	21	413	8	3/47	3/104	51.62	3.14	98.3	0	0
TN Walallawita	102.2	20	326	3	2/84	2/106	108.66	3.18	204.6	0	0
NA Sowter	68.0	7	237	2	1/15	1/42	118.50	3.48	204.0	0	0
NRT Gubbins	1.0	0	2	0	-	-	-	2.00	-	0	0
JM De Caires	3.0	0	7	0	-	-	-	2.33	-	0	0
MDE Holden	1.0	0	8	0	-	-	-	8.00	-	0	0

Bowling

Catches/Stumpings:
53 Simpson (inc 3st), 16 Robson, 19 White, 8 Eskinazi, 6 Andersson, Holden, 3 Handscomb, Hollman, Murtagh, Sowter, 2 Bamber, Cracknell, Walallawita, 1 Davies, de Caires, Gubbins, Harris, Helm

MIDDLESEX CRICKET

Batting

	Mat	Inns	NO	Runs	HS	Ave	SR	100	50	4s	6s
MK Andersson	4	4	3	133	44*	133.00	147.77	0	0	9	6
SS Eskinazi	4	4	0	201	130	50.25	104.14	1	0	20	5
SD Robson	4	4	0	169	76	42.25	99.41	0	2	21	0
MDE Holden	5	5	0	201	94	40.20	87.39	0	1	23	2
JLB Davies	5	5	0	164	70	32.80	106.49	0	2	18	2
RG White	6	5	0	140	55	28.00	67.30	0	1	11	0
JM De Caires	3	3	0	68	43	22.66	93.15	0	0	6	1
PSP Handscomb	6	6	0	130	75	21.66	94.20	0	1	15	0
V Chopra	3	3	0	55	45*	18.33	67.90	0	0	2	0
TN Walallawita	6	5	0	69	29	13.80	140.81	0	0	6	4
ER Bamber	6	4	1	37	21	12.33	82.22	0	0	4	0
JAR Harris	6	5	1	41	34	10.25	82.00	0	0	5	1
LBK Hollman	4	4	1	28	14*	9.33	80.00	0	0	3	0
JB Cracknell	1	1	0	2	2	2.00	33.33	0	0	0	0
TJ Murtagh	2	2	2	8	6*	-	133.33	0	0	1	0
TL Greatwood	1	1	1	7	7*	-	140.00	0	0	1	0

Bowling

	Overs	Mdns	Runs	Wkts	BBI	Ave	Econ	SR	4w	5w
TL Greatwood	6.0	1	30	2	2/30	15.00	5.00	18.0	0	0
TN Walallawita	55.0	2	287	4	2/54	71.75	5.21	82.5	0	0
JM De Caires	18.0	0	95	1	1/13	95.00	5.27	108.0	0	0
LBK Hollman	37.0	0	196	8	4/56	24.50	5.29	27.7	1	0
JAR Harris	50.0	2	300	7	2/45	42.85	6.00	42.8	0	0
TJ Murtagh	13.0	1	78	2	2/38	39.00	6.00	39.0	0	0
ER Bamber	49.2	0	297	10	3/41	29.70	6.02	29.6	0	0
SD Robson	13.0	0	93	1	1/26	93.00	7.15	78.0	0	0
MK Andersson	22.0	0	166	1	1/83	166.00	7.54	132.0	0	0
MDE Holden	1.0	0	11	0	-	-	11.00	-	0	0

Catches/Stumpings:
5 White (inc 1st), 3 Andersson, Handscomb, Robson, 2 de Caires, Eskinazi, Holden, 1 Bamber, Chopra, Davies, Harris, Hollman, Walallawita

www.middlesexccc.com / tel: 0207 289 1300

**MIDDLESEX
CRICKET**

	Mat	Inns	NO	Runs	HS	Ave	SR	100	50	4s	6s
SS Eskinazi	11	11	2	399	102*	44.33	140.49	1	3	51	5
CJ Green	7	6	3	107	26*	35.66	140.78	0	0	8	3
EJG Morgan	5	5	0	133	38	26.60	129.12	0	0	7	8
DJ Mitchell	8	8	0	209	58	26.12	144.13	0	1	11	12
PR Stirling	5	5	0	130	58	26.00	152.94	0	1	11	8
JB Cracknell	11	11	0	281	77	25.54	137.07	0	2	32	6
SD Robson	3	3	0	75	60	25.00	120.96	0	1	8	2
MDE Holden	8	7	1	120	50*	20.00	110.09	0	1	11	2
NA Sowter	11	9	4	96	37*	19.20	128.00	0	0	9	2
LBK Hollman	12	10	2	130	51	16.25	123.80	0	1	12	4
BC Cullen	12	6	3	43	20*	14.33	113.15	0	0	4	0
JA Simpson	12	12	2	143	62	14.30	126.54	0	1	8	8
JM De Caires	1	1	0	14	14	14.00	200.00	0	0	2	1
TG Helm	7	4	2	27	12	13.50	84.37	0	0	1	0
NRT Gubbins	3	2	0	24	24	12.00	92.30	0	0	0	1
V Chopra	1	1	0	12	12	12.00	80.00	0	0	0	0
Mujeeb Ur Rahman	6	3	1	13	13	6.50	100.00	0	0	0	1
ST Finn	13	4	2	8	4*	4.00	72.72	0	0	0	0
ER Bamber	5	1	1	3	3*	-	100.00	0	0	0	0
TJ Murtagh	2	-	-	-	-	-	-	-	-	-	-

Batting

	Overs	Mdns	Runs	Wkts	BBI	Ave	Econ	SR	4w	5w
NRT Gubbins	4.0	0	22	1	1/22	22.00	5.50	24.0	0	0
Mujeeb Ur Rahman	24.0	0	166	10	2/18	16.60	6.91	14.4	0	0
NA Sowter	40.0	0	300	15	3/13	20.00	7.50	16.0	0	0
PR Stirling	5.0	0	40	0	-	-	8.00	-	0	0
TJ Murtagh	6.0	0	49	0	-	-	8.16	-	0	0
TG Helm	26.0	0	215	5	2/30	43.00	8.26	31.2	0	0
LBK Hollman	23.0	0	196	9	2/10	21.77	8.52	15.3	0	0
BC Cullen	37.1	0	327	20	4/32	16.35	8.79	11.1	2	0
ST Finn	46.1	0	414	19	4/19	21.78	8.96	14.5	1	0
CJ Green	25.0	0	231	10	5/32	23.10	9.24	15.0	0	1
DJ Mitchell	10.0	0	94	8	3/24	11.75	9.40	7.5	0	0
ER Bamber	8.5	0	102	0	-	-	11.54	-	0	0

Bowling

Catches/Stumpings:
12 Simpson (inc 5st), 9 Holden, Hollman, 8 Finn, 6 Cracknell, Eskinazi, 4 Mitchell, Morgan, 3 Cullen, Green, 2 de Caires, Sowter, 1 Bamber, Robson, Stirling

NORTHAMPTONSHIRE

FORMED: 1878
HOME GROUND: County Ground, Northampton
ONE-DAY NAME: Northamptonshire Steelbacks
CAPTAIN: Adam Rossington (CC), Josh Cobb (RL50/T20)
2021 RESULTS: CC2: 4/6; RL50: 8/9 Group B; T20: 9/9 North Group
HONOURS: Gillette/NatWest/C&G/FP Trophy: (2) 1976, 1992; Benson & Hedges Cup: 1980; T20 Cup: (2) 2013, 2016

THE LOWDOWN

New head coach John Sadler has big shoes to fill in replacing David Ripley, who stepped down last September after 10 years in the job. Despite having a small squad, Northants have been one of the strongest white-ball counties under Ripley, winning two T20 trophies and remaining competitive in the Championship. The club take their place in Division One this season on account of their pre-pandemic promotion in 2019. But Northants did struggle last summer, not least in the T20 Blast where they finished bottom of their group. Ricardo Vasconcelos was again excellent across all formats, with Rob Keogh not far behind, but otherwise the batting was often wobbly. New Zealand opener Will Young should provide some stability in red-ball cricket this summer. The bowlers, led by the stalwart Ben Sanderson, fared better. Simon Kerrigan, still only 32, signed a new deal after taking 29 Championship wickets at 26, and there was a first pro contract for England U19 allrounder James Sales, son of Northants icon David. Western Australia pacer Matt Kelly has been signed for the first six Championship matches.

IN: Matt Kelly (Aus, CC), Will Young (NZ, CC/RL50), Jimmy Neesham (NZ, CC/T20)
OUT: Richard Levi (REL)

HEAD COACH: JOHN SADLER

A former Leicestershire batter, Sadler joined the Derbyshire backroom staff in 2014 and was briefly interim head coach before becoming Paul Nixon's deputy at Grace Road. Northants brought Sadler in as assistant coach in 2019 and offered him the top job after David Ripley resigned last year. Ripley has taken on a youth coaching role. Ben Smith, formerly of Leicestershire and Worcestershire, is the new batting coach, and Graeme White has agreed a player-coach role which will see him take charge of the Second XI while also acting as the club's fielding and spin-bowling coach.

COUNTY CHAMPIONSHIP AVERAGES 2021

Batting

	Mat	Inns	NO	Runs	HS	Ave	SR	100	50	4s	6s
R Vasconcelos	14	24	1	845	185*	36.73	61.05	2	2	114	3
AM Rossington	11	16	1	537	94	35.80	58.81	0	4	61	6
RI Keogh	14	24	2	766	126	34.81	56.19	2	4	100	0
LA Procter	13	21	2	597	93	31.42	39.19	0	5	62	2
GK Berg	9	10	3	216	69*	30.85	48.21	0	1	26	1
JJG Sales	3	6	2	112	53	28.00	43.07	0	1	17	0
SA Zaib	13	22	1	576	135	27.42	44.82	1	3	66	2
HOM Gouldstone	4	8	2	155	67*	25.83	33.76	0	1	20	0
EN Gay	9	17	0	391	101	23.00	50.32	1	1	57	1
TAI Taylor	11	17	2	316	50	21.06	45.33	0	1	43	2
SC Kerrigan	11	19	6	224	45*	17.23	33.33	0	0	27	1
WD Parnell	6	7	0	107	54	15.28	35.90	0	1	11	0
BJ Curran	7	10	0	148	36	14.80	48.05	0	0	20	0
CJ White	4	7	5	29	15*	14.50	51.78	0	0	4	0
CO Thurston	6	10	0	142	48	14.20	53.38	0	0	20	0
NL Buck	4	6	1	69	21*	13.80	38.12	0	0	11	1
BW Sanderson	13	17	3	72	20	5.14	40.00	0	0	10	0
AG Wakely	1	1	0	4	4	4.00	33.33	0	0	0	0
JJ Cobb	1	2	0	1	1	0.50	20.00	0	0	0	0

Bowling

	Overs	Mdns	Runs	Wkts	BBI	BBM	Ave	Econ	SR	5w	10w
EN Gay	5.0	0	22	1	1/8	1/8	22.00	4.40	30.0	0	0
WD Parnell	114.4	26	427	18	5/64	10/143	23.72	3.72	38.2	2	1
GK Berg	199.4	48	600	24	5/18	9/90	25.00	3.00	49.9	1	0
SC Kerrigan	298.5	57	766	29	5/39	7/75	26.41	2.56	61.8	2	0
BW Sanderson	435.2	117	1155	43	5/28	10/99	26.86	2.65	60.7	3	1
TAI Taylor	263.2	63	783	29	5/41	7/95	27.00	2.97	54.4	1	0
LA Procter	115.5	29	352	13	5/42	6/72	27.07	3.03	53.4	1	0
NL Buck	107.4	11	436	10	3/65	4/162	43.60	4.04	64.6	0	0
SA Zaib	43.1	6	139	3	2/32	2/66	46.33	3.22	86.3	0	0
JJG Sales	40.0	9	154	3	2/61	2/61	51.33	3.85	80.0	0	0
CJ White	94.0	10	319	5	4/40	4/40	63.80	3.39	112.8	0	0
RI Keogh	126.4	15	462	5	2/8	2/49	92.40	3.64	152.0	0	0

Catches/Stumpings:
33 Vasconcelos (inc 1st), 26 Rossington (inc 2st), 6 Curran, Taylor, 5 Gay, 4 Zaib, 3 Berg, Kerrigan, Thurston, 2 Procter, Sanderson, 1 Buck, Cobb, Keogh, Sales, Wakely

NORTHAMPTONSHIRE
STEELBACKS

Batting

	Mat	Inns	NO	Runs	HS	Ave	SR	100	50	4s	6s
TAI Taylor	7	4	2	145	65*	72.50	93.54	0	2	11	4
LA Procter	3	3	1	110	48	55.00	74.32	0	0	8	1
JJG Sales	3	3	2	47	28	47.00	70.14	0	0	1	0
EN Gay	8	8	3	189	84*	37.80	89.15	0	1	19	1
RI Keogh	8	6	1	160	52	32.00	103.22	0	1	17	2
R Vasconcelos	8	8	1	218	88	31.14	83.84	0	2	28	0
BJ Curran	8	7	1	182	94	30.33	88.78	0	2	18	1
SA Zaib	8	5	0	132	43	26.40	88.00	0	0	10	3
CO Thurston	4	2	1	25	21*	25.00	60.97	0	0	1	0
GG White	4	1	0	15	15	15.00	75.00	0	0	1	0
BW Sanderson	8	4	0	41	16	10.25	85.41	0	0	2	1
CJ White	7	3	1	20	10*	10.00	90.90	0	0	2	0
WD Parnell	5	2	0	15	9	7.50	62.50	0	0	2	0
FJ Heldreich	3	2	1	5	5	5.00	45.45	0	0	0	0
SC Kerrigan	4	3	0	5	3	1.66	27.77	0	0	0	0

Bowling

	Overs	Mdns	Runs	Wkts	BBI	Ave	Econ	SR	4w	5w
GG White	24.0	1	95	2	1/23	47.50	3.95	72.0	0	0
SA Zaib	22.0	1	92	5	3/37	18.40	4.18	26.4	0	0
RI Keogh	24.0	0	111	3	2/35	37.00	4.62	48.0	0	0
BW Sanderson	54.1	7	252	15	3/29	16.80	4.65	21.6	0	0
SC Kerrigan	38.5	2	191	6	4/48	31.83	4.91	38.8	1	0
CJ White	43.0	3	220	10	4/20	22.00	5.11	25.8	1	0
TAI Taylor	41.0	0	238	9	3/24	26.44	5.80	27.3	0	0
WD Parnell	31.0	0	180	3	1/39	60.00	5.80	62.0	0	0
LA Procter	8.0	0	48	3	3/40	16.00	6.00	16.0	0	0
EN Gay	3.0	0	19	0	-	-	6.33	-	0	0
JJG Sales	5.0	0	32	0	-	-	6.40	-	0	0
FJ Heldreich	20.0	0	150	3	2/69	50.00	7.50	40.0	0	0

Catches/Stumpings:
9 Vasconcelos (inc 1st), 3 Gay, Keogh, 2 Heldreich, Taylor, Thurston, C White, Zaib, 1 Curran, Kerrigan, Parnell, Procter, Sales, Sanderson

NORTHAMPTONSHIRE STEELBACKS

	Mat	Inns	NO	Runs	HS	Ave	SR	100	50	4s	6s
RI Keogh	12	12	5	347	56	49.57	125.72	0	3	22	8
R Vasconcelos	12	12	1	364	78*	33.09	117.79	0	2	44	4
JJ Cobb	6	6	0	185	62	30.83	165.17	0	1	21	7
SA Zaib	12	10	3	134	36	19.14	139.58	0	0	9	7
Mohammad Nabi	9	8	1	131	32	18.71	118.01	0	0	6	6
BJ Curran	4	4	0	71	62	17.75	154.34	0	1	11	1
AM Rossington	8	8	0	136	59	17.00	144.68	0	1	16	5
EN Gay	1	1	0	15	15	15.00	150.00	0	0	2	0
WD Parnell	11	10	1	129	25	14.33	105.73	0	0	14	1
BW Sanderson	8	3	1	21	9	10.50	61.76	0	0	1	0
RE Levi	5	5	0	46	30	9.20	100.00	0	0	4	2
TAI Taylor	12	8	2	53	20*	8.83	91.37	0	0	3	1
GG White	12	8	2	52	37	8.66	101.96	0	0	7	1
CO Thurston	4	2	0	11	7	5.50	78.57	0	0	1	0
NL Buck	3	2	2	26	26*	-	152.94	0	0	2	2
BD Glover	8	4	4	10	6*	-	76.92	0	0	1	0
FJ Heldreich	5	-	-	-	-	-	-	-	-	-	-

Batting

	Overs	Mdns	Runs	Wkts	BBI	Ave	Econ	SR	4w	5w
Mohammad Nabi	36.0	0	216	9	2/23	24.00	6.00	24.0	0	0
FJ Heldreich	18.0	0	117	5	2/17	23.40	6.50	21.6	0	0
JJ Cobb	9.0	0	68	2	2/19	34.00	7.55	27.0	0	0
GG White	43.4	0	355	15	4/26	23.66	8.12	17.4	1	0
WD Parnell	39.5	0	346	8	2/28	43.25	8.68	29.8	0	0
BW Sanderson	24.4	0	241	6	3/21	40.16	9.77	24.6	0	0
TAI Taylor	34.2	0	342	11	3/33	31.09	9.96	18.7	0	0
SA Zaib	2.0	0	20	0	-	-	10.00	-	0	0
BD Glover	16.2	0	173	4	1/21	43.25	10.59	24.5	0	0
NL Buck	7.0	0	77	0	-	-	11.00	-	0	0
RI Keogh	3.0	0	42	0	-	-	14.00	-	0	0

Bowling

Catches/Stumpings:
8 Vasconcelos (inc 2st), 6 Cobb, Taylor, 5 Parnell, Rossington (inc 2st), 4 G White, 3 Keogh, Nabi, Zaib, 1 Buck, Curran, Glover, Thurston

NOTTINGHAMSHIRE

FORMED: 1841

HOME GROUND: Trent Bridge, Nottingham

ONE-DAY NAME: Notts Outlaws

CAPTAIN: Steven Mullaney (CC), Haseeb Hameed (RL50), Dan Christian (T20)

2021 RESULTS: CC1: 3/6; RL50: 6/9 Group B; T20: Quarter-finalists

HONOURS: County Championship: (6) 1907, 1929, 1981, 1987, 2005, 2010; Gillette/NatWest/C&G/FP Trophy: 1987; Pro40/National League/CB40/YB40/RL50: (2) 2013, 2017; Benson & Hedges Cup: 1989; Sunday League: 1991; T20 Cup: 2017, 2020

THE LOWDOWN

Invariably one of the strongest teams on paper, Nottinghamshire are nothing if not volatile. They began last season without a four-day win since 2018 and finished it within four points of champions Warwickshire, cursing being dismissed for 155 and 127 in the crunch match against Hampshire at the Ageas Bowl. Notts start this season in Division Two on account of their dismal showing in 2019 (no wins and 10 defeats in 14 matches). They will be overwhelming favourites for promotion, largely because of a powerful international seam attack fortified by the return of former Aussie quick James Pattinson. Notts have also re-signed South Africa's Dane Paterson, who took 54 Championship wickets last summer but was still behind Luke Fletcher's 66. There is even the possibility that a vengeful Stuart Broad will appear more often after he was recently shunned by England. Runs shouldn't be a problem either, with Ben Slater, Ben Duckett and Joe Clarke all in good touch last summer and Haseeb Hameed returning to the fold after being dropped by England. The prospects of a third T20 trophy in six years are boosted by the return of 38-year-old Dan Christian as captain.

IN: Dane Paterson (SA), James Pattinson (Aus), Dan Christian (Aus, T20)
OUT: Ben Compton (Ken), Tom Barber (REL), Peter Trego (RET)

HEAD COACH: PETER MOORES

Moores scored 7,000 first-class runs and claimed 517 dismissals for Sussex between 1985 and 1998. He had two short spells as England head coach and won the Championship with Sussex in 2003 and Lancashire in 2011. The 59-year-old replaced Mick Newell (now Nottinghamshire's director of cricket) in 2016 and immediately led the club to the cup double as well as Championship promotion. Notts finished bottom of Division One in 2019 but added a third white-ball trophy in 2020. Moores signed a new three-year contract in September.

Batting

	Mat	Inns	NO	Runs	HS	Ave	SR	100	50	4s	6s
BT Slater	14	24	3	837	114*	39.85	44.23	2	5	114	2
H Hameed	11	19	1	679	114*	37.72	43.41	2	4	84	1
SA Northeast	2	3	0	112	65	37.33	45.52	0	1	19	0
BM Duckett	13	21	2	705	177*	37.10	68.91	1	4	99	0
JM Clarke	13	22	1	760	109	36.19	57.18	1	7	103	7
LW James	12	18	1	558	91	32.82	39.65	0	5	81	0
LA Patterson-White	14	20	3	538	101	31.64	55.98	1	3	87	1
TJ Moores	12	19	3	486	97	30.37	55.54	0	3	76	9
SJ Mullaney	14	22	0	657	117	29.86	55.44	1	3	94	13
D Schadendorf	1	1	0	24	24	24.00	41.37	0	0	1	0
JDM Evison	4	6	0	121	58	20.16	41.15	0	1	17	2
D Paterson	12	15	11	64	22	16.00	57.65	0	0	8	2
BA Hutton	8	11	0	174	51	15.81	46.77	0	1	26	0
ZJ Chappell	3	5	1	61	22	15.25	31.60	0	0	8	0
SCJ Broad	5	7	0	87	41	12.42	83.65	0	0	12	2
LJ Fletcher	13	17	5	140	51	11.66	47.13	0	1	19	3
BG Compton	3	5	0	55	20	11.00	41.98	0	0	9	0
JT Ball	1	1	0	4	4	4.00	28.57	0	0	1	0

Bowling

	Overs	Mdns	Runs	Wkts	BBI	BBM	Ave	Econ	SR	5w	10w
LJ Fletcher	420.5	135	984	66	7/37	10/57	14.90	2.33	38.2	4	1
SCJ Broad	150.0	34	368	23	4/37	6/70	16.00	2.45	39.1	0	0
JDM Evison	82.1	23	249	14	5/21	5/30	17.78	3.03	35.2	1	0
D Paterson	352.5	98	971	54	5/90	7/88	17.98	2.75	39.2	1	0
JT Ball	17.3	7	43	2	2/43	2/43	21.50	2.45	52.5	0	0
BA Hutton	254.0	75	679	29	5/62	7/148	23.41	2.67	52.5	2	0
LW James	139.0	27	424	14	4/51	6/54	30.28	3.05	59.5	0	0
LA Patterson-White	285.0	70	749	24	5/41	5/60	31.20	2.62	71.2	1	0
ZJ Chappell	100.0	21	306	6	3/64	3/128	51.00	3.06	100.0	0	0
SJ Mullaney	151.2	29	423	7	2/37	3/126	60.42	2.79	129.7	0	0
BT Slater	2.0	0	8	0	-	-	-	4.00	-	0	0
BM Duckett	3.0	0	17	0	-	-	-	5.66	-	0	0

Catches/Stumpings:
54 Moores (inc 2st), 15 Duckett, 11 Hameed, 8 Clarke, Hutton, Slater, 6 Mullaney, 4 Paterson, Patterson-White, Schadendorf, 2 Compton, Northeast, 1 Fletcher, James

Batting

	Mat	Inns	NO	Runs	HS	Ave	SR	100	50	4s	6s
BG Compton	1	1	0	71	71	71.00	70.29	0	1	5	0
BT Slater	8	8	1	395	86	56.42	90.80	0	4	51	2
H Hameed	2	2	0	107	103	53.50	109.18	1	0	10	1
M Montgomery	8	8	3	200	35	40.00	85.10	0	0	19	2
F Singh	3	2	1	27	21	27.00	117.39	0	0	5	0
JDM Evison	5	3	0	72	54	24.00	133.33	0	1	6	3
D Schadendorf	8	6	2	95	44*	23.75	110.46	0	0	6	4
SG Budinger	8	8	0	165	71	20.62	123.13	0	1	23	6
D Paterson	8	4	3	19	8*	19.00	111.76	0	0	0	2
BA Hutton	8	4	0	72	46	18.00	133.33	0	0	6	4
LW James	6	5	2	40	16*	13.33	75.47	0	0	5	0
PD Trego	8	8	0	95	39	11.87	77.86	0	0	5	4
SIM King	1	1	0	11	11	11.00	52.38	0	0	0	0
LJ Fletcher	4	2	1	10	5*	10.00	90.90	0	0	1	0
LA Patterson-White	8	6	0	51	27	8.50	68.00	0	0	3	1
TE Barber	3	1	1	0	0*	-	-	0	0	0	0

Bowling

	Overs	Mdns	Runs	Wkts	BBI	Ave	Econ	SR	4w	5w
F Singh	13.0	0	42	0	-	-	3.23	-	0	0
BA Hutton	38.0	2	185	6	2/22	30.83	4.86	38.0	0	0
PD Trego	16.0	0	80	2	1/19	40.00	5.00	48.0	0	0
LW James	9.0	0	48	5	5/48	9.60	5.33	10.8	0	1
LA Patterson-White	35.0	3	188	13	5/19	14.46	5.37	16.1	0	1
LJ Fletcher	22.0	2	131	6	4/30	21.83	5.95	22.0	1	0
TE Barber	8.0	0	49	1	1/33	49.00	6.12	48.0	0	0
D Paterson	31.0	1	211	8	3/25	26.37	6.80	23.2	0	0
M Montgomery	15.0	0	104	0	-	-	6.93	-	0	0
JDM Evison	23.0	2	163	4	2/33	40.75	7.08	34.5	0	0

Catches/Stumpings:
7 Schadendorf (inc 1st), 4 Hutton, Slater, Trego, 3 Paterson, 2 Evison, Hameed, Montgomery, 1 Budinger, Patterson-White

www.trentbridge.co.uk / tel: 0115 982 3000

Batting

	Mat	Inns	NO	Runs	HS	Ave	SR	100	50	4s	6s
AD Hales	15	15	4	482	101*	43.81	178.51	1	2	61	23
JM Clarke	12	12	1	408	136	37.09	180.53	1	1	36	23
BM Duckett	13	12	1	383	74*	34.81	158.26	0	3	47	10
SR Patel	15	13	3	309	64*	30.90	131.48	0	2	28	11
BT Slater	4	3	0	69	48	23.00	125.45	0	0	6	2
PD Trego	9	8	1	125	35	17.85	123.76	0	0	16	2
SJ Mullaney	15	13	2	169	43*	15.36	136.29	0	0	12	8
M Carter	15	7	4	40	23*	13.33	100.00	0	0	2	3
TJ Moores	13	11	0	145	48	13.18	112.40	0	0	7	5
SG Budinger	5	4	0	52	21	13.00	118.18	0	0	6	1
CG Harrison	15	8	3	53	22*	10.60	132.50	0	0	4	2
LJ Fletcher	13	8	2	36	23	6.00	97.29	0	0	3	1
D Paterson	6	3	1	10	6	5.00	90.90	0	0	2	0
LW James	4	2	0	8	7	4.00	100.00	0	0	1	0
JT Ball	9	2	2	18	18*	-	163.63	0	0	0	1
ZJ Chappell	2	1	1	2	2*	-	66.66	0	0	0	0

Bowling

	Overs	Mdns	Runs	Wkts	BBI	Ave	Econ	SR	4w	5w
SR Patel	52.0	1	345	16	3/4	21.56	6.63	19.5	0	0
CG Harrison	41.0	1	278	20	4/17	13.90	6.78	12.3	2	0
M Carter	53.0	0	372	18	3/17	20.66	7.01	17.6	0	0
SJ Mullaney	35.0	0	274	11	3/33	24.90	7.82	19.0	0	0
LJ Fletcher	41.0	0	372	13	3/31	28.61	9.07	18.9	0	0
JT Ball	29.4	0	278	18	4/11	15.44	9.37	9.8	1	0
ZJ Chappell	3.4	0	35	2	1/12	17.50	9.54	11.0	0	0
D Paterson	14.0	0	143	8	3/22	17.87	10.21	10.5	0	0
PD Trego	2.0	0	43	0	-	-	21.50	-	0	0

Catches/Stumpings:
13 Mullaney, 11 Moores (inc 6st), 9 Duckett, 8 Carter, Harrison, 7 Hales, Patel, 6 Clarke,
3 Budinger, Trego, 2 Ball, James, 1 Chappell, Paterson, Slater

TEAM PROFILE

SOMERSET CCC

FORMED: 1875
HOME GROUND: The Cooper Associates County Ground, Taunton
CAPTAIN: Tom Abell
2021 RESULTS: CC1: 6/6; RL50: 7/9 Group B; T20: Runners-up
HONOURS: Gillette/NatWest/C&G/FP Trophy: (3) 1979, 1983, 2001; Pro40/National League/CB40/YB40/RL50: 2019; Benson & Hedges Cup: (2) 1981, 1982; Sunday League: 1979; T20 Cup: 2005

THE LOWDOWN

It was, yes, another season in which Somerset finished runners-up, but reaching the T20 final for the first time in 10 years showed that they are contenders in all formats. Another tilt at the Championship looked likely only for the batting to fall to pieces in late summer: dismissed for less than 200 in six of their last eight innings. Of the frontline batters, only Tom Abell and Steve Davies averaged more than 25. The club have signed Australia opener Matt Renshaw until at least the end of August and, with Peter Siddle and Marchant de Lange also on the books, Somerset will have to pick two from three overseas players when selecting their Championship XI. Siddle completes a strong seam attack led by the irrepressible Craig Overton and the underrated Josh Davey, who hopes to be fit for the start of the season after undergoing surgery for a groin injury in November. With Lewis Gregory stepping down as T20 skipper, Abell now captains across all formats. In white-ball cricket all eyes will be on 20-year-old Will Smeed, Somerset's leading run-scorer in last year's T20 Blast before starring for Birmingham Phoenix in The Hundred.

IN: Matt Renshaw (Aus, CC/RL50), Peter Siddle (Aus)
OUT: Eddie Byrom (Gla), Sam Young (REL)

HEAD COACH: JASON KERR

A former Somerset allrounder, Kerr has been part of the coaching staff since 2005. He was promoted from bowling coach to head coach in 2017 and works alongside director of cricket Andy Hurry. Somerset were Championship runners-up in each of Kerr's first three seasons in charge, winning the One-Day Cup in 2019 and reaching T20 Finals Day last summer. Former Somerset seamer Steve Kirby looks after the bowlers. Jim Troughton has taken up a coaching role at Surrey after spending last summer at Taunton as a batting consultant.

COUNTY CHAMPIONSHIP AVERAGES 2021

	Mat	Inns	NO	Runs	HS	Ave	SR	100	50	4s	6s
L Gregory	9	10	2	389	107	48.62	62.14	1	3	56	5
DP Conway	2	3	0	121	88	40.33	52.83	0	1	19	0
TB Abell	12	20	2	711	132*	39.50	48.13	1	4	97	0
SM Davies	13	22	2	634	87	31.70	54.04	0	5	88	2
RE van der Merwe	6	8	0	241	88	30.12	71.09	0	2	28	5
Azhar Ali	3	6	0	177	60	29.50	44.47	0	2	23	1
JH Davey	12	16	7	238	75*	26.44	38.95	0	1	35	1
MJ Leach	10	15	4	276	49	25.09	48.16	0	0	37	2
GA Bartlett	11	16	1	373	100	24.86	49.14	1	2	53	2
C Overton	8	11	1	237	74	23.70	54.73	0	2	31	0
JC Hildreth	13	20	0	456	107	22.80	51.12	1	1	59	0
BGF Green	4	8	1	154	43	22.00	42.19	0	0	18	1
M de Lange	10	14	0	297	75	21.21	114.67	0	2	24	19
LP Goldsworthy	10	15	1	297	48	21.21	38.82	0	0	43	0
TA Lammonby	13	22	2	392	100	19.60	53.47	1	2	57	4
T Banton	8	14	1	245	51*	18.84	59.03	0	1	34	3
EJ Byrom	4	5	1	55	38	13.75	36.66	0	0	7	0
EO Leonard	1	2	1	10	6	10.00	55.55	0	0	2	0
JA Brooks	6	10	4	47	15	7.83	50.53	0	0	7	0
KL Aldridge	1	-	-	-	-	-	-	-	-	-	-

Batting

	Overs	Mdns	Runs	Wkts	BBI	BBM	Ave	Econ	SR	5w	10w
C Overton	270.3	93	650	42	5/25	8/64	15.47	2.40	38.6	4	0
JH Davey	292.2	84	781	35	5/30	7/62	22.31	2.67	50.1	2	0
RE van der Merwe	96.1	26	241	8	4/54	7/114	30.12	2.50	72.1	0	0
L Gregory	209.3	60	645	21	5/68	6/115	30.71	3.07	59.8	1	0
MJ Leach	241.0	77	562	18	6/43	7/66	31.22	2.33	80.3	1	0
M de Lange	231.5	49	685	20	4/55	5/76	34.25	2.95	69.5	0	0
JA Brooks	142.0	28	499	12	4/77	4/92	41.58	3.51	71.0	0	0
TB Abell	168.3	44	558	13	3/63	3/63	42.92	3.31	77.7	0	0
TA Lammonby	77.0	13	287	4	1/20	1/23	71.75	3.72	115.5	0	0
EO Leonard	18.0	2	85	1	1/68	1/85	85.00	4.72	108.0	0	0
BGF Green	40.0	11	93	1	1/29	1/29	93.00	2.32	240.0	0	0
LP Goldsworthy	24.0	8	45	0	-	-	-	1.87	-	0	0
KL Aldridge	22.0	2	101	0	-	-	-	4.59	-	0	0

Bowling

Catches/Stumpings:
38 Davies (inc 1st), 14 Hildreth, 11 Abell, 9 Overton, 7 Gregory, Lammonby, 5 Banton, 4 de Lange, van der Merwe, 3 Conway, 2 Ali, Bartlett, Davey, Green, Leach, 1 Byrom, Goldsworthy, Leonard

SOMERSET CCC

Batting

	Mat	Inns	NO	Runs	HS	Ave	SR	100	50	4s	6s
LP Goldsworthy	8	7	1	381	96	63.50	87.18	0	4	31	6
BGF Green	5	3	1	110	87	55.00	123.59	0	1	13	2
JC Hildreth	8	7	1	306	110	51.00	103.72	1	2	28	8
GW Thomas	2	2	0	82	75	41.00	89.13	0	1	5	4
SM Davies	8	7	0	269	94	38.42	103.46	0	2	36	3
GS Drissell	5	3	2	32	17*	32.00	91.42	0	0	2	1
GA Bartlett	6	5	0	159	108	31.80	98.75	1	0	8	9
JH Davey	5	4	1	70	53	23.33	90.90	0	1	4	2
KL Aldridge	6	3	1	27	12	13.50	67.50	0	0	1	0
M de Lange	3	3	1	26	20*	13.00	113.04	0	0	3	1
JEK Rew	2	2	0	26	20	13.00	81.25	0	0	3	0
SJ Young	8	7	0	73	25	10.42	64.03	0	0	5	3
EJ Byrom	7	6	1	49	18	9.80	59.75	0	0	4	0
S Baker	8	2	1	7	7*	7.00	25.00	0	0	0	0
EO Leonard	4	2	2	1	1*	-	100.00	0	0	0	0
JA Brooks	2	-	-	-	-	-	-	-	-	-	-
MJ Leach	1	-	-	-	-	-	-	-	-	-	-

Bowling

	Overs	Mdns	Runs	Wkts	BBI	Ave	Econ	SR	4w	5w
JA Brooks	17.0	2	88	3	2/64	29.33	5.17	34.0	0	0
BGF Green	34.3	2	179	8	3/64	22.37	5.18	25.8	0	0
LP Goldsworthy	40.0	0	210	3	1/17	70.00	5.25	80.0	0	0
GS Drissell	13.0	0	71	2	1/21	35.50	5.46	39.0	0	0
JH Davey	35.0	0	197	8	4/57	24.62	5.62	26.2	1	0
S Baker	54.4	2	330	10	3/46	33.00	6.03	32.8	0	0
KL Aldridge	30.0	0	209	6	3/39	34.83	6.96	30.0	0	0
MJ Leach	8.0	0	56	0	-	-	7.00	-	0	0
EO Leonard	22.0	0	166	3	2/84	55.33	7.54	44.0	0	0
M de Lange	18.0	0	153	1	1/67	153.00	8.50	108.0	0	0
GW Thomas	3.0	0	28	0	-	-	9.33	-	0	0

Catches/Stumpings:
10 Davies, 4 Byrom, Drissell 2 Baker, Bartlett, Goldsworthy, Hildreth, Leonard, 1 Aldridge, Green, Young

SOMERSET CCC

Batting

	Mat	Inns	NO	Runs	HS	Ave	SR	100	50	4s	6s
DP Conway	8	8	3	309	81*	61.80	125.60	0	4	41	2
TB Abell	6	6	1	295	78*	59.00	161.20	0	4	29	9
WCF Smeed	14	13	1	385	63*	32.08	132.30	0	1	34	19
JH Davey	8	4	3	29	16*	29.00	161.11	0	0	1	2
TA Lammonby	11	10	2	219	90	27.37	162.22	0	1	21	8
T Banton	10	10	1	243	107*	27.00	176.08	1	1	21	15
JC Hildreth	9	9	1	206	72*	25.75	132.05	0	1	25	8
BGF Green	14	8	2	129	43*	21.50	135.78	0	0	5	6
LP Goldsworthy	12	11	1	172	48	17.20	110.25	0	0	14	5
JA Brooks	9	3	2	17	10*	17.00	85.00	0	0	1	0
EJ Byrom	4	3	0	43	28	14.33	97.72	0	0	4	1
C Overton	11	7	3	51	16*	12.75	134.21	0	0	5	2
M de Lange	14	8	3	63	20	12.60	143.18	0	0	4	5
SM Davies	2	2	0	24	22	12.00	104.34	0	0	2	1
RE van der Merwe	7	6	1	46	25	9.20	124.32	0	0	4	1
L Gregory	11	7	0	64	24	9.14	91.42	0	0	5	0
GA Bartlett	3	3	0	23	14	7.66	100.00	0	0	1	1
MTC Waller	10	4	2	10	9	5.00	71.42	0	0	1	0
MJ Leach	2	-	-	-	-	-	-	-	-	-	-

Bowling

	Overs	Mdns	Runs	Wkts	BBI	Ave	Econ	SR	4w	5w
C Overton	37.0	1	264	13	3/28	20.30	7.13	17.0	0	0
RE van der Merwe	27.4	0	199	11	4/27	18.09	7.19	15.0	1	0
LP Goldsworthy	31.0	0	226	9	3/14	25.11	7.29	20.6	0	0
MJ Leach	8.0	0	60	5	3/28	12.00	7.50	9.6	0	0
JA Brooks	29.1	0	224	8	2/33	28.00	7.68	21.8	0	0
TA Lammonby	6.0	0	47	2	1/16	23.50	7.83	18.0	0	0
BGF Green	21.0	0	176	4	2/34	44.00	8.38	31.5	0	0
M de Lange	48.0	0	409	18	3/18	22.72	8.52	16.0	0	0
MTC Waller	28.0	0	241	5	2/26	48.20	8.60	33.6	0	0
JH Davey	25.5	0	253	13	4/34	19.46	9.79	11.9	1	0
L Gregory	23.0	0	226	12	5/24	18.83	9.82	11.5	1	1

Catches/Stumpings:

11 Banton (inc 3st), 10 Green, Overton, 8 Smeed, 7 Waller, 5 Conway, 4 Abell, Gregory, van der Merwe, 3 Goldsworthy, Lammonby, 2 Brooks, Byrom, de Lange, 1 Davey, Hildreth, Leach

TEAM PROFILE

FORMED: 1845
GROUND: The Kia Oval, London
CAPTAIN: Rory Burns (CC/RL50), Chris Jordan (T20)
2021 RESULTS: CC2: 5/6; RL50: Semi-finalists; T20: 5/9 South Group
HONOURS: Championship: (20) 1890, 1891, 1892, 1894, 1895, 1899, 1914, 1950, 1952, 1953, 1954, 1955, 1956, 1957, 1958, 1971, 1999, 2000, 2002, 2018; Gillette/NatWest/C&G/FP Trophy: 1982; Benson & Hedges Cup: (3) 1974, 1997, 2001; Pro40/National League/CB40/YB40/RL50: (2) 2003, 2011; Sunday League: 1996; T20 Cup: 2003

THE LOWDOWN

There's been quite a shake-up at The Oval following the loss of a string of distinguished players including Mark Stoneman, Rikki Clarke and Gareth Batty. In fact the indomitable Batty remains part of the furniture after he was appointed interim head coach when Vikram Solanki was lured away by the IPL. Chris Jordan has returned to the club that nurtured him and replaces Batty as T20 captain, while Aussie seamer Dan Worrall joins on a three-year contract and is not classed as overseas because he holds a UK passport. Seeing more of club captain Rory Burns, recently dropped by England, would be a major boon this summer. What of the crocked Currans? Sam should have recovered from a lower-back stress fracture by April but Tom faces a race to be fit for the T20 Blast after suffering a similar injury in January. The prolific Hashim Amla returns, but the big excitement is 21-year-old keeper-batter Jamie Smith, who cracked three red-ball hundreds last year. Jason Roy has taken a self-imposed break and will miss the start of the season, but Kemar Roach returns for the first five Championship matches.

IN: Chris Jordan (Sus), Cameron Steel (Dur), Dan Worrall (Aus, UK passport), Kemar Roach (WI, CC) , Sunil Narine (WI, T20)
OUT: Mark Stoneman (Mid), Jade Dernbach, Liam Plunkett (both REL), Gareth Batty, Rikki Clarke (both RET)

INTERIM HEAD COACH: GARETH BATTY

Surrey turned to Batty after Vikram Solanki left for the IPL earlier this year. The former England off-spinner retired at the end of last season and was initially appointed to work alongside Solanki and assistant coach Richard Johnson, who has since taken charge at Middlesex. Batty will be assisted by ex-Surrey allrounder Azhar Mahmood and former Warwickshire head coach Jim Troughton. The club will advertise for a permanent replacement for Solanki at the end of the season, a process to be overseen by new CEO Steve Elworthy.

www.kiaoval.com / tel: 0203 946 0100

	Mat	Inns	NO	Runs	HS	Ave	SR	100	50	4s	6s
OJ Pope	9	13	2	861	274	78.27	76.80	3	0	108	5
HM Amla	13	20	3	994	215*	58.47	44.21	3	2	105	1
RJ Burns	9	14	1	617	104*	47.46	50.57	1	7	83	2
BT Foakes	8	10	2	350	133	43.75	42.16	1	2	43	0
JL Smith	12	17	2	656	138	43.73	53.42	3	1	85	7
SA Abbott	1	1	0	40	40	40.00	47.05	0	0	1	2
WG Jacks	6	5	1	146	60	36.50	44.24	0	2	17	1
MD Stoneman	10	15	0	473	119	31.53	47.68	1	3	73	0
RS Patel	6	10	0	250	62	25.00	37.70	0	2	35	1
MP Dunn	1	1	0	23	23	23.00	115.00	0	0	2	1
J Overton	8	9	1	154	50	19.25	53.28	0	1	21	1
R Clarke	11	13	3	192	65	19.20	40.08	0	1	21	4
JPA Taylor	1	1	0	19	19	19.00	16.23	0	0	2	0
AAP Atkinson	2	4	1	52	41*	17.33	30.58	0	0	8	0
J Clark	12	14	1	208	61*	16.00	50.24	0	2	26	5
CT Steel	2	4	0	45	28	11.25	35.15	0	0	6	0
A Virdi	11	12	6	59	47	9.83	28.78	0	0	8	0
BBA Geddes	1	2	0	19	15	9.50	27.53	0	0	2	0
LJ Evans	2	3	0	21	11	7.00	50.00	0	0	3	0
KAJ Roach	5	3	1	13	8	6.50	22.03	0	0	2	0
RJW Topley	7	9	2	31	10	4.42	26.05	0	0	6	0
D Moriarty	4	3	0	12	8	4.00	16.43	0	0	2	0
JA Tattersall	1	1	0	4	4	4.00	11.42	0	0	0	0
R Ashwin	1	2	1	0	0*	0.00	0.00	0	0	0	0
KA Jamieson	1	1	1	0	0*	-	0.00	0	0	0	0

Batting

	Overs	Mdns	Runs	Wkts	BBI	BBM	Ave	Econ	SR	5w	10w
SA Abbott	15.0	8	27	2	2/5	2/27	13.50	1.80	45.0	0	0
R Ashwin	58.0	13	126	7	6/27	7/126	18.00	2.17	49.7	1	0
KAJ Roach	134.0	28	452	22	8/40	10/80	20.54	3.37	36.5	2	1
JPA Taylor	15.1	5	44	2	2/44	2/44	22.00	2.90	45.5	0	0
J Clark	276.0	36	904	32	6/21	6/54	28.25	3.27	51.7	2	0
D Moriarty	181.4	31	521	18	6/60	8/142	28.94	2.86	60.5	1	0
RJW Topley	199.3	46	616	21	5/66	6/126	29.33	3.08	57.0	1	0
A Virdi	299.4	48	961	28	6/171	7/142	34.32	3.20	64.2	1	0
AAP Atkinson	47.0	7	172	5	3/78	3/99	34.40	3.65	56.4	0	0
R Clarke	197.5	45	582	16	3/34	4/53	36.37	2.94	74.1	0	0
WG Jacks	64.0	9	216	4	1/7	1/33	54.00	3.37	96.0	0	0
J Overton	142.1	30	454	6	2/36	2/50	75.66	3.19	142.1	0	0
CT Steel	24.0	1	120	1	1/9	1/76	120.00	5.00	144.0	0	0
KA Jamieson	6.0	3	10	0	-	-	-	1.66	-	0	0
MD Stoneman	3.0	0	13	0	-	-	-	4.33	-	0	0
RJ Burns	7.0	1	22	0	-	-	-	3.14	-	0	0
RS Patel	23.0	5	80	0	-	-	-	3.47	-	0	0
MP Dunn	36.0	2	145	0	-	-	-	4.02	-	0	0

Bowling

Catches/Stumpings:
18 Foakes (inc 2st), 16 Smith (inc 1st), 13 Clarke, 6 Overton, Pope, 5 Burns, Tattersall, 4 Jacks, 3 Patel, 2 Amla, Clark, Evans, Moriarty, Stoneman, 1 Abbott, Ashwin, Dunn, Steel, Virdi

SURREY
COUNTY CRICKET CLUB

Batting

	Mat	Inns	NO	Runs	HS	Ave	SR	100	50	4s	6s
TH David	10	8	3	340	140*	68.00	150.44	2	1	27	20
JL Smith	10	7	2	315	85	63.00	80.35	0	3	27	11
RS Patel	10	8	1	386	131	55.14	113.19	2	1	33	16
MD Stoneman	9	8	2	329	117	54.83	79.27	1	1	33	5
R Clarke	9	5	0	165	82	33.00	89.67	0	1	17	5
BBA Geddes	4	4	1	84	32	28.00	90.32	0	0	10	2
NJH Kimber	3	1	0	16	16	16.00	55.17	0	0	3	0
HM Amla	4	3	0	47	29	15.66	57.31	0	0	6	0
C McKerr	10	4	2	30	20	15.00	53.57	0	0	2	0
AAP Atkinson	2	1	0	15	15	15.00	300.00	0	0	0	2
NMJ Reifer	10	5	0	63	28	12.60	91.30	0	0	6	1
MP Dunn	10	2	1	9	8*	9.00	30.00	0	0	0	0
OJ Pope	3	3	0	16	15	5.33	51.61	0	0	1	0
D Moriarty	10	3	1	8	5	4.00	44.44	0	0	1	0
CT Steel	5	3	1	5	4*	2.50	35.71	0	0	0	0
JPA Taylor	1	1	1	0	0*	-	-	0	0	0	0

Bowling

	Overs	Mdns	Runs	Wkts	BBI	Ave	Econ	SR	4w	5w
TH David	25.0	1	100	4	2/32	25.00	4.00	37.5	0	0
D Moriarty	81.5	7	357	15	4/30	23.80	4.36	32.7	1	0
JPA Taylor	6.0	0	27	1	1/27	27.00	4.50	36.0	0	0
R Clarke	61.3	2	282	4	1/16	70.50	4.58	92.2	0	0
CT Steel	45.0	1	220	10	4/33	22.00	4.88	27.0	2	0
RS Patel	9.4	0	51	2	1/5	25.50	5.27	29.0	0	0
C McKerr	64.2	0	386	18	4/64	21.44	6.00	21.4	1	0
MP Dunn	67.3	2	413	11	2/44	37.54	6.11	36.8	0	0
AAP Atkinson	16.0	1	113	5	4/43	22.60	7.06	19.2	1	0
NJH Kimber	12.0	0	87	2	2/57	43.50	7.25	36.0	0	0

Catches/Stumpings:
13 Smith (inc 2st), 6 David, 5 Moriarty, Patel, Reifer, Stoneman, 4 Clarke, Steel, 2 Dunn,
1 Atkinson, McKerr, Pope, Taylor

SURREY
COUNTY CRICKET CLUB

	Mat	Inns	NO	Runs	HS	Ave	SR	100	50	4s	6s
SM Curran	4	4	2	94	72*	47.00	159.32	0	1	6	6
TH David	2	2	1	45	25*	45.00	136.36	0	0	5	2
OJ Pope	5	5	1	168	60	42.00	141.17	0	2	15	1
WG Jacks	12	12	1	393	87	35.72	170.12	0	3	50	17
JJ Roy	4	4	0	139	64	34.75	147.87	0	1	16	5
JL Smith	13	12	3	297	60	33.00	125.84	0	3	29	5
TK Curran	4	1	0	25	25	25.00	250.00	0	0	1	2
LJ Evans	12	12	0	298	65	24.83	127.35	0	3	19	12
J Clark	10	7	3	97	37*	24.25	110.22	0	0	6	3
KA Jamieson	5	4	2	47	31	23.50	146.87	0	0	4	2
R Clarke	3	1	0	20	20	20.00	133.33	0	0	2	1
J Overton	12	10	1	134	28	14.88	167.50	0	0	8	10
RJ Burns	9	8	1	85	24	12.14	96.59	0	0	7	1
BBA Geddes	6	6	0	44	28	7.33	89.79	0	0	3	0
GJ Batty	13	2	1	7	4*	7.00	116.66	0	0	0	0
AAP Atkinson	8	5	2	9	5	3.00	52.94	0	0	0	0
JW Dernbach	2	1	0	2	2	2.00	100.00	0	0	0	0
HM Amla	1	1	0	0	0	0.00	0.00	0	0	0	0
D Moriarty	13	2	2	15	9*	-	150.00	0	0	1	1
MP Dunn	3	1	1	1	1*	-	33.33	0	0	0	0
C McKerr	2	-	-	-	-	-	-	-	-	-	-

Batting

	Overs	Mdns	Runs	Wkts	BBI	Ave	Econ	SR	4w	5w
D Moriarty	38.0	1	255	11	3/26	23.18	6.71	20.7	0	0
WG Jacks	21.0	2	141	4	2/7	35.25	6.71	31.5	0	0
GJ Batty	37.0	0	251	8	2/21	31.37	6.78	27.7	0	0
J Overton	17.0	0	136	4	2/14	34.00	8.00	25.5	0	0
R Clarke	3.0	0	25	0	-	-	8.33	-	0	0
AAP Atkinson	26.4	1	223	15	4/36	14.86	8.36	10.6	2	0
TK Curran	12.0	0	103	3	2/44	34.33	8.58	24.0	0	0
SM Curran	10.0	0	87	6	4/29	14.50	8.70	10.0	1	0
KA Jamieson	13.5	0	132	1	1/27	132.00	9.54	83.0	0	0
J Clark	25.3	0	263	5	1/20	52.60	10.31	30.6	0	0
C McKerr	2.3	0	26	0	-	-	10.40	-	0	0
JW Dernbach	3.0	0	40	0	-	-	13.33	-	0	0
MP Dunn	5.0	0	68	1	1/21	68.00	13.60	30.0	0	0

Bowling

Catches/Stumpings:
6 Burns, 5 Overton, 4 Clark, Smith 3 Atkinson, Clarke, Roy, 2 T Curran, Evans, Jacks, Pope,
1 Batty, S Curran, Dernbach, Dunn, Jamieson

SUSSEX

FORMED: 1839
HOME GROUND: The 1st Central County Ground, Hove
ONE-DAY NAME: Sussex Sharks
CAPTAIN: TBC (CC), Tom Haines (RL50), Luke Wright (T20)
2021 RESULTS: CC3: 6/6; RL50: 7/9 Group A; T20: Semi-finalists
HONOURS: Championship: (3) 2003, 2006, 2007; Gillette/NatWest/C&G/FP Trophy: (5) 1963, 1964, 1978, 1986, 2006; Pro40/National League/CB40/YB40/RL50: (2) 2008, 2009; Sunday League: 1982; T20 Cup: 2009

THE LOWDOWN

The Sussex faithful may well have been scratching their heads when casting their eye down the Championship XI last summer. Orr? Ibrahim? Sarro? Crocombe? Yet perhaps this will come to be seen as the year Sussex began nurturing success by boldly pitching their youngsters into battle. That they finished bottom of Division Three of the Championship came as no surprise, but there was a run to T20 Finals Day to lift spirits (where the names on the shirts were more familiar). It was quite a first season for head coach Ian Salisbury, who mid-season stripped the captain's armband from the experienced Ben Brown and gave it to 23-year-old batter Tom Haines. Brown went on to score 976 Championship runs (second only to Haines) but packed his bags and left for Hampshire last December. Chris Jordan and Phil Salt were other notable exits but Pakistan keeper Mohammad Rizwan has signed for the early season, with Aussie T20 star Josh Philippe to replace him in June. India's Cheteshwar Pujara will feature until at least the end of August after Travis Head had to cancel a deal to return as captain.

IN: Steven Finn (Mid), Fynn Hudson-Prentice (Der), Josh Philippe (Aus, CC/T20), Cheteshwar Pujara (Ind, CC/RL50), Mohammad Rizwan (Pak, CC/T20), Rashid Khan (Afg, T20)
OUT: Ben Brown (Ham), Chris Jordan (Sur), Phil Salt (Lan), Aaron Thomason (REL), Mitchell Claydon, Stuart Meaker (both RET)

HEAD COACH: IAN SALISBURY

The former England leggie moved up from spin-bowling coach to take charge of the four-day and 50-over sides following Jason Gillespie's departure in 2020, while James Kirtley looks after T20 affairs. Salisbury, who took 749 first-class wickets, had a brief spell in charge of Surrey before serving as the first full-time head coach of the England Physical Disability team. Grant Flower is the new batting coach and Mike Yardy has returned as Academy director.

COUNTY CHAMPIONSHIP AVERAGES 2021

	Mat	Inns	NO	Runs	HS	Ave	SR	100	50	4s	6s
BC Brown	12	21	2	976	157	51.36	59.65	4	2	115	2
TJ Haines	13	25	0	1176	156	47.04	52.71	3	6	143	1
WAT Beer	1	2	1	42	23*	42.00	37.50	0	0	2	0
AGH Orr	7	14	0	548	119	39.14	39.97	1	4	80	1
FJ Hudson-Prentice	3	5	1	145	67	36.25	60.92	0	1	21	0
OE Robinson	6	8	1	250	67	35.71	53.64	0	2	25	1
D Ibrahim	6	11	0	328	94	29.81	44.87	0	3	42	1
AD Thomason	9	17	2	379	78*	25.26	35.06	0	3	51	0
S van Zyl	9	17	0	422	113	24.82	50.96	1	3	59	2
JM Coles	2	4	1	72	36	24.00	56.69	0	0	10	0
GHS Garton	7	11	0	247	97	22.45	55.75	0	1	30	1
TGR Clark	7	13	2	240	54*	21.81	43.39	0	1	27	3
OJ Carter	6	12	1	235	51	21.36	37.72	0	1	31	1
JJ Carson	14	23	4	385	87	20.26	50.06	0	3	47	4
TM Head	6	11	1	183	49*	18.30	58.84	0	0	26	2
AD Lenham	1	2	0	29	20	14.50	41.42	0	0	3	0
SC Meaker	6	9	1	113	30*	14.12	46.50	0	0	18	0
DMW Rawlins	10	17	0	233	58	13.70	60.67	0	1	29	5
TI Hinley	1	2	0	20	19	10.00	43.47	0	0	3	0
HT Crocombe	9	17	2	83	46*	5.53	33.06	0	0	10	0
JA Atkins	5	9	5	21	10*	5.25	25.00	0	0	3	0
HD Ward	3	6	0	30	19	5.00	23.80	0	0	4	0
JP Sarro	3	6	3	8	7*	2.66	14.54	0	0	0	0
SF Hunt	6	10	4	12	7	2.00	13.18	0	0	1	0

Batting

	Overs	Mdns	Runs	Wkts	BBI	BBM	Ave	Econ	SR	5w	10w
JC Archer	18.0	4	43	3	2/29	3/43	14.33	2.38	36.0	0	0
OE Robinson	207.0	49	547	33	9/78	13/128	16.57	2.64	37.6	2	1
S van Zyl	11.0	2	22	1	1/10	1/10	22.00	2.00	66.0	0	0
WAT Beer	29.0	6	70	3	2/29	3/70	23.33	2.41	58.0	0	0
JA Atkins	137.4	14	469	20	5/51	5/75	23.45	3.40	41.3	2	0
ME Claydon	17.0	3	54	2	2/51	2/54	27.00	3.17	51.0	0	0
JJ Carson	449.4	65	1336	37	5/85	7/96	36.10	2.97	72.9	1	0
SF Hunt	127.5	18	487	13	3/47	4/72	37.46	3.80	59.0	0	0
HT Crocombe	211.0	29	756	20	4/92	5/83	37.80	3.58	63.3	0	0
GHS Garton	134.5	11	559	13	4/69	5/94	43.00	4.14	62.2	0	0
JP Sarro	43.0	3	220	4	2/53	2/71	55.00	5.11	64.5	0	0
SC Meaker	135.4	11	525	9	3/22	4/84	58.33	3.86	90.4	0	0
FJ Hudson-Prentice	58.2	5	204	2	2/49	3/110	68.00	3.49	116.6	0	0
AD Lenham	13.0	0	71	1	1/60	1/71	71.00	5.46	78.0	0	0
D Ibrahim	67.4	11	236	3	2/9	2/21	78.66	3.48	135.3	0	0
TM Head	27.4	4	109	1	1/23	1/23	109.00	3.93	166.0	0	0
TJ Haines	41.0	1	114	1	1/21	1/21	114.00	2.78	246.0	0	0
TGR Clark	33.0	3	120	1	1/37	1/41	120.00	3.63	198.0	0	0
DMW Rawlins	171.0	17	573	4	2/12	2/52	143.25	3.35	256.5	0	0

Bowling

Catches/Stumpings:
26 Brown (inc 3st), 16 Thomason, 14 Carter, 6 Clark, 4 Brown, Garton, van Zyl, 3 Carson, Head, Hudson-Prentice, Ibrahim, Rawlins, 2 Haines, Meaker, Robinson, Ward, 1 Orr, Sarro

SUSSEX
SHARKS

Batting

	Mat	Inns	NO	Runs	HS	Ave	SR	100	50	4s	6s
TM Head	7	7	2	291	56	58.20	111.92	0	3	25	8
BC Brown	5	5	0	252	105	50.40	95.81	1	1	24	1
TJ Haines	7	7	0	252	123	36.00	83.72	1	0	24	4
AGH Orr	5	5	0	144	108	28.80	68.57	1	0	10	5
D Wiese	5	5	0	132	36	26.40	126.92	0	0	12	6
TGR Clark	3	3	0	76	44	25.33	90.47	0	0	10	1
OJ Carter	7	7	1	151	59	25.16	95.56	0	2	13	4
JM Coles	7	6	1	95	32	19.00	66.43	0	0	10	1
WAT Beer	6	5	0	91	40	18.20	88.34	0	0	8	2
AD Lenham	7	5	2	47	16	15.66	82.45	0	0	3	1
HD Ward	2	2	0	24	20	12.00	82.75	0	0	5	0
D Ibrahim	7	5	0	59	46	11.80	62.76	0	0	4	0
HT Crocombe	4	4	2	16	9*	8.00	88.88	0	0	2	0
JP Sarro	5	1	1	4	4*	-	80.00	0	0	0	0

Bowling

	Overs	Mdns	Runs	Wkts	BBI	Ave	Econ	SR	4w	5w
JM Coles	48.4	0	217	8	3/27	27.12	4.45	36.5	0	0
WAT Beer	50.0	0	234	8	2/30	29.25	4.68	37.5	0	0
D Ibrahim	35.0	0	197	5	2/54	39.40	5.62	42.0	0	0
TM Head	16.0	0	93	2	2/35	46.50	5.81	48.0	0	0
AD Lenham	53.0	0	321	8	4/59	40.12	6.05	39.7	1	0
HT Crocombe	31.0	0	218	3	1/33	72.66	7.03	62.0	0	0
D Wiese	37.0	1	261	7	2/44	37.28	7.05	31.7	0	0
JP Sarro	26.0	1	189	4	2/41	47.25	7.26	39.0	0	0

Catches/Stumpings:
9 Carter (inc 2st), 3 Beer, Haines, Head, 2 Clark, Coles, Lenham, Wiese, 1 Brown, Ibrahim

www.sussexcricket.co.uk / tel: 0844 264 0202

SUSSEX SHARKS

Batting

	Mat	Inns	NO	Runs	HS	Ave	SR	100	50	4s	6s
Rashid Khan	3	3	2	57	27*	57.00	247.82	0	0	8	3
CJ Jordan	8	3	2	44	24*	44.00	157.14	0	0	2	3
LJ Wright	11	10	1	370	77	41.11	151.63	0	4	46	10
PD Salt	12	11	2	302	77*	33.55	147.31	0	3	31	12
RS Bopara	13	11	3	259	62*	32.37	122.16	0	3	24	5
GHS Garton	7	3	0	96	46	32.00	165.51	0	0	7	6
OE Robinson	5	1	0	31	31	31.00	163.15	0	0	4	0
DMW Rawlins	11	8	2	155	50*	25.83	155.00	0	1	9	10
TM Head	9	8	1	108	27	15.42	112.50	0	0	11	3
TS Mills	9	4	1	44	27	14.66	112.82	0	0	6	1
HD Ward	6	6	1	73	22	14.60	114.06	0	0	10	0
D Wiese	13	9	0	77	21	8.55	93.90	0	0	6	1
WAT Beer	13	5	2	25	11*	8.33	78.12	0	0	1	0
AD Thomason	5	2	0	16	8	8.00	80.00	0	0	1	1
AD Lenham	11	3	2	7	5*	7.00	35.00	0	0	0	0
ME Claydon	3	1	1	1	1*	-	100.00	0	0	0	0
OJ Carter	2	1	1	0	0*	-	0.00	0	0	0	0
JC Archer	1	-	-	-	-	-	-	-	-	-	-
HT Crocombe	1	-	-	-	-	-	-	-	-	-	-

Bowling

	Overs	Mdns	Runs	Wkts	BBI	Ave	Econ	SR	4w	5w
JC Archer	3.0	0	20	0	-	-	6.66	-	0	0
TM Head	1.0	0	7	0	-	-	7.00	-	0	0
RS Bopara	23.0	0	163	8	3/15	20.37	7.08	17.2	0	0
GHS Garton	24.0	1	174	11	3/19	15.81	7.25	13.0	0	0
AD Lenham	26.0	0	194	11	4/26	17.63	7.46	14.1	1	0
Rashid Khan	12.0	0	92	2	1/25	46.00	7.66	36.0	0	0
WAT Beer	36.0	1	280	9	2/20	31.11	7.77	24.0	0	0
D Wiese	24.4	0	193	11	2/16	17.54	7.82	13.4	0	0
TS Mills	30.0	0	240	17	3/20	14.11	8.00	10.5	0	0
CJ Jordan	26.0	0	211	8	3/30	26.37	8.11	19.5	0	0
DMW Rawlins	10.0	0	90	0	-	-	9.00	-	0	0
OE Robinson	16.2	0	152	5	2/15	30.40	9.30	19.6	0	0
ME Claydon	10.0	0	99	2	1/31	49.50	9.90	30.0	0	0
HT Crocombe	1.0	0	19	0	-	-	19.00	-	0	0

Catches/Stumpings:
9 Salt (inc 2st), 7 Wiese, 6 Head, 5 Jordan, Wright, 3 Beer, Bopara, Lenham, Robinson,
2 Carter, Garton, Khan, Rawlins, Thomason, Ward

TEAM PROFILE

FORMED: 1882
HOME GROUND: Edgbaston Stadium, Birmingham
T20 BLAST NAME: Birmingham Bears
CAPTAIN: Will Rhodes (CC/RL50), Carlos Brathwaite (T20)
2021 RESULTS: CC1: Winners; BWT: Winners; RL50: 5/9 Group B; T20: Quarter-finalists
HONOURS: Championship: (8) 1911, 1951, 1972, 1994, 1995, 2004, 2012, 2021; Bob Willis Trophy: 2021; Gillette/NatWest/C&G/FP Trophy: (5) 1966, 1968, 1989, 1993, 1995; Benson & Hedges Cup: (2) 1994, 2002; Pro40/National League/CB40/YB40/RL50: (2) 2010, 2016; Sunday League: (3) 1980, 1994, 1997; T20 Cup: 2014

THE LOWDOWN

To have won the Championship for an eighth time was some achievement for a Warwickshire side which in recent years has lost its lynchpins: Trott, Bell and Patel to name but three. They did it without 'big-name players', although that may soon change for someone like 22-year-old opener Rob Yates, whose four Championship centuries were three more than any other teammate managed. And yet the key to the batting was steadiness throughout: 10 players made at least one fifty. That list doesn't include Chris Benjamin, the young keeper-batter who made a hundred at Old Trafford on his Championship debut. Liam Norwell, free from injuries at last, stormed to 49 Championship wickets at 18 and there was no let up at the other end, whether it was Craig Miles (37 wickets), Will Rhodes (27) or Oliver Hannon-Dalby (24). Spinner Danny Briggs, signed from Sussex a year earlier to little fanfare, produced his best season in a white shirt (30 wickets at 22). A repeat this summer will be tough, particularly following the retirement of Tim Bresnan, but the return of West Indies heavyweight Carlos Brathwaite for the T20 Blast – this time as captain – boosts their chances in the shortest format.

IN: Alex Davies (Lan), Carlos Brathwaite (WI, T20)
OUT: Ed Pollock (Wor), Alex Thomson (Der), Tim Bresnan (RET)

FIRST-TEAM COACH: MARK ROBINSON

The ex-seamer, who took 584 first-class wickets, won the Championship in his first season after taking over from Jim Troughton in January 2021. Robinson claimed six trophies as Sussex coach between 2005 and 2015 before leading England Women to the 2017 World Cup triumph. Jonathan Trott has become assistant coach and Matt Mason, the former Worcestershire seamer, has replaced Graeme Welch as bowling coach.

Batting

	Mat	Inns	NO	Runs	HS	Ave	SR	100	50	4s	6s
RM Yates	13	23	2	793	132*	37.76	44.65	4	2	93	3
PJ Malan	6	10	1	339	141	37.66	59.05	1	1	37	2
DP Sibley	9	15	2	470	80	36.15	37.87	0	4	44	2
SR Hain	14	25	2	826	118	35.91	41.21	1	6	92	1
CG Benjamin	3	6	0	198	127	33.00	53.51	1	0	24	1
MJ Lamb	13	23	5	565	67	31.38	42.93	0	3	75	3
MGK Burgess	14	21	0	607	101	28.90	53.05	1	3	70	3
DR Briggs	12	19	4	411	66*	27.40	50.67	0	3	56	5
WMH Rhodes	14	26	6	633	91	26.37	47.62	0	5	77	6
TT Bresnan	10	15	2	311	68*	23.92	43.31	0	2	39	0
GH Vihari	3	6	0	100	52	16.66	38.75	0	1	11	0
OP Stone	4	5	1	63	43	15.75	37.27	0	0	10	0
JB Lintott	1	1	0	15	15	15.00	78.94	0	0	2	0
JG Bethell	1	2	0	23	15	11.50	52.27	0	0	5	0
CN Miles	11	16	2	146	25	10.42	29.97	0	0	11	0
LC Norwell	12	17	5	118	30*	9.83	48.36	0	0	14	3
OJ Hannon-Dalby	8	11	6	48	26	9.60	33.10	0	0	8	0
CR Woakes	2	3	0	19	10	6.33	55.88	0	0	4	0
CK Holder	2	3	1	6	6	3.00	42.85	0	0	1	0
RN Sidebottom	2	2	0	1	1	0.50	8.33	0	0	0	0
EA Brookes	1	-	-	-	-	-	-	-	-	-	-

Bowling

	Overs	Mdns	Runs	Wkts	BBI	BBM	Ave	Econ	SR	5w	10w
CR Woakes	72.3	23	205	12	3/26	6/66	17.08	2.82	36.2	0	0
LC Norwell	346.4	97	895	49	6/57	7/65	18.26	2.58	42.4	2	0
WMH Rhodes	178.0	51	481	26	5/23	6/84	18.50	2.70	41.0	1	0
CN Miles	277.4	62	807	37	5/30	6/55	21.81	2.90	45.0	2	0
DR Briggs	290.0	81	664	30	4/36	6/89	22.13	2.28	58.0	0	0
MJ Lamb	21.0	2	50	2	2/38	2/38	25.00	2.38	63.0	0	0
OJ Hannon-Dalby	258.5	73	698	24	5/76	7/121	29.08	2.69	64.7	1	0
OP Stone	124.3	20	395	13	4/89	6/154	30.38	3.17	57.4	0	0
TT Bresnan	163.0	57	417	12	3/35	4/71	34.75	2.55	81.5	0	0
RM Yates	47.0	7	108	3	2/54	2/54	36.00	2.29	94.0	0	0
CK Holder	45.0	9	177	2	1/23	2/108	88.50	3.93	135.0	0	0
GH Vihari	1.0	0	11	0	-	-	-	11.00	-	0	0
EA Brookes	7.0	2	22	0	-	-	-	3.14	-	0	0
JB Lintott	39.0	2	103	0	-	-	-	2.64	-	0	0
RN Sidebottom	46.0	9	113	0	-	-	-	2.45	-	0	0

Catches/Stumpings:
44 Burgess (inc 4st), 21 Yates, 18 Hain, 16 Bresnan, 13 Rhodes, 5 Lamb, 4 Briggs, 3 Miles, Vihari, 2 Hannon-Dalby, 1 Benjamin, Bethell, Lintott, Norwell, Sibley, Woakes

Batting

	Mat	Inns	NO	Runs	HS	Ave	SR	100	50	4s	6s
MJ Lamb	8	7	1	360	119*	60.00	96.77	1	2	32	3
CG Benjamin	1	1	0	50	50	50.00	87.71	0	1	3	3
DR Mousley	4	4	0	166	61	41.50	109.21	0	2	9	7
RM Yates	7	7	0	282	103	40.28	92.76	1	2	33	4
MGK Burgess	8	8	1	275	73	39.28	80.17	0	2	29	1
EJ Pollock	8	8	1	237	103*	33.85	92.57	1	0	29	5
WMH Rhodes	7	7	0	204	65	29.14	76.11	0	1	20	1
JG Bethell	8	7	1	141	66	23.50	94.63	0	1	9	4
EA Brookes	8	7	2	107	63	21.40	86.29	0	1	9	3
TT Bresnan	2	2	1	19	12	19.00	55.88	0	0	2	0
K Carver	5	3	2	18	13*	18.00	78.26	0	0	1	0
AM Chakrapani	2	2	0	22	18	11.00	56.41	0	0	1	0
KT van Vollenhoven	2	2	0	21	20	10.50	52.50	0	0	0	0
MS Johal	6	3	1	16	10*	8.00	64.00	0	0	0	0
GA Garrett	4	2	0	8	7	4.00	44.44	0	0	0	0
CN Miles	2	1	1	31	31*	-	100.00	0	0	2	1
RN Sidebottom	2	2	2	11	9*	-	68.75	0	0	1	0
J Bulpitt	3	-	-	-	-	-	-	-	-	-	-
LC Norwell	1	-	-	-	-	-	-	-	-	-	-

Bowling

	Overs	Mdns	Runs	Wkts	BBI	Ave	Econ	SR	4w	5w
LC Norwell	10.0	0	39	0	-	-	3.90	-	0	0
GA Garrett	27.0	1	135	5	3/50	27.00	5.00	32.4	0	0
K Carver	40.0	0	203	5	2/35	40.60	5.07	48.0	0	0
RM Yates	23.4	2	121	2	1/27	60.50	5.11	71.0	0	0
J Bulpitt	16.0	1	82	2	2/33	41.00	5.12	48.0	0	0
JG Bethell	57.0	0	301	11	4/36	27.36	5.28	31.0	1	0
MJ Lamb	28.0	1	151	4	4/35	37.75	5.39	42.0	1	0
MS Johal	41.4	2	228	7	2/35	32.57	5.47	35.7	0	0
WMH Rhodes	26.0	0	145	8	3/40	18.12	5.57	19.5	0	0
RN Sidebottom	16.4	1	97	2	1/41	48.50	5.82	50.0	0	0
DR Mousley	9.0	0	53	1	1/31	53.00	5.88	54.0	0	0
KT van Vollenhoven	7.0	0	45	0	-	-	6.42	-	0	0
TT Bresnan	18.0	0	117	1	1/64	117.00	6.50	108.0	0	0
EA Brookes	30.4	0	207	7	3/15	29.57	6.75	26.2	0	0
CN Miles	14.0	0	101	2	1/48	50.50	7.21	42.0	0	0

Catches/Stumpings:
12 Burgess (inc 2st), 8 E Brookes, 4 Rhodes, Yates, 2 Bethell, Johal, Lamb, Mousley, Pollock,
1 Bresnan, Sidebottom, van Vollenhoven

BIRMINGHAM BEARS

Batting

	Mat	Inns	NO	Runs	HS	Ave	SR	100	50	4s	6s
CG Benjamin	2	2	1	71	60*	71.00	165.11	0	1	9	2
SR Hain	14	13	3	398	83*	39.80	139.16	0	4	27	11
PJ Malan	3	3	0	85	63	28.33	126.86	0	1	7	3
CR Woakes	3	2	1	27	14	27.00	150.00	0	0	2	1
CR Brathwaite	11	10	2	183	52*	22.87	150.00	0	1	10	12
EJ Pollock	12	12	1	245	62	22.27	144.11	0	2	27	11
TT Bresnan	9	7	2	109	34*	21.80	122.47	0	0	8	6
JB Lintott	11	3	1	42	41	21.00	190.90	0	0	3	3
WMH Rhodes	14	13	0	258	79	19.84	134.37	0	1	23	8
AJ Hose	11	11	1	185	46*	18.50	133.09	0	0	23	7
DR Mousley	6	5	0	88	56	17.60	120.54	0	1	9	2
MJ Lamb	5	4	0	66	39	16.50	106.45	0	0	4	3
CN Miles	14	6	4	29	11*	14.50	78.37	0	0	2	0
KR Mayers	2	2	0	27	14	13.50	122.72	0	0	2	1
MGK Burgess	14	10	1	107	41	11.88	97.27	0	0	9	1
RM Yates	5	5	0	55	24	11.00	88.70	0	0	6	0
DR Briggs	13	8	5	26	7*	8.66	123.80	0	0	3	0
JG Bethell	3	3	1	12	7	6.00	85.71	0	0	0	1
RN Sidebottom	1	1	0	3	3	3.00	50.00	0	0	0	0
LC Norwell	1	1	0	0	0	0.00	0.00	0	0	0	0

Bowling

	Overs	Mdns	Runs	Wkts	BBI	Ave	Econ	SR	4w	5w
DR Mousley	10.0	0	70	2	1/3	35.00	7.00	30.0	0	0
DR Briggs	51.5	0	365	15	3/35	24.33	7.04	20.7	0	0
JB Lintott	43.0	0	304	15	4/20	20.26	7.06	17.2	1	0
CR Brathwaite	38.5	0	317	18	3/7	17.61	8.16	12.9	0	0
CN Miles	47.0	0	387	15	3/19	25.80	8.23	18.8	0	0
RM Yates	8.0	0	66	1	1/13	66.00	8.25	48.0	0	0
CR Woakes	11.0	0	97	3	2/38	32.33	8.81	22.0	0	0
TT Bresnan	31.3	0	280	16	4/26	17.50	8.88	11.8	1	0
MJ Lamb	1.0	0	9	0	-	-	9.00	-	0	0
WMH Rhodes	18.0	0	164	14	4/34	11.71	9.11	7.7	1	0
RN Sidebottom	4.0	0	37	1	1/37	37.00	9.25	24.0	0	0
JG Bethell	6.0	0	61	0	-	-	10.16	-	0	0
LC Norwell	2.1	0	31	0	-	-	14.30	-	0	0

Catches/Stumpings:
11 Hain, 10 Burgess (inc 6st), 9 Miles, Rhodes, 8 Lintott, 7 Hose, 4 Brathwaite, Lamb, Pollock, 2 Benjamin, Bresnan, Malan, Mousley, Woakes, 1 Bethell, Briggs, Sidebottom

TEAM PROFILE

FORMED: 1865
HOME GROUND: New Road, Worcester
ONE-DAY NAME: Worcestershire Rapids
CAPTAIN: Brett D'Oliveira
2021 RESULTS: CC3: 3/6; RL50: 5/9 Group A; T20: 5/9 North Group
HONOURS: Championship: (5) 1964, 1965, 1974, 1988, 1989; Gillette/NatWest/C&G/FP Trophy: 1994; Benson & Hedges Cup: 1991; Pro40/National League/CB40/YB40/RL50: 2007; Sunday League: (3) 1971, 1987, 1988; T20 Cup: 2018

THE LOWDOWN

Joe Leach has relinquished the captaincy after five difficult years in charge. The seam-bowling allrounder took Worcestershire to the Division Two title in his first year as skipper but was immediately hit by the Alex Hepburn rape case which left the club in turmoil. Leach has been a force of unity when Worcestershire needed it most – and their most reliable performer. It falls to Brett D'Oliveira, the new captain, to breathe life into a side which failed to make an impression across any format last summer. With the exception of Jake Libby (1,573 runs at 56 since joining the club) and Ed Barnard (now a genuine allrounder), there were no standout performers. The seam attack lacked edge without the injury-plagued Josh Tongue, and a red-ball spinner is sorely missing. Pakistan's Azhar Ali will shore up a shaky top-order this summer, but Daryl Mitchell has retired after nearly two decades in which he scored over 19,000 runs for the club and finished as their top T20 wicket-taker (101). After a long, dismal struggle with injury, England seamer Pat Brown hopes to be ready for the T20 Blast.

IN: Taylor Cornall, Ben Gibbon (both unattached), Ed Pollock (War), Azhar Ali (Pak, CC)
OUT: Ross Whiteley (Ham), Alex Milton (REL), Daryl Mitchell (RET)

FIRST-TEAM COACH: ALEX GIDMAN

The 41-year-old former allrounder was promoted from Second XI coach after playing a major role in the club's first T20 title in 2018, having joined the backroom staff earlier that year in the wake of Steve Rhodes' departure. A former Gloucestershire captain who scored nearly 11,000 first-class runs for his county, Gidman turned to coaching in 2016 after spending his last season as a player at New Road. Bowling coach Alan Richardson takes charge of the 50-over team while Gidman is with Birmingham Phoenix for The Hundred.

	Mat	Inns	NO	Runs	HS	Ave	SR	100	50	4s	6s
JD Libby	14	23	4	1075	180*	56.57	48.66	4	4	120	5
EG Barnard	13	18	3	746	128	49.73	51.16	2	3	90	0
JA Haynes	9	14	0	491	97	35.07	47.99	0	4	56	1
J Leach	13	19	5	377	84	26.92	55.19	0	1	48	4
BL D'Oliveira	14	21	2	480	71	25.26	51.22	0	3	58	2
OB Cox	14	21	2	413	60*	21.73	43.75	0	2	56	1
DKH Mitchell	14	23	1	470	113	21.36	43.19	1	3	64	0
MH Wessels	7	10	0	202	60	20.20	46.65	0	2	29	0
CAJ Morris	6	8	2	116	50	19.33	32.04	0	1	17	0
GH Roderick	7	11	2	167	42*	18.55	41.75	0	0	23	0
AS Joseph	6	8	0	148	61	18.50	61.15	0	1	20	3
TC Fell	12	19	0	324	69	17.05	37.07	0	2	53	0
JO Baker	5	7	2	84	61*	16.80	70.58	0	1	12	1
DY Pennington	10	14	4	156	56	15.60	44.95	0	1	20	2
JC Tongue	4	6	1	66	17	13.20	42.30	0	0	7	0
IS Sodhi	1	1	0	13	13	13.00	28.88	0	0	2	0
AW Finch	3	4	1	37	31	12.33	21.38	0	0	4	0
RA Whiteley	2	3	0	34	22	11.33	28.57	0	0	4	0

Batting

	Overs	Mdns	Runs	Wkts	BBI	BBM	Ave	Econ	SR	5w	10w
IS Sodhi	49.2	3	148	6	6/89	6/148	24.66	3.00	49.3	1	0
JC Tongue	115.5	18	358	14	5/39	7/98	25.57	3.09	49.6	1	0
J Leach	428.0	108	1141	38	5/68	9/136	30.02	2.66	67.5	1	0
DY Pennington	282.4	57	898	29	5/32	9/76	30.96	3.17	58.4	1	0
AW Finch	76.0	13	250	8	2/32	4/78	31.25	3.28	57.0	0	0
CAJ Morris	189.3	45	621	19	4/43	5/88	32.68	3.27	59.8	1	0
RA Whiteley	10.0	1	33	1	1/22	1/22	33.00	3.30	60.0	0	0
JO Baker	144.2	30	408	12	3/49	3/57	34.00	2.82	72.1	0	0
AS Joseph	158.0	21	574	15	2/22	4/106	38.26	3.63	63.2	0	0
EG Barnard	368.1	83	1052	25	4/43	5/88	42.08	2.85	88.3	0	0
BL D'Oliveira	253.4	29	808	15	3/95	3/95	53.86	3.18	101.4	0	0
DKH Mitchell	93.5	15	291	4	2/34	2/43	72.75	3.10	140.7	0	0
JD Libby	38.2	5	129	1	1/45	1/45	129.00	3.36	230.0	0	0

Bowling

Catches/Stumpings:
44 Cox (inc 2st), 13 Mitchell, 12 Barnard, 9 Fell, 8 Haynes, 6 Libby, 4 Baker, D'Oliveira,
3 Wessels, 2 Leach, 1 Pennington, Roderick, Whiteley

Batting

	Mat	Inns	NO	Runs	HS	Ave	SR	100	50	4s	6s
CAJ Morris	7	3	2	52	25*	52.00	74.28	0	0	3	2
JA Haynes	7	7	0	362	153	51.71	94.27	1	2	40	3
BL D'Oliveira	6	6	0	267	123	44.50	103.08	1	1	30	3
J Leach	7	7	3	169	88	42.25	109.03	0	1	15	8
JD Libby	7	7	0	239	76	34.14	84.45	0	2	11	2
JO Baker	7	7	4	84	25	28.00	89.36	0	0	8	2
TC Fell	7	7	0	172	58	24.57	83.90	0	2	14	3
JJ Dell	5	5	1	90	32	22.50	97.82	0	0	12	0
J Banton	3	3	0	56	33	18.66	78.87	0	0	1	2
EG Barnard	7	7	1	111	39*	18.50	75.00	0	0	6	0
AW Finch	7	3	1	25	23*	12.50	125.00	0	0	2	1
GH Roderick	7	7	0	78	23	11.14	66.10	0	0	2	2

Bowling

	Overs	Mdns	Runs	Wkts	BBI	Ave	Econ	SR	4w	5w
JD Libby	8.0	0	26	0	-	-	3.25	-	0	0
J Banton	12.0	0	55	4	3/15	13.75	4.58	18.0	0	0
BL D'Oliveira	36.3	0	184	7	3/8	26.28	5.04	31.2	0	0
J Leach	44.0	2	245	6	3/28	40.83	5.56	44.0	0	0
EG Barnard	47.0	1	265	9	2/25	29.44	5.63	31.3	0	0
AW Finch	37.0	1	222	6	2/54	37.00	6.00	37.0	0	0
JO Baker	45.2	1	273	7	2/53	39.00	6.02	38.8	0	0
CAJ Morris	43.0	1	266	4	1/31	66.50	6.18	64.5	0	0

Catches/Stumpings:
8 Roderick (inc 2st), 4 Leach, 3 Barnard, Haynes, Morris, 2 Banton, D'Oliveira, Fell, 1 Finch

www.wccc.co.uk / tel: 01905 748474

	Mat	Inns	NO	Runs	HS	Ave	SR	100	50	4s	6s
JD Libby	13	13	3	315	78*	31.50	108.24	0	2	20	1
OB Cox	13	12	3	275	61*	30.55	132.21	0	1	23	6
BL D'Oliveira	13	13	1	358	69	29.83	130.18	0	3	37	8
MH Wessels	11	11	0	300	77	27.27	132.15	0	1	33	6
MM Ali	4	4	0	106	52	26.50	145.20	0	1	10	6
RA Whiteley	13	11	2	237	42	26.33	127.41	0	0	17	10
DKH Mitchell	7	5	2	50	29	16.66	128.20	0	0	6	0
EG Barnard	13	9	2	106	43*	15.14	120.45	0	0	8	3
BJ Dwarshuis	13	9	5	52	15	13.00	94.54	0	0	4	0
JA Haynes	2	2	0	22	15	11.00	115.78	0	0	2	0
IS Sodhi	13	3	1	16	14	8.00	106.66	0	0	1	1
DY Pennington	11	3	2	8	4*	8.00	57.14	0	0	0	0
TC Fell	2	2	0	7	4	3.50	41.17	0	0	0	0
CAJ Morris	13	2	1	2	2*	2.00	50.00	0	0	0	0
JC Tongue	2	-	-	-	-	-	-	-	-	-	-

Batting

	Overs	Mdns	Runs	Wkts	BBI	Ave	Econ	SR	4w	5w
BL D'Oliveira	20.0	0	118	5	3/15	23.60	5.90	24.0	0	0
MM Ali	13.0	0	84	4	2/15	21.00	6.46	19.5	0	0
IS Sodhi	47.0	0	361	11	4/24	32.81	7.68	25.6	1	0
JC Tongue	5.0	0	41	1	1/12	41.00	8.20	30.0	0	0
DKH Mitchell	13.0	0	107	3	1/8	35.66	8.23	26.0	0	0
DY Pennington	31.0	3	260	13	4/24	20.00	8.38	14.3	1	0
EG Barnard	22.2	0	197	4	1/11	49.25	8.82	33.5	0	0
BJ Dwarshuis	47.0	0	419	15	4/31	27.93	8.91	18.8	1	0
CAJ Morris	41.5	0	398	17	3/21	23.41	9.51	14.7	0	0
JD Libby	2.0	0	23	0	-	-	11.50	-	0	0

Bowling

Catches/Stumpings:
8 Cox (inc 3st), Wessels, Whiteley, 7 D'Oliveira, 6 Sodhi, 5 Dwarshuis, 4 Mitchell, 3 Barnard, Morris, 2 Libby, 1 Ali, Pennington, Tongue

TEAM PROFILE

THE YORKSHIRE
COUNTY CRICKET CLUB

FORMED: 1863

HOME GROUND: Headingley Stadium, Leeds

ONE-DAY NAME: Yorkshire Vikings

CAPTAIN: Steven Patterson (CC), Dom Bess (RL50), David Willey (T20)

2021 RESULTS: CC1: 5/6; RL50: Quarter-finalists; T20: Quarter-finalists

HONOURS: County Championship: (33) 1893, 1896, 1898, 1900, 1901, 1902, 1905, 1908, 1912, 1919, 1922, 1923, 1924, 1925, 1931, 1932, 1933, 1935, 1937, 1938, 1939, 1946, 1949, 1959, 1960, 1962, 1963, 1966, 1967, 1968, 2001, 2014, 2015; Gillette/NatWest/C&G/FP Trophy: (3) 1965, 1969, 2002; Benson & Hedges Cup: 1987; Sunday League: 1983

THE LOWDOWN

After the darkest of winters, Yorkshire will be relieved to play some cricket. The entire backroom staff, including head coach Andrew Gale and director of cricket Martyn Moxon, were sacked in December following the club's report into racist abuse directed at their former player Azeem Rafiq. The chairman and CEO had resigned a month earlier. This after Yorkshire had initially played down the report and resisted calls for sweeping change. Ottis Gibson, the new head coach, knows the county scene well, has coaching experience at the highest level and, in the words of new Yorkshire chairman Lord Patel, "will help foster a culture of inclusion at the club". Darren Gough has taken Moxon's job until the end of the summer. But what of the players? Will they be cowed, or find strength in adversity? Yorkshire were strong across all formats last year, with five seamers taking 20 Championship wickets or more at an average of 25 or less. Middle-order batter Harry Brook and allrounder Jordan Thompson are stars in the making. As part of a tie-up with the PSL franchise Lahore Qalandars to "reduce barriers", Pakistan seamer Haris Rauf will appear during "a period of the 2022 season".

IN: Haris Rauf (Pak)

OUT: Mathew Pillans (REL)

HEAD COACH: OTTIS GIBSON

Yorkshire appointed the former West Indies fast bowler to replace Andrew Gale in January. Gibson took 659 first-class wickets in a 17-year career which included spells at three counties. He has been head coach of West Indies and South Africa between two spells as England's bowling coach. He will work with two new assistant coaches: ex-England seamer Kabir Ali and Alastair Maiden, former head of Academy at Leicestershire.

Batting

	Mat	Inns	NO	Runs	HS	Ave	SR	100	50	4s	6s
DJ Malan	2	3	0	220	199	73.33	58.20	1	0	26	2
GS Ballance	10	14	1	594	101*	45.69	50.04	1	4	68	8
DJ Willey	6	8	4	165	41*	41.25	52.71	0	0	15	4
A Lyth	14	22	1	819	153	39.00	51.80	3	3	117	4
HC Brook	14	22	1	797	118	37.95	61.97	2	5	110	4
JE Root	5	8	0	291	101	36.37	54.59	1	1	22	0
GCH Hill	7	11	0	263	71	23.90	36.83	0	2	35	1
DM Bess	14	20	1	399	56	21.00	39.97	0	2	50	0
JA Thompson	13	20	0	411	57	20.55	49.28	0	1	56	9
T Kohler-Cadmore	11	18	0	353	89	19.61	35.15	0	1	41	3
ML Revis	1	2	0	34	34	17.00	51.51	0	0	7	0
HG Duke	9	13	1	197	54	16.41	40.70	0	2	25	0
JA Tattersall	5	8	1	101	26	14.42	32.26	0	0	14	0
TW Loten	2	4	0	57	27	14.25	35.84	0	0	8	0
SA Patterson	13	17	2	191	47*	12.73	37.08	0	0	21	1
MD Fisher	5	7	2	55	17	11.00	36.91	0	0	6	0
BO Coad	10	13	5	84	33*	10.50	57.53	0	0	12	1
D Olivier	7	11	5	61	21	10.16	33.88	0	0	6	0
WAR Fraine	3	6	0	35	12	5.83	17.94	0	0	3	0
SA Northeast	2	2	0	4	3	2.00	13.79	0	0	0	0
DJ Leech	1	-	-	-	-	-	-	-	-	-	-

Bowling

	Overs	Mdns	Runs	Wkts	BBI	BBM	Ave	Econ	SR	5w	10w
ML Revis	9.0	2	19	2	2/19	2/19	9.50	2.11	27.0	0	0
GCH Hill	48.0	12	128	7	2/12	3/23	18.28	2.66	41.1	0	0
MD Fisher	121.0	29	393	20	5/41	9/64	19.65	3.24	36.3	1	0
JA Thompson	329.5	91	949	46	5/52	7/53	20.63	2.87	43.0	1	0
BO Coad	287.1	79	766	35	4/48	7/112	21.88	2.66	49.2	0	0
DJ Willey	148.3	30	479	20	5/61	6/82	23.95	3.22	44.5	1	0
SA Patterson	364.0	111	815	32	4/26	6/61	25.46	2.23	68.2	0	0
HC Brook	82.1	18	194	7	3/15	4/29	27.71	2.36	70.4	0	0
DM Bess	405.4	122	912	28	7/43	9/102	32.57	2.24	86.9	2	0
D Olivier	175.1	26	610	18	4/61	4/51	33.88	3.48	58.3	0	0
JE Root	27.0	4	74	1	1/26	1/32	74.00	2.74	162.0	0	0
A Lyth	13.0	8	6	0	-	-	-	0.46	-	0	0
DJ Leech	17.0	1	79	0	-	-	-	4.64	-	0	0

Catches/Stumpings:
31 Duke, 25 Lyth, 21 Kohler-Cadmore, 17 Brook, 16 Tattersall, 4 Bess, Root, Thompson,
3 Ballance, Patterson, 2 Malan, Northeast, 1 Fisher, Fraine, Hill, Olivier, Willey

Batting

	Mat	Inns	NO	Runs	HS	Ave	SR	100	50	4s	6s
MJ Waite	9	5	1	159	44	39.75	116.05	0	0	13	8
GCH Hill	9	7	1	222	90*	37.00	86.04	0	2	19	3
W Luxton	7	6	1	165	68	33.00	86.38	0	1	16	4
WAR Fraine	9	8	1	227	69*	32.42	113.50	0	1	29	5
ML Revis	9	7	1	186	58*	31.00	109.41	0	1	17	5
MW Pillans	7	3	1	61	40	30.50	70.93	0	0	5	1
HG Duke	9	7	0	206	125	29.42	79.23	1	0	19	1
GS Ballance	9	8	1	180	54	25.71	77.58	0	1	22	1
JA Tattersall	9	7	1	153	70	25.50	85.95	0	2	15	0
DM Bess	4	3	0	19	7	6.33	46.34	0	0	3	0
BO Coad	8	4	2	12	10	6.00	85.71	0	0	2	0
JR Sullivan	3	1	0	6	6	6.00	60.00	0	0	0	0
SA Patterson	1	1	0	1	1	1.00	33.33	0	0	0	0
JW Shutt	5	2	2	2	1*	-	11.76	0	0	0	0
D Olivier	1	-	-	-	-	-	-	-	-	-	-

Bowling

	Overs	Mdns	Runs	Wkts	BBI	Ave	Econ	SR	4w	5w
BO Coad	58.2	7	285	8	3/30	35.62	4.88	43.7	0	0
GCH Hill	47.0	2	249	10	3/47	24.90	5.29	28.2	0	0
ML Revis	43.0	3	229	5	2/43	45.80	5.32	51.6	0	0
JR Sullivan	14.0	0	79	5	4/11	15.80	5.64	16.8	1	0
DM Bess	32.1	2	188	1	1/28	188.00	5.84	193.0	0	0
MJ Waite	51.0	1	320	12	5/59	26.66	6.27	25.5	0	1
D Olivier	9.0	0	60	1	1/60	60.00	6.66	54.0	0	0
MW Pillans	34.0	0	251	8	4/26	31.37	7.38	25.5	2	0
JW Shutt	11.0	0	88	1	1/33	88.00	8.00	66.0	0	0

Catches/Stumpings:
9 Ballance, 5 Duke (inc 1st), Revis, Tattersall, 4 Fraine, 3 Shutt, 1 Bess, Coad, Hill, Luxton, Olivier, Pillans

VITALITY BLAST AVERAGES 2021

	Mat	Inns	NO	Runs	HS	Ave	SR	100	50	4s	6s	
JM Bairstow	4	4	0	295	112	73.75	175.59	1	2	26	18	
HC Brook	13	13	6	486	91*	69.42	149.07	0	2	41	20	
T Kohler-Cadmore	6	5	1	168	55	42.00	126.31	0	2	14	7	
DJ Willey	5	4	2	73	44	36.50	162.22	0	0	4	5	
JA Thompson	12	10	2	215	74	26.87	185.34	0	2	13	16	
WAR Fraine	7	7	4	79	22*	26.33	141.07	0	0	8	1	Batting
JE Root	4	4	0	97	49	24.25	105.43	0	0	9	0	
GS Ballance	9	8	1	159	55	22.71	128.22	0	1	16	6	
A Lyth	13	13	0	232	52	17.84	145.91	0	2	27	9	
DM Bess	9	4	2	32	24	16.00	110.34	0	0	4	0	
MD Stoneman	4	4	0	58	50	14.50	100.00	0	1	10	0	
MD Fisher	11	3	1	28	19	14.00	140.00	0	0	2	2	
GCH Hill	6	4	1	36	19*	12.00	85.71	0	0	1	2	
DJ Malan	4	4	0	41	23	10.25	105.12	0	0	7	0	
JA Tattersall	4	3	0	18	10	6.00	90.00	0	0	1	0	
MJ Waite	11	6	2	18	6*	4.50	90.00	0	0	0	1	
LH Ferguson	10	2	1	2	2	2.00	28.57	0	0	0	0	
SA Northeast	1	1	1	0	0*	-	-	0	0	0	0	
HG Duke	4	-	-	-	-	-	-	-	-	-	-	
JE Poysden	1	-	-	-	-	-	-	-	-	-	-	
AU Rashid	5	-	-	-	-	-	-	-	-	-	-	

	Overs	Mdns	Runs	Wkts	BBI	Ave	Econ	SR	4w	5w	
DM Bess	30.0	0	201	11	3/17	18.27	6.70	16.3	0	0	
LH Ferguson	37.0	1	269	14	4/24	19.21	7.27	15.8	1	0	
AU Rashid	20.0	0	149	5	3/32	29.80	7.45	24.0	0	0	
JE Root	11.0	0	89	3	1/19	29.66	8.09	22.0	0	0	Bowling
MD Fisher	36.4	0	321	12	2/15	26.75	8.75	18.3	0	0	
DJ Willey	18.0	0	161	7	3/44	23.00	8.94	15.4	0	0	
MJ Waite	28.3	1	264	9	2/17	29.33	9.26	19.0	0	0	
A Lyth	14.0	0	138	1	1/18	138.00	9.85	84.0	0	0	
JA Thompson	30.0	0	296	14	4/44	21.14	9.86	12.8	1	0	
JE Poysden	0.4	0	18	0	-	-	27.00	-	0	0	

Catches/Stumpings:
12 Lyth, 9 Brook, 7 Thompson, 5 Willey, 4 Ferguson, 3 Duke, Fisher, Fraine, Kohler-Cadmore,
2 Bairstow, Bess, Root, Stoneman, 1 Hill, Malan, Tattersall

Men's
Players

MOHAMMAD ABBAS   RHB / RMF / RO / W1

HAMPSHIRE

FULL NAME: Mohammad Abbas
BORN: March 10, 1990, Sialkot, Pakistan
SQUAD NO: 38
TEAMS: Pakistan, Hampshire, Khan Research Laboratories, Islamabad, Leicestershire, Multan Sultans, Pakistan Television, Rawalpindi, Sialkot, Southern Punjab, Sui Northern Gas Pipelines Limited
ROLE: Bowler
DEBUT: Test: 2017; ODI: 2019;
First-class: 2009; List A: 2009; T20: 2013

BEST BATTING: 40 Khan Research Laboratories vs Karachi Whites, Karachi, 2016
BEST BOWLING: 8-46 Khan Research Laboratories vs Karachi Whites, Karachi, 2016
COUNTY CAP: 2018 (Leicestershire)

TWITTER: @RealMAbbas226
NOTES: Hampshire have re-signed the Pakistan seamer to play Championship cricket for the first two months of the season. Abbas has been mopping up wickets for fun since his first venture in county cricket at Leicestershire in 2018 and 2019, claiming 79 Championship scalps at 20.67 across both seasons. He was due to play for Nottinghamshire in 2020 before the pandemic struck but was a sensation last summer for Hampshire, with a haul of 41 wickets at 15.87 in 10 matches. A late bloomer, the 32-year-old has emerged as one of the most skilful seamers in the world, becoming the joint-second-fastest to take 50 Test wickets for Pakistan (10 matches), behind only Yasir Shah (9)

Batting	Mat	Inns	NO	Runs	HS	Ave	SR	100	50	Ct	St
Tests	25	36	16	110	29	5.50	17.02	0	0	7	-
ODIs	3	-	-	-	-	-	-	-	-	0	-
First-class	132	187	73	759	40	6.65	27.36	0	0	36	-
List A	55	31	13	137	15*	7.61	53.10	0	0	13	-
T20s	32	10	7	32	15*	10.66	152.38	0	0	7	-

Bowling	Mat	Balls	Runs	Wkts	BBI	BBM	Ave	Econ	SR	5w	10
Tests	25	5134	2072	90	5/33	10/95	23.02	2.42	57.0	4	1
ODIs	3	162	153	1	1/44	1/44	153.00	5.66	162.0	0	0
First-class	132	25443	11207	539	8/46	14/93	20.79	2.64	47.2	38	11
List A	55	2693	2191	75	4/31	4/31	29.21	4.88	35.9	0	0
T20s	32	678	971	26	3/22	3/22	37.34	8.59	26.0	0	0

FULL NAME: Kyle John Abbott
BORN: June 18, 1987, Empangeni, KwaZulu-Natal, South Africa
SQUAD NO: 11
NICKNAME: Jimmy
TEAMS: South Africa, Hampshire, Boland, Dolphins, Durban Heat, Jafna Stallions, Kings XI Punjab, KwaZulu-Natal, Lahore Qalandars, Middlesex, Titans, Worcestershire
ROLE: Bowler
DEBUT: Test: 2013; ODI: 2013; T20I: 2013; First-class: 2009; List A: 2009; T20: 2011

HAMPSHIRE

BEST BATTING: 97* Hampshire vs Lancashire, Old Trafford, 2017
BEST BOWLING: 9-40 Hampshire vs Somerset, Southampton, 2019
COUNTY CAP: 2017 (Hampshire)

MOST EXCITING DAY AS A CRICKETER? Playing in the 2015 World Cup
CHILDHOOD SPORTING HERO? Lance Klusener
WHAT WOULD YOU DO IF YOU WERE IN CHARGE OF COUNTY CRICKET? Be more lenient on over-rates
FAVOURITE SMELL? A fire in the African bush
TWITTER: @Kyle_Abbott87

Batting	Mat	Inns	NO	Runs	HS	Ave	SR	100	50	Ct	St
Tests	11	14	0	95	17	6.78	28.10	0	0	4	-
ODIs	28	13	4	76	23	8.44	60.31	0	0	7	-
T20Is	21	6	4	23	9*	11.50	114.99	0	0	7	-
First-class	129	174	35	2649	97*	19.05	46.71	0	10	19	-
List A	112	55	22	536	56	16.24	81.33	0	1	29	-
T20s	156	54	30	324	30	13.50	117.81	0	0	33	-

Bowling	Mat	Balls	Runs	Wkts	BBI	BBM	Ave	Econ	SR	5w	10
Tests	11	2081	886	39	7/29	9/68	22.71	2.55	53.3	3	0
ODIs	28	1303	1051	34	4/21	4/21	30.91	4.83	38.3	0	0
T20Is	21	436	579	26	3/20	3/20	22.26	7.96	16.7	0	0
First-class	129	22237	10482	495	9/40	17/86	21.17	2.82	44.9	33	5
List A	112	5073	4414	149	5/43	5/43	29.62	5.22	34.0	1	0
T20s	156	3252	4484	157	5/14	5/14	28.56	8.27	20.7	1	0

TOM ABELL

RHB / RM / R0 / W0 / MVP49

SOMERSET

FULL NAME: Thomas Benjamin Abell
BORN: March 5, 1994, Taunton
SQUAD NO: 28
HEIGHT: 5ft 11in
NICKNAME: Sid
EDUCATION: Taunton School; University of Exeter
TEAMS: Somerset, Brisbane Heat, England Lions, Rangpur Rangers
ROLE: Batter
DEBUT: First-class: 2014; List A: 2015; T20: 2016

BEST BATTING: 135 Somerset vs Lancashire, Old Trafford, 2016
BEST BOWLING: 4-39 Somerset vs Warwickshire, Edgbaston, 2019
COUNTY CAP: 2018

WHO IS YOUR LOOKALIKE? Apparently it's the actor Eddie Redmayne… but I'm not so sure
FIRST CRICKET CLUB? Taunton CC, Somerset
WHAT WOULD YOU CHANGE ABOUT THE STRUCTURE OF THE COUNTY SEASON? Reinstate the Lord's final for 50-over cricket
WHO IS THE BEST BATTER/KEEPER/ALLROUNDER/BOWLER IN COUNTY CRICKET (EXCLUDING TEAMMATES)? Gary Ballance/Ben Foakes/Liam Dawson/Matthew Fisher
MOST UNDERRATED PLAYER IN COUNTY CRICKET? Sam Cook
WHAT WOULD A FLY ON THE WALL HEAR IN YOUR DRESSING ROOM? Tom Banton
MOST BEAUTIFUL THING YOU HAVE EVER SEEN? Jonny Wilkinson's drop goal
WHO WOULD YOU LEAST LIKE TO HAVE A NET WITH? Jack Brooks, because he gets me out for fun!
WHAT DO YOU MOST ENJOY LISTENING TO? Justin Bieber
WHAT MAKES YOU WORRY? The red Dukes ball
TWITTER: @tomabell1

Batting	Mat	Inns	NO	Runs	HS	Ave	SR	100	50	Ct	St
First-class	94	168	16	4957	135	32.61	48.78	8	28	67	-
List A	25	21	1	636	106	31.80	79.30	1	1	7	-
T20s	55	49	11	1286	101*	33.84	143.84	1	8	36	-

Bowling	Mat	Balls	Runs	Wkts	BBI	BBM	Ave	Econ	SR	5w	10
First-class	94	2721	1566	53	4/39	6/70	29.54	3.45	51.3	0	0
List A	25	36	26	2	2/19	2/19	13.00	4.33	18.0	0	0
T20s	55	60	100	2	1/11	1/11	50.00	10.00	30.0	0	0

COLIN ACKERMANN RHB / OB / R0 / W0 / MVP33

FULL NAME: Colin Niel Ackermann
BORN: April 4, 1991, George, Cape Province, South Africa
SQUAD NO: 48
HEIGHT: 6ft 1in
NICKNAME: Ackers
EDUCATION: Grey High School, Port Elizabeth; University of South Africa
TEAMS: Netherlands, Leicestershire, Eastern Province, South Africa U19, Warriors
ROLE: Allrounder
DEBUT: ODI: 2021; T20I: 2019; First-class: 2010; List A: 2010; T20: 2011

BEST BATTING: 196* Leicestershire vs Middlesex, Leicester, 2018
BEST BOWLING: 5-69 Leicestershire vs Sussex, Hove, 2019

WHO IS YOUR LOOKALIKE? Moises Henriques
FIRST CRICKET CLUB? Kibworth CC, Leicestershire
FAMILY TIES? My younger brother Travis Ackermann plays for South Western Districts in South Africa
BIGGEST INFLUENCE ON YOUR DEVELOPMENT AS A CRICKETER (EXCLUDING PARENTS)? Attending Grey High School, Port Elizabeth
WHO IS THE BEST BATTER/KEEPER/ALLROUNDER/BOWLER IN COUNTY CRICKET (EXCLUDING TEAMMATES)? Wayne Madsen/Ben Foakes/Ben Raine/Chris Rushworth
HOBBIES? Fishing
WHAT DO YOU MOST ENJOY LISTENING TO? Property podcasts
TWITTER: @ackers38

Batting	Mat	Inns	NO	Runs	HS	Ave	SR	100	50	Ct	St
ODIs	4	3	0	96	81	32.00	82.05	0	1	1	-
T20Is	14	14	3	300	43*	27.27	118.57	0	0	4	-
First-class	140	243	28	8728	196*	40.59	49.08	18	55	138	-
List A	87	79	14	2356	152*	36.24	78.87	2	16	56	
T20s	138	132	19	3108	79*	27.50	121.02	0	16	64	-

Bowling	Mat	Balls	Runs	Wkts	BBI	BBM	Ave	Econ	SR	5w	10
ODIs	4	114	81	2	1/10	1/10	40.50	4.26	57.0	0	0
T20Is	14	168	179	6	1/6	1/6	29.83	6.39	28.0	0	0
First-class	140	5579	3023	73	5/69	6/99	41.41	3.25	76.4	1	0
List A	87	2179	1744	44	4/48	4/48	39.63	4.80	49.5	0	0
T20s	138	1606	1944	69	7/18	7/18	28.17	7.26	23.2	1	0

SHAHEEN SHAH AFRIDI — LHB / LF / RO / WO

MIDDLESEX

FULL NAME: Shaheen Shah Afridi
BORN: April 06, 2000, Khyber Agency, Pakistan
SQUAD NO: 10
TEAMS: Pakistan, Middlesex, Baluchistan, Hampshire, Khan Research Laboratories, Khyber Pakhtunkhwa, Lahore Qalandars, Northern
ROLE: Bowler
DEBUT: Test: 2018; ODI: 2018; T20I: 2018; First-class: 2017; List A: 2018; T20: 2018

BEST BATTING: 25 Pakistanis vs Australia A, Perth, 2019
BEST BOWLING: 8-39 Khan Research Laboratories vs Rawalpindi, Rawalpindi, 2017

TWITTER: @iShaheenAfridi
NOTES: Middlesex supporters will be salivating over the prospect of watching the 2021 men's ICC Player of the Year taking the new ball at Lord's in the early season. Afridi has been signed to play both Championship and T20 cricket until mid-July, although Pakistan's rearranged ODI series against West Indies in June may curtail his involvement. The tall left-armer perfectly complements a strong Middlesex seam attack boasting the likes of Tim Murtagh, Ethan Bamber and Toby Roland-Jones. "Shaheen is a world-class pace bowler, and we are thrilled that he will be representing us in 2022," said Andrew Cornish, Middlesex's CEO. "His signature was highly sought-after, and the fact that he has chosen to join Middlesex is a massive coup for us as a club and speaks volumes of our ambitions"

Batting	Mat	Inns	NO	Runs	HS	Ave	SR	100	50	Ct	St
Tests	21	28	7	121	19	5.76	34.77	0	0	2	-
ODIs	28	15	9	87	19*	14.50	60.83	0	0	4	-
T20Is	39	4	3	19	10*	19.00	105.55	0	0	8	-
First-class	27	34	7	166	25	6.14	37.05	0	0	3	-
List A	33	17	10	90	19*	12.85	59.60	0	0	5	-
T20s	118	33	13	156	39*	7.80	96.89	0	0	27	-

Bowling	Mat	Balls	Runs	Wkts	BBI	BBM	Ave	Econ	SR	5w	10
Tests	21	4107	2055	86	6/51	10/94	23.89	3.00	47.7	4	1
ODIs	28	1419	1305	53	6/35	6/35	24.62	5.51	26.7	2	0
T20Is	39	860	1122	45	3/20	3/20	24.93	7.82	19.1	0	0
First-class	27	5176	2605	112	8/39	10/94	23.25	3.01	46.2	5	1
List A	33	1683	1566	58	6/35	6/35	27.00	5.58	29.0	2	0
T20s	118	2671	3438	163	6/19	6/19	21.09	7.72	16.3	4	0

QAIS AHMAD

RHB / LB

FULL NAME: Qais Ahmad Kamawal
BORN: August 15, 2000, Nangarhar, Afghanistan
SQUAD NO: 32
TEAMS: Afghanistan, Kent, Balkh Legends, Colombo Kings, Guyana Amazon Warriors, Hobart Hurricanes, Kabul Eagles, Melbourne Stars, Minister Group Dhaka, Quetta Gladiators, Speen Ghar Region, Rajshahi Kings, St Lucia Stars
ROLE: Bowler
DEBUT: Test: 2019; ODI: 2022; T20I: 2020; First-class: 2018; List A: 2018; T20: 2017

BEST BATTING: 50* Colombo Kings vs Dambulla Vikings, Hambantota, 2020 (T20)
BEST BOWLING: 5-18 Balkh Legends vs Kabul Zwanan, Sharjah, 2018 (T20)

TWITTER: @Qais_AhmadK
NOTES: Kent have re-signed the Afghan leg-spinner for this year's T20 Blast. Ahmad took 10 wickets in 12 appeareances for the Spitfires during their winning campaign in 2021, with an economy rate of just 6.65 runs per over. The 21-year-old burst onto the scene when he took 10 wickets on his first-class debut for Speen Ghar Region in 2018. He made his Test debut against Bangladesh during a famous victory at Chittagong in September 2019 but has not been able to secure a regular spot in Afghanistan's white-ball teams. He played his first ODI earlier this year and was recalled to the T20I side in March. Ahmad has starred in T20 leagues around the world and turned out for Melbourne Stars in the Big Bash over the winter

Batting	Mat	Inns	NO	Runs	HS	Ave	SR	100	50	Ct	St
Tests	1	2	0	23	14	11.50	56.09	0	0	0	-
ODIs	1	-	-	-	-	-	-	-	-	0	-
T20Is	2	2	1	8	8	8.00	88.88	0	0	0	-
First-class	12	17	2	226	46*	15.06	59.16	0	0	7	-
List A	14	8	2	118	36*	19.66	79.19	0	0	6	-
T20s	103	52	15	466	50*	12.59	124.26	0	1	28	-

Bowling	Mat	Balls	Runs	Wkts	BBI	BBM	Ave	Econ	SR	5w	10
Tests	1	54	28	1	1/22	1/28	28.00	3.11	54.0	0	0
ODIs	1	46	32	3	3/32	3/32	10.66	4.17	15.3	0	0
T20Is	2	36	46	4	3/25	3/25	11.50	7.66	9.0	0	0
First-class	12	2465	1395	68	7/41	13/127	20.51	3.39	36.2	5	3
List A	14	760	605	21	3/21	3/21	28.80	4.77	36.1	0	0
T20s	103	2127	2524	115	5/18	5/18	21.94	7.11	18.4	1	0

REHAN AHMED — RHB / LB / RO / WO

LEICESTERSHIRE

FULL NAME: Rehan Ahmed
BORN: August 13, 2004, Nottingham
SQUAD NO: 16
HEIGHT: 5ft 8in
NICKNAME: Ray
EDUCATION: Bluecoat School, Nottingham
TEAMS: Leicestershire, England U19
ROLE: Allrounder
DEBUT: List A: 2021

FIRST CRICKET CLUB? Thoresby Colliery CC, Mansfield, Nottinghamshire
WHAT WOULD YOU CHANGE ABOUT THE STRUCTURE OF THE COUNTY SEASON? Play more red-ball cricket in the middle of the summer – we either play four-day cricket in early season when it's freezing or late in the year when it's also cold
WHO IS THE BEST BATTER/KEEPER/ALLROUNDER/BOWLER IN COUNTY CRICKET (EXCLUDING TEAMMATES)? Jamie Smith/Harry Duke/Lyndon James/Luke Fletcher
MOST UNDERRATED PLAYER IN COUNTY CRICKET? Brett Hutton
MOST BEAUTIFUL THING YOU HAVE EVER SEEN? A BMW M8 in matt black
HOBBIES? Boxing
IF YOU COULD TURN BACK TIME... I'd change nothing! No regrets
WHO WOULD YOU MOST AND LEAST LIKE TO HAVE A NET WITH? Most – Sachin Tendulkar. Least – Shoaib Akhtar (scariest bowler alive)
MAKE ONE PREDICTION FOR THE FUTURE OF CRICKET: Another white-ball franchise tournament within the next five years
WHAT DO YOU MOST ENJOY LISTENING TO? Dave (rapper)
WHAT MAKES YOU WORRY? Not performing well
WHAT GIVES YOU JOY? Performing well
TWITTER: @RehanAhmed_16

Batting	Mat	Inns	NO	Runs	HS	Ave	SR	100	50	Ct	St
List A	7	6	4	89	40*	44.50	66.41	0	0	0	-

Bowling	Mat	Balls	Runs	Wkts	BBI	BBM	Ave	Econ	SR	5w	10
List A	7	332	318	5	2/25	2/25	63.60	5.74	66.4	0	0

BEN AITCHISON

RHB / RMF / R0 / W0

FULL NAME: Benjamin William Aitchison
BORN: July 6, 1999, Southport, Lancashire
SQUAD NO: 11
HEIGHT: 6ft 4in
NICKNAME: Biggen
EDUCATION: Merchant Taylors' School, Crosby
TEAMS: Derbyshire
ROLE: Bowler
DEBUT: First-class: 2020; List A: 2021

BEST BATTING: 50 Derbyshire vs Nottinghamshire, Derby, 2021
BEST BOWLING: 6-28 Derbyshire vs Durham, Derby, 2021

WHO IS YOUR LOOKALIKE? Eli Manning (former NFL player)
FIRST CRICKET CLUB? Formby CC, Liverpool
WHO IS THE BEST BATTER/KEEPER/ALLROUNDER/BOWLER IN COUNTY CRICKET (EXCLUDING TEAMMATES)? Ben Duckett/George Lavelle/Tim Bresnan/Tom Hartley
MOST UNDERRATED PLAYER IN COUNTY CRICKET? Tom Bailey
MOST BEAUTIFUL THING YOU HAVE EVER SEEN? The views from Sydney Harbour Bridge
HOBBIES? Golf
WHO WOULD YOU LEAST LIKE TO HAVE A NET WITH? Mark Wood – he's scary fast
MAKE ONE PREDICTION FOR THE FUTURE OF CRICKET: A T10 World Cup
WHAT DO YOU MOST ENJOY LISTENING TO? Podcasts
WHAT MAKES YOU WORRY? Bad weather
WHAT GIVES YOU JOY? Sport
GUILTY PLEASURE? Rom-coms
TWITTER: @Benaitchinson123

Batting	Mat	Inns	NO	Runs	HS	Ave	SR	100	50	Ct	St
First-class	16	21	4	208	50	12.23	48.03	0	1	14	-
List A	6	4	2	31	19	15.50	93.93	0	0	1	-

Bowling	Mat	Balls	Runs	Wkts	BBI	BBM	Ave	Econ	SR	5w	10
First-class	16	2122	1003	40	6/28	6/28	25.07	2.83	53.0	1	0
List A	6	177	205	2	2/51	2/51	102.50	6.94	88.5	0	0

KASEY ALDRIDGE

RHB / RFM / R0 / W0

SOMERSET

FULL NAME: Kasey Luke Aldridge
BORN: December 24, 2000, Bristol
SQUAD NO: 5
HEIGHT: 6ft 4in
NICKNAME: Fred
EDUCATION: Millfield School, Somerset
TEAMS: Somerset, England U19
ROLE: Allrounder
DEBUT: First-class: 2021; List A: 2021

FIRST CRICKET CLUB? Brislington CC, Bristol
BIGGEST INFLUENCE ON YOUR DEVELOPMENT AS A CRICKETER (EXCLUDING PARENTS)? My prep-school coach Dave Beal
WHAT WOULD A FLY ON THE WALL HEAR IN YOUR DRESSING ROOM? Darts
HOBBIES? Trying to hit the golf ball miles
WHO WOULD YOU MOST AND LEAST LIKE TO HAVE A NET WITH? Most – Andrew Flintoff. Least – Brett Lee
MAKE ONE PREDICTION FOR THE FUTURE OF CRICKET: Lewis Goldsworthy will play for England
WHAT DO YOU MOST ENJOY LISTENING TO? Eminem
WHAT MAKES YOU WORRY? Getting hit in the box
WHAT GIVES YOU JOY? Seeing the off pole out the ground
GUILTY PLEASURE? Domino's Pizza
TWITTER: @KaseyAldridge1

Batting	Mat	Inns	NO	Runs	HS	Ave	SR	100	50	Ct	St
First-class	1	-	-	-	-	-	-	-	-	0	-
List A	6	3	1	27	12	13.50	67.50	0	0	1	-

Bowling	Mat	Balls	Runs	Wkts	BBI	BBM	Ave	Econ	SR	5w	10
First-class	1	132	101	0	-	-	-	4.59	-	0	0
List A	6	180	209	6	3/39	3/39	34.83	6.96	30.0	0	0

FULL NAME: Azhar Ali
BORN: February 19, 1985, Lahore, Pakistan
SQUAD NO: TBC
TEAMS: Pakistan, Worcestershire,
Abbottabad Rhinos, Baluchistan Warriors,
Central Punjab, Khan Research Laboratories,
Lahore, Sui Northern Gas Pipelines Limited,
Punjab, Rawalpindi, Somerset
ROLE: Batter
DEBUT: Test: 2010; ODI: 2011;
First-class: 2002; List A: 2001; T20: 2006

WORCESTERSHIRE

BEST BATTING: 302* Pakistan vs West Indies, Dubai, 2016
BEST BOWLING: 4-34 Khan Research Laboratories vs Peshawar, Peshawar, 2003

TWITTER: @AzharAli_
NOTES: Worcestershire had to move fast to plug the gap left by Matthew Wade's unexpected
call-up to the IPL, and they alighted on Pakistan's well-travelled opener and former Test
captain. A veteran closing in on 100 Tests and holder of a Test triple-century, Azhar brings
great experience to a batting line-up which misfired last season, although his Championship
record during his time with Somerset was modest: 978 runs in 20 matches with just one
hundred. But he looked to be in good touch when compiling 185 against Australia at
Rawalpindi over the winter. "It is a fantastic signing and [head coach] Alex Gidman is
delighted," said Paul Pridgeon, chairman of Worcestershire's cricket steering group. "It
is excellent that we've got someone available to play County Championship cricket all
summer. It gives us that stability"

Batting	Mat	Inns	NO	Runs	HS	Ave	SR	100	50	Ct	St
Tests	91	169	11	6721	302*	42.53	41.87	18	34	65	-
ODIs	53	53	3	1845	102	36.90	74.45	3	12	8	-
First-class	225	392	33	14040	302*	39.10		41	63	150	-
List A	170	155	22	6278	132*	47.20		17	36	48	-
T20s	49	49	4	985	72	21.88	104.67	0	3	24	-

Bowling	Mat	Balls	Runs	Wkts	BBI	BBM	Ave	Econ	SR	5w	10
Tests	91	855	611	8	2/35	2/49	76.37	4.28	106.8	0	0
ODIs	53	258	260	4	2/26	2/26	65.00	6.04	64.5	0	0
First-class	225	3432	2148	48	4/34		44.75	3.75	71.5	0	0
List A	170	2514	2309	69	5/23	5/23	33.46	5.51	36.4	4	0
T20s	49	267	283	15	3/10	3/10	18.86	6.35	17.8	0	0

HASSAN ALI

RHB / RFM / R0 / W0

LANCASHIRE

FULL NAME: Hassan Ali
BORN: July 02, 1994, Mandi Bahauddin,
Pakistan
SQUAD NO: TBC
TEAMS: Pakistan, Lancashire, Central Punjab,
Comilla Victorians, Islamabad, St Kitts &
Nevis Patriots, Peshawar Zalmi, Sialkot
ROLE: Bowler
DEBUT: Test: 2017; ODI: 2016; T20I: 2016;
First-class: 2013; List A: 2013; T20: 2014

BEST BATTING: 106* Central Punjab vs Khyber Pakhtunkhwa, Karachi, 2021
BEST BOWLING: 8-107 Sialkot Stallions vs State Bank of Pakistan, Sialkot, 2014

TWITTER: @RealHa55an
NOTES: Lancashire have signed the Pakistan seamer for the first six games of the County
Championship. "Hassan is a high-quality player and has a fine record in first-class and Test-
match cricket," said Glen Chapple, Lancashire's head coach. "We believe that his red-ball
skills will complement our bowling attack nicely and that the experience he has gained at
international level can bring a lot into our dressing room." Hassan completes a powerful
Lancashire seam attack which includes James Anderson, Saqib Mahmood and Tom Bailey.
This will be the 27-year-old's first taste of county cricket and he has all the qualities to exploit
early-season English conditions much like his compatriot Mohammad Abbas has done
in recent years. Hassan is a regular for Pakistan in all formats of the game and has had a
devastating impact in Test cricket, taking 41 wickets at 16 last year

Batting	Mat	Inns	NO	Runs	HS	Ave	SR	100	50	Ct	St
Tests	17	25	5	299	30	14.95	81.47	0	0	6	-
ODIs	57	33	10	353	59	15.34	123.42	0	2	12	-
T20Is	48	17	10	119	23	17.00	188.88	0	0	11	-
First-class	56	82	22	1011	106*	16.85	76.47	1	3	20	-
List A	82	50	15	569	59	16.25	122.89	0	2	25	-
T20s	147	64	27	467	45	12.62	156.18	0	0	40	-

Bowling	Mat	Balls	Runs	Wkts	BBI	BBM	Ave	Econ	SR	5w	10
Tests	17	3012	1555	72	5/27	10/114	21.59	3.09	41.8	6	1
ODIs	57	2742	2610	89	5/34	5/34	29.32	5.71	30.8	4	0
T20Is	48	979	1359	60	4/18	4/18	22.65	8.32	16.3	0	0
First-class	56	10166	5659	244	8/107	11/94	23.19	3.33	41.6	16	4
List A	82	3964	3664	136	5/34	5/34	26.94	5.54	29.1	4	0
T20s	147	3173	4169	190	5/20	5/20	21.94	7.88	16.7	1	0

FULL NAME: Moeen Munir Ali
BORN: June 18, 1987, Birmingham
SQUAD NO: 8
HEIGHT: 6ft
NICKNAME: Brother Mo
EDUCATION: Moseley School, Birmingham
TEAMS: England, Worcestershire, Cape Town Blitz, Chennai Super Kings, Comilla Victorians, Matabeleland Tuskers, Multan Sultans, RC Bangalore, Warwickshire
ROLE: Allrounder
DEBUT: Test: 2014; ODI: 2014; T20I: 2014; First-class: 2005; List A: 2006; T20: 2007

BEST BATTING: 250 Worcestershire vs Glamorgan, Worcester, 2013
BEST BOWLING: 6-29 Worcestershire vs Lancashire, Old Trafford, 2012
COUNTY CAP: 2007 (Worcestershire)

FIRST CRICKET CLUB? Moseley Ashfield CC, Birmingham
FAMILY TIES? My cousin Kabir played for England and my brother Kadeer played for Worcestershire, Gloucestershire and Leicestershire
CHILDHOOD SPORTING HERO? Saeed Anwar
NOTES: Moeen has been retained by Chennai Super Kings for this year's IPL

Batting	Mat	Inns	NO	Runs	HS	Ave	SR	100	50	Ct	St
Tests	64	111	8	2914	155*	28.29	51.14	5	14	40	-
ODIs	112	89	14	1877	128	25.02	101.29	3	5	36	-
T20Is	49	44	10	637	72*	18.73	136.98	0	4	13	-
First-class	198	339	27	11334	250	36.32	55.04	20	69	120	-
List A	229	200	16	5172	158	28.10	101.67	11	20	69	-
T20s	216	204	20	4671	121*	25.38	140.90	2	25	71	-

Bowling	Mat	Balls	Runs	Wkts	BBI	BBM	Ave	Econ	SR	5w	10
Tests	64	11854	7149	195	6/53	10/112	36.66	3.61	60.7	5	1
ODIs	112	5056	4424	87	4/46	4/46	50.85	5.25	58.1	0	0
T20Is	49	649	854	33	3/24	3/24	25.87	7.89	19.6	0	0
First-class	198	24584	14490	382	6/29	12/96	37.93	3.53	64.3	12	2
List A	229	8167	7307	162	4/33	4/33	45.10	5.36	50.4	0	0
T20s	216	2992	3745	149	5/34	5/34	25.13	7.51	20.0	1	0

BEN ALLISON

RHB / RFM / R0 / W0

FULL NAME: Benjamin Michael John Allison
BORN: December 18, 1999, Colchester, Essex
SQUAD NO: 65
HEIGHT: 6ft 6in
NICKNAME: Pooey
EDUCATION: New Hall School, Chelmsford;
Chelmsford College
TEAMS: Essex, England U19, Gloucestershire
ROLE: Bowler
DEBUT: First-class: 2019; List A: 2021; T20: 2020

BEST BATTING: 52 Essex vs Durham, Chelmsford, 2021
BEST BOWLING: 3-109 Gloucestershire vs Derbyshire, Derby 2019

MOST EXCITING DAY AS A CRICKETER? Winning the T20 Blast in 2019, even though I wasn't playing
CHILDHOOD SPORTING HERO? Stuart Broad
BIGGEST INFLUENCE ON YOUR DEVELOPMENT AS A CRICKETER (EXCLUDING PARENTS)? My brothers
FAVOURITE SMELL? Petrol
GUILTY PLEASURE? Fizzy strawberry pencils

Batting	Mat	Inns	NO	Runs	HS	Ave	SR	100	50	Ct	St
First-class	3	4	0	69	52	17.25	33.65	0	1	1	-
List A	8	2	1	4	3	4.00	30.76	0	0	4	-
T20s	1	1	1	1*	-	100.00	0	0	2	-	

Bowling	Mat	Balls	Runs	Wkts	BBI	BBM	Ave	Econ	SR	5w	10
First-class	3	462	233	5	3/109	4/139	46.60	3.02	92.4	0	0
List A	8	343	351	7	2/33	2/33	50.14	6.13	49.0	0	0
T20s	1	18	32	1	1/32	1/32	32.00	10.66	18.0	0	0

TOM ALSOP

LHB / SLA / WK / R0 / W0

FULL NAME: Thomas Philip Alsop
BORN: November 27, 1995, High Wycombe, Buckinghamshire
SQUAD NO: 9
HEIGHT: 5ft 11in
NICKNAME: Lance
EDUCATION: Lavington School; The John Bentley School, Wiltshire
TEAMS: Hampshire, England Lions
ROLE: Batter/wicketkeeper
DEBUT: First-class: 2014; List A: 2014; T20: 2016

BEST BATTING: 150 Hampshire vs Warwickshire, Edgbaston, 2019
BEST BOWLING: 2-59 Hampshire vs Yorkshire, Headingley, 2016

WHO IS YOUR LOOKALIKE? Michael Fassbender and Damian Lewis (actors)
FIRST CRICKET CLUB? Bishop Canning CC, Wiltshire
WHAT WOULD YOU CHANGE ABOUT THE STRUCTURE OF THE COUNTY SEASON? I quite enjoyed the three-group system last year
WHO IS THE BEST BATTER/KEEPER/ALLROUNDER/BOWLER IN COUNTY CRICKET (EXCLUDING TEAMMATES)? Sam Northeast/Ben Foakes/Darren Stevens/Simon Harmer
MOST BEAUTIFUL THING YOU HAVE EVER SEEN? My Dalmatian
HOBBIES? Reading and audiobooks
WHO WOULD YOU MOST LIKE TO HAVE A NET WITH? Rohit Sharma
MAKE ONE PREDICTION FOR THE FUTURE OF CRICKET: Red-ball cricket will have a renaissance
WHAT DO YOU MOST ENJOY LISTENING TO? Nat King Cole
WHAT MAKES YOU WORRY? Not being present
WHAT GIVES YOU JOY? Seeing my dog wag her tail
GUILTY PLEASURE? Cadbury Fruit and Nut (big bar) with a cold glass of milk

Batting	Mat	Inns	NO	Runs	HS	Ave	SR	100	50	Ct	St
First-class	63	105	6	2563	150	25.88	45.38	4	14	79	-
List A	54	54	3	1703	130*	33.39	77.90	4	9	35	5
T20s	42	40	5	793	85	22.65	112.48	0	3	15	3

Bowling	Mat	Balls	Runs	Wkts	BBI	BBM	Ave	Econ	SR	5w	10
First-class	63	84	81	3	2/59	2/59	27.00	5.78	28.0	0	0
List A	54	-	-	-	-	-	-	-	-	-	-
T20s	42	-	-	-	-	-	-	-	-	-	-

HASHIM AMLA

RHB / OB / R0 / W0

FULL NAME: Hashim Mahomed Amla
BORN: March 31, 1983, Durban, South Africa
SQUAD NO: 1
HEIGHT: 6ft
TEAMS: South Africa, Surrey, Barbados Tridents, Cape Cobras, Derbyshire, Dolphins, Durban Heat, Essex, Hampshire, Khulna Tigers, Kings XI Punjab, KwaZulu-Natal, Nottinghamshire, Trinbago Knight Riders
ROLE: Batter
DEBUT: Test: 2004; ODI: 2008; T20I: 2009; First-class: 1999; List A: 2002; T20: 2004

BEST BATTING: 311* South Africa vs England, The Oval, 2012
BEST BOWLING: 1-10 South Africa A vs India A, Kimberley, 2002
COUNTY CAP: 2010 (Nottinghamshire)

TWITTER: @amlahash
NOTES: Amla signed a two-year contract with Surrey after calling time on his illustrious international career in August 2019. In 2020 he played only T20 cricket after his arrival was delayed by the pandemic, cracking three fifties to help Surrey reach Finals Day. The veteran hit a rich vein of form in red-ball cricket last summer, falling just six short of 1,000 Championship runs. Amla will fill one of the overseas slots at Surrey this summer and is expected to be available in all formats. The 39-year-old previously represented the county in 2013 and 2014 and has also had spells at Derbyshire, Essex, Hampshire and Nottinghamshire. He is still the only South African to have scored a Test triple-century – 311* against England at The Oval in 2012 – and is the fastest player to reach 7,000 ODI runs (150 innings)

Batting	Mat	Inns	NO	Runs	HS	Ave	SR	100	50	Ct	St
Tests	124	215	16	9282	311*	46.64	49.97	28	41	108	-
ODIs	181	178	14	8113	159	49.46	88.39	27	39	87	-
T20Is	44	44	6	1277	97*	33.60	132.05	0	8	19	-
First-class	251	418	34	18803	311*	48.96		55	90	188	-
List A	247	240	16	10020	159	44.73		30	52	108	-
T20s	164	163	15	4563	104*	30.83	126.04	2	30	39	-

Bowling	Mat	Balls	Runs	Wkts	BBI	BBM	Ave	Econ	SR	5w	10
Tests	124	54	37	0	-	-	-	4.11	-	0	0
ODIs	181	-	-	-	-	-	-	-	-	-	-
T20Is	44	-	-	-	-	-	-	-	-	-	-
First-class	251	393	277	1	1/10		277.00	4.22	393.0	0	0
List A	247	16	28	0	-	-	-	10.50	-	0	0
T20s	164	2	5	0	-	-	-	15.00	-	0	0

JAMES ANDERSON   LHB / RFM / R0 / W3

FULL NAME: James Michael Anderson
BORN: July 30, 1982, Burnley, Lancashire
SQUAD NO: 9
HEIGHT: 6ft 2in
NICKNAME: Jimmy
EDUCATION: St Theodore's Roman Catholic High School, Burnley
TEAMS: England, Lancashire, Auckland
ROLE: Bowler
DEBUT: Test: 2003; ODI: 2002; T20I: 2007; First-class: 2002; List A: 2000; T20: 2004

LANCASHIRE

BEST BATTING: 81 England vs India, Trent Bridge, 2014
BEST BOWLING: 7-19 Lancashire vs Kent, Old Trafford, 2021
COUNTY CAP: 2003; BENEFIT: 2012

FAMILY TIES? My dad played for Burnley CC
CHILDHOOD SPORTING HERO? Peter Martin
SURPRISING FACT ABOUT YOU? I'm allergic to mushrooms
TWITTER: @jimmy9

Batting	Mat	Inns	NO	Runs	HS	Ave	SR	100	50	Ct	St
Tests	169	239	103	1262	81	9.27	39.29	0	1	99	-
ODIs	194	79	43	273	28	7.58	48.66	0	0	53	-
T20Is	19	4	3	1	1*	1.00	50.00	0	0	3	-
First-class	270	348	145	1916	81	9.43		0	1	153	-
List A	261	105	63	376	28	8.95		0	0	68	-
T20s	44	10	6	23	16	5.75	88.46	0	0	8	-

Bowling	Mat	Balls	Runs	Wkts	BBI	BBM	Ave	Econ	SR	5w	10
Tests	169	36396	17014	640	7/42	11/71	26.58	2.80	56.8	31	3
ODIs	194	9584	7861	269	5/23	5/23	29.22	4.92	35.6	2	0
T20Is	19	422	552	18	3/23	3/23	30.66	7.84	23.4	0	0
First-class	270	53798	25334	1026	7/19		24.69	2.82	52.4	52	6
List A	261	12730	10230	358	5/23	5/23	28.57	4.82	35.5	2	0
T20s	44	933	1318	41	3/23	3/23	32.14	8.47	22.7	0	0

MARTIN ANDERSSON — RHB / RFM / RO / WO

MIDDLESEX

FULL NAME: Martin Kristoffer Andersson
BORN: September 6, 1996, Reading
SQUAD NO: 24
HEIGHT: 6ft 2in
NICKNAME: Pasty
EDUCATION: Reading Blue Coat School; University of Leeds
TEAMS: Middlesex, Derbyshire
ROLE: Allrounder
DEBUT: First-class: 2017; List A: 2021; T20: 2018

BEST BATTING: 92 Middlesex vs Hampshire, Radlett, 2020
BEST BOWLING: 4-25 Derbyshire vs Glamorgan, Derby, 2018

WHO IS YOUR LOOKALIKE? Max Verstappen
FIRST CRICKET CLUB? Reading CC, Berkshire
WHAT WOULD YOU CHANGE ABOUT THE STRUCTURE OF THE COUNTY SEASON? One-day cricket in April, four-day cricket in May/August/September and T20 in June/July
WHO IS THE BEST BATTER/KEEPER/ALLROUNDER/BOWLER IN COUNTY CRICKET (EXCLUDING TEAMMATES)? Marcus Harris/Ben Brown/Craig Overton/Simon Harmer
MOST UNDERRATED PLAYER IN COUNTY CRICKET? Tom Abell
WHAT WOULD A FLY ON THE WALL HEAR IN YOUR DRESSING ROOM? Tim Murtagh never shutting up
WHO WOULD YOU MOST AND LEAST LIKE TO HAVE A NET WITH? Hashim Amla/Shoaib Akhtar
MAKE ONE PREDICTION FOR THE FUTURE OF CRICKET: There will no longer be 18 counties
WHAT MAKES YOU WORRY? Shinning one in early April
SURPRISING FACT ABOUT YOU? My karaoke song of choice is Basshunter's "Now You're Gone" in Swedish
GUILTY PLEASURE? Eating Nutella from the jar
TWITTER: @MartinAnderss11

Batting	Mat	Inns	NO	Runs	HS	Ave	SR	100	50	Ct	St
First-class	26	48	3	860	92	19.11	55.44	0	5	15	-
List A	4	4	3	133	44*	133.00	147.77	0	0	3	-
T20s	11	11	1	95	24	9.50	101.06	0	0	8	-

Bowling	Mat	Balls	Runs	Wkts	BBI	BBM	Ave	Econ	SR	5w	10
First-class	26	2376	1405	55	4/25	7/98	25.54	3.54	43.2	0	0
List A	4	132	166	1	1/83	1/83	166.00	7.54	132.0	0	0
T20s	11	24	55	0	-	-	-	13.75	-	0	0

FULL NAME: Jofra Chioke Archer
BORN: April 1, 1995, Bridgetown, Barbados
SQUAD NO: 22
HEIGHT: 6ft 2in
NICKNAME: Jof
EDUCATION: Christ Church Foundation School, Bridgetown, Barbados
TEAMS: England, Sussex, Hobart Hurricanes, Khulna Titans, Quetta Gladiators, Rajasthan Royals, West Indies U19
ROLE: Bowler
DEBUT: Test: 2019; ODI: 2019; T20I: 2019; First-class: 2016; List A: 2016; T20: 2016

SUSSEX

BEST BATTING: 81* Sussex vs Northamptonshire, Northampton, 2017
BEST BOWLING: 7-67 Sussex vs Kent, Hove, 2017
COUNTY CAP: 2017

FIRST CRICKET CLUB? Pickwick CC, Bridgetown, Barbados
SURPRISING FACT ABOUT YOU? I'm ambidextrous
TWITTER: @JofraArcher

Batting	Mat	Inns	NO	Runs	HS	Ave	SR	100	50	Ct	St
Tests	13	20	0	155	30	7.75	50.65	0	0	2	-
ODIs	17	9	5	27	8*	6.75	79.41	0	0	5	-
T20Is	12	2	1	19	18*	19.00	190.00	0	0	4	-
First-class	43	63	10	1201	81*	22.66	66.94	0	6	21	-
List A	31	20	8	219	45	18.25	114.06	0	0	9	-
T20s	121	61	29	551	36	17.21	147.72	0	0	35	-

Bowling	Mat	Balls	Runs	Wkts	BBI	BBM	Ave	Econ	SR	5w	10
Tests	13	2609	1304	42	6/45	8/85	31.04	2.99	62.1	3	0
ODIs	17	911	720	30	3/27	3/27	24.00	4.74	30.3	0	0
T20Is	12	282	371	14	4/33	4/33	26.50	7.89	20.1	0	0
First-class	43	8856	4510	181	7/67	11/137	24.91	3.05	48.9	8	1
List A	31	1642	1365	51	5/42	5/42	26.76	4.98	32.1	1	0
T20s	121	2700	3446	153	4/18	4/18	22.52	7.65	17.6	0	0

JAMIE ATKINS

RHB / RFM / R0 / W0

SUSSEX

FULL NAME: Jamie Atkins
BORN: May 20, 2002, Redhill, Surrey
SQUAD NO: 32
HEIGHT: 6ft 6in
NICKNAME: J
EDUCATION: Eastbourne College
TEAMS: Sussex
ROLE: Bowler
DEBUT: First-class: 2021

BEST BATTING: 10* Sussex vs Yorkshire, Headingley, 2021
BEST BOWLING: 5-51 Sussex vs Kent, Canterbury, 2021

WHO IS YOUR LOOKALIKE? Miranda from the TV series of the same name
FIRST CRICKET CLUB? Roffey CC, Horsham
WHAT WOULD YOU CHANGE ABOUT THE STRUCTURE OF THE COUNTY SEASON? Play the final of the One-Day Cup at Lord's
BIGGEST INFLUENCE ON YOUR DEVELOPMENT AS A CRICKETER (EXCLUDING PARENTS)? James Kirtley at Sussex – he has trusted my bowling action
WHO IS THE BEST BATTER/KEEPER/ALLROUNDER/BOWLER IN COUNTY CRICKET (EXCLUDING TEAMMATES)? David Bedingham/Ben Foakes/Darren Stevens/Simon Harmer
MOST UNDERRATED PLAYER IN COUNTY CRICKET? Ben Coad
MOST BEAUTIFUL THING YOU HAVE EVER SEEN? Sunset on a beach in Florida
HOBBIES? The guitar
IF YOU COULD TURN BACK TIME... I would get into golf at a younger age
WHO WOULD YOU MOST LIKE TO HAVE A NET WITH? I would love to have a bowl at Ricky Ponting but I would not like to face Mitchell Johnson
MAKE ONE PREDICTION FOR THE FUTURE OF CRICKET: Five-over cricket becomes the norm
WHAT DO YOU MOST ENJOY LISTENING TO? Careless Whisper by George Michael
WHAT MAKES YOU WORRY? Whether I've forgotten to turn the oven off
TWITTER: @JamieAtkins2005

Batting	Mat	Inns	NO	Runs	HS	Ave	SR	100	50	Ct	St
First-class	5	9	5	21	10*	5.25	25.00	0	0	0	-

Bowling	Mat	Balls	Runs	Wkts	BBI	BBM	Ave	Econ	SR	5w	10
First-class	5	826	469	20	5/51	5/75	23.45	3.40	41.3	2	0

GUS ATKINSON

RHB / RMF / R0 / W0

FULL NAME: Angus Alexander Patrick Atkinson
BORN: January 19, 1998, Chelsea, London
SQUAD NO: 37
HEIGHT: 6ft 2in
NICKNAME: G-bus
EDUCATION: Northcote Lodge, London; Bradfield College, Berkshire
TEAMS: Surrey
ROLE: Bowler
DEBUT: First-class: 2020; List A: 2021; T20: 2020

BEST BATTING: 41* Surrey vs Northamptonshire, Northampton, 2021
BEST BOWLING: 3-78 Surrey vs Gloucestershire, Bristol, 2021

FIRST CRICKET CLUB? Spencer CC, London
BIGGEST INFLUENCE ON YOUR DEVELOPMENT AS A CRICKETER (EXCLUDING PARENTS)? Julian Wood, my school coach who believed in my ability before I did
WHO IS THE BEST BATTER/ALLROUNDER/BOWLER IN COUNTY CRICKET (EXCLUDING TEAMMATES)? Alastair Cook/Ryan Higgins/Chris Rushworth
MOST UNDERRATED PLAYER IN COUNTY CRICKET? Tom Lace
HOBBIES? Call of Duty (video game)
WHAT DO YOU MOST ENJOY LISTENING TO? Kid Cudi (rapper)
SURPRISING FACT ABOUT YOU? I had a rugby trial for Harlequins aged 13
TWITTER: @gus_atkinson1

Batting	Mat	Inns	NO	Runs	HS	Ave	SR	100	50	Ct	St
First-class	4	8	1	73	41*	10.42	34.43	0	0	0	-
List A	2	1	0	15	15	15.00	300.00	0	0	1	-
T20s	17	8	4	39	14	9.75	114.70	0	0	6	-

Bowling	Mat	Balls	Runs	Wkts	BBI	BBM	Ave	Econ	SR	5w	10
First-class	4	496	300	9	3/78	3/99	33.33	3.62	55.1	0	0
List A	2	96	113	5	4/43	4/43	22.60	7.06	19.2	0	0
T20s	17	286	423	22	4/36	4/36	19.22	8.87	13.0	0	0

HASSAN AZAD

LHB / OB / R1 / W0

LEICESTERSHIRE

FULL NAME: Mohammad Hassan Azad
BORN: January 7, 1994, Quetta, Balochistan, Pakistan
SQUAD NO: 42
HEIGHT: 5ft 10in
NICKNAME: Hass
EDUCATION: Bilborough Sixth Form College, Nottingham; Loughborough University
TEAMS: Leicestershire
ROLE: Batter
DEBUT: First-class: 2015

BEST BATTING: 152 Leicestershire vs Sussex, Leicester, 2021
BEST BOWLING: 1-15 Leicestershire vs Durham, Leicester, 2020

WHO IS YOUR LOOKALIKE? Freddie Mecury (so I've been told)
FIRST CRICKET CLUB? Underwood Miners' Welfare CC, Nottinghamshire
WHO IS THE BEST BATTER/KEEPER/ALLROUNDER/BOWLER IN COUNTY CRICKET (EXCLUDING TEAMMATES)? Jake Libby/Ben Foakes/Darren Stevens/Mohammad Abbas
MOST UNDERRATED PLAYER IN COUNTY CRICKET? Ryan Higgins
MOST BEAUTIFUL THING YOU HAVE EVER SEEN? Sunset over a rock pool on top of a waterfall at the end of a hike near Auckland in New Zealand
HOBBIES? Photography – I decided to get an SLR (single-lens reflex camera) a few years ago and now I can help my friends with their dating profiles!
IF YOU COULD TURN BACK TIME... I would have wafted outside off stump a little less
WHO WOULD YOU MOST AND LEAST LIKE TO HAVE A NET WITH? Most – Kumar Sangakkara (I tried my best to copy him when growing up and would love to pick his brain). Least – Steve Waugh (he doesn't have a reputation for being constructive with criticism!)
MAKE ONE PREDICTION FOR THE FUTURE OF CRICKET: A team will score 400 in a T20 by the year 2030
WHAT MAKES YOU WORRY? The idea that we have very little control over our lives beyond our own decisions
TWITTER: @Bat_Pad_Man

Batting	Mat	Inns	NO	Runs	HS	Ave	SR	100	50	Ct	St
First-class	41	66	7	2321	152	39.33	40.71	6	12	18	-

Bowling	Mat	Balls	Runs	Wkts	BBI	BBM	Ave	Econ	SR	5w	10
First-class	41	19	17	1	1/15	1/15	17.00	5.36	19.0	0	0

TOM BAILEY
RHB / RFM / R0 / W2 / MVP11

FULL NAME: Thomas Ernest Bailey
BORN: April 21, 1991, Preston, Lancashire
SQUAD NO: 8
HEIGHT: 6ft 4in
NICKNAME: Big Poppa
EDUCATION: Myerscough College, Lancashire
TEAMS: Lancashire, England Lions
ROLE: Bowler
DEBUT: First-class: 2012; List A: 2014; T20: 2015

BEST BATTING: 68 Lancashire vs Northamptonshire, Old Trafford, 2019
BEST BOWLING: 7-37 Lancashire vs Hampshire, Liverpool, 2021
COUNTY CAP: 2018

FIRST CRICKET CLUB? Vernon Carus CC, Lancashire
WHO IS THE BEST BATTER/KEEPER/ALLROUNDER/BOWLER IN COUNTY CRICKET (EXCLUDING TEAMMATES)? David Bedingham/Ben Foakes/Keith Barker/Simon Harmer
MOST UNDERRATED PLAYER IN COUNTY CRICKET? Ben Duckett
MOST BEAUTIFUL THING YOU HAVE EVER SEEN? A sunset in Goa, India
HOBBIES? Call of Duty (video game)
WHO WOULD YOU MOST LIKE TO HAVE A NET WITH? Michael Holding, to see how fast he was. Or Chris Gayle, to see how far he could hit the ball
MAKE ONE PREDICTION FOR THE FUTURE OF CRICKET: England will win the next Ashes
WHAT MAKES YOU WORRY? A dry forecast
TWITTER: @TomBaildog

Batting	Mat	Inns	NO	Runs	HS	Ave	SR	100	50	Ct	St
First-class	73	96	13	1505	68	18.13	51.87	0	7	15	-
List A	22	14	6	142	45	17.75	88.75	0	0	2	-
T20s	24	6	1	21	10	4.20	95.45	0	0	9	-

Bowling	Mat	Balls	Runs	Wkts	BBI	BBM	Ave	Econ	SR	5w	10
First-class	73	12835	6110	257	7/37	10/98	23.77	2.85	49.9	10	2
List A	22	1015	867	30	3/23	3/23	28.90	5.12	33.8	0	0
T20s	24	378	590	25	5/17	5/17	23.60	9.36	15.1	1	0

JONNY BAIRSTOW

RHB / WK / R3 / W0

YORKSHIRE

FULL NAME: Jonathan Marc Bairstow
BORN: September 26, 1989, Bradford
SQUAD NO: 21
NICKNAME: Bluey
EDUCATION: St Peter's School, York; Leeds Metropolitan University
TEAMS: England, Yorkshire, Peshawar Zalmi, Punjab Kings, Sunrisers Hyderabad
ROLE: Batter/wicketkeeper
DEBUT: Test: 2012; ODI: 2011; T20I: 2011; First-class: 2009; List A: 2009; T20: 2010

BEST BATTING: 246 Yorkshire vs Hampshire, Headingley, 2016

COUNTY CAP: 2011

FAMILY TIES? My father David played for Yorkshire and England
CHILDHOOD SPORTING HERO? Sachin Tendulkar
SURPRISING FACT ABOUT YOU? I played football for the Leeds United Academy for seven years
TWITTER: @jbairstow21
NOTES: Bairstow was bought by Punjab Kings for this year's IPL

Batting	Mat	Inns	NO	Runs	HS	Ave	SR	100	50	Ct	St
Tests	80	142	8	4575	167*	34.14	54.54	7	22	196	13
ODIs	89	81	8	3498	141*	47.91	105.01	11	14	45	3
T20Is	63	57	12	1190	86*	26.44	135.84	0	7	44	1
First-class	194	322	35	12329	246	42.95		26	64	487	24
List A	157	143	14	5420	174	42.01	103.93	14	24	96	9
T20s	166	153	26	3904	114	30.74	137.56	3	22	98	15

Bowling	Mat	Balls	Runs	Wkts	BBI	BBM	Ave	Econ	SR	5w	10
Tests	80	-	-	-	-	-	-	-	-	-	-
ODIs	89	-	-	-	-	-	-	-	-	-	-
T20Is	63	-	-	-	-	-	-	-	-	-	-
First-class	194	6	1	0	-	-	-	1.00	-	0	0
List A	157	-	-	-	-	-	-	-	-	-	-
T20s	166	-	-	-	-	-	-	-	-	-	-

JOSH BAKER RHB / SLA / R0 / W0

FULL NAME: Josh Oliver Baker
BORN: May 16, 2003, Redditch, Worcestershire
SQUAD NO: 33
HEIGHT: 6ft 4in
NICKNAME: Peperami
EDUCATION: Warkwood Middle School, Redditch; Malvern College
TEAMS: Worcestershire, England U19
ROLE: Bowler
DEBUT: First-class: 2021; List A: 2021

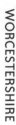

WORCESTERSHIRE

BEST BATTING: 61* Worcestershire vs Middlesex, Lord's, 2021
BEST BOWLING: 3-49 Worcestershire vs Sussex, Worcester, 2021

FIRST CRICKET CLUB? Astwood Bank CC, Redditch, Worcestershire
WHAT WOULD YOU CHANGE ABOUT THE STRUCTURE OF THE COUNTY SEASON? Have more time between matches
WHO IS THE BEST BATTER/KEEPER/ALLROUNDER/BOWLER IN COUNTY CRICKET (EXCLUDING TEAMMATES)? David Bedingham/John Simpson/Darren Stevens/James Sales
MOST BEAUTIFUL THING YOU HAVE EVER SEEN? A beach on St Kitts in the Caribbean
HOBBIES? Golf
WHO WOULD YOU MOST LIKE TO HAVE A NET WITH? Shane Warne (although he'd be too good for me)
MAKE ONE PREDICTION FOR THE FUTURE OF CRICKET: Cricket at the Olympics
WHAT MAKES YOU WORRY? Quick bowling
WHAT GIVES YOU JOY? Hitting sixes
TWITTER: @josh_baker03

Batting	Mat	Inns	NO	Runs	HS	Ave	SR	100	50	Ct	St
First-class	5	7	2	84	61*	16.80	70.58	0	1	4	-
List A	7	7	4	84	25	28.00	89.36	0	0	0	-

Bowling	Mat	Balls	Runs	Wkts	BBI	BBM	Ave	Econ	SR	5w	10
First-class	5	866	408	12	3/49	3/57	34.00	2.82	72.1	0	0
List A	7	272	273	7	2/53	2/53	39.00	6.02	38.8	0	0

SONNY BAKER

RHB / RFM / R0 / W0

SOMERSET

FULL NAME: Sonny Baker
BORN: March 13, 2003, Torbay, Devon
SQUAD NO: 16
HEIGHT: 6ft
NICKNAME: Bakes
EDUCATION: Torquay Boys' Grammar School; King's College, Taunton
TEAMS: Somerset, England U19
ROLE: Bowler
DEBUT: List A: 2021

FIRST CRICKET CLUB? Torquay CC, Devon
WHAT WOULD YOU CHANGE ABOUT THE STRUCTURE OF THE COUNTY SEASON? Create a larger gap between red-ball and T20 cricket
WHO IS THE BEST BATTER/KEEPER/ALLROUNDER/BOWLER IN COUNTY CRICKET (EXCLUDING TEAMMATES)? Tom Haines/Ben Cox/Ed Barnard/Chris Rushworth
HOBBIES? Rugby
IF YOU COULD TURN BACK TIME... I wouldn't have stressed so much over my GCSEs
WHO WOULD YOU MOST AND LEAST LIKE TO HAVE A NET WITH? Brett Lee for both – I'd love to talk fast bowling with him but facing that man would be brutal
MAKE ONE PREDICTION FOR THE FUTURE OF CRICKET: There will be ever more red-ball specialist batters
WHAT DO YOU MOST ENJOY LISTENING TO? Podcasts about human performance
WHAT GIVES YOU JOY? Bowling fast

Batting	Mat	Inns	NO	Runs	HS	Ave	SR	100	50	Ct	St
List A	8	2	1	7	7*	7.00	25.00	0	0	2	-

Bowling	Mat	Balls	Runs	Wkts	BBI	BBM	Ave	Econ	SR	5w	10
List A	8	328	330	10	3/46	3/46	33.00	6.03	32.8	0	0

GEORGE BALDERSON LHB / RM / R0 / W0

FULL NAME: George Philip Balderson
BORN: October 11, 2000, Manchester
SQUAD NO: 10
HEIGHT: 5ft 10in
NICKNAME: Baldy
EDUCATION: Cheadle Hulme High School,
Greater Manchester
TEAMS: Lancashire, England U19
ROLE: Allrounder
DEBUT: First-class: 2020; List A: 2021

LANCASHIRE

BEST BATTING: 77 Lancashire vs Nottinghamshire, Trent Bridge, 2021
BEST BOWLING: 3-21 Lancashire vs Hampshire, Liverpool, 2021

FIRST CRICKET CLUB? Cheadle Hulme CC, Greater Manchester. I'd watch my dad play there every Saturday
MOST EXCITING DAY AS A CRICKETER? Beating Derbyshire on the final day at Liverpool in 2020
CHILDHOOD SPORTING HERO? Jimmy Anderson
BIGGEST CRICKETING REGRET? Bowling leg-spin until I was 14
GUILTY PLEASURE? Taylor Swift
TWITTER: @BaldersonGeorge

Batting	Mat	Inns	NO	Runs	HS	Ave	SR	100	50	Ct	St
First-class	11	16	3	367	77	28.23	38.22	0	3	0	-
List A	6	4	2	46	19	23.00	71.87	0	0	1	-

Bowling	Mat	Balls	Runs	Wkts	BBI	BBM	Ave	Econ	SR	5w	10
First-class	11	1541	723	21	3/21	5/70	34.42	2.81	73.3	0	0
List A	6	162	136	5	3/25	3/25	27.20	5.03	32.4	0	0

JAKE BALL — RHB / RFM / R0 / W1

NOTTINGHAMSHIRE

FULL NAME: Jacob Timothy Ball
BORN: March 14, 1991, Mansfield, Nottinghamshire
SQUAD NO: 28
HEIGHT: 6ft 3in
NICKNAME: Yak
EDUCATION: Meden School, Mansfield
TEAMS: England, Nottinghamshire, Sydney Sixers
ROLE: Bowler
DEBUT: Test: 2016; ODI: 2016; T20I: 2018; First-class: 2011; List A: 2009; T20: 2011

BEST BATTING: 49* Nottinghamshire vs Warwickshire, Trent Bridge, 2015
BEST BOWLING: 6-49 Nottinghamshire vs Sussex, Trent Bridge, 2015
COUNTY CAP: 2016

WHO IS YOUR LOOKALIKE? Dr Alex (Love Island)
FIRST CRICKET CLUB? Welbeck Colliery CC, Nottinghamshire
FAMILY TIES? My uncle Bruce French played for England
WHAT WOULD YOU CHANGE ABOUT THE STRUCTURE OF THE COUNTY SEASON? Have fewer four-day games
WHAT WOULD A FLY ON THE WALL HEAR IN YOUR DRESSING ROOM? A lot of pointless conversations
MOST BEAUTIFUL THING YOU HAVE EVER SEEN? Lake Como
WHAT MAKES YOU WORRY? Everton in a relegation fight
SURPRISING FACT ABOUT YOU? I was a batter till the age of 15
TWITTER: @Jakeball30

Batting	Mat	Inns	NO	Runs	HS	Ave	SR	100	50	Ct	St
Tests	4	8	0	67	31	8.37	53.60	0	0	1	-
ODIs	18	6	2	38	28	9.50	77.55	0	0	5	-
T20Is	2	-	-	-	-	-	-	-	-	1	-
First-class	67	102	24	1024	49*	13.12	73.66	0	0	13	-
List A	96	38	15	198	28	8.60	99.00	0	0	19	-
T20s	93	17	11	53	18*	8.83	91.37	0	0	24	-

Bowling	Mat	Balls	Runs	Wkts	BBI	BBM	Ave	Econ	SR	5w	10
Tests	4	612	343	3	1/47	1/47	114.33	3.36	204.0	0	0
ODIs	18	947	980	21	5/51	5/51	46.66	6.20	45.0	1	0
T20Is	2	42	83	2	1/39	1/39	41.50	11.85	21.0	0	0
First-class	67	10191	5813	203	6/49	9/57	28.63	3.42	50.2	6	0
List A	96	4060	3984	118	5/51	5/51	33.76	5.88	34.4	1	0
T20s	93	1833	2717	116	4/11	4/11	23.42	8.89	15.8	0	0

GARY BALLANCE — LHB / LB / R4 / W0

FULL NAME: Gary Simon Ballance
BORN: November 22, 1989, Harare, Zimbabwe
SQUAD NO: 19
NICKNAME: Gazza
EDUCATION: Peterhouse School, Marondera, Zimbabwe; Harrow School, London
TEAMS: England, Yorkshire, Derbyshire, Mid West Rhinos, Zimbabwe U19
ROLE: Batter
DEBUT: Test: 2014; ODI: 2013; First-class: 2008; List A: 2006; T20: 2010

YORKSHIRE

BEST BATTING: 210 Mid West Rhinos vs Southern Rocks, Masvingo, 2011

COUNTY CAP: 2012 (Yorkshire)

NOTES: A close family friend of former Zimbabwe skipper David Houghton, Ballance signed for Derbyshire aged 16 before joining the Yorkshire Academy in 2008. He played for Zimbabwe at the 2006 U19 World Cup before qualifying to play for England. He made his Test debut at Sydney in the 2013/14 Ashes and hit three centuries the following summer to cement the No.3 spot but lost his place during the 2015 home series against Australia. His most recent Test was in 2017. The 32-year-old captained Yorkshire for one season but stood down in 2018 to take a break from cricket for personal reasons. He soon returned to action and went on to score 975 runs in 2019 to finish as the club's leading Championship run-scorer for the third season in a row. Ballance didn't play at all for Yorkshire in 2020 after suffering "heightened feelings of anxiety and stress" but was back on the field last summer, scoring a healthy 594 runs in 10 Championship matches

Batting	Mat	Inns	NO	Runs	HS	Ave	SR	100	50	Ct	St
Tests	23	42	2	1498	156	37.45	47.16	4	7	22	-
ODIs	16	15	1	297	79	21.21	67.04	0	2	8	-
First-class	170	276	25	11876	210	47.31	51.77	41	55	123	-
List A	119	110	15	4540	156	47.78	89.49	8	27	52	-
T20s	100	88	10	1807	79	23.16	122.67	0	7	46	-

Bowling	Mat	Balls	Runs	Wkts	BBI	BBM	Ave	Econ	SR	5w	10
Tests	23	12	5	0	-	-	-	2.50	-	0	0
ODIs	16	-	-	-	-	-	-	-	-	-	-
First-class	170	162	154	0	-	-	-	5.70	-	0	0
List A	119	-	-	-	-	-	-	-	-	-	-
T20s	100	-	-	-	-	-	-	-	-	-	-

ETHAN BAMBER — RHB / RMF / R0 / W1 / MVP37

MIDDLESEX

FULL NAME: Ethan Read Bamber
BORN: December 17, 1998, Westminster, London
SQUAD NO: 54
HEIGHT: 5ft 11in
NICKNAME: Sorry
EDUCATION: Mill Hill School, London; University of Exeter
TEAMS: Middlesex, England U19, Gloucestershire
ROLE: Bowler
DEBUT: First-class: 2018; List A: 2021; T20: 2019

BEST BATTING: 27* Middlesex vs Gloucestershire, Bristol, 2018
BEST BOWLING: 5-41 Middlesex vs Derbyshire, Lord's, 2021

WHO IS YOUR LOOKALIKE? Dobby from Harry Potter
FIRST CRICKET CLUB? North Middlesex CC, London
BIGGEST CRICKETING REGRET? Getting out with a shocking shot when the other batter was on 98
MOST UNDERRATED PLAYER IN COUNTY CRICKET? David Payne
WHAT WOULD A FLY ON THE WALL HEAR IN YOUR DRESSING ROOM? Incorrect crossword answers
MOST BEAUTIFUL THING YOU HAVE EVER SEEN? Marcus Smith's cross-field kick for Harlequins
HOBBIES? Cooking
WHO WOULD YOU MOST AND LEAST LIKE TO HAVE A NET WITH? Most and least – Dale Steyn. He's my hero but he also bowls too fast and short
MAKE ONE PREDICTION FOR THE FUTURE OF CRICKET: A franchise system instead of the counties
WHAT MAKES YOU WORRY? People's hatred for those who are different from them
GUILTY PLEASURE? Cereal
TWITTER: @etbamber

Batting	Mat	Inns	NO	Runs	HS	Ave	SR	100	50	Ct	St
First-class	26	44	11	311	27*	9.42	35.06	0	0	4	-
List A	6	4	1	37	21	12.33	82.22	0	0	1	-
T20s	5	1	1	3	3*	-	100.00	0	0	1	-

Bowling	Mat	Balls	Runs	Wkts	BBI	BBM	Ave	Econ	SR	5w	10
First-class	26	5054	2317	100	5/41	7/80	23.17	2.75	50.5	2	0
List A	6	296	297	10	3/41	3/41	29.70	6.02	29.6	0	0
T20s	5	53	102	0	-	-	-	11.54	-	0	0

TOM BANTON
RHB / WK / R0 / W0

FULL NAME: Thomas Banton
BORN: November 11, 1998, Chiltern, Buckinghamshire
SQUAD NO: 18
HEIGHT: 6ft 2in
EDUCATION: Bromsgrove School, Worcestershire; King's College, Taunton
TEAMS: England, Somerset, Brisbane Heat, Colombo Stars, Kolkata Knight Riders, Peshawar Zalmi, Quetta Gladiators
ROLE: Batter/wicketkeeper
DEBUT: ODI: 2020; T20I: 2019; First-class: 2018; List A: 2018; T20: 2017

BEST BATTING: 79 Somerset vs Hampshire, Taunton, 2019

FIRST CRICKET CLUB? Sutton Coldfield CC, Birmingham
WHAT WOULD YOU CHANGE ABOUT THE STRUCTURE OF THE COUNTY SEASON? Play less cricket
BIGGEST CRICKETING REGRET? Not playing for Somerset at the age of 10
WHO IS THE BEST BATTER/KEEPER/ALLROUNDER/BOWLER IN COUNTY CRICKET (EXCLUDING TEAMMATES)? Alastair Cook/Ben Foakes/Darren Stevens/Luke Fletcher
MOST UNDERRATED PLAYER IN COUNTY CRICKET? Ryan Higgins
MOST BEAUTIFUL THING YOU HAVE EVER SEEN? Mountains in Switzerland
HOBBIES? Hockey
WHO WOULD YOU MOST LIKE TO HAVE A NET WITH? AB de Villiers
WHAT GIVES YOU JOY? Time away from cricket
TWITTER: @tombanton18

Batting	Mat	Inns	NO	Runs	HS	Ave	SR	100	50	Ct	St
ODIs	6	5	0	134	58	26.80	92.41	0	1	2	-
T20Is	14	14	0	327	73	23.35	147.96	0	2	9	-
First-class	22	38	1	848	79	22.91	58.20	0	6	12	-
List A	24	22	0	658	112	29.90	87.50	2	4	16	1
T20s	75	74	3	1690	107*	23.80	149.16	2	10	39	6

Bowling	Mat	Balls	Runs	Wkts	BBI	BBM	Ave	Econ	SR	5w	10
ODIs	6	-	-	-	-	-	-	-	-	-	-
T20Is	14	-	-	-	-	-	-	-	-	-	-
First-class	22	-	-	-	-	-	-	-	-	-	-
List A	24	-	-	-	-	-	-	-	-	-	-
T20s	75	-	-	-	-	-	-	-	-	-	-

KEITH BARKER　　LHB / LFM / RO / W3

FULL NAME: Keith Hubert Douglas Barker
BORN: October 21, 1986, Manchester
SQUAD NO: 13
HEIGHT: 6ft 3in
NICKNAME: Barks
EDUCATION: Moorhead High School, Accrington; Preston College
TEAMS: Hampshire, England Lions, Warwickshire
ROLE: Allrounder
DEBUT: First-class: 2009; List A: 2009; T20: 2009

BEST BATTING: 125 Warwickshire vs Surrey, Guildford, 2013
BEST BOWLING: 7-46 Hampshire vs Nottinghamshire, Southampton, 2021
COUNTY CAP: 2013 (Warwickshire)

FIRST CRICKET CLUB? Enfield CC, Lancashire
BIGGEST INFLUENCE ON YOUR DEVELOPMENT AS A CRICKETER (EXCLUDING PARENTS)?
Dean Barker (brother) – we always played cricket as kids and I was determined to beat him every time. Never did though
WHO IS THE BEST BATTER/KEEPER/ALLROUNDER/BOWLER IN COUNTY CRICKET (EXCLUDING TEAMMATES)? Rob Yates/Alex Davies/Sam Curran/Chris Wright
MOST UNDERRATED PLAYER IN COUNTY CRICKET? Ben Mike
MOST BEAUTIFUL THING YOU HAVE EVER SEEN? My daughter
HOBBIES? Football
WHO WOULD YOU LEAST LIKE TO HAVE A NET WITH? Either Jeetan Patel or Rikki Clarke – both would get me out every other ball
SURPRISING FACT ABOUT YOU? I never scored a hundred for the Enfield first team

Batting	Mat	Inns	NO	Runs	HS	Ave	SR	100	50	Ct	St
First-class	139	188	32	4397	125	28.18	56.60	6	20	37	-
List A	62	39	11	560	56	20.00	94.59	0	1	14	-
T20s	65	35	7	383	46	13.67	111.01	0	0	17	-

Bowling	Mat	Balls	Runs	Wkts	BBI	BBM	Ave	Econ	SR	5w	10
First-class	139	22864	11079	445	7/46	10/70	24.89	2.90	51.3	18	1
List A	62	2342	2263	69	4/33	4/33	32.79	5.79	33.9	0	0
T20s	65	1206	1588	69	4/19	4/19	23.01	7.90	17.4	0	0

ED BARNARD — RHB / RMF / R0 / W0 / MVP16

FULL NAME: Edward George Barnard
BORN: November 20, 1995, Shrewsbury
SQUAD NO: 30
HEIGHT: 6ft
NICKNAME: Barndoor
EDUCATION: Meole Brace School, Shrewsbury; Shrewsbury School
TEAMS: Worcestershire, England Lions
ROLE: Allrounder
DEBUT: First-class: 2015; List A: 2015; T20: 2015

BEST BATTING: 128 Worcestershire vs Essex, Chelmsford, 2021
BEST BOWLING: 6-37 Worcestershire vs Somerset, Taunton, 2018

FIRST CRICKET CLUB? Shrewsbury CC, Shropshire. We were the National Knockout champions in 1983 and 2011
FAMILY TIES? Dad (Andy) played for Shropshire; brother (Mike) played for Shropshire and first-class cricket for Oxford MCCU; brother (Steve) played for Shropshire
WHO IS THE BEST BATTER/KEEPER/ALLROUNDER/BOWLER IN COUNTY CRICKET (EXCLUDING TEAMMATES)? David Bedingham/Ben Foakes/Ryan Higgins/Chris Rushworth
MOST UNDERRATED PLAYER IN COUNTY CRICKET? Sam Hain
HOBBIES? The Fantasy Premier League
WHAT MAKES YOU WORRY? Chris Rushworth's nip-backer
WHAT GIVES YOU JOY? Overthrows when I'm batting
TWITTER: @EdBarn95

Batting	Mat	Inns	NO	Runs	HS	Ave	SR	100	50	Ct	St
First-class	78	114	19	2858	128	30.08	53.03	2	15	52	-
List A	51	39	14	665	61	26.60	95.00	0	3	22	-
T20s	88	56	21	569	43*	16.25	130.80	0	0	46	-

Bowling	Mat	Balls	Runs	Wkts	BBI	BBM	Ave	Econ	SR	5w	10
First-class	78	12363	6528	230	6/37	11/89	28.38	3.16	53.7	5	1
List A	51	2190	2132	62	3/26	3/26	34.38	5.84	35.3	0	0
T20s	88	1342	1993	52	3/29	3/29	38.32	8.91	25.8	0	0

ED BARNES
RHB / RFM / R0 / W0

LEICESTERSHIRE

FULL NAME: Edward Barnes
BORN: November 26, 1997, York
SQUAD NO: 62
HEIGHT: 6ft
NICKNAME: Barnsey
EDUCATION: King James School, Knaresborough, North Yorkshire
TEAMS: Leicestershire, England U19, Yorkshire
ROLE: Bowler
DEBUT: First-class: 2020; List A: 2021; T20: 2020

BEST BATTING: 83* Leicestershire vs Somerset, Taunton, 2021
BEST BOWLING: 4-61 Leicestershire vs Hampshire, Southampton, 2021

FIRST CRICKET CLUB? Ouseburn CC, North Yorkshire
WHAT WOULD YOU CHANGE ABOUT THE STRUCTURE OF THE COUNTY SEASON? Introduce some day/night Championship cricket
BIGGEST INFLUENCE ON YOUR DEVELOPMENT AS A CRICKETER (EXCLUDING PARENTS)? Michael Vaughan. My first-ever cricket session was during a summer camp and Vaughan was there on the one day that I was there. That inspired me going forward
WHO IS THE BEST BATTER/KEEPER/ALLROUNDER/BOWLER IN COUNTY CRICKET (EXCLUDING TEAMMATES)? David Bedingham/John Simpson/Jordan Thompson/Sam Cook
HOBBIES? Leeds United
IF YOU COULD TURN BACK TIME... I'd learn another language
WHO WOULD YOU MOST AND LEAST LIKE TO HAVE A NET WITH? Most – Jacques Kallis, purely because he's one of the all-time greats. Least – Brett Lee, because of the fear factor
MAKE ONE PREDICTION FOR THE FUTURE OF CRICKET: It'll become like baseball
WHAT GIVES YOU JOY? Three points at Elland Road
GUILTY PLEASURE? Emmerdale

Batting	Mat	Inns	NO	Runs	HS	Ave	SR	100	50	Ct	St
First-class	12	13	4	263	83*	29.22	54.56	0	2	4	-
List A	8	4	2	53	33*	26.50	74.64	0	0	1	-
T20s	5	1	0	7	7	7.00	116.66	0	0	1	-

Bowling	Mat	Balls	Runs	Wkts	BBI	BBM	Ave	Econ	SR	5w	10
First-class	12	1418	831	21	4/61	4/61	39.57	3.51	67.5	0	0
List A	8	359	346	9	2/34	2/34	38.44	5.78	39.8	0	0
T20s	5	60	115	2	2/27	2/27	57.50	11.50	30.0	0	0

GEORGE BARTLETT

RHB / OB / R0 / W0

FULL NAME: George Anthony Bartlett
BORN: March 14, 1998, Frimley, Surrey
SQUAD NO: 14
HEIGHT: 6ft 1in
NICKNAME: GB
EDUCATION: Millfield School, Somerset
TEAMS: Somerset, England U19
ROLE: Batter
DEBUT: First-class: 2017; List A: 2019; T20: 2020

BEST BATTING: 137 Somerset vs Surrey, Guildford, 2019

FIRST CRICKET CLUB? Westlands CC, Yeovil, Somerset
MOST EXCITING DAY AS A CRICKETER? Winning the One-Day Cup at Lord's in 2019
CHILDHOOD SPORTING HERO? Marcus Trescothick
BIGGEST INFLUENCE ON YOUR DEVELOPMENT AS A CRICKETER (EXCLUDING PARENTS)? My school coaches
WHAT WOULD YOU DO IF YOU WERE IN CHARGE OF COUNTY CRICKET? Use Kookaburra balls in the County Championship and ban the shining of the cricket ball
FAVOURITE SMELL? Freshly cut grass
TWITTER: @georgebartlett9

Batting	Mat	Inns	NO	Runs	HS	Ave	SR	100	50	Ct	St
First-class	40	67	4	1711	137	27.15	53.73	5	5	10	-
List A	15	14	3	366	108	33.27	99.18	1	1	6	-
T20s	6	6	0	64	24	10.66	116.36	0	0	2	-

Bowling	Mat	Balls	Runs	Wkts	BBI	BBM	Ave	Econ	SR	5w	10
First-class	40	20	27	0	-	-	-	8.10	-	0	0
List A	15	-	-	-	-	-	-	-	-	-	-
T20s	6	-	-	-	-	-	-	-	-	-	-

SAM BATES

LHB / WK / R0 / W0

LEICESTERSHIRE

FULL NAME: Samuel David Bates
BORN: September 14, 1999, Leicester
SQUAD NO: 14
HEIGHT: 6ft 3in
NICKNAME: Bato
EDUCATION: Brookvale Groby,
Leicestershire; Gateway College, Leicester
TEAMS: Leicestershire
ROLE: Wicketkeeper
DEBUT: First-class: 2021

BEST BATTING: 6 Leicestershire vs Worcestershire, Worcester, 2021

WHO IS YOUR LOOKALIKE? Jordan Pickford
FIRST CRICKET CLUB? Newtown Linford CC, Leicestershire
BIGGEST INFLUENCE ON YOUR DEVELOPMENT AS A CRICKETER (EXCLUDING PARENTS)?
Dips Patel, currently the Leicestershire Second XI coach. He has spent countless hours
coaching me, and he never said no to a session whether it was 6am or 11pm
WHO IS THE BEST BATTER/KEEPER/ALLROUNDER/BOWLER IN COUNTY CRICKET
(EXCLUDING TEAMMATES)? Ollie Pope/Ben Foakes/Darren Stevens/Chris Rushworth
HOBBIES? Leicester City (I'm a season-ticket holder)
WHO WOULD YOU MOST LIKE TO HAVE A NET WITH? Kumar Sangakkara – to cover all
aspects of batting and keeping
MAKE ONE PREDICTION FOR THE FUTURE OF CRICKET: The birth of the five-over
competition
WHAT DO YOU MOST ENJOY LISTENING TO? Old-school rap
WHAT MAKES YOU WORRY? Jannik Vestergaard being picked in Leicester City's starting XI
TWITTER: @Batsey101

Batting	Mat	Inns	NO	Runs	HS	Ave	SR	100	50	Ct	St
First-class	1	2	0	6	6	3.00	25.00	0	0	2	1

Bowling	Mat	Balls	Runs	Wkts	BBI	BBM	Ave	Econ	SR	5w	10
First-class	1	-	-	-	-	-	-	-	-	-	-

AARON BEARD

LHB / RMF / RO / WO

FULL NAME: Aaron Paul Beard
BORN: October 15, 1997, Chelmsford
SQUAD NO: 14
HEIGHT: 5ft 11in
NICKNAME: Beardo
EDUCATION: The Boswells School, Chelmsford; Great Baddow High School, Chelmsford
TEAMS: Essex, England U19
ROLE: Bowler
DEBUT: First-class: 2016; List A: 2019; T20: 2019

BEST BATTING: 58* Essex vs Durham MCCU, Chelmsford, 2017
BEST BOWLING: 4-21 Essex vs Middlesex, Chelmsford, 2020

FIRST CRICKET CLUB? Writtle CC, Essex
MOST EXCITING DAY AS A CRICKETER? Taking 4-62 against Sri Lanka on my first-class debut in 2016
CHILDHOOD SPORTING HERO? David Beckham
BEST INNINGS YOU'VE SEEN? Dan Lawrence hitting 141 against Lancashire at Chelmsford in 2017. He batted out the final day to get Essex a draw after we had lost some early wickets
WHAT WOULD YOU DO IF YOU WERE IN CHARGE OF COUNTY CRICKET? Change the lbw rule: if it's hitting the stumps, it is out
TWITTER: @aaronbeard_14

Batting	Mat	Inns	NO	Runs	HS	Ave	SR	100	50	Ct	St
First-class	22	24	11	234	58*	18.00	44.23	0	1	5	-
List A	2	2	1	24	22*	24.00	120.00	0	0	0	-
T20s	10	3	1	26	13	13.00	152.94	0	0	1	-

Bowling	Mat	Balls	Runs	Wkts	BBI	BBM	Ave	Econ	SR	5w	10
First-class	22	2499	1498	49	4/21	7/45	30.57	3.59	51.0	0	0
List A	2	114	97	3	3/51	3/51	32.33	5.10	38.0	0	0
T20s	10	162	288	10	3/41	3/41	28.80	10.66	16.2	0	0

DAVID BEDINGHAM RHB / OB / R1 / W0 / MVP18

DURHAM

FULL NAME: David Guy Bedingham
BORN: April 22, 1994, George, Western Cape, South Africa
SQUAD NO: 5
HEIGHT: 6ft
NICKNAME: Bedders
EDUCATION: Wynberg Boys' High School, Cape Town; Stellenbosch University, Western Province
TEAMS: Durham, Boland, Cape Cobras, South Africa U19, Western Province
ROLE: Batter
DEBUT: First-class: 2013; List A: 2013; T20: 2015

BEST BATTING: 257 Durham vs Derbyshire, Chester-le-Street, 2021

WHO IS YOUR LOOKALIKE? Jim Carrey
FIRST CRICKET CLUB? Milnerton CC, Cape Town, South Africa
BIGGEST INFLUENCE ON YOUR DEVELOPMENT AS A CRICKETER (EXCLUDING PARENTS)?
Ashwell Prince – he really understood me and gave me the confidence to play my way
WHO IS THE BEST BATTER/KEEPER/ALLROUNDER/BOWLER IN COUNTY CRICKET
(EXCLUDING TEAMMATES)? Hashim Amla/Ben Cox/Matt Critchley/Sam Cook
MOST UNDERRATED PLAYER IN COUNTY CRICKET? Will Rhodes
WHO WOULD YOU MOST LIKE TO HAVE A NET WITH? Herschelle Gibbs – it would be good
to learn from a natural stroke-player, and to hear all his stories
MAKE ONE PREDICTION FOR THE FUTURE OF CRICKET: The USA will be a powerhouse
cricket nation in the next 15 years
WHAT DO YOU MOST ENJOY LISTENING TO? 1980s music after a four-day win
WHAT MAKES YOU WORRY? Life after death

Batting	Mat	Inns	NO	Runs	HS	Ave	SR	100	50	Ct	St
First-class	55	91	9	4033	257	49.18	61.27	11	16	50	-
List A	28	27	3	796	104*	33.16	92.23	2	6	9	-
T20s	47	43	1	904	73	21.52	130.63	0	6	11	1

Bowling	Mat	Balls	Runs	Wkts	BBI	BBM	Ave	Econ	SR	5w	10
First-class	55	18	18	0	-	-	-	6.00	-	0	0
List A	28	39	25	0	-	-	-	3.84	-	0	0
T20s	47	-	-	-	-	-	-	-	-	-	-

WILL BEER

RHB / LB

FULL NAME: William Andrew Thomas Beer
BORN: October 8, 1988, Crawley, Sussex
SQUAD NO: 18
HEIGHT: 5ft 10in
NICKNAME: Beery
EDUCATION: Reigate Grammar School;
Collyer's Sixth Form College, Horsham
TEAMS: Sussex, England U19
ROLE: Bowler
DEBUT: First-class: 2008; List A: 2009; T20:
2008

BEST BATTING: 37 Sussex vs Gloucestershire, Hove, 2014 (T20)
BEST BOWLING: 3-14 Sussex vs Glamorgan, Hove, 2014 (T20)

WHO IS YOUR LOOKALIKE? Jenson Button
FIRST CRICKET CLUB? Horsham CC, West Sussex
BIGGEST INFLUENCE ON YOUR DEVELOPMENT AS A CRICKETER (EXCLUDING PARENTS)?
Shane Warne – purely because I wanted so much to bowl like him
WHO IS THE BEST BATTER/KEEPER/ALLROUNDER/BOWLER IN COUNTY CRICKET
(EXCLUDING TEAMMATES)? James Vince/Ben Brown/Darren Stevens/Simon Harmer
MOST UNDERRATED PLAYER IN COUNTY CRICKET? Daniel Bell-Drummond
HOBBIES? Horse racing
WHO WOULD YOU MOST LIKE TO HAVE A NET WITH? Don Bradman, to see how good he
really was
MAKE ONE PREDICTION FOR THE FUTURE OF CRICKET: Tom Haines will score at least one
Test century
GUILTY PLEASURE? Dairy Milk Giant Buttons
TWITTER: @willbeer18
NOTES: Beer signed a T20-only contract with Sussex in November 2021

Batting	Mat	Inns	NO	Runs	HS	Ave	SR	100	50	Ct	St
First-class	28	36	8	797	97	28.46	36.37	0	4	6	-
List A	66	42	9	535	75	16.21	83.07	0	1	18	-
T20s	131	63	23	375	37	9.37	119.42	0	0	26	-

Bowling	Mat	Balls	Runs	Wkts	BBI	BBM	Ave	Econ	SR	5w	10
First-class	28	2928	1550	43	6/29	11/91	36.04	3.17	68.0	2	1
List A	66	2898	2480	62	3/27	3/27	40.00	5.13	46.7	0	0
T20s	131	2298	2867	106	3/14	3/14	27.04	7.48	21.6	0	0

DANIEL BELL-DRUMMOND RHB / RM / R1 / W0

KENT

FULL NAME: Daniel James Bell-Drummond
BORN: August 4, 1993, Lewisham, London
SQUAD NO: 23
HEIGHT: 5ft 11in
NICKNAME: DBD
EDUCATION: Millfield School, Somerset;
Anglia Ruskin University
TEAMS: Kent, Auckland, Colombo Kings,
England Lions, Rajshahi Kings
ROLE: Batter
DEBUT: First-class: 2011; List A: 2011; T20: 2011

BEST BATTING: 206* Kent vs Loughborough MCCU, Canterbury, 2016
BEST BOWLING: 3-47 Kent vs Middlesex, Canterbury, 2021
COUNTY CAP: 2015

FAMILY TIES? My father got me into cricket. I've always really enjoyed spending time at my local club Catford Wanderers CC
CHILDHOOD SPORTING HERO? Thierry Henry
TWITTER: @deebzz23
NOTES: Bell-Drummond was at the heart of Kent's T20 Blast triumph last summer, finishing as the club's leading run-scorer (492 runs, including six half-centuries) for the second season in a row and captaining the side for most of the tournament while Sam Billings was absent. As Kent's vice-captain, the 28-year-old has also frequently led the four-day side over the last two seasons. A stylish strokeplayer, Bell-Drummond had been tipped to open the batting for England since he was a teenager but hasn't been able to establish the sort of four-day consistency to match his form in the short formats, in which he is regarded as one of the best cricketers in the country

Batting	Mat	Inns	NO	Runs	HS	Ave	SR	100	50	Ct	St
First-class	127	218	18	6416	206*	32.08	50.38	11	32	49	-
List A	89	88	8	3381	171*	42.26	81.50	6	22	32	-
T20s	124	122	8	3562	112*	31.24	135.85	1	29	40	-

Bowling	Mat	Balls	Runs	Wkts	BBI	BBM	Ave	Econ	SR	5w	10
First-class	127	637	333	13	3/47	3/44	25.61	3.13	49.0	0	0
List A	89	155	121	5	2/22	2/22	24.20	4.68	31.0	0	0
T20s	124	105	179	5	2/19	2/19	35.80	10.22	21.0	0	0

CHRIS BENJAMIN   RHB / WK / R0 / W0

FULL NAME: Christopher Gavin Benjamin
BORN: April 29, 1999, Johannesburg, South Africa
SQUAD NO: 12
TEAMS: Warwickshire
ROLE: Wicketkeeper/batter
DEBUT: First-class: 2019; List A: 2021; T20: 2021

WARWICKSHIRE

BEST BATTING: 127 Warwickshire vs Lancashire, Old Trafford, 2021

NOTES: The 22-year-old batter-keeper burst on the scene last year and was rewarded with a three-year professional contract at Warwickshire in August. Benjamin had signed a rookie deal a month earlier after impressing as T20 captain of the club's Second XI, for whom he smashed a 66-ball 149 against Glamorgan at Newport. He went on to make an unbeaten 60 on his debut in the T20 Blast and was fast-tracked into the Birmingham Phoenix side for The Hundred. He also made a fifty in his maiden List-A match for the Bears. To prove that he's not just a short-format specialist, he went on to score a hundred on his Championship debut in August – 127 against Lancashire at Old Trafford. Benjamin, who graduated from Durham University with a first in Finance and Accounting last year, was born in South Africa and moved to the UK aged 18. As a British-passport holder, he qualifies as a local player. Paul Farbrace, Warwickshire's director of cricket, said: "Since signing his rookie contract, Chris has grabbed his opportunity with both hands and we believe that he has the opportunity to reach the higher echelons of the game"

Batting	Mat	Inns	NO	Runs	HS	Ave	SR	100	50	Ct	St
First-class	5	9	0	244	127	27.11	51.15	1	0	3	-
List A	1	1	0	50	50	50.00	87.71	0	1	0	-
T20s	11	9	5	183	60*	45.75	146.40	0	1	5	-
Bowling	Mat	Balls	Runs	Wkts	BBI	BBM	Ave	Econ	SR	5w	10
First-class	5	-	-	-	-	-	-	-	-	-	-
List A	1	-	-	-	-	-	-	-	-	-	-
T20s	11	-	-	-	-	-	-	-	-	-	-

GARETH BERG

RHB / RMF / RO / WO

FULL NAME: Gareth Kyle Berg
BORN: January 18, 1981, Cape Town, South Africa
SQUAD NO: 13
HEIGHT: 6ft
NICKNAME: Batman
EDUCATION: South African College School, Cape Town
TEAMS: Italy, Northamptonshire, Hampshire, Middlesex
ROLE: Allrounder
DEBUT: T20I: 2021; First-class: 2008; List A: 2008; T20: 2009

BEST BATTING: 130* Middlesex vs Leicestershire, Leicester, 2011
BEST BOWLING: 6-56 Hampshire vs Yorkshire, Southampton, 2016
COUNTY CAP: 2010 (Middlesex); 2016 (Hampshire)

WHO IS YOUR LOOKALIKE? Napoleon Dynamite
FIRST CRICKET CLUB? Alma Marist CC, Cape Town, South Africa
WHAT WOULD YOU CHANGE ABOUT THE STRUCTURE OF THE COUNTY SEASON? More focus on the red-ball game
BIGGEST INFLUENCE ON YOUR DEVELOPMENT AS A CRICKETER (EXCLUDING PARENTS)? My uncle Colin de Lucchi who taught me from the age of three
WHAT WOULD A FLY ON THE WALL HEAR IN YOUR DRESSING ROOM? "Let's hope the batsmen give us time to rest our legs"
MOST BEAUTIFUL THING YOU HAVE EVER SEEN? My children growing up
HOBBIES? Playing the piano
IF YOU COULD TURN BACK TIME... I would meet my wife earlier
WHO WOULD YOU MOST LIKE TO HAVE A NET WITH? Brian McMillan
WHAT MAKES YOU WORRY? If I forget to put out the rubbish
WHAT GIVES YOU JOY? Coaching at all levels
TWITTER: @Bergy646

Batting	Mat	Inns	NO	Runs	HS	Ave	SR	100	50	Ct	St
T20Is	6	6	2	39	12*	9.75	66.10	0	0	1	-
First-class	142	211	26	5227	130*	28.25	63.27	2	28	71	-
List A	103	77	13	1474	75	23.03	93.05	0	7	39	-
T20s	100	78	24	1122	90	20.77	122.35	0	3	25	-

Bowling	Mat	Balls	Runs	Wkts	BBI	BBM	Ave	Econ	SR	5w	10
T20Is	6	42	37	2	2/23	2/23	18.50	5.28	21.0	0	0
First-class	142	18630	9378	303	6/56	9/90	30.95	3.02	61.4	6	0
List A	103	3634	3184	97	5/26	5/26	32.82	5.25	37.4	1	0
T20s	100	1663	2200	76	4/20	4/20	28.94	7.93	21.8	0	0

DOM BESS

RHB / OB / R0 / W0 / MVP29

FULL NAME: Dominic Mark Bess
BORN: July 22, 1997, Exeter, Devon
SQUAD NO: 47
HEIGHT: 5ft 11in
NICKNAME: Moonhead
EDUCATION: Blundell's School, Tiverton, Devon
TEAMS: England, Yorkshire, Somerset
ROLE: Bowler
DEBUT: Test: 2018; First-class: 2016; List A: 2018; T20: 2016

BEST BATTING: 107 MCC vs Essex, Barbados, 2018
BEST BOWLING: 7-43 Yorkshire vs Northamptonshire, Northampton, 2021

FIRST CRICKET CLUB? Sidmouth CC, Devon. A beautiful coastal cricket club with a thatched roof
CHILDHOOD SPORTING HERO? Graeme Swann
BEST INNINGS YOU'VE SEEN? James Hildreth scoring a hundred on one leg against Nottinghamshire in 2016
TWITTER: @DomBess99

Batting	Mat	Inns	NO	Runs	HS	Ave	SR	100	50	Ct	St
Tests	14	19	5	319	57	22.78	44.92	0	1	3	-
First-class	66	99	15	1914	107	22.78	48.06	1	8	26	-
List A	19	15	1	119	24*	8.50	62.30	0	0	6	-
T20s	17	8	3	41	24	8.20	100.00	0	0	2	-

Bowling	Mat	Balls	Runs	Wkts	BBI	BBM	Ave	Econ	SR	5w	10
Tests	14	2502	1223	36	5/30	8/130	33.97	2.93	69.5	2	0
First-class	66	11461	5501	180	7/43	10/162	30.56	2.87	63.6	12	1
List A	19	841	804	12	3/35	3/35	67.00	5.73	70.0	0	0
T20s	17	336	417	16	3/17	3/17	26.06	7.44	21.0	0	0

JACOB BETHELL LHB / SLA / R0 / W0

WARWICKSHIRE

FULL NAME: Jacob Graham Bethell
BORN: October 23, 2003, Barbados
SQUAD NO: 2
HEIGHT: 5ft 10in
NICKNAME: Beth
EDUCATION: Harrison College, Barbados;
Rugby School, Warwickshire
TEAMS: Warwickshire, England U19
ROLE: Allrounder
DEBUT: First-class: 2021; List A: 2021; T20: 2021

BEST BATTING: 15 Warwickshire vs Yorkshire, Headingley, 2021

MOST EXCITING DAY AS A CRICKETER? The final day of the Bunbury Festival in 2018
CHILDHOOD SPORTING HERO? Sir Garry Sobers
BIGGEST INFLUENCE ON YOUR DEVELOPMENT AS A CRICKETER (EXCLUDING PARENTS)?
Michael Powell (former Warwickshire captain and director of cricket at Rugby School)
WHAT WOULD YOU DO IF YOU WERE IN CHARGE OF COUNTY CRICKET? Play more red-ball
matches, play more at outgrounds, and try to incentivise crowds for Championship games
FAVOURITE SMELL? New batting gloves

Batting	Mat	Inns	NO	Runs	HS	Ave	SR	100	50	Ct	St
First-class	1	2	0	23	15	11.50	52.27	0	0	1	-
List A	8	7	1	141	66	23.50	94.63	0	1	2	-
T20s	3	3	1	12	7	6.00	85.71	0	0	1	-
Bowling	Mat	Balls	Runs	Wkts	BBI	BBM	Ave	Econ	SR	5w	10
First-class	1	-	-	-	-	-	-	-	-	-	-
List A	8	342	301	11	4/36	4/36	27.36	5.28	31.0	0	0
T20s	3	36	61	0	-	-	-	10.16	-	0	0

SAM BILLINGS

RHB / WK / R0 / W0

FULL NAME: Samuel William Billings
BORN: June 15, 1991, Pembury, Kent
SQUAD NO: 7
HEIGHT: 6ft
NICKNAME: Bilbo
EDUCATION: Haileybury & Imperial College, Herts; Loughborough University
TEAMS: England, Kent, Chennai Super Kings, Delhi Capitals, Kolkata Knight Riders, Sydney Sixers, Sydney Thunder
ROLE: Batter/wicketkeeper
DEBUT: Test: 2022; ODI: 2015; T20I: 2015; First-class: 2011; List A: 2011; T20: 2011

KENT

BEST BATTING: 171 Kent vs Gloucestershire, Bristol, 2016

COUNTY CAP: 2015

FIRST CRICKET CLUB? Hartley Country Club, Dartford, Kent
WHO IS THE BEST BATTER/KEEPER/ALLROUNDER/BOWLER IN COUNTY CRICKET (EXCLUDING TEAMMATES)? Joe Clarke/Ben Foakes/Craig Overton/Simon Harmer
HOBBIES? Padel tennis
WHO WOULD YOU MOST LIKE TO HAVE A NET WITH? Ricky Ponting – best cricket eye I've ever come across
WHAT MAKES YOU WORRY? Getting ready to bat!
TWITTER: @sambillings
NOTES: Billings was bought by Kolkata Knight Riders for this year's IPL

Batting	Mat	Inns	NO	Runs	HS	Ave	SR	100	50	Ct	St
Tests	1	2	0	30	29	15.00	52.63	0	0	5	-
ODIs	25	20	2	607	118	33.72	92.38	1	4	18	-
T20Is	37	33	5	478	87	17.07	129.89	0	2	17	2
First-class	75	110	11	3357	171	33.90	60.29	6	15	178	11
List A	101	88	15	3044	175	41.69	103.96	7	20	87	8
T20s	215	201	30	4152	95*	24.28	131.64	0	24	119	21

Bowling	Mat	Balls	Runs	Wkts	BBI	BBM	Ave	Econ	SR	5w	10
Tests	1	-	-	-	-	-	-	-	-	-	-
ODIs	25	-	-	-	-	-	-	-	-	-	-
T20Is	37	-	-	-	-	-	-	-	-	-	-
First-class	75	1	4	0	-	-	-	24.00	-	0	0
List A	101	-	-	-	-	-	-	-	-	-	-
T20s	215	-	-	-	-	-	-	-	-	-	-

JACKSON BIRD

RHB / RFM / R0 / W0

KENT

FULL NAME: Jackson Munro Bird
BORN: December 11, 1986, Sydney, Australia
SQUAD NO: TBC
EDUCATION: St Pius X College, Chatswood, Sydney; Saint Ignatius' College Riverview, Sydney
TEAMS: Australia, Kent, Hampshire, Melbourne Stars, Nottinghamshire, Sydney Sixers, Tasmania
ROLE: Bowler
DEBUT: Test: 2012; First-class: 2011; List A: 2011; T20: 2012

BEST BATTING: 64 Tasmania vs Western Australia, Perth, 2021
BEST BOWLING: 7-18 Tasmania vs New South Wales, Hobart, 2021
COUNTY CAP: 2016 (Nottinghamshire)

TWITTER: @jbird431
NOTES: Tall, rangy and able to move the ball at decent pace, Bird comes across as an archetypal English seamer, and yet the Australian's record in his own conditions is significantly better than his indifferent returns in previous stints with Hampshire and Notts. Bird, who appeared in nine Tests without fully establishing himself, topped the wicket-taking charts for Tasmania in the 2020/21 Sheffield Shield, claiming 35 scalps at 22 apiece, and boasts an impressive overall tally of 319 wickets for his adopted state at an average of 21. The 35-year-old is available for Kent for the first six Championship games. "He is an experienced bowler who will strengthen our squad," said Paul Downton, Kent's director of cricket. "He is a proven wicket-taker who will also be a great mentor for our young seamers"

Batting	Mat	Inns	NO	Runs	HS	Ave	SR	100	50	Ct	St
Tests	9	9	6	43	19*	14.33	30.49	0	0	2	-
First-class	100	138	35	1265	64	12.28	59.33	0	3	51	-
List A	40	20	8	170	28*	14.16	100.00	0	0	16	-
T20s	78	22	13	76	14*	8.44	82.60	0	0	33	-

Bowling	Mat	Balls	Runs	Wkts	BBI	BBM	Ave	Econ	SR	5w	10
Tests	9	1934	1042	34	5/59	7/117	30.64	3.23	56.8	1	0
First-class	100	20529	10148	419	7/18	11/95	24.21	2.96	48.9	18	5
List A	40	2152	1715	51	6/25	6/25	33.62	4.78	42.1	1	0
T20s	78	1527	1932	65	4/31	4/31	29.72	7.59	23.4	0	0

ALEX BLAKE

LHB / RM

FULL NAME: Alexander James Blake
BORN: January 25, 1989, Farnborough, Kent
SQUAD NO: 10
HEIGHT: 6ft 2in
NICKNAME: TS
EDUCATION: Hayes Secondary School, Kent;
Leeds Metropolitan University
TEAMS: Kent, England U19
ROLE: Batter
DEBUT: First-class: 2008; List A: 2007; T20: 2010

KENT

BEST BATTING: 71* Kent vs Hampshire, Southampton, 2015 (T20)
BEST BOWLING: 1-17 Kent vs Gloucestershire, Canterbury, 2019 (T20)
COUNTY CAP: 2017

FIRST CRICKET CLUB? Bromley Town CC, London
MOST EXCITING DAY AS A CRICKETER? Receiving my county cap in 2017
CHILDHOOD SPORTING HERO? Ryan Giggs
WHAT WOULD YOU DO IF YOU WERE IN CHARGE OF COUNTY CRICKET? Introduce home
and away kits for white-ball cricket, put roofs on grounds to stop games being rained off
GUILTY PLEASURE? Listening to Little Mix
TWITTER: @aj_blake10
NOTES: The Kent batter is on a white-ball contract which runs until the end of the 2022 season

Batting	Mat	Inns	NO	Runs	HS	Ave	SR	100	50	Ct	St
First-class	46	72	6	1511	105*	22.89	55.61	1	6	25	-
List A	106	88	18	2125	116	30.35	100.14	1	12	53	-
T20s	141	122	29	1898	71*	20.40	134.32	0	9	80	-

Bowling	Mat	Balls	Runs	Wkts	BBI	BBM	Ave	Econ	SR	5w	10
First-class	46	210	138	3	2/9	2/9	46.00	3.94	70.0	0	0
List A	106	204	223	4	2/13	2/13	55.75	6.55	51.0	0	0
T20s	141	78	96	1	1/17	1/17	96.00	7.38	78.0	0	0

JACK BLATHERWICK

RHB / RFM / R0 / W0

LANCASHIRE

FULL NAME: Jack Morgan Blatherwick
BORN: June 4, 1998, Nottingham
SQUAD NO: 4
HEIGHT: 6ft 2in
NICKNAME: The Milkman
EDUCATION: Holgate Academy, Hucknall;
Central College, Nottingham
TEAMS: Lancashire, England U19,
Northamptonshire, Nottinghamshire
ROLE: Bowler
DEBUT: First-class: 2019; List A: 2018

BEST BATTING: 11 Lancashire vs Warwickshire, Lord's, 2021
BEST BOWLING: 4-28 Lancashire vs Somerset, Taunton, 2021

FIRST CRICKET CLUB? Kimberley Institute CC, Nottingham
FAMILY TIES? My uncle is the former Nottingham Forest defender Steve Blatherwick
BIGGEST INFLUENCE ON YOUR DEVELOPMENT AS A CRICKETER (EXCLUDING PARENTS)?
Mike Hendrick at Notts – old-school but really knowledgeable
WHO IS THE BEST BATTER/KEEPER/ALLROUNDER/BOWLER IN COUNTY CRICKET
(EXCLUDING TEAMMATES)? Zak Crawley/Ben Foakes/Lyndon James/Ollie Robinson
WHAT WOULD A FLY ON THE WALL HEAR IN YOUR DRESSING ROOM? Danny Lamb being on
the end of it
HOBBIES? Fishing
MAKE ONE PREDICTION FOR THE FUTURE OF CRICKET: Huge leagues in America
WHAT DO YOU MOST ENJOY LISTENING TO? Music from the 1970s and '80s
WHAT GIVES YOU JOY? Playing with all my pals on a cricket pitch
TWITTER: @BlatherwickJM

Batting	Mat	Inns	NO	Runs	HS	Ave	SR	100	50	Ct	St
First-class	6	7	2	23	11	4.60	27.71	0	0	1	-
List A	3	3	2	6	3*	6.00	28.57	0	0	1	-

Bowling	Mat	Balls	Runs	Wkts	BBI	BBM	Ave	Econ	SR	5w	10
First-class	6	605	428	11	4/28	6/95	38.90	4.24	55.0	0	0
List A	3	48	72	1	1/55	1/55	72.00	9.00	48.0	0	0

JOSH BOHANNON

RHB / RM / R0 / W0

FULL NAME: Joshua James Bohannon
BORN: April 9, 1997, Bolton, Lancashire
SQUAD NO: 20
HEIGHT: 5ft 9in
NICKNAME: Bosh
EDUCATION: Harper Green High School, Bolton
TEAMS: Lancashire, England Lions
ROLE: Batter
DEBUT: First-class: 2018; List A: 2018; T20: 2018

LANCASHIRE

BEST BATTING: 174 Lancashire vs Derbyshire, Old Trafford, 2019
BEST BOWLING: 3-46 Lancashire vs Hampshire, Southampton, 2018

WHO IS YOUR LOOKALIKE? Jonathan Trott
FIRST CRICKET CLUB? Farnworth CC, Greater Manchester
BIGGEST INFLUENCE ON YOUR DEVELOPMENT AS A CRICKETER (EXCLUDING PARENTS)? My girlfriend Lucy and her dad Ian
WHO IS THE BEST BATTER/KEEPER/ALLROUNDER/BOWLER IN COUNTY CRICKET (EXCLUDING TEAMMATES)? Adam Lyth/Ben Foakes/Darren Stevens/Simon Harmer
MOST UNDERRATED PLAYER IN COUNTY CRICKET? Rob Yates
IF YOU COULD TURN BACK TIME... I would listen more at school
WHAT MAKES YOU WORRY? Cricket nets
WHAT GIVES YOU JOY? Batting
SURPRISING FACT ABOUT YOU? I played junior cricket alongside Haseeb Hameed at Farnworth Social Circle CC (Bolton league)
GUILTY PLEASURE? Gogglebox
TWITTER: @joshbo97

Batting	Mat	Inns	NO	Runs	HS	Ave	SR	100	50	Ct	St
First-class	37	50	6	1935	174	43.97	47.49	3	12	19	-
List A	22	17	3	373	55*	26.64	81.44	0	2	4	-
T20s	22	14	5	112	35	12.44	100.90	0	0	11	-

Bowling	Mat	Balls	Runs	Wkts	BBI	BBM	Ave	Econ	SR	5w	10
First-class	37	1007	562	13	3/46	4/82	43.23	3.34	77.4	0	0
List A	22	150	208	1	1/33	1/33	208.00	8.32	150.0	0	0
T20s	22	-	-	-	-	-	-	-	-	-	-

RAVI BOPARA

RHB / RM

FULL NAME: Ravinder Singh Bopara
BORN: May 4, 1985, Forest Gate, London
SQUAD NO: 23
HEIGHT: 5ft 10in
NICKNAME: Puppy
EDUCATION: Brampton Manor, London
TEAMS: England, Sussex, Auckland, Essex, Gloucestershire, Karachi Kings, Kings XI Punjab, Multan Sultans, Peshawar Zalmi, Sunrisers Hyderabad, Sydney Sixers
ROLE: Allrounder
DEBUT: Test: 2007; ODI: 2007; T20I: 2008; First-class: 2002; List A: 2002; T20: 2003

BEST BATTING: 105* Essex vs Somerset, Chelmsford, 2010 (T20)
BEST BOWLING: 6-16 Karachi Kings vs Lahore Qalandars, Sharjah, 2016 (T20)
COUNTY CAP: 2005 (Essex); BENEFIT: 2015 (Essex)

MOST EXCITING DAY AS A CRICKETER? Playing against Sachin Tendulkar
CHILDHOOD SPORTING HERO? Sachin Tendulkar
BIGGEST INFLUENCE ON YOUR DEVELOPMENT AS A CRICKETER (EXCLUDING PARENTS)? Graham Gooch and Sachin Tendulkar
WHAT WOULD YOU DO IF YOU WERE IN CHARGE OF COUNTY CRICKET? Introduce a 10-over competition
FAVOURITE SMELL? Dog ears
SURPRISING FACT ABOUT YOU? I have a fast-food business
TWITTER: @ravibopara
NOTES: Bopara signed a T20-only contract with Sussex in August 2021

Batting	Mat	Inns	NO	Runs	HS	Ave	SR	100	50	Ct	St
Tests	13	19	1	575	143	31.94	52.89	3	0	6	-
ODIs	120	109	21	2695	101*	30.62	77.84	1	14	35	-
T20Is	38	35	10	711	65*	28.44	118.69	0	3	7	-
First-class	221	357	40	12821	229	40.44	51.54	31	55	118	-
List A	323	301	56	9845	201*	40.18		15	60	103	-
T20s	411	374	81	7987	105*	27.25	120.64	1	41	140	-

Bowling	Mat	Balls	Runs	Wkts	BBI	BBM	Ave	Econ	SR	5w	10
Tests	13	434	290	1	1/39	1/39	290.00	4.00	434.0	0	0
ODIs	120	1860	1523	40	4/38	4/38	38.07	4.91	46.5	0	0
T20Is	38	322	387	16	4/10	4/10	24.18	7.21	20.1	0	0
First-class	221	15462	9381	257	5/49		36.50	3.64	60.1	3	0
List A	323	8097	7197	248	5/63	5/63	29.02	5.33	32.6	1	0
T20s	411	5040	6317	245	6/16	6/16	25.78	7.52	20.5	1	0

SCOTT BORTHWICK LHB / LB / R3 / W0 / MVP12

FULL NAME: Scott George Borthwick
BORN: April 19, 1990, Sunderland, County Durham
SQUAD NO: 16
HEIGHT: 5ft 10in
NICKNAME: Badger
EDUCATION: Farringdon Community Sports College, Sunderland
TEAMS: England, Durham, Chilaw Marians, Surrey, Wellington
ROLE: Allrounder
DEBUT: Test: 2014; ODI: 2011; T20I: 2011; First-class 2009; List A: 2009; T20: 2008

DURHAM

BEST BATTING: 216 Durham vs Middlesex, Chester-le-Street, 2014
BEST BOWLING: 6-70 Durham vs Surrey, The Oval, 2013
COUNTY CAP: 2018 (Surrey)

FIRST CRICKET CLUB? Eppleton CC, Sunderland. I made my first-team debut aged 13 and got a 44-ball duck (on a poor pitch)
MOST EXCITING DAY AS A CRICKETER? Making my England debut
CHILDHOOD SPORTING HERO? Shane Warne
BIGGEST INFLUENCE ON YOUR DEVELOPMENT AS A CRICKETER (EXCLUDING PARENTS)? Geoff Cook – he was Academy director when I joined Durham, and he was head coach when I made my first-team debut
GUILTY PLEASURE? Eating Galaxy chocolate while playing Football Manager
TWITTER: @Borthwick16

Batting	Mat	Inns	NO	Runs	HS	Ave	SR	100	50	Ct	St
Tests	1	2	0	5	4	2.50	26.31	0	0	2	-
ODIs	2	2	0	18	15	9.00	112.50	0	0	0	-
T20Is	1	1	0	14	14	14.00	87.50	0	0	1	-
First-class	182	305	25	9762	216	34.86	52.28	20	51	235	-
List A	108	79	12	1610	87	24.02	78.72	0	10	42	-
T20s	106	55	18	650	62	17.56	100.15	0	1	50	-

Bowling	Mat	Balls	Runs	Wkts	BBI	BBM	Ave	Econ	SR	5w	10
Tests	1	78	82	4	3/33	4/82	20.50	6.30	19.5	0	0
ODIs	2	54	72	0	-	-	-	8.00	-	0	0
T20Is	1	24	15	1	1/15	1/15	15.00	3.75	24.0	0	0
First-class	182	13026	8556	220	6/70	8/84	38.89	3.94	59.2	3	0
List A	108	3237	3196	79	5/38	5/38	40.45	5.92	40.9	1	0
T20s	106	1388	1865	74	4/18	4/18	25.20	8.06	18.7	0	0

NAT BOWLEY

LHB / OB / R0 / W0

FULL NAME: Nathan John Bowley
BORN: August 3, 2001, Nottingham
SQUAD NO: 33
HEIGHT: 6ft 3in
NICKNAME: Natty B
EDUCATION: Woodbrook Vale School, Loughborough; Loughborough College
TEAMS: Leicestershire
ROLE: Bowler

WHO IS YOUR LOOKALIKE? Nicklas Bendtner
FIRST CRICKET CLUB? Loughborough Outwoods CC, Leicestershire
WHAT WOULD YOU CHANGE ABOUT THE STRUCTURE OF THE COUNTY SEASON? Increase the amount of red-ball cricket in the middle of the summer
BIGGEST INFLUENCE ON YOUR DEVELOPMENT AS A CRICKETER (EXCLUDING PARENTS)? Dips Patel (Leicestershire Second XI coach) and Jigar Naik (spin-bowling coach) – I have worked with both of them since I was 13
WHO IS THE BEST BATTER/KEEPER/ALLROUNDER/BOWLER IN COUNTY CRICKET (EXCLUDING TEAMMATES)? Ollie Pope/Ben Foakes/Darren Stevens/Simon Harmer
MOST UNDERRATED PLAYER IN COUNTY CRICKET? George Hill
WHAT WOULD A FLY ON THE WALL HEAR IN YOUR DRESSING ROOM? A lot of football chat
MOST BEAUTIFUL THING YOU HAVE EVER SEEN? Sunset from the top of Bradgate Park in Charnwood Forest, Leicestershire
IF YOU COULD TURN BACK TIME... I would stop Claudio Ranieri from being sacked as Leicester City manager
WHO WOULD YOU MOST LIKE TO HAVE A NET WITH? Graeme Swann (my sporting hero)
WHAT DO YOU MOST ENJOY LISTENING TO? Cheesy singalongs
SURPRISING FACT ABOUT YOU? I once put on my Leicester City shirt for a cup final on Football Manager (video game)
GUILTY PLEASURE? One Direction
TWITTER: @nat_bowley

JAMES BRACEY

LHB / WK / R0 / W0

FULL NAME: James Robert Bracey
BORN: May 3, 1997, Bristol
SQUAD NO: 25
HEIGHT: 6ft 1in
NICKNAME: Bob
EDUCATION: The Ridings High School, Bristol; SGS Filton College; Loughborough University
TEAMS: England, Gloucestershire
ROLE: Batter/wicketkeeper
DEBUT: Test: 2021; First-class: 2016; List A: 2019; T20: 2019

BEST BATTING: 156 Gloucestershire vs Glamorgan, Cardiff, 2017

COUNTY CAP: 2016

FIRST CRICKET CLUB? Winterbourne CC, Bristol
FAMILY TIES? My older brother Sam has played first-class cricket for Cardiff MCCU
CHILDHOOD SPORTING HERO? Rickie Lambert – Bristol Rovers legend
SURPRISING FACT ABOUT YOU? I was probably the only child ever who did not like Ketchup or baked beans
TWITTER: @bobbybracey114

Batting	Mat	Inns	NO	Runs	HS	Ave	SR	100	50	Ct	St
Tests	2	3	0	8	8	2.66	29.62	0	0	6	-
First-class	53	92	8	2937	156	34.96	46.96	7	14	88	-
List A	14	14	1	648	113*	49.84	103.84	1	5	13	1
T20s	30	26	3	425	64	18.47	122.83	0	1	9	10

Bowling	Mat	Balls	Runs	Wkts	BBI	BBM	Ave	Econ	SR	5w	10
Tests	2	-	-	-	-	-	-	-	-	-	-
First-class	53	60	35	0	-	-	-	3.50	-	0	0
List A	14	18	23	1	1/23	1/23	23.00	7.66	18.0	0	0
T20s	30	-	-	-	-	-	-	-	-	-	-

CARLOS BRATHWAITE

RHB / RMF

WARWICKSHIRE

FULL NAME: Carlos Ricardo Brathwaite
BORN: July 18, 1988, Christ Church, Barbados
SQUAD NO: 26
TEAMS: West Indies, Warwickshire,
Antigua Hawksbills, Barbados, Barisal
Bulls, Combined Campuses & Colleges,
Delhi Daredevils, Jamaica Tallawahs, Kent,
Khulna Titans, Kolkata Knight Riders, Multan
Sultans, St Kitts & Nevis Patriots, Sunrisers
Hyderabad, Sydney Sixers
ROLE: Allrounder
DEBUT: Test: 2015; ODI: 2011; T20I: 2011;
First-class: 2011; List A: 2011; T20: 2011

BEST BATTING: 64* Khulna Titans vs Dhaka Dynamites, Mirpur, 2017 (T20)
BEST BOWLING: 4-15 St Kitts & Nevis Patriots vs Barbados Tridents, Bridgetown, 2017 (T20)

TWITTER: @CRBrathwaite26
NOTES: The former Windies T20 skipper and global short-format star has re-joined the
Birmingham Bears for the Blast and will captain the side this summer. The 33-year-old
played in 11 of the club's 15 games last summer. "Carlos has been a great addition to the
dressing room. He is popular with all of the squad," said Paul Farbrace, Warwickshire's
director of cricket. "His experience of playing in and winning some of the biggest short-form
tournaments in the world has been invaluable in supporting the development of our young
players." Brathwaite's extraordinary innings in the 2016 World T20 final, when he belted
Ben Stokes for four consecutive sixes to seal the trophy for West Indies at Eden Gardens, has
gone down in legend

Batting	Mat	Inns	NO	Runs	HS	Ave	SR	100	50	Ct	St
Tests	3	5	1	181	69	45.25	63.73	0	3	0	-
ODIs	44	37	3	559	101	16.44	91.04	1	1	11	-
T20Is	41	27	6	310	37*	14.76	113.13	0	0	19	-
First-class	39	64	9	1522	109	27.67		1	9	20	-
List A	92	78	11	1350	113	20.14		2	4	31	-
T20s	223	172	39	2122	64*	15.95	135.76	0	4	92	-

Bowling	Mat	Balls	Runs	Wkts	BBI	BBM	Ave	Econ	SR	5w	10
Tests	3	408	242	1	1/30	1/139	242.00	3.55	408.0	0	0
ODIs	44	1825	1766	43	5/27	5/27	41.06	5.80	42.4	1	0
T20Is	41	700	1013	31	3/20	3/20	32.67	8.57	22.8	0	0
First-class	39	4472	2098	88	7/90	9/61	23.84	2.81	50.8	2	0
List A	92	3500	3018	105	5/27	5/27	28.74	5.17	33.3	1	0
T20s	223	3937	5354	199	4/15	4/15	26.90	8.15	19.7	0	0

DANNY BRIGGS — RHB / SLA / R0 / W0 / MVP24

FULL NAME: Danny Richard Briggs
BORN: April 30, 1991, Newport, Isle of Wight
SQUAD NO: 14
HEIGHT: 6ft 2in
NICKNAME: Briggsy
EDUCATION: Carisbrooke High School, Isle of Wight
TEAMS: England, Warwickshire, Adelaide Strikers, Hampshire, Sussex
ROLE: Bowler
DEBUT: ODI: 2012; T20I: 2012; First-class: 2009; List A: 2009; T20: 2010

BEST BATTING: 120* Sussex vs South Africa A, Arundel, 2017
BEST BOWLING: 6-45 England Lions vs Windward Islands, Roseau, 2011
COUNTY CAP: 2012 (Hampshire); 2021 (Warwickshire)

FIRST CRICKET CLUB? Ventnor CC, Isle of Wight
MOST EXCITING DAY AS A CRICKETER? It's a toss-up between my England debut, playing in T20 Finals Day, and winning the Championship
CHILDHOOD SPORTING HERO? Shane Warne
BIGGEST INFLUENCE ON YOUR DEVELOPMENT AS A CRICKETER (EXCLUDING PARENTS)?
Sam Garaway – my first coach who made me fall in love with the game
TWITTER: @DannyBriggs19

Batting	Mat	Inns	NO	Runs	HS	Ave	SR	100	50	Ct	St
ODIs	1	-	-	-	-	-	-	-	-	0	-
T20Is	7	1	1	0	0*	-	-	0	0	1	-
First-class	121	158	42	2182	120*	18.81		1	4	42	-
List A	107	56	24	402	37*	12.56	93.27	0	0	34	-
T20s	201	52	34	189	35*	10.50	112.50	0	0	33	-

Bowling	Mat	Balls	Runs	Wkts	BBI	BBM	Ave	Econ	SR	5w	10
ODIs	1	60	39	2	2/39	2/39	19.50	3.90	30.0	0	0
T20Is	7	108	199	5	2/25	2/25	39.80	11.05	21.6	0	0
First-class	121	20496	10112	303	6/45	9/96	33.37	2.96	67.6	8	0
List A	107	4916	4188	112	4/32	4/32	37.39	5.11	43.8	0	0
T20s	201	4079	4919	219	5/19	5/19	22.46	7.23	18.6	1	0

STUART BROAD — LHB / RFM / R0 / W0

NOTTINGHAMSHIRE

FULL NAME: Stuart Christopher John Broad
BORN: June 24, 1986, Nottingham
SQUAD NO: 8
HEIGHT: 6ft 6in
NICKNAME: Broady
EDUCATION: Oakham School, Rutland
TEAMS: England, Nottinghamshire, Hobart Hurricanes, Kings XI Punjab, Leicestershire
ROLE: Bowler
DEBUT: Test: 2007; ODI: 2006; T20I: 2006; First-class: 2005; List A: 2005; T20: 2006

BEST BATTING: 169 England vs Pakistan, Lord's, 2010
BEST BOWLING: 8-15 England vs Australia, Trent Bridge, 2015
COUNTY CAP: 2007 (Leicestershire); 2008 (Notts); BENEFIT: 2019 (Notts)

WHO IS YOUR LOOKALIKE? Draco Malfoy from Harry Potter
FIRST CRICKET CLUB? Egerton Park CC, Melton Mowbray, Leicestershire
FAMILY TIES? My father Chris played for England, Nottinghamshire and Gloucestershire and is now an ICC match official
WHO IS THE BEST BATTER/KEEPER/ALLROUNDER/BOWLER IN COUNTY CRICKET (EXCLUDING TEAMMATES)? Joe Root/Ben Foakes/Ben Stokes/James Anderson
WHAT WOULD A FLY ON THE WALL HEAR IN YOUR DRESSING ROOM? Joe Clarke talking HOBBIES? Wine and golf
WHO WOULD YOU MOST LIKE TO HAVE A NET WITH? Ian Botham, though I can't imagine him netting
WHAT DO YOU MOST ENJOY LISTENING TO? Silence
TWITTER: @StuartBroad8

Batting	Mat	Inns	NO	Runs	HS	Ave	SR	100	50	Ct	St
Tests	152	224	39	3412	169	18.44	64.68	1	13	51	-
ODIs	121	68	25	529	45*	12.30	74.61	0	0	27	-
T20Is	56	26	10	118	18*	7.37	100.00	0	0	21	-
First-class	242	343	59	5469	169	19.25	63.04	1	25	87	-
List A	151	80	28	620	45*	11.92	75.88	0	0	32	-
T20s	85	32	12	152	18*	7.60	102.01	0	0	26	-

Bowling	Mat	Balls	Runs	Wkts	BBI	BBM	Ave	Econ	SR	5w	10
Tests	152	30575	14932	537	8/15	11/121	27.80	2.93	56.9	19	3
ODIs	121	6109	5364	178	5/23	5/23	30.13	5.26	34.3	1	0
T20Is	56	1173	1491	65	4/24	4/24	22.93	7.62	18.0	0	0
First-class	242	45502	22888	854	8/15		26.80	3.01	53.2	31	4
List A	151	7496	6591	216	5/23	5/23	30.51	5.27	34.7	1	0
T20s	85	1788	2144	100	4/24	4/24	21.44	7.19	17.8	0	0

HARRY BROOK   RHB / RMF / R0 / W0 / MVP9

FULL NAME: Harry Cherrington Brook
BORN: February 22, 1999, Keighley, Yorkshire
SQUAD NO: 88
HEIGHT: 6ft
EDUCATION: Sedbergh School, Cumbria
TEAMS: England, Yorkshire, Hobart Hurricanes, Lahore Qalandars
ROLE: Batter
DEBUT: T20I: 2022; First-class: 2016; List A: 2017; T20: 2018

BEST BATTING: 124 Yorkshire vs Essex, Chelmsford, 2018
BEST BOWLING: 3-15 Yorkshire vs Glamorgan, Cardiff, 2021

MOST EXCITING DAY AS A CRICKETER? My first-class debut for Yorkshire against Pakistan A at Headingley in 2016
CHILDHOOD SPORTING HERO? Jacques Kallis
SURPRISING FACT ABOUT YOU? I love Tinder
GUILTY PLEASURE? Peaky Blinders
TWITTER: @harry_brook88

Batting	Mat	Inns	NO	Runs	HS	Ave	SR	100	50	Ct	St
T20Is	1	1	0	10	10	10.00	76.92	0	0	0	-
First-class	48	78	2	2100	124	27.63	60.74	4	11	36	-
List A	15	12	1	343	103	31.18	99.42	1	1	4	-
T20s	61	59	15	1549	102*	35.20	146.82	1	4	38	-

Bowling	Mat	Balls	Runs	Wkts	BBI	BBM	Ave	Econ	SR	5w	10
T20Is	1	-	-	-	-	-	-	-	-	-	-
First-class	48	837	379	8	3/15	4/29	47.37	2.71	104.6	0	0
List A	15	18	19	0	-	-	-	6.33	-	0	0
T20s	61	12	26	1	1/13	1/13	26.00	13.00	12.0	0	0

ETHAN BROOKES

RHB / RMF / R0 / W0

WARWICKSHIRE

FULL NAME: Ethan Alexander Brookes
BORN: May 23, 2001, Solihull, Warwickshire
SQUAD NO: 77
HEIGHT: 6ft 2in
NICKNAME: Eth
EDUCATION: Solihull School
TEAMS: Warwickshire
ROLE: Bowler
DEBUT: First-class: 2019; List A: 2021

BEST BATTING: 15* Warwickshire vs Glamorgan, Cardiff, 2020

FIRST CRICKET CLUB? Olton & West Warwicks CC, Solihull
MOST EXCITING DAY AS A CRICKETER? Playing at Lord's for the English Schools Cricket Association, making my first-team debut for Warwickshire in the County Championship in 2019, and winning the County Championship last summer
CHILDHOOD SPORTING HERO? Andrew Flintoff
BIGGEST INFLUENCE ON YOUR DEVELOPMENT AS A CRICKETER (EXCLUDING PARENTS)? Dave Cowper – my very first coach who helped me with the fundamentals
WHAT WOULD YOU DO IF YOU WERE IN CHARGE OF COUNTY CRICKET? Introduce the Decision Review System
FAVOURITE SMELL? Fresh paint
GUILTY PLEASURE? Call of Duty (video game)
TWITTER: @ethanbrookes2

Batting	Mat	Inns	NO	Runs	HS	Ave	SR	100	50	Ct	St
First-class	3	3	1	21	15*	10.50	52.50	0	0	0	-
List A	8	7	2	107	63	21.40	86.29	0	1	8	-

Bowling	Mat	Balls	Runs	Wkts	BBI	BBM	Ave	Econ	SR	5w	10
First-class	3	132	76	0	-	-	-	3.45	-	0	0
List A	8	184	207	7	3/15	3/15	29.57	6.75	26.2	0	0

HENRY BROOKES

RHB / RFM / R0 / W0

FULL NAME: Henry James Hamilton Brookes
BORN: August 21, 1999, Solihull, Warwickshire
SQUAD NO: 10
HEIGHT: 6ft 4in
EDUCATION: Tudor Grange Academy, Solihull
TEAMS: Warwickshire, England Lions
ROLE: Bowler
DEBUT: First-class: 2017; List A: 2018; T20: 2018

WARWICKSHIRE

BEST BATTING: 84 Warwickshire vs Kent, Edgbaston, 2019
BEST BOWLING: 4-54 Warwickshire vs Northamptonshire, Edgbaston, 2018

FIRST CRICKET CLUB? Olton & West Warwicks CC, Solihull
FAMILY TIES? My brother Ben has played age-group cricket for Warwickshire and my other brother Ethan plays with me at the club
MOST EXCITING DAY AS A CRICKETER? Winning the County Championship with Warwickshire last year
CHILDHOOD SPORTING HERO? Andrew Flintoff
BIGGEST INFLUENCE ON YOUR DEVELOPMENT AS A CRICKETER (EXCLUDING PARENTS)? My grandad – what a hero
TWITTER: @BrookesHenry

Batting	Mat	Inns	NO	Runs	HS	Ave	SR	100	50	Ct	St
First-class	19	29	3	488	84	18.76	50.88	0	3	8	-
List A	12	5	2	13	12*	4.33	108.33	0	0	1	-
T20s	24	11	2	94	31*	10.44	120.51	0	0	3	-

Bowling	Mat	Balls	Runs	Wkts	BBI	BBM	Ave	Econ	SR	5w	10
First-class	19	3117	2066	55	4/54	8/119	37.56	3.97	56.6	0	0
List A	12	551	601	17	3/50	3/50	35.35	6.54	32.4	0	0
T20s	24	526	778	31	3/26	3/26	25.09	8.87	16.9	0	0

JACK BROOKS

RHB / RFM / R0 / W4

SOMERSET

FULL NAME: Jack Alexander Brooks
BORN: June 4, 1984, Oxford
SQUAD NO: 70
HEIGHT: 6ft 2in
NICKNAME: Headband Warrior
EDUCATION: Wheatley Park School, South Oxfordshire
TEAMS: Somerset, England Lions, Northamptonshire, Yorkshire
ROLE: Bowler
DEBUT: First-class: 2009; List A: 2009; T20: 2010

BEST BATTING: 109* Yorkshire vs Lancashire, Old Trafford, 2017
BEST BOWLING: 6-65 Yorkshire vs Middlesex, Lord's, 2016
COUNTY CAP: 2012 (Northamptonshire); 2013 (Yorkshire)

FIRST CRICKET CLUB? Tiddington CC, Oxfordshire
WHAT WOULD YOU CHANGE ABOUT THE STRUCTURE OF THE COUNTY SEASON? Schedule Championship cricket for the summer holidays. And play less cricket
BIGGEST INFLUENCE ON YOUR DEVELOPMENT AS A CRICKETER (EXCLUDING PARENTS)? My brother Nathan – he was 10 years older than me and never let me win
WHO IS THE BEST BATTER/KEEPER/ALLROUNDER/BOWLER IN COUNTY CRICKET (EXCLUDING TEAMMATES)? Alastair Cook/Ben Foakes/Darren Stevens/Darren Stevens
MOST UNDERRATED PLAYER IN COUNTY CRICKET? Luke Fletcher
WHAT WOULD A FLY ON THE WALL HEAR IN YOUR DRESSING ROOM? Apples being crunched
HOBBIES? Nature-watching
IF YOU COULD TURN BACK TIME... I'd prevent the rise of social media
WHO WOULD YOU MOST AND LEAST LIKE TO HAVE A NET WITH? I'd least like to face Curtly Ambrose… but I'd love to bowl at him
GUILTY PLEASURE? A sausage roll
TWITTER: @brooksyferret

Batting	Mat	Inns	NO	Runs	HS	Ave	SR	100	50	Ct	St
First-class	139	175	62	1874	109*	16.58	58.67	1	5	32	-
List A	38	15	5	49	10	4.90	52.12	0	0	4	-
T20s	65	13	8	76	33*	15.20	118.75	0	0	18	-

Bowling	Mat	Balls	Runs	Wkts	BBI	BBM	Ave	Econ	SR	5w	10
First-class	139	22839	13384	487	6/65	9/84	27.48	3.51	46.8	20	0
List A	38	1686	1364	40	3/30	3/30	34.10	4.85	42.1	0	0
T20s	65	1204	1506	55	5/21	5/21	27.38	7.50	21.8	1	0

BEN BROWN RHB / WK / R1 / W0

FULL NAME: Ben Christopher Brown
BORN: November 23, 1988, Crawley, Sussex
SQUAD NO: 10
HEIGHT: 5ft 8in
NICKNAME: Goblin
EDUCATION: Ardingly College, West Sussex; Manchester Metropolitan University
TEAMS: Hampshire, England U19, Sussex
ROLE: Batter/wicketkeeper
DEBUT: First-class: 2007; List A: 2007; T20: 2008

BEST BATTING: 163 Sussex vs Durham, Hove, 2014
BEST BOWLING: 1-48 Sussex vs Essex, Colchester, 2016
COUNTY CAP: 2014 (Sussex)

WHO IS YOUR LOOKALIKE? Dermot O'Leary (TV presenter)
FIRST CRICKET CLUB? Balcombe CC, West Sussex
WHAT WOULD YOU CHANGE ABOUT THE STRUCTURE OF THE COUNTY SEASON? Have the Championship fixtures more evenly spread across the summer
MOST UNDERRATED PLAYER IN COUNTY CRICKET? Chris Rushworth – he'd take a lot of Test wickets in English conditions
MOST BEAUTIFUL THING YOU HAVE EVER SEEN? My new-born son
HOBBIES? I've just studied for a Masters in Sporting Directorship so hobbies have taken a back seat!
MAKE ONE PREDICTION FOR THE FUTURE OF CRICKET: Lots more players specialising in one format very early in their careers
WHAT DO YOU MOST ENJOY LISTENING TO? Rod Stewart, Elton John, Queen, Chuck Berry, Fleetwood Mac
WHAT MAKES YOU WORRY? My son!
TWITTER: @Ben_brown26

Batting	Mat	Inns	NO	Runs	HS	Ave	SR	100	50	Ct	St
First-class	157	250	36	8649	163	40.41	61.28	22	44	434	21
List A	79	63	13	1354	105	27.08	89.90	1	9	68	12
T20s	82	65	9	840	68	15.00	112.00	0	1	41	7

Bowling	Mat	Balls	Runs	Wkts	BBI	BBM	Ave	Econ	SR	5w	10
First-class	157	120	109	1	1/48	1/48	109.00	5.45	120.0	0	0
List A	79	-	-	-	-	-	-	-	-	-	-
T20s	82	-	-	-	-	-	-	-	-	-	-

PAT BROWN

RHB / RFM / R0 / W0

FULL NAME: Patrick Rhys Brown
BORN: August 23, 1998, Peterborough, Cambridgeshire
SQUAD NO: 36
HEIGHT: 6ft 2in
NICKNAME: Brownfish
EDUCATION: Bourne Grammar School, Lincolnshire; University of Worcester
TEAMS: England, Worcestershire, Peshawar Zalmi
ROLE: Bowler
DEBUT: T20I: 2019; First-class: 2017; List A: 2018; T20: 2017

BEST BATTING: 5* Worcestershire vs Sussex, Worcester, 2017
BEST BOWLING: 2-15 Worcestershire vs Gloucestershire, Worcester, 2017

FIRST CRICKET CLUB? Market Deeping CC, Lincolnshire
BIGGEST INFLUENCE ON YOUR DEVELOPMENT AS A CRICKETER (EXCLUDING PARENTS)?
Ross Dewar, my strength and conditioning coach at Worcestershire
WHAT WOULD A FLY ON THE WALL HEAR IN YOUR DRESSING ROOM? Flying darts
IF YOU COULD TURN BACK TIME... I'd change the result of the 2019 T20 Blast final
WHO WOULD YOU MOST LIKE TO HAVE A NET WITH? Brett Lee
SURPRISING FACT ABOUT YOU? I'm not as grumpy as I seem when I am bowling
TWITTER: @patbrowny6

Batting	Mat	Inns	NO	Runs	HS	Ave	SR	100	50	Ct	St
T20Is	4	1	1	4	4*	-	44.44	0	0	2	-
First-class	5	6	4	14	5*	7.00	25.00	0	0	2	-
List A	10	2	1	3	3	3.00	42.85	0	0	3	-
T20s	56	10	7	22	7*	7.33	57.89	0	0	13	-

Bowling	Mat	Balls	Runs	Wkts	BBI	BBM	Ave	Econ	SR	5w	10
T20Is	4	78	128	3	1/29	1/29	42.66	9.84	26.0	0	0
First-class	5	376	266	7	2/15	3/70	38.00	4.24	53.7	0	0
List A	10	418	438	12	3/53	3/53	36.50	6.28	34.8	0	0
T20s	56	1097	1651	66	4/21	4/21	25.01	9.03	16.6	0	0

NICK BROWNE

LHB / LB / R3 / W0

FULL NAME: Nicholas Laurence Joseph Browne
BORN: March 24, 1991, Leytonstone, Essex
SQUAD NO: 10
HEIGHT: 6ft 3in
NICKNAME: Orse
EDUCATION: Trinity Catholic High School, London
TEAMS: Essex
ROLE: Batter
DEBUT: First-class: 2013; List A: 2015; T20: 2015

BEST BATTING: 255 Essex vs Derbyshire, Chelmsford, 2016

COUNTY CAP: 2015

FIRST CRICKET CLUB? South Woodford CC, London. My parents met each other at the club
MOST EXCITING DAY AS A CRICKETER? Winning the County Championship on the last day at Taunton in 2019
CHILDHOOD SPORTING HERO? Marcus Trescothick
BIGGEST INFLUENCE ON YOUR DEVELOPMENT AS A CRICKETER (EXCLUDING PARENTS)? My two older brothers, both of whom I played club cricket with
WHAT WOULD YOU DO IF YOU WERE IN CHARGE OF COUNTY CRICKET? Keep with an elite first division with eight teams, with two overseas players per county like for this season
FAVOURITE SMELL? Fresh leather
TWITTER: @NickBrowne4

Batting	Mat	Inns	NO	Runs	HS	Ave	SR	100	50	Ct	St
First-class	109	176	12	6197	255	37.78	47.54	16	28	79	-
List A	22	19	0	560	99	29.47	87.77	0	3	8	1
T20s	14	12	2	165	38	16.50	114.58	0	0	6	-

Bowling	Mat	Balls	Runs	Wkts	BBI	BBM	Ave	Econ	SR	5w	10
First-class	109	268	175	0	-	-	-	3.91	-	0	0
List A	22	-	-	-	-	-	-	-	-	-	-
T20s	14	-	-	-	-	-	-	-	-	-	-

NATHAN BUCK

RHB / RFM / R0 / W0

NORTHAMPTONSHIRE

FULL NAME: Nathan Liam Buck
BORN: April 26, 1991, Leicester
SQUAD NO: 11
HEIGHT: 6ft 3in
EDUCATION: Ashby Grammar School,
Ashby-de-la-Zouch
TEAMS: Northamptonshire, England Lions,
Lancashire, Leicestershire
ROLE: Bowler
DEBUT: First-class: 2009; List A: 2009;
T20: 2010

BEST BATTING: 53 Northamptonshire vs Glamorgan, Cardiff, 2019
BEST BOWLING: 6-34 Northamptonshire vs Durham, Chester-le-Street, 2017
COUNTY CAP: 2011 (Leicestershire)

FIRST CRICKET CLUB? Grace Dieu Park CC, Leicestershire. I got hit into the forest on many occasions
BIGGEST CRICKETING REGRET? Not getting "off 'em" on debut
WHO IS THE BEST BATTER/KEEPER/ALLROUNDER/BOWLER IN COUNTY CRICKET (EXCLUDING TEAMMATES)? Darren Stevens can keep too
MOST UNDERRATED PLAYER IN COUNTY CRICKET? Tim Murtagh
MOST BEAUTIFUL THING YOU HAVE EVER SEEN? Ben Sanderson's best-man's speech
HOBBIES? Archery
MAKE ONE PREDICTION FOR THE FUTURE OF CRICKET: Lunches will be replaced by protein shakes
WHAT DO YOU MOST ENJOY LISTENING TO? The sound of people rushing to put their pads on
SURPRISING FACT ABOUT YOU? I got seven A stars and three As in my GCSEs
TWITTER: @nathanbuck17

Batting	Mat	Inns	NO	Runs	HS	Ave	SR	100	50	Ct	St
First-class	100	140	38	1475	53	14.46		0	3	18	-
List A	61	29	11	141	21	7.83	72.30	0	0	13	-
T20s	66	21	13	96	26*	12.00	102.12	0	0	14	-

Bowling	Mat	Balls	Runs	Wkts	BBI	BBM	Ave	Econ	SR	5w	10
First-class	100	15286	9135	269	6/34	8/107	33.95	3.58	56.8	8	0
List A	61	2527	2632	69	4/39	4/39	38.14	6.24	36.6	0	0
T20s	66	1279	1885	71	4/26	4/26	26.54	8.84	18.0	0	0

SOL BUDINGER

LHB / OB / WK / R0 / W0

FULL NAME: Soloman George Budinger
BORN: August 21, 1999, Colchester, Essex
SQUAD NO: 1
HEIGHT: 6ft
NICKNAME: Lord
EDUCATION: The Southport School, Queensland, Australia
TEAMS: Nottinghamshire
ROLE: Batter
DEBUT: List A: 2021; T20: 2021

WHO IS YOUR LOOKALIKE? Brad Pitt
FIRST CRICKET CLUB? Coomera Hope Island CC, Queensland, Australia
BIGGEST INFLUENCE ON YOUR DEVELOPMENT AS A CRICKETER (EXCLUDING PARENTS)?
Ant Botha, Nottinghamshire assistant coach. He developed me from a club player to a pro cricketer, so I wouldn't be where I am now without him
MOST UNDERRATED PLAYER IN COUNTY CRICKET? Ben Slater
MOST BEAUTIFUL THING YOU HAVE EVER SEEN? Safari in Africa
HOBBIES? Golf
IF YOU COULD TURN BACK TIME... I would study harder at school
WHO WOULD YOU LEAST LIKE TO HAVE A NET WITH? Mitchell Johnson
WHAT DO YOU MOST ENJOY LISTENING TO? Rock and roll
WHAT MAKES YOU WORRY? Not knowing
WHAT GIVES YOU JOY? Cricket
GUILTY PLEASURE? Pizza
TWITTER: @lordbudinger

Batting	Mat	Inns	NO	Runs	HS	Ave	SR	100	50	Ct	St
List A	8	8	0	165	71	20.62	123.13	0	1	1	-
T20s	5	4	0	52	21	13.00	118.18	0	0	3	-

Bowling	Mat	Balls	Runs	Wkts	BBI	BBM	Ave	Econ	SR	5w	10
List A	8	-	-	-	-	-	-	-	-	-	-
T20s	5	-	-	-	-	-	-	-	-	-	-

MICHAEL BURGESS RHB / WK / R0 / W0

WARWICKSHIRE

FULL NAME: Michael Gregory Kerran Burgess
BORN: July 8, 1994, Epsom
SQUAD NO: 61
HEIGHT: 6ft 1in
NICKNAME: Burge
EDUCATION: Cranleigh School, Surrey; Loughborough University
TEAMS: Warwickshire, Leicestershire, Sussex
ROLE: Wicketkeeper/batter
DEBUT: First-class: 2014; List A: 2015; T20: 2016

BEST BATTING: 146 Sussex vs Nottinghamshire, Hove, 2017

COUNTY CAP: 2021 (Warwickshire)

FIRST CRICKET CLUB? Reigate Priory CC, Surrey
BIGGEST INFLUENCE ON YOUR DEVELOPMENT AS A CRICKETER (EXCLUDING PARENTS)?
Russell Cobb, head coach at Loughborough MCCU. He's a great man-manager and a very relaxed personality
BEST INNINGS YOU'VE SEEN? Brendon McCullum's last Test innings when he scored the fastest-ever Test hundred (54 balls) against Australia at Christchurch in 2016
BIGGEST CRICKETING REGRET? Not learning to bowl mystery spin
WHAT WOULD YOU DO IF YOU WERE IN CHARGE OF COUNTY CRICKET? Go for a three-division Championship, ban all cricket when it's colder than 10 degrees
TWITTER: @mgkburgess

Batting	Mat	Inns	NO	Runs	HS	Ave	SR	100	50	Ct	St
First-class	53	77	4	2474	146	33.89	63.28	3	13	91	6
List A	27	25	1	638	73	26.58	90.11	0	4	20	3
T20s	52	42	9	491	56	14.87	112.10	0	1	21	12

Bowling	Mat	Balls	Runs	Wkts	BBI	BBM	Ave	Econ	SR	5w	10
First-class	53	36	14	0	-	-	-	2.33	-	0	0
List A	27	-	-	-	-	-	-	-	-	-	-
T20s	52	-	-	-	-	-	-	-	-	-	-

RORY BURNS

LHB / RM / R6 / W0

FULL NAME: Rory Joseph Burns
BORN: August 26, 1990, Epsom, Surrey
SQUAD NO: 17
HEIGHT: 5ft 10in
NICKNAME: Fong
EDUCATION: Whitgift School, Croydon, London; City of London Freemens's; Cardiff Metropolitan University
TEAMS: England, Surrey
ROLE: Batter
DEBUT: Test: 2018; First-class: 2011; List A: 2012; T20: 2012

BEST BATTING: 219* Surrey vs Hampshire, The Oval, 2017
BEST BOWLING: 1-18 Surrey vs Middlesex, Lord's, 2013
COUNTY CAP: 2014

FIRST CRICKET CLUB? Banstead CC, Surrey
WHO IS THE BEST BATTER/KEEPER/ALLROUNDER/BOWLER IN COUNTY CRICKET (EXCLUDING TEAMMATES)? Steven Davies/Ben Cox/Craig Overton/Simon Harmer
WHAT WOULD A FLY ON THE WALL HEAR IN YOUR DRESSING ROOM? The coffee machine
MOST BEAUTIFUL THING YOU HAVE EVER SEEN? My wife and daughter
HOBBIES? Golf
WHO WOULD YOU MOST LIKE TO HAVE A NET WITH? Brian Lara
SURPRISING FACT ABOUT YOU? I have a strong whisky collection at home

Batting	Mat	Inns	NO	Runs	HS	Ave	SR	100	50	Ct	St
Tests	32	59	0	1789	133	30.32	43.80	3	11	24	-
First-class	159	277	15	10791	219*	41.18	48.73	21	63	133	-
List A	57	55	6	1722	95	35.14	84.78	0	12	29	-
T20s	63	53	9	725	56*	16.47	119.63	0	2	27	1

Bowling	Mat	Balls	Runs	Wkts	BBI	BBM	Ave	Econ	SR	5w	10
Tests	32	-	-	-	-	-	-	-	-	-	-
First-class	159	228	149	2	1/18	1/18	74.50	3.92	114.0	0	0
List A	57	-	-	-	-	-	-	-	-	-	-
T20s	63	-	-	-	-	-	-	-	-	-	-

WILL BUTTLEMAN — RHB / WK / R0 / W0

FULL NAME: William Edward Lewis Buttleman
BORN: April 20, 2000, Chelmsford
SQUAD NO: 9
HEIGHT: 6ft 1in
NICKNAME: Butterz
EDUCATION: Felsted School, Essex
TEAMS: Essex
ROLE: Wicketkeeper
DEBUT: First-class: 2019; List A: 2021; T20: 2021

BEST BATTING: 0 Essex vs Yorkshire, Headingley, 2019

FIRST CRICKET CLUB? Cloghams CC, Essex
MOST EXCITING DAY AS A CRICKETER? Making my first-class debut in 2019
CHILDHOOD SPORTING HERO? Rickie Fowler
BIGGEST INFLUENCE ON YOUR DEVELOPMENT AS A CRICKETER (EXCLUDING PARENTS)?
Northern District CC in Sydney (apart from Essex of course!)
WHAT WOULD YOU DO IF YOU WERE IN CHARGE OF COUNTY CRICKET? Introduce home and away kit
FAVOURITE SMELL? Wagamama
GUILTY PLEASURE? Jelly
TWITTER: @Will_Buttleman

Batting	Mat	Inns	NO	Runs	HS	Ave	SR	100	50	Ct	St
First-class	1	1	0	0	0	0.00	0.00	0	0	3	-
List A	5	5	0	48	23	9.60	51.06	0	0	3	-
T20s	9	9	1	158	56*	19.75	119.69	0	1	2	1

Bowling	Mat	Balls	Runs	Wkts	BBI	BBM	Ave	Econ	SR	5w	10
First-class	1	-	-	-	-	-	-	-	-	-	-
List A	5	-	-	-	-	-	-	-	-	-	-
T20s	9	-	-	-	-	-	-	-	-	-	-

JOS BUTTLER   RHB / WK / R0 / W0

FULL NAME: Joseph Charles Buttler
BORN: September 8, 1990, Taunton
SQUAD NO: 6
NICKNAME: Jose
EDUCATION: King's College, Taunton
TEAMS: England, Lancashire, Comilla Victorians, Melbourne Renegades, Mumbai Indians, Rajasthan Royals, Somerset, Sydney Thunder
ROLE: Batter/wicketkeeper
DEBUT: Test: 2014; ODI: 2012; T20I: 2011; First-class: 2009; List A: 2009; T20: 2009

BEST BATTING: 152 England vs Pakistan, Southampton, 2020

COUNTY CAP: 2013 (Somerset), 2018 (Lancashire)

TWITTER: @josbuttler
NOTES: One of English cricket's most ferocious hitters, Buttler's international and T20 duties have restricted him to just 16 Championship appearances since he left Somerset to join Lancashire in 2013. Called up for England's limited-overs squads in 2012, he made his Test debut two years later but it wasn't until his maiden hundred in 2018 that he became a regular in the red-ball side. Buttler was in vintage form in 2020, scoring a magnificent 152 against Pakistan at the Ageas Bowl, but he was left out of England's squad for the recent tour to the Caribbean following the Ashes debacle. There is no denying his extraordinary skills in the shorter forms, of which perhaps the best example was his 46-ball ODI hundred against Pakistan in Dubai in 2015 – the fastest by an England player. And, not forgetting, he is also a World Cup winner. Buttler has been retained by Rajasthan Royals for the 2022 IPL

Batting	Mat	Inns	NO	Runs	HS	Ave	SR	100	50	Ct	St
Tests	57	100	9	2907	152	31.94	54.18	2	18	153	1
ODIs	148	123	23	3872	150	38.72	118.66	9	20	181	32
T20Is	88	80	18	2140	101*	34.51	141.16	1	15	39	10
First-class	122	199	16	5888	152	32.17	57.20	7	33	274	3
List A	219	183	43	6038	150	43.12	119.46	11	36	233	37
T20s	298	276	50	7335	124	32.45	144.02	2	50	163	34

Bowling	Mat	Balls	Runs	Wkts	BBI	BBM	Ave	Econ	SR	5w	10
Tests	57	-	-	-	-	-	-	-	-	-	-
ODIs	148	-	-	-	-	-	-	-	-	-	-
T20Is	88	-	-	-	-	-	-	-	-	-	-
First-class	122	12	11	0	-	-	-	5.50	-	0	0
List A	219	-	-	-	-	-	-	-	-	-	-
T20s	298	-	-	-	-	-	-	-	-	-	-

EDDIE BYROM

LHB / OB / RO / WO

GLAMORGAN

FULL NAME: Edward James Byrom
BORN: June 17, 1997, Harare, Zimbabwe
SQUAD NO: 97
HEIGHT: 6ft
NICKNAME: Muta
EDUCATION: King's College, Taunton
TEAMS: Glamorgan, Rising Stars, Somerset
ROLE: Batter
DEBUT: First-class: 2017; List A: 2021; T20: 2019

BEST BATTING: 152 Rising Stars vs Bulawayo Metropolitan Tuskers, Kwekwe, 2017
BEST BOWLING: 2-64 Glamorgan vs Surrey, The Oval, 2021

WHO IS YOUR LOOKALIKE? Miguel Almirón (footballer)
FIRST CRICKET CLUB? Taunton St Andrews CC, Somerset
WHAT WOULD YOU CHANGE ABOUT THE STRUCTURE OF THE COUNTY SEASON? Have two
fewer Championship and 50-over games
WHO IS THE BEST BATTER/KEEPER/ALLROUNDER/BOWLER IN COUNTY CRICKET
(EXCLUDING TEAMMATES)? James Vince/Ben Foakes/Craig Overton/Craig Overton
MOST UNDERRATED PLAYER IN COUNTY CRICKET? Tom Abell
WHAT WOULD A FLY ON THE WALL HEAR IN YOUR DRESSING ROOM? Marnus Labuschagne
MOST BEAUTIFUL THING YOU HAVE EVER SEEN? Victoria Falls, Zimbabwe
HOBBIES? Playing the guitar
WHO WOULD YOU MOST LIKE TO HAVE A NET WITH? Kumar Sangakkara, because I want to
bat like him
MAKE ONE PREDICTION FOR THE FUTURE OF CRICKET: 50-over cricket will decline
WHAT MAKES YOU WORRY? Batting
TWITTER: @EddieByrom

Batting	Mat	Inns	NO	Runs	HS	Ave	SR	100	50	Ct	St
First-class	34	61	3	1585	152	27.32	44.46	3	5	17	-
List A	7	6	1	49	18	9.80	59.75	0	0	4	-
T20s	18	16	1	269	54*	17.93	153.71	0	1	4	-
Bowling	Mat	Balls	Runs	Wkts	BBI	BBM	Ave	Econ	SR	5w	10
First-class	34	162	107	2	2/64	2/64	53.50	3.96	81.0	0	0
List A	7	-	-	-	-	-	-	-	-	-	-
T20s	18	-	-	-	-	-	-	-	-	-	-

FULL NAME: Harry Robert Charles Came
BORN: August 27, 1998, Hampshire
SQUAD NO: 4
HEIGHT: 5ft 8in
NICKNAME: Hazza, Cameo
EDUCATION: Bradfield College, Berkshire
TEAMS: Derbyshire, Hampshire
ROLE: Batter
DEBUT: First-class: 2019; List A: 2021; T20: 2021

DERBYSHIRE

BEST BATTING: 45 Derbyshire vs Sussex, Hove, 2021

WHO IS YOUR LOOKALIKE? Ethan Payne (internet personality)
FIRST CRICKET CLUB? Odiham & Greywell CC, Hampshire
BIGGEST CRICKETING REGRET? Getting run out for 99 for the Hampshire Academy when I was 16 years old
WHO IS THE BEST BATTER/KEEPER/ALLROUNDER/BOWLER IN COUNTY CRICKET (EXCLUDING TEAMMATES)? James Vince/Ben Foakes/Darren Stevens/Sam Cook
MOST UNDERRATED PLAYER IN COUNTY CRICKET? Gus Atkinson
WHAT WOULD A FLY ON THE WALL HEAR IN YOUR DRESSING ROOM? A lot of coffee chat
MOST BEAUTIFUL THING YOU HAVE EVER SEEN? A flat white from BEAR (speciality coffee shop) in Derby
IF YOU COULD TURN BACK TIME... I'd change the last over of the 2016 World T20 final
WHO WOULD YOU MOST LIKE TO HAVE A NET WITH? Muttiah Muralitharan – just to see if I could pick him
WHAT MAKES YOU WORRY? A slice on the first tee
WHAT GIVES YOU JOY? Coffee
TWITTER: @HarryCame4

Batting	Mat	Inns	NO	Runs	HS	Ave	SR	100	50	Ct	St
First-class	8	11	1	140	45	14.00	37.23	0	0	2	-
List A	7	6	0	141	57	23.50	85.45	0	1	0	-
T20s	11	11	0	207	56	18.81	119.65	0	1	5	-

Bowling	Mat	Balls	Runs	Wkts	BBI	BBM	Ave	Econ	SR	5w	10
First-class	8	-	-	-	-	-	-	-	-	-	-
List A	7	-	-	-	-	-	-	-	-	-	-
T20s	11	-	-	-	-	-	-	-	-	-	-

JACK CAMPBELL · RHB / LMF / R0 / W0

DURHAM

FULL NAME: Jack Oliver Ian Campbell
BORN: November 11, 1999, Portsmouth
SQUAD NO: 21
HEIGHT: 6ft 7in
NICKNAME: Jacko
EDUCATION: Churcher's College, Petersfield, Hampshire
TEAMS: Durham, England U19
ROLE: Bowler
DEBUT: First-class: 2019; List A: 2021; T20: 2021

BEST BATTING: 2 Durham MCCU vs Durham, Chester-le-Street, 2019
BEST BOWLING: 1-43 Durham vs Leicestershire, Leicester, 2019

FIRST CRICKET CLUB? Steep CC, Hampshire
MOST EXCITING DAY AS A CRICKETER? Making my first-class debut in 2019
CHILDHOOD SPORTING HERO? Andrew Flintoff
BIGGEST INFLUENCE ON YOUR DEVELOPMENT AS A CRICKETER (EXCLUDING PARENTS)? My old club captain who pushed me to play in the first team when I was 12 to prepare me for playing at a higher level
WHAT WOULD YOU DO IF YOU WERE IN CHARGE OF COUNTY CRICKET? Give the bowlers a chance by giving them a new ball after 40 overs
GUILTY PLEASURE? White chocolate
TWITTER: @jack_campbell11

Batting	Mat	Inns	NO	Runs	HS	Ave	SR	100	50	Ct	St
First-class	3	4	2	2	2	1.00	9.52	0	0	0	-
List A	5	-	-	-	-	-	-	-	-	1	-
T20s	2	1	0	6	6	6.00	75.00	0	0	0	-

Bowling	Mat	Balls	Runs	Wkts	BBI	BBM	Ave	Econ	SR	5w	10
First-class	3	468	261	1	1/43	1/87	261.00	3.34	468.0	0	0
List A	5	210	226	6	3/58	3/58	37.66	6.45	35.0	0	0
T20s	2	12	21	1	1/21	1/21	21.00	10.50	12.0	0	0

LUKAS CAREY

RHB / RFM / R0 / W0

FULL NAME: Lukas John Carey
BORN: July 17, 1997, Carmarthen, Wales
SQUAD NO: 17
EDUCATION: Pontarddulais Comprehensive School, Swansea; Gower College Swansea
TEAMS: Glamorgan
ROLE: Bowler
DEBUT: First-class: 2016; List A: 2017; T20: 2017

GLAMORGAN

BEST BATTING: 62* Glamorgan vs Derbyshire, Swansea, 2019
BEST BOWLING: 4-54 Glamorgan vs Middlesex, Cardiff, 2019

TWITTER: @LukasCarey
NOTES: A graduate from Glamorgan's Academy who hails from Robert Croft's club Pontarddulais, Carey is another talented local product. He made a promising start to his Glamorgan career in 2016, picking up seven wickets against Northants with his skiddy fast-medium seamers on his first-class debut, before his breakthrough season in 2017 (35 wickets in 10 Championship matches as well as a maiden first-class fifty). Carey featured regularly in all three formats in 2018 and 2019 but a side strain restricted the 23-year-old to just one appearance the following summer. He played only three Championship matches last season but was an ever-present in the club's triumphant One-Day Cup side, taking 12 wickets at an average of 29.33

Batting	Mat	Inns	NO	Runs	HS	Ave	SR	100	50	Ct	St
First-class	33	46	6	631	62*	15.77	77.51	0	3	5	-
List A	28	15	9	175	39	29.16	98.31	0	0	4	-
T20s	9	3	2	7	5	7.00	70.00	0	0	2	-

Bowling	Mat	Balls	Runs	Wkts	BBI	BBM	Ave	Econ	SR	5w	10
First-class	33	5145	3009	87	4/54	7/151	34.58	3.50	59.1	0	0
List A	28	1194	1107	24	2/24	2/24	46.12	5.56	49.7	0	0
T20s	9	138	209	4	1/15	1/15	52.25	9.08	34.5	0	0

KIRAN CARLSON   RHB / OB / R0 / W0

GLAMORGAN

FULL NAME: Kiran Shah Carlson
BORN: May 16, 1998, Cardiff
SQUAD NO: 5
HEIGHT: 5ft 11in
NICKNAME: Dink
EDUCATION: Whitchurch High School,
Cardiff; Cardiff University
TEAMS: Glamorgan
ROLE: Batter
DEBUT: First-class: 2016; List A: 2016; T20: 2017

BEST BATTING: 191 Glamorgan vs Gloucestershire, Cardiff, 2017
BEST BOWLING: 5-28 Glamorgan vs Northamptonshire, Northampton, 2016
COUNTY CAP: 2021

FIRST CRICKET CLUB? Cardiff CC
WHAT WOULD YOU CHANGE ABOUT THE STRUCTURE OF THE COUNTY SEASON? Have
more red-ball cricket in the middle of the summer
WHO IS THE BEST BATTER/KEEPER/ALLROUNDER/BOWLER IN COUNTY CRICKET
(EXCLUDING TEAMMATES)? David Bedingham/Ben Foakes/Darren Stevens/Sam Cook
MOST UNDERRATED PLAYER IN COUNTY CRICKET? Jake Libby
WHAT WOULD A FLY ON THE WALL HEAR IN YOUR DRESSING ROOM? Joe Cooke talking
about the need to close fridge doors
MOST BEAUTIFUL THING YOU HAVE EVER SEEN? Wales winning the rugby Grand Slam in 2019
HOBBIES? Rock climbing
WHO WOULD YOU MOST AND LEAST LIKE TO HAVE A NET WITH? Most – Sachin Tendulkar.
Least – Shoaib Akhtar
MAKE ONE PREDICTION FOR THE FUTURE OF CRICKET: A club World Cup
SURPRISING FACT ABOUT YOU? I'm half-Indian
TWITTER: @kiran_carlson

Batting	Mat	Inns	NO	Runs	HS	Ave	SR	100	50	Ct	St
First-class	48	83	6	2430	191	31.55	59.29	7	9	19	-
List A	27	25	2	573	82	24.91	97.61	0	4	9	-
T20s	34	30	1	480	58	16.55	129.03	0	1	13	-

Bowling	Mat	Balls	Runs	Wkts	BBI	BBM	Ave	Econ	SR	5w	10
First-class	48	531	338	7	5/28	5/78	48.28	3.81	75.8	1	0
List A	27	42	47	1	1/30	1/30	47.00	6.71	42.0	0	0
T20s	34	1	1	0	-	-	-	6.00	-	0	0

BRYDON CARSE   RHB / RFM / R0 / W0 / MVP47

FULL NAME: Brydon Alexander Carse
BORN: July 31, 1995, Port Elizabeth, South Africa
SQUAD NO: 99
HEIGHT: 6ft 2in
NICKNAME: Cheesy
EDUCATION: Pearson High School, Port Elizabeth
TEAMS: England, Durham, Eastern Province
ROLE: Bowler
DEBUT: ODI: 2021; First-class: 2016; List A: 2019; T20: 2014

DURHAM

BEST BATTING: 77* Durham vs Northamptonshire, Chester-le-Street, 2019
BEST BOWLING: 6-26 Durham vs Middlesex, Lord's, 2019

FIRST CRICKET CLUB? Union CC, South Africa
FAMILY TIES? My dad James played for Northamptonshire, Rhodesia, Eastern Province, Border and Western Province
MOST EXCITING DAY AS A CRICKETER? Winning at Lord's with Durham
CHILDHOOD SPORTING HERO? Mark Boucher
BIGGEST INFLUENCE ON YOUR DEVELOPMENT AS A CRICKETER (EXCLUDING PARENTS)? Geoff Cook (former Durham head coach)
WHAT WOULD YOU DO IF YOU WERE IN CHARGE OF COUNTY CRICKET? Allow a free hit for no-balls in four-day cricket
FAVOURITE SMELL? A leg of lamb in the slow cooker
GUILTY PLEASURE? Thai Sweet Chilli Sensations
TWITTER: @CarseBrydon

Batting	Mat	Inns	NO	Runs	HS	Ave	SR	100	50	Ct	St
ODIs	3	2	1	43	31	43.00	82.69	0	0	0	-
First-class	33	41	10	804	77*	25.93	48.81	0	2	5	-
List A	10	3	1	45	31	22.50	76.27	0	0	2	-
T20s	40	29	11	390	51	21.66	146.06	0	1	13	-

Bowling	Mat	Balls	Runs	Wkts	BBI	BBM	Ave	Econ	SR	5w	10
ODIs	3	150	136	6	5/61	5/61	22.66	5.44	25.0	1	0
First-class	33	4463	2814	95	6/26	8/119	29.62	3.78	46.9	5	0
List A	10	395	359	16	5/61	5/61	22.43	5.45	24.6	1	0
T20s	40	648	949	21	3/30	3/30	45.19	8.78	30.8	0	0

JACK CARSON

RHB / OB / R0 / W0

SUSSEX

FULL NAME: Jack Joshua Carson
BORN: December 3, 2000, Craigavon, County Armagh, Northern Ireland
SQUAD NO: 16
HEIGHT: 6ft 2in
NICKNAME: Carse
EDUCATION: Bainbridge Academy, County Down, Northern Ireland; Hurstpierpoint College, West Sussex
TEAMS: Sussex
ROLE: Bowler
DEBUT: First-class: 2020

BEST BATTING: 87 Sussex vs Worcestershire, Worcester, 2021
BEST BOWLING: 5-85 Sussex vs Yorkshire, Hove, 2021

WHO IS YOUR LOOKALIKE? Otis from Sex Education (TV series)
FIRST CRICKET CLUB? Waringstown CC, Craigavon, Northern Ireland
WHAT WOULD YOU CHANGE ABOUT THE STRUCTURE OF THE COUNTY SEASON? Change the 50-over competition into an FA Cup-style knockout
BIGGEST INFLUENCE ON YOUR DEVELOPMENT AS A CRICKETER (EXCLUDING PARENTS)? Ian Salisbury – he has made me into a better bowler in a technical sense but also helped me to manage my emotions
WHO IS THE BEST BATTER/KEEPER/ALLROUNDER/BOWLER IN COUNTY CRICKET (EXCLUDING TEAMMATES)? Zak Crawley/Ben Foakes/Darren Stevens/Simon Harmer
MOST UNDERRATED PLAYER IN COUNTY CRICKET? Tim Murtagh
MOST BEAUTIFUL THING YOU HAVE EVER SEEN? A well-poured Guinness
HOBBIES? Golf
WHO WOULD YOU MOST LIKE TO HAVE A NET WITH? The ex-Sussex and Glamorgan player Tony Cottey. He's my landlord so it'd be great to have a bowl at him with bragging rights up for grabs
MAKE ONE PREDICTION FOR THE FUTURE OF CRICKET: The resurgence of Test cricket
WHAT DO YOU MOST ENJOY LISTENING TO? Drum and bass
GUILTY PLEASURE? Medical dramas on TV
TWITTER: @_jackcarson11

Batting	Mat	Inns	NO	Runs	HS	Ave	SR	100	50	Ct	St
First-class	19	32	4	445	87	15.89	47.34	0	3	5	-

Bowling	Mat	Balls	Runs	Wkts	BBI	BBM	Ave	Econ	SR	5w	10
First-class	19	3587	1811	55	5/85	7/96	32.92	3.02	65.2	2	0

MATT CARTER RHB / OB / R0 / W0

FULL NAME: Matthew Carter
BORN: May 26, 1996, Lincoln
SQUAD NO: 20
HEIGHT: 6ft 6in
NICKNAME: Long Plod
EDUCATION: Branston Community Academy, Lincolnshire
TEAMS: Nottinghamshire, England Lions
ROLE: Bowler
DEBUT: First-class: 2015; List A: 2018; T20: 2018

BEST BATTING: 33 Nottinghamshire vs Sussex, Hove, 2017
BEST BOWLING: 7-56 Nottinghamshire vs Somerset, Taunton, 2015

FIRST CRICKET CLUB? Market Rasen CC, Lincolnshire
FAMILY TIES? My dad and oldest brother played at village level. My brother Andrew played for Notts, Derby and Hampshire before retiring in 2016
MOST EXCITING DAY AS A CRICKETER? Taking seven wickets in the first innings on my first-class debut
CHILDHOOD SPORTING HERO? Andrew Flintoff
SURPRISING FACT ABOUT YOU? Any chance I get, whether for an hour or a full day, it's spent with the dog in the middle of a field shooting. I've had a lot of swimming achievements but now I'm scared of swimming

Batting	Mat	Inns	NO	Runs	HS	Ave	SR	100	50	Ct	St
First-class	17	27	2	241	33	9.64	48.68	0	0	16	-
List A	16	10	1	65	21*	7.22	76.47	0	0	5	-
T20s	45	16	7	110	23*	12.22	125.00	0	0	19	-

Bowling	Mat	Balls	Runs	Wkts	BBI	BBM	Ave	Econ	SR	5w	10
First-class	17	3546	1989	50	7/56	10/195	39.78	3.36	70.9	2	1
List A	16	701	625	23	4/40	4/40	27.17	5.34	30.4	0	0
T20s	45	868	1079	50	3/14	3/14	21.58	7.45	17.3	0	0

OLI CARTER

RHB / WK / R0 / W0

SUSSEX

FULL NAME: Oliver James Carter
BORN: November 2, 2001, Eastbourne, Sussex
SQUAD NO: 11
HEIGHT: 5ft 8in
NICKNAME: Tiger
EDUCATION: Eastbourne College
TEAMS: Sussex
ROLE: Wicketkeeper
DEBUT: First-class: 2021; List A: 2021; T20: 2021

BEST BATTING: 51 Sussex vs Derbyshire, Hove, 2021

WHO IS YOUR LOOKALIKE? Joe Exotic (The Tiger King)
FIRST CRICKET CLUB? Barcombe CC, East Sussex
WHO IS THE BEST BATTER/KEEPER/ALLROUNDER/BOWLER IN COUNTY CRICKET (EXCLUDING TEAMMATES)? Joe Root/Ben Foakes/Ben Stokes/Simon Harmer
MOST UNDERRATED PLAYER IN COUNTY CRICKET? Ben Cox
MOST BEAUTIFUL THING YOU HAVE EVER SEEN? St James' Park
HOBBIES? Playing Nomination Whist with the fellas
IF YOU COULD TURN BACK TIME... I'd have had a mullet earlier
MAKE ONE PREDICTION FOR THE FUTURE OF CRICKET: International T10 cricket
WHAT MAKES YOU WORRY? The thought of Newcastle getting relegated
WHAT GIVES YOU JOY? Watching outtakes from the TV series After Life
TWITTER: @OliCarter11

Batting	Mat	Inns	NO	Runs	HS	Ave	SR	100	50	Ct	St
First-class	6	12	1	235	51	21.36	37.72	0	1	14	-
List A	7	7	1	151	59	25.16	95.56	0	2	7	2
T20s	2	1	1	0	0*	-	0.00	0	0	1	1

Bowling	Mat	Balls	Runs	Wkts	BBI	BBM	Ave	Econ	SR	5w	10
First-class	6	-	-	-	-	-	-	-	-	-	-
List A	7	-	-	-	-	-	-	-	-	-	-
T20s	2	-	-	-	-	-	-	-	-	-	-

ZAK CHAPPELL

RHB / RFM / R0 / W0

FULL NAME: Zachariah John Chappell
BORN: August 21, 1996, Grantham, Lincolnshire
SQUAD NO: 32
HEIGHT: 6ft 5in
NICKNAME: Smasher
EDUCATION: Stamford School, Lincolnshire
TEAMS: Nottinghamshire, England Lions, Gloucestershire, Leicestershire
ROLE: Bowler
DEBUT: First-class: 2015; List A: 2015; T20: 2015

NOTTINGHAMSHIRE

BEST BATTING: 96 Leicestershire vs Derbyshire, Derby, 2015
BEST BOWLING: 6-44 Leicestershire vs Northamptonshire, Northampton, 2018

FIRST CRICKET CLUB? Stamford Town CC, Lincolnshire
MOST EXCITING DAY AS A CRICKETER? When a swarm of bees took over the ground in India
CHILDHOOD SPORTING HERO? Brett Lee
WHAT WOULD YOU CHANGE ABOUT THE STRUCTURE OF THE COUNTY SEASON? Have fewer games in the County Championship
SURPRISING FACT ABOUT YOU? I can walk on my hands
WHAT GIVES YOU JOY? Good coffee
FAVOURITE SMELL? A shed
GUILTY PLEASURE? Hot cross buns
TWITTER: @ZakkChappell

Batting	Mat	Inns	NO	Runs	HS	Ave	SR	100	50	Ct	St
First-class	26	39	7	659	96	20.59	52.38	0	2	5	-
List A	17	14	6	141	59*	17.62	64.38	0	1	2	-
T20s	18	11	3	69	16	8.62	127.77	0	0	7	-

Bowling	Mat	Balls	Runs	Wkts	BBI	BBM	Ave	Econ	SR	5w	10
First-class	26	3445	2106	59	6/44	6/53	35.69	3.66	58.3	1	0
List A	17	731	765	17	3/45	3/45	45.00	6.27	43.0	0	0
T20s	18	307	497	15	3/23	3/23	33.13	9.71	20.4	0	0

BEN CHARLESWORTH

LHB / RM / RO / WO

FULL NAME: Ben Geoffrey Charlesworth
BORN: November 19, 2000, Oxford
SQUAD NO: 64
HEIGHT: 6ft 3in
NICKNAME: Charlie
EDUCATION: St Edward's School, Oxford
TEAMS: Gloucestershire, England U19
ROLE: Allrounder
DEBUT: First-class: 2018; List A: 2019

BEST BATTING: 77* Gloucestershire vs Middlesex, Bristol, 2018
BEST BOWLING: 3-25 Gloucestershire vs Middlesex, Bristol, 2018
COUNTY CAP: 2018

FIRST CRICKET CLUB? Abingdon Vale CC, Oxfordshire. It was 10 minutes down the road from my house. I played and trained there from the age of five to 16
FAMILY TIES? My brother Luke Charlesworth plays for Gloucestershire Second XI
CHILDHOOD SPORTING HERO? Kumar Sangakkara
WHAT WOULD YOU DO IF YOU WERE IN CHARGE OF COUNTY CRICKET? Introduce free hits in red-ball cricket to bring more excitement into the longer format – and to punish bowlers for no-balls
BIGGEST CRICKETING REGRET? Not speaking to Eoin Morgan in 2018 when I played against Middlesex. I could have learned a thing or two by having a chat with him
TWITTER: @Ben_1289

Batting	Mat	Inns	NO	Runs	HS	Ave	SR	100	50	Ct	St
First-class	18	27	2	529	77*	21.16	38.11	0	4	5	-
List A	7	7	1	274	99*	45.66	81.06	0	2	1	-

Bowling	Mat	Balls	Runs	Wkts	BBI	BBM	Ave	Econ	SR	5w	10
First-class	18	441	271	8	3/25	3/25	33.87	3.68	55.1	0	0
List A	7	12	13	0	-	-	-	6.50	-	0	0

DAN CHRISTIAN

RHB / RM

FULL NAME: Daniel Trevor Christian
BORN: May 4, 1983, Sydney, Australia
SQUAD NO: 54
HEIGHT: 6ft
EDUCATION: St Gregory's College, Sydney
TEAMS: Australia, Notts, Gloucestershire, Hampshire, Hobart Hurricanes, Melbourne Renegades, Middlesex, Rising Pune Supergiant, RC Bangalore, South Australia, Sydney Sixers, Victoria
ROLE: Allrounder
DEBUT: ODI: 2012; T20I: 2010; First-class: 2008; List A: 2006; T20: 2006

NOTTINGHAMSHIRE

BEST BATTING: 129 Middlesex vs Kent, Canterbury, 2014 (T20)
BEST BOWLING: 5-14 Hobart Hurricanes vs Adelaide Strikers, Hobart, 2017 (T20)
COUNTY CAP: 2013 (Gloucestershire); 2015 (Nottinghamshire)

WHO IS YOUR LOOKALIKE? Chris Hemsworth (actor)
FIRST CRICKET CLUB? Narrandera CC, New South Wales, Australia
BIGGEST CRICKETING REGRET? Not nailing down a spot in the Australia team
WHO IS THE BEST BATTER/KEEPER/ALLROUNDER/BOWLER IN COUNTY CRICKET (EXCLUDING TEAMMATES)? James Vince/Sam Billings/Darren Stevens/Chris Jordan
MOST BEAUTIFUL THING YOU HAVE EVER SEEN? My daughter Harper
IF YOU COULD TURN BACK TIME... I'd change the lbw law
WHO WOULD YOU LEAST LIKE TO HAVE A NET WITH? Shaun Tait – too fast
MAKE ONE PREDICTION FOR THE FUTURE OF CRICKET: No more 50-over cricket
TWITTER: @danchristian54

Batting	Mat	Inns	NO	Runs	HS	Ave	SR	100	50	Ct	St
ODIs	20	18	5	273	39	21.00	88.92	0	0	10	-
T20Is	23	14	6	118	39	14.75	126.88	0	0	6	-
First-class	83	141	17	3783	131*	30.50	53.77	5	16	90	-
List A	120	108	21	2844	117	32.68	101.64	2	14	43	-
T20s	380	327	88	5540	129	23.17	138.84	2	16	171	-

Bowling	Mat	Balls	Runs	Wkts	BBI	BBM	Ave	Econ	SR	5w	10
ODIs	20	727	595	20	5/31	5/31	29.75	4.91	36.3	1	0
T20Is	23	279	398	13	3/27	3/27	30.61	8.55	21.4	0	0
First-class	83	10301	5679	163	5/24	9/87	34.84	3.30	63.1	3	0
List A	120	3896	3585	107	6/48	6/48	33.50	5.52	36.4	3	0
T20s	380	5607	7864	272	5/14	5/14	28.91	8.41	20.6	2	0

GRAHAM CLARK

RHB / LB / R0 / W0

DURHAM

FULL NAME: Graham Clark
BORN: March 16, 1993, Whitehaven, Cumbria
SQUAD NO: 7
HEIGHT: 6ft 1in
NICKNAME: Schnoz
EDUCATION: St Benedict's Catholic High School, Whitehaven
TEAMS: Durham
ROLE: Batter
DEBUT: First-class: 2015; List A: 2015; T20: 2015

BEST BATTING: 109 Durham vs Glamorgan, Chester-le-Street, 2017
BEST BOWLING: 1-10 Durham vs Sussex, Arundel, 2018

WHO IS YOUR LOOKALIKE? Shrek
FIRST CRICKET CLUB? Cleator CC, Cumbria
WHAT WOULD YOU CHANGE ABOUT THE STRUCTURE OF THE COUNTY SEASON? Increase Championship games to 16 for each team
WHO IS THE BEST BATTER/KEEPER/ALLROUNDER/BOWLER IN COUNTY CRICKET (EXCLUDING TEAMMATES)? Joe Clarke/Ben Foakes/Darren Stevens/Simon Harmer
MOST UNDERRATED PLAYER IN COUNTY CRICKET? Alex Davies
WHAT WOULD A FLY ON THE WALL HEAR IN YOUR DRESSING ROOM? Irrelevant conversations
MOST BEAUTIFUL THING YOU HAVE EVER SEEN? Probably should say my girlfriend… but it would be the scenery of Queenstown (New Zealand)
IF YOU COULD TURN BACK TIME… I'd change the outcome of last year's RL50 final!
WHO WOULD YOU LEAST LIKE TO HAVE A NET WITH? Steve Harmison
MAKE ONE PREDICTION FOR THE FUTURE OF CRICKET: The Hundred will rival the IPL
WHAT MAKES YOU WORRY? When my career will come to an end
WHAT GIVES YOU JOY? Taking my dog for a walk
TWITTER: @GrahamClark16

Batting	Mat	Inns	NO	Runs	HS	Ave	SR	100	50	Ct	St
First-class	37	67	2	1626	109	25.01	51.34	1	10	25	-
List A	41	41	2	1311	141*	33.61	89.06	4	3	15	-
T20s	71	70	4	1594	91*	24.15	143.47	0	9	30	-

Bowling	Mat	Balls	Runs	Wkts	BBI	BBM	Ave	Econ	SR	5w	10
First-class	37	95	58	2	1/10	1/10	29.00	3.66	47.5	0	0
List A	41	54	50	4	3/18	3/18	12.50	5.55	13.5	0	0
T20s	71	26	66	0	-	-	-	15.23	-	0	0

FULL NAME: Jordan Clark
BORN: October 14, 1990, Whitehaven, Cumbria
SQUAD NO: 8
HEIGHT: 6ft 4in
EDUCATION: Sedbergh School, Cumbria
TEAMS: Surrey, Hobart Hurricanes, Lancashire
ROLE: Allounder
DEBUT: First-class: 2015; List A: 2010; T20: 2011

BEST BATTING: 140 Lancashire vs Surrey, The Oval, 2017
BEST BOWLING: 6-21 Surrey vs Hampshire, The Oval, 2021

FAMILY TIES? My younger brother Graham plays for Durham. My older brother Darren has played Minor Counties with Cumberland and together with my dad won the National Village Cup with Cleator CC in 2013
MOST EXCITING DAY AS A CRICKETER? Taking a hat-trick against Yorkshire in the Championship match at Old Trafford in 2018
FAVOURITE SMELL? Fish
GUILTY PLEASURE? Sweet and salty popcorn
TWITTER: @Clarksy16

Batting	Mat	Inns	NO	Runs	HS	Ave	SR	100	50	Ct	St
First-class	64	90	9	2100	140	25.92	54.15	1	12	9	-
List A	51	39	8	954	79*	30.77	99.89	0	5	8	-
T20s	101	72	26	1013	60	22.02	131.72	0	1	36	-

Bowling	Mat	Balls	Runs	Wkts	BBI	BBM	Ave	Econ	SR	5w	10
First-class	64	7346	4298	131	6/21	7/97	32.80	3.51	56.0	4	0
List A	51	1452	1536	34	4/34	4/34	45.17	6.34	42.7	0	0
T20s	101	1178	1775	58	4/22	4/22	30.60	9.04	20.3	0	0

TOM CLARK

LHB / RM / R0 / W0

SUSSEX

FULL NAME: Thomas Geoffrey Reeves Clark
BORN: July 2, 2001, Haywards Heath, Sussex
SQUAD NO: 27
HEIGHT: 6ft 2in
EDUCATION: Ardingly College, West Sussex
TEAMS: Sussex, England U19
ROLE: Batter
DEBUT: First-class: 2019; List A: 2021

BEST BATTING: 65 Sussex vs Kent, Canterbury, 2020
BEST BOWLING: 1-37 Sussex vs Kent, Hove, 2021

WHO IS YOUR LOOKALIKE? Michael McIntyre
FIRST CRICKET CLUB? Horsham CC, West Sussex
WHAT WOULD YOU CHANGE ABOUT THE STRUCTURE OF THE COUNTY SEASON? Play most four-day cricket in the middle of the summer
BIGGEST INFLUENCE ON YOUR DEVELOPMENT AS A CRICKETER (EXCLUDING PARENTS)? My brothers – they taught me the game
WHO IS THE BEST BATTER/KEEPER/ALLROUNDER/BOWLER IN COUNTY CRICKET (EXCLUDING TEAMMATES)? Joe Clarke/Ben Foakes/Darren Stevens/Luke Fletcher
MOST UNDERRATED PLAYER IN COUNTY CRICKET? Ben Brown
WHO WOULD YOU MOST AND LEAST LIKE TO HAVE A NET WITH? Most – Brian Lara, the best left-hander there ever was. Least – Curtly Ambrose, I imagine he'd be horrible to face
MAKE ONE PREDICTION FOR THE FUTURE OF CRICKET: Tom Haines to be the next Marcus Trescothick
WHAT DO YOU MOST ENJOY LISTENING TO? Sports podcasts
WHAT MAKES YOU WORRY? Manchester United
WHAT GIVES YOU JOY? Being top of our Fantasy Premier League table
GUILTY PLEASURE? Pringles
TWITTER: @tomclark2702

Batting	Mat	Inns	NO	Runs	HS	Ave	SR	100	50	Ct	St
First-class	12	22	2	363	65	18.15	42.35	0	2	8	-
List A	3	3	0	76	44	25.33	90.47	0	0	2	-

Bowling	Mat	Balls	Runs	Wkts	BBI	BBM	Ave	Econ	SR	5w	10
First-class	12	198	120	1	1/37	1/41	120.00	3.63	198.0	0	0
List A	3	-	-	-	-	-	-	-	-	-	-

JOE CLARKE — RHB / WK / R1 / W0

FULL NAME: Joseph Michael Clarke
BORN: May 26, 1996, Shrewsbury, Shropshire
SQUAD NO: 33
HEIGHT: 6ft
EDUCATION: Llanfyllin High School, Powys
TEAMS: Nottinghamshire, England Lions, Karachi Kings, Melbourne Stars, Perth Scorchers, Worcestershire
ROLE: Batter
DEBUT: First-class: 2015; List A: 2015; T20: 2015

NOTTINGHAMSHIRE

BEST BATTING: 194 Worcestershire vs Derbyshire, Worcester, 2016

COUNTY CAP: 2021 (Nottinghamshire)

FIRST CRICKET CLUB? Oswestry CC, Shropshire
CHILDHOOD SPORTING HERO? Adam Gilchrist
BEST INNINGS YOU'VE SEEN? Callum Ferguson's 192 for Worcestershire against Leicestershire in the 2018 One-Day Cup. Pure skill, and so good to watch from the other end
BIGGEST CRICKETING REGRET? Being not out overnight before Bank Holiday Monday
SURPRISING FACT ABOUT YOU? I can speak (some) Welsh
TWITTER: @joeclarke10

Batting	Mat	Inns	NO	Runs	HS	Ave	SR	100	50	Ct	St
First-class	93	160	11	5609	194	37.64	60.46	18	23	44	-
List A	62	59	5	1846	139	34.18	92.81	4	9	22	2
T20s	114	111	7	2946	136	28.32	152.24	3	18	36	4

Bowling	Mat	Balls	Runs	Wkts	BBI	BBM	Ave	Econ	SR	5w	10
First-class	93	12	22	0	-	-	-	11.00	-	0	0
List A	62	-	-	-	-	-	-	-	-	-	-
T20s	114	-	-	-	-	-	-	-	-	-	-

YORKSHIRE

BEN COAD   RHB / RMF / R0 / W1

FULL NAME: Benjamin Oliver Coad
BORN: January 10, 1994, Harrogate, Yorkshire
SQUAD NO: 10
HEIGHT: 6ft 3in
NICKNAME: Hench
EDUCATION: Thirsk School & Sixth Form College, North Yorkshire
TEAMS: Yorkshire
ROLE: Bowler
DEBUT: First-class: 2016; List A: 2013; T20: 2015

BEST BATTING: 48 Yorkshire vs Surrey, Scarborough, 2019
BEST BOWLING: 6-25 Yorkshire vs Lancashire, Headingley, 2017
COUNTY CAP: 2018

FIRST CRICKET CLUB? Studley Royal CC, Ripon, North Yorkshire
FAMILY TIES? My brothers played representative cricket at junior levels. My dad played Minor Counties for Suffolk
MOST EXCITING DAY AS A CRICKETER? My second T20 game in 2015, playing against Warwickshire at home in front of a very good crowd and managing to take two wickets and winning the game against the defending champions
SURPRISING FACT ABOUT YOU? I'm a Newcastle United fan
TWITTER: @bencoad10

Batting	Mat	Inns	NO	Runs	HS	Ave	SR	100	50	Ct	St
First-class	48	63	21	603	48	14.35	64.42	0	0	2	-
List A	25	10	7	27	10	9.00	71.05	0	0	6	-
T20s	12	4	1	14	7	4.66	56.00	0	0	6	-

Bowling	Mat	Balls	Runs	Wkts	BBI	BBM	Ave	Econ	SR	5w	10
First-class	48	8613	3896	192	6/25	10/102	20.29	2.71	44.8	9	2
List A	25	1114	1033	28	4/63	4/63	36.89	5.56	39.7	0	0
T20s	12	217	323	13	3/40	3/40	24.84	8.93	16.6	0	0

JOSH COBB

RHB / LB / R0 / W0

FULL NAME: Joshua James Cobb
BORN: August 17, 1990, Leicester
SQUAD NO: 4
HEIGHT: 6ft
NICKNAME: Lord
EDUCATION: Oakham School, Rutland
TEAMS: Northamptonshire, Barisal Bulls, Central Districts, Dhaka Gladiators, England U19, Leicestershire, Prime Doleshwar Sporting Club, Sylhet Superstars
ROLE: Batter
DEBUT: First-class: 2007; List A: 2008; T20: 2008

BEST BATTING: 148* Leicestershire vs Middlesex, Lord's, 2008
BEST BOWLING: 2-11 Leicestershire vs Gloucestershire, Leicester, 2011
COUNTY CAP: 2018 (Northamptonshire)

WHO IS YOUR LOOKALIKE? Simon Mignolet (footballer)
FIRST CRICKET CLUB? Kibworth CC, Leicestershire
FAMILY TIES? My dad Russell played for Leicestershire
WHAT WOULD YOU CHANGE ABOUT THE STRUCTURE OF THE COUNTY SEASON? Have a three-division Championship – 10 games for each county, fresher players
BIGGEST INFLUENCE ON YOUR DEVELOPMENT AS A CRICKETER (EXCLUDING PARENTS)? Paul Nixon, my first captain
WHO IS THE BEST BATTER/KEEPER/ALLROUNDER/BOWLER IN COUNTY CRICKET (EXCLUDING TEAMMATES)? Joe Clarke/Ben Foakes/Ryan Higgins/Ollie Robinson
WHAT MAKES YOU WORRY? Fitness testing
SURPRISING FACT ABOUT YOU? At Oakham I was a member of the debating society and took an active interest in historical and modern British politics. I take a number of books and papers with me to away games which keep me busy during rain delays, much to the dismay of my teammates
TWITTER: @Cobby24

Batting	Mat	Inns	NO	Runs	HS	Ave	SR	100	50	Ct	St
First-class	127	218	22	5156	148*	26.30	50.28	4	30	54	-
List A	99	94	7	3330	146*	38.27	91.45	7	21	29	-
T20s	167	158	16	3548	103	24.98	133.08	1	20	78	-

Bowling	Mat	Balls	Runs	Wkts	BBI	BBM	Ave	Econ	SR	5w	10
First-class	127	2716	1607	18	2/11	2/11	89.27	3.55	150.8	0	0
List A	99	1758	1712	35	3/34	3/34	48.91	5.84	50.2	0	0
T20s	167	1548	2025	61	4/22	4/22	33.19	7.84	25.3	0	0

IAN COCKBAIN
RHB / RM / R0 / W0

GLOUCESTERSHIRE

FULL NAME: Ian Andrew Cockbain
BORN: February 17, 1987, Liverpool
SQUAD NO: 28
HEIGHT: 6ft
NICKNAME: Gramps
EDUCATION: Maghull High School, Sefton, Merseyside; Liverpool John Moores University
TEAMS: Gloucestershire, Adelaide Strikers, Karachi Kings
ROLE: Batter
DEBUT: First-class: 2011; List A: 2011; T20: 2011

BEST BATTING: 151* Gloucestershire vs Surrey, Bristol, 2014
BEST BOWLING: 1-23 Gloucestershire vs Durham MCCU, Bristol, 2016
COUNTY CAP: 2011; BENEFIT: 2019

WHO IS YOUR LOOKALIKE? Martin Keown
FIRST CRICKET CLUB? Bootle CC, Merseyside
BIGGEST INFLUENCE ON YOUR DEVELOPMENT AS A CRICKETER (EXCLUDING PARENTS)? My grandad – he spent hours and hours throwing balls to me as a kid while we were watching Dad play
WHO IS THE BEST BATTER/KEEPER/ALLROUNDER/BOWLER IN COUNTY CRICKET (EXCLUDING TEAMMATES)? Joe Root/Ben Cox/Darren Stevens/Liam Norwell
MOST UNDERRATED PLAYER IN COUNTY CRICKET? Liam Norwell
IF YOU COULD TURN BACK TIME... I would have tried to become a pro golfer
WHO WOULD YOU MOST LIKE TO HAVE A NET WITH? Ricky Ponting, my hero when I was growing up
WHAT DO YOU MOST ENJOY LISTENING TO? Soul or jazz
WHAT MAKES YOU WORRY? Not being able to support my family
WHAT GIVES YOU JOY? Seeing and listening to my son have a belly laugh

Batting	Mat	Inns	NO	Runs	HS	Ave	SR	100	50	Ct	St
First-class	57	97	7	2684	151*	29.82	43.02	5	15	36	-
List A	68	59	11	1633	108*	34.02	88.36	2	10	41	-
T20s	144	136	27	3681	123	33.77	132.07	1	20	69	-

Bowling	Mat	Balls	Runs	Wkts	BBI	BBM	Ave	Econ	SR	5w	10
First-class	57	47	44	1	1/23	1/23	44.00	5.61	47.0	0	0
List A	68	-	-	-	-	-	-	-	-	-	-
T20s	144	-	-	-	-	-	-	-	-	-	-

MICHAEL COHEN

LHB / LFM / R0 / W0

FULL NAME: Michael Alexander Robert Cohen
BORN: August 4, 1998, Cape Town, South Africa
SQUAD NO: 8
HEIGHT: 5ft 10in
NICKNAME: Uncoh
EDUCATION: Reddam House Constantia, Cape Town; University of South Africa
TEAMS: Derbyshire, Cape Cobras, South Africa U19, Western Province
ROLE: Bowler
DEBUT: First-class: 2017; List A: 2018; T20: 2017

BEST BATTING: 30* Derbyshire vs Nottinghamshire, Trent Bridge, 2020
BEST BOWLING: 5-40 Western Province vs South Western Districts, Rondesbosch, 2018

WHO IS YOUR LOOKALIKE? Mario
FIRST CRICKET CLUB? Western Province CC, Cape Town
WHAT WOULD YOU CHANGE ABOUT THE STRUCTURE OF THE COUNTY SEASON? Have more county cricket played in August to allow for more breathing room between fixtures and a greater chance for fans to watch during the peak of summer
WHO IS THE BEST BATTER/KEEPER/ALLROUNDER/BOWLER IN COUNTY CRICKET (EXCLUDING TEAMMATES)? Joe Root/Dane Vilas/Darren Stevens/Luke Fletcher
MOST UNDERRATED PLAYER IN COUNTY CRICKET? Fynn Hudson-Prentice
HOBBIES? Playing the guitar, which serves as a welcome change from trying to evade balls launched at me
WHO WOULD YOU MOST AND LEAST LIKE TO HAVE A NET WITH? Most – Wasim Akram (my boyhood hero). Least – Shaun Tait
MAKE ONE PREDICTION FOR THE FUTURE OF CRICKET: The emergence of ambidextrous batters
WHAT DO YOU MOST ENJOY LISTENING TO? Metal/hard rock
WHAT MAKES YOU WORRY? The idea that a Kookaburra ball will be used in county cricket
GUILTY PLEASURE? Fluffy socks

Batting	Mat	Inns	NO	Runs	HS	Ave	SR	100	50	Ct	St
First-class	22	28	15	172	30*	13.23	30.71	0	0	2	-
List A	4	1	0	16	16	16.00	123.07	0	0	1	-
T20s	12	5	4	22	7*	22.00	115.78	0	0	0	-

Bowling	Mat	Balls	Runs	Wkts	BBI	BBM	Ave	Econ	SR	5w	10
First-class	22	2828	1777	68	5/40	9/70	26.13	3.77	41.5	3	0
List A	4	192	160	3	1/17	1/17	53.33	5.00	64.0	0	0
T20s	12	202	289	9	2/17	2/17	32.11	8.58	22.4	0	0

JAMES COLES   RHB / SLA / R0 / W0

SUSSEX

FULL NAME: James Matthew Coles
BORN: April 2, 2004, Aylesbury, Buckinghamshire
SQUAD NO: 30
HEIGHT: 6ft 1in
NICKNAME: Roller
EDUCATION: Magdalen College School, Oxford
TEAMS: Sussex, England U19
ROLE: Allrounder
DEBUT: First-class: 2020; List A: 2021

BEST BATTING: 36 Sussex vs Kent, Canterbury, 2021
BEST BOWLING: 2-32 Sussex vs Surrey, The Oval, 2020

WHO IS YOUR LOOKALIKE? Ostreicher from American Pie
FIRST CRICKET CLUB? Aston Rowant CC, Chinnor, Oxfordshire
WHAT WOULD YOU CHANGE ABOUT THE STRUCTURE OF THE COUNTY SEASON? Play a bigger proportion of the Championship from June onwards so that the games are played on better pitches more closely aligned to the international game
WHO IS THE BEST BATTER/KEEPER/ALLROUNDER/BOWLER IN COUNTY CRICKET (EXCLUDING TEAMMATES)? Ben Brown/Ben Cox/Danny Lamb/Simon Harmer
MOST BEAUTIFUL THING YOU HAVE EVER SEEN? The Grand Canyon in Arizona
HOBBIES? Fishing
WHO WOULD YOU MOST AND LEAST LIKE TO HAVE A NET WITH? Most – Hashim Amla. Least – David Warner
MAKE ONE PREDICTION FOR THE FUTURE OF CRICKET: The growth of the game in America
WHAT DO YOU MOST ENJOY LISTENING TO? Chilled hip-hop
WHAT GIVES YOU JOY? Making other people smile

Batting	Mat	Inns	NO	Runs	HS	Ave	SR	100	50	Ct	St
First-class	3	6	1	93	36	18.60	51.38	0	0	0	-
List A	7	6	1	95	32	19.00	66.43	0	0	2	-

Bowling	Mat	Balls	Runs	Wkts	BBI	BBM	Ave	Econ	SR	5w	10
First-class	3	210	127	3	2/32	3/35	42.33	3.62	70.0	0	0
List A	7	292	217	8	3/27	3/27	27.12	4.45	36.5	0	0

BEN COMPTON

LHB / OB / R0 / W0

FULL NAME: Benjamin Garnet Compton
BORN: March 29, 1994, Durban, South Africa
SQUAD NO: 2
HEIGHT: 6ft 1in
NICKNAME: Compo
EDUCATION: Clifton College, Durban; The Open University, Milton Keynes
TEAMS: Kent, Mountaineers, Nottinghamshire
ROLE: Batter
DEBUT: First-class: 2019; List A: 2021

BEST BATTING: 109* Mountaineers vs Tuskers, Harare, 2022

WHO IS YOUR LOOKALIKE? Prince Harry
FIRST CRICKET CLUB? Wimbledon CC, London
MOST BEAUTIFUL THING YOU HAVE EVER SEEN? Victoria Falls, Zimbabwe
HOBBIES? Writing, film, travel
IF YOU COULD TURN BACK TIME... I'd have stopped anyone from putting pineapple on pizza
WHO WOULD YOU MOST AND LEAST LIKE TO HAVE A NET WITH? Most – Nick Compton. Least – Nick Compton. He's got a great insight into batting but he's my cousin so he'd tell me I'm useless
MAKE ONE PREDICTION FOR THE FUTURE OF CRICKET: USA will become a big player
WHAT GIVES YOU JOY? Coffee in the morning
GUILTY PLEASURE? Chocolate brownies

Batting	Mat	Inns	NO	Runs	HS	Ave	SR	100	50	Ct	St
First-class	10	18	5	577	109*	44.38	46.01	2	2	9	-
List A	9	8	0	432	110	54.00	78.40	2	2	5	-

Bowling	Mat	Balls	Runs	Wkts	BBI	BBM	Ave	Econ	SR	5w	10
First-class	10	-	-	-	-	-	-	-	-	-	-
List A	9	-	-	-	-	-	-	-	-	-	-

SAM CONNERS — RHB / RFM / R0 / W0

DERBYSHIRE

FULL NAME: Samuel Conners
BORN: February 13, 1999, Nottingham
SQUAD NO: 59
HEIGHT: 6ft
NICKNAME: Sammy
EDUCATION: George Spencer Academy, Nottingham
TEAMS: Derbyshire, England U19
ROLE: Bowler
DEBUT: First-class: 2019; List A: 2019; T20: 2020

BEST BATTING: 39 Derbyshire vs Kent, Derby, 2021
BEST BOWLING: 5-83 Derbyshire vs Durham, Chester-le-Street, 2021

WHO IS YOUR LOOKALIKE? Jimmy Anderson
FIRST CRICKET CLUB? Attenborough CC, Nottingham
BIGGEST INFLUENCE ON YOUR DEVELOPMENT AS A CRICKETER (EXCLUDING PARENTS)?
Steve Kirby, our former bowling coach
MOST UNDERRATED PLAYER IN COUNTY CRICKET? Matt Critchley
WHAT WOULD A FLY ON THE WALL HEAR IN YOUR DRESSING ROOM? Discussions about golf-swing techniques
MOST BEAUTIFUL THING YOU HAVE EVER SEEN? My chip in for an eagle
IF YOU COULD TURN BACK TIME... I'd have improved my batting
WHO WOULD YOU MOST AND LEAST LIKE TO HAVE A NET WITH? Most – Jimmy Anderson (to learn). Least – Chris Gayle (he'd smack me)
MAKE ONE PREDICTION FOR THE FUTURE OF CRICKET: Matt Critchley to play for England
WHAT DO YOU MOST ENJOY LISTENING TO? Dance music
WHAT MAKES YOU WORRY? Facing real fast bowling
WHAT GIVES YOU JOY? Seeing the off stump cartwheeling
TWITTER: @SamConners7

Batting	Mat	Inns	NO	Runs	HS	Ave	SR	100	50	Ct	St
First-class	17	22	6	179	39	11.18	31.79	0	0	1	-
List A	3	1	0	4	4	4.00	200.00	0	0	2	-
T20s	6	1	1	2	2*	-	100.00	0	0	0	-

Bowling	Mat	Balls	Runs	Wkts	BBI	BBM	Ave	Econ	SR	5w	10
First-class	17	2143	1191	40	5/83	7/87	29.77	3.33	53.5	1	0
List A	3	138	150	2	1/45	1/45	75.00	6.52	69.0	0	0
T20s	6	72	120	3	2/38	2/38	40.00	10.00	24.0	0	0

FULL NAME: Alastair Nathan Cook
BORN: December 25, 1984, Gloucester
SQUAD NO: 26
HEIGHT: 6ft 2in
NICKNAME: Chef
EDUCATION: Bedford School
TEAMS: England, Essex
ROLE: Batter
DEBUT: Test: 2006; ODI: 2006; T20I: 2007;
First-class: 2003; List A: 2003; T20: 2005

ESSEX

BEST BATTING: 294 England vs India, Edgbaston, 2011
BEST BOWLING: 3-13 Essex vs Northamptonshire, Chelmsford, 2005
COUNTY CAP: 2005; BENEFIT: 2014

FIRST CRICKET CLUB? Maldon CC, Essex. Both of my brothers also played for the club
FAMILY TIES? Dad played for the local club side and was a very good opening bat, while my mum made the teas
CHILDHOOD SPORTING HERO? Graham Gooch – I watched him playing for Essex at Chelmsford

Batting	Mat	Inns	NO	Runs	HS	Ave	SR	100	50	Ct	St
Tests	161	291	16	12472	294	45.35	46.95	33	57	175	-
ODIs	92	92	4	3204	137	36.40	77.13	5	19	36	-
T20Is	4	4	0	61	26	15.25	112.96	0	0	1	-
First-class	324	568	42	24841	294	47.22	50.78	69	117	349	-
List A	178	176	13	6510	137	39.93	80.46	13	38	73	-
T20s	32	30	2	892	100*	31.85	127.61	1	5	13	-

Bowling	Mat	Balls	Runs	Wkts	BBI	BBM	Ave	Econ	SR	5w	10
Tests	161	18	7	1	1/6	1/6	7.00	2.33	18.0	0	0
ODIs	92	-	-	-	-	-	-	-	-	-	-
T20Is	4	-	-	-	-	-	-	-	-	-	-
First-class	324	288	216	7	3/13		30.85	4.50	41.1	0	0
List A	178	18	10	0	-	-	-	3.33	-	0	0
T20s	32	-	-	-	-	-	-	-	-	-	-

SAM COOK

RHB / RFM / R0 / W1 / MVP8

FULL NAME: Samuel James Cook
BORN: August 4, 1997, Chelmsford, Essex
SQUAD NO: 16
HEIGHT: 6ft 2in
NICKNAME: Little Chef
EDUCATION: Great Baddow High School,
Chelmsford; Loughborough University
TEAMS: Essex, England Lions
ROLE: Bowler
DEBUT: First-class: 2016; List A: 2018; T20: 2018

BEST BATTING: 37* Essex vs Yorkshire, Headingley, 2019
BEST BOWLING: 7-23 Essex vs Kent, Canterbury, 2019
COUNTY CAP: 2020

FIRST CRICKET CLUB? Writtle CC, Essex
CHILDHOOD SPORTING HERO? Cristiano Ronaldo
BIGGEST INFLUENCE ON YOUR DEVELOPMENT AS A CRICKETER (EXCLUDING PARENTS)?
Ryan ten Doeschate and Anthony McGrath
WHAT WOULD YOU DO IF YOU WERE IN CHARGE OF COUNTY CRICKET? Introduce
pyrotechnics at Championship games
FAVOURITE SMELL? Vetiver and lavender diffuser
TWITTER: @samcook09

Batting	Mat	Inns	NO	Runs	HS	Ave	SR	100	50	Ct	St
First-class	47	48	17	266	37*	8.58	38.27	0	0	4	-
List A	12	4	2	9	6	4.50	69.23	0	0	1	-
T20s	29	12	7	28	18	5.60	100.00	0	0	4	-

Bowling	Mat	Balls	Runs	Wkts	BBI	BBM	Ave	Econ	SR	5w	10
First-class	47	7389	3298	162	7/23	12/65	20.35	2.67	45.6	10	2
List A	12	582	457	11	3/37	3/37	41.54	4.71	52.9	0	0
T20s	29	552	784	32	4/15	4/15	24.50	8.52	17.2	0	0

CHRIS COOKE
RHB / WK / R0 / W0

FULL NAME: Christopher Barry Cooke
BORN: May 30, 1986, Johannesburg, South Africa
SQUAD NO: 46
HEIGHT: 5ft 11in
NICKNAME: Jelly
EDUCATION: Bishops School, Cape Town; University of Cape Town
TEAMS: Glamorgan, Western Province
ROLE: Batter/wicketkeeper
DEBUT: First-class: 2009; List A: 2009; T20: 2011

GLAMORGAN

BEST BATTING: 205* Glamorgan vs Surrey, The Oval, 2021

COUNTY CAP: 2016

FIRST CRICKET CLUB? Cape Town CC, South Africa
MOST EXCITING DAY AS A CRICKETER? Playing in the one-day final at Lord's in 2013
CHILDHOOD SPORTING HERO? Jonty Rhodes
WHAT WOULD YOU DO IF YOU WERE IN CHARGE OF COUNTY CRICKET? Bring back the 40-over format, trial Kookaburra balls in the County Championship, push for T20 cricket to be an Olympic sport
GUILTY PLEASURE? A glass of Pinotage with biltong
TWITTER: @Cooky_24

Batting	Mat	Inns	NO	Runs	HS	Ave	SR	100	50	Ct	St
First-class	103	174	26	5588	205*	37.75	53.76	8	33	197	7
List A	88	81	9	2607	161	36.20	98.34	3	14	54	5
T20s	128	111	22	2022	72	22.71	135.34	0	6	79	11

Bowling	Mat	Balls	Runs	Wkts	BBI	BBM	Ave	Econ	SR	5w	10
First-class	103	18	19	0	-	-	-	6.33	-	0	0
List A	88	-	-	-	-	-	-	-	-	-	-
T20s	128	-	-	-	-	-	-	-	-	-	-

JOE COOKE   LHB / RMF / R0 / W0

FULL NAME: Joe Michael Cooke
BORN: May 30, 1997, Hemel Hempstead, Hertfordshire
SQUAD NO: 57
HEIGHT: 6ft 3in
EDUCATION: Parmiter's School, Watford; Durham University
TEAMS: Glamorgan
ROLE: Allrounder
DEBUT: First-class: 2017; List A: 2021

BEST BATTING: 68 Glamorgan vs Surrey, The Oval, 2021
BEST BOWLING: 1-26 Durham MCCU vs Warwickshire, Edgbaston, 2018

WHO IS YOUR LOOKALIKE? Mason Mount
FIRST CRICKET CLUB? Kings Langley CC, Hertfordshire
BIGGEST INFLUENCE ON YOUR DEVELOPMENT AS A CRICKETER (EXCLUDING PARENTS)?
Shane Burger – he helped me make the changes that led to me becoming a professional while I was training with KwaZulu Natal Inland in South Africa
WHO IS THE BEST BATTER/KEEPER/ALLROUNDER/BOWLER IN COUNTY CRICKET (EXCLUDING TEAMMATES)? Alastair Cook/Ben Foakes/Ben Stokes/James Anderson
MOST UNDERRATED PLAYER IN COUNTY CRICKET? Ryan Higgins
HOBBIES? Basketball
WHO WOULD YOU LEAST LIKE TO HAVE A NET WITH? Curtly Ambrose
WHAT DO YOU MOST ENJOY LISTENING TO? The sounds of the rainforest
TWITTER: @cooke_joe

Batting	Mat	Inns	NO	Runs	HS	Ave	SR	100	50	Ct	St
First-class	14	19	2	279	68	16.41	34.19	0	1	14	-
List A	10	8	3	174	66*	34.80	119.17	0	1	4	-

Bowling	Mat	Balls	Runs	Wkts	BBI	BBM	Ave	Econ	SR	5w	10
First-class	14	534	359	3	1/26	1/26	119.66	4.03	178.0	0	0
List A	10	377	286	20	5/61	5/61	14.30	4.55	18.8	1	0

TAYLOR CORNALL   LHB / SLA / R0 / W0

FULL NAME: Taylor Ryan Cornall
BORN: October 9, 1998, Lytham St Anne's,
Lancashire
SQUAD NO: 57
HEIGHT: 6ft
NICKNAME: Tails
EDUCATION: ASK Lytham, Lancashire;
University of Leeds
TEAMS: Worcestershire, Lancashire
ROLE: Batter
DEBUT: First-class: 2019; List A: 2021

BEST BATTING: 19 Leeds/Bradford MCCU vs Derbyshire, Derby, 2019

FIRST CRICKET CLUB? Thornton Cleveleys CC, Blackpool, Lancashire
WHAT WOULD YOU CHANGE ABOUT THE STRUCTURE OF THE COUNTY SEASON? I would
have independent groundsmen
MOST UNDERRATED PLAYER IN COUNTY CRICKET? Danny Lamb
WHAT WOULD A FLY ON THE WALL HEAR IN YOUR DRESSING ROOM?
"One-hundred-and-eighty!"
MOST BEAUTIFUL THING YOU HAVE EVER SEEN? The Lake District
HOBBIES? Betting on the horses
WHO WOULD YOU MOST AND LEAST LIKE TO HAVE A NET WITH? Most – Marnus
Labuschagne. Least – Stuart Broad
MAKE ONE PREDICTION FOR THE FUTURE OF CRICKET: The County Championship will
become a day/night competition
WHAT DO YOU MOST ENJOY LISTENING TO? Country music
WHAT MAKES YOU WORRY? Not putting in enough effort
WHAT GIVES YOU JOY? Life

Batting	Mat	Inns	NO	Runs	HS	Ave	SR	100	50	Ct	St
First-class	2	4	0	43	19	10.75	37.39	0	0	2	-
List A	2	2	2	30	23*	-	130.43	0	0	2	-

Bowling	Mat	Balls	Runs	Wkts	BBI	BBM	Ave	Econ	SR	5w	10
First-class	2	-	-	-	-	-	-	-	-	-	-
List A	2	-	-	-	-	-	-	-	-	-	-

PAUL COUGHLIN

RHB / RFM / R0 / W0

DURHAM

FULL NAME: Paul Coughlin
BORN: October 23, 1992, Sunderland
SQUAD NO: 23
HEIGHT: 6ft 2in
NICKNAME: Coggers
EDUCATION: St Robert of Newminster
Catholic School, Sunderland
TEAMS: Durham, England Lions,
Nottinghamshire
ROLE: Allrounder
DEBUT: First-class: 2012; List A: 2012; T20: 2014

BEST BATTING: 90 Durham vs Derbyshire, Chester-le-Street, 2020
BEST BOWLING: 5-49 Durham vs Northamptonshire, Chester-le-Street, 2017

FAMILY TIES? My younger brother Josh has played for Durham. My uncle Tommy Harland
played for the club when it was a Minor County. A different uncle had a homemade net in
his back garden when I was a kid, and that's how I got into cricket
MOST EXCITING DAY AS A CRICKETER? Winning the One-Day Cup at Lord's in 2014
CHILDHOOD SPORTING HERO? Andrew Flintoff
SURPRISING FACT ABOUT YOU? I started out aiming to be a wicketkeeper. Then I tried
myself as a batter. But I ended up being more of a bowler
TWITTER: @Coughlin92

Batting	Mat	Inns	NO	Runs	HS	Ave	SR	100	50	Ct	St
First-class	46	71	8	1571	90	24.93	55.14	0	8	25	-
List A	27	18	4	177	22	12.64	95.67	0	0	7	-
T20s	47	32	9	555	53	24.13	136.02	0	1	13	-

Bowling	Mat	Balls	Runs	Wkts	BBI	BBM	Ave	Econ	SR	5w	10
First-class	46	5823	3409	101	5/49	10/133	33.75	3.51	57.6	3	1
List A	27	977	915	18	3/36	3/36	50.83	5.61	54.2	0	0
T20s	47	691	1111	50	5/42	5/42	22.22	9.64	13.8	1	0

BEN COX

RHB / WK / R0 / W0

FULL NAME: Oliver Benjamin Cox
BORN: February 2, 1992, Wordsley, Stourbridge, Worcestershire
SQUAD NO: 10
HEIGHT: 5ft 10in
NICKNAME: Cocko
EDUCATION: Bromsgrove School, Worcestershire
TEAMS: Worcestershire, Boost Defenders, Otago
ROLE: Wicketkeeper
DEBUT: First-class: 2009; List A: 2010; T20: 2010

BEST BATTING: 124 Worcestershire vs Gloucestershire, Cheltenham, 2017

FIRST CRICKET CLUB? Belbroughton CC, Worcestershire – a tiny village club which I had to leave because I couldn't get in the first team as a wicketkeeper
WHAT WOULD YOU CHANGE ABOUT THE STRUCTURE OF THE COUNTY SEASON?
Implement a red-ball North vs South competition to take place at the same time as The Hundred
BIGGEST INFLUENCE ON YOUR DEVELOPMENT AS A CRICKETER (EXCLUDING PARENTS)?
Steve Rhodes – he taught me pretty much everything there is to know about wicketkeeping and the work that it takes to be a professional sportsman
WHO IS THE BEST BATTER/KEEPER/ALLROUNDER/BOWLER IN COUNTY CRICKET
(EXCLUDING TEAMMATES)? Joe Clarke/Ben Foakes/Darren Stevens/Chris Rushworth
HOBBIES? Selling funky sports socks
IF YOU COULD TURN BACK TIME... I wouldn't get a three-year ban from entering Australia
WHO WOULD YOU MOST LIKE TO HAVE A NET WITH? Saeed Ajmal
WHAT MAKES YOU WORRY? Everything
TWITTER: @bencox10

Batting	Mat	Inns	NO	Runs	HS	Ave	SR	100	50	Ct	St
First-class	135	217	29	5177	124	27.53	58.87	4	28	372	15
List A	74	58	9	1371	122*	27.97	97.16	1	5	80	9
T20s	133	117	43	2060	61*	27.83	125.68	0	5	58	30
Bowling	Mat	Balls	Runs	Wkts	BBI	BBM	Ave	Econ	SR	5w	10
First-class	135	-	-	-	-	-	-	-	-	-	-
List A	74	-	-	-	-	-	-	-	-	-	-
T20s	133	-	-	-	-	-	-	-	-	-	-

JORDAN COX

RHB / WK / R0 / W0

KENT

FULL NAME: Jordan Matthew Cox
BORN: October 21, 2000, Portsmouth
SQUAD NO: 22
HEIGHT: 5ft 11in
EDUCATION: Felsted School, Essex
TEAMS: Kent, England U19, Hobart Hurricanes
ROLE: Batter/wicketkeeper
DEBUT: First-class: 2019; List A: 2019; T20: 2019

BEST BATTING: 238* Kent vs Sussex, Canterbury, 2020

FIRST CRICKET CLUB? Sandwich Town CC, Dover, Kent
WHAT WOULD A FLY ON THE WALL HEAR IN YOUR DRESSING ROOM? The sound of Old Dover Road
HOBBIES? Golf
WHO WOULD YOU MOST AND LEAST LIKE TO HAVE A NET WITH? Most – AB de Villiers, so that I could learn to become a 360-degree player. Least – Jofra Archer, so that I don't get my head knocked off
MAKE ONE PREDICTION FOR THE FUTURE OF CRICKET: One type of ball used for all cricket all over the world
WHAT MAKES YOU WORRY? Losing people who are important to me
WHAT GIVES YOU JOY? Family

Batting	Mat	Inns	NO	Runs	HS	Ave	SR	100	50	Ct	St
First-class	20	33	3	974	238*	32.46	47.16	1	4	17	-
List A	1	1	0	21	21	21.00	80.76	0	0	1	-
T20s	30	25	9	510	64	31.87	131.10	0	3	21	4

Bowling	Mat	Balls	Runs	Wkts	BBI	BBM	Ave	Econ	SR	5w	10
First-class	20	6	3	0	-	-	-	3.00	-	0	0
List A	1	-	-	-	-	-	-	-	-	-	-
T20s	30	-	-	-	-	-	-	-	-	-	-

JOE CRACKNELL

RHB / WK / R0 / W0

FULL NAME: Joseph Benjamin Cracknell
BORN: March 16, 2000, Enfield, London
SQUAD NO: 48
HEIGHT: 5ft 11in
NICKNAME: Crackers
EDUCATION: London Oratory School;
Durham University
TEAMS: Middlesex
ROLE: Batter/wicketkeeper
DEBUT: First-class: 2021; List A: 2021;
T20: 2020

MIDDLESEX

BEST BATTING: 13 Middlesex vs Leicestershire, Northwood, 2021

WHO IS YOUR LOOKALIKE? Megamind (from the film of the same name)
FIRST CRICKET CLUB? North Middlesex CC, London
WHAT WOULD YOU CHANGE ABOUT THE STRUCTURE OF THE COUNTY SEASON? More T20 cricket
MOST BEAUTIFUL THING YOU HAVE EVER SEEN? Glow worms in a cave in New Zealand
HOBBIES? Darts – my favourite day out is the World Championship at Ally Pally
IF YOU COULD TURN BACK TIME... I'd engage more in GCSE Maths
WHO WOULD YOU MOST AND LEAST LIKE TO HAVE A NET WITH? Most – Piers Morgan, because I'd love to see him get bounced. Least – WG Grace, because he would bat all day no matter how many times he was out
MAKE ONE PREDICTION FOR THE FUTURE OF CRICKET: An American franchise league to be bigger than the IPL within the next 10 years
WHAT DO YOU MOST ENJOY LISTENING TO? Rain on a window pane
WHAT MAKES YOU WORRY? The nip-backer cannoning into my front shin
TWITTER: @cracknell_joe

Batting	Mat	Inns	NO	Runs	HS	Ave	SR	100	50	Ct	St
First-class	1	2	0	20	13	10.00	40.81	0	0	2	-
List A	1	1	0	2	2	2.00	33.33	0	0	0	-
T20s	18	18	0	459	77	25.50	139.51	0	3	8	-

Bowling	Mat	Balls	Runs	Wkts	BBI	BBM	Ave	Econ	SR	5w	10
First-class	1	-	-	-	-	-	-	-	-	-	-
List A	1	-	-	-	-	-	-	-	-	-	-
T20s	18	-	-	-	-	-	-	-	-	-	-

MASON CRANE

RHB / LB / R0 / W0

FULL NAME: Mason Sidney Crane
BORN: February 18, 1997, Shoreham-by-Sea, Sussex
SQUAD NO: 32
HEIGHT: 5ft 10in
NICKNAME: Mase
EDUCATION: Lancing College, West Sussex
TEAMS: England, Hampshire, New South Wales
ROLE: Bowler
DEBUT: Test: 2018; T20I: 2017; First-class: 2015; List A: 2015; T20: 2015

BEST BATTING: 29 Hampshire vs Somerset, Taunton, 2017
BEST BOWLING: 5-35 Hampshire vs Warwickshire, Southampton, 2015

WHO IS YOUR LOOKALIKE? Brad Pitt
FIRST CRICKET CLUB? Worthing CC, West Sussex
BIGGEST INFLUENCE ON YOUR DEVELOPMENT AS A CRICKETER (EXCLUDING PARENTS)?
Two brilliant coaches: Raj Maru (director of cricket at Lancing College) and Stuart MacGill
WHO IS THE BEST BATTER/KEEPER/ALLROUNDER/BOWLER IN COUNTY CRICKET
(EXCLUDING TEAMMATES)? Dawid Malan/Ben Foakes/Craig Overton/Ollie Robinson
MOST UNDERRATED PLAYER IN COUNTY CRICKET? Ben Sanderson
MOST BEAUTIFUL THING YOU HAVE EVER SEEN? Thierry Henry being through on goal circa 2003/04
WHO WOULD YOU MOST LIKE TO HAVE A NET WITH? Don Bradman
MAKE ONE PREDICTION FOR THE FUTURE OF CRICKET: Five5
GUILTY PLEASURE? Singing in the car
TWITTER: @masoncrane32

Batting	Mat	Inns	NO	Runs	HS	Ave	SR	100	50	Ct	St
Tests	1	2	0	6	4	3.00	54.54	0	0	0	-
T20Is	2	-	-	-	-	-	-	-	-	0	-
First-class	48	65	20	511	29	11.35	32.96	0	0	11	-
List A	39	16	12	112	28*	28.00	82.96	0	0	14	-
T20s	56	16	14	59	12*	29.50	81.94	0	0	12	-

Bowling	Mat	Balls	Runs	Wkts	BBI	BBM	Ave	Econ	SR	5w	10
Tests	1	288	193	1	1/193	1/193	193.00	4.02	288.0	0	0
T20Is	2	48	62	1	1/38	1/38	62.00	7.75	48.0	0	0
First-class	48	7743	4923	119	5/35	6/69	41.36	3.81	65.0	3	0
List A	39	1982	2009	67	4/30	4/30	29.98	6.08	29.5	0	0
T20s	56	1165	1413	64	3/15	3/15	22.07	7.27	18.2	0	0

ZAK CRAWLEY

RHB / RM / R0 / W0

FULL NAME: Zak Crawley
BORN: February 3, 1998, Bromley, Kent
SQUAD NO: 16
HEIGHT: 6ft 5in
EDUCATION: Tonbridge School, Kent
TEAMS: England, Kent
ROLE: Batter
DEBUT: Test: 2019; ODI: 2021; First-class: 2017;
List A: 2017; T20: 2018

BEST BATTING: 267 England vs Pakistan, Southampton, 2020

COUNTY CAP: 2019

FIRST CRICKET CLUB? Holmesdale CC, Sevenoaks, Kent
MOST EXCITING DAY AS A CRICKETER? The final day of the Cape Town Test in January 2020
CHILDHOOD SPORTING HERO? Tiger Woods
BIGGEST INFLUENCE ON YOUR DEVELOPMENT AS A CRICKETER (EXCLUDING PARENTS)?
Rob Key
WHAT WOULD YOU DO IF YOU WERE IN CHARGE OF COUNTY CRICKET? Ban the second
new ball, make the use of the heavy roller compulsory
TWITTER: @zakcrawley

Batting	Mat	Inns	NO	Runs	HS	Ave	SR	100	50	Ct	St
Tests	18	32	0	903	267	28.21	54.03	1	5	21	-
ODIs	3	3	1	97	58*	48.50	114.11	0	1	4	-
First-class	69	120	3	3678	267	31.43	57.37	5	23	64	-
List A	26	25	2	840	120	36.52	75.94	1	5	15	-
T20s	38	36	2	1096	108*	32.23	150.96	1	5	12	-
Bowling	Mat	Balls	Runs	Wkts	BBI	BBM	Ave	Econ	SR	5w	10
Tests	18	-	-	-	-	-	-	-	-	-	-
ODIs	3	-	-	-	-	-	-	-	-	-	-
First-class	69	66	33	0	-	-	-	3.00	-	0	0
List A	26	12	17	0	-	-	-	8.50	-	0	0
T20s	38	-	-	-	-	-	-	-	-	-	-

MATT CRITCHLEY

RHB / LB / R1 / W0 / MVP2

ESSEX

FULL NAME: Matthew James John Critchley
BORN: August 13, 1996, Preston, Lancashire
SQUAD NO: 20
HEIGHT: 6ft 2in
NICKNAME: Critch
EDUCATION: St Michael's CE High School, Chorley; Cardinal Newman College, Preston; University of Derby
TEAMS: Essex, Derbyshire, England Lions
ROLE: Allrounder
DEBUT: First-class: 2015; List A: 2015; T20: 2016

BEST BATTING: 137* Derbyshire vs Northamptonshire, Derby, 2015
BEST BOWLING: 6-73 Derbyshire vs Leicestershire, Leicester, 2020
COUNTY CAP: 2019 (Derbyshire)

FIRST CRICKET CLUB? Chorley CC, Lancashire
CHILDHOOD SPORTING HERO? Shane Warne
BIGGEST INFLUENCE ON YOUR DEVELOPMENT AS A CRICKETER (EXCLUDING PARENTS)?
Stuart MacGill – I worked with him in Australia and he has an amazing knowledge of leg-spin
WHAT WOULD YOU DO IF YOU WERE IN CHARGE OF COUNTY CRICKET? Make tea longer
GUILTY PLEASURE? McDonald's
TWITTER: @mattcritchley96

Batting	Mat	Inns	NO	Runs	HS	Ave	SR	100	50	Ct	St
First-class	67	114	13	3254	137*	32.21	59.01	4	18	42	-
List A	43	34	9	685	64*	27.40	103.47	0	2	6	-
T20s	77	60	11	963	80*	19.65	118.74	0	2	27	-

Bowling	Mat	Balls	Runs	Wkts	BBI	BBM	Ave	Econ	SR	5w	10
First-class	67	7342	4908	114	6/73	10/194	43.05	4.01	64.4	3	1
List A	43	1530	1674	31	4/48	4/48	54.00	6.56	49.3	0	0
T20s	77	1230	1580	59	4/36	4/36	26.77	7.70	20.8	0	0

HENRY CROCOMBE

RHB / RFM / R0 / W0

FULL NAME: Henry Thomas Crocombe
BORN: September 20, 2001, Eastbourne, Sussex
SQUAD NO: 14
HEIGHT: 6ft 2in
NICKNAME: Crocs
EDUCATION: Bede's Senior School, Hailsham, East Sussex
TEAMS: Sussex
ROLE: Bowler
DEBUT: First-class: 2020; List A: 2021; T20: 2021

BEST BATTING: 46* Sussex vs Northamptonshire, Hove, 2021
BEST BOWLING: 4-92 Sussex vs Derbyshire, Hove, 2021

FIRST CRICKET CLUB? Hellingly CC, Hailsham, East Sussex
WHAT WOULD YOU CHANGE ABOUT THE STRUCTURE OF THE COUNTY SEASON? Red-ball cricket to be spread out more evenly across the season
BIGGEST INFLUENCE ON YOUR DEVELOPMENT AS A CRICKETER (EXCLUDING PARENTS)? James Kirtley, Sussex's former pace-bowling coach who is now the club's T20 coach. He has passed on all the knowledge I have needed to be the player I am now
WHO IS THE BEST BATTER/KEEPER/ALLROUNDER/BOWLER IN COUNTY CRICKET (EXCLUDING TEAMMATES)? Joe Root/Ben Foakes/Ben Stokes/Simon Harmer
WHAT WOULD A FLY ON THE WALL HEAR IN YOUR DRESSING ROOM? Indoor cricket
MOST BEAUTIFUL THING YOU HAVE EVER SEEN? Space
WHO WOULD YOU LEAST LIKE TO HAVE A NET WITH? Shoaib Akhtar
WHAT MAKES YOU WORRY? Fast bowlers
TWITTER: @CrocombeHenry

Batting	Mat	Inns	NO	Runs	HS	Ave	SR	100	50	Ct	St
First-class	13	25	6	128	46*	6.73	30.26	0	0	1	-
List A	4	4	2	16	9*	8.00	88.88	0	0	0	-
T20s	1	-	-	-	-	-	-	-	-	0	-

Bowling	Mat	Balls	Runs	Wkts	BBI	BBM	Ave	Econ	SR	5w	10
First-class	13	1692	1001	23	4/92	5/83	43.52	3.54	73.5	0	0
List A	4	186	218	3	1/33	1/33	72.66	7.03	62.0	0	0
T20s	1	6	19	0	-	-	-	19.00	-	0	0

LANCASHIRE

FULL NAME: Steven John Croft
BORN: October 11, 1984, Blackpool
SQUAD NO: 15
HEIGHT: 5ft 11in
NICKNAME: Crofty
EDUCATION: Highfield High School, Blackpool; Myerscough College, Lancashire
TEAMS: Lancashire, Auckland, Northern Districts
ROLE: Batter
DEBUT: First-class: 2005; List A: 2003; T20: 2006

BEST BATTING: 156 Lancashire vs Northamptonshire, Old Trafford, 2014
BEST BOWLING: 6-41 Lancashire vs Worcestershire, Old Trafford, 2012
COUNTY CAP: 2010; BENEFIT: 2018

FIRST CRICKET CLUB? Blackpool CC, Lancashire
WHO IS THE BEST BATTER/KEEPER/ALLROUNDER/BOWLER IN COUNTY CRICKET (EXCLUDING TEAMMATES)? Joe Clarke/Ben Foakes/Steven Mullaney/Ben Sanderson
MOST UNDERRATED PLAYER IN COUNTY CRICKET? Callum Parkinson
MOST BEAUTIFUL THING YOU HAVE EVER SEEN? My three girls
HOBBIES? Call of Duty (video game)
WHO WOULD YOU MOST LIKE TO HAVE A NET WITH? VVS Laxman
WHAT MAKES YOU WORRY? Danny Lamb shaking his head
SURPRISING FACT ABOUT YOU? I grew up in Sri Lanka and learnt the game there
TWITTER: @Stevenjcroft

Batting	Mat	Inns	NO	Runs	HS	Ave	SR	100	50	Ct	St
First-class	191	289	29	8792	156	33.81	50.31	14	52	190	-
List A	164	145	25	4435	127	36.95		3	32	84	-
T20s	209	191	45	4388	94*	30.05	122.77	0	24	123	-

Bowling	Mat	Balls	Runs	Wkts	BBI	BBM	Ave	Econ	SR	5w	10
First-class	191	5507	3057	72	6/41	9/105	42.45	3.33	76.4	1	0
List A	164	2865	2642	64	4/24	4/24	41.28	5.53	44.7	0	0
T20s	209	1780	2198	78	3/6	3/6	28.17	7.40	22.8	0	0

BLAKE CULLEN

RHB / RFM / R0 / W0

FULL NAME: Blake Carlton Cullen
BORN: February 19, 2002, Isleworth, London
SQUAD NO: 19
HEIGHT: 6ft 3in
NICKNAME: The Professor
EDUCATION: Hampton School, London
TEAMS: Middlesex, England U19
ROLE: Bowler
DEBUT: First-class: 2020; T20: 2021

BEST BATTING: 34 Middlesex vs Sussex, Radlett, 2020
BEST BOWLING: 3-30 Middlesex vs Surrey, The Oval, 2021

FIRST CRICKET CLUB? Wycombe House CC, London
WHO IS THE BEST BATTER/KEEPER/ALLROUNDER/BOWLER IN COUNTY CRICKET
(EXCLUDING TEAMMATES)? James Vince/Ben Brown/Darren Stevens/Ollie Robinson
MOST UNDERRATED PLAYER IN COUNTY CRICKET? Tom Haines
IF YOU COULD TURN BACK TIME...I'd be a leg-spinning allrounder
MAKE ONE PREDICTION FOR THE FUTURE OF CRICKET: Hitting the ball out the ground will
be worth more than six runs
GUILTY PLEASURE? Bowling an unnecessary inswinger

Batting	Mat	Inns	NO	Runs	HS	Ave	SR	100	50	Ct	St
First-class	6	8	0	104	34	13.00	30.40	0	0	1	-
T20s	20	10	5	61	20*	12.20	115.09	0	0	4	-

Bowling	Mat	Balls	Runs	Wkts	BBI	BBM	Ave	Econ	SR	5w	10
First-class	6	836	503	13	3/30	4/114	38.69	3.61	64.3	0	0
T20s	20	343	531	30	4/32	4/32	17.70	9.28	11.4	0	0

TOM CULLEN

RHB / WK / R0 / W0

GLAMORGAN

FULL NAME: Thomas Nicholas Cullen
BORN: January 4, 1992, Perth, Australia
SQUAD NO: 54
HEIGHT: 5ft 11in
NICKNAME: TC
EDUCATION: Aquinas College, Perth; Cardiff Metropolitan University
TEAMS: Glamorgan
ROLE: Wicketkeeper
DEBUT: First-class: 2015; List A: 2021; T20: 2021

BEST BATTING: 63 Glamorgan vs Northamptonshire, Northampton, 2019

WHO IS YOUR LOOKALIKE? David Warner
FIRST CRICKET CLUB? South Perth CC, Western Australia
WHO IS THE BEST BATTER/KEEPER/ALLROUNDER/BOWLER IN COUNTY CRICKET
(EXCLUDING TEAMMATES)? Alastair Cook/Sam Billings/Ryan Higgins/Michael Hogan (sorry, he is a teammate, but he just is the best)
MOST UNDERRATED PLAYER IN COUNTY CRICKET? Tom Abell
WHAT WOULD A FLY ON THE WALL HEAR IN YOUR DRESSING ROOM? Gibberish about Welsh rugby
IF YOU COULD TURN BACK TIME... I wouldn't have given up cricket for two years when I was 17 to chase a football dream
WHO WOULD YOU MOST AND LEAST LIKE TO HAVE A NET WITH? Most – Ricky Ponting (greatest of all time). Least – Kevin Pietersen, because he'd probably just call me average for the entire session
MAKE ONE PREDICTION FOR THE FUTURE OF CRICKET: Test and four-day cricket will go full circle and regain its lure as the most attractive form of the game
TWITTER: @thomascullen186

Batting	Mat	Inns	NO	Runs	HS	Ave	SR	100	50	Ct	St
First-class	20	31	3	582	63	20.78	41.01	0	4	50	1
List A	10	8	3	175	58*	35.00	79.18	0	1	18	1
T20s	1	1	0	5	5	5.00	55.55	0	0	1	-

Bowling	Mat	Balls	Runs	Wkts	BBI	BBM	Ave	Econ	SR	5w	10
First-class	20	-	-	-	-	-	-	-	-	-	-
List A	10	-	-	-	-	-	-	-	-	-	-
T20s	1	-	-	-	-	-	-	-	-	-	-

BEN CURRAN

LHB / OB / R0 / W0

FULL NAME: Benjamin Jack Curran
BORN: June 7, 1996, Northampton
SQUAD NO: 57
HEIGHT: 5ft 9in
NICKNAME: Lord
EDUCATION: Wellington College, Berkshire
TEAMS: Northamptonshire, Southern Rocks
ROLE: Batter
DEBUT: First-class: 2018; List A: 2019; T20: 2018

BEST BATTING: 83* Northamptonshire vs Sussex, Northampton, 2018

WHO IS YOUR LOOKALIKE? Alec Baldwin (actor), so people say
FIRST CRICKET CLUB? Weybridge CC, Surrey
FAMILY TIES? My dad Kevin played for Zimbabwe, Gloucestershire and Northamptonshire. My older brother Tom and younger brother Sam both play for Surrey
WHAT WOULD YOU CHANGE ABOUT THE STRUCTURE OF THE COUNTY SEASON? Have the three competitions in three separate blocks
WHO IS THE BEST BATTER/KEEPER/ALLROUNDER/BOWLER IN COUNTY CRICKET (EXCLUDING TEAMMATES)? Hashim Amla/Ben Foakes/Chris Woakes/Simon Harmer
HOBBIES? Cage diving with sharks
WHO WOULD YOU MOST LIKE TO HAVE A NET WITH? Steve Smith
TWITTER: @curranjb_57

Batting	Mat	Inns	NO	Runs	HS	Ave	SR	100	50	Ct	St
First-class	27	45	4	1201	83*	29.29	51.65	0	7	19	-
List A	16	15	1	481	94	34.35	88.74	0	4	4	-
T20s	9	9	0	125	62	13.88	127.55	0	1	3	-

Bowling	Mat	Balls	Runs	Wkts	BBI	BBM	Ave	Econ	SR	5w	10
First-class	27	24	19	0	-	-	-	4.75	-	0	0
List A	16	6	6	0	-	-	-	6.00	-	0	0
T20s	9	-	-	-	-	-	-	-	-	-	-

SAM CURRAN
LHB / LMF / R0 / W0

SURREY

FULL NAME: Samuel Matthew Curran
BORN: June 3, 1998, Northampton
SQUAD NO: 58
HEIGHT: 5ft 11in
NICKNAME: Junior
EDUCATION: Wellington College, Berkshire
TEAMS: England, Surrey, Auckland, Chennai Super Kings, Kings XI Punjab
ROLE: Allrounder
DEBUT: Test: 2018; ODI: 2018; T20I: 2019; First-class: 2015; List A: 2015; T20: 2015

BEST BATTING: 96 Surrey vs Lancashire, The Oval, 2016
BEST BOWLING: 7-58 Surrey vs Durham, Chester-le-Street, 2016
COUNTY CAP: 2018

CHILDHOOD SPORTING HERO? Brian Lara
FAMILY TIES? My father Kevin played for Zimbabwe, and my brother Tom plays with me at Surrey. Ben, my other brother, plays for Northants. We have always been a competitive family
TWITTER: @CurranSM

Batting	Mat	Inns	NO	Runs	HS	Ave	SR	100	50	Ct	St
Tests	24	38	5	815	78	24.69	64.12	0	3	5	-
ODIs	11	7	2	141	95*	28.20	85.97	0	1	2	-
T20Is	16	10	5	91	24	18.20	159.64	0	0	0	-
First-class	74	114	14	2732	96	27.32	60.45	0	18	19	-
List A	60	39	7	721	95*	22.53	85.42	0	2	22	-
T20s	109	82	22	1236	72*	20.60	136.42	0	6	28	-

Bowling	Mat	Balls	Runs	Wkts	BBI	BBM	Ave	Econ	SR	5w	10
Tests	24	3091	1669	47	4/58	5/92	35.51	3.23	65.7	0	0
ODIs	11	442	430	12	5/48	5/48	35.83	5.83	36.8	1	0
T20Is	16	276	365	16	3/28	3/28	22.81	7.93	17.2	0	0
First-class	74	10730	6001	200	7/58	10/101	30.00	3.35	53.6	7	1
List A	60	2662	2469	78	5/48	5/48	31.65	5.56	34.1	1	0
T20s	109	2021	2906	103	4/11	4/11	28.21	8.62	19.6	0	0

FULL NAME: Thomas Kevin Curran
BORN: March 12, 1995, Cape Town, South Africa
SQUAD NO: 59
HEIGHT: 6ft
NICKNAME: TC
EDUCATION: Wellington College, Berkshire
TEAMS: England, Surrey, Delhi Capitals, Kolkata Knight Riders, Rajasthan Royals, Sydney Sixers, Tshwane Spartans
ROLE: Bowler
DEBUT: Test: 2017; ODI: 2017; T20I: 2017; First-class: 2014; List A: 2013; T20: 2014

SURREY

BEST BATTING: 60 Surrey vs Leicestershire, Leicester, 2015
BEST BOWLING: 7-20 Surrey vs Gloucestershire, The Oval, 2015
COUNTY CAP: 2016

CHILDHOOD SPORTING HERO? Hamilton Masakadza
FAMILY TIES? My father Kevin played for Northants and Zimbabwe, my brother Sam also plays for Surrey, and my other younger brother Ben is at Northants
TWITTER: @_TC59

Batting	Mat	Inns	NO	Runs	HS	Ave	SR	100	50	Ct	St
Tests	2	3	1	66	39	33.00	55.00	0	0	0	-
ODIs	28	17	9	303	47*	37.87	94.39	0	0	5	-
T20Is	30	13	7	64	14*	10.66	114.28	0	0	8	-
First-class	59	81	11	1241	60	17.72	50.75	0	5	20	-
List A	86	56	21	739	47*	21.11	93.54	0	0	26	-
T20s	156	89	31	1145	62	19.74	133.76	0	3	46	-

Bowling	Mat	Balls	Runs	Wkts	BBI	BBM	Ave	Econ	SR	5w	10
Tests	2	396	200	2	1/65	1/82	100.00	3.03	198.0	0	0
ODIs	28	1308	1290	34	5/35	5/35	37.94	5.91	38.4	1	0
T20Is	30	588	907	29	4/36	4/36	31.27	9.25	20.2	0	0
First-class	59	10341	5613	195	7/20	10/176	28.78	3.25	53.0	7	1
List A	86	3909	3633	126	5/16	5/16	28.83	5.57	31.0	3	0
T20s	156	3077	4553	182	4/22	4/22	25.01	8.87	16.9	0	0

SCOTT CURRIE RHB / RMF / R0 / W0

HAMPSHIRE

FULL NAME: Scott William Currie
BORN: May 2, 2001, Poole, Dorset
SQUAD NO: 44
HEIGHT: 6ft 5in
NICKNAME: Ruby
EDUCATION: St Edward's RC & COFE School, Poole
TEAMS: Hampshire, England U19
ROLE: Bowler
DEBUT: First-class: 2020; List A: 2021; T20: 2020

BEST BATTING: 38 Hampshire vs Kent, Canterbury, 2020
BEST BOWLING: 4-109 Hampshire vs Surrey, The Oval, 2021

WHO IS YOUR LOOKALIKE? Jeff Hornacek (NBA coach and former player)
FIRST CRICKET CLUB? Poole Town CC, Dorset
WHO IS THE BEST BATTER/KEEPER/ALLROUNDER/BOWLER IN COUNTY CRICKET (EXCLUDING TEAMMATES)? Hashim Amla/Ben Cox/Simon Harmer/Tom Bailey
MOST UNDERRATED PLAYER IN COUNTY CRICKET? Ben Sanderson
MOST BEAUTIFUL THING YOU HAVE EVER SEEN? Paul Scholes on the edge of the 18-yard box
IF YOU COULD TURN BACK TIME... I'd change the result of Game Six of the 1998 NBA Finals
WHO WOULD YOU MOST AND LEAST LIKE TO HAVE A NET WITH? Most – Malcolm Marshall, Hampshire's best-ever. Least – Glen Chapple, because he was relentless
MAKE ONE PREDICTION FOR THE FUTURE OF CRICKET: Someone will develop a method to prevent footholes appearing at the crease
WHAT DO YOU MOST ENJOY LISTENING TO? My old man
WHAT MAKES YOU WORRY? AFC Bournemouth
WHAT GIVES YOU JOY? AFC Bournemouth

Batting	Mat	Inns	NO	Runs	HS	Ave	SR	100	50	Ct	St
First-class	2	4	0	43	38	10.75	41.34	0	0	3	-
List A	5	4	2	17	8	8.50	65.38	0	0	5	-
T20s	13	7	4	7	3	2.33	46.66	0	0	3	-

Bowling	Mat	Balls	Runs	Wkts	BBI	BBM	Ave	Econ	SR	5w	10
First-class	2	269	167	7	4/109	4/109	23.85	3.72	38.4	0	0
List A	5	111	132	6	3/58	3/58	22.00	7.13	18.5	0	0
T20s	13	222	302	20	4/24	4/24	15.10	8.16	11.1	0	0

ANUJ DAL

RHB / RM / R0 / W0

FULL NAME: Anuj Kailash Dal
BORN: July 8, 1996, Newcastle-under-Lyme, Staffordshire
SQUAD NO: 65
HEIGHT: 5ft 9in
NICKNAME: Nuj
EDUCATION: Nottingham High School
TEAMS: Derbyshire
ROLE: Batter
DEBUT: First-class: 2018; List A: 2019; T20: 2018

BEST BATTING: 106 Derbyshire vs Leicestershire, Derby, 2021
BEST BOWLING: 3-11 Derbyshire vs Sussex, Derby, 2019

FIRST CRICKET CLUB? Kimberley Institute CC, Nottinghamshire
WHAT WOULD YOU CHANGE ABOUT THE STRUCTURE OF THE COUNTY SEASON? Reduce the number of matches
BIGGEST INFLUENCE ON YOUR DEVELOPMENT AS A CRICKETER (EXCLUDING PARENTS)? Mal Loye, assistant coach at Derbyshire
WHO IS THE BEST BATTER/KEEPER/ALLROUNDER/BOWLER IN COUNTY CRICKET (EXCLUDING TEAMMATES)? Sam Robson/John Simpson/Darren Stevens/Liam Norwell
MOST UNDERRATED PLAYER IN COUNTY CRICKET? Matt Milnes
MOST BEAUTIFUL THING YOU HAVE EVER SEEN? Universal Studios Florida (theme park)
HOBBIES? Riding rollercoasters and spending time with my dog
WHO WOULD YOU MOST LIKE TO HAVE A NET WITH? Jos Buttler
WHAT DO YOU MOST ENJOY LISTENING TO? Podcasts about finance
WHAT MAKES YOU WORRY? Cricket!
WHAT GIVES YOU JOY? Going on theme-park holidays with my brother
GUILTY PLEASURE? A bag of Haribo after a tough day in the field
TWITTER: @AnujDal

Batting	Mat	Inns	NO	Runs	HS	Ave	SR	100	50	Ct	St
First-class	27	43	7	843	106	23.41	46.36	1	4	17	-
List A	12	9	2	103	52	14.71	109.57	0	1	4	-
T20s	21	16	6	159	35	15.90	121.37	0	0	7	-

Bowling	Mat	Balls	Runs	Wkts	BBI	BBM	Ave	Econ	SR	5w	10
First-class	27	1300	574	20	3/11	4/74	28.70	2.64	65.0	0	0
List A	12	78	95	0	-	-	-	7.30	-	0	0
T20s	21	6	8	0	-	-	-	8.00	-	0	0

AJEET DALE

RHB / RFM / R0 / W0

GLOUCESTERSHIRE

FULL NAME: Ajeet Singh Dale
BORN: July 3, 2000, Slough, Berkshire
SQUAD NO: 39
HEIGHT: 6ft 1in
NICKNAME: AJ
EDUCATION: Hall Grove School, Bagshot, Surrey; Wellington College, Berkshire
TEAMS: Gloucestershire, Hampshire
ROLE: Bowler
DEBUT: First-class: 2020

BEST BATTING: 6 Hampshire vs Sussex, Hove, 2020
BEST BOWLING: 3-20 Hampshire vs Sussex, Hove, 2020

MOST EXCITING DAY AS A CRICKETER? Making my first-class debut in 2020 against Sussex at Hove in the Bob Willis Trophy
CHILDHOOD SPORTING HERO? Sachin Tendulkar
BIGGEST INFLUENCE ON YOUR DEVELOPMENT AS A CRICKETER (EXCLUDING PARENTS)? Nheem Amin – head coach at the Counties Cricket Academy. He taught me the game when I was very young and helped me to enjoy playing it
WHAT WOULD YOU DO IF YOU WERE IN CHARGE OF COUNTY CRICKET? Create a tournament to play in the winter, improve diversity at both grassroots and elite level, have music played between overs in non-televised white-ball games
FAVOURITE SMELL? A pair of new trainers
GUILTY PLEASURE? Married at First Sight (TV series)

Batting	Mat	Inns	NO	Runs	HS	Ave	SR	100	50	Ct	St
First-class	2	4	1	7	6	2.33	13.46	0	0	0	-

Bowling	Mat	Balls	Runs	Wkts	BBI	BBM	Ave	Econ	SR	5w	10
First-class	2	126	73	4	3/20	3/35	18.25	3.47	31.5	0	0

FULL NAME: Robin James Das
BORN: February 27, 2002, Leytonstone, Essex
SQUAD NO: 47
EDUCATION: Brentwood School, Essex
TEAMS: Essex
ROLE: Batter
DEBUT: T20: 2020

ESSEX

NOTES: Another Essex discovery from the ever-fruitful east London conveyor belt, the Leytonstone-born right-hander is a British Bangladeshi who's come through the pathway ranks at the club while starring for the mighty Wanstead & Snaresbrook CC. He made his senior T20 debut at the back-end of 2020 but didn't feature for the first team last term. He will be hoping that his excellent late-summer form for the Second XI – for whom he debuted as a 16-year-old – carries into this campaign and he gets his chance in the first team. Academy director Barry Hyam, speaking in 2020, was full of praise: "He showed excellent form in both red-ball and white-ball cricket although perhaps leaning slightly towards white-ball cricket. He is a strong lad who strikes the ball really cleanly and is pretty switched-on to work out different situations in the game"

Batting	Mat	Inns	NO	Runs	HS	Ave	SR	100	50	Ct	St
T20s	1	1	0	7	7	7.00	87.50	0	0	0	-

Bowling	Mat	Balls	Runs	Wkts	BBI	BBM	Ave	Econ	SR	5w	10
T20s	1	-	-	-	-	-	-	-	-	-	-

JOSH DAVEY — RHB / RFM / R0 / W0 / MVP38

SOMERSET

FULL NAME: Joshua Henry Davey
BORN: August 3, 1990, Aberdeen, Scotland
SQUAD NO: 38
HEIGHT: 6ft
NICKNAME: JD
EDUCATION: Culford School, Bury St Edmunds; Oxford Brookes University
TEAMS: Scotland, Somerset, Hampshire, Middlesex
ROLE: Bowler
DEBUT: ODI: 2010; T20I: 2012; First-class: 2010; List A: 2010; T20: 2010

BEST BATTING: 75* Somerset vs Leicestershire, Taunton, 2021
BEST BOWLING: 5-21 Somerset vs Yorkshire, Taunton, 2019
COUNTY CAP: 2021 (Somerset)

FIRST CRICKET CLUB? Bury St Edmunds CC, Suffolk
MOST EXCITING DAY AS A CRICKETER? Beating Hampshire in the One-Day Cup final at Lord's in 2019
BEST INNINGS YOU'VE SEEN? Chris Gayle's 151 not out against Kent at Taunton in 2015
TWITTER: @JoshDavey38

Batting	Mat	Inns	NO	Runs	HS	Ave	SR	100	50	Ct	St
ODIs	31	28	6	497	64	22.59	66.98	0	2	10	-
T20Is	28	15	7	111	24	13.87	130.58	0	0	14	-
First-class	50	77	19	1076	75*	18.55	43.84	0	4	15	-
List A	91	72	17	1280	91	23.27	67.90	0	6	27	-
T20s	64	35	19	267	24	16.68	128.98	0	0	30	-

Bowling	Mat	Balls	Runs	Wkts	BBI	BBM	Ave	Econ	SR	5w	10
ODIs	31	1301	1082	49	6/28	6/28	22.08	4.99	26.5	2	0
T20Is	28	593	791	34	4/18	4/18	23.26	8.00	17.4	0	0
First-class	50	6670	3090	140	5/21	8/51	22.07	2.77	47.6	4	0
List A	91	3374	3008	113	6/28	6/28	26.61	5.34	29.8	2	0
T20s	64	1084	1570	75	4/18	4/18	20.93	8.69	14.4	0	0

TIM DAVID

RHB / OB

FULL NAME: Timothy Hays David
BORN: March 16, 1996, Singapore
SQUAD NO: TBC
TEAMS: Singapore, Lancashire, Hobart Hurricanes, Lahore Qalandars, Multan Sultans, Mumbai Indians, Perth Scorchers, Royal Challengers Bangalore, St Lucia Kings, Surrey, Tasmania
ROLE: Batter
DEBUT: T20I: 2019; List A: 2019; T20: 2018

BEST BATTING: 92* Singapore vs Malyasia, Bangkok, 2020 (T20)
BEST BOWLING: 1-4 Multan Sultans vs Islamabad United, Lahore, 2022 (T20)

TWITTER: @timdavid8
NOTES: The Australian-raised Singapore international has become hot property on the T20 circuit after his big-hitting exploits around the globe. David made his presence felt during a brief spell with Surrey last summer, crunching two centuries and a fifty in eight One-Day Cup knocks before joining Southern Brave for the latter stages of their triumphant Hundred campaign. Lancashire fought off competition to secure his services for the Blast this summer and David will form part of a formidable batting unit which also includes Jos Buttler, Liam Livingstone and fellow new arrival Phil Salt. His burgeoning reputation was confirmed when Mumbai Indians forked out £1.14m for him at the 2022 IPL auction, making him the highest paid Aussie in the tournament. David has made 14 T20I appearances for Singapore but George Bailey, Australia's chief selector, has admitted he is in contention for a T20 World Cup berth later this year. An exceptional fielder and handy off-break bowler, David's T20 batting strike rate is the 10th-best in the history of the format

Batting	Mat	Inns	NO	Runs	HS	Ave	SR	100	50	Ct	St
T20Is	14	14	2	558	92*	46.50	158.52	0	4	12	-
List A	16	14	5	745	140*	82.77	123.14	2	5	12	-
T20s	89	83	25	1965	92*	33.87	159.36	0	9	48	-

Bowling	Mat	Balls	Runs	Wkts	BBI	BBM	Ave	Econ	SR	5w	10
T20Is	14	164	255	5	1/18	1/18	51.00	9.32	32.8	0	0
List A	16	216	151	9	3/26	3/26	16.77	4.19	24.0	0	0
T20s	89	330	493	8	1/4	1/4	61.62	8.96	41.2	0	0

ALEX DAVIES

RHB / WK / R1 / W0

FULL NAME: Alexander Luke Davies
BORN: August 23, 1994, Darwen, Lancashire
SQUAD NO: TBC
HEIGHT: 5ft 8in
NICKNAME: Davo
EDUCATION: Queen Elizabeth's Grammar School, Blackburn
TEAMS: Warwickshire, England Lions, Lancashire
ROLE: Batter/wicketkeeper
DEBUT: First-class: 2012; List A: 2011; T20: 2014

BEST BATTING: 147 Lancashire vs Northamptonshire, Northampton, 2019

COUNTY CAP: 2017 (Lancashire)

FIRST CRICKET CLUB? Darwen CC, Lancashire
MOST EXCITING DAY AS A CRICKETER? T20 Finals Day in 2015
CHILDHOOD SPORTING HERO? Sachin Tendulkar
FAVOURITE SMELL? Lunch at Old Trafford at 12.55 when you're in the field
TWITTER: @aldavies23

Batting	Mat	Inns	NO	Runs	HS	Ave	SR	100	50	Ct	St
First-class	94	143	8	4773	147	35.35	57.37	5	33	181	19
List A	49	46	3	1380	147	32.09	90.49	1	7	48	11
T20s	88	82	12	1901	94*	27.15	128.35	0	14	49	10

Bowling	Mat	Balls	Runs	Wkts	BBI	BBM	Ave	Econ	SR	5w	10
First-class	94	6	6	0	-	-	-	6.00	-	0	0
List A	49	-	-	-	-	-	-	-	-	-	-
T20s	88	-	-	-	-	-	-	-	-	-	-

FULL NAME: Jack Leo Benjamin Davies
BORN: March 30, 2000, Reading
SQUAD NO: 23
HEIGHT: 5ft 8in
NICKNAME: Davo
EDUCATION: Wellington College, Berkshire
TEAMS: Middlesex, England U19
ROLE: Batter/wicketkeeper
DEBUT: First-class: 2020; List A: 2021;
T20: 2020

MIDDLESEX

BEST BATTING: 24 Middlesex vs Hampshire, Lord's, 2021

WHO IS YOUR LOOKALIKE? Sam Prince from Made In Chelsea
FIRST CRICKET CLUB? Henley CC, Oxfordshire
WHAT WOULD YOU CHANGE ABOUT THE STRUCTURE OF THE COUNTY SEASON? Anything to have more games played at Lord's
BIGGEST CRICKETING REGRET? All those leaves when I've had my pads blown off
MOST UNDERRATED PLAYER IN COUNTY CRICKET? Rob Yates
WHAT WOULD A FLY ON THE WALL HEAR IN YOUR DRESSING ROOM? Robbie White getting excited about getting seven across on the crossword
MOST BEAUTIFUL THING YOU HAVE EVER SEEN? Sunset in Brighton
HOBBIES? Rackets
WHAT GIVES YOU JOY? Watching Tim Murtagh and Ethan Bamber in tandem with a dark-red Dukes
GUILTY PLEASURE? Mamma Mia
TWITTER: @daviesjlb

Batting	Mat	Inns	NO	Runs	HS	Ave	SR	100	50	Ct	St
First-class	3	5	0	48	24	9.60	26.37	0	0	1	-
List A	5	5	0	164	70	32.80	106.49	0	2	1	-
T20s	4	4	0	48	23	12.00	106.66	0	0	0	-

Bowling	Mat	Balls	Runs	Wkts	BBI	BBM	Ave	Econ	SR	5w	10
First-class	3	-	-	-	-	-	-	-	-	-	-
List A	5	-	-	-	-	-	-	-	-	-	-
T20s	4	-	-	-	-	-	-	-	-	-	-

STEVEN DAVIES — LHB / WK / R6 / W0

SOMERSET

FULL NAME: Steven Michael Davies
BORN: June 17, 1986, Bromsgrove, Worcestershire
SQUAD NO: 11
HEIGHT: 6ft
NICKNAME: Davos
EDUCATION: King Charles High School, Kidderminster
TEAMS: England, Somerset, Surrey, Worcestershire
ROLE: Batter/wicketkeeper
DEBUT: ODI: 2009; T20I: 2009; First-class: 2005; List A: 2003; T20: 2006

BEST BATTING: 200* Surrey vs Glamorgan, Cardiff, 2015

COUNTY CAP: 2011 (Surrey); 2017 (Somerset)

FIRST CRICKET CLUB? Victoria Carpets CC, Kidderminster, Worcestershire
WHO IS THE BEST BATTER/KEEPER/ALLROUNDER/BOWLER IN COUNTY CRICKET (EXCLUDING TEAMMATES)? Alastair Cook/Ben Foakes/Darren Stevens/Chris Rushworth
HOBBIES? Snooker. Wonderful sport
WHO WOULD YOU MOST LIKE TO HAVE A NET WITH? Ricky Ponting – best bloke ever
MAKE ONE PREDICTION FOR THE FUTURE OF CRICKET: Fewer formats
WHAT MAKES YOU WORRY? Green pitches
SURPRISING FACT ABOUT YOU? I'm a session harp player
GUILTY PLEASURE? Pop music
TWITTER: @SteveDavies43

Batting	Mat	Inns	NO	Runs	HS	Ave	SR	100	50	Ct	St
ODIs	8	8	0	244	87	30.50	105.62	0	1	8	-
T20Is	5	5	0	102	33	20.40	124.39	0	0	2	1
First-class	244	406	39	14051	200*	38.28	60.25	25	67	588	34
List A	192	180	14	5914	127*	35.62		0	9	37	157	42
T20s	153	144	8	2850	99*	20.95	141.01	0	16	69	23

Bowling	Mat	Balls	Runs	Wkts	BBI	BBM	Ave	Econ	SR	5w	10
ODIs	8	-	-	-	-	-	-	-	-	-	-
T20Is	5	-	-	-	-	-	-	-	-	-	-
First-class	244	0	0	0	-	-	-	-	-	0	0
List A	192	0	0	0	-	-	-	-	-	0	0
T20s	153	-	-	-	-	-	-	-	-	-	-

WILL DAVIS

RHB / RFM / R0 / W0

FULL NAME: William Samuel Davis
BORN: March 6, 1996, Stafford
SQUAD NO: 44
HEIGHT: 6ft 2in
NICKNAME: Spaceman
EDUCATION: Stafford Grammar School
TEAMS: Leicestershire, Derbyshire, England U19
ROLE: Bowler
DEBUT: First-class: 2015; List A: 2016; T20: 2019

LEICESTERSHIRE

BEST BATTING: 42 Leicestershire vs Kent, Leicester, 2021
BEST BOWLING: 7-146 Derbyshire vs Glamorgan, Colwyn Bay, 2016

MOST EXCITING DAY AS A CRICKETER? Taking my maiden five-wicket haul in first-class cricket against Glamorgan at Colwyn Bay in 2016
CHILDHOOD SPORTING HERO? Cristiano Ronaldo
SURPRISING FACT ABOUT YOU? I have to turn at the end of my bowling mark before running in
TWITTER: @W_Davis44
NOTES: The former Derbyshire and England U19 seamer was an important part of the bowling attack which helped the Foxes reach the quarter-finals of the T20 Blast in 2020 but he has struggled with injuries, making just six appeareances in white-ball cricket last year. The 26-year-old enjoyed his best season with the red ball in 2019, taking 29 wickets at 32.89

Batting	Mat	Inns	NO	Runs	HS	Ave	SR	100	50	Ct	St
First-class	32	43	15	336	42	12.00	47.45	0	0	6	-
List A	8	4	2	47	15*	23.50	77.04	0	0	1	-
T20s	21	7	4	6	4*	2.00	35.29	0	0	8	-

Bowling	Mat	Balls	Runs	Wkts	BBI	BBM	Ave	Econ	SR	5w	10
First-class	32	4702	2739	87	7/146	8/87	31.48	3.49	54.0	2	0
List A	8	309	361	8	2/40	2/40	45.12	7.00	38.6	0	0
T20s	21	311	455	16	3/24	3/24	28.43	8.77	19.4	0	0

LIAM DAWSON RHB / SLA / R1 / W0 / MVP43

HAMPSHIRE

FULL NAME: Liam Andrew Dawson
BORN: March 1, 1990, Swindon
SQUAD NO: 8
HEIGHT: 5ft 8in
NICKNAME: Lemmy
EDUCATION: The John Bentley School, Wiltshire
TEAMS: England, Hampshire, Comilla Victorians, Essex, Islamabad United, Mountaineers, Peshawar Zalmi, Rangpur Riders
ROLE: Allrounder
DEBUT: Test: 2016; ODI: 2016; T20I: 2016; First-class: 2007; List A: 2007; T20: 2008

BEST BATTING: 169 Hampshire vs Somerset, Southampton, 2011
BEST BOWLING: 7-51 Mountaineers vs Mashonaland Eagles, Mutare Sports Club, 2011
COUNTY CAP: 2013 (Hampshire)

FIRST CRICKET CLUB? Goatacre CC, Wiltshire
FAMILY TIES? I got into the game watching my dad play for Goatacre CC in Wiltshire. My brother Brad has played Minor Counties for Wiltshire
WHAT WOULD YOU CHANGE ABOUT THE STRUCTURE OF THE COUNTY SEASON? Play less four-day cricket
MAKE ONE PREDICTION FOR THE FUTURE OF CRICKET: There will be only 10 counties
WHAT DO YOU MOST ENJOY LISTENING TO? Coldplay
WHAT MAKES YOU WORRY? The unknown
TWITTER: @daws128

Batting	Mat	Inns	NO	Runs	HS	Ave	SR	100	50	Ct	St
Tests	3	6	2	84	66*	21.00	42.63	0	1	2	-
ODIs	3	2	0	14	10	7.00	82.35	0	0	0	-
T20Is	8	4	1	23	10	7.66	121.05	0	0	2	-
First-class	164	267	29	7812	169	32.82	49.65	10	42	164	-
List A	160	130	23	3529	113*	32.98	95.32	3	18	72	-
T20s	190	143	33	2096	82	19.05	114.22	0	5	77	-
Bowling	Mat	Balls	Runs	Wkts	BBI	BBM	Ave	Econ	SR	5w	10
Tests	3	526	298	7	2/34	4/101	42.57	3.39	75.1	0	0
ODIs	3	84	96	3	2/70	2/70	32.00	6.85	28.0	0	0
T20Is	8	150	177	5	3/27	3/27	35.40	7.08	30.0	0	0
First-class	164	16083	7844	223	7/51	8/129	35.17	2.92	72.1	4	0
List A	160	6206	4890	162	6/47	6/47	30.18	4.72	38.3	1	0
T20s	190	3101	3735	138	5/17	5/17	27.06	7.22	22.4	1	0

JOSH DE CAIRES

RHB / RM / R0 / W0

FULL NAME: Joshua Michael de Caires
BORN: April 25, 2002, Paddington, London
SQUAD NO: 99
HEIGHT: 6ft
EDUCATION: St Albans School, Hertfordshire; University of Leeds
TEAMS: Middlesex
ROLE: Batter
DEBUT: First-class: 2021; List A: 2021; T20: 2021

MIDDLESEX

BEST BATTING: 17 Middlesex vs Leicestershire, Northwood, 2021

WHO IS YOUR LOOKALIKE? My dad (Mike Atherton)
FIRST CRICKET CLUB? Radlett CC, Hertfordshire
MOST UNDERRATED PLAYER IN COUNTY CRICKET? Ethan Bamber
MOST BEAUTIFUL THING YOU HAVE EVER SEEN? Max Holden with a fresh haircut
HOBBIES? Playing golf badly
WHO WOULD YOU MOST AND LEAST LIKE TO HAVE A NET WITH? Brian Lara – just to watch him bat
MAKE ONE PREDICTION FOR THE FUTURE OF CRICKET: Blake Cullen to play for England
WHAT DO YOU MOST ENJOY LISTENING TO? Michael Holding on commentary
WHAT MAKES YOU WORRY? Being told to field at second slip
GUILTY PLEASURE? Shadow batting
TWITTER: @josh_decaires

Batting	Mat	Inns	NO	Runs	HS	Ave	SR	100	50	Ct	St
First-class	2	4	0	28	17	7.00	26.66	0	0	1	-
List A	3	3	0	68	43	22.66	93.15	0	0	2	-
T20s	1	1	0	14	14	14.00	200.00	0	0	2	-

Bowling	Mat	Balls	Runs	Wkts	BBI	BBM	Ave	Econ	SR	5w	10
First-class	2	18	7	0	-	-	-	2.33	-	0	0
List A	3	108	95	1	1/13	1/13	95.00	5.27	108.0	0	0
T20s	1	-	-	-	-	-	-	-	-	-	-

MARCHANT DE LANGE   RHB / RF / R0 / W0 / MVP30

SOMERSET

FULL NAME: Marchant de Lange
BORN: October 13, 1990, Tzaneen, Transvaal, South Africa
SQUAD NO: 90
HEIGHT: 6ft 7in
NICKNAME: Shanna
TEAMS: South Africa, Somerset, Dambulla Giants, Durban Heat, Easterns, Free State, Glamorgan, Islamabad United, Knights, Kolkata Knight Riders, Mumbai Indians, Titans
ROLE: Bowler
DEBUT: Test: 2011; ODI: 2012; T20I: 2012; First-class: 2010; List A: 2010; T20: 2011

BEST BATTING: 113 Glamorgan vs Northamptonshire, Northampton, 2020
BEST BOWLING: 7-23 Knights vs Titans, Centurion, 2016

FIRST CRICKET CLUB? Tzaneen CC, Limpopo, South Africa
MOST EXCITING DAY AS A CRICKETER? Making my international debut for South Africa
CHILDHOOD SPORTING HERO? Brett Lee
SURPRISING FACT ABOUT YOU? I love art
GUILTY PLEASURE? Cupcakes
TWITTER: @Marchant90

Batting	Mat	Inns	NO	Runs	HS	Ave	SR	100	50	Ct	St
Tests	2	2	0	9	9	4.50	47.36	0	0	1	-
ODIs	4	-	-	-	-	-	-	-	-	0	-
T20Is	6	-	-	-	-	-	-	-	-	1	-
First-class	95	128	17	1878	113	16.91	80.42	1	5	40	-
List A	98	69	19	776	58*	15.52	108.22	0	2	25	-
T20s	130	56	23	372	28*	11.27	129.61	0	0	31	-

Bowling	Mat	Balls	Runs	Wkts	BBI	BBM	Ave	Econ	SR	5w	10
Tests	2	448	277	9	7/81	8/126	30.77	3.70	49.7	1	0
ODIs	4	209	198	10	4/46	4/46	19.80	5.68	20.9	0	0
T20Is	6	140	228	7	2/26	2/26	32.57	9.77	20.0	0	0
First-class	95	17105	10071	334	7/23	11/62	30.15	3.53	51.2	11	2
List A	98	4792	4426	170	5/49	5/49	26.03	5.54	28.1	4	0
T20s	130	2534	3673	144	5/20	5/20	25.50	8.69	17.5	1	0

JOSH DELL

RHB / RM / R0 / W0

FULL NAME: Joshua Jamie Dell
BORN: September 26, 1997, Tenbury Wells, Worcestershire
SQUAD NO: 52
HEIGHT: 6ft 3in
NICKNAME: Dellboy
EDUCATION: Abberley Hall School, Worcestershire; Cheltenham College
TEAMS: Worcestershire, England U19
ROLE: Batter
DEBUT: First-class: 2019; List A: 2018

BEST BATTING: 61 Worcestershire vs Durham, Worcester, 2019

FIRST CRICKET CLUB? Ombersley CC, Worcestershire. I've been playing there since I was 11
WHO IS THE BEST BATTER/BOWLER IN COUNTY CRICKET (EXCLUDING TEAMMATES)? David Bedingham/Chris Rushworth
MOST UNDERRATED PLAYER IN COUNTY CRICKET? Tom Kohler-Cadmore
WHAT WOULD A FLY ON THE WALL HEAR IN YOUR DRESSING ROOM? Ben Cox's terrible music
MOST BEAUTIFUL THING YOU HAVE EVER SEEN? The top of Joe Leach's head
HOBBIES? Making podcasts
WHO WOULD YOU MOST LIKE TO HAVE A NET WITH? Kevin Pietersen
GUILTY PLEASURE? A cup of tea and some Jammie Dodgers

Batting	Mat	Inns	NO	Runs	HS	Ave	SR	100	50	Ct	St
First-class	7	12	0	158	61	13.16	31.47	0	1	5	-
List A	6	6	1	136	46	27.20	99.27	0	0	1	-

Bowling	Mat	Balls	Runs	Wkts	BBI	BBM	Ave	Econ	SR	5w	10
First-class	7	-	-	-	-	-	-	-	-	-	-
List A	6	-	-	-	-	-	-	-	-	-	-

JOE DENLY

RHB / LB / R4 / W0

KENT

FULL NAME: Joseph Liam Denly
BORN: March 16, 1986, Canterbury, Kent
SQUAD NO: 6
HEIGHT: 6ft
NICKNAME: Denners
EDUCATION: Chaucer Technology School, Canterbury
TEAMS: England, Kent, Barisal Burners, Brisbane Heat, Kolkata Knight Riders, Lahore Qalandars, Middlesex, Sydney Sixers
ROLE: Batter
DEBUT: Test: 2019; ODI: 2009; T20I: 2009; First-class: 2004; List A: 2004; T20: 2004

BEST BATTING: 227 Kent vs Worcestershire, Worcester, 2017
BEST BOWLING: 4-36 Kent vs Derbyshire, Derby, 2018
COUNTY CAP: 2008 (Kent); 2012 (Middlesex); **BENEFIT:** 2019 (Kent)

FIRST CRICKET CLUB? Whitstable CC, Kent
WHO IS THE BEST BATTER/KEEPER/ALLROUNDER/BOWLER IN COUNTY CRICKET (EXCLUDING TEAMMATES)? Alastair Cook/Ben Foakes/Craig Overton/Chris Rushworth
WHAT WOULD A FLY ON THE WALL HEAR IN YOUR DRESSING ROOM? Sam Billings
IF YOU COULD TURN BACK TIME... I'd change a few of my hairstyle choices
WHO WOULD YOU MOST LIKE TO HAVE A NET WITH? Matthew Hayden – I loved watching him when I was growing up
MAKE ONE PREDICTION FOR THE FUTURE OF CRICKET: Franchises in all formats
WHAT MAKES YOU WORRY? The kids
WHAT GIVES YOU JOY? The kids
TWITTER: @joed1986

Batting	Mat	Inns	NO	Runs	HS	Ave	SR	100	50	Ct	St
Tests	15	28	0	827	94	29.53	39.64	0	6	7	-
ODIs	16	13	0	446	87	34.30	70.90	0	4	7	-
T20Is	13	12	2	125	30	12.50	105.93	0	0	4	-
First-class	221	380	25	12720	227	35.83	54.86	29	64	88	-
List A	159	150	16	4902	150*	36.58	76.83	8	26	54	-
T20s	247	239	18	5771	127	26.11	121.41	4	31	95	-

Bowling	Mat	Balls	Runs	Wkts	BBI	BBM	Ave	Econ	SR	5w	10
Tests	15	390	219	2	2/42	2/42	109.50	3.36	195.0	0	0
ODIs	16	102	101	1	1/24	1/24	101.00	5.94	102.0	0	0
T20Is	13	72	93	7	4/19	4/19	13.28	7.75	10.2	0	0
First-class	221	5632	2984	72	4/36	6/114	41.44	3.17	78.2	0	0
List A	159	1406	1199	47	4/35	4/35	25.51	5.11	29.9	0	0
T20s	247	837	1085	45	4/19	4/19	24.11	7.77	18.6	0	0

CHRIS DENT

LHB / SLA / R4 / W0

FULL NAME: Christopher David James Dent
BORN: January 20, 1991, Bristol
SQUAD NO: 15
HEIGHT: 5ft 9in
NICKNAME: Denty
EDUCATION: Backwell School, North Somerset; SGS Filton College, Bristol
TEAMS: Gloucestershire, England U19
ROLE: Batter
DEBUT: First-class: 2010; List A: 2009; T20: 2010

GLOUCESTERSHIRE

BEST BATTING: 268 Gloucestershire vs Glamorgan, Bristol, 2015
BEST BOWLING: 2-21 Gloucestershire vs Sussex, Hove, 2016
COUNTY CAP: 2010

FIRST CRICKET CLUB? Cleeve CC, Somerset
MOST EXCITING DAY AS A CRICKETER? The 2015 Lord's one-day final
CHILDHOOD SPORTING HERO? Brian Lara
BIGGEST CRICKETING REGRET? Every time I was out in the 90s trying to hit a six
WHAT WOULD YOU DO IF YOU WERE IN CHARGE OF COUNTY CRICKET? Introduce a new rule which says that if you hit the ball against the stumps at the other end, it's worth five runs (unless the bowler touches it)
FAVOURITE SMELL? Jean Paul Gaultier
GUILTY PLEASURE? Double cream
TWITTER: @cdent15

Batting	Mat	Inns	NO	Runs	HS	Ave	SR	100	50	Ct	St
First-class	159	286	25	9711	268	37.20	51.59	18	58	165	-
List A	77	72	6	2136	151*	32.36	93.47	4	6	27	-
T20s	69	63	7	1337	87	23.87	130.43	0	7	26	-

Bowling	Mat	Balls	Runs	Wkts	BBI	BBM	Ave	Econ	SR	5w	10
First-class	159	1238	831	9	2/21	2/21	92.33	4.02	137.5	0	0
List A	77	438	412	12	4/43	4/43	34.33	5.64	36.5	0	0
T20s	69	120	168	5	1/4	1/4	33.60	8.40	24.0	0	0

SEAN DICKSON

RHB / RM / R0 / W0

FULL NAME: Sean Robert Dickson
BORN: September 2, 1991, Johannesburg, South Africa
SQUAD NO: 58
HEIGHT: 5ft 11in
NICKNAME: Dicko
EDUCATION: King Edward VII School, Johannesburg; University of Pretoria
TEAMS: Durham, Kent, Northerns
ROLE: Batter
DEBUT: First-class: 2013; List A: 2013; T20: 2014

BEST BATTING: 318 Kent vs Northamptonshire, Beckenham, 2017
BEST BOWLING: 1-15 Northerns vs Griqualand West, Centurion, 2015

FIRST CRICKET CLUB? Old Park Sports Club, Johannesburg
BIGGEST INFLUENCE ON YOUR DEVELOPMENT AS A CRICKETER (EXCLUDING PARENTS)?
Jimmy Cook (former South Africa and Somerset batter). He coached me as a junior
WHO IS THE BEST BATTER/KEEPER/ALLROUNDER/BOWLER IN COUNTY CRICKET
(EXCLUDING TEAMMATES)? Joe Clarke/Ben Cox/Darren Stevens/Sam Cook
MOST UNDERRATED PLAYER IN COUNTY CRICKET? Alex Thomson
WHAT WOULD A FLY ON THE WALL HEAR IN YOUR DRESSING ROOM? Loads of South
African accents
MOST BEAUTIFUL THING YOU HAVE EVER SEEN? A rainbow
HOBBIES? Making furniture
WHO WOULD YOU LEAST LIKE TO HAVE A NET WITH? James Pattinson, because he is such
an angry man
WHAT MAKES YOU WORRY? My outside edge
GUILTY PLEASURE? Cheese
TWITTER: @Seano_146

Batting	Mat	Inns	NO	Runs	HS	Ave	SR	100	50	Ct	St
First-class	77	129	10	3912	318	32.87	49.81	10	15	63	-
List A	51	46	5	1285	103*	31.34	82.00	1	9	15	-
T20s	32	26	6	568	53	28.40	124.56	0	3	17	-

Bowling	Mat	Balls	Runs	Wkts	BBI	BBM	Ave	Econ	SR	5w	10
First-class	77	96	53	2	1/15	2/40	26.50	3.31	48.0	0	0
List A	51	12	20	0	-	-	-	10.00	-	0	0
T20s	32	6	9	1	1/9	1/9	9.00	9.00	6.0	0	0

ANEURIN DONALD   RHB / OB / R1 / W0

FULL NAME: Aneurin Henry Thomas Donald
BORN: December 20, 1996, Swansea
SQUAD NO: 12
HEIGHT: 6ft 3in
NICKNAME: Don
EDUCATION: Pontarddulais Comprehensive
School, Swansea; Gower College Swansea
TEAMS: Hampshire, Glamorgan, England U19
ROLE: Batter
DEBUT: First-class: 2014; List A: 2015; T20: 2015

BEST BATTING: 234 Glamorgan vs Derbyshire, Colwyn Bay, 2016

FAMILY TIES? My grand-uncle Bernard Hedges scored Glamorgan's first one-day century
MOST EXCITING DAY AS A CRICKETER? Hard to choose between the last Lord's one-day final
in 2019 and making a first-class double hundred at Colwyn Bay in 2016
CHILDHOOD SPORTING HERO? Gavin Henson
BIGGEST INFLUENCE ON YOUR DEVELOPMENT AS A CRICKETER (EXCLUDING PARENTS)?
Jacques Rudolph – he passed on a lot of wisdom about batting and life while I was at
Glamorgan
FAVOURITE SMELL? Welsh salt-marsh lamb
GUILTY PLEASURE? Slogging a red Dukes
TWITTER: @AneurinDonald12

Batting	Mat	Inns	NO	Runs	HS	Ave	SR	100	50	Ct	St
First-class	48	86	5	2610	234	32.22	73.31	3	15	35	-
List A	30	27	1	424	57	16.30	82.65	0	2	13	-
T20s	54	49	3	927	76	20.15	136.52	0	5	33	-

Bowling	Mat	Balls	Runs	Wkts	BBI	BBM	Ave	Econ	SR	5w	10
First-class	48	-	-	-	-	-	-	-	-	-	-
List A	30	-	-	-	-	-	-	-	-	-	-
T20s	54	-	-	-	-	-	-	-	-	-	-

DAN DOUTHWAITE · RHB / RMF / R0 / W0

GLAMORGAN

FULL NAME: Daniel Alexander Douthwaite
BORN: February 8, 1997, Kingston-upon-Thames, Surrey
SQUAD NO: 88
HEIGHT: 6ft 1in
NICKNAME: Jugs
EDUCATION: Reed's School, Cobham, Surrey; Cardiff Metropolitan University
TEAMS: Glamorgan, Warwickshire
ROLE: Allrounder
DEBUT: First-class: 2019; List A: 2018; T20: 2018

BEST BATTING: 100* Cardiff MCCU vs Sussex, Hove, 2019
BEST BOWLING: 4-48 Glamorgan vs Derbyshire, Derby, 2019

FIRST CRICKET CLUB? Stoke d'Abernon CC, Cobham, Surrey
BIGGEST INFLUENCE ON YOUR DEVELOPMENT AS A CRICKETER (EXCLUDING PARENTS)? Keith Medlycott at Surrey
WHO IS THE BEST BATTER/KEEPER/ALLROUNDER/BOWLER IN COUNTY CRICKET (EXCLUDING TEAMMATES)? Ollie Pope/Ben Foakes/Darren Stevens/Darren Stevens
MOST UNDERRATED PLAYER IN COUNTY CRICKET? Ryan Higgins
HOBBIES? Fishing
IF YOU COULD TURN BACK TIME... I'd bet on Leicester City winning the Premier League in 2016
WHO WOULD YOU MOST AND LEAST LIKE TO HAVE A NET WITH? Most – Andrew Flintoff (idolised him as a kid). Least – Brett Lee (just too quick)
MAKE ONE PREDICTION FOR THE FUTURE OF CRICKET: More day/night matches in four-day cricket
WHAT MAKES YOU WORRY? Pace bowlers
WHAT GIVES YOU JOY? Full balls
TWITTER: @DanDouthwaite

Batting	Mat	Inns	NO	Runs	HS	Ave	SR	100	50	Ct	St
First-class	27	41	3	1085	100*	28.55	53.26	1	6	7	-
List A	4	4	2	99	52*	49.50	147.76	0	1	2	-
T20s	29	26	5	346	53	16.47	132.56	0	1	5	-

Bowling	Mat	Balls	Runs	Wkts	BBI	BBM	Ave	Econ	SR	5w	10
First-class	27	2955	2156	52	4/48	6/137	41.46	4.37	56.8	0	0
List A	4	138	126	5	3/43	3/43	25.20	5.47	27.6	0	0
T20s	29	364	536	20	3/28	3/28	26.80	8.83	18.2	0	0

GEORGE DRISSELL

RHB / OB / R0 / W0

FULL NAME: George Samuel Drissell
BORN: January 20, 1999, Bristol
SQUAD NO: 8
HEIGHT: 6ft 2in
NICKNAME: Dris, Lemon, Lethal
EDUCATION: Bedminster Down Secondary School, Bristol; SGS Filton College, Bristol
TEAMS: Durham, Gloucestershire, Somerset
ROLE: Allrounder
DEBUT: First-class: 2017; List A: 2018

BEST BATTING: 19 Gloucestershire vs Warwickshire, Edgbaston, 2018
BEST BOWLING: 4-83 Gloucestershire vs Glamorgan, Newport, 2019
COUNTY CAP: 2017 (Gloucestershire)

WHO IS YOUR LOOKALIKE? Ross Barkley apparently…
FIRST CRICKET CLUB? Bedminster CC, Bristol
WHAT WOULD YOU CHANGE ABOUT THE STRUCTURE OF THE COUNTY SEASON? Seems pretty good to me the way it is
WHO IS THE BEST BATTER/KEEPER/ALLROUNDER/BOWLER IN COUNTY CRICKET (EXCLUDING TEAMMATES)? Alastair Cook/Ben Cox/Ryan Higgins/Sam Cook
MOST UNDERRATED PLAYER IN COUNTY CRICKET? Chris Dent
MOST BEAUTIFUL THING YOU HAVE EVER SEEN? Bristol City 2, Manchester United 1. Korey Smith in the 93rd minute. Doesn't get much better than that
HOBBIES? Golf – a beautifully frustrating game. Seems like that's a common theme…
IF YOU COULD TURN BACK TIME… I fell off a treadmill once and it went a bit viral on Twitter. It wasn't one of my finest moments
WHO WOULD YOU LEAST LIKE TO HAVE A NET WITH? Brett Lee
WHAT DO YOU MOST ENJOY LISTENING TO? House music
WHAT MAKES YOU WORRY? Bristol City
TWITTER: @georgedris8

Batting	Mat	Inns	NO	Runs	HS	Ave	SR	100	50	Ct	St
First-class	7	11	0	77	19	7.00	30.19	0	0	0	-
List A	6	4	2	32	17*	16.00	86.48	0	0	4	-

Bowling	Mat	Balls	Runs	Wkts	BBI	BBM	Ave	Econ	SR	5w	10
First-class	7	817	504	8	4/83	4/174	63.00	3.70	102.1	0	0
List A	6	120	116	2	1/21	1/21	58.00	5.80	60.0	0	0

LEUS DU PLOOY — LHB / SLA / R0 / W0

DERBYSHIRE

FULL NAME: Jacobus Leus du Plooy
BORN: January 12, 1995, Pretoria, South Africa
SQUAD NO: 76
HEIGHT: 5ft 11in
NICKNAME: Dups
EDUCATION: Afrikaanse Hoër Seunskool (Affies), Pretoria; University of South Africa
TEAMS: Derbyshire, Free State, Knights, Northerns, South Western Districts, Titans
ROLE: Batter
DEBUT: First-class: 2015; List A: 2014; T20: 2014

BEST BATTING: 186 South Western Districts vs Northern Cape, Kimberley, 2022
BEST BOWLING: 3-76 Northerns vs Western Province, Pretoria, 2019

WHO IS YOUR LOOKALIKE? Heinz Winkler (chef)
FIRST CRICKET CLUB? Tuks CC, Pretoria, South Africa
WHAT WOULD YOU CHANGE ABOUT THE STRUCTURE OF THE COUNTY SEASON? Schedule The Hundred and RL50 comp at different times – all players should be available
WHAT WOULD A FLY ON THE WALL HEAR IN YOUR DRESSING ROOM? People playing football-volleyball
MOST BEAUTIFUL THING YOU HAVE EVER SEEN? A leopard at Kruger National Park
HOBBIES? Playing the guitar and learning Spanish
IF YOU COULD TURN BACK TIME... I'd explore and live more freely
WHO WOULD YOU MOST AND LEAST LIKE TO HAVE A NET WITH? Most – Kumar Sangakkara. Least – Shoaib Akhtar
MAKE ONE PREDICTION FOR THE FUTURE OF CRICKET: The IPL will be more important than winning a World Cup (I truly hope that won't be the case)
WHAT DO YOU MOST ENJOY LISTENING TO? Alternative folk
WHAT GIVES YOU JOY? Fist-pumping Wayne Madsen
GUILTY PLEASURE? Häagen-Dazs Salted Caramel ice cream

Batting	Mat	Inns	NO	Runs	HS	Ave	SR	100	50	Ct	St
First-class	74	120	15	4543	186	43.26	49.15	13	24	58	-
List A	45	42	10	1865	155	58.28	87.51	5	10	23	-
T20s	68	62	15	1515	92	32.23	124.69	0	9	26	-

Bowling	Mat	Balls	Runs	Wkts	BBI	BBM	Ave	Econ	SR	5w	10
First-class	74	1751	1243	25	3/76	3/76	49.72	4.25	70.0	0	0
List A	45	399	389	11	3/19	3/19	35.36	5.84	36.2	0	0
T20s	68	170	221	13	4/15	4/15	17.00	7.80	13.0	0	0

BEN DUCKETT   LHB / OB / WK / R2 / W0 / MVP32

FULL NAME: Ben Matthew Duckett
BORN: October 17, 1994, Farnborough, Kent
SQUAD NO: 17
HEIGHT: 5ft 9in
NICKNAME: Ducky
EDUCATION: Millfield School, Somerset; Winchester House School; Stowe School
TEAMS: England, Nottinghamshire, Brisbane Heat, Hobart Hurricanes, Northamptonshire, Islamabad United
ROLE: Batter
DEBUT: Test: 2016; ODI: 2016; T20I: 2019; First-class: 2013; List A: 2013; T20: 2012

NOTTINGHAMSHIRE

BEST BATTING: 282* Northamptonshire vs Sussex, Northampton, 2016
BEST BOWLING: 1-21 Northamptonshire vs Kent, Beckenham, 2017
COUNTY CAP: 2016 (Northamptonshire); 2018 (Nottinghamshire)

FIRST CRICKET CLUB? Glastonbury CC, Somerset
WHAT WOULD YOU CHANGE ABOUT THE STRUCTURE OF THE COUNTY SEASON? Nothing – the structure this year is great and I can't wait
MOST UNDERRATED PLAYER IN COUNTY CRICKET? Rob Keogh
MOST BEAUTIFUL THING YOU HAVE EVER SEEN? Woburn Golf Club
WHO WOULD YOU MOST LIKE TO HAVE A NET WITH? Brian Lara, because he was my idol growing up. I always turned on the TV when he was batting
MAKE ONE PREDICTION FOR THE FUTURE OF CRICKET: The Hundred will be the best competition in the world
WHAT MAKES YOU WORRY? The nipping Dukes ball
TWITTER: @benduckett11

Batting	Mat	Inns	NO	Runs	HS	Ave	SR	100	50	Ct	St
Tests	4	7	0	110	56	15.71	57.89	0	1	1	-
ODIs	3	3	0	123	63	41.00	80.92	0	2	0	-
T20Is	1	1	0	9	9	9.00	128.57	0	0	0	-
First-class	108	185	10	6845	282*	39.11	71.44	19	30	86	3
List A	73	68	7	2341	220*	38.37	99.49	3	16	38	3
T20s	145	138	21	3419	96	29.22	134.60	0	22	69	2

Bowling	Mat	Balls	Runs	Wkts	BBI	BBM	Ave	Econ	SR	5w	10
Tests	4	-	-	-	-	-	-	-	-	-	-
ODIs	3	-	-	-	-	-	-	-	-	-	-
T20Is	1	-	-	-	-	-	-	-	-	-	-
First-class	108	107	84	1	1/21	1/32	84.00	4.71	107.0	0	0
List A	73	-	-	-	-	-	-	-	-	-	-
T20s	145	-	-	-	-	-	-	-	-	-	-

SURREY

MATT DUNN

LHB / RFM / R0 / W0

FULL NAME: Matthew Peter Dunn
BORN: May 5, 1992, Egham, Surrey
SQUAD NO: 4
HEIGHT: 6ft 1in
NICKNAME: Dunny
EDUCATION: Bishopsgate School; Bearwood College, Wokingham
TEAMS: Surrey, England U19
ROLE: Bowler
DEBUT: First-class: 2010; List A: 2011; T20: 2013

BEST BATTING: 31* Surrey vs Kent, Guildford, 2014
BEST BOWLING: 5-43 Surrey vs Somerset, Guildford, 2019

WHO IS YOUR LOOKALIKE? Rob Beckett (comedian)
FIRST CRICKET CLUB? Egham CC, Surrey
BIGGEST CRICKETING REGRET? Not working on my batting from a younger age
HOBBIES? Breakdancing
WHO WOULD YOU LEAST LIKE TO HAVE A NET WITH? Fidel Edwards – he once broke my rib
WHAT GIVES YOU JOY? I absolutely love coffee
SURPRISING FACT ABOUT YOU? I lived in Norway when I was younger
TWITTER: @MatthewDunn05

Batting	Mat	Inns	NO	Runs	HS	Ave	SR	100	50	Ct	St
First-class	43	50	22	197	31*	7.03	21.62	0	0	10	-
List A	11	2	1	9	8*	9.00	30.00	0	0	3	-
T20s	23	4	2	4	2	2.00	50.00	0	0	5	-

Bowling	Mat	Balls	Runs	Wkts	BBI	BBM	Ave	Econ	SR	5w	10
First-class	43	6511	4237	117	5/43	8/128	36.21	3.90	55.6	4	0
List A	11	441	445	13	2/32	2/32	34.23	6.05	33.9	0	0
T20s	23	405	618	27	3/8	3/8	22.88	9.15	15.0	0	0

NED ECKERSLEY RHB / WK / R1 / W0

FULL NAME: Edmund James Holden Eckersley
BORN: August 9, 1989, Oxford
SQUAD NO: 66
HEIGHT: 6ft
NICKNAME: Steady
EDUCATION: St Benedict's School, Ealing, London
TEAMS: Durham, Leicestershire, Mountaineers
ROLE: Batter/wicketkeeper
DEBUT: First-class: 2011; List A: 2008; T20: 2011

BEST BATTING: 158 Leicestershire vs Derbyshire, Derby, 2017
BEST BOWLING: 2-29 Leicestershire vs Lancashire, Old Trafford, 2013
COUNTY CAP: 2013 (Leicestershire)

FIRST CRICKET CLUB? Ealing CC, London
CHILDHOOD SPORTING HERO? Tiger Woods
BIGGEST INFLUENCE ON YOUR DEVELOPMENT AS A CRICKETER (EXCLUDING PARENTS)? My former coach, the late Bob Jones. He grew my love of cricket
WHAT WOULD YOU DO IF YOU WERE IN CHARGE OF COUNTY CRICKET? Make each side play 10 Championship matches in the season, find a way to encourage better pitches, change the minimum salary for young players
GUILTY PLEASURE? The odd negroni
TWITTER: @nedeckersley

Batting	Mat	Inns	NO	Runs	HS	Ave	SR	100	50	Ct	St
First-class	139	241	19	7171	158	32.30	50.49	16	27	248	4
List A	46	43	6	1091	108	29.48	87.98	1	5	28	1
T20s	78	66	15	848	50*	16.62	111.57	0	1	25	7

Bowling	Mat	Balls	Runs	Wkts	BBI	BBM	Ave	Econ	SR	5w	10
First-class	139	112	74	2	2/29	2/29	37.00	3.96	56.0	0	0
List A	46	-	-	-	-	-	-	-	-	-	-
T20s	78	-	-	-	-	-	-	-	-	-	-

STEVIE ESKINAZI RHB / WK / R0 / W0

FULL NAME: Stephen Sean Eskinazi
BORN: March 28, 1994, Johannesburg, South Africa
SQUAD NO: 28
HEIGHT: 6ft 2in
NICKNAME: Eski
EDUCATION: Christ Church Grammar School, Perth; University of Western Australia; University of Hertfordshire
TEAMS: Middlesex
ROLE: Batter
DEBUT: First-class: 2015; List A: 2018; T20: 2016

BEST BATTING: 179 Middlesex vs Warwickshire, Edgbaston, 2017

COUNTY CAP: 2018

WHO IS YOUR LOOKALIKE? Henry Cavill (actor)
FIRST CRICKET CLUB? Fair Oak CC, Hampshire
WHO IS THE BEST BATTER/KEEPER/ALLROUNDER/BOWLER IN COUNTY CRICKET (EXCLUDING TEAMMATES)? Joe Clarke/Ben Brown/Craig Overton/James Anderson
WHAT WOULD A FLY ON THE WALL HEAR IN YOUR DRESSING ROOM? Philosophical, astute debate about the current topics which really matter
MOST BEAUTIFUL THING YOU HAVE EVER SEEN? Sunset at Oia on the Greek island of Santorini
HOBBIES? Barista (Level 2 qualification!)
WHO WOULD YOU MOST LIKE TO HAVE A NET WITH? Jacques Kallis
WHAT DO YOU MOST ENJOY LISTENING TO? Ziggy Alberts (Australian singer)
WHAT MAKES YOU WORRY? Letting people down
GUILTY PLEASURE? Whole bags of sweets
TWITTER: @seskinazi

Batting	Mat	Inns	NO	Runs	HS	Ave	SR	100	50	Ct	St
First-class	65	116	7	3478	179	31.90	52.14	7	14	60	-
List A	21	20	2	697	130	38.72	94.06	2	1	8	-
T20s	50	47	5	1524	102*	36.28	137.42	1	12	23	-

Bowling	Mat	Balls	Runs	Wkts	BBI	BBM	Ave	Econ	SR	5w	10
First-class	65	12	4	0	-	-	-	2.00	-	0	0
List A	21	-	-	-	-	-	-	-	-	-	-
T20s	50	-	-	-	-	-	-	-	-	-	-

ALEX EVANS

LHB / RFM / R0 / W0

FULL NAME: Huw Alexander Evans
BORN: August 9, 2000, Bedford
SQUAD NO: 72
HEIGHT: 6ft 2in
NICKNAME: Prince
EDUCATION: Bedford Modern School;
Loughborough University
TEAMS: Leicestershire
ROLE: Bowler
DEBUT: First-class: 2019

BEST BATTING: 15 Leicestershire vs Yorkshire, Headingley, 2020
BEST BOWLING: 3-49 Loughborough MCCU vs Kent, Canterbury, 2019

FIRST CRICKET CLUB? Ampthill Town CC, Bedfordshire
BIGGEST INFLUENCE ON YOUR DEVELOPMENT AS A CRICKETER (EXCLUDING PARENTS)?
Tom Smith, former Lancashire cricketer and now Second XI coach at Leicestershire
MOST UNDERRATED PLAYER IN COUNTY CRICKET? Jake Libby
MOST BEAUTIFUL THING YOU HAVE EVER SEEN? The view from the top of Snowdon
HOBBIES? Golf
MAKE ONE PREDICTION FOR THE FUTURE OF CRICKET: Leicestershire to win the treble
GUILTY PLEASURE? A Guinness
TWITTER: @HuwAlexEvans

Batting	Mat	Inns	NO	Runs	HS	Ave	SR	100	50	Ct	St
First-class	9	14	5	61	15	6.77	49.19	0	0	1	-
Bowling	Mat	Balls	Runs	Wkts	BBI	BBM	Ave	Econ	SR	5w	10
First-class	9	1178	666	14	3/49	4/79	47.57	3.39	84.1	0	0

LAURIE EVANS

RHB / RM / R0 / W0

SURREY

FULL NAME: Laurie John Evans
BORN: October 12, 1987, Lambeth, London
SQUAD NO: 10
HEIGHT: 6ft
NICKNAME: Loz
EDUCATION: Whitgift School; The John Fisher School, Purley; Durham University
TEAMS: Surrey, Colombo Kings, England Lions, Multan Sultans, Northamptonshire, Perth Scorchers, Rajshahi Kings, St Kitts & Nevis Patriots, Sussex, Warwickshire
ROLE: Batter
DEBUT: First-class: 2007; List A: 2009; T20: 2009

BEST BATTING: 108* Colombo Kings vs Jaffna Stallions, Hambantota, 2020 (T20)
BEST BOWLING: 1-5 Warwickshire vs Gloucestershire, Cheltenham, 2013 (T20)

MOST EXCITING DAY AS A CRICKETER? Winning the T20 Blast with Warwickshire in 2014
CHILDHOOD SPORTING HERO? Jonny Wilkinson
WHAT WOULD YOU DO IF YOU WERE IN CHARGE OF COUNTY CRICKET? Reduce the amount of games, use DRS for TV games, offer free entry for kids
FAVOURITE SMELL? Petrol
GUILTY PLEASURE? Wine
TWITTER: @laurieevans32
NOTES: Evans signed a new white-ball contract with Surrey in March

Batting	Mat	Inns	NO	Runs	HS	Ave	SR	100	50	Ct	St
First-class	73	125	6	3495	213*	29.36	46.43	6	18	58	-
List A	63	57	11	1735	134*	37.71	96.98	3	5	25	-
T20s	199	181	44	4695	108*	34.27	134.64	2	33	78	1

Bowling	Mat	Balls	Runs	Wkts	BBI	BBM	Ave	Econ	SR	5w	10
First-class	73	366	270	2	1/29	1/29	135.00	4.42	183.0	0	0
List A	63	54	82	1	1/29	1/29	82.00	9.11	54.0	0	0
T20s	199	22	35	1	1/5	1/5	35.00	9.54	22.0	0	0

SAM EVANS

RHB / OB / RO / WO

FULL NAME: Samuel Thomes Evans
BORN: December 20, 1997, Leicester
SQUAD NO: 21
HEIGHT: 5ft 8in
NICKNAME: Smevs
EDUCATION: Lancaster Boys School, Leicester; Wyggeston & Queen Elizabeth I College; Loughborough University
TEAMS: Leicestershire
ROLE: Batter
DEBUT: First-class: 2017; List A: 2018

BEST BATTING: 138 Leicestershire vs Surrey, The Oval, 2021

WHO IS YOUR LOOKALIKE? Donkey from Shrek
FIRST CRICKET CLUB? Leicester Ivanhoe CC, Leicester
WHAT WOULD YOU CHANGE ABOUT THE STRUCTURE OF THE COUNTY SEASON? Play the 50-over competition at the beginning of the season
BIGGEST INFLUENCE ON YOUR DEVELOPMENT AS A CRICKETER (EXCLUDING PARENTS)? Trevor Ward – he helped me a lot at Leicester Ivanhoe CC
WHO IS THE BEST BATTER/KEEPER/ALLROUNDER/BOWLER IN COUNTY CRICKET (EXCLUDING TEAMMATES)? James Vince/Ben Foakes/Darren Stevens/Kyle Abbott
MOST UNDERRATED PLAYER IN COUNTY CRICKET? Sam Cook
MOST BEAUTIFUL THING YOU HAVE EVER SEEN? Mossman Gorge, Queensland, Australia
HOBBIES? Coffee
WHAT MAKES YOU WORRY? Losing my hair
WHAT GIVES YOU JOY? Dogs, nature, and socialising
GUILTY PLEASURE? A Galaxy Caramel
TWITTER: @SamEvans97

Batting	Mat	Inns	NO	Runs	HS	Ave	SR	100	50	Ct	St
First-class	23	36	1	988	138	28.22	39.19	4	2	8	-
List A	2	1	0	20	20	20.00	71.42	0	0	0	-

Bowling	Mat	Balls	Runs	Wkts	BBI	BBM	Ave	Econ	SR	5w	10
First-class	23	54	46	0	-	-	-	5.11	-	0	0
List A	2	-	-	-	-	-	-	-	-	-	-

JOEY EVISON

RHB / RM / R0 / W0

FULL NAME: Joseph David Michael Evison
BORN: November 14, 2001, Peterborough, Cambridgeshire
SQUAD NO: 90
HEIGHT: 6ft 2in
NICKNAME: Evo
EDUCATION: Stamford School, Lincolnshire
TEAMS: Nottinghamshire, England U19
ROLE: Allrounder
DEBUT: First-class: 2019; List A: 2021

BEST BATTING: 58 Nottinghamshire vs Yorkshire, Trent Bridge, 2021
BEST BOWLING: 5-21 Nottinghamshire vs Durham, Chester-le-Street, 2021

WHO IS YOUR LOOKALIKE? Ben Stokes
FIRST CRICKET CLUB? Bourne CC, Lincolnshire
WHAT WOULD YOU CHANGE ABOUT THE STRUCTURE OF THE COUNTY SEASON? Bring back pink-ball matches
WHO IS THE BEST BATTER/KEEPER/ALLROUNDER/BOWLER IN COUNTY CRICKET (EXCLUDING TEAMMATES)? David Bedingham/Ben Foakes/Jordan Thompson/Chris Rushworth
MOST UNDERRATED PLAYER IN COUNTY CRICKET? Jamie Porter
MOST BEAUTIFUL THING YOU HAVE EVER SEEN? Jonny Wilkinson's drop goal in the 2003 World Cup
IF YOU COULD TURN BACK TIME... I would back Leicester City to win the 2015/16 Premier League
MAKE ONE PREDICTION FOR THE FUTURE OF CRICKET: A Test batsman who is just as good batting right-handed as left-handed
WHAT MAKES YOU WORRY? Being late
WHAT GIVES YOU JOY? My dogs
GUILTY PLEASURE? M&S pancakes
TWITTER: @EvisonJoey

Batting	Mat	Inns	NO	Runs	HS	Ave	SR	100	50	Ct	St
First-class	6	10	0	247	58	24.70	49.40	0	1	2	-
List A	5	3	0	72	54	24.00	133.33	0	1	2	-

Bowling	Mat	Balls	Runs	Wkts	BBI	BBM	Ave	Econ	SR	5w	10
First-class	6	684	356	18	5/21	5/30	19.77	3.12	38.0	1	0
List A	5	138	163	4	2/33	2/33	40.75	7.08	34.5	0	0

TOM FELL   RHB / OB / R1 / W0

FULL NAME: Thomas Charles Fell
BORN: October 17, 1993, Hillingdon, Middlesex
SQUAD NO: 29
HEIGHT: 6ft 1in
NICKNAME: Lord
EDUCATION: Tettenhall College, Wolverhampton; Oakham School, Rutland; Oxford Brookes University
TEAMS: Worcestershire
ROLE: Batter
DEBUT: First-class: 2013; List A: 2013; T20: 2018

BEST BATTING: 171 Worcestershire vs Middlesex, Worcester, 2015

COUNTY CAP: 2013

WHO IS YOUR LOOKALIKE? Joe Leach
FIRST CRICKET CLUB? Wolverhampton CC, West Midlands
WHAT WOULD YOU CHANGE ABOUT THE STRUCTURE OF THE COUNTY SEASON? Play more Championship cricket in June, July and August, turn the 50-over competition into a knockout which includes National (formerly Minor) Counties
BIGGEST INFLUENCE ON YOUR DEVELOPMENT AS A CRICKETER (EXCLUDING PARENTS)? Steve Rhodes, former Worcestershire coach. He gave me my first contract and the opportunity to play first-team cricket so early in my career
WHO IS THE BEST BATTER/KEEPER/ALLROUNDER/BOWLER IN COUNTY CRICKET (EXCLUDING TEAMMATES)? Joe Clarke/Ben Foakes/Darren Stevens/Simon Harmer
MOST UNDERRATED PLAYER IN COUNTY CRICKET? Sam Cook
WHAT DO YOU MOST ENJOY LISTENING TO? The Ricky Gervais Show (podcast)
WHAT MAKES YOU WORRY? Out of bounds right
WHAT GIVES YOU JOY? Walking the dogs to a pub
TWITTER: @TomFell_29

Batting	Mat	Inns	NO	Runs	HS	Ave	SR	100	50	Ct	St
First-class	96	162	7	4468	171	28.82	48.55	6	19	73	-
List A	52	51	5	1541	116*	33.50	80.42	1	13	18	-
T20s	9	7	0	69	28	9.85	88.46	0	0	2	-

Bowling	Mat	Balls	Runs	Wkts	BBI	BBM	Ave	Econ	SR	5w	10
First-class	96	20	17	0	-	-	-	5.10	-	0	0
List A	52	-	-	-	-	-	-	-	-	-	-
T20s	9	-	-	-	-	-	-	-	-	-	-

ADAM FINCH

RHB / RFM / R0 / W0

WORCESTERSHIRE

FULL NAME: Adam William Finch
BORN: May 28, 2000, Wordsley, Stourbridge, Worcestershire
SQUAD NO: 61
HEIGHT: 6ft 4in
EDUCATION: Kingswinford School, West Midlands; Oldswinford Hospital Sixth Form College, Stourbridge
TEAMS: Worcestershire, England U19, Surrey
ROLE: Bowler
DEBUT: First-class: 2019; List A: 2021; T20: 2020

BEST BATTING: 31 Worcestershire vs Warwickshire, Worcester, 2021
BEST BOWLING: 4-38 Surrey vs Essex, Chelmsford, 2020

WHO IS YOUR LOOKALIKE? Johnny Bravo (from the animated comedy TV series of the same name)
FIRST CRICKET CLUB? Himley CC, Staffordshire
BIGGEST INFLUENCE ON YOUR DEVELOPMENT AS A CRICKETER (EXCLUDING PARENTS)? Paul Pridgeon, former Worcestershire seamer who worked with the Academy to help bring through young players
WHO IS THE BEST BATTER/KEEPER/ALLROUNDER/BOWLER IN COUNTY CRICKET (EXCLUDING TEAMMATES)? David Bedingham/Ben Foakes/Darren Stevens/Kyle Abbott
MOST UNDERRATED PLAYER IN COUNTY CRICKET? Liam Norwell
MOST BEAUTIFUL THING YOU HAVE EVER SEEN? Queenstown in New Zealand
HOBBIES? Golf
WHO WOULD YOU MOST LIKE TO HAVE A NET WITH? Glenn McGrath
TWITTER: @Adamfinch00

Batting	Mat	Inns	NO	Runs	HS	Ave	SR	100	50	Ct	St
First-class	14	19	7	127	31	10.58	23.87	0	0	1	-
List A	7	3	1	25	23*	12.50	125.00	0	0	1	-
T20s	5	1	1	3	3*	-	60.00	0	0	0	-

Bowling	Mat	Balls	Runs	Wkts	BBI	BBM	Ave	Econ	SR	5w	10
First-class	14	1965	1147	28	4/38	4/78	40.96	3.50	70.1	0	0
List A	7	222	222	6	2/54	2/54	37.00	6.00	37.0	0	0
T20s	5	96	147	4	1/22	1/22	36.75	9.18	24.0	0	0

FULL NAME: Steven Thomas Finn
BORN: April 4, 1989, Watford, Hertfordshire
SQUAD NO: 44
HEIGHT: 6ft 8in
NICKNAME: Cyril
EDUCATION: Parmiter's School, Watford
TEAMS: England, Sussex, Islamabad United, Middlesex, Otago
ROLE: Bowler
DEBUT: Test: 2010; ODI: 2011; T20I: 2011; First-class: 2005; List A: 2007; T20: 2008

BEST BATTING: 56 England vs New Zealand, Dunedin, 2013
BEST BOWLING: 9-37 Middlesex vs Worcestershire, Worcester, 2010
COUNTY CAP: 2009 (Middlesex)

FIRST CRICKET CLUB? Langleybury CC, Hertfordshire
MOST EXCITING DAY AS A CRICKETER? The 2015 Ashes Test at Edgbaston
CHILDHOOD SPORTING HERO? Glenn McGrath
BIGGEST INFLUENCE ON YOUR DEVELOPMENT AS A CRICKETER (EXCLUDING PARENTS)?
Angus Fraser – we had lots of chats about bowling in my early years
WHAT WOULD YOU DO IF YOU WERE IN CHARGE OF COUNTY CRICKET? Change the rule about a bouncer being a wide – it should be a no-ball!
TWITTER: @finnysteve

Batting	Mat	Inns	NO	Runs	HS	Ave	SR	100	50	Ct	St
Tests	36	47	22	279	56	11.16	30.96	0	1	8	-
ODIs	69	30	13	136	35	8.00	60.98	0	0	15	-
T20Is	21	3	3	14	8*	-	73.68	0	0	6	-
First-class	159	195	63	1283	56	9.71	39.94	0	2	49	-
List A	144	59	25	411	42*	12.08	67.48	0	0	33	-
T20s	130	28	20	78	11*	9.75	85.71	0	0	40	-

Bowling	Mat	Balls	Runs	Wkts	BBI	BBM	Ave	Econ	SR	5w	10
Tests	36	6412	3800	125	6/79	9/187	30.40	3.55	51.2	5	0
ODIs	69	3550	2996	102	5/33	5/33	29.37	5.06	34.8	2	0
T20Is	21	480	583	20	3/16	3/16	21.59	7.28	17.7	0	0
First-class	159	28086	16247	563	9/37		28.85	3.47	49.8	15	1
List A	144	6821	5847	201	5/33	5/33	29.08	5.14	33.9	3	0
T20s	130	2644	3567	162	5/16	5/16	22.01	8.09	16.3	1	0

MATTHEW FISHER

RHB / RFM / R0 / W0

YORKSHIRE

FULL NAME: Matthew David Fisher
BORN: November 9, 1997, York
SQUAD NO: 7
HEIGHT: 6ft 2in
NICKNAME: Nemo
EDUCATION: Easingwold School, North Yorkshire
TEAMS: Yorkshire, England Lions
ROLE: Bowler
DEBUT: First-class: 2015; List A: 2013; T20: 2015

BEST BATTING: 47* Yorkshire vs Kent, Headingley, 2019
BEST BOWLING: 5-41 Yorkshire vs Somerset, Scarborough, 2021

BIGGEST INFLUENCE ON YOUR DEVELOPMENT AS A CRICKETER (EXCLUDING PARENTS)?
Tony Pickersgill, the former age-group bowling coach at Yorkshire. He helped make my bowling technically sound and adapted to a high level at a young age
WHAT WOULD YOU DO IF YOU WERE IN CHARGE OF COUNTY CRICKET? Make boundaries bigger, have six stumps in T20 cricket, blindfold the batsmen (batters' game)
SURPRISING FACT ABOUT YOU? I'm deaf in one ear
GUILTY PLEASURE? Gogglebox on TV
TWITTER: @9M_Fisher

Batting	Mat	Inns	NO	Runs	HS	Ave	SR	100	50	Ct	St
First-class	22	28	5	312	47*	13.56	30.37	0	0	7	-
List A	34	18	10	228	36*	28.50	98.70	0	0	10	-
T20s	39	12	5	61	19	8.71	129.78	0	0	12	-

Bowling	Mat	Balls	Runs	Wkts	BBI	BBM	Ave	Econ	SR	5w	10
First-class	22	3249	1750	63	5/41	9/64	27.77	3.23	51.5	2	0
List A	34	1384	1366	32	3/32	3/32	42.68	5.92	43.2	0	0
T20s	39	743	1128	43	5/22	5/22	26.23	9.10	17.2	1	0

FULL NAME: Luke Jack Fletcher
BORN: September 18, 1988, Nottingham
SQUAD NO: 19
HEIGHT: 6ft 6in
NICKNAME: Fletch
EDUCATION: Henry Mellish Comprehensive School, Nottingham
TEAMS: Nottinghamshire, Derbyshire, England U19, Surrey, Wellington
ROLE: Bowler
DEBUT: First-class: 2008; List A: 2008; T20: 2009

NOTTINGHAMSHIRE

BEST BATTING: 92 Nottinghamshire vs Hampshire, Southampton, 2009
BEST BOWLING: 7-37 Nottinghamshire vs Worcestershire, Trent Bridge, 2021
COUNTY CAP: 2014 (Nottinghamshire)

WHO IS YOUR LOOKALIKE? Shrek
FIRST CRICKET CLUB? Bulwell CC, Nottinghamshire
WHAT WOULD YOU CHANGE ABOUT THE STRUCTURE OF THE COUNTY SEASON? Fewer games
BIGGEST CRICKETING REGRET? Getting out on 92 – twice
WHO IS THE BEST BATTER/KEEPER/ALLROUNDER/BOWLER IN COUNTY CRICKET (EXCLUDING TEAMMATES)? Alastair Cook/Ben Foakes/Darren Stevens/Simon Harmer
MOST UNDERRATED PLAYER IN COUNTY CRICKET? Will Rhodes
WHO WOULD YOU MOST LIKE TO HAVE A NET WITH? Andrew Flintoff
WHAT MAKES YOU WORRY? My kids
WHAT GIVES YOU JOY? My kids
GUILTY PLEASURE? Toblerone
TWITTER: @fletcherluke

Batting	Mat	Inns	NO	Runs	HS	Ave	SR	100	50	Ct	St
First-class	130	191	33	2169	92	13.72	46.82	0	5	29	-
List A	79	42	17	505	53*	20.20	112.47	0	1	13	-
T20s	93	36	13	155	27	6.73	108.39	0	0	9	-

Bowling	Mat	Balls	Runs	Wkts	BBI	BBM	Ave	Econ	SR	5w	10
First-class	130	22245	10638	409	7/37	10/57	26.00	2.86	54.3	10	1
List A	79	3244	3067	87	5/56	5/56	35.25	5.67	37.2	1	0
T20s	93	1865	2585	102	5/43	5/43	25.34	8.31	18.2	1	0

BEN FOAKES

RHB / WK / R0 / W0

FULL NAME: Benjamin Thomas Foakes
BORN: February 15, 1993, Colchester, Essex
SQUAD NO: 7
HEIGHT: 6ft 2in
EDUCATION: Tendring Technology College, Essex
TEAMS: England, Surrey, Essex
ROLE: Wicketkeeper/batter
DEBUT: Test: 2018; ODI: 2019; T20I: 2019; First-class: 2011; List A: 2013; T20: 2014

BEST BATTING: 141* Surrey vs Hampshire, Southampton, 2016

COUNTY CAP: 2016 (Surrey)

WHO IS YOUR LOOKALIKE? Adrian Grenier (actor)
FIRST CRICKET CLUB? Frinton-on-Sea CC, Essex
WHAT WOULD YOU CHANGE ABOUT THE STRUCTURE OF THE COUNTY SEASON? Not have Championship matches randomly scheduled in the middle of the T20 competition
MOST UNDERRATED PLAYER IN COUNTY CRICKET? Tom Bailey
MOST BEAUTIFUL THING YOU HAVE EVER SEEN? Exuma, Bahamas
WHO WOULD YOU MOST LIKE TO HAVE A NET WITH? Kumar Sangakkara
WHAT GIVES YOU JOY? Travel
SURPRISING FACT ABOUT YOU? I once had a tooth glued back together after being involved in a car crash. Later, while I was batting, it came unstuck and was dangling, so I tore it out at lunch and batted with no front teeth

Batting	Mat	Inns	NO	Runs	HS	Ave	SR	100	50	Ct	St
Tests	8	16	3	410	107	31.53	46.75	1	1	14	5
ODIs	1	1	1	61	61*	-	80.26	0	1	2	1
T20Is	1	-	-	-	-	-	-	-	-	1	-
First-class	124	196	33	6282	141*	38.53	51.10	11	34	255	29
List A	73	63	11	1941	92	37.32	86.49	0	18	86	11
T20s	77	52	12	856	75*	21.40	124.05	0	4	38	10

Bowling	Mat	Balls	Runs	Wkts	BBI	BBM	Ave	Econ	SR	5w	10
Tests	8	-	-	-	-	-	-	-	-	-	-
ODIs	1	-	-	-	-	-	-	-	-	-	-
T20Is	1	-	-	-	-	-	-	-	-	-	-
First-class	124	6	6	0	-	-	-	6.00	-	0	0
List A	73	-	-	-	-	-	-	-	-	-	-
T20s	77	-	-	-	-	-	-	-	-	-	-

WILL FRAINE

RHB / RM / RO / WO

FULL NAME: William Alan Richard Fraine
BORN: June 13, 1996, Huddersfield
SQUAD NO: 31
EDUCATION: Silcoates School, Wakefield,
West Yorkshire; Bromsgrove Sixth Form
College, Worcestershire; Durham University
TEAMS: Yorkshire, Eagles, Nottinghamshire
ROLE: Batter
DEBUT: First-class: 2017; List A: 2018; T20: 2018

YORKSHIRE

BEST BATTING: 106 Yorkshire vs Surrey, Scarborough, 2019

NOTES: The top-order batter turned down an offer from Nottinghamshire to sign for his home county Yorkshire in October 2018. "There's always that pull of being a Yorkie lad," he said upon joining the White Rose. Fraine was born in Huddersfield and played for Yorkshire's age-group sides up to U19 level. After moving to a boarding school in Bromsgrove, Fraine played Second XI cricket for Worcestershire and Nottinghamshire. He made his first-class debut for Durham MCCU in 2016 but had to wait another three years to score his maiden hundred – 106 against Surrey at Scarborough. He underwent knee surgery before the start of the 2020 season but still managed to feature for Yorkshire in the Bob Willis Trophy and the T20 Blast. He played in all three competitions last summer without nailing down a place in any format

Batting	Mat	Inns	NO	Runs	HS	Ave	SR	100	50	Ct	St
First-class	23	37	1	829	106	23.02	41.78	1	2	11	-
List A	13	11	2	254	69*	28.22	114.41	0	1	5	-
T20s	26	25	8	321	44*	18.88	150.70	0	0	17	-

Bowling	Mat	Balls	Runs	Wkts	BBI	BBM	Ave	Econ	SR	5w	10
First-class	23	24	25	0	-	-	-	6.25	-	0	0
List A	13	-	-	-	-	-	-	-	-	-	-
T20s	26	-	-	-	-	-	-	-	-	-	-

JAMES FULLER

RHB / RFM / R0 / W0

FULL NAME: James Kerr Fuller
BORN: January 24, 1990, Cape Town, South Africa
SQUAD NO: 26
HEIGHT: 6ft 2in
NICKNAME: Foz
EDUCATION: Westlake Boys High School, Auckland; University of Otago
TEAMS: Hampshire, Auckland, England Lions, Gloucestershire, Middlesex, Otago
ROLE: Bowler
DEBUT: First-class: 2010; List A: 2011; T20: 2011

BEST BATTING: 93 Middlesex vs Somerset, Taunton, 2016
BEST BOWLING: 6-24 Otago vs Wellington, Dunedin, 2013
COUNTY CAP: 2011 (Gloucestershire)

FIRST CRICKET CLUB? North Shore CC, Auckland, New Zealand
MOST EXCITING DAY AS A CRICKETER? The Glorious Glosters winning the 2015 one-day trophy
CHILDHOOD SPORTING HERO? Shane Bond
SURPRISING FACT ABOUT YOU? I have held my breath for over three minutes and 30 seconds
TWITTER: @James_Fuller246

Batting	Mat	Inns	NO	Runs	HS	Ave	SR	100	50	Ct	St
First-class	59	78	10	1334	93	19.61	63.91	0	6	23	-
List A	69	55	17	884	55*	23.26	103.63	0	2	23	-
T20s	112	75	25	1038	53*	20.76	141.22	0	2	48	-

Bowling	Mat	Balls	Runs	Wkts	BBI	BBM	Ave	Econ	SR	5w	10
First-class	59	8864	5294	162	6/24	10/79	32.67	3.58	54.7	5	1
List A	69	2641	2610	79	6/35	6/35	33.03	5.92	33.4	1	0
T20s	112	1646	2454	97	6/28	6/28	25.29	8.94	16.9	1	0

GEORGE GARRETT

RHB / RMF / R0 / W0

FULL NAME: George Anthony Garrett
BORN: March 4, 2000, Harpenden, Hertfordshire
SQUAD NO: 44
HEIGHT: 6ft 4in
NICKNAME: Gazza
EDUCATION: Shrewsbury School; University of Birmingham
TEAMS: Warwickshire
ROLE: Bowler
DEBUT: First-class: 2019; List A: 2021; T20: 2019

BEST BATTING: 24 Warwickshire vs Essex, Edgbaston, 2019
BEST BOWLING: 2-53 Warwickshire vs Nottinghamshire, Trent Bridge, 2019

WHO IS YOUR LOOKALIKE? Francis Bourgeois (social media personality)
FIRST CRICKET CLUB? Harpenden CC, Hertfordshire
WHAT WOULD YOU CHANGE ABOUT THE STRUCTURE OF THE COUNTY SEASON? Set up an FA-Cup-style one-day competition which includes National (formerly Minor) Counties
WHO IS THE BEST BATTER/KEEPER/ALLROUNDER/BOWLER IN COUNTY CRICKET (EXCLUDING TEAMMATES)? Joe Clarke/Ben Foakes/Ryan Higgins/Michael Hogan
MOST UNDERRATED PLAYER IN COUNTY CRICKET? Sam Cook
MOST BEAUTIFUL THING YOU HAVE EVER SEEN? Lord's when the sun is out
HOBBIES? Reading
IF YOU COULD TURN BACK TIME... I'd have far more regulation on social media companies
WHO WOULD YOU MOST LIKE TO HAVE A NET WITH? Glenn McGrath
MAKE ONE PREDICTION FOR THE FUTURE OF CRICKET: Olympic T20 cricket
WHAT GIVES YOU JOY? Couple of beers down the pub with friends and family
TWITTER: @Georgegarrett14

Batting	Mat	Inns	NO	Runs	HS	Ave	SR	100	50	Ct	St
First-class	3	4	2	32	24	16.00	35.16	0	0	0	-
List A	4	2	0	8	7	4.00	44.44	0	0	0	-
T20s	2	-	-	-	-	-	-	-	-	0	-

Bowling	Mat	Balls	Runs	Wkts	BBI	BBM	Ave	Econ	SR	5w	10
First-class	3	509	302	8	2/53	4/125	37.75	3.55	63.6	0	0
List A	4	162	135	5	3/50	3/50	27.00	5.00	32.4	0	0
T20s	2	24	39	1	1/19	1/19	39.00	9.75	24.0	0	0

GEORGE GARTON

LHB / LF / R0 / W0

SUSSEX

FULL NAME: George Henry Simmons Garton
BORN: April 15, 1997, Brighton
SQUAD NO: 15
HEIGHT: 6ft 1in
NICKNAME: Garts
EDUCATION: Hurstpierpoint College, West Sussex
TEAMS: England, Sussex, Adelaide Strikers, Royal Challengers Bangalore
ROLE: Bowler
DEBUT: T20I: 2022; First-class: 2016; List A: 2016; T20: 2016

BEST BATTING: 97 Sussex vs Glamorgan, Cardiff, 2021
BEST BOWLING: 5-26 Sussex vs Essex, Hove, 2020

FIRST CRICKET CLUB? Preston Nomads CC, West Sussex
MOST EXCITING DAY AS A CRICKETER? Playing my first game for England Lions
CHILDHOOD SPORTING HERO? I didn't have one
BEST INNINGS YOU'VE SEEN? Phil Salt's Championship hundred against Derbyshire at Hove in 2018 – that was some serious ball-striking
WHAT WOULD YOU DO IF YOU WERE IN CHARGE OF COUNTY CRICKET? Remove the limit on bouncers
FAVOURITE SMELL? A bonfire
GUILTY PLEASURE? Cadbury Dairy Milk
TWITTER: @george_garton

Batting	Mat	Inns	NO	Runs	HS	Ave	SR	100	50	Ct	St
T20Is	1	1	0	2	2	2.00	50.00	0	0	0	-
First-class	24	34	6	569	97	20.32	55.89	0	4	14	-
List A	24	11	2	103	38	11.44	86.55	0	0	11	-
T20s	51	25	8	295	46	17.35	131.11	0	0	14	-

Bowling	Mat	Balls	Runs	Wkts	BBI	BBM	Ave	Econ	SR	5w	10
T20Is	1	24	57	1	1/57	1/57	57.00	14.25	24.0	0	0
First-class	24	2804	1890	53	5/26	9/76	35.66	4.04	52.9	1	0
List A	24	942	993	29	4/43	4/43	34.24	6.32	32.4	0	0
T20s	51	899	1307	56	4/16	4/16	23.33	8.72	16.0	0	0

EMILIO GAY

LHB / RM / R0 / W0

FULL NAME: Emilio Nico Gay
BORN: April 14, 2000, Bedford
SQUAD NO: 19
HEIGHT: 6ft 2in
NICKNAME: Nico
EDUCATION: Rushmoor School, Bedford;
Bedford School
TEAMS: Northamptonshire
ROLE: Batter
DEBUT: First-class: 2019; List A: 2021; T20: 2021

BEST BATTING: 101 Northamptonshire vs Kent, Canterbury, 2021
BEST BOWLING: 1-8 Northamptonshire vs Kent, Northampton, 2021

WHO IS YOUR LOOKALIKE? Michael B Jordan (actor)
FIRST CRICKET CLUB? Bedford CC, Bedfordshire
WHAT WOULD YOU CHANGE ABOUT THE STRUCTURE OF THE COUNTY SEASON? Have
three divisions for the County Championship
BIGGEST INFLUENCE ON YOUR DEVELOPMENT AS A CRICKETER (EXCLUDING PARENTS)?
Jack Mousley – my coach at Bedfordshire
WHAT WOULD A FLY ON THE WALL HEAR IN YOUR DRESSING ROOM? Players talking about
other players and coaches (good and bad)
MOST BEAUTIFUL THING YOU HAVE EVER SEEN? People in the Caribbean living in poverty
and enjoying life
WHO WOULD YOU MOST AND LEAST LIKE TO HAVE A NET WITH? Most – Sachin Tendulkar.
Least – Chris Lynn
WHAT MAKES YOU WORRY? Relationship issues
GUILTY PLEASURE? Reality TV shows
TWITTER: @emilio_nico1

Batting	Mat	Inns	NO	Runs	HS	Ave	SR	100	50	Ct	St
First-class	14	23	1	512	101	23.27	48.94	1	2	10	-
List A	8	8	3	189	84*	37.80	89.15	0	1	3	-
T20s	1	1	0	15	15	15.00	150.00	0	0	0	-

Bowling	Mat	Balls	Runs	Wkts	BBI	BBM	Ave	Econ	SR	5w	10
First-class	14	30	22	1	1/8	1/8	22.00	4.40	30.0	0	0
List A	8	18	19	0	-	-	-	6.33	-	0	0
T20s	1	-	-	-	-	-	-	-	-	-	-

BEN GEDDES

RHB / R0 / W0

FULL NAME: Benedict Brodie Albert Geddes
BORN: July 31, 2001, Epsom, Surrey
SQUAD NO: 14
HEIGHT: 6ft 2in
NICKNAME: Geddo
EDUCATION: St John's School, Leatherhead
TEAMS: Surrey
ROLE: Batter
DEBUT: First-class: 2021; List A: 2021; T20: 2021

BEST BATTING: 15 Surrey vs Hampshire, Southampton, 2021

FIRST CRICKET CLUB? Ashtead CC, Surrey
WHO IS THE BEST BATTER/KEEPER/ALLROUNDER/BOWLER IN COUNTY CRICKET (EXCLUDING TEAMMATES)? Joe Root/Ben Foakes/Ben Stokes/James Anderson
MOST UNDERRATED PLAYER IN COUNTY CRICKET? Sam Cook
HOBBIES? Golf
WHO WOULD YOU MOST AND LEAST LIKE TO HAVE A NET WITH? Most – AB de Villiers. Least – Muttiah Muralitharan
WHAT GIVES YOU JOY? Straight drives on the golf course
TWITTER: @BenGeddes123

Batting	Mat	Inns	NO	Runs	HS	Ave	SR	100	50	Ct	St
First-class	1	2	0	19	15	9.50	27.53	0	0	0	-
List A	4	4	1	84	32	28.00	90.32	0	0	0	-
T20s	6	6	0	44	28	7.33	89.79	0	0	0	-

Bowling	Mat	Balls	Runs	Wkts	BBI	BBM	Ave	Econ	SR	5w	10
First-class	1	-	-	-	-	-	-	-	-	-	-
List A	4	-	-	-	-	-	-	-	-	-	-
T20s	6	-	-	-	-	-	-	-	-	-	-

BEN GIBBON

RHB / LFM / R0 / W0

FULL NAME: Benjamin James Gibbon
BORN: June 9, 2000, Chester, Cheshire
SQUAD NO: TBC
HEIGHT: 6ft 3in
EDUCATION: Ellesmere College, Shropshire;
Myerscough College, Lancashire
TEAMS: Worcestershire
ROLE: Bowler

WHO IS YOUR LOOKALIKE? Chris Hemsworth (actor)
FIRST CRICKET CLUB? Tattenhall CC, Cheshire
WHO IS THE BEST BATTER/KEEPER/ALLROUNDER/BOWLER IN COUNTY CRICKET
(EXCLUDING TEAMMATES)? Rob Yates/Ben Foakes/Luke Wood/Luke Fletcher
HOBBIES? Biking and golf
WHO WOULD YOU LEAST LIKE TO HAVE A NET WITH? Steve Smith
MAKE ONE PREDICTION FOR THE FUTURE OF CRICKET: More franchise competitions around
the world
WHAT DO YOU MOST ENJOY LISTENING TO? Pop music
NOTES: The Pears signed the promising left-arm seamer on a two-year deal last September
after he impressed for the club's Second XI. Gibbon cut his teeth in the National Counties
Championship and was named Cheshire's Bowler of the Year for 2021. He has also played
for Lancashire's Second XI. "I've been looking to sign a contract for a long time, and I'm
delighted that the hard work has paid off," said Gibbon. "I've been earning a living working
on construction sites doing the building work. It is hard graft, and I'm happy not to have to
do it anymore. Every time I was at work, I was thinking, 'I'd much rather be a professional
cricketer'." Paul Pridgeon, chairman of Worcestershire's cricket steering group, added:
"Ben brings something different to our group of bowlers in being a left-armer, and I know
Alex Gidman [the head coach] and Alan Richardson [the bowling coach] are quite excited
about him"

OLIVER GIBSON

RHB / RFM / R0 / W0

DURHAM

FULL NAME: Oliver James Gibson
BORN: July 7, 2000, Northallerton, Yorkshire
SQUAD NO: 73
HEIGHT: 5ft 11in
NICKNAME: Gibbo
EDUCATION: Queen Elizabeth Grammar
School, Hexham, Northumberland;
Derwentside Sixth Form College, Consett,
County Durham
TEAMS: Durham
ROLE: Bowler

NOTES: A seamer who has come through the Durham Academy, Gibson has featured in matchday squads in the County Championship and the T20 Blast but is still awaiting his first-team debut. Gibson signed with the county in November 2019 after making three appearances in the previous year's Second XI Championship. He also played a handful of Second XI Trophy matches in a Durham side which reached the final, where they lost to Kent, and took seven wickets at 16.57 in four second-team T20 games. Since then the 20-year-old has been a regular performer in the club's Second XI and he signed a new one-year deal with Durham last October. Gibson has played club cricket for Shotley Bridge CC in the north-west of County Durham, home of his boyhood hero Paul Collingwood, before turning out for Burnopfield CC last summer

NATHAN GILCHRIST

RHB / RFM / R0 / W0

FULL NAME: Nathan Nicholas Gilchrist
BORN: June 11, 2000, Harare, Zimbabwe
SQUAD NO: 17
HEIGHT: 6ft 5in
NICKNAME: Gilly
EDUCATION: St Stithians School, Johannesburg; King's College, Taunton
TEAMS: Kent, Somerset
ROLE: Bowler
DEBUT: First-class: 2020; List A: 2021

BEST BATTING: 25 Kent vs Surrey, The Oval, 2020
BEST BOWLING: 5-38 Kent vs Worcestershire, Canterbury, 2021

FIRST CRICKET CLUB? Staplegrove CC, Somerset. The cricket field was right next to a herd of cows
WHAT WOULD YOU CHANGE ABOUT THE STRUCTURE OF THE COUNTY SEASON? Start and finish each tournament in one block
WHO IS THE BEST BATTER/KEEPER/ALLROUNDER/BOWLER IN COUNTY CRICKET (EXCLUDING TEAMMATES)? David Bedingham/Ben Foakes/Craig Overton/Simon Harmer
MOST UNDERRATED PLAYER IN COUNTY CRICKET? James Hildreth
WHAT WOULD A FLY ON THE WALL HEAR IN YOUR DRESSING ROOM? Zak Crawley's horrendous jokes
MOST BEAUTIFUL THING YOU HAVE EVER SEEN? Victoria Falls, Zimbabwe
HOBBIES? Fashion
WHO WOULD YOU MOST AND LEAST LIKE TO HAVE A NET WITH? Dale Steyn because he's my sporting idol/Shoaib Akhtar because he'd take my head off!
MAKE ONE PREDICTION FOR THE FUTURE OF CRICKET: The Hundred will become an Olympic sport
WHAT DO YOU MOST ENJOY LISTENING TO? Hip-hop
WHAT MAKES YOU WORRY? Global warming
TWITTER: @nathgilchrist

Batting	Mat	Inns	NO	Runs	HS	Ave	SR	100	50	Ct	St
First-class	10	10	1	90	25	10.00	35.85	0	0	2	-
List A	6	4	1	19	8	6.33	86.36	0	0	0	-

Bowling	Mat	Balls	Runs	Wkts	BBI	BBM	Ave	Econ	SR	5w	10
First-class	10	1015	672	30	5/38	8/74	22.40	3.97	33.8	1	0
List A	6	153	181	8	5/45	5/45	22.62	7.09	19.1	1	0

RICHARD GLEESON

RHB / RFM

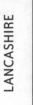

FULL NAME: Richard James Gleeson
BORN: December 2, 1987, Blackpool
SQUAD NO: 11
HEIGHT: 6ft 4in
NICKNAME: Granddaddy
EDUCATION: Baines High School,
Lancashire; University of Cumbria
TEAMS: Lancashire, England Lions,
Melbourne Renegades, Northamptonshire,
Rangpur Riders
ROLE: Bowler
DEBUT: First-class: 2015; List A: 2016; T20: 2016

BEST BATTING: 7* Northamptonshire vs Worcestershire, Worcester, 2016 (T20)
BEST BOWLING: 3-12 Northamptonshire v Warwickshire, Edgbaston, 2016 (T20)

FIRST CRICKET CLUB? Blackpool CC, Lancashire
FAMILY TIES? My father ran the bar at our local cricket club, my sister ran the kitchen, and my brother-in-law was the first XI captain
WHO IS THE BEST BATTER/KEEPER/BOWLER IN COUNTY CRICKET (EXCLUDING TEAMMATES)? Alastair Cook/Ben Cox/Liam Norwell
MOST UNDERRATED PLAYER IN COUNTY CRICKET? Ben Foakes
HOBBIES? Fishing
IF YOU COULD TURN BACK TIME... I wouldn't change my bowling action
MAKE ONE PREDICTION FOR THE FUTURE OF CRICKET: A resurgence for Test cricket
WHAT DO YOU MOST ENJOY LISTENING TO? Oasis
WHAT MAKES YOU WORRY? Practising yorkers in the nets against batters
SURPRISING FACT ABOUT YOU? I am a published poet
TWITTER: @RicGleeson
NOTES: Gleeson has signed a T20-only contract with Lancashire for 2022

Batting	Mat	Inns	NO	Runs	HS	Ave	SR	100	50	Ct	St
First-class	34	39	16	259	31	11.26	34.07	0	0	8	-
List A	21	13	5	53	13	6.62	42.06	0	0	3	-
T20s	52	12	7	24	7*	4.80	82.75	0	0	11	-

Bowling	Mat	Balls	Runs	Wkts	BBI	BBM	Ave	Econ	SR	5w	10
First-class	34	5526	3053	143	6/43	10/113	21.34	3.31	38.6	10	1
List A	21	841	816	28	5/47	5/47	29.14	5.82	30.0	1	0
T20s	52	1009	1346	50	3/12	3/12	26.92	8.00	20.1	0	0

BRANDON GLOVER

RHB / RFM / R0 / W0

FULL NAME: Brandon Dale Glover
BORN: April 3, 1997, Johannesburg, SA
SQUAD NO: 20
HEIGHT: 6ft 2in
NICKNAME: The Camel
EDUCATION: St Stithians College, Johannesburg; Stellenbosch University, Western Province
TEAMS: Netherlands, Northamptonshire, Boland, South Africa U19
ROLE: Bowler
DEBUT: ODI: 2019; T20I: 2019; First-class: 2016; List A: 2017; T20: 2019

BEST BATTING: 12* Boland vs Gauteng, Paarl, 2019
BEST BOWLING: 4-83 Boland vs Free State, Bloemfontein, 2017

WHO IS YOUR LOOKALIKE? Tobey Maguire (mainly when I was younger)
FIRST CRICKET CLUB? Old Parks Sports Club, Johannesburg
WHAT WOULD YOU CHANGE ABOUT THE STRUCTURE OF THE COUNTY SEASON? Don't allow The Hundred to overlap with the 50-over competition so that all players can play in both
BIGGEST INFLUENCE ON YOUR DEVELOPMENT AS A CRICKETER (EXCLUDING PARENTS)? Along with my school coaches, simply watching Brett Lee and Dale Steyn made me want to break down their bowling actions and try to copy them myself
MOST BEAUTIFUL THING YOU HAVE EVER SEEN? The first pint after lockdown
WHAT MAKES YOU WORRY? When I have to cook for everyone
WHAT GIVES YOU JOY? Bowling

Batting	Mat	Inns	NO	Runs	HS	Ave	SR	100	50	Ct	St
ODIs	6	4	3	21	18	21.00	60.00	0	0	2	-
T20Is	21	6	3	2	1*	0.66	18.18	0	0	3	-
First-class	10	15	6	38	12*	4.22	30.64	0	0	1	-
List A	11	9	5	76	27	19.00	65.51	0	0	2	-
T20s	35	11	8	12	6*	4.00	48.00	0	0	7	-

Bowling	Mat	Balls	Runs	Wkts	BBI	BBM	Ave	Econ	SR	5w	10
ODIs	6	330	298	8	3/43	3/43	37.25	5.41	41.2	0	0
T20Is	21	426	481	30	4/12	4/12	16.03	6.77	14.2	0	0
First-class	10	1320	827	24	4/83	5/104	34.45	3.75	55.0	0	0
List A	11	506	459	11	3/43	3/43	41.72	5.44	46.0	0	0
T20s	35	626	809	41	4/12	4/12	19.73	7.75	15.2	0	0

BILLY GODLEMAN

LHB / LB / R2 / W0

DERBYSHIRE

FULL NAME: Billy Ashley Godleman
BORN: February 11, 1989, Camden, London
SQUAD NO: 1
HEIGHT: 6ft 2in
NICKNAME: Chief
EDUCATION: Islington Green School, London
TEAMS: Derbyshire, Essex, Middlesex
ROLE: Batter
DEBUT: First-class: 2005; List A: 2007; T20: 2006

BEST BATTING: 227 Derbyshire vs Glamorgan, Swansea, 2019

COUNTY CAP: 2015 (Derbyshire)

FIRST CRICKET CLUB? Brondesbury CC, London
WHAT WOULD YOU CHANGE ABOUT THE STRUCTURE OF THE COUNTY SEASON? More Championship cricket in the middle of the summer
BIGGEST INFLUENCE ON YOUR DEVELOPMENT AS A CRICKETER (EXCLUDING PARENTS)? David Houghton (former Derbyshire coach) – he has that rare skill of keeping things simple
WHO IS THE BEST BATTER/KEEPER/ALLROUNDER/BOWLER IN COUNTY CRICKET (EXCLUDING TEAMMATES)? Tom Westley/Adam Wheater/Matt Critchley/Simon Harmer
MOST BEAUTIFUL THING YOU HAVE EVER SEEN? My baby daughter
WHO WOULD YOU MOST LIKE TO HAVE A NET WITH? Shane Warne and Glenn McGrath – to experience what it was like to face them together
MAKE ONE PREDICTION FOR THE FUTURE OF CRICKET: Matt Critchley to play for England
WHAT DO YOU MOST ENJOY LISTENING TO? Wayne Madsen talking cricket
WHAT MAKES YOU WORRY? Not having enough sleep

Batting	Mat	Inns	NO	Runs	HS	Ave	SR	100	50	Ct	St
First-class	173	311	15	9559	227	32.29	47.13	22	44	105	-
List A	71	69	8	2687	137	44.04	79.02	7	12	23	-
T20s	96	90	7	1867	92	22.49	114.82	0	12	43	-

Bowling	Mat	Balls	Runs	Wkts	BBI	BBM	Ave	Econ	SR	5w	10
First-class	173	30	35	0	-	-	-	7.00	-	0	0
List A	71	-	-	-	-	-	-	-	-	-	-
T20s	96	-	-	-	-	-	-	-	-	-	-

G

FULL NAME: Zafar Gohar Khan
BORN: February 01, 1995, Lahore, Pakistan
SQUAD NO: 77
TEAMS: Pakistan, Gloucestershire, Central Punjab, Islamabad United, Lahore Blues, Lahore Qalandars, State Bank of Pakistan, Sui Southern Gas Corporation, Zarai Taraqiati Bank Limited
ROLE: Bowler
DEBUT: Test: 2021; ODI: 2015; First-class: 2013; List A: 2013; T20: 2013

GLOUCESTERSHIRE

BEST BATTING: 100* Central Punjab vs Baluchistan, Quetta, 2019
BEST BOWLING: 7-79 Central Punjab vs Northern, Faisalabad, 2019

TWITTER: @iamzafargohar
NOTES: Gloucestershire fans will be delighted by the return of Zafar Gohar, who excelled during a brief spell with the club last year. Having made his Test debut against New Zealand in January 2021 – six years after playing his first ODI – the Pakistani left-arm spinner arrived at Bristol in late August and collected 20 wickets in four Championship matches at an average of 14.35, including a career-best match haul of 11-101 versus Durham. His bowling strike rate of 35.2 was the best of any spinner in the competition. He re-joins the club as a retained player for the first few months of the season and will turn full-time for August and September, meaning he will be available for selection from the first match of the season on a pay-by-appearance basis until the end of July

Batting	Mat	Inns	NO	Runs	HS	Ave	SR	100	50	Ct	St
Tests	1	2	0	71	37	35.50	56.34	0	0	0	-
ODIs	1	1	0	15	15	15.00	100.00	0	0	0	-
First-class	51	72	9	1415	100*	22.46	48.34	1	5	22	-
List A	59	47	9	504	53	13.26	82.48	0	1	13	-
T20s	61	30	13	255	32*	15.00	119.15	0	0	19	-

Bowling	Mat	Balls	Runs	Wkts	BBI	BBM	Ave	Econ	SR	5w	10
Tests	1	192	159	0	-	-	-	4.96	-	0	0
ODIs	1	60	54	2	2/54	2/54	27.00	5.40	30.0	0	0
First-class	51	11378	5651	189	7/79	11/101	29.89	2.97	60.2	10	3
List A	59	2968	2455	87	5/56	5/56	28.21	4.96	34.1	1	0
T20s	61	1199	1544	67	4/14	4/14	23.04	7.72	17.8	0	0

LEWIS GOLDSWORTHY

RHB / SLA / R0 / W0

SOMERSET

FULL NAME: Lewis Peter Goldsworthy
BORN: January 8, 2001, Cornwall
SQUAD NO: 44
HEIGHT: 5ft 7in
NICKNAME: Golders
EDUCATION: Cambourne Science & International Academy, Cornwall; Millfield School, Somerset
TEAMS: Somerset, England U19
ROLE: Allrounder
DEBUT: First-class: 2021; List A: 2021; T20: 2020

BEST BATTING: 48 Somerset vs Surrey, The Oval, 2021

FIRST CRICKET CLUB? Troon CC, Cornwall
WHO IS THE BEST BATTER/KEEPER/BOWLER IN COUNTY CRICKET (EXCLUDING TEAMMATES)? Ollie Pope/Ben Foakes/Darren Stevens
MOST UNDERRATED PLAYER IN COUNTY CRICKET? Jordan Cox
WHAT WOULD A FLY ON THE WALL HEAR IN YOUR DRESSING ROOM? Debate about the Fantasy Premier League
MOST BEAUTIFUL THING YOU HAVE EVER SEEN? St Ives, Cornwall
WHO WOULD YOU MOST LIKE TO HAVE A NET WITH? Monty Panesar
WHAT MAKES YOU WORRY? When Mohamed Salah misses
TWITTER: @lewisgoldsworthy

Batting	Mat	Inns	NO	Runs	HS	Ave	SR	100	50	Ct	St
First-class	10	15	1	297	48	21.21	38.82	0	0	1	-
List A	8	7	1	381	96	63.50	87.18	0	4	2	-
T20s	15	12	2	210	48	21.00	113.51	0	0	4	-

Bowling	Mat	Balls	Runs	Wkts	BBI	BBM	Ave	Econ	SR	5w	10
First-class	10	144	45	0	-	-	-	1.87	-	0	0
List A	8	240	210	3	1/17	1/17	70.00	5.25	80.0	0	0
T20s	15	252	312	14	3/14	3/14	22.28	7.42	18.0	0	0

DOMINIC GOODMAN — RHB / RMF / R0 / W0

FULL NAME: Dominic Charles Goodman
BORN: October 23, 2000, Ashford, Kent
SQUAD NO: 83
HEIGHT: 6ft 5in
NICKNAME: Len
EDUCATION: Dr Challenor's Grammar School, Amersham, Buckinghamshire; University of Exeter
TEAMS: Gloucestershire
ROLE: Bowler
DEBUT: First-class: 2021

BEST BATTING: 9* Gloucestershire vs Hampshire, Southampton, 2021
BEST BOWLING: 2-19 Gloucestershire vs Somerset, Taunton, 2021

MOST EXCITING DAY AS A CRICKETER? Being 12th man when Gloucestershire pulled off a fourth-day victory at Derby
CHILDHOOD SPORTING HERO? Andrew Flintoff
BIGGEST INFLUENCE ON YOUR DEVELOPMENT AS A CRICKETER (EXCLUDING PARENTS)? Tim Hancock – he brought me through the Gloucestershire Academy
WHAT WOULD YOU DO IF YOU WERE IN CHARGE OF COUNTY CRICKET? Introduce day/night Championship fixtures at the beginning and end of the season, free entry for children to T20 Blast games
FAVOURITE SMELL? A flat white early in the morning
GUILTY PLEASURE? Pringles
TWITTER: @dominic_goodman

Batting	Mat	Inns	NO	Runs	HS	Ave	SR	100	50	Ct	St
First-class	4	5	3	20	9*	10.00	17.24	0	0	0	-

Bowling	Mat	Balls	Runs	Wkts	BBI	BBM	Ave	Econ	SR	5w	10
First-class	4	624	252	5	2/19	3/55	50.40	2.42	124.8	0	0

ANDY GORVIN

RHB / RMF / R0 / W0

FULL NAME: Andrew William Gorvin
BORN: May 10, 1997, Winchester, Hampshire
SQUAD NO: 11
HEIGHT: 5ft 9in
NICKNAME: Gorv
EDUCATION: Portsmouth High School;
Cardiff Metropolitan University
TEAMS: Glamorgan
ROLE: Bowler
DEBUT: List A: 2021

WHO IS YOUR LOOKALIKE? Owen Farrell
FIRST CRICKET CLUB? Hayling Island CC, Hampshire
WHAT WOULD YOU CHANGE ABOUT THE STRUCTURE OF THE COUNTY SEASON? Play more
Championship matches during the height of the summer
WHO IS THE BEST BATTER/KEEPER/BOWLER IN COUNTY CRICKET (EXCLUDING
TEAMMATES)? James Vince/Ben Foakes/Sam Cook
MOST UNDERRATED PLAYER IN COUNTY CRICKET? Keith Barker
MOST BEAUTIFUL THING YOU HAVE EVER SEEN? The Great Wall of China
HOBBIES? Tennis and golf
WHO WOULD YOU MOST AND LEAST LIKE TO HAVE A NET WITH? Most – Sachin Tendulkar.
Least – Mitchell Johnson (don't think he'd hold back when bowling to a Pom in the nets)
MAKE ONE PREDICTION FOR THE FUTURE OF CRICKET: Red-ball cricket will have a
resurgence in this country
WHAT MAKES YOU WORRY? I don't worry too much, apart from perhaps about family and
friends
WHAT GIVES YOU JOY? Playing golf on a warm, sunny, calm day
TWITTER: @gorv97

Batting	Mat	Inns	NO	Runs	HS	Ave	SR	100	50	Ct	St
List A	4	1	1	12	12*	-	66.66	0	0	1	-

Bowling	Mat	Balls	Runs	Wkts	BBI	BBM	Ave	Econ	SR	5w	10
List A	4	108	74	1	1/11	1/11	74.00	4.11	108.0	0	0

BEN GREEN
RHB / RFM / R0 / W0

FULL NAME: Benjamin George Frederick Green
BORN: September 28, 1997, Exeter, Devon
SQUAD NO: 54
HEIGHT: 6ft 2in
NICKNAME: Neil
EDUCATION: St Peter's Preparatory School, Lympstone, Devon; Exeter School
TEAMS: Somerset, England U19
ROLE: Allrounder
DEBUT: First-class: 2018; List A: 2018; T20: 2016

BEST BATTING: 54 Somerset vs Glamorgan, Taunton, 2020
BEST BOWLING: 1-8 Somerset vs Hampshire, Southampton, 2018

WHO IS YOUR LOOKALIKE? Freddie Prinze Jr (actor)
FIRST CRICKET CLUB? Clyst St George CC, East Devon
WHO IS THE BEST BATTER/KEEPER/ALLROUNDER/BOWLER IN COUNTY CRICKET (EXCLUDING TEAMMATES)? Alastair Cook/Ben Foakes/Darren Stevens/Chris Rushworth
MOST UNDERRATED PLAYER IN COUNTY CRICKET? Jake Libby
WHAT WOULD A FLY ON THE WALL HEAR IN YOUR DRESSING ROOM? Max Waller
MOST BEAUTIFUL THING YOU HAVE EVER SEEN? Serpentine Falls, Western Australia
HOBBIES? Golf
WHO WOULD YOU MOST LIKE TO HAVE A NET WITH? Andrew Flintoff
TWITTER: @Ben_Green28

Batting	Mat	Inns	NO	Runs	HS	Ave	SR	100	50	Ct	St
First-class	9	17	1	324	54	20.25	40.00	0	1	5	-
List A	8	6	3	145	87	48.33	109.02	0	1	1	-
T20s	18	11	3	165	43*	20.62	132.00	0	0	12	-

Bowling	Mat	Balls	Runs	Wkts	BBI	BBM	Ave	Econ	SR	5w	10
First-class	9	282	110	2	1/8	1/17	55.00	2.34	141.0	0	0
List A	8	273	249	9	3/64	3/64	27.66	5.47	30.3	0	0
T20s	18	180	265	8	4/26	4/26	33.12	8.83	22.5	0	0

LEWIS GREGORY

RHB / RFM / R0 / W1

SOMERSET

FULL NAME: Lewis Gregory
BORN: May 24, 1992, Plymouth, Devon
SQUAD NO: 24
HEIGHT: 6ft
NICKNAME: Mowgli
EDUCATION: Hele's School, Plymouth
TEAMS: England, Somerset, Brisbane Heat, Islamabad United, Karachi Kings, Peshawar Zalmi, Rangpur Rangers
ROLE: Allrounder
DEBUT: ODI: 2021; T20I: 2019; First-class: 2011; List A: 2010; T20: 2011

BEST BATTING: 137 Somerset vs Middlesex, Lord's, 2017
BEST BOWLING: 6-32 Somerset vs Kent, Canterbury, 2019
COUNTY CAP: 2015

MOST EXCITING DAY AS A CRICKETER? Taking my maiden first-class five-wicket haul at Lord's and scoring my maiden first-class hundred at the same ground
CHILDHOOD SPORTING HERO? Tiger Woods
SURPRISING FACT ABOUT YOU? I'm a black belt in taekwondo
TWITTER: @Lewisgregory23

Batting	Mat	Inns	NO	Runs	HS	Ave	SR	100	50	Ct	St
ODIs	3	2	0	117	77	58.50	100.86	0	1	0	-
T20Is	9	7	1	45	15	7.50	109.75	0	0	0	-
First-class	98	142	15	2958	137	23.29	58.41	3	11	56	-
List A	79	59	6	1323	105*	24.96	100.83	1	8	27	-
T20s	157	123	29	1943	76*	20.67	139.18	0	5	70	-

Bowling	Mat	Balls	Runs	Wkts	BBI	BBM	Ave	Econ	SR	5w	10
ODIs	3	114	97	4	3/44	3/44	24.25	5.10	28.5	0	0
T20Is	9	78	117	2	1/10	1/10	58.50	9.00	39.0	0	0
First-class	98	14285	7745	303	6/32	11/53	25.56	3.25	47.1	15	2
List A	79	3062	3038	110	4/23	4/23	27.61	5.95	27.8	0	0
T20s	157	2390	3584	134	5/24	5/24	26.74	8.99	17.8	1	0

GAVIN GRIFFITHS

RHB / RFM / R0 / W0

FULL NAME: Gavin Timothy Griffiths
BORN: November 19, 1993, Ormskirk, Lancashire
SQUAD NO: 93
HEIGHT: 6ft 2in
NICKNAME: Gavlar
EDUCATION: St Michael's CE High School, Chorley; St Mary's College, Crosby
TEAMS: Leicestershire, England U19, Hampshire, Lancashire
ROLE: Bowler
DEBUT: First-class: 2017; List A: 2014; T20: 2015

BEST BATTING: 40 Leicestershire vs Middlesex, Leicester, 2018
BEST BOWLING: 6-49 Leicestershire vs Durham, Chester-le-Street, 2018

WHO IS YOUR LOOKALIKE? Gareth Gates (singer)
FIRST CRICKET CLUB? Ormskirk CC, Lancashire
WHAT WOULD YOU CHANGE ABOUT THE STRUCTURE OF THE COUNTY SEASON? Introduce a week-long break in the middle of the season
BIGGEST INFLUENCE ON YOUR DEVELOPMENT AS A CRICKETER (EXCLUDING PARENTS)? John Stanworth, Lancashire Academy director
WHO IS THE BEST BATTER/KEEPER/ALLROUNDER/BOWLER IN COUNTY CRICKET (EXCLUDING TEAMMATES)? James Vince/Ben Foakes/Darren Stevens/Tom Bailey
MOST UNDERRATED PLAYER IN COUNTY CRICKET? Ben Raine
WHAT WOULD A FLY ON THE WALL HEAR IN YOUR DRESSING ROOM? Callum Parkinson moaning
MAKE ONE PREDICTION FOR THE FUTURE OF CRICKET: There will be no umpires in T20 cricket – it will all be video-based with a referee on the field
WHAT DO YOU MOST ENJOY LISTENING TO? Coldplay
SURPRISING FACT ABOUT YOU? I have played chess for England
GUILTY PLEASURE? Singing in the car
TWITTER: @Gavvlar

Batting	Mat	Inns	NO	Runs	HS	Ave	SR	100	50	Ct	St
First-class	31	42	16	370	40	14.23	35.10	0	0	4	-
List A	26	12	8	39	15*	9.75	41.05	0	0	11	-
T20s	60	20	17	56	12	18.66	88.88	0	0	12	-

Bowling	Mat	Balls	Runs	Wkts	BBI	BBM	Ave	Econ	SR	5w	10
First-class	31	4141	2324	67	6/49	10/83	34.68	3.36	61.8	1	1
List A	26	1174	1175	33	4/30	4/30	35.60	6.00	35.5	0	0
T20s	60	992	1457	53	4/24	4/24	27.49	8.81	18.7	0	0

NICK GUBBINS

LHB / LB / R1 / W0

HAMPSHIRE

FULL NAME: Nicholas Richard Trail Gubbins
BORN: December 31, 1993, Richmond, Surrey
SQUAD NO: 31
HEIGHT: 6ft
NICKNAME: Cathy
EDUCATION: Radley College, Oxfordshire; University of Leeds
TEAMS: Hampshire, England Lions, Middlesex, Tuskers
ROLE: Batter
DEBUT: First-class: 2013; List A: 2014; T20: 2015

BEST BATTING: 201* Middlesex vs Lancashire, Lord's, 2016
BEST BOWLING: 4-41 Tuskers vs Eagles, Harare, 2022
COUNTY CAP: 2016 (Middlesex)

WHO IS YOUR LOOKALIKE? Doctor Cathy Speed (physician)
FIRST CRICKET CLUB? Stirlands CC, Chichester, West Sussex
FAMILY TIES? My dad played one ODI for Singapore
WHAT WOULD YOU CHANGE ABOUT THE STRUCTURE OF THE COUNTY SEASON?
Better pitches plus fewer matches equals higher-quality cricket and better preparation for the Test team
WHO IS THE BEST BATTER/KEEPER/ALLROUNDER/BOWLER IN COUNTY CRICKET (EXCLUDING TEAMMATES)? Sam Robson/John Simpson/Ryan Higgins/Tim Murtagh
MOST UNDERRATED PLAYER IN COUNTY CRICKET? Gary Ballance
MOST BEAUTIFUL THING YOU HAVE EVER SEEN? The Big Five in Africa
MAKE ONE PREDICTION FOR THE FUTURE OF CRICKET: 50-over cricket will subside… there will be only Test and T20 cricket
WHAT MAKES YOU WORRY? Hospitals
WHAT GIVES YOU JOY? Chelsea FC
GUILTY PLEASURE? Oreo ice cream
TWITTER: @ngubbins18

Batting	Mat	Inns	NO	Runs	HS	Ave	SR	100	50	Ct	St
First-class	93	166	4	5517	201*	34.05	50.03	11	32	38	-
List A	63	62	3	2385	141	40.42	94.75	6	14	12	-
T20s	39	35	0	515	53	14.71	117.31	0	1	15	-

Bowling	Mat	Balls	Runs	Wkts	BBI	BBM	Ave	Econ	SR	5w	10
First-class	93	239	115	5	4/41	4/41	23.00	2.88	47.8	0	0
List A	63	90	81	4	4/38	4/38	20.25	5.40	22.5	0	0
T20s	39	30	30	1	1/22	1/22	30.00	6.00	30.0	0	0

BROOKE GUEST

RHB / WK / R0 / W0

FULL NAME: Brooke David Guest
BORN: May 14, 1997, Whitworth Park, Manchester
SQUAD NO: 29
HEIGHT: 5ft 11in
NICKNAME: Guesty
EDUCATION: Kent Street Senior High School, Perth; Murdoch University, Perth
TEAMS: Derbyshire, Australia U19, Lancashire
ROLE: Wicketkeeper
DEBUT: First-class: 2018; List A: 2019; T20: 2020

BEST BATTING: 116 Derbyshire vs Leicestershire, Derby, 2021

FIRST CRICKET CLUB? South Perth CC, Australia
BIGGEST INFLUENCE ON YOUR DEVELOPMENT AS A CRICKETER (EXCLUDING PARENTS)? Wayne Andrews was my first batting coach and he helped me through junior cricket in Western Australia
MOST BEAUTIFUL THING YOU HAVE EVER SEEN? The Scottish countryside
WHO WOULD YOU MOST LIKE TO HAVE A NET WITH? Michael Hussey (he was called Mr Cricket for a reason)
WHAT DO YOU MOST ENJOY LISTENING TO? Podcasts
WHAT GIVES YOU JOY? Winning
GUILTY PLEASURE? Chocolate

Batting	Mat	Inns	NO	Runs	HS	Ave	SR	100	50	Ct	St
First-class	15	24	1	525	116	22.82	42.27	1	1	31	3
List A	9	8	0	211	74	26.37	78.14	0	1	4	2
T20s	16	15	9	173	34*	28.83	134.10	0	0	13	1

Bowling	Mat	Balls	Runs	Wkts	BBI	BBM	Ave	Econ	SR	5w	10
First-class	15	-	-	-	-	-	-	-	-	-	-
List A	9	-	-	-	-	-	-	-	-	-	-
T20s	16	-	-	-	-	-	-	-	-	-	-

RAHMANULLAH GURBAZ

RHB / WK

FULL NAME: Rahmanullah Gurbaz
BORN: November 28, 2001, Afghanistan
SQUAD NO: TBC
TEAMS: Afghanistan, Leicestershire, Islamabad United, Jaffna Kings, Kabul Region, Kandy Tuskers, Khulna Tigers, Mis Ainak Knights, Multan Sultans, Paktia Royals
ROLE: Wicketkeeper/batter
DEBUT: ODI: 2021; T20I: 2019; First-class: 2018; List A: 2017; T20: 2017

BEST BATTING: 99 Kabul Eagles vs Amo Sharks, Kabul, 2020 (T20)

TWITTER: @RGurbaz_21
NOTES: A hard-hitting top-order batter, Rahmanullah joins his Afghanistan teammate Naveen-ul-Haq for Leicestershire's T20 Blast campaign. After smashing a century on his ODI debut against Ireland in January 2021, an innings which included nine sixes, the youngster is making his mark in both international white-ball formats and he showed glimpses of his talent at last year's T20 World Cup when he blitzed 46 in a thumping victory over Scotland. He has also kept wicket for his country, giving the Foxes another option behind the stumps. Paul Nixon, Leicestershire's head coach, said: "We have been keeping a very close eye on Rahmanullah for a couple of years now. He is one of the most exciting young players in the modern game, his 360-degree clean power-hitting ability is to be marvelled at. He has a class and a raw power fused into his game and it creates match-winning abilities"

Batting	Mat	Inns	NO	Runs	HS	Ave	SR	100	50	Ct	St
ODIs	9	9	1	428	127	53.50	91.84	3	0	6	2
T20Is	20	20	0	534	87	26.70	137.62	0	3	7	1
First-class	12	19	0	941	153	49.52	72.38	1	7	16	5
List A	38	34	5	1232	128	42.48	97.70	5	3	36	7
T20s	69	68	1	1620	99	24.17	151.82	0	10	37	5
Bowling	Mat	Balls	Runs	Wkts	BBI	BBM	Ave	Econ	SR	5w	10
ODIs	9	-	-	-	-	-	-	-	-	-	-
T20Is	20	-	-	-	-	-	-	-	-	-	-
First-class	12	-	-	-	-	-	-	-	-	-	-
List A	38	-	-	-	-	-	-	-	-	-	-
T20s	69	-	-	-	-	-	-	-	-	-	-

SAM HAIN — RHB / RM / R0 / W0 / MVP48

FULL NAME: Samuel Robert Hain
BORN: July 16, 1995, Hong Kong
SQUAD NO: 16
HEIGHT: 6ft
NICKNAME: Ched
EDUCATION: The Southport School, Queensland, Australia
TEAMS: Warwickshire, Australia U19, England Lions
ROLE: Batter
DEBUT: First-class: 2014; List A: 2013; T20: 2016

WARWICKSHIRE

BEST BATTING: 208 Warwickshire vs Northamptonshire, Edgbaston, 2014

COUNTY CAP: 2018

MOST EXCITING DAY AS A CRICKETER? Winning the One-Day Cup in 2016 and the County Championship last summer
CHILDHOOD SPORTING HERO? Bryson DeChambeau
TWITTER: @Sammiehain

Batting	Mat	Inns	NO	Runs	HS	Ave	SR	100	50	Ct	St
First-class	95	151	14	4924	208	35.94	45.56	11	28	90	-
List A	58	56	9	2810	161*	59.78	86.46	10	15	22	-
T20s	81	78	14	2386	95	37.28	128.14	0	17	49	-
Bowling	Mat	Balls	Runs	Wkts	BBI	BBM	Ave	Econ	SR	5w	10
First-class	95	42	31	0	-	-	-	4.42	-	0	0
List A	58	-	-	-	-	-	-	-	-	-	-
T20s	81	-	-	-	-	-	-	-	-	-	-

TOM HAINES

LHB / RM / R1 / W0

SUSSEX

FULL NAME: Thomas Jacob Haines
BORN: October 28, 1998, Crawley, West Sussex
SQUAD NO: 20
HEIGHT: 5ft 11in
NICKNAME: Hainus
EDUCATION: Tanbridge House School, Horsham; Hurstpierpoint College, West Sussex
TEAMS: Sussex
ROLE: Batter
DEBUT: First-class: 2016; List A: 2021

BEST BATTING: 156 Sussex vs Middlesex, Hove, 2021
BEST BOWLING: 1-9 Sussex vs Durham, Chester-le-Street, 2019
COUNTY CAP: 2021

WHO IS YOUR LOOKALIKE? Bruno Fernandes (footballer)
FIRST CRICKET CLUB? Brockham Green CC, Surrey
BIGGEST INFLUENCE ON YOUR DEVELOPMENT AS A CRICKETER (EXCLUDING PARENTS)?
Former Sussex batsman Jeremy Heath. He coached me from the age of 10 and I still speak to him now
BIGGEST CRICKETING REGRET? Not bowling leggies
MOST UNDERRATED PLAYER IN COUNTY CRICKET? Ben Brown
MOST BEAUTIFUL THING YOU HAVE EVER SEEN? Lucas Moura's hat-trick for Spurs against Ajax in the 2019 Champions League semi-final
IF YOU COULD TURN BACK TIME... I'd change the result of the 2019 Champions League final
WHO WOULD YOU MOST LIKE TO HAVE A NET WITH? Brian Lara
WHAT GIVES YOU JOY? Sport
GUILTY PLEASURE? Jaffa Cakes
TWITTER: @tomhaines

Batting	Mat	Inns	NO	Runs	HS	Ave	SR	100	50	Ct	St
First-class	34	60	1	2008	156	34.03	51.06	5	8	8	-
List A	7	7	0	252	123	36.00	83.72	1	0	3	-

Bowling	Mat	Balls	Runs	Wkts	BBI	BBM	Ave	Econ	SR	5w	10
First-class	34	1050	480	10	1/9	2/73	48.00	2.74	105.0	0	0
List A	7	-	-	-	-	-	-	-	-	-	-

ALEX HALES
RHB / RM

FULL NAME: Alexander Daniel Hales
BORN: January 3, 1989, Hillingdon, London
SQUAD NO: 10
HEIGHT: 6ft 5in
EDUCATION: Chesham High School, Buckinghamshire
TEAMS: England, Nottinghamshire, Adelaide Strikers, Hobart Hurricanes, Kolkata Knight Riders, Melbourne Renegades, Sunrisers, Sydney Thunder, Worcestershire
ROLE: Batter
DEBUT: Test: 2015; ODI: 2014; T20I: 2011; First-class: 2008; List A: 2008; T20: 2009

BEST BATTING: 116* England vs Sri Lanka, Chittagong, 2014 (T20)

COUNTY CAP: 2011 (Nottinghamshire)

FIRST CRICKET CLUB? Denham CC, Buckinghamshire. We lived in a bungalow on the cricket ground
CHILDHOOD SPORTING HERO? Dominic Cork
TWITTER: @AlexHales1
NOTES: Hales made his most recent first-class appearance back in 2017 and now plays white-ball cricket only. He turned out for Sydney Thunder in the Big Bash over the winter

Batting	Mat	Inns	NO	Runs	HS	Ave	SR	100	50	Ct	St
Tests	11	21	0	573	94	27.28	43.84	0	5	8	-
ODIs	70	67	3	2419	171	37.79	95.72	6	14	27	-
T20Is	60	60	7	1644	116*	31.01	136.65	1	8	32	-
First-class	107	182	6	6655	236	37.81	59.06	13	38	84	-
List A	175	169	6	6260	187*	38.40	99.09	17	32	66	-
T20s	336	333	27	9471	116*	30.95	146.08	5	58	161	-

Bowling	Mat	Balls	Runs	Wkts	BBI	BBM	Ave	Econ	SR	5w	10
Tests	11	18	2	0	-	-	-	0.66	-	0	0
ODIs	70	-	-	-	-	-	-	-	-	-	-
T20Is	60	-	-	-	-	-	-	-	-	-	-
First-class	107	311	173	3	2/63	2/63	57.66	3.33	103.6	0	0
List A	175	4	10	0	-	-	-	15.00	-	0	0
T20s	336	3	7	0	-	-	-	14.00	-	0	0

HASEEB HAMEED

RHB / LB / R1 / W0

NOTTINGHAMSHIRE

FULL NAME: Haseeb Hameed
BORN: January 17, 1997, Bolton, Lancashire
SQUAD NO: 99
HEIGHT: 6ft
NICKNAME: Has
EDUCATION: Bolton School
TEAMS: England, Nottinghamshire, Lancashire
ROLE: Batter
DEBUT: Test: 2016; First-class: 2015; List A: 2017

BEST BATTING: 122 Lancashire vs Nottinghamshire, Trent Bridge, 2015

COUNTY CAP: 2016 (Lancashire); 2020 (Nottinghamshire)

FIRST CRICKET CLUB? Tonge CC, Bolton
WHAT WOULD YOU CHANGE ABOUT THE STRUCTURE OF THE COUNTY SEASON?
No red-ball cricket in April or September!
BIGGEST INFLUENCE ON YOUR DEVELOPMENT AS A CRICKETER (EXCLUDING PARENTS)?
John Stanworth at Lancashire
WHO IS THE BEST BATTER/KEEPER/ALLROUNDER/BOWLER IN COUNTY CRICKET
(EXCLUDING TEAMMATES)? Alastair Cook/Ben Foakes/Darren Stevens/Luke Fletcher
WHAT WOULD A FLY ON THE WALL HEAR IN YOUR DRESSING ROOM? Skeleton Move by
Master G
MOST BEAUTIFUL THING YOU HAVE EVER SEEN? The Taj Mahal
HOBBIES? Football
GUILTY PLEASURE? Dandelion and burdock (drink)
TWITTER: @HaseebHameed97

Batting	Mat	Inns	NO	Runs	HS	Ave	SR	100	50	Ct	St
Tests	10	19	1	439	82	24.38	32.02	0	4	7	-
First-class	87	147	13	4203	122	31.36	37.88	8	24	57	-
List A	21	21	3	663	103	36.83	81.85	1	4	5	-

Bowling	Mat	Balls	Runs	Wkts	BBI	BBM	Ave	Econ	SR	5w	10
Tests	10	-	-	-	-	-	-	-	-	-	-
First-class	87	42	21	0	-	-	-	3.00	-	0	0
List A	21	-	-	-	-	-	-	-	-	-	-

MILES HAMMOND

LHB / OB / R0 / W0

FULL NAME: Miles Arthur Halhead Hammond
BORN: January 11, 1996, Cheltenham, Gloucestershire
SQUAD NO: 88
HEIGHT: 6ft 1in
NICKNAME: Hammer
EDUCATION: St Edward's School, Oxford; University of the Arts London
TEAMS: Gloucestershire, England U19
ROLE: Batter
DEBUT: First-class: 2013; List A: 2013; T20: 2013

BEST BATTING: 123* Gloucestershire vs Middlesex, Bristol, 2018
BEST BOWLING: 2-37 Gloucestershire vs Leicestershire, Leicester, 2021
COUNTY CAP: 2013

FIRST CRICKET CLUB? Cumnor CC, Oxford
WHAT WOULD YOU CHANGE ABOUT THE STRUCTURE OF THE COUNTY SEASON? Have fewer games in April and May
BIGGEST CRICKETING REGRET? Choosing initially to bowl off-spin
WHO IS THE BEST BATTER/KEEPER/ALLROUNDER/BOWLER IN COUNTY CRICKET (EXCLUDING TEAMMATES)? Hashim Amla/Ben Foakes/Darren Stevens/Simon Harmer
HOBBIES? Drawing
WHO WOULD YOU LEAST LIKE TO HAVE A NET WITH? Matt Taylor – he has my number every time
WHAT GIVES YOU JOY? Putting birdies
SURPRISING FACT ABOUT YOU? I wear my house key around my neck
TWITTER: @hammo125

Batting	Mat	Inns	NO	Runs	HS	Ave	SR	100	50	Ct	St
First-class	36	63	5	1561	123*	26.91	43.70	2	9	34	-
List A	8	6	0	185	95	30.83	73.12	0	1	1	-
T20s	60	54	3	1181	63	23.15	137.96	0	3	25	-

Bowling	Mat	Balls	Runs	Wkts	BBI	BBM	Ave	Econ	SR	5w	10
First-class	36	586	453	5	2/37	2/37	90.60	4.63	117.2	0	0
List A	8	114	97	5	2/18	2/18	19.40	5.10	22.8	0	0
T20s	60	12	17	0	-	-	-	8.50	-	0	0

PETER HANDSCOMB RHB / WK / RO / WO

FULL NAME: Peter Stephen Patrick Handscomb
BORN: April 26, 1991, Melbourne, Australia
SQUAD NO: 29
HEIGHT: 6ft 4in
EDUCATION: Deakin University, Melbourne
TEAMS: Australia, Middlesex, Durham, Gloucestershire, Hobart Hurricanes, Melbourne Stars, Rising Pune Supergiants, Victoria, Yorkshire
ROLE: Batter/wicketkeeper
DEBUT: Test: 2016; ODI: 2017; T20I: 2019; First-class: 2011; List A: 2011; T20: 2012

BEST BATTING: 215 Victoria vs New South Wales, Sydney, 2016

COUNTY CAP: 2015 (Gloucestershire)

TWITTER: @phandscomb54

NOTES: The Australian batter-wicketkeeper returns to Middlesex to complete his two-year deal with the club and is due to captain the side in the County Championship and One-Day Cup. Handscomb's appereances for the club in 2021 were limited on account of the Sheffield Shield beginning earlier than usual. He struggled badly in seven Championship matches, making just one-half century in 13 innings, and did not fare much better in the One-Day Cup. Born to British parents but raised in Australia, Handscomb passed 50 in each of his first four Test matches, including two centuries, but hasn't played for Australia in any format since 2019. The Victorian captains his state side in the Sheffield Shield and has had previous county stints with Gloucestershire (2015), Yorkshire (2017) and Durham (2018)

Batting	Mat	Inns	NO	Runs	HS	Ave	SR	100	50	Ct	St
Tests	16	29	5	934	110	38.91	49.83	2	4	28	-
ODIs	22	20	1	632	117	33.26	97.38	1	4	14	-
T20Is	2	2	1	33	20*	33.00	100.00	0	0	0	-
First-class	131	221	15	7779	215	37.76	52.69	17	44	205	4
List A	123	113	14	3687	140	37.24	90.50	4	22	109	5
T20s	111	98	23	1732	103*	23.09	118.46	1	5	53	13

Bowling	Mat	Balls	Runs	Wkts	BBI	BBM	Ave	Econ	SR	5w	10
Tests	16	-	-	-	-	-	-	-	-	-	-
ODIs	22	-	-	-	-	-	-	-	-	-	-
T20Is	2	-	-	-	-	-	-	-	-	-	-
First-class	131	66	79	0	-	-	-	7.18	-	0	0
List A	123	-	-	-	-	-	-	-	-	-	-
T20s	111	-	-	-	-	-	-	-	-	-	-

OLIVER HANNON-DALBY   LHB / RMF / R0 / W0

FULL NAME: Oliver James Hannon-Dalby
BORN: June 20, 1989, Halifax, Yorkshire
SQUAD NO: 20
HEIGHT: 6ft 8in
NICKNAME: Owl Face
EDUCATION: Brooksbank School, West Yorkshire; Leeds Metropolitan University
TEAMS: Warwickshire, Yorkshire
ROLE: Bowler
DEBUT: First-class: 2008; List A: 2011; T20: 2012

BEST BATTING: 40 Warwickshire vs Somerset, Taunton, 2014
BEST BOWLING: 6-33 Warwickshire vs Gloucestershire, Bristol, 2020

FIRST CRICKET CLUB? Copley CC, West Yorkshire
MOST EXCITING DAY AS A CRICKETER? T20 Finals Day in 2014 and winning the Championship last summer
CHILDHOOD SPORTING HERO? Alan Shearer
BIGGEST INFLUENCE ON YOUR DEVELOPMENT AS A CRICKETER (EXCLUDING PARENTS)? Fred Hemmingway, my first coach at Copley CC
WHAT WOULD YOU DO IF YOU WERE IN CHARGE OF COUNTY CRICKET? All grounds to have Lord's-standard teas, compulsory pre-season tours to Barbados, do something to help the bowlers in white-ball cricket
FAVOURITE SMELL? The top of my dog's head
TWITTER: @OHD_20

Batting	Mat	Inns	NO	Runs	HS	Ave	SR	100	50	Ct	St
First-class	83	102	37	497	40	7.64	27.38	0	0	10	-
List A	43	15	9	91	21*	15.16	95.78	0	0	14	-
T20s	60	12	7	53	14*	10.60	96.36	0	0	12	-

Bowling	Mat	Balls	Runs	Wkts	BBI	BBM	Ave	Econ	SR	5w	10
First-class	83	13147	6805	224	6/33	12/110	30.37	3.10	58.6	8	1
List A	43	1978	2075	65	5/27	5/27	31.92	6.29	30.4	1	0
T20s	60	1252	1829	75	4/20	4/20	24.38	8.76	16.6	0	0

SIMON HARMER   RHB / OB / R0 / W4 / MVP1

ESSEX

FULL NAME: Simon Ross Harmer
BORN: February 10, 1989, Pretoria, SA
SQUAD NO: 11
HEIGHT: 6ft 2in
NICKNAME: Big Red
EDUCATION: Pretoria Boys High School;
Nelson Mandela Metropolitan University,
Port Elizabeth
TEAMS: South Africa, Essex, Border, Eastern
Province, Jozi Stars, Titans, Warriors
ROLE: Bowler
DEBUT: Test: 2015; First-class: 2009; List A:
2010; T20: 2011

BEST BATTING: 102* Essex vs Surrey, The Oval, 2018
BEST BOWLING: 9-80 Essex vs Derbyshire, Chelmsford, 2021
COUNTY CAP: 2018

FIRST CRICKET CLUB? Pretoria High School Old Boys CC, South Africa
MOST EXCITING DAY AS A CRICKETER? Making my international debut for South Africa at
Newlands
CHILDHOOD SPORTING HERO? Jacques Kallis
WHAT WOULD YOU DO IF YOU WERE IN CHARGE OF COUNTY CRICKET? Create a revenue-
share model, like the one Cricket Australia implements, to commercialise the image rights
of county players; make it mandatory that every county has a director of cricket to bridge
the gap between the changeroom and the boardroom; allow overseas players who sign
multi-year deals the choice of a tier-two or tier-five visa so they can have similar rights to
their colleagues
TWITTER: @Simon_Harmer_

Batting	Mat	Inns	NO	Runs	HS	Ave	SR	100	50	Ct	St
Tests	5	6	1	58	13	11.60	33.33	0	0	1	-
First-class	172	250	49	4781	102*	23.78	47.92	2	24	172	-
List A	93	78	25	1136	44*	21.43	99.38	0	0	63	-
T20s	124	73	24	874	43	17.83	127.03	0	0	62	-

Bowling	Mat	Balls	Runs	Wkts	BBI	BBM	Ave	Econ	SR	5w	10
Tests	5	1148	588	20	4/61	7/153	29.40	3.07	57.4	0	0
First-class	172	41446	19590	743	9/80	14/128	26.36	2.83	55.7	43	10
List A	93	4440	3651	96	4/42	4/42	38.03	4.93	46.2	0	0
T20s	124	2336	2944	105	4/19	4/19	28.03	7.56	22.2	0	0

JAMES HARRIS

RHB / RMF / RO / W3

FULL NAME: James Alexander Russell Harris
BORN: May 16, 1990, Morriston, Swansea
SQUAD NO: TBC
HEIGHT: 6ft 1in
NICKNAME: Bones
EDUCATION: Pontarddulais Comprehensive School, Swansea; Gorseinon College, Swansea
TEAMS: Glamorgan, England Lions, Kent, Middlesex
ROLE: Bowler
DEBUT: First-class: 2007; List A: 2007; T20: 2008

BEST BATTING: 87* Glamorgan vs Nottinghamshire, Swansea, 2007
BEST BOWLING: 9-34 Middlesex vs Durham, Lord's, 2015
COUNTY CAP: 2010 (Glamorgan); 2015 (Middlesex)

FIRST CRICKET CLUB? Pontarddulais CC, South Wales
WHAT WOULD YOU CHANGE ABOUT THE STRUCTURE OF THE COUNTY SEASON?
Somehow spread the Championship more evenly across the season
BIGGEST INFLUENCE ON YOUR DEVELOPMENT AS A CRICKETER (EXCLUDING PARENTS)?
Glamorgan legend Alan Jones – he taught me the values of the game that have shaped me into the cricketer I am today
MOST BEAUTIFUL THING YOU HAVE EVER SEEN? The view of Cape Town and Table Mountain from the top of Lion's Head
HOBBIES? Road cycling (I'm pretty obsessed)
MAKE ONE PREDICTION FOR THE FUTURE OF CRICKET: A country's Test and T20 XIs will be completely different
WHAT MAKES YOU WORRY? Leaving my bike outside a cafe
WHAT GIVES YOU JOY? Exploring outdoors with my other half and the puppy
GUILTY PLEASURE? An almond croissant
TWITTER: @James_Harris9

Batting	Mat	Inns	NO	Runs	HS	Ave	SR	100	50	Ct	St
First-class	153	224	52	3952	87*	22.97		0	18	44	-
List A	70	42	9	458	117	13.87	74.47	1	0	15	-
T20s	58	28	13	164	18	10.93	104.45	0	0	8	-

Bowling	Mat	Balls	Runs	Wkts	BBI	BBM	Ave	Econ	SR	5w	10
First-class	153	26275	14586	508	9/34	13/103	28.71	3.33	51.7	15	2
List A	70	3026	2948	95	4/38	4/38	31.03	5.84	31.8	0	0
T20s	58	1030	1594	48	4/23	4/23	33.20	9.28	21.4	0	0

MARCUS HARRIS

LHB / **OB** / **R0** / **W0**

GLOUCESTERSHIRE

FULL NAME: Marcus Sinclair Harris
BORN: July 21, 1992, Perth, Australia
SQUAD NO: TBC
TEAMS: Australia, Gloucestershire,
Leicestershire, Melbourne Renegades, Perth
Scorchers, Victoria, Western Australia
ROLE: Batter
DEBUT: Test: 2018; First-class: 2011; List A: 2011;
T20: 2014

BEST BATTING: 250* Victoria vs New South Wales, Melbourne, 2018

TWITTER: @MarcusHarris14
NOTES: Gloucestershire have signed the Australian Test opener on a two-year contract to play across all formats. Harris was outstanding for Leicestershire last summer, his first in county cricket, scoring three centuries in eight Championship matches and adding a fourth in the One-Day Cup. The left-hander turned down a new contract with the Foxes in order to make the move to Bristol. Harris first made waves in 2011 when aged 18 he scored 157 for Western Australia in his third first-class match, but it was only after his move to Victoria five years later that he began to fulfil his talent. He scored a career-best 250 not out against New South Wales in the 2018/19 Sheffield Shield and made his Test debut that season. Harris hasn't been able to nail down a spot in the Test team but featured in the first four matches of this winter's Ashes before being losing his place for the final game at Hobart

Batting	Mat	Inns	NO	Runs	HS	Ave	SR	100	50	Ct	St
Tests	14	26	2	607	79	25.29	45.91	0	3	8	-
First-class	122	219	15	8068	250*	39.54	53.25	19	34	61	-
List A	52	51	3	1590	127	33.12	86.98	2	8	13	-
T20s	48	47	1	970	85	21.08	122.47	0	4	17	-

Bowling	Mat	Balls	Runs	Wkts	BBI	BBM	Ave	Econ	SR	5w	10
Tests	14	-	-	-	-	-	-	-	-	-	-
First-class	122	78	64	0	-	-	-	4.92	-	0	0
List A	52	-	-	-	-	-	-	-	-	-	-
T20s	48	-	-	-	-	-	-	-	-	-	-

CALVIN HARRISON
RHB / LB / R0 / W0

FULL NAME: Calvin Grant Harrison
BORN: April 29, 1998, Durban, South Africa
SQUAD NO: 31
HEIGHT: 6ft 3in
EDUCATION: King's College, Taunton; Oxford Brookes University
TEAMS: Nottinghamshire, Hampshire
ROLE: Allrounder
DEBUT: First-class: 2019; T20: 2020

BEST BATTING: 37* Oxford MCCU vs Middlesex, Northwood, 2019
BEST BOWLING: 1-30 Oxford MCCU vs Middlesex, Northwood, 2019

FIRST CRICKET CLUB? Onslow CC, Wellington, New Zealand
NOTES: Born in South Africa and raised in New Zealand before studying at King's College, Taunton, Harrison's career exploded into life last summer after a series of eye-catching performances for Nottinghamshire in the T20 Blast, claiming 20 scalps in 15 appearances to top the Outlaws' wicket-taking charts. That led to a late call-up for Manchester Originals in The Hundred and a two-year contract extension at Trent Bridge. All this after his career appeared to be going nowhere in particular. Released by Somerset after coming through their Academy, the tall leg-spinning allrounder had trialled unsuccessfully at several clubs, representing six county Second XIs before getting his big break when he thumped 121 from 166 deliveries while playing for Oxford UCCE in a warm-up match against Notts in March 2021. Interest piqued, Notts wanted a closer look at Harrison, who last year completed an undergraduate Psychology degree at Oxford Brookes. Their curiosity has been well rewarded

Batting	Mat	Inns	NO	Runs	HS	Ave	SR	100	50	Ct	St
First-class	2	3	1	65	37*	32.50	38.23	0	0	1	-
T20s	23	13	4	92	23	10.22	126.02	0	0	14	-

Bowling	Mat	Balls	Runs	Wkts	BBI	BBM	Ave	Econ	SR	5w	10
First-class	2	162	113	3	1/30	2/72	37.66	4.18	54.0	0	0
T20s	23	334	412	23	4/17	4/17	17.91	7.40	14.5	0	0

TOM HARTLEY

RHB / SLA / R0 / W0

FULL NAME: Tom William Hartley
BORN: May 3, 1998, Ormskirk, Lancashire
SQUAD NO: 2
HEIGHT: 6ft 4in
NICKNAME: TDF
EDUCATION: Merchant Taylors' School, Crosby, Merseyside
TEAMS: Lancashire
ROLE: Bowler
DEBUT: First-class: 2020; T20: 2020

BEST BATTING: 25 Lancashire vs Northamptonshire, Old Trafford, 2021
BEST BOWLING: 4-42 Lancashire vs Kent, Old Trafford, 2021

FIRST CRICKET CLUB? Ormskirk CC, Lancashire
WHAT WOULD YOU CHANGE ABOUT THE STRUCTURE OF THE COUNTY SEASON? Bring in five-day matches, play more games at outgrounds, play more games against southern counties, and less mixing of white- and red-ball cricket
BIGGEST INFLUENCE ON YOUR DEVELOPMENT AS A CRICKETER (EXCLUDING PARENTS)? My captain at Ormskirk CC – for giving me plenty of overs in my younger years
WHO IS THE BEST BATTER/KEEPER/ALLROUNDER/BOWLER IN COUNTY CRICKET (EXCLUDING TEAMMATES)? David Bedingham/Ben Foakes/Darren Stevens/Simon Harmer
MOST UNDERRATED PLAYER IN COUNTY CRICKET? Callum Parkinson
WHAT WOULD A FLY ON THE WALL HEAR IN YOUR DRESSING ROOM? Conversations about fantasy football
MOST BEAUTIFUL THING YOU HAVE EVER SEEN? The view from Table Mountain in Cape Town
HOBBIES? Gardening
WHO WOULD YOU MOST LIKE TO HAVE A NET WITH? Daniel Vettori
WHAT MAKES YOU WORRY? Not taking wickets
WHAT GIVES YOU JOY? Giving batters a send-off
GUILTY PLEASURE? Chocolate Digestives
TWITTER: @tomhartley100

Batting	Mat	Inns	NO	Runs	HS	Ave	SR	100	50	Ct	St
First-class	7	8	4	96	25	24.00	27.82	0	0	4	-
T20s	32	11	6	46	16*	9.20	95.83	0	0	8	-

Bowling	Mat	Balls	Runs	Wkts	BBI	BBM	Ave	Econ	SR	5w	10
First-class	7	1164	467	10	4/42	4/42	46.70	2.40	116.4	0	0
T20s	32	622	724	25	4/16	4/16	28.96	6.98	24.8	0	0

JAMES HAYES — RHB / RFM / R0 / W0

FULL NAME: James Philip Henry Hayes
BORN: June 27, 2001, Haywards Heath, Sussex
SQUAD NO: TBC
HEIGHT: 6ft 3in
EDUCATION: King's College, Taunton; Richard Huish College
TEAMS: Nottinghamshire
ROLE: Bowler

WHO IS YOUR LOOKALIKE? Ron Weasley (character in Harry Potter)
FIRST CRICKET CLUB? Cuckfield CC, West Sussex
WHAT WOULD YOU CHANGE ABOUT THE STRUCTURE OF THE COUNTY SEASON? Have more rest days between Championship matches
WHO IS THE BEST BATTER/KEEPER/ALLROUNDER/BOWLER IN COUNTY CRICKET (EXCLUDING TEAMMATES)? Tom Haines/Ben Foakes/Darren Stevens/Simon Harmer
MOST UNDERRATED PLAYER IN COUNTY CRICKET? Tom Abell
MOST BEAUTIFUL THING YOU HAVE EVER SEEN? A pub at the end of a four-hour walk
HOBBIES? Call of Duty (video game)
IF YOU COULD TURN BACK TIME...I would bowl leg-spin
WHO WOULD YOU MOST AND LEAST LIKE TO HAVE A NET WITH? Most – Ian Botham. Least – Joel Garner
MAKE ONE PREDICTION FOR THE FUTURE OF CRICKET: Domination of the white ball
WHAT DO YOU MOST ENJOY LISTENING TO? The sound of stumps being knocked out the ground
WHAT MAKES YOU WORRY? The prospect of playing less red-ball cricket
WHAT GIVES YOU JOY? Nicking someone off

JACK HAYNES   RHB / OB / R0 / W0

FULL NAME: Jack Alexander Haynes
BORN: January 30, 2001, Worcester
SQUAD NO: 17
HEIGHT: 6ft 1in
NICKNAME: Clunesy
EDUCATION: Malvern College
TEAMS: Worcestershire, England U19
ROLE: Batter
DEBUT: First-class: 2019; List A: 2018; T20: 2020

BEST BATTING: 97 Worcestershire vs Derbyshire, Worcester, 2021

WHO IS YOUR LOOKALIKE? Martin Clunes
FIRST CRICKET CLUB? Ombersley CC, Worcestershire
FAMILY TIES? My father Gavin played more than 200 matches for Worcestershire in the
1990s and my older brother Josh plays for Leeds/Bradford MCCU
WHO IS THE BEST BATTER/KEEPER/ALLROUNDER/BOWLER IN COUNTY CRICKET
(EXCLUDING TEAMMATES)? David Bedingham/Ben Foakes/Darren Stevens/Simon Harmer
MOST UNDERRATED PLAYER IN COUNTY CRICKET? Joe Clarke
HOBBIES? Horse racing
WHO WOULD YOU MOST LIKE TO HAVE A NET WITH? Graeme Hick – Worcester legend
MAKE ONE PREDICTION FOR THE FUTURE OF CRICKET: More and more international teams
TWITTER: @jack_haynes1

Batting	Mat	Inns	NO	Runs	HS	Ave	SR	100	50	Ct	St
First-class	19	30	2	895	97	31.96	49.33	0	6	10	-
List A	8	8	0	395	153	49.37	93.60	1	2	4	-
T20s	9	9	0	171	41	19.00	134.64	0	0	2	-

Bowling	Mat	Balls	Runs	Wkts	BBI	BBM	Ave	Econ	SR	5w	10
First-class	19	-	-	-	-	-	-	-	-	-	-
List A	8	-	-	-	-	-	-	-	-	-	-
T20s	9	-	-	-	-	-	-	-	-	-	-

TOM HELM — RHB / RFM / R0 / W0

FULL NAME: Thomas George Helm
BORN: May 7, 1994, Aylesbury, Buckinghamshire
SQUAD NO: 7
HEIGHT: 6ft 4in
NICKNAME: Cheddy
EDUCATION: The Misbourne School, Buckinghamshire
TEAMS: Middlesex, England Lions, Glamorgan
ROLE: Bowler
DEBUT: First-class: 2013; List A: 2013; T20: 2016

BEST BATTING: 52 Middlesex vs Derbyshire, Lord's, 2018
BEST BOWLING: 5-36 Middlesex vs Worcestershire, Worcester, 2019
COUNTY CAP: 2019 (Middlesex)

WHO IS YOUR LOOKALIKE? Zac Efron
FIRST CRICKET CLUB? Chesham CC, Buckinghamshire
FAMILY TIES? My brother Sam played Minor Counties for Buckinghamshire
WHAT WOULD YOU CHANGE ABOUT THE STRUCTURE OF THE COUNTY SEASON? Start in May and play through October
MOST UNDERRATED PLAYER IN COUNTY CRICKET? Tim Murtagh
WHAT WOULD A FLY ON THE WALL HEAR IN YOUR DRESSING ROOM? A cracking insight into Ethan Bamber's cooking
MOST BEAUTIFUL THING YOU HAVE EVER SEEN? A "green timed finesse" (FIFA 22 videogame)
IF YOU COULD TURN BACK TIME... I'd change the thickness of my hair
WHO WOULD YOU LEAST LIKE TO HAVE A NET WITH? Angus Fraser – he would just tell me how good he is!
WHAT DO YOU MOST ENJOY LISTENING TO? My neighbours upstairs arguing
TWITTER: @tomhelm7

Batting	Mat	Inns	NO	Runs	HS	Ave	SR	100	50	Ct	St
First-class	34	49	10	608	52	15.58	45.85	0	1	10	-
List A	40	24	8	206	30	12.87	71.28	0	0	15	-
T20s	57	24	14	120	28*	12.00	99.17	0	0	5	-

Bowling	Mat	Balls	Runs	Wkts	BBI	BBM	Ave	Econ	SR	5w	10
First-class	34	5224	2772	87	5/36	7/140	31.86	3.18	60.0	3	0
List A	40	1816	1742	56	5/33	5/33	31.10	5.75	32.4	2	0
T20s	57	1102	1622	64	5/11	5/11	25.34	8.83	17.2	1	0

BEURAN HENDRICKS — LHB / LFM / R0 / W0

LEICESTERSHIRE

FULL NAME: Beuran Eric Hendricks
BORN: June 08, 1990, Bellville, Cape Town, South Africa
SQUAD NO: TBC
TEAMS: South Africa, Leicestershire, Cape Cobras, Gauteng, Jozi Stars, Kings XI Punjab, Lions, Nelson Mandela Bay Giants, Western Province
ROLE: Bowler
DEBUT: Test: 2020; ODI: 2019; T20I: 2014; First-class: 2010; List A: 2010; T20: 2011

BEST BATTING: 68 Lions vs Dolphins, Johannesburg, 2018
BEST BOWLING: 7-29 Lions vs Cape Cobras, Johannesburg, 2020

TWITTER: @Beuran_H13
NOTES: The South African left-arm seamer is ready for his first taste of county cricket after signing a deal with the Foxes which includes the County Championship and One-Day Cup. Hendricks made his Test debut against England at Johannesburg in 2020, taking 5-64 in the second innings, but since then he hasn't been seen in whites for South Africa. He's featured more recently in the Proteas' white-ball set-up but wasn't part of their T20 World Cup plans. "I would like to thank Claude Henderson [director of cricket] and the club for this great opportunity," Hendricks said. "I am very much looking forward to working with Paul Nixon [head coach] and Colin Ackermann [captain] and I cannot wait to meet up with the rest of the squad"

Batting	Mat	Inns	NO	Runs	HS	Ave	SR	100	50	Ct	St
Tests	1	2	1	9	5*	9.00	50.00	0	0	0	-
ODIs	8	3	1	6	3	3.00	31.57	0	0	2	-
T20Is	19	5	2	18	12*	6.00	78.26	0	0	4	-
First-class	99	115	36	765	68	9.68	37.94	0	1	26	-
List A	80	42	21	168	24	8.00	59.57	0	0	18	-
T20s	94	19	10	41	12*	4.55	70.68	0	0	18	-

Bowling	Mat	Balls	Runs	Wkts	BBI	BBM	Ave	Econ	SR	5w	10
Tests	1	231	175	6	5/64	6/175	29.16	4.54	38.5	1	0
ODIs	8	276	249	5	3/59	3/59	49.80	5.41	55.2	0	0
T20Is	19	409	627	25	4/14	4/14	25.08	9.19	16.3	0	0
First-class	99	14675	8076	332	7/29	11/63	24.32	3.30	44.2	19	2
List A	80	3503	3373	104	5/31	5/31	32.43	5.77	33.6	2	0
T20s	94	1959	2718	122	6/29	6/29	22.27	8.32	16.0	1	0

MATT HENRY

RHB / RFM / R0 / W1

FULL NAME: Matthew James Henry
BORN: December 14, 1991, Christchurch, New Zealand
SQUAD NO: 24
HEIGHT: 6ft 2in
NICKNAME: Henaz
EDUCATION: St Bede's College, Christchurch
TEAMS: New Zealand, Kent, Derbyshire, Canterbury, Kings XI Punjab, Worcestershire
ROLE: Bowler
DEBUT: Test: 2015; ODI: 2014; T20I: 2014; First-class: 2011; List A: 2011; T20: 2011

BEST BATTING: 81 Kent vs Derbyshire, Derby, 2018
BEST BOWLING: 7-23 New Zealand vs South Africa, Christchurch, 2022
COUNTY CAP: 2018 (Kent)

TWITTER: @Matthenry014
NOTES: The Kiwi seamer returns for a second spell at Kent and will be available for the seven Championship games of the season from mid-July, as well as for the One-Day Cup. Henry was devastating when he appeared for the county in 2018, taking 75 wickets in 11 Championship matches to help inspire Kent to promotion. He has previously played for Derbyshire and Worcestershire. An established international, Henry starred in New Zealand's run to the World Cup final in 2019 and recorded a first-class best of 7-23 on his home ground at Hagley Oval in Christchurch during the Test series against South Africa earlier this year

Batting	Mat	Inns	NO	Runs	HS	Ave	SR	100	50	Ct	St
Tests	16	20	5	294	66	19.60	73.68	0	2	6	-
ODIs	55	21	7	211	48*	15.07	100.00	0	0	17	-
T20Is	6	2	1	10	10	10.00	200.00	0	0	1	-
First-class	80	104	17	1740	81	20.00	77.16	0	6	33	-
List A	133	71	19	654	48*	12.57	107.74	0	0	49	-
T20s	100	60	25	470	44	13.42	158.78	0	0	36	-

Bowling	Mat	Balls	Runs	Wkts	BBI	BBM	Ave	Econ	SR	5w	10
Tests	16	3691	1938	51	7/23	9/55	38.00	3.15	72.3	1	0
ODIs	55	2877	2538	98	5/30	5/30	25.89	5.29	29.3	2	0
T20Is	6	132	191	7	3/44	3/44	27.28	8.68	18.8	0	0
First-class	80	16893	8505	349	7/23	12/73	24.36	3.02	48.4	16	3
List A	133	6655	5815	215	6/45	6/45	27.04	5.24	30.9	4	0
T20s	100	2019	2912	102	4/43	4/43	28.54	8.65	19.7	0	0

RYAN HIGGINS RHB / OB / R0 / W2 / MVP17

GLOUCESTERSHIRE

FULL NAME: Ryan Francis Higgins
BORN: January 6, 1995, Harare, Zimbabwe
SQUAD NO: 29
HEIGHT: 5ft 11in
NICKNAME: Fizzer
EDUCATION: Peterhouse School, Marondera, Zimbabwe; Bradfield College, Reading
TEAMS: Gloucestershire, England U19, Middlesex
ROLE: Allrounder
DEBUT: First-class: 2017; List A: 2014; T20: 2014

BEST BATTING: 199 Gloucestershire vs Leicestershire, Leicester, 2019
BEST BOWLING: 7-42 Gloucestershire vs Warwickshire, Bristol, 2020
COUNTY CAP: 2018 (Gloucestershire)

FIRST CRICKET CLUB? Falkland CC, Berkshire
MOST EXCITING DAY AS A CRICKETER? T20 Finals Day in 2020
CHILDHOOD SPORTING HERO? Michael Hussey
BIGGEST CRICKETING REGRET? My time in Sydney – I did not take the game seriously out there
WHAT WOULD YOU DO IF YOU WERE IN CHARGE OF COUNTY CRICKET? Make four-day cricket free to watch, introduce music in Championship cricket, encourage the private ownership of counties (like in football's Premier League)
GUILTY PLEASURE? Popcorn
TWITTER: @ryanhiggins21

Batting	Mat	Inns	NO	Runs	HS	Ave	SR	100	50	Ct	St
First-class	51	80	10	2162	199	30.88	62.83	5	7	15	-
List A	33	29	5	680	81*	28.33	97.00	0	3	5	-
T20s	87	77	24	1346	77*	25.39	133.00	0	4	21	-

Bowling	Mat	Balls	Runs	Wkts	BBI	BBM	Ave	Econ	SR	5w	10
First-class	51	9019	3889	178	7/42	11/96	21.84	2.58	50.6	7	1
List A	33	915	845	24	4/50	4/50	35.20	5.54	38.1	0	0
T20s	87	1006	1495	62	5/13	5/13	24.11	8.91	16.2	1	0

JAMES HILDRETH

RHB / RM / R7 / W0

FULL NAME: James Charles Hildreth
BORN: September 9, 1984, Milton Keynes, Buckinghamshire
SQUAD NO: 25
HEIGHT: 5ft 10in
NICKNAME: Hildy
EDUCATION: Millfield School, Somerset
TEAMS: Somerset, England Lions
ROLE: Batter
DEBUT: First-class: 2003; List A: 2003; T20: 2004

BEST BATTING: 303* Somerset vs Warwickshire, Taunton, 2009
BEST BOWLING: 2-39 Somerset vs Hampshire, Taunton, 2009
COUNTY CAP: 2007; BENEFIT: 2017

MOST EXCITING DAY AS A CRICKETER? Winning the T20 Cup in 2005, captaining England Lions and captaining Somerset
CHILDHOOD SPORTING HERO? Ricky Ponting
SURPRISING FACT ABOUT YOU? I'm a big MK Dons fan
TWITTER: @dreth25

Batting	Mat	Inns	NO	Runs	HS	Ave	SR	100	50	Ct	St
First-class	280	460	31	17738	303*	41.34		47	78	247	-
List A	220	206	37	6087	159	36.01		8	29	81	-
T20s	205	192	33	3900	107*	24.52	124.64	1	17	73	-

Bowling	Mat	Balls	Runs	Wkts	BBI	BBM	Ave	Econ	SR	5w	10
First-class	280	576	492	6	2/39		82.00	5.12	96.0	0	0
List A	220	150	185	6	2/26	2/26	30.83	7.40	25.0	0	0
T20s	205	169	247	10	3/24	3/24	24.70	8.76	16.9	0	0

LEWIS HILL

RHB / WK / R0 / W0

LEICESTERSHIRE

FULL NAME: Lewis John Hill
BORN: October 5, 1990, Leicester
SQUAD NO: 23
HEIGHT: 5ft 8in
NICKNAME: Hilly
EDUCATION: Hastings High School, Hinckley; John Cleveland College, Hinckley
TEAMS: Leicestershire
ROLE: Wicketkeeper
DEBUT: First-class: 2015; List A: 2012; T20: 2015

BEST BATTING: 145 Leicestershire vs Sussex, Leicester, 2021

WHO IS YOUR LOOKALIKE? Apparently George Ford (rugby player)
FIRST CRICKET CLUB? Lutterworth CC, Leicestershire
FAMILY TIES? My dad and brother both play for Lutterworth CC
WHO IS THE BEST BATTER/KEEPER/ALLROUNDER/BOWLER IN COUNTY CRICKET (EXCLUDING TEAMMATES)? Tom Abell/Ben Foakes/Lewis Gregory/Mohammad Abbas
MOST UNDERRATED PLAYER IN COUNTY CRICKET? Saif Zaib
WHO WOULD YOU MOST LIKE TO HAVE A NET WITH? Shane Warne
MAKE ONE PREDICTION FOR THE FUTURE OF CRICKET: It'll still be going strong 30 years from now
SURPRISING FACT ABOUT YOU? I was targeted by armed robbers twice while working at my local newsagents
TWITTER: @ljhill23

Batting	Mat	Inns	NO	Runs	HS	Ave	SR	100	50	Ct	St
First-class	55	93	10	2403	145	28.95	52.66	4	10	99	3
List A	49	44	2	1168	118	27.80	94.42	3	4	27	2
T20s	65	51	9	776	59	18.47	123.76	0	2	24	2

Bowling	Mat	Balls	Runs	Wkts	BBI	BBM	Ave	Econ	SR	5w	10
First-class	55	36	28	0	-	-	-	4.66	-	0	0
List A	49	-	-	-	-	-	-	-	-	-	-
T20s	65	-	-	-	-	-	-	-	-	-	-

TOM HINLEY

LHB / SLW / R0 / W0

FULL NAME: Tom Ian Hinley
BORN: February 5, 2003, Frimley, Surrey
SQUAD NO: 42
HEIGHT: 6ft 1in
NICKNAME: Hinners
EDUCATION: Warden Park Academy, West Sussex; Eastbourne College; Loughborough University
TEAMS: Sussex
ROLE: Allrounder
DEBUT: First-class: 2021

BEST BATTING: 19 Sussex vs Leicestershire, Leicester, 2021

WHO IS YOUR LOOKALIKE? There was a guy called Victor who featured in my GCSE Spanish textbook and he looked identical to me

FIRST CRICKET CLUB? Lindfield CC, West Sussex

WHO IS THE BEST BATTER/KEEPER/ALLROUNDER/BOWLER IN COUNTY CRICKET (EXCLUDING TEAMMATES)? James Vince/Ben Foakes/Darren Stevens/Simon Harmer

MOST UNDERRATED PLAYER IN COUNTY CRICKET? Ethan Bamber

WHAT WOULD A FLY ON THE WALL HEAR IN YOUR DRESSING ROOM? "Good old Sussex by the Sea…" (when we've won)

MOST BEAUTIFUL THING YOU HAVE EVER SEEN? The jungle in Sri Lanka seen from a hotel window

HOBBIES? The Xbox

WHO WOULD YOU MOST LIKE TO HAVE A NET WITH? Shane Warne

MAKE ONE PREDICTION FOR THE FUTURE OF CRICKET: Sussex will be one of the strongest counties in the country

WHAT DO YOU MOST ENJOY LISTENING TO? Indie rock

WHAT MAKES YOU WORRY? The exams I have coming up

WHAT GIVES YOU JOY? Playing cricket with people I like

TWITTER: @hinnersjnr

Batting	Mat	Inns	NO	Runs	HS	Ave	SR	100	50	Ct	St
First-class	1	2	0	20	19	10.00	43.47	0	0	0	-

Bowling	Mat	Balls	Runs	Wkts	BBI	BBM	Ave	Econ	SR	5w	10
First-class	1	36	35	0	-	-	-	5.83	-	0	0

MICHAEL HOGAN   RHB / RMF / R0 / W3

FULL NAME: Michael Garry Hogan
BORN: May 31, 1981, Newcastle, Australia
SQUAD NO: 31
HEIGHT: 6ft 5in
NICKNAME: Hulk
TEAMS: Glamorgan, Hobart Hurricanes,
Western Australia
ROLE: Bowler
DEBUT: First-class: 2009; List A: 2009;
T20: 2010

BEST BATTING: 57 Glamorgan vs Lancashire, Colwyn Bay, 2015
BEST BOWLING: 7-92 Glamorgan vs Gloucestershire, Bristol, 2013
COUNTY CAP: 2013

MOST EXCITING DAY AS A CRICKETER? Defending three when I was bowling the final over
in a T20 game against Kent a few years ago
CHILDHOOD SPORTING HERO? Glenn McGrath
SURPRISING FACT ABOUT YOU? I'm very boring
TWITTER: @hoges31
NOTES: In December the Western Australian seamer announced that this summer –
Hogan's 10th at Glamorgan – will be his last as a professional cricketer. The 41-year-old
took his 600th first-class wicket in 2020 and was in fine form last summer, finishing as the
club's leading wicket-taker in the Championship and playing a lead role in Glamorgan's
triumphant One-Day Cup campaign. After being delayed because of the pandemic, Hogan
has been granted a testimonial for his final season in Cardiff. "I'm 41 and need to spend
more time with my family, I've missed out on a lot with the kids and it's probably the right
time for me and for the club to look to the future," said Hogan. "I'm incredibly happy with
my form, it's been nice to play at such a great club, but time moves on, there's always a
replacement and hopefully someone else will have a successful 10 or 15 year career with
Glamorgan"

Batting	Mat	Inns	NO	Runs	HS	Ave	SR	100	50	Ct	St
First-class	172	239	95	2361	57	16.39	84.86	0	4	81	-
List A	79	30	20	187	27	18.70	82.74	0	0	28	-
T20s	97	21	13	78	17*	9.75	102.63	0	0	41	-

Bowling	Mat	Balls	Runs	Wkts	BBI	BBM	Ave	Econ	SR	5w	10
First-class	172	34750	15623	636	7/92	10/87	24.56	2.69	54.6	24	2
List A	79	3959	3218	118	5/44	5/44	27.27	4.87	33.5	1	0
T20s	97	1966	2565	105	5/17	5/17	24.42	7.82	18.7	1	0

MAX HOLDEN

LHB / OB / R0 / W0

FULL NAME: Max David Edward Holden
BORN: December 18, 1997, Cambridge
SQUAD NO: 4
HEIGHT: 6ft 1in
NICKNAME: Pepsi
EDUCATION: Sawston Village College, Cambridge; Hills Road Sixth Form College, Cambridge
TEAMS: Middlesex, England Lions, Northamptonshire
ROLE: Batter
DEBUT: First-class: 2017; List A: 2017; T20: 2018

BEST BATTING: 153 Northamptonshire vs Kent, Beckenham, 2017
BEST BOWLING: 2-59 Northamptonshire vs Kent, Beckenham, 2017

WHO IS YOUR LOOKALIKE? Taylor Lautner (actor)
FIRST CRICKET CLUB? Cambridge St Giles CC, Cambridgeshire
WHAT WOULD YOU CHANGE ABOUT THE STRUCTURE OF THE COUNTY SEASON? Nothing – I love the game the way it is
WHO IS THE BEST BATTER/KEEPER/ALLROUNDER/BOWLER IN COUNTY CRICKET (EXCLUDING TEAMMATES)? Ollie Pope/Ben Foakes/Lewis Gregory/Ollie Robinson
MOST UNDERRATED PLAYER IN COUNTY CRICKET? Wayne Madsen
WHAT WOULD A FLY ON THE WALL HEAR IN YOUR DRESSING ROOM? Tim Murtagh
MOST BEAUTIFUL THING YOU HAVE EVER SEEN? The view from the top of Table Mountain in Cape Town
WHO WOULD YOU MOST AND LEAST LIKE TO HAVE A NET WITH? Most – Steve Smith (to chat about batting theory). Least – Tim Murtagh (he gets me out every other ball)
WHAT MAKES YOU WORRY? Disorganisation
GUILTY PLEASURE? Harry Potter
TWITTER: @maxholden_4

Batting	Mat	Inns	NO	Runs	HS	Ave	SR	100	50	Ct	St
First-class	53	97	5	2356	153	25.60	46.21	3	9	21	-
List A	16	15	1	613	166	43.78	89.61	1	3	4	-
T20s	24	23	3	539	102*	26.95	128.63	1	2	16	-

Bowling	Mat	Balls	Runs	Wkts	BBI	BBM	Ave	Econ	SR	5w	10
First-class	53	642	460	5	2/59	3/94	92.00	4.29	128.4	0	0
List A	16	126	104	1	1/29	1/29	104.00	4.95	126.0	0	0
T20s	24	6	12	0	-	-	-	12.00	-	0	0

IAN HOLLAND

RHB / RM / R0 / W0

HAMPSHIRE

FULL NAME: Ian Gabriel Holland
BORN: October 3, 1990, Wisconsin, USA
SQUAD NO: 22
HEIGHT: 6ft
NICKNAME: Dutchy
EDUCATION: Ringwood Secondary College, Melbourne
TEAMS: USA, Hampshire, Northamptonshire, Victoria
ROLE: Allrounder
DEBUT: ODI: 2019; T20I: 2021; First-class: 2016; List A: 2017; T20: 2017

BEST BATTING: 146* Hampshire vs Middlesex, Southampton, 2021
BEST BOWLING: 6-60 Hampshire vs Surrey, Arundel, 2020

WHO IS YOUR LOOKALIKE? Hugh Jackman (actor)
FIRST CRICKET CLUB? Ringwood CC, Melbourne
WHAT WOULD YOU CHANGE ABOUT THE STRUCTURE OF THE COUNTY SEASON? Reduce the schedule by about 20 per cent so that players have more time between games
MOST UNDERRATED PLAYER IN COUNTY CRICKET? Josh Davey
WHO WOULD YOU LEAST LIKE TO HAVE A NET WITH? Malcolm Marshall
GUILTY PLEASURE? Doughnuts
TWITTER: @IanHolland22

Batting	Mat	Inns	NO	Runs	HS	Ave	SR	100	50	Ct	St
ODIs	8	8	0	244	75	30.50	76.48	0	2	3	-
T20Is	6	3	1	47	39*	23.50	90.38	0	0	1	-
First-class	45	72	7	1752	146*	26.95	46.34	3	9	21	-
List A	28	27	6	465	75	22.14	82.30	0	3	10	-
T20s	23	18	9	238	65	26.44	114.97	0	1	5	-

Bowling	Mat	Balls	Runs	Wkts	BBI	BBM	Ave	Econ	SR	5w	10
ODIs	8	275	209	7	3/11	3/11	29.85	4.56	39.2	0	0
T20Is	6	138	89	10	2/3	2/3	8.90	3.86	13.8	0	0
First-class	45	4442	1926	63	6/60	7/77	30.57	2.60	70.5	1	0
List A	28	987	893	25	4/12	4/12	35.72	5.42	39.4	0	0
T20s	23	331	342	15	2/3	2/3	22.80	6.19	22.0	0	0

LUKE HOLLMAN

LHB / LB / RO / WO

FULL NAME: Luke Barnaby Kurt Hollman
BORN: September 16, 2000, Islington, London
SQUAD NO: 56
HEIGHT: 6ft 3in
NICKNAME: Donny
EDUCATION: Acland Burghley School, Camden, London
TEAMS: Middlesex, England U19
ROLE: Allrounder
DEBUT: First-class: 2021; List A: 2021; T20: 2020

BEST BATTING: 46 Middlesex vs Worcestershire, Lord's, 2021
BEST BOWLING: 5-65 Middlesex vs Sussex, Hove, 2021

WHO IS YOUR LOOKALIKE? Ole Gunnar Solskjaer
FIRST CRICKET CLUB? North Middlesex CC, London
WHAT WOULD YOU CHANGE ABOUT THE STRUCTURE OF THE COUNTY SEASON? Play more red-ball cricket in high summer
WHO IS THE BEST BATTER/KEEPER/ALLROUNDER/BOWLER IN COUNTY CRICKET (EXCLUDING TEAMMATES)? Jamie Smith/Adam Wheater/Craig Overton/Simon Harmer
MOST UNDERRATED PLAYER IN COUNTY CRICKET? Callum Parkinson
MOST BEAUTIFUL THING YOU HAVE EVER SEEN? Sunset at Rum Point on Grand Cayman
IF YOU COULD TURN BACK TIME... I'd create a better structure for a T20 Champions League
MAKE ONE PREDICTION FOR THE FUTURE OF CRICKET: Pakistan and India will play Test matches against each other
WHAT MAKES YOU WORRY? When I overthink things
WHAT GIVES YOU JOY? Playing cricket

Batting	Mat	Inns	NO	Runs	HS	Ave	SR	100	50	Ct	St
First-class	6	9	1	176	46	22.00	39.19	0	0	3	-
List A	4	4	1	28	14*	9.33	80.00	0	0	1	-
T20s	19	17	5	269	51	22.41	131.21	0	1	11	-

Bowling	Mat	Balls	Runs	Wkts	BBI	BBM	Ave	Econ	SR	5w	10
First-class	6	634	363	13	5/65	10/155	27.92	3.43	48.7	2	1
List A	4	222	196	8	4/56	4/56	24.50	5.29	27.7	0	0
T20s	19	282	359	18	3/18	3/18	19.94	7.63	15.6	0	0

ALEX HORTON

RHB / WK / R0 / W0

FULL NAME: Alex Jack Horton
BORN: January 7, 2004, Newport, Monmouthshire
SQUAD NO: 12
HEIGHT: 5ft 10in
NICKNAME: Horts
EDUCATION: St Edward's School, Oxford
TEAMS: Glamorgan, England U19
ROLE: Wicketkeeper/batter

WHO IS YOUR LOOKALIKE? Supposedly it's Victor Lindelöf (footballer)
FIRST CRICKET CLUB? Newbridge CC, Monmouthshire, Wales
WHO IS THE BEST BATTER/KEEPER/ALLROUNDER/BOWLER IN COUNTY CRICKET (EXCLUDING TEAMMATES)? Alex Lees/Ben Foakes/Chris Woakes/James Anderson
MOST UNDERRATED PLAYER IN COUNTY CRICKET? Tom Prest (England U19 captain)
MOST BEAUTIFUL THING YOU HAVE EVER SEEN? A bird's eye view of the Dominican Republic as I was flying over it
HOBBIES? Golf
IF YOU COULD TURN BACK TIME... I wouldn't have played that one time for Blackwood CC when I was 12...
WHO WOULD YOU MOST AND LEAST LIKE TO HAVE A NET WITH? Most – Viv Richards. Least – Virat Kohli
MAKE ONE PREDICTION FOR THE FUTURE OF CRICKET: It will become more and more a white-ball game – though I hope not!
WHAT MAKES YOU WORRY? Exams
WHAT GIVES YOU JOY? Sport
TWITTER: @AlexQuidge12

ADAM HOSE   RHB / RM / R0 / W0

FULL NAME: Adam John Hose
BORN: October 25, 1992, Newport, Isle of Wight
SQUAD NO: 21
HEIGHT: 6ft 5in
NICKNAME: Pipe
EDUCATION: Carisbrooke School, Newport
TEAMS: Warwickshire, Somerset, Wellington
ROLE: Batter
DEBUT: First-class: 2016; List A: 2015; T20: 2015

BEST BATTING: 111 Warwickshire vs Nottinghamshire, Edgbaston, 2019

FIRST CRICKET CLUB? Ventnor CC, Isle of Wight
MOST EXCITING DAY AS A CRICKETER? T20 Finals Day with Birmingham Bears in 2017
CHILDHOOD SPORTING HERO? Kevin Pietersen
BEST INNINGS YOU'VE SEEN? Roelof van der Merwe's 165 not out to beat Surrey in the 2017 One-Day Cup. We were chasing 291 and it wasn't looking good at 22-5…
FAVOURITE SMELL? A Sunday roast
GUILTY PLEASURE? Caramel Digestives
TWITTER: @adamhose21

Batting	Mat	Inns	NO	Runs	HS	Ave	SR	100	50	Ct	St
First-class	19	35	1	746	111	21.94	44.99	1	4	5	-
List A	29	24	1	761	101*	33.08	90.27	1	4	16	-
T20s	65	64	6	1642	119	28.31	144.16	1	9	30	-

Bowling	Mat	Balls	Runs	Wkts	BBI	BBM	Ave	Econ	SR	5w	10
First-class	19	-	-	-	-	-	-	-	-	-	-
List A	29	-	-	-	-	-	-	-	-	-	-
T20s	65	-	-	-	-	-	-	-	-	-	-

BENNY HOWELL RHB / RM / R0 / W0

FULL NAME: Benny Alexander Cameron Howell
BORN: October 5, 1988, Bordeaux, France
SQUAD NO: 13
HEIGHT: 5ft 11in
NICKNAME: Novak
EDUCATION: The Oratory School, Reading
TEAMS: Gloucestershire, Hampshire, Chattogram Challengers, Khulna Titans, Melbourne Renegades, Peshawar Zalmi, Punjab Kings, Rangpur Riders
ROLE: Allrounder
DEBUT: First-class: 2011; List A: 2010; T20: 2011

BEST BATTING: 163 Gloucestershire vs Glamorgan, Cardiff, 2017
BEST BOWLING: 5-57 Gloucestershire vs Leicestershire, Leicester, 2013
COUNTY CAP: 2012 (Gloucestershire)

FIRST CRICKET CLUB? Stoke Row CC, Oxfordshire
MOST EXCITING DAY AS A CRICKETER? The 2015 one-day final at Lord's
CHILDHOOD SPORTING HERO? Steve Waugh
BIGGEST INFLUENCE ON YOUR DEVELOPMENT AS A CRICKETER (EXCLUDING PARENTS)?
In a general sense, all baseball pitchers – they have incredible skills that are honed over thousands of hours of practice
WHAT WOULD YOU DO IF YOU WERE IN CHARGE OF COUNTY CRICKET? Organise a winter competition, encourage an objective review of umpire performances
GUILTY PLEASURE? A nightly ritual serving of natural yoghurt, peanut butter, hazelnut butter, banana and berries
TWITTER: @bennyhowell510
NOTES: Howell was handed his first IPL contract when he was bought by Punjab Kings for this year's tournament

Batting	Mat	Inns	NO	Runs	HS	Ave	SR	100	50	Ct	St
First-class	86	136	13	3378	163	27.46	54.35	2	18	52	-
List A	86	72	14	2050	122	35.34	90.70	1	13	27	-
T20s	157	130	37	2122	57	22.81	129.46	0	6	63	-

Bowling	Mat	Balls	Runs	Wkts	BBI	BBM	Ave	Econ	SR	5w	10
First-class	86	6455	3222	96	5/57	8/96	33.56	2.99	67.2	1	0
List A	86	3043	2640	76	3/37	3/37	34.73	5.20	40.0	0	0
T20s	157	2938	3516	163	5/18	5/18	21.57	7.18	18.0	1	0

FYNN HUDSON-PRENTICE   RHB / RMF / R0 / W0 / MVP20

FULL NAME: Fynn Jake Hudson-Prentice
BORN: January 12, 1996, Haywards Heath, Sussex
SQUAD NO: 33
HEIGHT: 6ft
NICKNAME: Jack Sparrow
EDUCATION: Warden Park School, Cuckfield, West Sussex; Bede's Senior School, Hailsham, East Sussex
TEAMS: Sussex, Derbyshire
ROLE: Allrounder
DEBUT: First-class: 2015; List A: 2014; T20: 2019

BEST BATTING: 99 Derbyshire vs Middlesex, Derby, 2019
BEST BOWLING: 5-68 Derbyshire vs Nottinghamshire, Trent Bridge, 2021

WHO IS YOUR LOOKALIKE? Captain Jack Sparrow
FIRST CRICKET CLUB? St Andrews CC, Burgess Hill, West Sussex
BIGGEST INFLUENCE ON YOUR DEVELOPMENT AS A CRICKETER (EXCLUDING PARENTS)?
Steve Kirby – he has been a great friend, mentor and coach over the last four years of my career, helping me to where I am now
WHO IS THE BEST BATTER/KEEPER/ALLROUNDER/BOWLER IN COUNTY CRICKET (EXCLUDING TEAMMATES)? Ollie Pope/Ben Foakes/Darren Stevens/Simon Harmer
MOST UNDERRATED PLAYER IN COUNTY CRICKET? Luis Reece
MOST BEAUTIFUL THING YOU HAVE EVER SEEN? The views from the Southern Alps in New Zealand
HOBBIES? Golf, golf, golf
WHO WOULD YOU MOST LIKE TO HAVE A NET WITH? Andrew Flintoff
WHAT DO YOU MOST ENJOY LISTENING TO? The High Performance Podcast
TWITTER: @fynnhudson33

Batting	Mat	Inns	NO	Runs	HS	Ave	SR	100	50	Ct	St
First-class	27	45	7	925	99	24.34	59.06	0	4	7	-
List A	10	8	2	328	93	54.66	112.71	0	3	2	-
T20s	27	19	3	244	41	15.25	121.39	0	0	8	-

Bowling	Mat	Balls	Runs	Wkts	BBI	BBM	Ave	Econ	SR	5w	10
First-class	27	2582	1373	47	5/68	8/76	29.21	3.19	54.9	1	0
List A	10	307	339	6	3/37	3/37	56.50	6.62	51.1	0	0
T20s	27	450	697	28	3/36	3/36	24.89	9.29	16.0	0	0

ALEX HUGHES

RHB / RM / R0 / W0

DERBYSHIRE

FULL NAME: Alex Lloyd Hughes
BORN: September 29, 1991, Wordsley, Staffordshire
SQUAD NO: 18
HEIGHT: 6ft
NICKNAME: Yozza
EDUCATION: Ounsdale High School, Wolverhampton; University of Worcester
TEAMS: Derbyshire
ROLE: Allrounder
DEBUT: First-class: 2013; List A: 2012; T20: 2011

BEST BATTING: 142 Derbyshire vs Gloucestershire, Bristol, 2017
BEST BOWLING: 4-46 Derbyshire vs Glamorgan, Derby, 2014
COUNTY CAP: 2017

WHO IS YOUR LOOKALIKE? Jude Law
FIRST CRICKET CLUB? Wombourne CC, Staffordshire
WHAT WOULD YOU CHANGE ABOUT THE STRUCTURE OF THE COUNTY SEASON? Play the first two months of the season in Barbados or Dubai
WHO IS THE BEST BATTER/KEEPER/ALLROUNDER/BOWLER IN COUNTY CRICKET (EXCLUDING TEAMMATES)? Adam Lyth/Ben Cox/Matt Critchley/Chris Rushworth
MOST UNDERRATED PLAYER IN COUNTY CRICKET? Ben Raine
MOST BEAUTIFUL THING YOU HAVE EVER SEEN? The straight left hand of Conor McGregor (martial artist)
IF YOU COULD TURN BACK TIME... Everything happens for a reason...
WHO WOULD YOU MOST LIKE TO HAVE A NET WITH? Some numpty so I can smack it everywhere
WHAT DO YOU MOST ENJOY LISTENING TO? 50 Cent (rapper)
WHAT GIVES YOU JOY? Everything! Peace and love to you all
GUILTY PLEASURE? Call of Duty (video game)
TWITTER: @Yozza18

Batting	Mat	Inns	NO	Runs	HS	Ave	SR	100	50	Ct	St
First-class	78	136	12	3401	142	27.42	45.62	6	13	54	-
List A	71	49	8	894	96*	21.80	92.73	0	3	30	-
T20s	89	68	17	869	43*	17.03	121.87	0	0	36	-

Bowling	Mat	Balls	Runs	Wkts	BBI	BBM	Ave	Econ	SR	5w	10
First-class	78	3687	1897	37	4/46	4/75	51.27	3.08	99.6	0	0
List A	71	2027	1898	43	4/44	4/44	44.13	5.61	47.1	0	0
T20s	89	1415	1903	54	4/42	4/42	35.24	8.06	26.2	0	0

SEAN HUNT

RHB / LFM / R0 / W0

FULL NAME: Sean Frank Hunt
BORN: December 7, 2001, Guildford, Surrey
SQUAD NO: 21
HEIGHT: 6ft 5in
NICKNAME: Hunty
EDUCATION: Howard of Effingham School, Surrey
TEAMS: Sussex
ROLE: Bowler
DEBUT: First-class: 2021

BEST BATTING: 7 Sussex vs Lancashire, Old Trafford, 2021
BEST BOWLING: 3-47 Sussex vs Lancashire, Old Trafford, 2021

WHO IS YOUR LOOKALIKE? Sean Dyche (football manager)
FIRST CRICKET CLUB? Horsley & Send CC, West Horsley, Surrey
WHAT WOULD YOU CHANGE ABOUT THE STRUCTURE OF THE COUNTY SEASON? Play all the T20 Blast in one uninterrupted block
BIGGEST INFLUENCE ON YOUR DEVELOPMENT AS A CRICKETER (EXCLUDING PARENTS)? Geoff Arnold, my former bowling coach at Surrey
WHO IS THE BEST BATTER/KEEPER/ALLROUNDER/BOWLER IN COUNTY CRICKET (EXCLUDING TEAMMATES)? James Vince/Ben Foakes/Darren Stevens/Simon Harmer
MOST UNDERRATED PLAYER IN COUNTY CRICKET? Ethan Bamber
MOST BEAUTIFUL THING YOU HAVE EVER SEEN? A Guinness
WHO WOULD YOU MOST AND LEAST LIKE TO HAVE A NET WITH? Most – Pat Cummins. Least – Steve Smith
MAKE ONE PREDICTION FOR THE FUTURE OF CRICKET: Test cricket will keep going strong
WHAT DO YOU MOST ENJOY LISTENING TO? Frankie Stew & Harvey Gunn
WHAT MAKES YOU WORRY? A 3ft putt
TWITTER: @seanhunt139

Batting	Mat	Inns	NO	Runs	HS	Ave	SR	100	50	Ct	St
First-class	6	10	4	12	7	2.00	13.18	0	0	0	-

Bowling	Mat	Balls	Runs	Wkts	BBI	BBM	Ave	Econ	SR	5w	10
First-class	6	767	487	13	3/47	4/72	37.46	3.80	59.0	0	0

LIAM HURT

RHB / RFM / R0 / W0

FULL NAME: Liam Jack Hurt
BORN: March 15, 1994, Preston, Lancashire
SQUAD NO: 22
HEIGHT: 6ft 3in
NICKNAME: Tyrone
EDUCATION: Balshaw's CE High School, Leyland, Lancashire
TEAMS: Lancashire, Leicestershire
ROLE: Bowler
DEBUT: First-class: 2019; List A: 2015; T20: 2019

BEST BATTING: 38 Lancashire vs Leicestershire, Leicester, 2019
BEST BOWLING: 4-27 Lancashire vs Durham, Chester-le-Street, 2020

WHO IS YOUR LOOKALIKE? Anthony Joshua (boxer) or Ashley Banjo (dancer/TV personality)
FIRST CRICKET CLUB? Leyland CC, Lancashire
MAKE ONE PREDICTION FOR THE FUTURE OF CRICKET: Players will be bought and sold mid-season
WHAT DO YOU MOST ENJOY LISTENING TO? Matt Parkinson
WHAT MAKES YOU WORRY? George Lavelle's dancing
GUILTY PLEASURE? Watching Friends
TWITTER: @LiamHurt

Batting	Mat	Inns	NO	Runs	HS	Ave	SR	100	50	Ct	St
First-class	3	3	0	41	38	13.66	42.70	0	0	0	-
List A	12	6	3	49	15*	16.33	84.48	0	0	4	-
T20s	7	1	0	0	0	0.00	0.00	0	0	4	-

Bowling	Mat	Balls	Runs	Wkts	BBI	BBM	Ave	Econ	SR	5w	10
First-class	3	438	248	7	4/27	5/71	35.42	3.39	62.5	0	0
List A	12	468	461	15	3/55	3/55	30.73	5.91	31.2	0	0
T20s	7	114	185	6	3/22	3/22	30.83	9.73	19.0	0	0

BRETT HUTTON

RHB / RMF / R0 / W0

FULL NAME: Brett Alan Hutton
BORN: February 6, 1993, Doncaster, Yorkshire
SQUAD NO: 16
HEIGHT: 6ft 3in
NICKNAME: Bert
EDUCATION: Worksop College, Nottinghamshire
TEAMS: Nottinghamshire, England U19, Northamptonshire
ROLE: Bowler
DEBUT: First-class: 2011; List A: 2011; T20: 2016

NOTTINGHAMSHIRE

BEST BATTING: 74 Nottinghamshire vs Durham, Trent Bridge, 2016
BEST BOWLING: 8-57 Northamptonshire vs Gloucestershire, Northampton, 2018
COUNTY CAP: 2021 (Nottinghamshire)

WHO IS YOUR LOOKALIKE? Teen Wolf
FIRST CRICKET CLUB? Worksop CC, Nottinghamshire
WHAT WOULD YOU CHANGE ABOUT THE STRUCTURE OF THE COUNTY SEASON? More red-ball cricket in the middle of the summer
MOST UNDERRATED PLAYER IN COUNTY CRICKET? Ben Sanderson
MOST BEAUTIFUL THING YOU HAVE EVER SEEN? Barbados
IF YOU COULD TURN BACK TIME... I'd take golf lessons as a kid
WHO WOULD YOU MOST AND LEAST LIKE TO HAVE A NET WITH? Brett Lee – both the most and least I'd like to have a net with. It would be great to have faced him even though he bowls too fast to bat against
WHAT DO YOU MOST ENJOY LISTENING TO? Country music
WHAT MAKES YOU WORRY? Money
WHAT GIVES YOU JOY? Golf
GUILTY PLEASURE? Cutting the grass
TWITTER: @BrettAH26

Batting	Mat	Inns	NO	Runs	HS	Ave	SR	100	50	Ct	St
First-class	66	100	12	1554	74	17.65	43.49	0	5	43	-
List A	23	15	5	245	46	24.50	102.08	0	0	9	-
T20s	9	7	4	50	18*	16.66	106.38	0	0	3	-

Bowling	Mat	Balls	Runs	Wkts	BBI	BBM	Ave	Econ	SR	5w	10
First-class	66	10901	5860	222	8/57	10/106	26.39	3.22	49.1	11	2
List A	23	956	961	22	3/72	3/72	43.68	6.03	43.4	0	0
T20s	9	172	255	5	2/28	2/28	51.00	8.89	34.4	0	0

COLIN INGRAM — LHB / LB / R0 / W0

GLAMORGAN

FULL NAME: Colin Alexander Ingram
BORN: July 3, 1985, Port Elizabeth, SA
SQUAD NO: 41
HEIGHT: 5ft 10in
NICKNAME: Stingray
EDUCATION: Woodbridge College, Eastern Cape, South Africa
TEAMS: South Africa, Glamorgan, Adelaide Strikers, Delhi Daredevils, Eastern Province, Hobart Hurricanes, Somerset, Warriors
ROLE: Batter
DEBUT: ODI: 2010; T20I: 2010; First-class: 2004; List A: 2005; T20: 2007

BEST BATTING: 190 Eastern Province vs KwaZulu-Natal, Port Elizabeth, 2009
BEST BOWLING: 4-16 Eastern Province vs Boland, Port Elizabeth, 2006
COUNTY CAP: 2017 (Glamorgan)

WHO IS YOUR LOOKALIKE? Russell Crowe
FIRST CRICKET CLUB? Old Grey CC, Port Elizabeth, South Africa
WHO IS THE BEST BATTER/ALLROUNDER/BOWLER IN COUNTY CRICKET (EXCLUDING TEAMMATES)? James Vince/Ben Stokes or Darren Stevens/David Payne
MOST UNDERRATED PLAYER IN COUNTY CRICKET? Jamie Overton
MOST BEAUTIFUL THING YOU HAVE EVER SEEN? A sunrise over water with a rod in hand
HOBBIES? I enjoy building things and working with wood – have made the odd table and kid's jungle gym
IF YOU COULD TURN BACK TIME... I'd have changed many things… but let the past be the past and let's crack on
WHO WOULD YOU MOST LIKE TO HAVE A NET WITH? Mark Ramprakash
TWITTER: @CAIngram41

Batting	Mat	Inns	NO	Runs	HS	Ave	SR	100	50	Ct	St
ODIs	31	29	3	843	124	32.42	82.32	3	3	12	-
T20Is	9	9	1	210	78	26.25	129.62	0	1	2	-
First-class	112	197	17	6675	190	37.08		14	30	75	-
List A	186	178	18	7584	142	47.40	90.13	18	48	65	-
T20s	309	301	42	7569	127*	29.22	137.71	4	46	96	-

Bowling	Mat	Balls	Runs	Wkts	BBI	BBM	Ave	Econ	SR	5w	10
ODIs	31	6	17	0	-	-	-	17.00	-	0	0
T20Is	9	-	-	-	-	-	-	-	-	-	-
First-class	112	3516	2132	50	4/16	5/50	42.64	3.63	70.3	0	0
List A	186	1482	1345	40	4/39	4/39	33.62	5.44	37.0	0	0
T20s	309	949	1247	38	4/32	4/32	32.81	7.88	24.9	0	0

WILL JACKS RHB / OB / R0 / W0

FULL NAME: William George Jacks
BORN: November 21, 1998, Chertsey, Surrey
SQUAD NO: 9
HEIGHT: 6ft 2in
NICKNAME: Jacko
EDUCATION: St George's College, Weybridge
TEAMS: Surrey, Chattogram Challengers, England Lions, Hobart Hurricanes, Islamabad United
ROLE: Batter
DEBUT: First-class: 2018; List A: 2018; T20: 2018

BEST BATTING: 120 Surrey vs Kent, Beckenham, 2019
BEST BOWLING: 1-7 Surrey vs Gloucestershire, The Oval, 2021

FIRST CRICKET CLUB? Valley End CC, Surrey
MOST EXCITING DAY AS A CRICKETER? Winning the County Championship in 2018
CHILDHOOD SPORTING HERO? Kevin Pietersen
WHAT WOULD YOU DO IF YOU WERE IN CHARGE OF COUNTY CRICKET? Play more T20 games on the weekend
TWITTER: @Wjacks9

Batting	Mat	Inns	NO	Runs	HS	Ave	SR	100	50	Ct	St
First-class	30	44	5	1142	120	29.28	49.76	1	9	32	-
List A	22	21	0	506	121	24.09	95.65	1	2	13	-
T20s	77	70	5	1724	92*	26.52	154.48	0	12	29	-

Bowling	Mat	Balls	Runs	Wkts	BBI	BBM	Ave	Econ	SR	5w	10
First-class	30	552	320	4	1/7	1/33	80.00	3.47	138.0	0	0
List A	22	482	423	11	2/32	2/32	38.45	5.26	43.8	0	0
T20s	77	413	499	19	4/15	4/15	26.26	7.24	21.7	0	0

LYNDON JAMES

RHB / RMF / R0 / W0

NOTTINGHAMSHIRE

FULL NAME: Lyndon Wallace James
BORN: December 27, 1998, Worksop, Nottinghamshire
SQUAD NO: 45
HEIGHT: 6ft 3in
NICKNAME: LJ
EDUCATION: Oakham School, Rutland
TEAMS: Nottinghamshire
ROLE: Allrounder
DEBUT: First-class: 2018; List A: 2019; T20: 2021

BEST BATTING: 91 Nottinghamshire vs Lancashire, Trent Bridge, 2021
BEST BOWLING: 4-51 Nottinghamshire vs Essex, Trent Bridge, 2021

FIRST CRICKET CLUB? Ordsall Bridon CC, Nottinghamshire
BIGGEST INFLUENCE ON YOUR DEVELOPMENT AS A CRICKETER (EXCLUDING PARENTS)?
My brother – because of all the back-yard cricket we played together
MOST BEAUTIFUL THING YOU HAVE EVER SEEN? Beautiful downtown Bramall Lane
IF YOU COULD TURN BACK TIME… I wouldn't have bottled a hundred last season
WHO WOULD YOU MOST AND LEAST LIKE TO HAVE A NET WITH? Most – Kevin Pietersen.
Least – Marnus Labuschagne
WHAT MAKES YOU WORRY? Facing the GOAT (Darren Stevens) on a nipper
WHAT GIVES YOU JOY? Hitting fairways and greens
GUILTY PLEASURE? Call of Duty (video game)
TWITTER: @LyndonJames27

Batting	Mat	Inns	NO	Runs	HS	Ave	SR	100	50	Ct	St
First-class	15	22	2	635	91	31.75	40.99	0	5	2	-
List A	7	6	2	40	16*	10.00	71.42	0	0	1	-
T20s	4	2	0	8	7	4.00	100.00	0	0	2	-

Bowling	Mat	Balls	Runs	Wkts	BBI	BBM	Ave	Econ	SR	5w	10
First-class	15	1146	601	20	4/51	6/54	30.05	3.14	57.3	0	0
List A	7	54	48	5	5/48	5/48	9.60	5.33	10.8	1	0
T20s	4	-	-	-	-	-	-	-	-	-	-

KEATON JENNINGS — LHB / RM / R1 / W0

FULL NAME: Keaton Kent Jennings
BORN: June 19, 1992, Johannesburg, South Africa
SQUAD NO: 1
HEIGHT: 6ft 4in
NICKNAME: Jet
EDUCATION: King Edward VII School; University of South Africa
TEAMS: England, Lancashire, Durham, Gauteng, South Africa U19
ROLE: Batter
DEBUT: Test: 2016; First-class: 2011; List A: 2012; T20: 2014

BEST BATTING: 221* Durham vs Yorkshire, Chester-le-Street, 2016
BEST BOWLING: 3-37 Durham vs Sussex, Chester-le-Street, 2017
COUNTY CAP: 2018 (Lancashire)

FIRST CRICKET CLUB? Pirates CC, Johannesburg, South Africa
FAMILY TIES? My brother Dylan, uncle Kenneth and father Ray have all played first-class cricket in South Africa
BIGGEST INFLUENCE ON YOUR DEVELOPMENT AS A CRICKETER (EXCLUDING PARENTS)? Andy Flower
MOST BEAUTIFUL THING YOU HAVE EVER SEEN? A Kumar Sangakkara cover-drive
HOBBIES? Studying for a Masters in Business
WHO WOULD YOU MOST AND LEAST LIKE TO HAVE A NET WITH? Most – Mike Hussey, loved watching him when I was growing up. Least – Mark Wood, because he bowls too fast!
WHAT DO YOU MOST ENJOY LISTENING TO? Foo Fighters
TWITTER: @JetJennings

Batting	Mat	Inns	NO	Runs	HS	Ave	SR	100	50	Ct	St
Tests	17	32	1	781	146*	25.19	42.49	2	1	17	-
First-class	148	254	17	8078	221*	34.08	45.10	20	31	121	-
List A	73	72	14	2404	139	41.44	81.27	4	17	31	-
T20s	70	51	17	1252	108	36.82	121.90	1	5	15	-

Bowling	Mat	Balls	Runs	Wkts	BBI	BBM	Ave	Econ	SR	5w	10
Tests	17	73	55	0	-	-	-	4.52	-	0	0
First-class	148	1761	988	30	3/37	4/48	32.93	3.36	58.7	0	0
List A	73	690	670	11	2/19	2/19	60.90	5.82	62.7	0	0
T20s	70	510	628	22	4/37	4/37	28.54	7.38	23.1	0	0

MANRAJ JOHAL
RHB / RFM / R0 / W0

WARWICKSHIRE

FULL NAME: Manraj Singh Johal
BORN: October 12, 2001, Birmingham
SQUAD NO: 5
HEIGHT: 6ft 1in
NICKNAME: Manny
EDUCATION: Oldbury Academy; Sandwell College, West Midlands
TEAMS: Warwickshire
ROLE: Bowler
DEBUT: First-class: 2021; List A: 2021

BEST BATTING: 19 Warwickshire vs Lancashire, Lord's, 2021
BEST BOWLING: 3-29 Warwickshire vs Lancashire, Lord's, 2021

FIRST CRICKET CLUB? Olton & West Warwickshire CC
MOST EXCITING DAY AS A CRICKETER? The day I heard that I was signing my first contract as a professional with Warwickshire
CHILDHOOD SPORTING HERO? Brett Lee
BIGGEST INFLUENCE ON YOUR DEVELOPMENT AS A CRICKETER (EXCLUDING PARENTS)? Kadeer Ali, the former Worcestershire batsman and now their Second XI coach. He helped me to join a Premier League club which was so important for my development. I also played with him in a couple of Minor Counties games for Staffordshire
NOTES: The Staffordshire seamer became a professional in October 2020 after signing his first contract with Warwickshire. Johal, who plays his club cricket for West Bromwich Dartmouth CC in the Birmingham & District Premier League, has worked his way through the ranks since first representing Warwickshire at U11 level. Manraj made his first-class debut last summer, taking four wickets in the Bob Willis Trophy final at Lord's, and also featured in the One-Day Cup

Batting	Mat	Inns	NO	Runs	HS	Ave	SR	100	50	Ct	St
First-class	1	1	0	19	19	19.00	73.07	0	0	0	-
List A	6	3	1	16	10*	8.00	64.00	0	0	2	-

Bowling	Mat	Balls	Runs	Wkts	BBI	BBM	Ave	Econ	SR	5w	10
First-class	1	108	59	4	3/29	4/59	14.75	3.27	27.0	0	0
List A	6	250	228	7	2/35	2/35	32.57	5.47	35.7	0	0

MICHAEL JONES

RHB / OB / R0 / W0

FULL NAME: Michael Alexander Jones
BORN: January 5, 1998, Ormskirk, Lancashire
SQUAD NO: 10
HEIGHT: 6ft 3in
NICKNAME: Conqs
EDUCATION: Ormskirk School; Myerscough College, Preston; Edge Hill University, Ormskirk
TEAMS: Scotland, Durham
ROLE: Batter
DEBUT: ODI: 2018; First-class: 2018; List A: 2018

BEST BATTING: 82 Durham vs Nottinghamshire, Trent Bridge, 2020

MOST EXCITING DAY AS A CRICKETER? The World Cup Qualifier between Scotland and West Indies at Harare in 2018. We fell five runs short of a win which would have meant qualification for the 2019 World Cup
CHILDHOOD SPORTING HERO? Steven Gerrard
WHAT WOULD YOU DO IF YOU WERE IN CHARGE OF COUNTY CRICKET? Introduce free hits for no-balls in first-class cricket
FAVOURITE SMELL? Sauvage by Christian Dior
GUILTY PLEASURE? Sugar doughnuts
TWITTER: @mikejones04

Batting	Mat	Inns	NO	Runs	HS	Ave	SR	100	50	Ct	St
ODIs	8	8	0	281	87	35.12	70.07	0	3	3	-
First-class	13	21	1	443	82	22.15	40.12	0	3	4	-
List A	8	8	0	281	87	35.12	70.07	0	3	3	-

Bowling	Mat	Balls	Runs	Wkts	BBI	BBM	Ave	Econ	SR	5w	10
ODIs	8	-	-	-	-	-	-	-	-	-	-
First-class	13	-	-	-	-	-	-	-	-	-	-
List A	8	-	-	-	-	-	-	-	-	-	-

ROB JONES

RHB / LB / R0 / W0

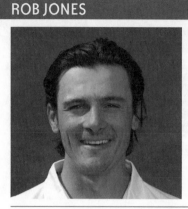

FULL NAME: Robert Peter Jones
BORN: November 3, 1995, Warrington, Cheshire
SQUAD NO: 12
HEIGHT: 5ft 11in
NICKNAME: Jonah
EDUCATION: Bridgewater High School, Warrington; Priestley College
TEAMS: Lancashire, England U19
ROLE: Batter
DEBUT: First-class: 2016; List A: 2018; T20: 2017

BEST BATTING: 122 Lancashire vs Middlesex, Lord's, 2019
BEST BOWLING: 1-4 Lancashire vs Northamptonshire, Old Trafford, 2021

WHO IS YOUR LOOKALIKE? Johnny Depp
FIRST CRICKET CLUB? Stretton CC, Warrington, Cheshire
BIGGEST INFLUENCE ON YOUR DEVELOPMENT AS A CRICKETER (EXCLUDING PARENTS)?
Bob Milne – he have me a chance at the Cheshire Academy
MOST BEAUTIFUL THING YOU HAVE EVER SEEN? The mountain of Tryfan in Snowdonia on a clear day
HOBBIES? Hiking, collecting whisky
WHAT GIVES YOU JOY? Whisky
GUILTY PLEASURE? Birdwatching
TWITTER: @robpeterjones

Batting	Mat	Inns	NO	Runs	HS	Ave	SR	100	50	Ct	St
First-class	39	56	5	1374	122	26.94	38.62	2	6	38	-
List A	20	16	3	425	72	32.69	72.89	0	3	9	-
T20s	21	14	8	238	61*	39.66	119.59	0	1	9	-

Bowling	Mat	Balls	Runs	Wkts	BBI	BBM	Ave	Econ	SR	5w	10
First-class	39	108	49	2	1/4	1/4	24.50	2.72	54.0	0	0
List A	20	122	122	2	1/3	1/3	61.00	6.00	61.0	0	0
T20s	21	6	10	0	-	-	-	10.00	-	0	0

CHRIS JORDAN

RHB / RFM / R0 / W1

FULL NAME: Christopher James Jordan
BORN: October 4, 1988, Christ Church, Barbados
SQUAD NO: 34
HEIGHT: 6ft
EDUCATION: Combermere School, Barbados; Dulwich College, London
TEAMS: England, Surrey, Barbados, Chennai Super Kings, Kings XI Punjab, Perth Scorchers, Sunrisers, Sussex, Sydney Sixers
ROLE: Allrounder
DEBUT: Test: 2014; ODI: 2013; T20I: 2013; First-class: 2007; List A: 2007; T20: 2008

BEST BATTING: 166 Sussex vs Northamptonshire, Northampton, 2019
BEST BOWLING: 7-43 Barbados vs Combined Campuses & Colleges, Bridgetown, 2013
COUNTY CAP: 2014 (Sussex)

FIRST CRICKET CLUB? Spartan Juniors CC, Barbados
TWITTER: @ChrisJordan94
NOTES: After nearly a decade at Sussex, Jordan has re-joined the club which released him back in 2013. "I am extremely pleased to be returning to the place where it all started for me at the age of 17," he said. "I return having evolved not only as a cricketer but as a person and I'm looking forward to continuing that evolution." Jordan has also been snapped up by Chennai Super Kings for this year's IPL

Batting	Mat	Inns	NO	Runs	HS	Ave	SR	100	50	Ct	St
Tests	8	11	1	180	35	18.00	56.25	0	0	14	-
ODIs	34	23	9	170	38*	12.14	88.08	0	0	19	-
T20Is	75	43	19	358	36	14.91	132.10	0	0	40	-
First-class	114	159	23	3443	166	25.31		3	15	137	-
List A	84	56	15	634	55	15.46		0	1	45	-
T20s	264	153	62	1308	45*	14.37	121.78	0	0	141	-

Bowling	Mat	Balls	Runs	Wkts	BBI	BBM	Ave	Econ	SR	5w	10
Tests	8	1530	752	21	4/18	7/50	35.80	2.94	72.8	0	0
ODIs	34	1618	1611	45	5/29	5/29	35.80	5.97	35.9	1	0
T20Is	75	1559	2250	80	4/6	4/6	28.12	8.65	19.4	0	0
First-class	114	18986	10730	335	7/43	9/58	32.02	3.39	56.6	10	0
List A	84	3798	3633	121	5/28	5/28	30.02	5.73	31.3	2	0
T20s	264	5262	7507	272	4/6	4/6	27.59	8.55	19.3	0	0

ESHUN KALLEY

RHB / RMF / R0 / W0

ESSEX

FULL NAME: Eshun Singh Kalley
BORN: November 23, 2001, Ilford, Essex
SQUAD NO: 30
EDUCATION: Barking Abbey School, Essex
TEAMS: Essex
ROLE: Bowler

NOTES: Kalley has been handed his first professional contract by Essex as the club look to bolster their seam-bowling stocks. Another Academy graduate from the Essex talent factory, he'll be hoping to follow Jack Plom and Ben Allison into the first-team picture and he did his chances no harm last campaign with a solid showing for the Second XI, taking 11 red-ball wickets at 25, while also turning out for Hertfordshire in the National Counties Championship, taking a five-for in his first appearance

MATT KELLY

RHB / RMF / R0 / W0

FULL NAME: Matthew Liam Kelly
BORN: December 07, 1994, Claremont, Western Australia, Australia
SQUAD NO: TBC
TEAMS: Northamptonshire, Australia U19, Perth Scorchers, Western Australia
ROLE: Bowler
DEBUT: First-class: 2017; List A: 2017; T20: 2018

BEST BATTING: 89 Western Australia vs New South Wales, Adelaide, 2020
BEST BOWLING: 6-67 Western Australia vs South Australia, Perth, 2019

NOTES: Northants have secured the Western Australian's signature for their first six Championship games. A strapping 6ft 3in seamer with a reputation for bowling long spells, Kelly has all the components to thrive in county cricket and will form a slippery new-ball attack with Ben Sanderson. While Kelly's white-ball traits are well known – a Perth Scorchers stalwart, he was snapped up by Kolkata Knight Riders in 2019 – it's his red-ball attributes which have attracted Northants; Kelly took more wickets than Mitchell Starc, Peter Siddle and Michael Neser in the 2020/21 Sheffield Shield season, picking up 20 at 34.25 apiece. "Matt possesses a fantastic skillset that we feel is well suited to English conditions and will complement our bowling attack nicely," said Chris Liddle, Northants's bowling coach. "He's got a great record in red-ball cricket and we think he's a perfect fit for what we need. I can't wait to get him over here and see what he can bring to the group"

Batting	Mat	Inns	NO	Runs	HS	Ave	SR	100	50	Ct	St
First-class	35	47	11	578	89	16.05	42.62	0	1	15	-
List A	18	8	2	50	16	8.33	72.46	0	0	10	-
T20s	27	10	4	63	23*	10.50	126.00	0	0	8	-

Bowling	Mat	Balls	Runs	Wkts	BBI	BBM	Ave	Econ	SR	5w	10
First-class	35	6578	3131	105	6/67	8/96	29.81	2.85	62.6	5	0
List A	18	789	674	25	4/25	4/25	26.96	5.12	31.5	0	0
T20s	27	584	787	41	4/25	4/25	19.19	8.08	14.2	0	0

ROB KEOGH   RHB / OB / R0 / W0

FULL NAME: Robert Ian Keogh
BORN: October 21, 1991, Dunstable, Bedfordshire
SQUAD NO: 14
HEIGHT: 6ft 2in
NICKNAME: Keezy
EDUCATION: Queensbury Upper School, Dunstable; Dunstable College
TEAMS: Northamptonshire
ROLE: Allrounder
DEBUT: First-class: 2012; List A: 2010; T20: 2011

BEST BATTING: 221 Northamptonshire vs Hampshire, Southampton, 2013
BEST BOWLING: 9-52 Northamptonshire vs Glamorgan, Northampton, 2016
COUNTY CAP: 2019

WHO IS YOUR LOOKALIKE? Olivier Giroud
FIRST CRICKET CLUB? Dunstable Town CC, Bedfordshire
WHO IS THE BEST BATTER/KEEPER/ALLROUNDER IN COUNTY CRICKET (EXCLUDING TEAMMATES)? David Bedingham/Jordan Cox/Darren Stevens
WHAT WOULD A FLY ON THE WALL HEAR IN YOUR DRESSING ROOM? Wannabe boxing commentary and some bad jokes
MOST BEAUTIFUL THING YOU HAVE EVER SEEN? A Rolex Daytona
IF YOU COULD TURN BACK TIME... I'd have begun playing golf at a younger age
WHO WOULD YOU LEAST LIKE TO HAVE A NET WITH? As a bowler, Emilio Gay – he bats for too long and I'd want to go home! As a batsman, Chris Rushworth – he would get me out all the time
WHAT DO YOU MOST ENJOY LISTENING TO? Dubai Beach Club Playlist
WHAT GIVES YOU JOY? Watches, golf and dogs
GUILTY PLEASURE? Peanut M&Ms
TWITTER: @RobKeogh91

Batting	Mat	Inns	NO	Runs	HS	Ave	SR	100	50	Ct	St
First-class	97	159	10	4453	221	29.88	50.91	11	14	25	-
List A	54	48	4	1432	134	32.54	88.94	2	12	12	-
T20s	71	48	15	921	59*	27.90	117.77	0	4	29	-

Bowling	Mat	Balls	Runs	Wkts	BBI	BBM	Ave	Econ	SR	5w	10
First-class	97	7358	4333	94	9/52	13/125	46.09	3.53	78.2	1	1
List A	54	1146	1036	11	2/26	2/26	94.18	5.42	104.1	0	0
T20s	71	318	439	16	3/30	3/30	27.43	8.28	19.8	0	0

SIMON KERRIGAN

RHB / SLA / RO / W2

FULL NAME: Simon Christopher Kerrigan
BORN: May 10, 1989, Preston, Lancashire
SQUAD NO: 10
HEIGHT: 5ft 9in
NICKNAME: Kegs
EDUCATION: Corpus Christi High School, Lancashire; Preston College; Edge Hill University, Ormskirk
TEAMS: England, Northamptonshire, Lancashire
ROLE: Bowler
DEBUT: Test: 2013; First-class: 2010; List A: 2011; T20: 2010

BEST BATTING: 62* Lancashire vs Hampshire, Southport, 2013
BEST BOWLING: 9-51 Lancashire vs Hampshire, Liverpool, 2011
COUNTY CAP: 2013 (Lancashire)

WHO IS YOUR LOOKALIKE? An umpa lumpa
FIRST CRICKET CLUB? Grimsargh CC, Preston, Lancashire
WHAT WOULD YOU CHANGE ABOUT THE STRUCTURE OF THE COUNTY SEASON? Play the RL50 as a knockout competition and include the National (formerly Minor) Counties. Use a Kookaburra ball in red-ball cricket during the months of April and September
BIGGEST INFLUENCE ON YOUR DEVELOPMENT AS A CRICKETER (EXCLUDING PARENTS)? John Stanworth (Lancashire Academy) and Peter Moores – both are brilliant coaches and man-managers
HOBBIES? Loading the dishwasher
WHO WOULD YOU MOST AND LEAST LIKE TO HAVE A NET WITH? Most – Murali Kartik, a genius. Least – Shane Watson (I would come out in a rash if I was to bowl to him)
WHAT MAKES YOU WORRY? The lack of reliable baseload power in Mozambique
WHAT GIVES YOU JOY? Birra Moretti
TWITTER: @Kegs10

Batting	Mat	Inns	NO	Runs	HS	Ave	SR	100	50	Ct	St
Tests	1	1	1	1	1*	-	8.33	0	0	0	-
First-class	117	142	48	1283	62*	13.64	36.85	0	3	40	-
List A	39	18	6	35	10	2.91	45.45	0	0	12	-
T20s	24	4	4	9	4*	-	180.00	0	0	11	-

Bowling	Mat	Balls	Runs	Wkts	BBI	BBM	Ave	Econ	SR	5w	10
Tests	1	48	53	0	-	-	-	6.62	-	0	0
First-class	117	22578	10699	354	9/51	12/192	30.22	2.84	63.7	15	3
List A	39	1689	1493	34	4/48	4/48	43.91	5.30	49.6	0	0
T20s	24	516	595	20	3/17	3/17	29.75	6.91	25.8	0	0

RASHID KHAN

RHB / LB

FULL NAME: Rashid Khan Arman
BORN: September 20, 1998, Nangarhar, Afghanistan
SQUAD NO: 1
TEAMS: Afghanistan, Sussex, Adelaide Strikers, Durban Heat, Guyana Amazon Warriors, Kabul Zwanan, Lahore Qalandars, Quetta Gladiators, Sunrisers Hyderabad
ROLE: Bowler
DEBUT: Test: 2018; ODI: 2015; T20I: 2015; First-class: 2016; List A: 2015; T20: 2015

BEST BATTING: 56* Kabul Zwanan vs Balkh Legends, Sharjah, 2018 (T20)
BEST BOWLING: 6-17 Adelaide Strikers vs Brisbane Heat, Brisbane, 2022 (T20)

TWITTER: @rashidkhan_19
NOTES: Sussex have re-signed the 23-year-old leg-spinner for a fourth T20 Blast campaign. Rashid was the first Afghan to sign for an English county when he joined Sussex ahead of the 2018 season and he played a huge part in taking the club to the final of that year's competition. He impressed again in 2019 and in all has taken 26 wickets in 23 matches at an economy rate of 7.07. Possessing a lethal googly, Rashid is the biggest talent to emerge from Afghanistan and has played in the major T20 leagues all over the world

Batting	Mat	Inns	NO	Runs	HS	Ave	SR	100	50	Ct	St
Tests	5	7	0	106	51	15.14	79.69	0	1	0	-
ODIs	80	63	10	1069	60*	20.16	103.38	0	5	25	-
T20Is	58	29	13	183	33	11.43	118.83	0	0	20	-
First-class	9	11	1	231	52	23.10	77.00	0	2	0	-
List A	82	64	10	1090	60*	20.18	104.00	0	5	26	-
T20s	311	176	57	1422	56*	11.94	145.10	0	1	89	-

Bowling	Mat	Balls	Runs	Wkts	BBI	BBM	Ave	Econ	SR	5w	10
Tests	5	1534	760	34	7/137	11/104	22.35	2.97	45.1	4	2
ODIs	80	4074	2821	151	7/18	7/18	18.68	4.15	26.9	4	0
T20Is	58	1316	1357	105	5/3	5/3	12.92	6.18	12.5	2	0
First-class	9	2713	1287	69	8/74	12/122	18.65	2.84	39.3	8	3
List A	82	4181	2909	155	7/18	7/18	18.76	4.17	26.9	4	0
T20s	311	7157	7571	435	6/17	6/17	17.40	6.34	16.4	4	0

FEROZE KHUSHI

RHB / OB / R0 / W0

FULL NAME: Feroze Isa Nazir Khushi
BORN: June 23, 1999, Whipps Cross, Essex
SQUAD NO: 23
HEIGHT: 6ft 1in
NICKNAME: Fink
EDUCATION: Kelmscott School, Walthamstow, London
TEAMS: Essex
ROLE: Batter
DEBUT: First-class: 2020; List A: 2021; T20: 2020

BEST BATTING: 66 Essex vs Surrey, Chelmsford, 2020

MOST EXCITING DAY AS A CRICKETER? When I hit six sixes in the last over of a school match when we needed 30 runs to win
CHILDHOOD SPORTING HERO? Shahid Afridi
SURPRISING FACT ABOUT YOU? I went to the same school as Fabrice Muamba
NOTES: The 22-year-old batter broke into the senior team in 2020, playing in four matches of Essex's triumphant campaign in the Bob Willis Trophy. Khushi made 45 on his first-class debut against Kent at Chelmsford and followed it up with 66 versus Surrey at the same ground. Last summer he made his List A debut and scored one hundred and a half-century in five innings during the One-Day Cup. In December he agreed a contract that will keep him at the club until the end of 2023 season. Khushi first signed for Essex in October 2017 after a number of impressive performances for the club's Second XI

Batting	Mat	Inns	NO	Runs	HS	Ave	SR	100	50	Ct	St
First-class	4	5	0	125	66	25.00	54.34	0	1	5	-
List A	5	5	0	234	109	46.80	86.98	1	1	2	-
T20s	3	3	0	19	17	6.33	95.00	0	0	0	-

Bowling	Mat	Balls	Runs	Wkts	BBI	BBM	Ave	Econ	SR	5w	10
First-class	4	-	-	-	-	-	-	-	-	-	-
List A	5	-	-	-	-	-	-	-	-	-	-
T20s	3	-	-	-	-	-	-	-	-	-	-

LOUIS KIMBER   RHB / OB / WK / R0 / W0

LEICESTERSHIRE

FULL NAME: Louis Philip James Kimber
BORN: February 24, 1997, Scunthorpe, Lincolnshire
SQUAD NO: 17
HEIGHT: 6ft 3in
NICKNAME: Melmo
EDUCATION: William Farr Church of England School, Lincoln; Loughborough University
TEAMS: Leicestershire
ROLE: Batter
DEBUT: First-class: 2019; List A: 2021; T20: 2021

BEST BATTING: 71 Leicestershire vs Worcestershire, Worcester, 2021
BEST BOWLING: 1-34 Loughborough MCCU vs Kent, Canterbury, 2019

WHO IS YOUR LOOKALIKE? Nick Kimber (my brother who plays for Surrey)
FIRST CRICKET CLUB? Lindum CC, Lincolnshire
WHO IS THE BEST BATTER/KEEPER/ALLROUNDER/BOWLER IN COUNTY CRICKET (EXCLUDING TEAMMATES)? Joe Root/Ben Foakes/Ben Stokes/James Anderson
MOST UNDERRATED PLAYER IN COUNTY CRICKET? Tom Abell
WHAT WOULD A FLY ON THE WALL HEAR IN YOUR DRESSING ROOM? Conversations about fantasy football
MOST BEAUTIFUL THING YOU HAVE EVER SEEN? Palm Beach, Sydney, Australia
IF YOU COULD TURN BACK TIME... I'd watch the Arsenal Invincibles of 2003/04
WHO WOULD YOU LEAST LIKE TO HAVE A NET WITH? Mitchell Johnson
MAKE ONE PREDICTION FOR THE FUTURE OF CRICKET: No more umpires
WHAT DO YOU MOST ENJOY LISTENING TO? Hybrid Minds
WHAT MAKES YOU WORRY? Heights
WHAT GIVES YOU JOY? Shooting below my handicap
TWITTER: @lkimber17

Batting	Mat	Inns	NO	Runs	HS	Ave	SR	100	50	Ct	St
First-class	6	9	1	250	71	31.25	46.72	0	3	7	-
List A	8	6	0	197	85	32.83	104.78	0	2	1	-
T20s	9	6	0	102	53	17.00	137.83	0	1	6	-

Bowling	Mat	Balls	Runs	Wkts	BBI	BBM	Ave	Econ	SR	5w	10
First-class	6	159	101	2	1/34	1/34	50.50	3.81	79.5	0	0
List A	8	-	-	-	-	-	-	-	-	-	-
T20s	9	-	-	-	-	-	-	-	-	-	-

NICK KIMBER

RHB / RMF / R0 / W0

FULL NAME: Nicholas John Henry Kimber
BORN: January 16, 2001, Lincoln
SQUAD NO: 12
HEIGHT: 6ft 2in
NICKNAME: Kimbo
EDUCATION: William Farr Church of England School, Lincoln; Oakham School, Rutland
TEAMS: Surrey, England U19
ROLE: Bowler
DEBUT: List A: 2021

SURREY

FIRST CRICKET CLUB? Lindum CC, Lincolnshire
FAMILY TIES? My older brother Louis plays for Leicestershire, and my other older brother James has played Minor Counties for Lincolnshire as well as for Notts Second XI
WHAT WOULD YOU CHANGE ABOUT THE STRUCTURE OF THE COUNTY SEASON? Play more pink-ball cricket and set up a franchise system
BIGGEST INFLUENCE ON YOUR DEVELOPMENT AS A CRICKETER (EXCLUDING PARENTS)? Neil Johnson, the former Zimbabwe allrounder and now director of cricket at Oakham School. He taught me a lot about the game and how to play it properly
HOBBIES? Video games
WHO WOULD YOU MOST AND LEAST LIKE TO HAVE A NET WITH? Most – Stuart Broad (my hero growing up). Least – Brett Lee
WHAT DO YOU MOST ENJOY LISTENING TO? Hip-hop
WHAT GIVES YOU JOY? Cricket
GUILTY PLEASURE? Doughnuts
TWITTER: @NKimber11

Batting	Mat	Inns	NO	Runs	HS	Ave	SR	100	50	Ct	St
List A	3	1	0	16	16	16.00	55.17	0	0	0	-

Bowling	Mat	Balls	Runs	Wkts	BBI	BBM	Ave	Econ	SR	5w	10
List A	3	72	87	2	2/57	2/57	43.50	7.25	36.0	0	0

SAMMY KING RHB / RMF / R0 / W0

NOTTINGHAMSHIRE

FULL NAME: Samuel Isaac Michael King
BORN: January 12, 2003, Nottingham
SQUAD NO: 94
HEIGHT: 6ft 4in
NICKNAME: Kingy
EDUCATION: Nottingham High School;
University of Nottingham
TEAMS: Nottinghamshire
ROLE: Allrounder
DEBUT: List A: 2021

WHO IS YOUR LOOKALIKE? Michele Morrone (actor)
FIRST CRICKET CLUB? Gedling Colliery CC, Nottingham
WHAT WOULD YOU CHANGE ABOUT THE STRUCTURE OF THE COUNTY SEASON?
Have more T20 cricket
WHO IS THE BEST BATTER/KEEPER/ALLROUNDER/BOWLER IN COUNTY CRICKET
(EXCLUDING TEAMMATES)? Hashim Amla/Ben Foakes/Tom Abell/Marchant de Lange
WHAT WOULD A FLY ON THE WALL HEAR IN YOUR DRESSING ROOM? "Shush Jevison,
enough from you"
MOST BEAUTIFUL THING YOU HAVE EVER SEEN? James Hayes failing a front squat
HOBBIES? Being social
WHO WOULD YOU MOST AND LEAST LIKE TO HAVE A NET WITH? Most – Muttiah
Muralitharan, to see how good he was. Least – Marchant de Lange, because he's rapid
MAKE ONE PREDICTION FOR THE FUTURE OF CRICKET: More money
WHAT MAKES YOU WORRY? Exams

Batting	Mat	Inns	NO	Runs	HS	Ave	SR	100	50	Ct	St
List A	1	1	0	11	11	11.00	52.38	0	0	0	-

Bowling	Mat	Balls	Runs	Wkts	BBI	BBM	Ave	Econ	SR	5w	10
List A	1	-	-	-	-	-	-	-	-	-	-

FRED KLAASSEN

RHB / LMF / R0 / W0

FULL NAME: Frederick Jack Klaassen
BORN: November 13, 1992, Haywards Heath, Sussex
SQUAD NO: 18
HEIGHT: 6ft 5in
NICKNAME: TFD
EDUCATION: University of Otago, Dunedin, New Zealand
TEAMS: Netherlands, Kent
ROLE: Bowler
DEBUT: ODI: 2018; T20I: 2018; First-class: 2019; List A: 2017; T20: 2018

BEST BATTING: 14* Kent vs Loughborough MCCU, Canterbury, 2019
BEST BOWLING: 4-44 Kent vs Middlesex, Canterbury, 2020

WHO IS YOUR LOOKALIKE? Roddy from the film Flushed Away
FIRST CRICKET CLUB? Cornwall CC, Auckland, New Zealand
WHAT WOULD YOU CHANGE ABOUT THE STRUCTURE OF THE COUNTY SEASON? Include Scotland, Ireland and Netherlands in the 50-over competition
WHO IS THE BEST BATTER/KEEPER/ALLROUNDER/BOWLER IN COUNTY CRICKET (EXCLUDING TEAMMATES)? David Bedingham/Ben Foakes/Lewis Gregory/David Payne
MOST UNDERRATED PLAYER IN COUNTY CRICKET? Chris Dent
MOST BEAUTIFUL THING YOU HAVE EVER SEEN? Steven Gerrard's goal against Olympiakos in the 2004/05 Champions League
MAKE ONE PREDICTION FOR THE FUTURE OF CRICKET: No more 50-over cricket
WHAT DO YOU MOST ENJOY LISTENING TO? Jazz
WHAT MAKES YOU WORRY? Flat pitches
TWITTER: @freddieklaassen

Batting	Mat	Inns	NO	Runs	HS	Ave	SR	100	50	Ct	St
ODIs	10	7	1	41	13	6.83	53.24	0	0	3	-
T20Is	24	9	3	34	13	5.66	85.00	0	0	11	-
First-class	5	8	3	45	14*	9.00	17.44	0	0	3	-
List A	27	19	8	98	16*	8.90	60.86	0	0	12	-
T20s	68	16	7	57	13	6.33	95.00	0	0	27	-

Bowling	Mat	Balls	Runs	Wkts	BBI	BBM	Ave	Econ	SR	5w	10
ODIs	10	576	351	20	3/23	3/23	17.55	3.65	28.8	0	0
T20Is	24	470	625	22	3/31	3/31	28.40	7.97	21.3	0	0
First-class	5	689	422	9	4/44	4/80	46.88	3.67	76.5	0	0
List A	27	1342	1066	41	3/23	3/23	26.00	4.76	32.7	0	0
T20s	68	1330	1915	73	4/17	4/17	26.23	8.63	18.2	0	0

TOM KOHLER-CADMORE   RHB / OB / R1 / W0

FULL NAME: Tom Kohler-Cadmore
BORN: August 19, 1994, Chatham, Kent
SQUAD NO: 32
HEIGHT: 6ft 2in
NICKNAME: Pepsi
EDUCATION: Malvern College, Worcestershire
TEAMS: Yorkshire, England Lions, Jaffna Kings, Peshawar Zalmi, Quetta Gladiators, Worcestershire
ROLE: Batter
DEBUT: First-class: 2014; List A: 2013; T20: 2014

BEST BATTING: 176 Yorkshire vs Leeds/Bradford MCCU, Weetwood, 2019

COUNTY CAP: 2019 (Yorkshire)

MOST EXCITING DAY AS A CRICKETER? My first Roses match
BIGGEST INFLUENCE ON YOUR DEVELOPMENT AS A CRICKETER (EXCLUDING PARENTS)?
My school coaches Noel Brett and Mark Hardinges – they put in so many hours of training with me, as did my Worcester coaches
WHAT WOULD YOU DO IF YOU WERE IN CHARGE OF COUNTY CRICKET? Go back to 40-over cricket, play the first month of the season somewhere warm
SURPRISING FACT ABOUT YOU? I've been called the songbird of my generation by people who have heard me sing
TWITTER: @tomkcadmore

Batting	Mat	Inns	NO	Runs	HS	Ave	SR	100	50	Ct	St
First-class	77	126	8	3812	176	32.30	52.65	9	16	108	-
List A	56	54	1	1808	164	34.11	86.79	3	10	29	-
T20s	108	107	10	2907	127	29.96	139.02	1	22	60	-

Bowling	Mat	Balls	Runs	Wkts	BBI	BBM	Ave	Econ	SR	5w	10
First-class	77	-	-	-	-	-	-	-	-	-	-
List A	56	-	-	-	-	-	-	-	-	-	-
T20s	108	-	-	-	-	-	-	-	-	-	-

MARNUS LABUSCHAGNE

RHB / LB / R0 / W0

FULL NAME: Marnus Labuschagne
BORN: June 22, 1994, Klerksdorp, North West Province, South Africa
SQUAD NO: 99
TEAMS: Australia, Glamorgan, Brisbane Heat, Queensland
ROLE: Batter
DEBUT: Test: 2018; ODI: 2020; First-class: 2014; List A: 2015; T20: 2017

BEST BATTING: 215 Australia vs New Zealand, Sydney, 2020
BEST BOWLING: 3-45 Australia vs Pakistan, Abu Dhabi, 2018

TWITTER: @marnus3cricket

NOTES: Labuschagne initially signed a two-year contract for Glamorgan in November 2019 but extended his deal to run until the end of 2022 after not being able to join up with the Welsh county during the pandemic-hit 2020 season. The Australian batter will be available across all formats, subject to international commitments. Labuschagne made a huge impact in his first season at Cardiff in 2019, scoring five centuries and five fifties in 10 Championship matches before playing a starring role for Australia in the Ashes. He was less effective in six red-ball appeareances last summer but finished as the club's leading run-scorer in the T20 Blast. Only Ricky Ponting, Matthew Hayden and Wally Hammond have scored more runs in an Australian Test summer than Labuschagne's 897 in five Tests during the 2019/20 season down under. The 27-year-old was ranked No.1 in the ICC's Test batting rankings as of March 2022

Batting	Mat	Inns	NO	Runs	HS	Ave	SR	100	50	Ct	St
Tests	23	40	1	2220	215	56.92	53.77	6	12	20	-
ODIs	13	12	0	473	108	39.41	91.13	1	3	4	-
First-class	105	184	14	7841	215	46.12	54.02	21	41	95	-
List A	55	54	2	1868	135	35.92	87.65	2	15	23	-
T20s	25	24	2	666	93*	30.27	127.34	0	4	13	-

Bowling	Mat	Balls	Runs	Wkts	BBI	BBM	Ave	Econ	SR	5w	10
Tests	23	894	540	12	3/45	5/119	45.00	3.62	74.5	0	0
ODIs	13	24	36	0	-	-	-	9.00	-	0	0
First-class	105	4968	3131	64	3/45	5/77	48.92	3.78	77.6	0	0
List A	55	599	647	9	3/46	3/46	71.88	6.48	66.5	0	0
T20s	25	294	443	21	3/13	3/13	21.09	9.04	14.0	0	0

TOM LACE

RHB / WK / R0 / W0

FULL NAME: Thomas Cresswell Lace
BORN: May 27, 1998, Hammersmith
SQUAD NO: 8
HEIGHT: 5ft 9in
NICKNAME: Lacey
EDUCATION: Millfield School, Somerset;
Royal Holloway, University of London
TEAMS: Gloucestershire, Derbyshire,
Middlesex
ROLE: Batter
DEBUT: First-class: 2018; List A: 2019

BEST BATTING: 143 Derbyshire vs Glamorgan, Swansea, 2019

FIRST CRICKET CLUB? Sheen Park Colts, Wycombe, Buckinghamshire
MOST EXCITING DAY AS A CRICKETER? Making my first-class debut for Derbyshire in 2019
CHILDHOOD SPORTING HERO? Frank Lampard
WHAT WOULD YOU DO IF YOU WERE IN CHARGE OF COUNTY CRICKET? Make the morning football warm-up compulsory
FAVOURITE SMELL? When you walk past a Subway
GUILTY PLEASURE? The Greatest Showman (musical)
TWITTER: @tom_lace

Batting	Mat	Inns	NO	Runs	HS	Ave	SR	100	50	Ct	St
First-class	33	61	5	1730	143	30.89	45.05	4	7	22	-
List A	15	13	0	205	48	15.76	68.79	0	0	3	-

Bowling	Mat	Balls	Runs	Wkts	BBI	BBM	Ave	Econ	SR	5w	10
First-class	33	-	-	-	-	-	-	-	-	-	-
List A	15	12	20	2	2/20	2/20	10.00	10.00	6.0	0	0

SURANGA LAKMAL

RHB / RMF / R0 / W0

FULL NAME: Ranasinghe Arachchige
Suranga Lakmal
BORN: March 10, 1987, Matara, Sri Lanka
SQUAD NO: 82
TEAMS: Sri Lanka, Derbyshire, Jaffna Kings,
Kandy Crusaders, Tamil Union Cricket &
Athletic Club, Western Troopers
ROLE: Bowler
DEBUT: Test: 2010; ODI: 2009; T20I: 2011;
First-class: 2008; List A: 2007; T20: 2008

BEST BATTING: 58* Tamil Union Cricket & Athletic Club vs Sri Lanka Navy SC, Welisara, 2013
BEST BOWLING: 6-68 Tamil Union Cricket & Athletic Club vs Nondescripts CC, Colombo, 2013

TWITTER: @surangalk1987
NOTES: The Sri Lankan seamer will be reunited with his former coach Mickey Arthur after signing a two-year deal with Derbyshire that covers all formats. Lakmal, who recently retired from international cricket, is the fourth-highest wicket-taker in Sri Lanka's Test history and his experience and ability to swing the ball both ways should make him a formidable opponent in county cricket. "Suranga is among Sri Lanka's all-time greats with the ball and it's brilliant to be able to bring him to Derbyshire for the next two seasons," said Arthur. "We have big ambitions for the project at Derbyshire and Suranga's decision to retire from international cricket and commit to the club shows he's as excited about those plans as the other players and coaches"

Batting	Mat	Inns	NO	Runs	HS	Ave	SR	100	50	Ct	St
Tests	69	107	25	928	42	11.31	48.25	0	0	22	-
ODIs	86	48	22	244	26	9.38	60.39	0	0	20	-
T20Is	11	6	3	7	5*	2.33	63.63	0	0	3	-
First-class	129	168	36	1510	58*	11.43	53.45	0	1	46	-
List A	170	92	45	436	38*	9.27	65.36	0	0	42	-
T20s	66	31	16	143	33	9.53	109.16	0	0	18	-

Bowling	Mat	Balls	Runs	Wkts	BBI	BBM	Ave	Econ	SR	5w	10
Tests	69	12335	6186	170	5/47	7/80	36.38	3.00	72.5	4	0
ODIs	86	3881	3534	109	4/13	4/13	32.42	5.46	35.6	0	0
T20Is	11	208	330	8	2/26	2/26	41.25	9.51	26.0	0	0
First-class	129	20075	11049	346	6/68	9/134	31.93	3.30	58.0	9	0
List A	170	7609	6712	235	5/31	5/31	28.56	5.29	32.3	3	0
T20s	66	1275	1716	69	5/34	5/34	24.86	8.07	18.4	1	0

DANNY LAMB RHB / RFM / R0 / W0 / MVP35

LANCASHIRE

FULL NAME: Daniel John Lamb
BORN: September 7, 1995, Preston, Lancashire
SQUAD NO: 26
HEIGHT: 6ft
NICKNAME: Sherman
EDUCATION: St Michael's CE High School, Chorley; Cardinal Newman College, Preston; Edge Hill University, Ormskirk
TEAMS: Lancashire
ROLE: Allrounder
DEBUT: First-class: 2018; List A: 2017; T20: 2017

BEST BATTING: 125 Lancashire vs Kent, Canterbury, 2021
BEST BOWLING: 4-55 Lancashire vs Yorkshire, Headingley, 2020

WHO IS YOUR LOOKALIKE? Chuck Sherman from American Pie apparently
FIRST CRICKET CLUB? Hoghton CC, Lancashire
WHO IS THE BEST BATTER/KEEPER/BOWLER IN COUNTY CRICKET (EXCLUDING TEAMMATES)? James Vince/Ben Foakes/Simon Harmer
MOST BEAUTIFUL THING YOU HAVE EVER SEEN? The view from the summit of Bowfell in the Lake District
HOBBIES? Hiking (completing the Wainwrights)
WHAT GIVES YOU JOY? The Lake District
SURPRISING FACT ABOUT YOU? I was Blackburn Rovers Academy goalkeeper from U9 to U16 level
TWITTER: @lamby236

Batting	Mat	Inns	NO	Runs	HS	Ave	SR	100	50	Ct	St
First-class	19	25	4	575	125	27.38	43.65	1	3	7	-
List A	9	6	3	152	86*	50.66	131.03	0	1	5	-
T20s	34	16	8	170	29*	21.25	111.11	0	0	3	-

Bowling	Mat	Balls	Runs	Wkts	BBI	BBM	Ave	Econ	SR	5w	10
First-class	19	2418	1218	41	4/55	7/72	29.70	3.02	58.9	0	0
List A	9	436	406	14	5/30	5/30	29.00	5.58	31.1	1	0
T20s	34	558	769	28	3/23	3/23	27.46	8.26	19.9	0	0

MATT LAMB RHB / RM / R0 / W0

FULL NAME: Matthew James Lamb
BORN: July 19, 1996, Wolverhampton, Staffordshire
SQUAD NO: 7
HEIGHT: 6ft 4in
NICKNAME: Jon
EDUCATION: North Bromsgrove High School, Worcestershire
TEAMS: Warwickshire
ROLE: Batter
DEBUT: First-class: 2016; List A: 2017; T20: 2019

BEST BATTING: 173 Warwickshire vs Essex, Edgbaston, 2019
BEST BOWLING: 2-38 Warwickshire vs Worcestershire, Worcester, 2021

FIRST CRICKET CLUB? Barnt Green CC, Worcestershire
MOST EXCITING DAY AS A CRICKETER? Beating Middlesex at Lord's in 2017 inside three days after we were bowled out for 126 on the first day
CHILDHOOD SPORTING HERO? Paul Gascoigne
BIGGEST INFLUENCE ON YOUR DEVELOPMENT AS A CRICKETER (EXCLUDING PARENTS)? Former wicketkeeper/batsman Tony Frost, now Warwickshire's batting coach. He has supported me on and off the field
WHAT WOULD YOU DO IF YOU WERE IN CHARGE OF COUNTY CRICKET? No run-outs for backing up, and 12 runs if you hit it out the ground
SURPRISING FACT ABOUT YOU? I was about to quit cricket until I was luckily selected for a Second XI game against Worcestershire in September 2015 and managed to score 142
GUILTY PLEASURE? Homemade cheesecake
TWITTER: @Lamb_Matt

Batting	Mat	Inns	NO	Runs	HS	Ave	SR	100	50	Ct	St
First-class	33	56	7	1356	173	27.67	41.69	1	7	11	-
List A	11	10	1	421	119*	46.77	95.68	1	2	3	-
T20s	10	9	2	168	39	24.00	120.00	0	0	4	-

Bowling	Mat	Balls	Runs	Wkts	BBI	BBM	Ave	Econ	SR	5w	10
First-class	33	488	304	8	2/38	2/38	38.00	3.73	61.0	0	0
List A	11	174	160	4	4/35	4/35	40.00	5.51	43.5	0	0
T20s	10	6	9	0	-	-	-	9.00	-	0	0

SOMERSET

FULL NAME: Thomas Alexander Lammonby
BORN: June 2, 2000, Exeter, Devon
SQUAD NO: 15
HEIGHT: 6ft
NICKNAME: Lammers
EDUCATION: Exeter School
TEAMS: Somerset, England U19, Hobart Hurricanes, Karachi Kings
ROLE: Batter
DEBUT: First-class: 2020; T20: 2019

BEST BATTING: 116 Somerset vs Essex, Lord's, 2020
BEST BOWLING: 1-4 Somerset vs Gloucestershire, Taunton

WHO IS YOUR LOOKALIKE? Sam Maunder (rugby union player)
FIRST CRICKET CLUB? Exeter CC, Devon
BIGGEST CRICKETING REGRET? Not playing at the 2018 U19 World Cup because of injury
WHO IS THE BEST BATTER/KEEPER/BOWLER IN COUNTY CRICKET (EXCLUDING TEAMMATES)? Joe Clarke/Ben Foakes/Simon Harmer
MOST UNDERRATED PLAYER IN COUNTY CRICKET? Tom Hartley
WHAT WOULD A FLY ON THE WALL HEAR IN YOUR DRESSING ROOM? Lots of talk about hairlines
HOBBIES? Squash – as a kid I played in competitions all around the country
WHO WOULD YOU MOST AND LEAST LIKE TO HAVE A NET WITH? Most – Ricky Ponting. Least – Morné Morkel
MAKE ONE PREDICTION FOR THE FUTURE OF CRICKET: It will grow in Europe
WHAT MAKES YOU WORRY? Spiders
GUILTY PLEASURE? Chocolate eclairs
TWITTER: @TomLammonby

Batting	Mat	Inns	NO	Runs	HS	Ave	SR	100	50	Ct	St
First-class	19	33	4	851	116	29.34	52.49	4	2	11	-
T20s	42	33	8	492	90	19.68	150.45	0	1	13	-

Bowling	Mat	Balls	Runs	Wkts	BBI	BBM	Ave	Econ	SR	5w	10
First-class	19	534	325	6	1/4	1/4	54.16	3.65	89.0	0	0
T20s	42	192	320	11	2/32	2/32	29.09	10.00	17.4	0	0

GEORGE LAVELLE

LHB / WK / R0 / W0

FULL NAME: George Isaac Davies Lavelle
BORN: March 24, 2000, Ormskirk, Lancashire
SQUAD NO: 24
HEIGHT: 5ft 8in
NICKNAME: Spizza
EDUCATION: Merchant Taylors' School, Crosby, Merseyside
TEAMS: Lancashire, England U19
ROLE: Wicketkeeper/batter
DEBUT: First-class: 2020; List A: 2021; T20: 2020

BEST BATTING: 32 Lancashire vs Nottinghamshire, Trent Bridge, 2021

WHO IS YOUR LOOKALIKE? Michael Owen
FIRST CRICKET CLUB? Ormskirk CC, Lancashire
WHO IS THE BEST BATTER/KEEPER/ALLROUNDER/BOWLER IN COUNTY CRICKET (EXCLUDING TEAMMATES)? James Vince/Ben Cox/Simon Harmer/Luke Fletcher
WHAT WOULD A FLY ON THE WALL HEAR IN YOUR DRESSING ROOM? Jack Blatherwick singing
MOST BEAUTIFUL THING YOU HAVE EVER SEEN? Yosemite National Park, California
WHO WOULD YOU MOST LIKE TO HAVE A NET WITH? Ian Bell
WHAT MAKES YOU WORRY? Who I select for my fantasy football team
WHAT GIVES YOU JOY? Mo Salah
TWITTER: Glavelle_181

Batting	Mat	Inns	NO	Runs	HS	Ave	SR	100	50	Ct	St
First-class	3	5	0	56	32	11.20	50.90	0	0	7	-
List A	7	4	0	100	52	25.00	96.15	0	1	6	1
T20s	2	2	0	18	12	9.00	90.00	0	0	0	-

Bowling	Mat	Balls	Runs	Wkts	BBI	BBM	Ave	Econ	SR	5w	10
First-class	3	-	-	-	-	-	-	-	-	-	-
List A	7	-	-	-	-	-	-	-	-	-	-
T20s	2	-	-	-	-	-	-	-	-	-	-

DAN LAWRENCE　　　　　　　　　　RHB / LB / R1 / W0

ESSEX

FULL NAME: Daniel William Lawrence
BORN: July 12, 1997, Whipps Cross, Essex
SQUAD NO: 28
EDUCATION: Trinity Catholic High School,
Woodford Green, London
TEAMS: England, Essex, Brisbane Heat
ROLE: Batter
DEBUT: Test: 2021; First-class: 2015; List A:
2016; T20: 2015

BEST BATTING: 161 Essex vs Surrey, The Oval, 2015
BEST BOWLING: 2-28 Essex vs Durham, Chelmsford, 2021
COUNTY CAP: 2017

FAMILY TIES? My dad is the groundsman at Chingford CC and played at the club for many years. My great uncle played for England
CHILDHOOD SPORTING HERO? David Beckham
TWITTER: @DanLawrence288
NOTES: Lawrence has been on England's radar ever since he made 161 as a 17-year-old in 2015 in his second Championship appearance. The following year he passed 1,000 first-class runs in his first full season at Chelmsford and was the Cricket Writers' Young Player of the Year in 2017 after contributing three hundreds to Essex's title-winning campaign. He made his England Lions debut that year. Lawrence was a key contributor when Essex won the Championship-T20 double in 2019 and impressed hugely during the England Lions tour to Australia the following winter. He hasn't been able to nail down a place in the England side since making his Test debut in Sri Lanka in January 2021 but was recalled to the national side for the recent tour of the West Indies

Batting	Mat	Inns	NO	Runs	HS	Ave	SR	100	50	Ct	St
Tests	8	15	2	354	81*	27.23	49.03	0	3	1	-
First-class	93	147	16	5073	161	38.72	53.23	11	26	64	-
List A	28	25	0	670	115	26.80	89.09	1	4	9	-
T20s	74	67	9	1575	86	27.15	140.12	0	9	24	-

Bowling	Mat	Balls	Runs	Wkts	BBI	BBM	Ave	Econ	SR	5w	10
Tests	8	36	33	1	1/16	1/16	33.00	5.50	36.0	0	0
First-class	93	1033	610	17	2/26	2/8	35.88	3.54	60.7	0	0
List A	28	573	597	11	3/35	3/35	54.27	6.25	52.0	0	0
T20s	74	450	580	26	3/21	3/21	22.30	7.73	17.3	0	0

JACK LEACH

LHB / SLA / R0 / W3

FULL NAME: Matthew Jack Leach
BORN: June 22, 1991, Taunton, Somerset
SQUAD NO: 17
HEIGHT: 6ft
NICKNAME: Nut
EDUCATION: Bishop Fox's Community School; Richard Huish College; Cardiff Metropolitan University
TEAMS: England, Somerset
ROLE: Bowler
DEBUT: Test: 2018; First-class: 2012; List A: 2012; T20: 2021

SOMERSET

BEST BATTING: 92 England vs Ireland, Lord's, 2019
BEST BOWLING: 8-85 Somerset vs Essex, Taunton, 2018
COUNTY CAP: 2017

FIRST CRICKET CLUB? Taunton Deane CC, Somerset
BEST INNINGS YOU'VE SEEN? Marcus Trescothick's 13-ball fifty in a T20 in 2010
WHAT WOULD YOU DO IF YOU WERE IN CHARGE OF COUNTY CRICKET? Change the lbw law so that you can be given out even if you are hit outside the line
SURPRISING FACT ABOUT YOU? I wrote a letter to Marcus Trescothick asking for advice when I was about 10 years old. He sent me a long reply and I still have the letter. What a man
TWITTER: @jackleach1991

Batting	Mat	Inns	NO	Runs	HS	Ave	SR	100	50	Ct	St
Tests	19	34	10	324	92	13.50	36.94	0	1	9	-
First-class	110	155	39	1518	92	13.08	37.33	0	3	44	-
List A	17	5	2	22	18	7.33	44.00	0	0	9	-
T20s	2	-	-	-	-	-	-	-	-	1	-

Bowling	Mat	Balls	Runs	Wkts	BBI	BBM	Ave	Econ	SR	5w	10
Tests	19	4146	2180	68	5/83	8/153	32.05	3.15	60.9	2	0
First-class	110	20596	9384	351	8/85	12/102	26.73	2.73	58.6	22	3
List A	17	872	697	21	3/7	3/7	33.19	4.79	41.5	0	0
T20s	2	48	60	5	3/28	3/28	12.00	7.50	9.6	0	0

JOE LEACH

RHB / RMF / R0 / W3 / MVP31

WORCESTERSHIRE

FULL NAME: Joseph Leach
BORN: October 30, 1990, Stafford
SQUAD NO: 23
HEIGHT: 6ft
NICKNAME: SSB
EDUCATION: Shrewsbury School; University of Leeds
TEAMS: Worcestershire
ROLE: Allrounder
DEBUT: First-class: 2012; List A: 2012; T20: 2013

BEST BATTING: 114 Worcestershire vs Gloucestershire, Cheltenham, 2013
BEST BOWLING: 6-73 Worcestershire vs Warwickshire, Edgbaston, 2015
COUNTY CAP: 2012

WHO IS YOUR LOOKALIKE? Neil Ruddock (ex-footballer)
FIRST CRICKET CLUB? Stone CC, Staffordshire. Never play on the back foot at Stone!
BIGGEST INFLUENCE ON YOUR DEVELOPMENT AS A CRICKETER (EXCLUDING PARENTS)?
Grandpa – for endlessly throwing me balls in the nets
BIGGEST CRICKETING REGRET? Being injured for T20 Finals Day in 2018
WHO IS THE BEST BATTER/KEEPER/ALLROUNDER/BOWLER IN COUNTY CRICKET
(EXCLUDING TEAMMATES)? Wayne Madsen/Ben Foakes/Darren Stevens/Chris Rushworth
MOST UNDERRATED PLAYER IN COUNTY CRICKET? Matt Milnes
WHAT WOULD A FLY ON THE WALL HEAR IN YOUR DRESSING ROOM? A lot of stick being
aimed at Jake Libby and Charlie Morris
MOST BEAUTIFUL THING YOU HAVE EVER SEEN? The Rocky Mountains at Banff, Canada
WHAT DO YOU MOST ENJOY LISTENING TO? The Quickly Kevin, Will He Score? podcast
GUILTY PLEASURE? Escape to the Country on TV
TWITTER: @joeleach230

Batting	Mat	Inns	NO	Runs	HS	Ave	SR	100	50	Ct	St
First-class	106	157	22	3296	114	24.41	62.51	2	19	25	-
List A	45	35	11	708	88	29.50	102.01	0	2	17	-
T20s	54	33	8	261	24	10.44	113.47	0	0	10	-

Bowling	Mat	Balls	Runs	Wkts	BBI	BBM	Ave	Econ	SR	5w	10
First-class	106	17742	9756	368	6/73	10/122	26.51	3.29	48.2	14	1
List A	45	1971	1964	49	4/30	4/30	40.08	5.97	40.2	0	0
T20s	54	849	1355	52	5/33	5/33	26.05	9.57	16.3	1	0

KENT

FULL NAME: Jack Andrew Leaning
BORN: October 18, 1993, Bristol
SQUAD NO: 34
HEIGHT: 6ft
EDUCATION: Archbishop Holgate's School, York; York College
TEAMS: Kent, England U19, Yorkshire
ROLE: Batter
DEBUT: First-class: 2013; List A: 2012; T20: 2013

BEST BATTING: 220* Kent vs Sussex, Canterbury, 2020
BEST BOWLING: 2-20 Yorkshire vs Hampshire, Southampton, 2019
COUNTY CAP: 2016 (Yorkshire); 2021 (Kent)

WHO IS YOUR LOOKALIKE? Bruno Fernandes (footballer)
FIRST CRICKET CLUB? Heworth CC, York, North Yorkshire
WHAT WOULD YOU CHANGE ABOUT THE STRUCTURE OF THE COUNTY SEASON?
More Championship cricket in the middle of the summer
WHO IS THE BEST BATTER/KEEPER/BOWLER IN COUNTY CRICKET (EXCLUDING
TEAMMATES)? Gary Ballance/Ben Foakes/Simon Harmer
MOST UNDERRATED PLAYER IN COUNTY CRICKET? Ollie Robinson (Kent)
WHAT WOULD A FLY ON THE WALL HEAR IN YOUR DRESSING ROOM? Stevo talking us
through every wicket he's ever taken
MOST BEAUTIFUL THING YOU HAVE EVER SEEN? The view from the top of the Sydney
Harbour Bridge
IF YOU COULD TURN BACK TIME... I would have tried to become a golfer
WHO WOULD YOU MOST LIKE TO HAVE A NET WITH? Shane Warne in his prime
WHAT DO YOU MOST ENJOY LISTENING TO? The roar of the crowd when it's a full house
TWITTER: @JackLeaning1

Batting	Mat	Inns	NO	Runs	HS	Ave	SR	100	50	Ct	St
First-class	86	137	17	3979	220*	33.15	42.51	6	22	72	-
List A	54	46	7	1123	131*	28.79	79.64	2	5	26	-
T20s	77	67	16	1474	81*	28.90	133.27	0	6	38	-

Bowling	Mat	Balls	Runs	Wkts	BBI	BBM	Ave	Econ	SR	5w	10
First-class	86	1335	813	14	2/20	2/25	58.07	3.65	95.3	0	0
List A	54	345	327	10	5/22	5/22	32.70	5.68	34.5	1	0
T20s	77	132	168	8	3/15	3/15	21.00	7.63	16.5	0	0

ALEX LEES

LHB / LB / R2 / W0

DURHAM

FULL NAME: Alexander Zak Lees
BORN: April 14, 1993, Halifax, Yorkshire
SQUAD NO: 19
HEIGHT: 6ft 3in
NICKNAME: Leesy
EDUCATION: Holy Trinity Senior School, Halifax
TEAMS: Durham, Yorkshire
ROLE: Batter
DEBUT: First-class: 2010; List A: 2011; T20: 2013

BEST BATTING: 275* Yorkshire vs Derbyshire, Chesterfield, 2013
BEST BOWLING: 2-51 Yorkshire vs Middlesex, Lord's, 2016
COUNTY CAP: 2014 (Yorkshire)

CHILDHOOD SPORTING HERO? Brian Lara
FIRST CRICKET CLUB? Bradshaw & Illingworth CC, Halifax
SURPRISING FACT ABOUT YOU? I do a bit of magic on the side
TWITTER: @aleesy14
NOTES: Lees joined Durham in August 2018 following a tough couple of seasons at Yorkshire. The left-handed opener has since recovered the form of his early career, falling narrowly short of 1,000 first-class runs in 2019 and also impressing in 50-over cricket. He was outstanding for Durham the next year, finishing as the club's top run-scorer in both the Bob Willis Trophy and the T20 Blast. Following another consistent season in 2021, Lees received his first call-up to the Test squad for England's recent tour of the Caribbean.

Batting	Mat	Inns	NO	Runs	HS	Ave	SR	100	50	Ct	St
First-class	128	219	14	7153	275*	34.89	46.80	17	36	89	-
List A	63	58	6	2095	126*	40.28	78.25	4	16	22	-
T20s	56	53	6	1350	77*	28.72	121.18	0	8	20	-

Bowling	Mat	Balls	Runs	Wkts	BBI	BBM	Ave	Econ	SR	5w	10
First-class	128	67	96	3	2/51	2/51	32.00	8.59	22.3	0	0
List A	63	-	-	-	-	-	-	-	-	-	-
T20s	56	-	-	-	-	-	-	-	-	-	-

ARCHIE LENHAM

RHB / LB / RO / WO

FULL NAME: Archie David Lenham
BORN: July 23, 2004, Eastbourne, Sussex
SQUAD NO: 41
HEIGHT: 5ft 7in
NICKNAME: Catch
EDUCATION: Bede's Senior School,
Hailsham, East Sussex
TEAMS: Sussex, England U19
ROLE: Bowler
DEBUT: First-class: 2021; List A: 2021; T20: 2021

BEST BATTING: 20 Sussex vs Worcestershire, Worcester, 2021
BEST BOWLING: 1-60 Sussex vs Worcestershire, Worcester, 2021

FIRST CRICKET CLUB? Eastbourne CC, East Sussex
FAMILY TIES? My grandfather Les Lenham played for Sussex in the 1950s and '60s, and my dad Neil played for the club in the 1980s and '90s
WHO IS THE BEST BATTER/KEEPER/ALLROUNDER/BOWLER IN COUNTY CRICKET (EXCLUDING TEAMMATES)? James Vince/Ben Cox/Samit Patel/Simon Harmer
MOST UNDERRATED PLAYER IN COUNTY CRICKET? Alex Davies
MOST BEAUTIFUL THING YOU HAVE EVER SEEN? Views of the glacier at Les Deux Alpes in France
HOBBIES? Golf
WHO WOULD YOU MOST LIKE TO HAVE A NET WITH? Shane Warne, the best leg-spinner of all time
MAKE ONE PREDICTION FOR THE FUTURE OF CRICKET: England to win the 2022 T20 World Cup
WHAT GIVES YOU JOY? Playing sport

Batting	Mat	Inns	NO	Runs	HS	Ave	SR	100	50	Ct	St
First-class	1	2	0	29	20	14.50	41.42	0	0	0	-
List A	7	5	2	47	16	15.66	82.45	0	0	2	-
T20s	11	3	2	7	5*	7.00	35.00	0	0	3	-

Bowling	Mat	Balls	Runs	Wkts	BBI	BBM	Ave	Econ	SR	5w	10
First-class	1	78	71	1	1/60	1/71	71.00	5.46	78.0	0	0
List A	7	318	321	8	4/59	4/59	40.12	6.05	39.7	0	0
T20s	11	156	194	11	4/26	4/26	17.63	7.46	14.1	0	0

NED LEONARD
RHB / RFM / R0 / W0

SOMERSET

FULL NAME: Edward Owen Leonard
BORN: August 15, 2002, Hammersmith, London
SQUAD NO: 19
HEIGHT: 6ft 2in
NICKNAME: Deadly
EDUCATION: Millfield School, Somerset
TEAMS: Somerset, England U19
ROLE: Bowler
DEBUT: First-class: 2021; List A: 2021

BEST BATTING: 6 Somerset vs Lancashire, Taunton, 2021
BEST BOWLING: 1-68 Somerset vs Lancashire, Taunton, 2021

MOST EXCITING DAY AS A CRICKETER? Signing my first professional contract at Somerset
CHILDHOOD SPORTING HERO? Jonny Wilkinson
BIGGEST INFLUENCE ON YOUR DEVELOPMENT AS A CRICKETER (EXCLUDING PARENTS)?
Mark Garaway – director of cricket at Millfield School
WHAT WOULD YOU DO IF YOU WERE IN CHARGE OF COUNTY CRICKET? Remove the free-hit rule from T20 and one-day formats, allow three bouncers per over
FAVOURITE SMELL? A wood fire in the pub
TWITTER: @n_leoand

Batting	Mat	Inns	NO	Runs	HS	Ave	SR	100	50	Ct	St
First-class	1	2	1	10	6	10.00	55.55	0	0	1	-
List A	4	2	2	1	1*	-	100.00	0	0	2	-

Bowling	Mat	Balls	Runs	Wkts	BBI	BBM	Ave	Econ	SR	5w	10
First-class	1	108	85	1	1/68	1/85	85.00	4.72	108.0	0	0
List A	4	132	166	3	2/84	2/84	55.33	7.54	44.0	0	0

FULL NAME: Jacob Daniel Libby
BORN: January 3, 1993, Plymouth, Devon
SQUAD NO: 2
HEIGHT: 5ft 8in
NICKNAME: Libs
EDUCATION: Plymouth College; Truro College, Cornwall; Cardiff Metropolitan University
TEAMS: Worcestershire, Northamptonshire, Nottinghamshire
ROLE: Batter
DEBUT: First-class: 2014; List A: 2019; T20: 2018

WORCESTERSHIRE

BEST BATTING: 184 Worcestershire vs Glamorgan, Worcester, 2020
BEST BOWLING: 2-45 Worcestershire vs Glamorgan, Worcester, 2020

FIRST CRICKET CLUB? Menheniot & Looe CC, Cornwall
WHAT WOULD YOU CHANGE ABOUT THE STRUCTURE OF THE COUNTY SEASON? Play the first few rounds in the West Indies!
BIGGEST INFLUENCE ON YOUR DEVELOPMENT AS A CRICKETER (EXCLUDING PARENTS)? Sean Hooper – my old coach from Cornwall who I still seek advice from to this day
MOST UNDERRATED PLAYER IN COUNTY CRICKET? Brett Hutton
MOST BEAUTIFUL THING YOU HAVE EVER SEEN? Wineglass Bay in Tasmania
IF YOU COULD TURN BACK TIME... I would have got more Labradors
MAKE ONE PREDICTION FOR THE FUTURE OF CRICKET: The game in England will be played with a Kookaburra ball
WHAT DO YOU MOST ENJOY LISTENING TO? That Peter Crouch Podcast
WHAT MAKES YOU WORRY? The Dukes ball in April
WHAT GIVES YOU JOY? Scoring first-class hundreds
TWITTER: @JakeLibby1

Batting	Mat	Inns	NO	Runs	HS	Ave	SR	100	50	Ct	St
First-class	75	130	11	4176	184	35.09	44.32	10	18	29	-
List A	14	12	0	356	76	29.66	89.44	0	3	1	-
T20s	42	36	7	1002	78*	34.55	125.56	0	5	12	-

Bowling	Mat	Balls	Runs	Wkts	BBI	BBM	Ave	Econ	SR	5w	10
First-class	75	778	471	7	2/45	2/45	67.28	3.63	111.1	0	0
List A	14	48	26	0	-	-	-	3.25	-	0	0
T20s	42	54	77	1	1/11	1/11	77.00	8.55	54.0	0	0

ARRON LILLEY

RHB / OB

FULL NAME: Arron Mark Lilley
BORN: April 1, 1991, Tameside, Lancashire
SQUAD NO: 7
HEIGHT: 6ft 2in
NICKNAME: Bigshow
EDUCATION: Mossley Hollins High School, Tameside; Ashton Sixth Form
TEAMS: Leicestershire, Lancashire
ROLE: Allrounder
DEBUT: First-class: 2013; List A: 2012; T20: 2013

BEST BATTING: 99* Leicestershire vs Yorkshire, Leicester, 2021 (T20)
BEST BOWLING: 3-26 Leicestershire vs Durham, Leicester, 2021 (T20)

WHO IS YOUR LOOKALIKE? Tyson Fury
FIRST CRICKET CLUB? Micklehurst CC, Greater Manchester. My grandad and dad played there before me
WHAT WOULD YOU CHANGE ABOUT THE STRUCTURE OF THE COUNTY SEASON? Play more Twenty20!
WHO IS THE BEST BATTER/KEEPER/ALLROUNDER/BOWLER IN COUNTY CRICKET (EXCLUDING TEAMMATES)? Joe Clarke/Ben Foakes/Darren Stevens/Matt Parkinson
MOST UNDERRATED PLAYER IN COUNTY CRICKET? Tom Bailey
MOST BEAUTIFUL THING YOU HAVE EVER SEEN? My dog Hector
HOBBIES? Golf
WHO WOULD YOU MOST AND LEAST LIKE TO HAVE A NET WITH? Most – Shane Warne. Least – David Warner
MAKE ONE PREDICTION FOR THE FUTURE OF CRICKET: England will be No.1 in all formats by the year 2025
TWITTER: @Arronlilley20
NOTES: Lilley signed a three-year white-ball contract in December 2020

Batting	Mat	Inns	NO	Runs	HS	Ave	SR	100	50	Ct	St
First-class	16	20	5	444	63	29.60	88.27	0	2	5	-
List A	27	18	2	262	46	16.37	127.18	0	0	14	-
T20s	108	79	10	1415	99*	20.50	150.21	0	3	59	-

Bowling	Mat	Balls	Runs	Wkts	BBI	BBM	Ave	Econ	SR	5w	10
First-class	16	2721	1428	43	5/23	6/151	33.20	3.14	63.2	2	0
List A	27	774	715	19	4/30	4/30	37.63	5.54	40.7	0	0
T20s	108	1256	1571	49	3/26	3/26	32.06	7.50	25.6	0	0

GEORGE LINDE   LHB / SLA / R0 / W0

FULL NAME: George Fredrik Linde
BORN: December 04, 1991, Cape Town, South Africa
SQUAD NO: 27
TEAMS: South Africa, Kent, Cape Cobras, Cape Town Blitz, South Western Districts, Western Province
ROLE: Allrounder
DEBUT: Test: 2019; ODI: 2021; T20I: 2020; First-class: 2012; List A: 2012; T20: 2012

BEST BATTING: 148* Cape Cobras vs Titans, Cape Town, 2020
BEST BOWLING: 7-29 Cape Cobras vs Knights, Cape Town, 2021

TWITTER: @gflinde

NOTES: Kent have signed the South African allrounder on a two-year deal as an overseas player. A tall left-arm orthodox spinner and very capable lower-order batter, Linde is expected to be available across all competitions. He took Test-best figures of 5-64 in the most recent of his three Test appearances but has found himself on the periphery of the international set-up in recent times. "This is an exciting opportunity for me to play county cricket for the first time in my career," said Linde, who was named South Africa's domestic four-day cricketer of the year for 2021. "I'm really looking forward to wearing the Kent shirt with pride and to make my own mark on this club's history." Paul Downton, Kent's director of cricket, added: "We have long identified the need for an experienced, high-quality spin bowler to balance our side in all formats, and the fact that George is an accomplished left-handed middle-order batter makes his addition to the squad even more exciting"

Batting	Mat	Inns	NO	Runs	HS	Ave	SR	100	50	Ct	St
Tests	3	6	0	135	37	22.50	52.94	0	0	0	-
ODIs	2	2	1	27	18	27.00	93.10	0	0	3	-
T20Is	14	11	1	111	29	11.10	130.58	0	0	6	-
First-class	61	89	9	2453	148*	30.66	65.15	4	12	33	-
List A	64	58	11	1173	93*	24.95	103.25	0	8	28	-
T20s	106	81	24	974	52*	17.08	135.09	0	2	29	-

Bowling	Mat	Balls	Runs	Wkts	BBI	BBM	Ave	Econ	SR	5w	10
Tests	3	473	252	9	5/64	5/68	28.00	3.19	52.5	1	0
ODIs	2	90	72	3	2/32	2/32	24.00	4.80	30.0	0	0
T20Is	14	288	340	15	3/23	3/23	22.66	7.08	19.2	0	0
First-class	61	11016	5310	222	7/29	11/131	23.91	2.89	49.6	15	3
List A	64	2891	2562	89	6/47	6/47	28.78	5.31	32.4	2	0
T20s	106	2101	2537	110	4/19	4/19	23.06	7.24	19.1	0	0

JAKE LINTOTT

RHB / SLW / RO / WO

WARWICKSHIRE

FULL NAME: Jacob Benedict Lintott
BORN: April 22, 1993, Taunton, Somerset
SQUAD NO: 23
HEIGHT: 5ft 11in
NICKNAME: Linsanity
EDUCATION: Queen's College, Taunton
TEAMS: Warwickshire, Barbados Royals, Fortune Barisal, Gloucestershire, Hampshire
ROLE: Bowler
DEBUT: First-class: 2021; T20: 2017

BEST BATTING: 15 Warwickshire vs Worcestershire, Worcester, 2021

WHO IS YOUR LOOKALIKE? Fabien Barthez (ex-footballer)
FIRST CRICKET CLUB? Taunton St Andrews CC, Somerset
WHAT WOULD YOU CHANGE ABOUT THE STRUCTURE OF THE COUNTY SEASON?
RL50: three regions, 10 games per team plus knockout stages, played in April/May.
Championship: three divisions (10 games each), played in June and September. T20: three
regions (10 games plus knockout stages) played in July. The Hundred: played in August.
Everyone's a winner – higher-quality Championship cricket (played in the warmer months
and with fewer games), everyone plays in the 50-over comp, T20 and The Hundred during
the school holidays
BIGGEST INFLUENCE ON YOUR DEVELOPMENT AS A CRICKETER (EXCLUDING PARENTS)?
Piers McBride, my county age-group coach at Somerset. He has been very supportive of me
since I was 13 and still works with me now at my club Clevedon CC
MOST BEAUTIFUL THING YOU HAVE EVER SEEN? The Wharf Bar on Manly Beach (Sydney)
on a Sunday afternoon
WHO WOULD YOU MOST LIKE TO HAVE A NET WITH? Shane Warne (my childhood hero)
GUILTY PLEASURE? Exeter City FC
TWITTER: @lintott23

Batting	Mat	Inns	NO	Runs	HS	Ave	SR	100	50	Ct	St
First-class	1	1	0	15	15	15.00	78.94	0	0	1	-
T20s	41	17	6	104	41	9.45	107.21	0	0	22	-

Bowling	Mat	Balls	Runs	Wkts	BBI	BBM	Ave	Econ	SR	5w	10
First-class	1	234	103	0	-	-	-	2.64	-	0	0
T20s	41	848	972	48	4/20	4/20	20.25	6.87	17.6	0	0

LANCASHIRE

FULL NAME: Liam Stephen Livingstone
BORN: August 4, 1993, Barrow-in-Furness, Cumbria
SQUAD NO: 7
HEIGHT: 6ft 2in
EDUCATION: Chetwynde School, Barrow-in-Furness
TEAMS: England, Lancashire, Cape Town Blitz, Karachi Kings, Perth Scorchers, Peshawar Zalmi, Punjab Kings, Rajasthan Royals
ROLE: Batter
DEBUT: ODI: 2021; T20I: 2018; First-class: 2016; List A: 2015; T20: 2015

BEST BATTING: 224 Lancashire vs Warwickshire, Old Trafford, 2017
BEST BOWLING: 6-52 Lancashire vs Surrey, Old Trafford, 2017
COUNTY CAP: 2017

FIRST CRICKET CLUB? Barrow CC, Cumbria
FAMILY TIES? My father and brother played low-level club cricket
MOST EXCITING DAY AS A CRICKETER? Winning the T20 Blast in 2015
CHILDHOOD SPORTING HERO? Andrew Flintoff – he was so good to watch as a young kid.
Shane Warne – I was a leg-spinner growing up
SURPRISING FACT ABOUT YOU? I once scored 350 in a club game
TWITTER: @liaml4893
NOTES: Livingstone was signed by Punjab Kings for the 2022 IPL

Batting	Mat	Inns	NO	Runs	HS	Ave	SR	100	50	Ct	St
ODIs	3	3	1	72	36	36.00	112.50	0	0	1	-
T20Is	17	13	1	285	103	23.75	158.33	1	0	8	-
First-class	62	94	14	3069	224	38.36	59.45	7	15	74	-
List A	58	49	4	1624	129	36.08	100.00	1	10	26	-
T20s	167	158	14	4110	103	28.54	144.05	2	23	71	-

Bowling	Mat	Balls	Runs	Wkts	BBI	BBM	Ave	Econ	SR	5w	10
ODIs	3	18	20	1	1/20	1/20	20.00	6.66	18.0	0	0
T20Is	17	198	235	12	2/15	2/15	19.58	7.12	16.5	0	0
First-class	62	3375	1554	43	6/52	6/52	36.13	2.76	78.4	1	0
List A	58	1323	1154	24	3/51	3/51	48.08	5.23	55.1	0	0
T20s	167	1124	1482	69	4/17	4/17	21.47	7.91	16.2	0	0

DAVID LLOYD — RHB / OB / R0 / W0 / MVP39

GLAMORGAN

FULL NAME: David Liam Lloyd
BORN: June 15, 1992, St Asaph, Denbighshire, Wales
SQUAD NO: 73
HEIGHT: 5ft 9in
NICKNAME: Dai
EDUCATION: Darland High School, Wrexham; Shrewsbury School
TEAMS: Glamorgan
ROLE: Batter
DEBUT: First-class: 2012; List A: 2014; T20: 2014

BEST BATTING: 121 Glamorgan vs Surrey, The Oval, 2021
BEST BOWLING: 4-11 Glamorgan vs Kent, Cardiff, 2021

WHO IS YOUR LOOKALIKE? Sergio Ramos
FIRST CRICKET CLUB? Brymbo CC, Clwyd, Wales
WHAT WOULD YOU CHANGE ABOUT THE STRUCTURE OF THE COUNTY SEASON?
Have more four-day cricket in the middle of the season
BIGGEST INFLUENCE ON YOUR DEVELOPMENT AS A CRICKETER (EXCLUDING PARENTS)?
Paul Pridgeon, the former Worcestershire seamer
BIGGEST CRICKETING REGRET? Getting 97 not out in a T20 against Kent in 2016
WHO IS THE BEST BATTER/ALLROUNDER/BOWLER IN COUNTY CRICKET (EXCLUDING
TEAMMATES)? Joe Clarke/Darren Stevens/Ryan Higgins
MOST UNDERRATED PLAYER IN COUNTY CRICKET? Chris Dent
WHAT DO YOU MOST ENJOY LISTENING TO? Foals (British rock band)
WHAT MAKES YOU WORRY? Runs
SURPRISING FACT ABOUT YOU? I have a degree in Economics
GUILTY PLEASURE? Wrexham AFC
TWITTER: @lloyddl2010

Batting	Mat	Inns	NO	Runs	HS	Ave	SR	100	50	Ct	St
First-class	83	141	13	3767	121	29.42	60.39	5	16	41	-
List A	46	40	2	942	92	24.78	85.24	0	5	12	-
T20s	67	61	2	1407	97*	23.84	131.25	0	8	18	-

Bowling	Mat	Balls	Runs	Wkts	BBI	BBM	Ave	Econ	SR	5w	10
First-class	83	5368	3370	82	4/11	6/32	41.09	3.76	65.4	0	0
List A	46	745	741	17	5/53	5/53	43.58	5.96	43.8	1	0
T20s	67	102	152	6	2/13	2/13	25.33	8.94	17.0	0	0

JAMES LOGAN — LHB / SLA / R0 / W0

KENT

FULL NAME: James Edwin Graham Logan
BORN: October 12, 1997, Wakefield, Yorkshire
SQUAD NO: 11
HEIGHT: 6ft 1in
NICKNAME: Logi
EDUCATION: Normanton Freestone High School, West Yorkshire; Pontefract New College
TEAMS: Kent, Yorkshire
ROLE: Bowler
DEBUT: First-class: 2018; List A: 2021; T20: 2021

BEST BATTING: 21 Kent vs Leicestershire, Leicester, 2021
BEST BOWLING: 4-22 Yorkshire vs Warwickshire, York, 2019

WHO IS YOUR LOOKALIKE? Roman Kemp (TV personality)
FIRST CRICKET CLUB? Altofts CC, Normanton, West Yorkshire
WHO IS THE BEST BATTER/KEEPER/ALLROUNDER/BOWLER IN COUNTY CRICKET (EXCLUDING TEAMMATES)? David Bedingham/Ben Foakes/Simon Harmer/Luke Fletcher
MOST UNDERRATED PLAYER IN COUNTY CRICKET? Ryan Higgins
HOBBIES? Call of Duty (video game)
IF YOU COULD TURN BACK TIME... I'd go to university
WHO WOULD YOU MOST LIKE TO HAVE A NET WITH? Ravindra Jadeja
MAKE ONE PREDICTION FOR THE FUTURE OF CRICKET: Four-day Test matches
WHAT DO YOU MOST ENJOY LISTENING TO? Football podcasts
WHAT MAKES YOU WORRY? Injuries
WHAT GIVES YOU JOY? Leeds United (when they win)

Batting	Mat	Inns	NO	Runs	HS	Ave	SR	100	50	Ct	St
First-class	6	9	2	84	21	12.00	24.00	0	0	2	-
List A	6	4	2	46	17*	23.00	69.69	0	0	0	-
T20s	2	-	-	-	-	-	-	-	-	1	-

Bowling	Mat	Balls	Runs	Wkts	BBI	BBM	Ave	Econ	SR	5w	10
First-class	6	481	204	12	4/22	5/47	17.00	2.54	40.0	0	0
List A	6	198	207	3	2/45	2/45	69.00	6.27	66.0	0	0
T20s	2	24	18	2	1/4	1/4	9.00	4.50	12.0	0	0

YORKSHIRE

FULL NAME: Adam Lyth
BORN: September 25, 1987, Whitby, Yorkshire
SQUAD NO: 9
HEIGHT: 5ft 9in
NICKNAME: Budge
EDUCATION: Caedmon School; Whitby Community School
TEAMS: England, Yorkshire, Multan Sultans, Rangpur Riders
ROLE: Batter
DEBUT: Test: 2015;
First-class: 2007; List A: 2006; T20: 2008

BEST BATTING: 251 Yorkshire vs Lancashire, Old Trafford, 2014
BEST BOWLING: 2-9 Yorkshire vs Middlesex, Scarborough, 2016
COUNTY CAP: 2010; BENEFIT: 2021

WHO IS YOUR LOOKALIKE? Alan Shearer
FIRST CRICKET CLUB? Scarborough CC, North Yorkshire
FAMILY TIES? My brother and dad played for Scarborough and my grandad played for Whitby CC
BIGGEST INFLUENCE ON YOUR DEVELOPMENT AS A CRICKETER (EXCLUDING PARENTS)? Phil Hart, my former coach at Scarborough
MOST UNDERRATED PLAYER IN COUNTY CRICKET? Luke Fletcher
MOST BEAUTIFUL THING YOU HAVE EVER SEEN? Whitby sea front
WHO WOULD YOU MOST LIKE TO HAVE A NET WITH? Shane Warne
WHAT DO YOU MOST ENJOY LISTENING TO? U2
WHAT MAKES YOU WORRY? Nothing
SURPRISING FACT ABOUT YOU? I had trials with Manchester City
GUILTY PLEASURE? Whisky
TWITTER: @lythy09

Batting	Mat	Inns	NO	Runs	HS	Ave	SR	100	50	Ct	St
Tests	7	13	0	265	107	20.38	50.09	1	0	8	-
First-class	195	326	16	11713	251	37.78		27	61	261	-
List A	122	115	8	3765	144	35.18	93.84	5	18	55	-
T20s	142	133	3	3265	161	25.11	144.02	1	20	79	-

Bowling	Mat	Balls	Runs	Wkts	BBI	BBM	Ave	Econ	SR	5w	10
Tests	7	6	0	0	-	-	-	-	-	0	0
First-class	195	2905	1705	36	2/9	2/9	47.36	3.52	80.6	0	0
List A	122	360	373	6	2/27	2/27	62.16	6.21	60.0	0	0
T20s	142	512	654	25	5/31	5/31	26.16	7.66	20.4	1	0

WAYNE MADSEN

RHB / OB / R5 / W0

FULL NAME: Wayne Lee Madsen
BORN: January 2, 1984, Durban, South Africa
SQUAD NO: 77
HEIGHT: 5ft 11in
NICKNAME: Psycho
EDUCATION: Highbury Preparatory School;
Kearsney College; University of South Africa
TEAMS: Derbyshire, Dolphins, KwaZulu-
Natal, Multan Sultans, Peshawar Zalmi
ROLE: Batter
DEBUT: First-class: 2004; List A: 2004; T20: 2010

BEST BATTING: 231* Derbyshire vs Northamptonshire, Northampton, 2012
BEST BOWLING: 3-45 KwaZulu-Natal vs Eastern Province, Port Elizabeth, 2008
COUNTY CAP: 2011; **BENEFIT:** 2017

WHO IS YOUR LOOKALIKE? Robin Van Persie
FIRST CRICKET CLUB? Crusaders CC, Durban, South Africa. I got a golden duck on debut
**WHO IS THE BEST BATTER/KEEPER/ALLROUNDER/BOWLER IN COUNTY CRICKET
(EXCLUDING TEAMMATES)?** Zak Crawley/Ben Foakes/Darren Stevens/Chris Rushworth
MOST UNDERRATED PLAYER IN COUNTY CRICKET? Ben Sanderson
WHAT WOULD A FLY ON THE WALL HEAR IN YOUR DRESSING ROOM? The whoosh of a flip-
flop flying through the air!
HOBBIES? Gardening
IF YOU COULD TURN BACK TIME... I'd change the world's use of plastic
WHO WOULD YOU MOST AND LEAST LIKE TO HAVE A NET WITH? Most – Sachin Tendulkar
(to pick his brains). Least – Mark Footitt (he'd never land it in my half of the pitch)
WHAT DO YOU MOST ENJOY LISTENING TO? The High Performance Podcast
WHAT MAKES YOU WORRY? The Russian on a green one (that's Chris Rushworth)
GUILTY PLEASURE? Amarula (South African liqueur)
TWITTER: @waynemadders77

Batting	Mat	Inns	NO	Runs	HS	Ave	SR	100	50	Ct	St
First-class	200	357	24	12852	231*	38.59	51.49	32	66	219	-
List A	105	97	17	3323	138	41.53	89.93	6	19	69	-
T20s	125	122	21	3018	86*	29.88	133.12	0	20	43	-

Bowling	Mat	Balls	Runs	Wkts	BBI	BBM	Ave	Econ	SR	5w	10
First-class	200	3348	1842	37	3/45		49.78	3.30	90.4	0	0
List A	105	668	573	16	3/27	3/27	35.81	5.14	41.7	0	0
T20s	125	492	645	19	2/20	2/20	33.94	7.86	25.8	0	0

SAQIB MAHMOOD

RHB / RFM / R0 / W0

LANCASHIRE

FULL NAME: Saqib Mahmood
BORN: February 25, 1997, Birmingham
SQUAD NO: 25
HEIGHT: 6ft 3in
NICKNAME: Saq
EDUCATION: Matthew Moss High School, Rochdale
TEAMS: England, Lancashire, Peshawar Zalmi, Sydney Thunder
ROLE: Bowler
DEBUT: ODI: 2020; T20I: 2019; First-class: 2016; List A: 2016; T20: 2015

BEST BATTING: 34 Lancashire vs Middlesex, Old Trafford, 2019
BEST BOWLING: 5-47 Lancashire vs Yorkshire, Old Trafford, 2021

TWITTER: @SaqMahmood25
NOTES: One of the quickest bowlers on the circuit, Mahmood made his full Lancashire debut in 2015 before having a big impact at the 2016 U19 World Cup, becoming a regular for England Lions. Injuries and the tough competition for places initially limited his opportunities for his county, but the 25-year-old was exceptional in 2019 – particularly in the One-Day Cup in which he took 28 wickets at 18.50 to be named Player of the Tournament. Mahmood made his T20 international debut for England later that year, followed by his ODI debut in February 2020. He was overlooked for last year's T20 World Cup but returned to the side earlier this year and was called up for the Test series in the Caribbean in March

Batting	Mat	Inns	NO	Runs	HS	Ave	SR	100	50	Ct	St
ODIs	7	2	0	20	12	10.00	64.51	0	0	1	-
T20Is	12	7	4	22	7*	7.33	78.57	0	0	2	-
First-class	26	31	13	227	34	12.61	30.92	0	0	4	-
List A	34	14	6	137	45	17.12	84.56	0	0	8	-
T20s	59	18	12	56	11*	9.33	76.71	0	0	11	-

Bowling	Mat	Balls	Runs	Wkts	BBI	BBM	Ave	Econ	SR	5w	10
ODIs	7	365	279	14	4/42	4/42	19.92	4.58	26.0	0	0
T20Is	12	228	398	7	3/33	3/33	56.85	10.47	32.5	0	0
First-class	26	3760	1981	70	5/47	6/96	28.30	3.16	53.7	1	0
List A	34	1667	1545	64	6/37	6/37	24.14	5.56	26.0	3	0
T20s	59	1130	1666	74	4/14	4/14	22.51	8.84	15.2	0	0

DAWID MALAN

LHB / LB / R3 / W0

FULL NAME: Dawid Johannes Malan
BORN: September 3, 1987, Roehampton
SQUAD NO: 29
HEIGHT: 6ft
EDUCATION: Paarl Boys' High School;
University of South Africa
TEAMS: England, Yorkshire, Comilla
Warriors, Boland, Hobart Hurricanes,
Khulna Titans, Middlesex, Islamabad United,
Peshawar Zalmi, Punjab Kings
ROLE: Batter
DEBUT: Test: 2017; ODI: 2019; T20I: 2017;
First-class: 2006; List A: 2006; T20: 2006

BEST BATTING: 219 Yorkshire vs Derbyshire, Headingley, 2020
BEST BOWLING: 5-61 Middlesex vs Lancashire, Liverpool, 2012
COUNTY CAP: 2010 (Middlesex); 2020 (Yorkshire); BENEFIT: 2019 (Middlesex)

FAMILY TIES? My dad Dawid played for Transvaal B and Western Province B and my brother
Charl played for MCC Young Cricketers and Loughborough MCCU
CHILDHOOD SPORTING HERO? Gary Kirsten
SURPRISING FACT ABOUT YOU? I love to go to the cinema by myself
TWITTER: @DJMalan29

Batting	Mat	Inns	NO	Runs	HS	Ave	SR	100	50	Ct	St
Tests	22	39	0	1074	140	27.53	40.96	1	9	13	-
ODIs	6	6	2	158	68*	39.50	87.77	0	2	3	-
T20Is	36	35	5	1239	103*	41.30	137.20	1	11	14	-
First-class	200	342	21	12131	219	37.79	52.44	27	63	204	-
List A	154	150	23	5269	185*	41.48	83.90	10	27	54	-
T20s	253	247	37	6775	117	32.26	127.42	5	40	91	-

Bowling	Mat	Balls	Runs	Wkts	BBI	BBM	Ave	Econ	SR	5w	10
Tests	22	222	131	2	2/33	2/33	65.50	3.54	111.0	0	0
ODIs	6	-	-	-	-	-	-	-	-	-	-
T20Is	36	12	27	1	1/27	1/27	27.00	13.50	12.0	0	0
First-class	200	4159	2516	63	5/61	5/61	39.93	3.62	66.0	1	0
List A	154	1347	1310	40	4/25	4/25	32.75	5.83	33.6	0	0
T20s	253	567	722	23	2/10	2/10	31.39	7.64	24.6	0	0

SHAN MASOOD — LHB / RM / RO / WO

DERBYSHIRE

FULL NAME: Shan Masood Khan
BORN: October 14, 1989, Kuwait
SQUAD NO: 94
TEAMS: Pakistan, Derbyshire, Baluchistan, Islamabad, Multan Sultans, National Bank of Pakistan, Sindh, Southern Punjab, United Bank Limited
ROLE: Batter
DEBUT: Test: 2013; ODI: 2019; First-class: 2007; List A: 2008; T20: 2011

BEST BATTING: 199 Islamabad vs Karachi Whites, Islamabad, 2013
BEST BOWLING: 2-52 Durham MCCU vs Warwickshire, 2011, Durham

TWITTER: @shani_official

NOTES: Mickey Arthur made swift use of his contacts after taking on the role of head of cricket at Derbyshire, snapping up Shan Masood for the entirety of the 2022 season. Arthur knows the southpaw opener well from his time as coach of Pakistan and he will hope that Masood can add some solidity to a batting unit which registered only five Championship hundreds last summer. He certainly brings quality, having scored three Test centuries between December 2019 and August 2020, including an eight-hour 156 against England at Old Trafford. Masood has slipped out of the international reckoning since, playing the most recent of his 25 Tests in January 2021. He will be available for Derbyshire across all formats. The 32-year-old is familiar with life in the UK having lived a stone's throw from Lord's in his teenage years, and later studied Economics at Durham University. "Playing county cricket is something I've always wanted to do," he said, "so when Mickey approached me to join Derbyshire, I jumped at the chance. He's perhaps been the greatest influence in my career and I'm looking forward to working with him again"

Batting	Mat	Inns	NO	Runs	HS	Ave	SR	100	50	Ct	St
Tests	25	47	0	1378	156	29.31	45.26	4	6	16	-
ODIs	5	5	0	111	50	22.20	76.55	0	1	1	-
First-class	136	233	11	7942	199	35.77	48.37	18	37	82	-
List A	97	95	16	4540	182*	57.46	82.72	14	26	26	-
T20s	93	91	2	2226	103*	25.01	123.39	1	13	35	-

Bowling	Mat	Balls	Runs	Wkts	BBI	BBM	Ave	Econ	SR	5w	10
Tests	25	144	92	2	1/6	1/6	46.00	3.83	72.0	0	0
ODIs	5	-	-	-	-	-	-	-	-	-	-
First-class	136	875	607	8	2/52	2/52	75.87	4.16	109.3	0	0
List A	97	24	17	2	2/0	2/0	8.50	4.25	12.0	0	0
T20s	93	-	-	-	-	-	-	-	-	-	-

BEN MCDERMOTT

RHB / WK

FULL NAME: Benjamin Reginald McDermott
BORN: December 12, 1994, Brisbane, Australia
SQUAD NO: 28
HEIGHT: 6ft
TEAMS: Australia, Hampshire, Brisbane Heat, Derbyshire, Hobart Hurricanes, Melbourne Renegades, Queensland, Tasmania
ROLE: Batter/wicketkeeper
DEBUT: ODI: 2021; T20I: 2018; First-class: 2014; List A: 2014; T20: 2014

BEST BATTING: 127 Hobart Hurricanes vs Melbourne Renegades, Melbourne, 2021 (T20)

TWITTER: @benmcdermott100
NOTES: Hampshire have signed the explosive keeper-batter for the whole of this summer's T20 Blast campaign. McDermott is the son of former Australian fast bowler Craig. He made his Big Bash debut for Brisbane Heat in 2014 at the age of 19 before switching to Hobart Hurricanes ahead of the 2016/17 campaign. The 27-year-old made his T20I debut for Australia in October 2018 and was recently recalled to the side after finishing as the leading run-scorer in the 2021/22 Big Bash. McDermott was signed by Derbyshire on a white-ball contract for the 2020 season, deferred to last summer in the wake of the pandemic. In the end he made just two first-class appeareances for the county after being called up by Australia

Batting	Mat	Inns	NO	Runs	HS	Ave	SR	100	50	Ct	St
ODIs	2	2	0	28	28	14.00	56.00	0	0	0	-
T20Is	22	20	3	247	53	14.52	92.85	0	1	12	-
First-class	44	78	9	2288	107*	33.15	42.98	2	16	32	-
List A	28	28	2	1239	133	47.65	80.09	4	7	27	-
T20s	96	91	16	2386	127	31.81	132.11	3	11	48	3

Bowling	Mat	Balls	Runs	Wkts	BBI	BBM	Ave	Econ	SR	5w	10
ODIs	2	-	-	-	-	-	-	-	-	-	-
T20Is	22	-	-	-	-	-	-	-	-	-	-
First-class	44	102	75	0	-	-	-	4.41	-	0	0
List A	28	-	-	-	-	-	-	-	-	-	-
T20s	96	-	-	-	-	-	-	-	-	-	-

JAMIE MCILROY — RHB / LFM / R0 / W0

GLAMORGAN

FULL NAME: Jamie Peter McIlroy
BORN: June 19, 1994, Hereford
SQUAD NO: 35
HEIGHT: 6ft 3in
NICKNAME: Macca
EDUCATION: Builth Wells High School,
Powys; Coleg Powys, Newtown
TEAMS: Glamorgan
ROLE: Bowler
DEBUT: First-class: 2021

BEST BOWLING: 1-12 Glamorgan vs Yorkshire, Headingley, 2021

FIRST CRICKET CLUB? Builth Wells CC, Powys
MOST EXCITING DAY AS A CRICKETER? Hard to choose between winning the Minor
Counties national knockout cup with Herefordshire and signing my first professional
contract at Glamorgan
CHILDHOOD SPORTING HERO? Ryan Giggs
BIGGEST INFLUENCE ON YOUR DEVELOPMENT AS A CRICKETER (EXCLUDING PARENTS)?
Ed Price, my former Herefordshire U17 coach. He was the first person to teach me how to
correctly swing a ball and control it with the wrist position
WHAT WOULD YOU DO IF YOU WERE IN CHARGE OF COUNTY CRICKET? Come up with
more incentives to entice spectators, push to get more games on the television
GUILTY PLEASURE? A Greggs sausage roll
TWITTER: @Jamiemcilroy94

Batting	Mat	Inns	NO	Runs	HS	Ave	SR	100	50	Ct	St
First-class	2	1	0	0	0	0.00	0.00	0	0	0	-

Bowling	Mat	Balls	Runs	Wkts	BBI	BBM	Ave	Econ	SR	5w	10
First-class	2	228	131	1	1/12	1/38	131.00	3.44	228.0	0	0

CONOR MCKERR RHB / RFM / R0 / W0

FULL NAME: Conor McKerr
BORN: January 19, 1998, Johannesburg, South Africa
SQUAD NO: 83
HEIGHT: 6ft 6in
NICKNAME: Tree
EDUCATION: St John's College, Johannesburg
TEAMS: Surrey, Derbyshire, South Africa U19
ROLE: Bowler
DEBUT: First-class: 2017; List A: 2019; T20: 2021

BEST BATTING: 29 Surrey vs Yorkshire, The Oval, 2018
BEST BOWLING: 5-54 Derbyshire vs Northamptonshire, Northampton, 2017

WHO IS YOUR LOOKALIKE? Ron Swanson (character from Parks and Recreation TV series)
FIRST CRICKET CLUB? Randburg CC, Johannesburg
WHAT WOULD YOU CHANGE ABOUT THE STRUCTURE OF THE COUNTY SEASON?
Each format to be started and finished in one block
BIGGEST INFLUENCE ON YOUR DEVELOPMENT AS A CRICKETER (EXCLUDING PARENTS)?
Alec Stewart – he gave me the chance to be a professional cricketer
WHO IS THE BEST BATTER/KEEPER/ALLROUNDER/BOWLER IN COUNTY CRICKET
(EXCLUDING TEAMMATES)? Jamie Smith/Ben Foakes/Liam Livingstone/Kyle Abbott
MOST BEAUTIFUL THING YOU HAVE EVER SEEN? Clouds moving in reverse
WHO WOULD YOU MOST LIKE TO HAVE A NET WITH? Graeme Smith
MAKE ONE PREDICTION FOR THE FUTURE OF CRICKET: Test cricket will always be the
pinnacle of the game
WHAT DO YOU MOST ENJOY LISTENING TO? Country music
WHAT MAKES YOU WORRY? The thought that we live in a simulation
GUILTY PLEASURE? Muffins
TWITTER: @cemckerr83

Batting	Mat	Inns	NO	Runs	HS	Ave	SR	100	50	Ct	St
First-class	14	15	4	133	29	12.09	41.43	0	0	2	-
List A	16	10	4	86	26*	14.33	72.26	0	0	4	-
T20s	9	3	1	8	7*	4.00	88.88	0	0	2	-

Bowling	Mat	Balls	Runs	Wkts	BBI	BBM	Ave	Econ	SR	5w	10
First-class	14	1705	1054	38	5/54	10/141	27.73	3.70	44.8	2	1
List A	16	697	720	26	4/64	4/64	27.69	6.19	26.8	0	0
T20s	9	141	217	5	2/23	2/23	43.40	9.23	28.2	0	0

MATTIE MCKIERNAN

RHB / LB / R0 / W0

DERBYSHIRE

FULL NAME: Matthew Henry McKiernan
BORN: June 14, 1994, Wigan, Lancashire
SQUAD NO: 21
HEIGHT: 6ft 1in
NICKNAME: Macca
EDUCATION: Lowton High School, Leigh, Greater Manchester; St John Rigby College, Wigan; Edge Hill University, Ormskirk
TEAMS: Derbyshire
ROLE: Bowler
DEBUT: First-class: 2019; List A: 2021; T20: 2018

BEST BATTING: 52 Derbyshire vs Lancashire, Liverpool, 2020
BEST BOWLING: 2-3 Derbyshire vs Nottinghamshire, Trent Bridge, 2020

WHO IS YOUR LOOKALIKE? Harry Potter (when I'm wearing my glasses)
FIRST CRICKET CLUB? Leigh CC, Wigan
BIGGEST INFLUENCE ON YOUR DEVELOPMENT AS A CRICKETER (EXCLUDING PARENTS)? Karl Brown, ex-Lancashire. I've played club cricket with him for many years
WHO IS THE BEST BATTER/KEEPER/ALLROUNDER/BOWLER IN COUNTY CRICKET (EXCLUDING TEAMMATES)? James Vince/Ben Foakes/Matt Critchley/Simon Harmer
MOST UNDERRATED PLAYER IN COUNTY CRICKET? Darren Stevens
MOST BEAUTIFUL THING YOU HAVE EVER SEEN? The Sagrada Família in Barcelona
HOBBIES? Fantasy football
WHO WOULD YOU MOST LIKE TO HAVE A NET WITH? Kane Williamson – just love watching him bat
MAKE ONE PREDICTION FOR THE FUTURE OF CRICKET: There'll be more ambidextrous bowlers
WHAT DO YOU MOST ENJOY LISTENING TO? Anything that's in the charts
TWITTER: @MattieMcKiernan

Batting	Mat	Inns	NO	Runs	HS	Ave	SR	100	50	Ct	St
First-class	4	7	0	133	52	19.00	30.64	0	1	7	-
List A	7	6	1	113	38	22.60	129.88	0	0	4	-
T20s	13	11	2	79	25	8.77	119.69	0	0	4	-

Bowling	Mat	Balls	Runs	Wkts	BBI	BBM	Ave	Econ	SR	5w	10
First-class	4	86	64	2	2/3	2/16	32.00	4.46	43.0	0	0
List A	7	174	200	3	1/26	1/26	66.66	6.89	58.0	0	0
T20s	13	180	217	6	3/9	3/9	36.16	7.23	30.0	0	0

LEWIS MCMANUS

RHB / WK / R0 / W0

FULL NAME: Lewis David McManus
BORN: October 9, 1994, Poole, Dorset
SQUAD NO: 18
HEIGHT: 5ft 8in
NICKNAME: Lewy
EDUCATION: Claysmore School,
Bournemouth; University of Exeter
TEAMS: Hampshire, England U19
ROLE: Wicketkeeper/batter
DEBUT: First-class: 2015; List A: 2016; T20: 2016

BEST BATTING: 132* Hampshire vs Surrey, Southampton, 2016

WHO IS YOUR LOOKALIKE? Anyone tall
FIRST CRICKET CLUB? Broadstone CC, Poole, Dorset
WHAT WOULD YOU CHANGE ABOUT THE STRUCTURE OF THE COUNTY SEASON?
Make sure the formats don't overlap
WHO IS THE BEST BATTER/KEEPER/ALLROUNDER/BOWLER IN COUNTY CRICKET
(EXCLUDING TEAMMATES)? Joe Root/Ben Foakes/Lewis Gregory/Ollie Robinson
WHAT WOULD A FLY ON THE WALL HEAR IN YOUR DRESSING ROOM? Kyle Abbott's tunes!
WHO WOULD YOU MOST LIKE TO HAVE A NET WITH? AB de Villiers
MAKE ONE PREDICTION FOR THE FUTURE OF CRICKET: Hampshire will win the Championship
WHAT MAKES YOU WORRY? Being late
SURPRISING FACT ABOUT YOU? I once saw James Tomlinson take a one-handed catch at
fine-leg while holding a banana in the other hand during a first-class game
TWITTER: @lewis_mcmanus

Batting	Mat	Inns	NO	Runs	HS	Ave	SR	100	50	Ct	St
First-class	55	77	8	1876	132*	27.18	47.62	1	9	122	13
List A	37	30	6	563	50	23.45	90.22	0	1	27	8
T20s	61	51	11	674	60*	16.85	130.36	0	2	27	15

Bowling	Mat	Balls	Runs	Wkts	BBI	BBM	Ave	Econ	SR	5w	10
First-class	55	-	-	-	-	-	-	-	-	-	-
List A	37	-	-	-	-	-	-	-	-	-	-
T20s	61	-	-	-	-	-	-	-	-	-	-

DUSTIN MELTON

RHB / RFM / R0 / W0

DERBYSHIRE

FULL NAME: Dustin Renton Melton
BORN: April 11, 1995, Harare, Zimbabwe
SQUAD NO: 13
HEIGHT: 6ft 4in
NICKNAME: Dusty
EDUCATION: Pretoria Boys High School;
University of Pretoria
TEAMS: Derbyshire
ROLE: Bowler
DEBUT: First-class: 2019; T20: 2020

BEST BATTING: 15 Derbyshire vs Essex, Chelmsford, 2021
BEST BOWLING: 4-22 Derbyshire vs Leicestershire, Leicester, 2020

FIRST CRICKET CLUB? Tuks CC, Pretoria, South Africa
WHO IS THE BEST BATTER/KEEPER/ALLROUNDER/BOWLER IN COUNTY CRICKET
(EXCLUDING TEAMMATES)? Harry Brook/Jordan Cox/Matt Critchley/Chris Rushworth
MOST UNDERRATED PLAYER IN COUNTY CRICKET? Matt Critchley
WHAT WOULD A FLY ON THE WALL HEAR IN YOUR DRESSING ROOM? Quite a few South
African accents
MOST BEAUTIFUL THING YOU HAVE EVER SEEN? The Great Barrier Reef
IF YOU COULD TURN BACK TIME... I would have learnt to bowl with both arms
WHO WOULD YOU MOST AND LEAST LIKE TO HAVE A NET WITH? Most – Aiden Markram.
We played school and club cricket together, and it was always a good challenge playing and
training together. Least – Matthew Hayden. He'd be hell bent on smashing the ball back at me
MAKE ONE PREDICTION FOR THE FUTURE OF CRICKET: America will have a growing
influence on the sport
WHAT DO YOU MOST ENJOY LISTENING TO? Small up-and-coming bands
WHAT MAKES YOU WORRY? Facing 90mph bouncers
GUILTY PLEASURE? Video games
TWITTER: @Dusty_Melts

Batting	Mat	Inns	NO	Runs	HS	Ave	SR	100	50	Ct	St
First-class	11	15	6	51	15	5.66	47.66	0	0	3	-
T20s	4	-	-	-	-	-	-	-	-	4	-

Bowling	Mat	Balls	Runs	Wkts	BBI	BBM	Ave	Econ	SR	5w	10
First-class	11	1169	772	19	4/22	5/47	40.63	3.96	61.5	0	0
T20s	4	78	124	4	2/37	2/37	31.00	9.53	19.5	0	0

BEN MIKE

RHB / RFM / R0 / W0

FULL NAME: Benjamin Wentworth Munro Mike
BORN: August 24, 1998, Nottingham
SQUAD NO: 8
HEIGHT: 6ft 1in
NICKNAME: Benny
EDUCATION: Loughborough Grammar School
TEAMS: Leicestershire, Warwickshire
ROLE: Bowler
DEBUT: First-class: 2018; List A: 2018; T20: 2019

BEST BATTING: 74 Leicestershire vs Surrey, Leicester, 2021
BEST BOWLING: 5-37 Leicestershire vs Sussex, Hove, 2018

WHO IS YOUR LOOKALIKE? Youri Tielemans (footballer)
FIRST CRICKET CLUB? Radcliffe-on-Trent CC, Nottingham
WHAT WOULD YOU CHANGE ABOUT THE STRUCTURE OF THE COUNTY SEASON?
Schedule one pink-ball round of Championship matches
BIGGEST INFLUENCE ON YOUR DEVELOPMENT AS A CRICKETER (EXCLUDING PARENTS)?
Dips Patel at Leicestershire and Brad Spencer in Perth
BIGGEST CRICKETING REGRET? Trying to be perfect
MOST BEAUTIFUL THING YOU HAVE EVER SEEN? Sunset over the west coast of Barbados
HOBBIES? Fashion
WHO WOULD YOU MOST LIKE TO HAVE A NET WITH? Viv Richards
WHAT DO YOU MOST ENJOY LISTENING TO? Soca music
GUILTY PLEASURE? Tesco cookies after a day's play
TWITTER: @benmike_

Batting	Mat	Inns	NO	Runs	HS	Ave	SR	100	50	Ct	St
First-class	28	43	4	887	74	22.74	47.23	0	6	6	-
List A	10	9	1	159	41	19.87	67.65	0	0	1	-
T20s	28	21	7	270	37	19.28	142.85	0	0	11	-

Bowling	Mat	Balls	Runs	Wkts	BBI	BBM	Ave	Econ	SR	5w	10
First-class	28	3432	2315	63	5/37	9/94	36.74	4.04	54.4	1	0
List A	10	299	376	10	3/34	3/34	37.60	7.54	29.9	0	0
T20s	28	232	424	15	4/22	4/22	28.26	10.96	15.4	0	0

CRAIG MILES — RHB / RFM / R0 / W3 / MVP44

WARWICKSHIRE

FULL NAME: Craig Neil Miles
BORN: July 20, 1994, Swindon, Wiltshire
SQUAD NO: 18
HEIGHT: 6ft 4in
NICKNAME: Milo
EDUCATION: Bradon Forest School, Purton, Wiltshire; SGS Filton College, Bristol
TEAMS: Warwickshire, Gloucestershire
ROLE: Bowler
DEBUT: First-class: 2011; List A: 2011; T20: 2013

BEST BATTING: 62* Gloucestershire vs Worcestershire, Cheltenham, 2014
BEST BOWLING: 6-63 Gloucestershire vs Northamptonshire, Northampton, 2015
COUNTY CAP: 2011 (Gloucestershire)

FIRST CRICKET CLUB? Purton CC, Swindon
FAMILY TIES? My older brother Adam has played for Cardiff MCCU and for New Zealand side Otago in first-class cricket
MOST EXCITING DAY AS A CRICKETER? Beating Surrey in the 2015 One-Day Cup final at Lord's when I was with Gloucestershire
CHILDHOOD SPORTING HERO? Wayne Rooney
WHAT WOULD YOU DO IF YOU WERE IN CHARGE OF COUNTY CRICKET? Allow the second new ball after 60 overs, bring back the 40-over format
SURPRISING FACT ABOUT YOU? I played football for Swindon Town Academy until I was 13
TWITTER: @cmiles34

Batting	Mat	Inns	NO	Runs	HS	Ave	SR	100	50	Ct	St
First-class	89	125	21	1624	62*	15.61	43.89	0	5	24	-
List A	39	16	4	146	31*	12.16	80.21	0	0	5	-
T20s	27	11	6	42	11*	8.40	82.35	0	0	13	-

Bowling	Mat	Balls	Runs	Wkts	BBI	BBM	Ave	Econ	SR	5w	10
First-class	89	14127	8600	323	6/63	10/121	26.62	3.65	43.7	17	1
List A	39	1637	1733	46	4/29	4/29	37.67	6.35	35.5	0	0
T20s	27	547	738	30	3/19	3/19	24.60	8.09	18.2	0	0

TYMAL MILLS

RHB / LF

FULL NAME: Tymal Solomon Mills
BORN: August 12, 1992, Dewsbury, Yorkshire
SQUAD NO: 7
HEIGHT: 6ft 1in
EDUCATION: Mildenhall College of Technology, Suffolk; University of East London
TEAMS: England, Sussex, Essex, Hobart Hurricanes, Mumbai Indians, Perth Scorchers, Peshawar Zalmi, RC Bangalore
ROLE: Bowler
DEBUT: T20I: 2016; First-class: 2011; List A: 2011; T20: 2012

BEST BATTING: 27 Sussex vs Gloucestershire, Hove, 2021 (T20)
BEST BOWLING: 4-22 Sussex vs Middlesex, Lord's, 2015 (T20)

WHO IS YOUR LOOKALIKE? My wife says I'm better looking than Vin Diesel (actor)
FIRST CRICKET CLUB? Tuddenham CC, Suffolk
WHAT WOULD YOU CHANGE ABOUT THE STRUCTURE OF THE COUNTY SEASON?
Reduce the T20 Blast to 10 group games rather than 14
HOBBIES? I'm a big NFL fan
IF YOU COULD TURN BACK TIME... "If I could find a way I'd take back those words that have hurt you. And you'd stay." (Cher)
WHO WOULD YOU MOST AND LEAST LIKE TO HAVE A NET WITH? Most – my best mate and former teammate Tom Craddock. Least – my mum (terrible bowler)
WHAT GIVES YOU JOY? My daughter
GUILTY PLEASURE? Watching terrible TV shows with my wife
TWITTER: @tmills15
NOTES: Mills plays for Sussex on a white-ball-only contract

Batting	Mat	Inns	NO	Runs	HS	Ave	SR	100	50	Ct	St
T20Is	12	3	2	1	1*	1.00	33.33	0	0	1	-
First-class	32	38	15	260	31*	11.30	57.77	0	0	9	-
List A	23	9	5	7	3*	1.75	31.81	0	0	3	-
T20s	156	31	15	111	27	6.93	97.36	0	0	22	-

Bowling	Mat	Balls	Runs	Wkts	BBI	BBM	Ave	Econ	SR	5w	10
T20Is	12	250	339	11	3/27	3/27	30.81	8.13	22.7	0	0
First-class	32	3531	2008	55	4/25	5/79	36.50	3.41	64.2	0	0
List A	23	790	787	22	3/23	3/23	35.77	5.97	35.9	0	0
T20s	156	3207	4181	176	4/22	4/22	23.75	7.82	18.2	0	0

MATT MILNES RHB / RFM / R0 / W1 / MVP19

KENT

FULL NAME: Matthew Edward Milnes
BORN: July 29, 1994, Nottingham
SQUAD NO: 8
HEIGHT: 6ft 1in
NICKNAME: Mad Dog
EDUCATION: West Bridgford School,
Nottinghamshire; Durham University
TEAMS: Kent, England Lions,
Nottinghamshire
ROLE: Bowler
DEBUT: First-class: 2014; List A: 2019; T20: 2019

BEST BATTING: 78 Kent vs Yorkshire, Canterbury, 2021
BEST BOWLING: 6-53 Kent vs Leicestershire, Leicester, 2021
COUNTY CAP: 2021 (Kent)

WHO IS YOUR LOOKALIKE? Lee Evans but I can't see why…
FIRST CRICKET CLUB? Plumtree CC, Nottinghamshire
WHAT WOULD YOU CHANGE ABOUT THE STRUCTURE OF THE COUNTY SEASON? T20 to be
played in one block with the knockout stage straight after the group stage
WHO IS THE BEST BATTER/KEEPER/ALLROUNDER/BOWLER IN COUNTY CRICKET
(EXCLUDING TEAMMATES)? Tom Abell/Ben Foakes/Lewis Gregory/Sam Cook
MOST UNDERRATED PLAYER IN COUNTY CRICKET? Ricardo Vasconcelos – didn't know
much about him until playing against him last year. Serious player
WHAT WOULD A FLY ON THE WALL HEAR IN YOUR DRESSING ROOM? Nathan Gilchrist
telling us all how good he is
HOBBIES? Football – you can't beat being on the terraces for a non-league game
IF YOU COULD TURN BACK TIME… I'd be a left-arm spinner who bats No.5
WHAT MAKES YOU WORRY? The thought of starting a game without having my run-up measured
TWITTER: @mmilnes84

Batting	Mat	Inns	NO	Runs	HS	Ave	SR	100	50	Ct	St
First-class	35	52	15	632	78	17.08	40.80	0	1	15	-
List A	12	7	1	101	26	16.83	112.22	0	0	5	-
T20s	29	10	6	24	13*	6.00	141.17	0	0	9	-

Bowling	Mat	Balls	Runs	Wkts	BBI	BBM	Ave	Econ	SR	5w	10
First-class	35	5558	3155	119	6/53	9/77	26.51	3.40	46.7	4	0
List A	12	575	647	19	5/79	5/79	34.05	6.75	30.2	1	0
T20s	29	563	838	32	5/22	5/22	26.18	8.93	17.5	1	0

MATTHEW MONTGOMERY　　　RHB / OB / R0 / W0

FULL NAME: Matthew Montgomery
BORN: May 10, 2000, Johannesburg, South Africa
SQUAD NO: TBC
HEIGHT: 6ft
NICKNAME: Monty
EDUCATION: Clifton College, Durban, South Africa; Loughborough University
TEAMS: Nottinghamshire, KwaZulu-Natal, South Africa U19
ROLE: Batter

BEST BATTING: 50* KwaZulu-Natal vs South Western Districts, Oudtshoorn, 2019

FIRST CRICKET CLUB? Delta CC, Durban, South Africa
WHAT WOULD YOU CHANGE ABOUT THE STRUCTURE OF THE COUNTY SEASON? Have less of a clash between the different formats
MOST BEAUTIFUL THING YOU HAVE EVER SEEN? The Gary Player Country Club Golf Course in Sun City, South Africa
IF YOU COULD TURN BACK TIME... I would invest in Bitcoin
WHO WOULD YOU MOST AND LEAST LIKE TO HAVE A NET WITH? Most – AB de Villiers (my childhood hero). Least – Shoaib Akhtar
MAKE ONE PREDICTION FOR THE FUTURE OF CRICKET: Franchise red-ball cricket
WHAT DO YOU MOST ENJOY LISTENING TO? Podcasts

Batting	Mat	Inns	NO	Runs	HS	Ave	SR	100	50	Ct	St
First-class	4	6	1	175	50*	35.00	41.27	0	1	4	-
List A	12	12	4	421	104	52.62	80.19	1	1	3	-
T20s	2	1	1	30	30*	-	115.38	0	0	0	-

Bowling	Mat	Balls	Runs	Wkts	BBI	BBM	Ave	Econ	SR	5w	10
First-class	4	-	-	-	-	-	-	-	-	-	-
List A	12	132	128	0	-	-	-	5.81	-	0	0
T20s	2	-	-	-	-	-	-	-	-	-	-

TOM MOORES

LHB / WK / R0 / W0

NOTTINGHAMSHIRE

FULL NAME: Thomas James Moores
BORN: September 4, 1996, Brighton, Sussex
SQUAD NO: 23
HEIGHT: 5ft 9in
EDUCATION: Loughborough Grammar School; Millfield School, Somerset
TEAMS: Nottinghamshire, England Lions, Jaffna Stallions, Kandy Warriors, Lancashire, Multan Sultans
ROLE: Wicketkeeper/batter
DEBUT: First-class: 2016; List A: 2016; T20: 2016

BEST BATTING: 106 Nottinghamshire vs Yorkshire, Trent Bridge, 2020

COUNTY CAP: 2021 (Nottinghamshire)

FIRST CRICKET CLUB? Barrow Town CC, Leicestershire. The club gave me my first opportunity to play men's cricket
FAMILY TIES? My father Peter played for Sussex and was England head coach. He's now my coach at Nottinghamshire
CHILDHOOD SPORTING HERO? Adam Gilchrist
TWITTER: @tommoores23

Batting	Mat	Inns	NO	Runs	HS	Ave	SR	100	50	Ct	St
First-class	51	85	4	1858	106	22.93	50.20	2	5	143	4
List A	21	19	3	566	76	35.37	113.65	0	5	18	5
T20s	93	80	17	1412	80*	22.41	133.20	0	6	49	16
Bowling	Mat	Balls	Runs	Wkts	BBI	BBM	Ave	Econ	SR	5w	10
First-class	51	-	-	-	-	-	-	-	-	-	-
List A	21	-	-	-	-	-	-	-	-	-	-
T20s	93	-	-	-	-	-	-	-	-	-	-

EOIN MORGAN

LHB / RM / R1 / W0

FULL NAME: Eoin Joseph Gerard Morgan
BORN: September 10, 1986, Dublin
SQUAD NO: 16
HEIGHT: 5ft 9in
NICKNAME: Moggie
EDUCATION: Catholic University School, Dublin; Dulwich College, London
TEAMS: England, Ireland, Middlesex, Karachi Kings, Kolkata Knight Riders, RC Bangalore, Sunrisers, Sydney Thunder
ROLE: Batter
DEBUT: Test: 2010; ODI: 2006; T20I: 2009; First-class: 2004; List A: 2003; T20: 2006

BEST BATTING: 209* Ireland vs UAE, Abu Dhabi, 2007
BEST BOWLING: 2-24 Middlesex vs Nottinghamshire, Lord's, 2007
COUNTY CAP: 2008; BENEFIT: 2020

TWITTER: @Eoin16

NOTES: An Irishman by birth, Morgan switched his allegiance to England after he was named in their provisional squad for the 2009 World T20. He made his Test debut in 2010 and scored two hundreds, but ultimately his unorthodox technique was exposed in the longer form of the game and he played the last of his 16 Tests in 2012. He was handed the ODI captaincy in 2014 and has transformed England's limited-overs cricket, leading the side to a euphoric victory in the 2019 World Cup. Morgan also leads the T20I side and captains Middlesex in the T20 Blast. He hasn't played four-day cricket since 2019. Despite captaining the Kolkata Knight Riders to the final of the IPL in 2021, Morgan went unsold at this year's auction

Batting	Mat	Inns	NO	Runs	HS	Ave	SR	100	50	Ct	St
Tests	16	24	1	700	130	30.43	54.77	2	3	11	-
ODIs	246	228	34	7701	148	39.69	91.25	14	47	87	-
T20Is	115	107	21	2458	91	28.58	136.17	0	14	46	-
First-class	102	169	18	5042	209*	33.39	51.02	11	24	76	1
List A	377	347	49	11654	161	39.10	91.03	22	68	127	-
T20s	355	333	50	7476	91	26.41	131.31	0	37	155	-

Bowling	Mat	Balls	Runs	Wkts	BBI	BBM	Ave	Econ	SR	5w	10
Tests	16	-	-	-	-	-	-	-	-	-	-
ODIs	246	-	-	-	-	-	-	-	-	-	-
T20Is	115	-	-	-	-	-	-	-	-	-	-
First-class	102	120	94	2	2/24	2/24	47.00	4.70	60.0	0	0
List A	377	42	49	0	-	-	-	7.00	-	0	0
T20s	355	-	-	-	-	-	-	-	-	-	-

SURREY

DANIEL MORIARTY

LHB / SLA / RO / W0

FULL NAME: Daniel Thornhill Moriarty
BORN: December 2, 1999, Reigate, Surrey
SQUAD NO: 21
HEIGHT: 6ft 2in
NICKNAME: Mozza
EDUCATION: Rondesbosch Boy's High School, Cape Town
TEAMS: Surrey, South Africa U19
ROLE: Bowler
DEBUT: First-class: 2020; List A: 2021; T20: 2020

BEST BATTING: 8 Surrey vs Essex, The Oval, 2021
BEST BOWLING: 6-60 Surrey vs Sussex, The Oval, 2020

WHO IS YOUR LOOKALIKE? Graeme Smith
FIRST CRICKET CLUB? Western Province CC, Cape Town
BIGGEST INFLUENCE ON YOUR DEVELOPMENT AS A CRICKETER (EXCLUDING PARENTS)?
Gareth Batty – he has helped me understand my game in more depth
WHO IS THE BEST BATTER/KEEPER/ALLROUNDER/BOWLER IN COUNTY CRICKET
(EXCLUDING TEAMMATES)? David Bedingham/Ben Foakes/Darren Stevens/Simon Harmer
MOST UNDERRATED PLAYER IN COUNTY CRICKET? Michael Pepper
MOST BEAUTIFUL THING YOU HAVE EVER SEEN? Sunrise after hiking up Lion's Head
mountain in Cape Town
WHO WOULD YOU MOST LIKE TO HAVE A NET WITH? Daniel Vettori
MAKE ONE PREDICTION FOR THE FUTURE OF CRICKET: It will become more skilful,
competitive and will be played at a higher intensity
WHAT DO YOU MOST ENJOY LISTENING TO? Audiobooks
WHAT MAKES YOU WORRY? Failure
GUILTY PLEASURE? Strawberry whey

Batting	Mat	Inns	NO	Runs	HS	Ave	SR	100	50	Ct	St
First-class	6	6	0	13	8	2.16	13.54	0	0	2	-
List A	10	3	1	8	5	4.00	44.44	0	0	5	-
T20s	26	2	2	15	9*	-	150.00	0	0	1	-

Bowling	Mat	Balls	Runs	Wkts	BBI	BBM	Ave	Econ	SR	5w	10
First-class	6	1680	863	35	6/60	11/224	24.65	3.08	48.0	4	1
List A	10	491	357	15	4/30	4/30	23.80	4.36	32.7	0	0
T20s	26	498	566	28	3/25	3/25	20.21	6.81	17.7	0	0

JACK MORLEY

LHB / SLA / R0 / W0

FULL NAME: Jack Peter Morley
BORN: June 25, 2001, Rochdale, Lancashire
SQUAD NO: 18
HEIGHT: 5ft 11in
NICKNAME: Morles
EDUCATION: Siddal Moor Sports College, Heywood, Greater Manchester; Myerscough College, Preston, Lancashire
TEAMS: Lancashire, England U19
ROLE: Bowler
DEBUT: First-class: 2020; List A: 2021

BEST BATTING: 3 Lancashire vs Derbyshire, Liverpool, 2020
BEST BOWLING: 4-62 Lancashire vs Derbyshire, Liverpool, 2020

FIRST CRICKET CLUB? Heywood CC, Rochdale
MOST EXCITING DAY AS A CRICKETER? Day four of my first-class debut against Derbyshire at Liverpool in 2020, when I took four wickets to help us win the game
BIGGEST INFLUENCE ON YOUR DEVELOPMENT AS A CRICKETER (EXCLUDING PARENTS)?
My cousin Tom Hardman – he got me into playing cricket from a young age
FAVOURITE SMELL? A barbecue
TWITTER: @jackmorley196

Batting	Mat	Inns	NO	Runs	HS	Ave	SR	100	50	Ct	St
First-class	1	1	0	3	3	3.00	6.52	0	0	0	-
List A	7	2	1	6	6	6.00	54.54	0	0	2	-

Bowling	Mat	Balls	Runs	Wkts	BBI	BBM	Ave	Econ	SR	5w	10
First-class	1	240	71	5	4/62	5/71	14.20	1.77	48.0	0	0
List A	7	336	224	9	2/22	2/22	24.88	4.00	37.3	0	0

CHARLIE MORRIS — RHB / RMF / R0 / W2

FULL NAME: Charles Andrew John Morris
BORN: July 6, 1992, Hereford
SQUAD NO: 31
HEIGHT: 6ft
NICKNAME: Bishop
EDUCATION: Kingswood School, Bath; King's College, Taunton; Oxford Brookes University
TEAMS: Worcestershire
ROLE: Bowler
DEBUT: First-class: 2012; List A: 2013; T20: 2013

BEST BATTING: 53* Worcestershire vs Australians, Worcester, 2019
BEST BOWLING: 7-45 Worcestershire vs Leicestershire, Leicester, 2019

FIRST CRICKET CLUB? Yelverton CC, Devon
MOST EXCITING DAY AS A CRICKETER? Playing in T20 Finals Day in 2019
WHAT WOULD YOU DO IF YOU WERE IN CHARGE OF COUNTY CRICKET? Encourage counties to play more Second XI fixtures at county grounds, use a Dukes ball for all Second XI matches, continue to fund the MCC Universities scheme (I owe so much to the MCCU system for giving me my break in the professional game and I'd like to see others continue to have that opportunity)
GUILTY PLEASURE? Whisky
TWITTER: @morris_9

Batting	Mat	Inns	NO	Runs	HS	Ave	SR	100	50	Ct	St
First-class	69	91	49	570	53*	13.57	30.33	0	2	12	-
List A	41	21	14	110	25*	15.71	65.47	0	0	9	-
T20s	26	6	4	8	4	4.00	66.66	0	0	6	-

Bowling	Mat	Balls	Runs	Wkts	BBI	BBM	Ave	Econ	SR	5w	10
First-class	69	12230	6400	216	7/45	9/109	29.62	3.13	56.6	7	0
List A	41	1661	1645	44	4/33	4/33	37.38	5.94	37.7	0	0
T20s	26	499	790	28	3/21	3/21	28.21	9.49	17.8	0	0

DAN MOUSLEY

LHB / OB / R0 / W0

FULL NAME: Daniel Richard Mousley
BORN: July 8, 2001, Birmingham
SQUAD NO: 80
HEIGHT: 6ft 2in
NICKNAME: Mouse
EDUCATION: Bablake School, Coventry
TEAMS: Warwickshire, England U19
ROLE: Batter
DEBUT: First-class: 2019; List A: 2021; T20: 2020

WARWICKSHIRE

BEST BATTING: 71 Warwickshire vs Glamorgan, Cardiff, 2020

FIRST CRICKET CLUB? Nether Whitacre CC, Coleshill, Warwickshire
MOST EXCITING DAY AS A CRICKETER? The group match against Australia during the 2020 U19 World Cup in South Africa. It went down to the last ball of the match, just a shame we didn't come out on top
CHILDHOOD SPORTING HERO? Andrew Flintoff
BIGGEST INFLUENCE ON YOUR DEVELOPMENT AS A CRICKETER (EXCLUDING PARENTS)? My uncles who threw balls at me in the garden and in the nets every weekend and every training session – that made me very competitive
WHAT WOULD YOU DO IF YOU WERE IN CHARGE OF COUNTY CRICKET? Have more first-class cricket, more evening games, and more TV games
FAVOURITE SMELL? Petrol
TWITTER: @danmousley80

Batting	Mat	Inns	NO	Runs	HS	Ave	SR	100	50	Ct	St
First-class	3	5	0	152	71	30.40	49.19	0	1	1	-
List A	9	9	0	338	105	37.55	95.48	1	2	6	-
T20s	9	8	1	189	58*	27.00	123.52	0	2	3	-

Bowling	Mat	Balls	Runs	Wkts	BBI	BBM	Ave	Econ	SR	5w	10
First-class	3	54	37	0	-	-	-	4.11	-	0	0
List A	9	252	178	7	3/32	3/32	25.42	4.23	36.0	0	0
T20s	9	72	92	3	1/3	1/3	30.66	7.66	24.0	0	0

WIAAN MULDER

RHB / RFM / R0 / W0

FULL NAME: Pieter Willem Adriaan Mulder
BORN: February 19, 1998, Johannesburg, South Africa
SQUAD NO: TBC
TEAMS: South Africa, Leicestershire, Gauteng, Kent, Lions, Tshwane Spartans
ROLE: Allrounder
DEBUT: Test: 2019; ODI: 2017; T20I: 2021; First-class: 2016; List A: 2017; T20: 2016

BEST BATTING: 146 Lions vs Knights, Bloemfontein, 2019
BEST BOWLING: 7-25 Lions vs Dolphins, Potchefstroom, 2016

TWITTER: @wiaan_m
NOTES: Leicestershire have re-signed the South African allrounder as an overseas player for this summer's County Championship and One-Day Cup. This will be Mulder's second stint in county cricket after a brief spell with Kent in 2019. He had been due to play for the Foxes last year only for international committments to scupper the deal. A brisk seamer and hard-hitting batter, Mulder made his ODI debut in October 2017 at the age of 19 before earning his Test cap a little over a year later. He now features regurlarly in all three formats for his country and is likely to be needed by the South Africa during their tour of the UK between July and September this summer

Batting	Mat	Inns	NO	Runs	HS	Ave	SR	100	50	Ct	St
Tests	8	13	0	205	36	15.76	41.66	0	0	13	-
ODIs	12	10	4	81	19*	13.50	81.00	0	0	5	-
T20Is	5	3	1	51	36	25.50	115.90	0	0	4	-
First-class	46	76	14	2101	146	33.88	51.46	5	7	37	-
List A	37	31	8	498	66	21.65	87.21	0	1	10	-
T20s	43	34	14	515	63	25.75	127.47	0	4	17	-

Bowling	Mat	Balls	Runs	Wkts	BBI	BBM	Ave	Econ	SR	5w	10
Tests	8	846	416	14	3/1	5/108	29.71	2.95	60.4	0	0
ODIs	12	354	341	10	2/59	2/59	34.10	5.77	35.4	0	0
T20Is	5	66	90	5	2/10	2/10	18.00	8.18	13.2	0	0
First-class	46	5726	3123	118	7/25	8/79	26.46	3.27	48.5	1	0
List A	37	1287	1153	37	3/32	3/32	31.16	5.37	34.7	0	0
T20s	43	571	782	29	2/10	2/10	26.96	8.21	19.6	0	0

STEVEN MULLANEY RHB / RM / R1 / W0 / MVP22

FULL NAME: Steven John Mullaney
BORN: November 19, 1986, Warrington, Cheshire
SQUAD NO: 5
HEIGHT: 5ft 8in
NICKNAME: Mull
EDUCATION: St Mary's Catholic High School, Greater Manchester
TEAMS: Nottinghamshire, England Lions, Lancashire
ROLE: Allrounder
DEBUT: First-class: 2006; List A: 2006; T20: 2006

BEST BATTING: 179 Nottinghamshire vs Warwickshire, Trent Bridge, 2019
BEST BOWLING: 5-32 Nottinghamshire vs Gloucestershire, Trent Bridge, 2017
COUNTY CAP: 2013 (Nottinghamshire)

FIRST CRICKET CLUB? Golborne CC, Cheshire
BIGGEST INFLUENCE ON YOUR DEVELOPMENT AS A CRICKETER (EXCLUDING PARENTS)?
Peter Moores – he makes it fun and makes you better as a player and a person
WHO IS THE BEST BATTER/ALLROUNDER/BOWLER IN COUNTY CRICKET (EXCLUDING TEAMMATES)? Jamie Smith/George Balderson/Chris Rushworth
MOST UNDERRATED PLAYER IN COUNTY CRICKET? Callum Parkinson
MOST BEAUTIFUL THING YOU HAVE EVER SEEN? Las Vegas
HOBBIES? Rugby League
WHO WOULD YOU MOST LIKE TO HAVE A NET WITH? Kane Williamson – I would love to chat to him about leadership and batting
WHAT MAKES YOU WORRY? Life after cricket
GUILTY PLEASURE? Karaoke
TWITTER: @mull05

Batting	Mat	Inns	NO	Runs	HS	Ave	SR	100	50	Ct	St
First-class	157	263	9	8384	179	33.00	58.00	16	45	148	-
List A	123	91	17	2611	124	35.28	103.32	2	19	57	-
T20s	158	112	27	1464	55	17.22	141.31	0	2	78	-

Bowling	Mat	Balls	Runs	Wkts	BBI	BBM	Ave	Econ	SR	5w	10
First-class	157	8885	4507	120	5/32	7/46	37.55	3.04	74.0	1	0
List A	123	3981	3458	100	4/29	4/29	34.58	5.21	39.8	0	0
T20s	158	2457	3232	114	4/19	4/19	28.35	7.89	21.5	0	0

MIDDLESEX

FULL NAME: Timothy James Murtagh
BORN: August 2, 1981, Lambeth, London
SQUAD NO: 34
HEIGHT: 6ft
NICKNAME: Murts
EDUCATION: The John Fisher School, London; St Mary's College, Twickenham
TEAMS: Ireland, Middlesex, England U19, Surrey
ROLE: Bowler
DEBUT: Test: 2018; ODI: 2012; T20I: 2012; First-class: 2000; List A: 2000; T20: 2003

BEST BATTING: 74* Surrey vs Middlesex, The Oval, 2004
BEST BOWLING: 7-82 Middlesex vs Derbyshire, Derby, 2009
COUNTY CAP: 2008 (Middlesex); BENEFIT: 2015 (Middlesex)

WHO IS YOUR LOOKALIKE? Frank Lampard
FIRST CRICKET CLUB? Purley CC, London
BIGGEST CRICKETING REGRET? Missing the 2015 World Cup through injury
WHO IS THE BEST BATTER/KEEPER/ALLROUNDER/BOWLER IN COUNTY CRICKET
(EXCLUDING TEAMMATES)? Alastair Cook/Ben Cox/Craig Overton/Ollie Robinson
MOST UNDERRATED PLAYER IN COUNTY CRICKET? Ryan Higgins
MOST BEAUTIFUL THING YOU HAVE EVER SEEN? The birth of my children
WHAT MAKES YOU WORRY? Liverpool FC
WHAT GIVES YOU JOY? Liverpool FC
GUILTY PLEASURE? Bubble baths
TWITTER: @tjmurtagh

Batting	Mat	Inns	NO	Runs	HS	Ave	SR	100	50	Ct	St
Tests	3	6	2	109	54*	27.25	82.57	0	1	0	-
ODIs	58	36	12	188	23*	7.83	63.08	0	0	16	-
T20Is	14	5	3	26	12*	13.00	104.00	0	0	3	-
First-class	248	333	97	4285	74*	18.15		0	11	68	-
List A	213	129	47	828	35*	10.09		0	0	55	-
T20s	109	39	14	227	40*	9.08	106.07	0	0	23	-

Bowling	Mat	Balls	Runs	Wkts	BBI	BBM	Ave	Econ	SR	5w	10
Tests	3	570	213	13	5/13	6/65	16.38	2.24	43.8	1	0
ODIs	58	3020	2290	74	5/21	5/21	30.94	4.54	40.8	1	0
T20Is	14	268	324	13	3/23	3/23	24.92	7.25	20.6	0	0
First-class	248	43852	21915	899	7/82		24.37	2.99	48.7	38	4
List A	213	9850	8211	277	5/21	5/21	29.64	5.00	35.5	1	0
T20s	109	2128	2895	113	6/24	6/24	25.61	8.16	18.8	1	0

TAWANDA MUYEYE

RHB / OB / R0 / W0

FULL NAME: Tawanda Sean Muyeye
BORN: March 05, 2001, Harare, Zimbabwe
SQUAD NO: 14
HEIGHT: 6ft
EDUCATION: Eastbourne College, East Sussex; The Open University, Milton Keynes
TEAMS: Kent
ROLE: Batter
DEBUT: First-class: 2021; List A: 2021

BEST BATTING: 89 Kent vs Middlesex, Canterbury, 2021

WHO IS YOUR LOOKALIKE? Either Idris Elba (actor) or Marcus Rashford
FIRST CRICKET CLUB? Mountaineers, Mutare, Zimbabwe
WHAT WOULD YOU CHANGE ABOUT THE STRUCTURE OF THE COUNTY SEASON?
Increase the amount of second XI cricket so that players have more opportunity to improve and a better chance of being selected for the first team
WHO IS THE BEST BATTER/KEEPER/ALLROUNDER/BOWLER IN COUNTY CRICKET (EXCLUDING TEAMMATES)? Joe Clarke/Ben Foakes/Ryan Higgins/Ollie Robinson
MOST UNDERRATED PLAYER IN COUNTY CRICKET? Tom Abell
WHAT WOULD A FLY ON THE WALL HEAR IN YOUR DRESSING ROOM? Jordan Cox telling us that the ball is doing all sorts out in the middle
MOST BEAUTIFUL THING YOU HAVE EVER SEEN? My Air Jordans
HOBBIES? Reading
IF YOU COULD TURN BACK TIME... I'd have had more fun at school and been more adventurous in my teenage years
MAKE ONE PREDICTION FOR THE FUTURE OF CRICKET: The IPL will lose its appeal because salaries elsewhere will be so high
WHAT MAKES YOU WORRY? Not doing my university work
TWITTER: @tawanda_muyeye

Batting	Mat	Inns	NO	Runs	HS	Ave	SR	100	50	Ct	St
First-class	4	6	2	142	89	35.50	50.53	0	1	0	-
List A	8	7	1	140	30	23.33	99.29	0	0	1	-

Bowling	Mat	Balls	Runs	Wkts	BBI	BBM	Ave	Econ	SR	5w	10
First-class	4	-	-	-	-	-	-	-	-	-	-
List A	8	36	16	0	-	-	-	2.66	-	0	0

SUNIL NARINE   RHB / OB

FULL NAME: Sunil Philip Narine
BORN: May 26, 1988, Arima, Trinidad &
Tobago
SQUAD NO: TBC
HEIGHT: 5ft 10in
TEAMS: West Indies, Surrey, Comilla Victorians,
Dhaka Dynamites, Guyana Amazon Warriors,
Kolkata Knight Riders, Lahore Qalandars,
Melbourne Renegades, Sydney Sixers,
Trinbago Knight Riders, Trinidad & Tobago
ROLE: Bowler
DEBUT: Test: 2012; ODI: 2011; T20I: 2012;
First-class: 2009; List A: 2011; T20: 2011

BEST BATTING: 79 Trinbago Knight Riders vs Babados Tridents, Port of Spain, 2017 (T20)
BEST BOWLING: 5-19 Kolkata Knight Riders vs Kings XI Punjab, Kolkata, 2012 (T20)

NOTES: Surrey have signed the West Indian mystery spinner for this summer's T20 Blast.
Narine is a familiar face on the global T20 circuit, having won two IPLs with the Kolkata
Knight Riders and three Caribbean Premier League titles. He has featured only sporadically
for West Indies and hasn't played any international cricket since 2019. The last of his six Test
matches was in 2013. "I'm thrilled to have the opportunity to play for Surrey in the Blast this
year," said Narine. "It's one of the few competitions around the world I haven't experienced.
The stint I enjoyed with Oval Invincibles in 2021 [in The Hundred] gave me a taste of how
unique playing in front of a packed Oval crowd really is"

Batting	Mat	Inns	NO	Runs	HS	Ave	SR	100	50	Ct	St
Tests	6	7	2	40	22*	8.00	43.47	0	0	2	-
ODIs	65	45	12	363	36	11.00	82.31	0	0	14	-
T20Is	51	23	8	155	30	10.33	112.31	0	0	7	-
First-class	13	18	6	213	40*	17.75		0	0	10	-
List A	100	69	17	625	51	12.01		0	1	22	-
T20s	391	235	45	2926	79	15.40	146.74	0	11	83	-

Bowling	Mat	Balls	Runs	Wkts	BBI	BBM	Ave	Econ	SR	5w	10
Tests	6	1650	851	21	6/91	8/223	40.52	3.09	78.5	2	0
ODIs	65	3540	2435	92	6/27	6/27	26.46	4.12	38.4	2	0
T20Is	51	1102	1105	52	4/12	4/12	21.25	6.01	21.1	0	0
First-class	13	3023	1398	65	8/17	13/39	21.50	2.77	46.5	8	3
List A	100	5481	3399	163	6/9	6/9	20.85	3.72	33.6	6	0
T20s	391	8928	8990	429	5/19	5/19	20.95	6.04	20.8	1	0

JIMMY NEESHAM LHB / RM

FULL NAME: James Douglas Sheahan Neesham
BORN: September 17, 1990, Auckland, New Zealand
SQUAD NO: TBC
TEAMS: New Zealand, Northamptonshire, Auckland, Delhi Daredevils, Derbyshire, Essex, Guyana Amazon Warriors, Kent, Kings XI Punjab, Mumbai Indians, Otago, Rajasthan Royals, Trinbago Knight Riders, Wellington
ROLE: Allrounder
DEBUT: Test: 2014; ODI: 2013; T20I: 2012; First-class: 2010; List A: 2010; T20: 2010

BEST BATTING: 59* Otago vs Auckland, Queenstown, 2012 (T20)
BEST BOWLING: 4-24 Wellington vs Otago, Wellington, 2018 (T20)

TWITTER: @JimmyNeesh
NOTES: The Steelbacks have snapped up the hard-hitting Kiwi allrounder for the T20 Blast, with the terms of the deal also allowing him to feature in the County Championship fixture against Warwickshire in late June. Northants will be Neesham's fourth county after previous spells with Derbyshire, Kent and, Essex, for whom he made 13 Blast appearances last season. He brings a wealth of short-format experience and starred in the T20 World Cup last year, bludgeoning 27 from 11 deliveries to defeat England in the semi-finals. A popular figure in the game who isn't afraid to put his head above the parapet on Twitter, Neesham hit centuries in each of his first two Test matches but hasn't represented the Black Caps in the longer format since 2017

Batting	Mat	Inns	NO	Runs	HS	Ave	SR	100	50	Ct	St
Tests	12	22	1	709	137*	33.76	66.32	2	4	12	-
ODIs	66	56	10	1320	97*	28.69	97.63	0	6	24	-
T20Is	38	29	10	416	48*	21.89	151.82	0	0	11	-
First-class	67	112	10	3249	147	31.85	71.37	5	17	67	-
List A	129	113	22	3087	120*	33.92	102.38	2	18	51	-
T20s	182	143	39	2376	59*	22.84	136.94	0	5	61	-

Bowling	Mat	Balls	Runs	Wkts	BBI	BBM	Ave	Econ	SR	5w	10
Tests	12	1076	675	14	3/42	3/42	48.21	3.76	76.8	0	0
ODIs	66	2115	2139	68	5/27	5/27	31.45	6.06	31.1	2	0
T20Is	38	381	586	21	3/16	3/16	27.90	9.22	18.1	0	0
First-class	67	7059	4012	123	5/65	6/82	32.61	3.41	57.3	2	0
List A	129	4205	4059	145	5/27	5/27	27.99	5.79	29.0	4	0
T20s	182	2670	4015	158	4/24	4/24	25.41	9.02	16.8	0	0

MICHAEL NESER RHB / RMF / R0 / W0

FULL NAME: Michael Gertges Neser
BORN: March 29, 1990, Pretoria, South Africa
SQUAD NO: 30
TEAMS: Australia, Glamorgan, Adelaide Strikers, Brisbane Heat, Kings XI Punjab, Queensland
ROLE: Bowler
DEBUT: Test: 2021; ODI: 2018; First-class: 2010; List A: 2010; T20: 2011

BEST BATTING: 121 Queensland vs Tasmania, Adelaide, 2020
BEST BOWLING: 6-57 Queensland vs Tasmania, Hobart, 2017

NOTES: The Australian seamer signed a new two-year contract with Glamorgan last June after making his debut for the club earlier in the year. Neser was outstanding across five Championship games last summer, taking 23 wickets at 16.78. "Cardiff is a beautiful city, and I couldn't think of anywhere better to play over the next two years," said Neser after putting pen to paper. "As a team [we] played some really good cricket [last] season and there's plenty of young talent which bodes well for the future." The 32-year-old made his two ODI appearances against England in 2018 and has been on the fringes of the Australian squad for a number of years, belatedly making his Test debut during last winter's Ashes. Born in South Africa but relocated to Australia's Gold Coast aged 10, Neser has been a prolific wicket-taker in the Sheffield Shield for Queensland and scored his maiden first-class hundred against Tasmania in December 2020

Batting	Mat	Inns	NO	Runs	HS	Ave	SR	100	50	Ct	St
Tests	1	2	0	38	35	19.00	102.70	0	0	0	-
ODIs	2	2	0	8	6	4.00	50.00	0	0	0	-
First-class	72	99	13	2107	121	24.50	53.04	1	11	29	-
List A	59	45	13	747	122	23.34	87.06	1	2	18	-
T20s	78	50	18	424	40*	13.25	114.28	0	0	36	-

Bowling	Mat	Balls	Runs	Wkts	BBI	BBM	Ave	Econ	SR	5w	10
Tests	1	144	61	2	1/28	2/61	30.50	2.54	72.0	0	0
ODIs	2	100	120	2	2/46	2/46	60.00	7.19	50.0	0	0
First-class	72	12540	5944	244	6/57	8/76	24.36	2.84	51.3	7	0
List A	59	2708	2399	69	4/41	4/41	34.76	5.31	39.2	0	0
T20s	78	1514	2134	79	3/24	3/24	27.01	8.45	19.1	0	0

ARON NIJJAR LHB / SLA / R0 / W0

FULL NAME: Aron Stuart Singh Nijjar
BORN: September 24, 1994, Goodmayes, Essex
SQUAD NO: 24
EDUCATION: Ilford County High School
TEAMS: Essex
ROLE: Bowler
DEBUT: First-class: 2015; List A: 2015; T20: 2018

BEST BATTING: 53 Essex vs Northamptonshire, Chelmsford, 2015
BEST BOWLING: 2-28 Essex vs Cambridge MCCU, Cambridge, 2019

TWITTER: @aronnijjar
NOTES: The left-arm orthodox spinner was a regular fixture in Essex's T20 side for the first time in 2020, doing a steady job in nine of the club's 10 matches after Australian leggie Adam Zampa was forced to cancel his Blast contract because of travel restrictions. Nijjar had already done a fine job of replacing Zampa on T20 Finals Day the previous year to help Essex lift the trophy. The 27-year-old is yet to establish himself in the first-class game, having played only twice in the Championship since making a handful of appearances in 2015, but was an ever-present for the Eagles in both shorter formats last summer. He penned a new two-year deal with the club last December. "I've really enjoyed playing an important role in the side [last] season, especially being trusted with the ball during key overs of the match," he said. "I feel my game has developed over the past few years and having world-class spinners at the club has allowed me to learn and continue broadening my skills"

Batting	Mat	Inns	NO	Runs	HS	Ave	SR	100	50	Ct	St
First-class	14	16	5	239	53	21.72	44.58	0	1	3	-
List A	13	9	5	136	32*	34.00	113.33	0	0	7	-
T20s	25	12	5	75	27*	10.71	120.96	0	0	12	-

Bowling	Mat	Balls	Runs	Wkts	BBI	BBM	Ave	Econ	SR	5w	10
First-class	14	1253	806	19	2/28	3/48	42.42	3.85	65.9	0	0
List A	13	649	558	13	2/26	2/26	42.92	5.15	49.9	0	0
T20s	25	561	685	25	3/22	3/22	27.40	7.32	22.4	0	0

SAM NORTHEAST   RHB / OB / R4 / W0

FULL NAME: Sam Alexander Northeast
BORN: October 16, 1989, Ashford, Kent
SQUAD NO: TBC
HEIGHT: 5ft 11in
NICKNAME: Chumley
EDUCATION: Harrow School, London
TEAMS: Glamorgan, England Lions, Hampshire, Kent, Nottinghamshire, Yorkshire
ROLE: Batter
DEBUT: First-class: 2007; List A: 2007; T20: 2010

BEST BATTING: 191 Kent vs Derbyshire, Canterbury, 2016
BEST BOWLING: 1-60 Kent vs Gloucestershire, Cheltenham, 2013
COUNTY CAP: 2012 (Kent)

WHO IS YOUR LOOKALIKE? Nick Knight
FIRST CRICKET CLUB? Sandwich Town CC, Kent
WHAT WOULD YOU CHANGE ABOUT THE STRUCTURE OF THE COUNTY SEASON?
Less cricket, more rest time
WHO IS THE BEST BATTER/KEEPER/ALLROUNDER/BOWLER IN COUNTY CRICKET
(EXCLUDING TEAMMATES)? Hashim Amla/Ben Foakes/Ben Stokes/Ollie Robinson
MOST UNDERRATED PLAYER IN COUNTY CRICKET? Ben Brown
MOST BEAUTIFUL THING YOU HAVE EVER SEEN? My daughter
HOBBIES? Anything sport-related
IF YOU COULD TURN BACK TIME... I'd change a lot
WHO WOULD YOU MOST LIKE TO HAVE A NET WITH? Ricky Ponting
MAKE ONE PREDICTION FOR THE FUTURE OF CRICKET: Franchises taking over the
county game
WHAT DO YOU MOST ENJOY LISTENING TO? Two Hacks, One Pro (cricket podcast)
WHAT MAKES YOU WORRY? World War Three
TWITTER: @sanortheast

Batting	Mat	Inns	NO	Runs	HS	Ave	SR	100	50	Ct	St
First-class	182	306	23	10839	191	38.30	55.41	25	56	89	-
List A	106	98	10	2986	132	33.93	77.13	4	17	38	-
T20s	127	117	13	2966	114	28.51	127.78	1	20	33	-

Bowling	Mat	Balls	Runs	Wkts	BBI	BBM	Ave	Econ	SR	5w	10
First-class	182	178	147	1	1/60	1/60	147.00	4.95	178.0	0	0
List A	106	-	-	-	-	-	-	-	-	-	-
T20s	127	-	-	-	-	-	-	-	-	-	-

LIAM NORWELL

RHB / RFM / R0 / W3

FULL NAME: Liam Connor Norwell
BORN: December 27, 1991, Bournemouth
SQUAD NO: 24
HEIGHT: 6ft 3in
NICKNAME: Pasty
EDUCATION: Redruth School, Cornwall
TEAMS: Warwickshire, England Lions, Gloucestershire
ROLE: Bowler
DEBUT: First-class: 2011; List A: 2012; T20: 2012

BEST BATTING: 102 Gloucestershire vs Derbyshire, Bristol, 2016
BEST BOWLING: 8-43 Gloucestershire vs Leicestershire, Leicester, 2017
COUNTY CAP: 2011 (Gloucestershire)

FIRST CRICKET CLUB? Redruth CC, Cornwall
WHAT WOULD YOU CHANGE ABOUT THE STRUCTURE OF THE COUNTY SEASON?
Bring back a white-ball knockout competition with a Lord's final and split Championship into two divisions of nine teams (rather than one of 10 and one of eight)
BIGGEST CRICKETING REGRET? Not learning enough from the senior players in the first years of my career
WHO IS THE BEST BATTER/KEEPER/ALLROUNDER/BOWLER IN COUNTY CRICKET (EXCLUDING TEAMMATES)? James Vince/Ben Foakes/Tom Abell/Sam Cook
MOST UNDERRATED PLAYER IN COUNTY CRICKET? Graeme van Buuren
MAKE ONE PREDICTION FOR THE FUTURE OF CRICKET: The Championship will soon be reduced to 10 games a year for each county
WHAT MAKES YOU WORRY? Bad coffee
GUILTY PLEASURE? Angel Delight
TWITTER: @LCNorwell

Batting	Mat	Inns	NO	Runs	HS	Ave	SR	100	50	Ct	St
First-class	87	114	42	995	102	13.81	46.00	1	2	18	-
List A	18	10	2	47	16	5.87	69.11	0	0	2	-
T20s	26	6	5	5	2*	5.00	62.50	0	0	10	-

Bowling	Mat	Balls	Runs	Wkts	BBI	BBM	Ave	Econ	SR	5w	10
First-class	87	15232	8202	325	8/43	10/65	25.23	3.23	46.8	14	3
List A	18	840	755	23	6/52	6/52	32.82	5.39	36.5	2	0
T20s	26	459	737	13	3/27	3/27	56.69	9.63	35.3	0	0

KENT

FULL NAME: Marcus Kevin O'Riordan
BORN: January 25, 1998, Pembury, Kent
SQUAD NO: 55
HEIGHT: 5ft 10in
NICKNAME: Ray
EDUCATION: Holmewood House School, Tunbridge Wells; Tonbridge School
TEAMS: Kent
ROLE: Allrounder
DEBUT: First-class: 2019; List A: 2021; T20: 2019

BEST BATTING: 52* Kent vs Hampshire, Canterbury, 2020
BEST BOWLING: 3-50 Kent vs Sussex, Canterbury, 2020

FIRST CRICKET CLUB? Tunbridge Wells CC, Kent
WHAT WOULD YOU CHANGE ABOUT THE STRUCTURE OF THE COUNTY SEASON?
Introduce a 32-team FA Cup-style knockout competition (50 overs or T20) consisting of first-class counties, National Counties and qualifying club sides. Offer promotion to the County Championship for National Counties. Play the 50-over competition at the start of the season to break up the Championship block
BIGGEST INFLUENCE ON YOUR DEVELOPMENT AS A CRICKETER (EXCLUDING PARENTS)?
Andy Whittall, my housemaster at Tonbridge School. He suggested I start bowling off-spin instead of medium pace
WHO IS THE BEST BATTER/KEEPER/ALLROUNDER/BOWLER IN COUNTY CRICKET
(EXCLUDING TEAMMATES)? James Vince/Ben Foakes/Matt Critchley/Simon Harmer
HOBBIES? Hockey

Batting	Mat	Inns	NO	Runs	HS	Ave	SR	100	50	Ct	St
First-class	13	17	3	377	52*	26.92	43.83	0	1	5	-
List A	5	4	1	119	60	39.66	85.61	0	1	2	-
T20s	3	2	1	15	13*	15.00	93.75	0	0	1	-

Bowling	Mat	Balls	Runs	Wkts	BBI	BBM	Ave	Econ	SR	5w	10
First-class	13	715	433	10	3/50	4/72	43.30	3.63	71.5	0	0
List A	5	126	157	1	1/77	1/77	157.00	7.47	126.0	0	0
T20s	3	60	55	3	2/24	2/24	18.33	5.50	20.0	0	0

FULL NAME: Duanne Olivier
BORN: May 9, 1992, Groblersdal, Limpopo, South Africa
SQUAD NO: 74
HEIGHT: 6ft 4in
NICKNAME: Doozle
TEAMS: South Africa, Yorkshire, Derbyshire, Free State, Gauteng, Jaffna Stallions, Jozi Stars, Knights
ROLE: Bowler
DEBUT: Test: 2017; ODI: 2019; First-class: 2011; List A: 2011; T20: 2011

BEST BATTING: 72 Free State vs Namibia, Bloemfontein, 2014
BEST BOWLING: 6-37 South Africa vs Pakistan, Centurion, 2018
COUNTY CAP: 2020 (Yorkshire)

MOST EXCITING DAY AS A CRICKETER? Making my Test debut against Sri Lanka at Johannesburg in 2017
CHILDHOOD SPORTING HERO? Allan Donald
BIGGEST INFLUENCE ON YOUR DEVELOPMENT AS A CRICKETER (EXCLUDING PARENTS)? My wife – she always pushes me to be better and inspires me every day
WHAT WOULD YOU DO IF YOU WERE IN CHARGE OF COUNTY CRICKET? Offer free entrance for everybody for the first game of the season, create more events which involve the local community, have a day in which the local cricket, football and rugby-league sides play against one another in each of those three sports
TWITTER: @Duanne992

Batting	Mat	Inns	NO	Runs	HS	Ave	SR	100	50	Ct	St
Tests	13	16	8	38	10*	4.75	23.75	0	0	2	-
ODIs	2	-	-	-	-	-	-	-	-	0	-
First-class	129	166	59	1366	72	12.76	42.17	0	3	37	-
List A	50	25	10	201	25*	13.40	65.68	0	0	8	-
T20s	56	17	11	85	15*	14.16	87.62	0	0	8	-

Bowling	Mat	Balls	Runs	Wkts	BBI	BBM	Ave	Econ	SR	5w	10
Tests	13	1908	1219	56	6/37	11/96	21.76	3.83	34.0	3	1
ODIs	2	114	124	3	2/73	2/73	41.33	6.52	38.0	0	0
First-class	129	22000	11882	511	6/37	11/96	23.25	3.24	43.0	26	4
List A	50	2067	1837	64	4/34	4/34	28.70	5.33	32.2	0	0
T20s	56	1092	1569	66	4/28	4/28	23.77	8.62	16.5	0	0

FELIX ORGAN

RHB / OB / R0 / W0

FULL NAME: Felix Spencer Organ
BORN: June 2, 1999, Sydney, Australia
SQUAD NO: 3
HEIGHT: 5ft 10in
NICKNAME: Fe
EDUCATION: Canford School, Dorset
TEAMS: Hampshire, England U19
ROLE: Allrounder
DEBUT: First-class: 2017; List A: 2018; T20: 2020

BEST BATTING: 100 Hampshire vs Kent, Southampton, 2019
BEST BOWLING: 5-25 Hampshire vs Surrey, Southampton, 2019

WHO IS YOUR LOOKALIKE? Mason Crane
FIRST CRICKET CLUB? St Cross Symondians CC, Winchester, Hampshire
MOST UNDERRATED PLAYER IN COUNTY CRICKET? Rob Yates
WHAT WOULD A FLY ON THE WALL HEAR IN YOUR DRESSING ROOM? Aneurin Donald
talking about PGA Tour Standard golf swings
MOST BEAUTIFUL THING YOU HAVE EVER SEEN? My hole in one
IF YOU COULD TURN BACK TIME... I would not have slashed at so many wide ones
WHO WOULD YOU MOST LIKE TO HAVE A NET WITH? Nathan Lyon
MAKE ONE PREDICTION FOR THE FUTURE OF CRICKET: Hampshire will win the County
Championship
WHAT MAKES YOU WORRY? Putin
WHAT GIVES YOU JOY? Liverpool FC

Batting	Mat	Inns	NO	Runs	HS	Ave	SR	100	50	Ct	St
First-class	18	29	0	589	100	20.31	41.92	1	3	11	-
List A	11	7	0	120	79	17.14	67.03	0	1	5	-
T20s	3	3	0	21	9	7.00	91.30	0	0	0	-

Bowling	Mat	Balls	Runs	Wkts	BBI	BBM	Ave	Econ	SR	5w	10
First-class	18	875	420	23	5/25	5/25	18.26	2.88	38.0	1	0
List A	11	287	219	5	2/43	2/43	43.80	4.57	57.4	0	0
T20s	3	48	54	3	2/21	2/21	18.00	6.75	16.0	0	0

ALI ORR

LHB / RM / RO / WO

FULL NAME: Alastair Graham Hamilton Orr
BORN: April 6, 2001, Eastbourne, Sussex
SQUAD NO: 6
HEIGHT: 6ft
EDUCATION: Bede's Senior School, Hailsham, East Sussex; Loughborough University
TEAMS: Sussex
ROLE: Batter
DEBUT: First-class: 2021; List A: 2021

SUSSEX

BEST BATTING: 119 Sussex vs Kent, Canterbury, 2021

WHO IS YOUR LOOKALIKE? Tom Clark
FIRST CRICKET CLUB? Eastbourne CC, East Sussex
WHO IS THE BEST BATTER/KEEPER/ALLROUNDER/BOWLER IN COUNTY CRICKET (EXCLUDING TEAMMATES)? Alastair Cook/Ben Foakes/Darren Stevens/James Anderson
MOST UNDERRATED PLAYER IN COUNTY CRICKET? Louis Kimber
MOST BEAUTIFUL THING YOU HAVE EVER SEEN? The Taj Mahal in India
HOBBIES? Golf – I recently started playing and absolutely love it
IF YOU COULD TURN BACK TIME... I would change the final lap of the final Grand Prix at Abu Dhabi in 2021
WHO WOULD YOU MOST AND LEAST LIKE TO HAVE A NET WITH? Most – Alastair Cook. Least – Shaun Tait
MAKE ONE PREDICTION FOR THE FUTURE OF CRICKET: Sussex will win the County Championship by 2030
WHAT DO YOU MOST ENJOY LISTENING TO? Coldplay
WHAT MAKES YOU WORRY? Not knowing what's going to happen

Batting	Mat	Inns	NO	Runs	HS	Ave	SR	100	50	Ct	St
First-class	7	14	0	548	119	39.14	39.97	1	4	1	-
List A	5	5	0	144	108	28.80	68.57	1	0	0	-
Bowling	Mat	Balls	Runs	Wkts	BBI	BBM	Ave	Econ	SR	5w	10
First-class	7	-	-	-	-	-	-	-	-	-	-
List A	5	-	-	-	-	-	-	-	-	-	-

CRAIG OVERTON RHB / RFM / R0 / W1 / MVP6

SOMERSET

FULL NAME: Craig Overton
BORN: April 10, 1994, Barnstaple, Devon
SQUAD NO: 12
HEIGHT: 6ft 5in
NICKNAME: Goober
EDUCATION: West Buckland School, Devon
TEAMS: England, Somerset
ROLE: Allrounder
DEBUT: Test: 2017; ODI: 2018; First-class: 2012;
List A: 2012; T20: 2014

BEST BATTING: 138 Somerset vs Hampshire, Taunton, 2016
BEST BOWLING: 6-24 Somerset vs Cardiff MCCU, Taunton, 2019
COUNTY CAP: 2016

WHO IS YOUR LOOKALIKE? My brother Jamie, and Michael Phelps
FIRST CRICKET CLUB? North Devon CC, Bideford
BIGGEST CRICKETING REGRET? Not winning the Championship
WHO IS THE BEST BATTER/KEEPER/ALLROUNDER/BOWLER IN COUNTY CRICKET
(EXCLUDING TEAMMATES)? Alastair Cook/Ben Cox/Simon Harmer/Chris Rushworth
MOST UNDERRATED PLAYER IN COUNTY CRICKET? Ryan Higgins
WHAT WOULD A FLY ON THE WALL HEAR IN YOUR DRESSING ROOM?
"One-hundred-and-eighty!"
MOST BEAUTIFUL THING YOU HAVE EVER SEEN? The Valley of Rocks, Devon
IF YOU COULD TURN BACK TIME... I'd change the finale of the 2010 County Championship
WHAT MAKES YOU WORRY? I'm not really a worrier
TWITTER: @craigoverton12

Batting	Mat	Inns	NO	Runs	HS	Ave	SR	100	50	Ct	St
Tests	6	11	2	167	41*	18.55	43.15	0	0	4	-
ODIs	4	2	1	18	18*	18.00	100.00	0	0	4	-
First-class	106	155	20	2927	138	21.68	63.01	1	13	81	-
List A	72	52	17	774	66*	22.11	116.39	0	2	33	-
T20s	63	34	14	322	35*	16.10	119.70	0	0	35	-

Bowling	Mat	Balls	Runs	Wkts	BBI	BBM	Ave	Econ	SR	5w	10
Tests	6	1082	571	17	3/14	6/61	33.58	3.16	63.6	0	0
ODIs	4	194	181	4	2/23	2/23	45.25	5.59	48.5	0	0
First-class	106	17801	8738	374	6/24	9/51	23.36	2.94	47.5	13	0
List A	72	3330	2946	94	5/18	5/18	31.34	5.30	35.4	1	0
T20s	63	1188	1763	58	3/17	3/17	30.39	8.90	20.4	0	0

FULL NAME: Jamie Overton
BORN: April 10, 1994, Barnstaple, Devon
SQUAD NO: 88
HEIGHT: 6ft 5in
NICKNAME: J
EDUCATION: West Buckland School, Devon
TEAMS: Surrey, England Lions, Northamptonshire, Somerset
ROLE: Bowler
DEBUT: First-class: 2012; List A: 2012; T20: 2015

BEST BATTING: 120 Somerset vs Warwickshire, Edgbaston, 2020
BEST BOWLING: 6-95 Somerset vs Middlesex, Taunton, 2013

WHO IS YOUR LOOKALIKE? Craig Overton
FIRST CRICKET CLUB? North Devon CC
FAMILY TIES? My dad played for Devon and my twin brother Craig plays for Somerset
WHAT WOULD YOU CHANGE ABOUT THE STRUCTURE OF THE COUNTY SEASON? Not have first-class games during the white-ball competitions
BIGGEST INFLUENCE ON YOUR DEVELOPMENT AS A CRICKETER (EXCLUDING PARENTS)? Clifford Dark, my club coach at North Devon CC. He offered me the opportunity to play at a higher age-group level and gave me lots of confidence
MOST UNDERRATED PLAYER IN COUNTY CRICKET? Ryan Higgins
MOST BEAUTIFUL THING YOU HAVE EVER SEEN? Watching horses galloping on a crisp winter morning
HOBBIES? Horse racing
WHO WOULD YOU MOST LIKE TO HAVE A NET WITH? Wasim Akram
MAKE ONE PREDICTION FOR THE FUTURE OF CRICKET: Test cricket will be a four-day format
TWITTER: @JamieOverton

Batting	Mat	Inns	NO	Runs	HS	Ave	SR	100	50	Ct	St
First-class	77	108	22	1660	120	19.30	79.46	1	9	44	-
List A	42	31	8	399	40*	17.34	114.65	0	0	19	-
T20s	70	38	13	401	40*	16.04	168.48	0	0	39	-

Bowling	Mat	Balls	Runs	Wkts	BBI	BBM	Ave	Econ	SR	5w	10
First-class	77	9827	5773	185	6/95	8/143	31.20	3.52	53.1	4	0
List A	42	1662	1742	57	4/42	4/42	30.56	6.28	29.1	0	0
T20s	70	1135	1795	59	5/47	5/47	30.42	9.48	19.2	1	0

CALLUM PARKINSON   RHB / SLA / R0 / W1 / MVP7

LEICESTERSHIRE

FULL NAME: Callum Francis Parkinson
BORN: October 24, 1996, Bolton, Lancashire
SQUAD NO: 10
HEIGHT: 5ft 8in
NICKNAME: Parky
EDUCATION: Bolton School; Canon Slade School, Bolton
TEAMS: Leicestershire, Derbyshire
ROLE: Bowler
DEBUT: First-class: 2016; List A: 2017; T20: 2017

BEST BATTING: 75 Leicestershire vs Kent, Canterbury, 2017
BEST BOWLING: 8-148 Leicestershire vs Worcestershire, Worcester, 2017

WHO IS YOUR LOOKALIKE? Matt Parkinson
FIRST CRICKET CLUB? Heaton CC, Bolton
WHO IS THE BEST BATTER/KEEPER/ALLROUNDER/BOWLER IN COUNTY CRICKET
(EXCLUDING TEAMMATES)? Joe Clarke/John Simpson/Ryan Higgins/Simon Harmer
MOST UNDERRATED PLAYER IN COUNTY CRICKET? Ben Raine
WHAT WOULD A FLY ON THE WALL HEAR IN YOUR DRESSING ROOM? Ben Mike and Harry
Swindells arguing with each other
HOBBIES? Watching Bolton Wanderers home and away
WHO WOULD YOU MOST AND LEAST LIKE TO HAVE A NET WITH? Most – Daniel Vettori.
Least – Dale Steyn
MAKE ONE PREDICTION FOR THE FUTURE OF CRICKET: Afghanistan will win the men's
World Cup within the next 10 years
WHAT DO YOU MOST ENJOY LISTENING TO? Chris Wright's cricketing opinions
WHAT MAKES YOU WORRY? Thinking how cold it'll be in April when we're fielding
GUILTY PLEASURE? The Notebook (rom-com film)
TWITTER: @cal_parky

Batting	Mat	Inns	NO	Runs	HS	Ave	SR	100	50	Ct	St
First-class	41	60	10	888	75	17.76	38.79	0	1	6	-
List A	13	11	3	222	52*	27.75	87.40	0	1	2	-
T20s	68	37	19	233	27*	12.94	104.01	0	0	13	-

Bowling	Mat	Balls	Runs	Wkts	BBI	BBM	Ave	Econ	SR	5w	10
First-class	41	7085	3792	104	8/148	10/108	36.46	3.21	68.1	4	2
List A	13	552	589	4	1/34	1/34	147.25	6.40	138.0	0	0
T20s	68	1367	1734	73	4/20	4/20	23.75	7.61	18.7	0	0

MATT PARKINSON
RHB / LB / R0 / W0

FULL NAME: Matthew William Parkinson
BORN: October 24, 1996, Bolton, Lancashire
SQUAD NO: 28
HEIGHT: 5ft 9in
NICKNAME: Daddy
EDUCATION: Canon Slade School, Bolton
TEAMS: England, Lancashire
ROLE: Bowler
DEBUT: ODI: 2020; T20I: 2019; First-class: 2016;
List A: 2018; T20: 2017

LANCASHIRE

BEST BATTING: 21* Lancashire vs Northamptonshire, Old Trafford, 2021
BEST BOWLING: 7-126 Lancashire vs Kent, Canterbury, 2021
COUNTY CAP: 2019

WHO IS YOUR LOOKALIKE? Callum Parkinson
FIRST CRICKET CLUB? Heaton CC, Bolton
BIGGEST INFLUENCE ON YOUR DEVELOPMENT AS A CRICKETER (EXCLUDING PARENTS)?
Stuart MacGill and Jeetan Patel
MOST BEAUTIFUL THING YOU HAVE EVER SEEN? Whitsunday Islands, Queensland, Australia
HOBBIES? Reading
MAKE ONE PREDICTION FOR THE FUTURE OF CRICKET: White-ball cricket only
WHAT DO YOU MOST ENJOY LISTENING TO? Country music
WHAT MAKES YOU WORRY? New seasons
WHAT GIVES YOU JOY? Coffee
TWITTER: @mattypark96

Batting	Mat	Inns	NO	Runs	HS	Ave	SR	100	50	Ct	St
ODIs	5	1	1	7	7*	-	87.50	0	0	1	-
T20Is	4	2	0	5	5	2.50	83.33	0	0	0	-
First-class	32	38	18	153	21*	7.65	33.04	0	0	7	-
List A	30	12	9	50	15*	16.66	55.55	0	0	5	-
T20s	67	11	4	24	7*	3.42	75.00	0	0	7	-

Bowling	Mat	Balls	Runs	Wkts	BBI	BBM	Ave	Econ	SR	5w	10
ODIs	5	208	203	5	2/28	2/28	40.60	5.85	41.6	0	0
T20Is	4	84	133	6	4/47	4/47	22.16	9.50	14.0	0	0
First-class	32	5146	2382	102	7/126	10/165	23.35	2.77	50.4	4	1
List A	30	1510	1318	47	5/51	5/51	28.04	5.23	32.1	2	0
T20s	67	1429	1789	103	4/9	4/9	17.36	7.51	13.8	0	0

RISHI PATEL

RHB / LB / R0 / W0

LEICESTERSHIRE

FULL NAME: Rishi Ketan Patel
BORN: July 26, 1998, Chigwell, Essex
SQUAD NO: 26
HEIGHT: 6ft 2in
NICKNAME: Yogi
EDUCATION: Brentwood School, Essex
TEAMS: Leicestershire, Essex
ROLE: Batter
DEBUT: First-class: 2019; List A: 2019; T20: 2021

BEST BATTING: 44 Leicestershire vs Gloucestershire, Bristol, 2021

FIRST CRICKET CLUB? Ilford CC, London
WHAT WOULD YOU CHANGE ABOUT THE STRUCTURE OF THE COUNTY SEASON? More red-ball cricket at the peak of summer
MOST UNDERRATED PLAYER IN COUNTY CRICKET? Joe Clarke
WHAT WOULD A FLY ON THE WALL HEAR IN YOUR DRESSING ROOM? Lots of talk about coffee
MOST BEAUTIFUL THING YOU HAVE EVER SEEN? Sunset over a lake in Vietnam
HOBBIES? Golf, squash, pub quizzes
WHO WOULD YOU MOST LIKE TO HAVE A NET WITH? Sachin Tendulkar – just to watch his methods and talk to him about his mental approach
MAKE ONE PREDICTION FOR THE FUTURE OF CRICKET: Test cricket will never die
WHAT DO YOU MOST ENJOY LISTENING TO? Podcasts about different sportsmen
WHAT MAKES YOU WORRY? Being late to training
TWITTER: @Rishikpatel26

Batting	Mat	Inns	NO	Runs	HS	Ave	SR	100	50	Ct	St
First-class	12	17	0	313	44	18.41	48.45	0	0	10	-
List A	11	11	1	384	118	38.40	94.81	1	1	5	-
T20s	14	12	1	175	35	15.90	127.73	0	0	7	-

Bowling	Mat	Balls	Runs	Wkts	BBI	BBM	Ave	Econ	SR	5w	10
First-class	12	-	-	-	-	-	-	-	-	-	-
List A	11	-	-	-	-	-	-	-	-	-	-
T20s	14	-	-	-	-	-	-	-	-	-	-

RYAN PATEL

LHB / RMF / R0 / W0

FULL NAME: Ryan Patel
BORN: October 26, 1997, Sutton, Surrey
SQUAD NO: 26
HEIGHT: 5ft 10in
NICKNAME: Pat
EDUCATION: Whitgift School, Croydon
TEAMS: Surrey, England U19
ROLE: Allrounder
DEBUT: First-class: 2017; List A: 2019; T20: 2019

BEST BATTING: 100* Surrey vs Essex, The Oval, 2019
BEST BOWLING: 6-5 Surrey vs Somerset, Guildford, 2018

WHO IS YOUR LOOKALIKE? Sanjeev Baskhar (TV presenter)
FIRST CRICKET CLUB? Old Rutlishians CC, London
BIGGEST INFLUENCE ON YOUR DEVELOPMENT AS A CRICKETER (EXCLUDING PARENTS)?
Sid Lahiri, director of the Rajasthan Royals Academy in Cobham who has also worked with
Surrey age-group sides
GUILTY PLEASURE? Beer

Batting	Mat	Inns	NO	Runs	HS	Ave	SR	100	50	Ct	St
First-class	32	52	4	1176	100*	24.50	38.95	1	4	17	-
List A	13	11	2	443	131	49.22	110.47	2	1	6	-
T20s	7	3	1	7	5*	3.50	70.00	0	0	1	-

Bowling	Mat	Balls	Runs	Wkts	BBI	BBM	Ave	Econ	SR	5w	10
First-class	32	1485	853	15	6/5	6/12	56.86	3.44	99.0	1	0
List A	13	130	133	4	2/65	2/65	33.25	6.13	32.5	0	0
T20s	7	21	36	0	-	-	-	10.28	-	0	0

SAMIT PATEL

RHB / SLA / R4 / W0 / MVP36

NOTTINGHAMSHIRE

FULL NAME: Samit Rohit Patel
BORN: November 30, 1984, Leicester
SQUAD NO: 21
HEIGHT: 5ft 8in
NICKNAME: Slippery
EDUCATION: Worksop College
TEAMS: England, Nottinghamshire, Dambulla
Viiking, Galle Gladiators, Glamorgan, Lahore
Qalandars, Melbourne Renegades, St Lucia
Kings, Wellington
ROLE: Allrounder
DEBUT: Test: 2012; ODI: 2008; T20I: 2011;
First-class: 2002; List A: 2002; T20: 2003

BEST BATTING: 257* Nottinghamshire vs Gloucestershire, Bristol, 2017
BEST BOWLING: 7-68 Nottinghamshire vs Hampshire, Southampton, 2011
COUNTY CAP: 2008 (Nottinghamshire); BENEFIT: 2017 (Nottinghamshire)

FIRST CRICKET CLUB? Kimberley Institute CC, Nottinghamshire
WHAT WOULD YOU CHANGE ABOUT THE STRUCTURE OF THE COUNTY SEASON? Play each
format in one block and play fewer four-day matches
WHO IS THE BEST BATTER/KEEPER/ALLROUNDER/BOWLER IN COUNTY CRICKET
(EXCLUDING TEAMMATES)? James Vince/Ben Foakes/Lewis Gregory/Craig Overton
MOST UNDERRATED PLAYER IN COUNTY CRICKET? Alex Davies
MOST BEAUTIFUL THING YOU HAVE EVER SEEN? The Taj Mahal, Table Mountain, and the
Pitons on St Lucia
HOBBIES? I have a property portfolio that I am looking to expand
WHO WOULD YOU LEAST LIKE TO HAVE A NET WITH? Patrick Patterson
TWITTER: @Samitpatel21

Batting	Mat	Inns	NO	Runs	HS	Ave	SR	100	50	Ct	St
Tests	6	9	0	151	42	16.77	44.67	0	0	3	-
ODIs	36	22	7	482	70*	32.13	93.23	0	1	7	-
T20Is	18	14	2	189	67	15.75	109.24	0	1	3	-
First-class	231	376	20	12692	257*	35.65	62.71	26	64	140	-
List A	245	212	34	6270	136*	35.22	85.38	8	33	70	-
T20s	351	295	63	5962	90*	25.69	125.91	0	32	101	-

Bowling	Mat	Balls	Runs	Wkts	BBI	BBM	Ave	Econ	SR	5w	10
Tests	6	858	421	7	2/27	3/164	60.14	2.94	122.5	0	0
ODIs	36	1187	1091	24	5/41	5/41	45.45	5.51	49.4	1	0
T20Is	18	252	321	7	2/6	2/6	45.85	7.64	36.0	0	0
First-class	231	26909	13650	357	7/68		38.23	3.04	75.3	5	1
List A	245	8319	7491	225	6/13	6/13	33.29	5.40	36.9	2	0
T20s	351	6321	7631	290	4/5	4/5	26.31	7.24	21.7	0	0

DANE PATERSON — RHB / RFM / R0 / W0 / MVP34

FULL NAME: Dane Paterson
BORN: April 4, 1989, Cape Town, South Africa
SQUAD NO: 4
TEAMS: South Africa, Nottinghamshire, Cape Cobras, Dolphins, Eastern Province, Jozi Stars, KwaZulu-Natal, Paarl Rocks, South Western Districts, Western Province
ROLE: Bowler
DEBUT: Test: 2020; ODI: 2017; T20I: 2017; First-class: 2009; List A: 2009; T20: 2013

NOTTINGHAMSHIRE

BEST BATTING: 59 KwaZulu-Natal vs Free State, Bloemfontein, 2013
BEST BOWLING: 7-20 Western Province vs Free State, Rondebosch, 2013

TWITTER: @DanePaterson44
NOTES: Notts wasted little time tying Paterson down for another season after the South African seamer impressed for the club last summer. A stocky, bustling right-armer, his components are well suited to Trent Bridge's juicy conditions, as was demonstrated by last term's tally of 54 first-class wickets at less than 18 runs per wicket. "When overseas players commit themselves fully to a club and deliver consistently on the field, we've seen many times before how valuable they can be in the county game," said Peter Moores, the Notts head coach. With senior appearances for the Proteas in all formats, Paterson offers versatility to a high-quality seam attack and adaptability with both red and white ball. He was unlucky not to be included in South Africa's squad for New Zealand earlier this year after a fruitful campaign for Warriors in South Africa, which featured a spell of 7-25 in their opening fixture

Batting	Mat	Inns	NO	Runs	HS	Ave	SR	100	50	Ct	St
Tests	2	4	3	43	39*	43.00	87.75	0	0	1	-
ODIs	4	-	-	-	-	-	-	-	-	2	-
T20Is	8	2	1	5	4*	5.00	250.00	0	0	1	-
First-class	117	146	43	1302	59	12.64	73.85	0	1	44	-
List A	91	36	10	302	29	11.61	105.96	0	0	29	-
T20s	97	32	14	158	24*	8.77	132.77	0	0	26	-

Bowling	Mat	Balls	Runs	Wkts	BBI	BBM	Ave	Econ	SR	5w	10
Tests	2	347	166	4	2/86	3/104	41.50	2.87	86.7	0	0
ODIs	4	209	217	4	3/44	3/44	54.25	6.22	52.2	0	0
T20Is	8	179	265	9	4/32	4/32	29.44	8.88	19.8	0	0
First-class	117	18791	9710	417	7/20	10/62	23.28	3.10	45.0	15	1
List A	91	4318	3743	123	5/19	5/19	30.43	5.20	35.1	1	0
T20s	97	1930	2546	101	4/24	4/24	25.20	7.91	19.1	0	0

STEVEN PATTERSON RHB / RMF / R0 / W2

YORKSHIRE

FULL NAME: Steven Andrew Patterson
BORN: October 3, 1983, Beverley, Yorkshire
SQUAD NO: 17
HEIGHT: 6ft 4in
NICKNAME: Dead Man
EDUCATION: Malet Lambert School, Hull; St Mary's Sixth Form College, Hull; University of Leeds
TEAMS: Yorkshire
ROLE: Bowler
DEBUT: First-class: 2005; List A: 2003; T20: 2009

BEST BATTING: 63* Yorkshire vs Warwickshire, Edgbaston, 2016
BEST BOWLING: 6-40 Yorkshire vs Essex, Chelmsford, 2018
COUNTY CAP: 2012; BENEFIT: 2017

FIRST CRICKET CLUB? Hull CC, East Yorkshire
FAMILY TIES? My grandad played for Durham before World War II
WHAT WOULD YOU CHANGE ABOUT THE STRUCTURE OF THE COUNTY SEASON?
Play everyone twice in the County Championship
WHO IS THE BEST BATTER/KEEPER/ALLROUNDER/BOWLER IN COUNTY CRICKET
(EXCLUDING TEAMMATES)? Ollie Pope/Ben Foakes/Craig Overton/Ollie Robinson
MOST UNDERRATED PLAYER IN COUNTY CRICKET? Josh Davey
IF YOU COULD TURN BACK TIME... I'd spend more time with my dad
WHO WOULD YOU MOST AND LEAST LIKE TO HAVE A NET WITH? Most – Glenn McGrath.
Just to watch him bowl, as he was my favourite bowler as a child. Least – Kumar Sangakkara,
because he was so good and we could never get him out

Batting	Mat	Inns	NO	Runs	HS	Ave	SR	100	50	Ct	St
First-class	172	207	45	2568	63*	15.85	39.27	0	4	34	-
List A	97	41	21	250	25*	12.50		0	0	17	-
T20s	63	9	4	9	3*	1.80	42.85	0	0	10	-

Bowling	Mat	Balls	Runs	Wkts	BBI	BBM	Ave	Econ	SR	5w	10
First-class	172	27870	12466	452	6/40	8/94	27.57	2.68	61.6	8	0
List A	97	4116	3524	122	6/32	6/32	28.88	5.13	33.7	2	0
T20s	63	1290	1811	61	4/30	4/30	29.68	8.42	21.1	0	0

LIAM PATTERSON-WHITE LHB / SLA / R0 / W0

FULL NAME: Liam Anthony Patterson-White
BORN: November 8, 1998, Sunderland, County Durham
SQUAD NO: 87
HEIGHT: 6ft
NICKNAME: Patto
EDUCATION: Worksop College, Nottinghamshire
TEAMS: Nottinghamshire, England U19
ROLE: Allrounder
DEBUT: First-class: 2019; List A: 2021

BEST BATTING: 101 Nottinghamshire vs Somerset, Taunton, 2021
BEST BOWLING: 5-41 Nottinghamshire vs Hampshire, Southampton, 2021

FIRST CRICKET CLUB? Bashford Mill CC, Nottingham
MOST EXCITING DAY AS A CRICKETER? Making my professional debut in 2019
CHILDHOOD SPORTING HERO? James Taylor
BIGGEST INFLUENCE ON YOUR DEVELOPMENT AS A CRICKETER (EXCLUDING PARENTS)?
Ant Botha – assistant coach at Nottinghamshire. He helped me when working with the Academy and Second XI teams and continues to back me, showing why I deserve to represent Nottinghamshire
FAVOURITE SMELL? A scented candle
TWITTER: @LiamPattersonW2

Batting	Mat	Inns	NO	Runs	HS	Ave	SR	100	50	Ct	St
First-class	20	29	5	662	101	27.58	50.15	1	4	7	-
List A	8	6	0	51	27	8.50	68.00	0	0	1	-

Bowling	Mat	Balls	Runs	Wkts	BBI	BBM	Ave	Econ	SR	5w	10
First-class	20	2747	1296	46	5/41	6/107	28.17	2.83	59.7	2	0
List A	8	210	188	13	5/19	5/19	14.46	5.37	16.1	1	0

DAVID PAYNE

RHB / LFM / R0 / W0

GLOUCESTERSHIRE

FULL NAME: David Alan Payne
BORN: February 15, 1991, Poole, Dorset
SQUAD NO: 14
HEIGHT: 6ft 3in
NICKNAME: Sid
EDUCATION: Lytchett Minster Secondary &
Sixth Form, Poole, Dorset
TEAMS: Gloucestershire, England U19
ROLE: Bowler
DEBUT: First-class: 2011; List A: 2009; T20: 2010

BEST BATTING: 67* Gloucestershire vs Glamorgan, Cardiff, 2016
BEST BOWLING: 6-26 Gloucestershire vs Leicestershire, Bristol, 2011
COUNTY CAP: 2011

FIRST CRICKET CLUB? Parley CC, Dorset
WHAT WOULD YOU CHANGE ABOUT THE STRUCTURE OF THE COUNTY SEASON?
Divide the Championship into three divisions of six teams, each to play 10 matches with a
two-up/two-down system
WHO IS THE BEST BATTER/KEEPER/ALLROUNDER/BOWLER IN COUNTY CRICKET
(EXCLUDING TEAMMATES)? Joe Clarke/Ben Foakes/Matt Critchley/Craig Overton
MOST UNDERRATED PLAYER IN COUNTY CRICKET? Benny Howell
MOST BEAUTIFUL THING YOU HAVE EVER SEEN? New Zealand
WHAT DO YOU MOST ENJOY LISTENING TO? Heart FM
WHAT MAKES YOU WORRY? How good batters are becoming
TWITTER: @sidpayne7

Batting	Mat	Inns	NO	Runs	HS	Ave	SR	100	50	Ct	St
First-class	109	134	42	1754	67*	19.06	46.59	0	6	37	-
List A	66	27	17	171	36*	17.10	76.68	0	0	19	-
T20s	109	24	14	49	10	4.90	85.96	0	0	20	-
Bowling	Mat	Balls	Runs	Wkts	BBI	BBM	Ave	Econ	SR	5w	10
First-class	109	17713	9132	311	6/26	11/87	29.36	3.09	56.9	6	1
List A	66	2867	2746	110	7/29	7/29	24.96	5.74	26.0	3	0
T20s	109	2178	3091	133	5/24	5/24	23.24	8.51	16.3	1	0

DILLON PENNINGTON

RHB / RFM / R0 / W0

FULL NAME: Dillon Young Pennington
BORN: February 26, 1999, Shrewsbury, Shropshire
SQUAD NO: 22
HEIGHT: 6ft 4in
NICKNAME: Dill
EDUCATION: Wrekin College, Shropshire; University of Worcester
TEAMS: Worcestershire, England U19
ROLE: Bowler
DEBUT: First-class: 2018; List A: 2018; T20: 2018

WORCESTERSHIRE

BEST BATTING: 56 Worcestershire vs Essex, Chelmsford, 2021
BEST BOWLING: 5-32 Worcestershire vs Derbyshire, Worcester, 2021

FIRST CRICKET CLUB? Shrewsbury CC, Shropshire
BIGGEST CRICKETING REGRET? Being injured a lot of the time and causing hell for the Worcestershire backroom staff
MOST UNDERRATED PLAYER IN COUNTY CRICKET? Ryan Higgins
WHAT WOULD A FLY ON THE WALL HEAR IN YOUR DRESSING ROOM? Ben Cox
HOBBIES? Golf. But I am terrible – spend a lot of time in the trees
WHO WOULD YOU MOST LIKE TO HAVE A NET WITH? Kevin Pietersen
WHAT DO YOU MOST ENJOY LISTENING TO? Old hits
TWITTER: @DillonPenning14

Batting	Mat	Inns	NO	Runs	HS	Ave	SR	100	50	Ct	St
First-class	25	40	9	309	56	9.96	41.14	0	1	6	-
List A	3	2	1	7	4*	7.00	28.00	0	0	2	-
T20s	36	11	7	35	10*	8.75	87.50	0	0	10	-

Bowling	Mat	Balls	Runs	Wkts	BBI	BBM	Ave	Econ	SR	5w	10
First-class	25	4049	2225	70	5/32	9/76	31.78	3.29	57.8	1	0
List A	3	156	178	8	5/67	5/67	22.25	6.84	19.5	1	0
T20s	36	616	925	36	4/9	4/9	25.69	9.00	17.1	0	0

MICHAEL PEPPER

RHB / WK / R0 / W0

FULL NAME: Michael-Kyle Steven Pepper
BORN: June 25, 1998, Harlow, Essex
SQUAD NO: 19
HEIGHT: 6ft 2in
NICKNAME: Peps
EDUCATION: The Perse School, Cambridge
TEAMS: Essex
ROLE: Wicketkeeper/batter
DEBUT: First-class: 2018; List A: 2021; T20: 2018

BEST BATTING: 92 Essex vs Durham, Chester-le-Street, 2021

FIRST CRICKET CLUB? Wendens Ambo CC, Saffron Walden
NOTES: The 23-year-old wicketkeeper/batter signed his first contract with the club in September 2018 after making his Championship and T20 debuts earlier that summer. As understudy to Adam Wheater, he was sidelined after appendix surgery in the early part of the 2019 season and made just one Championship appearance. He was the Eagles's leading run-scorer in the T20 Blast XI last summer and also played five Championship matches, making a career-best 92 against Durham at Chester-le-Street. The former Cambridgeshire keeper signed a new deal last November. "I feel like 2021 was a big season for me," said Pepper. "I managed to break into the first team and play regular cricket, which was what I set out to do from a personal perspective. Next year I'll be targeting more runs and more victories, which will hopefully lead to the side bringing some more silverware back to Chelmsford"

Batting	Mat	Inns	NO	Runs	HS	Ave	SR	100	50	Ct	St
First-class	9	13	0	265	92	20.38	48.98	0	2	9	-
List A	5	3	0	40	34	13.33	67.79	0	0	0	-
T20s	22	21	6	362	55*	24.13	119.86	0	1	11	-

Bowling	Mat	Balls	Runs	Wkts	BBI	BBM	Ave	Econ	SR	5w	10
First-class	9	-	-	-	-	-	-	-	-	-	-
List A	5	-	-	-	-	-	-	-	-	-	-
T20s	22	-	-	-	-	-	-	-	-	-	-

KEEGAN PETERSEN RHB / LB / WK / R0 / W0

FULL NAME: Keegan Darryl Petersen
BORN: August 08, 1993, Paarl, South Africa
SQUAD NO: TBC
TEAMS: South Africa, Durham, Boland, Cape Cobras, Dolphins, Knights, KwaZulu-Natal Coastal, Northern Cape
ROLE: Batter
DEBUT: Test: 2021; First-class: 2012; List A: 2012; T20: 2013

DURHAM

BEST BATTING: 225* Boland vs North West, Paarl, 2013
BEST BOWLING: 3-49 Knights vs Dolphins, Durban, 2017

TWITTER: @KeeganKP
NOTES: Going by his sparkling performances across a breakout series against India last winter, South Africa's latest batting star will bring some much-desired class to Durham's top order. Elevated to bat at No.3 against India's seam attack and confronted with a series of juicy tracks, he made three high-quality fifties across the final two Tests, claiming the Player of the Match award in the decider at Cape Town with scores of 72 and 82. Petersen, a wristy strokemaker who shares more than a batting position with his predecessor Hashim Amla, is yet to experience English county cricket but has enjoyed stints in club cricket with Stroud CC in Gloucestershire. He is available for the first half of the Championship campaign and will meet up with the squad ahead of their match against Leicestershire in the second week of the full season, before joining the South African tourists for the latter part of the season

Batting	Mat	Inns	NO	Runs	HS	Ave	SR	100	50	Ct	St
Tests	5	9	0	320	82	35.55	54.42	0	3	11	-
First-class	107	178	16	6713	225*	41.43	53.04	17	32	84	4
List A	66	62	8	1780	134*	32.96	71.91	3	11	27	-
T20s	54	47	12	910	66*	26.00	100.22	0	3	25	1

Bowling	Mat	Balls	Runs	Wkts	BBI	BBM	Ave	Econ	SR	5w	10
Tests	5	-	-	-	-	-	-	-	-	-	-
First-class	107	342	327	3	3/49	3/49	109.00	5.73	114.0	0	0
List A	66	166	145	3	1/18	1/18	48.33	5.24	55.3	0	0
T20s	54	42	69	0	-	-	-	9.85	-	0	0

TOBY PETTMAN

RHB / RFM / R0 / W0

NOTTINGHAMSHIRE

FULL NAME: Toby Henry Somerville Pettman
BORN: May 11, 1998, Kingston-upon-Thames, Surrey
SQUAD NO: 15
HEIGHT: 6ft 7in
NICKNAME: Tobe
EDUCATION: Tonbridge School, Kent; Jesus College, Oxford
TEAMS: Nottinghamshire
ROLE: Bowler
DEBUT: First-class: 2017

BEST BATTING: 54* Oxford University vs Cambridge University, Oxford, 2018
BEST BOWLING: 5-19 Oxford University vs Cambridge University, Cambridge, 2019

WHO IS YOUR LOOKALIKE? Brett Staniland (Love Island)
FIRST CRICKET CLUB? Withyham CC, East Sussex
WHAT WOULD YOU CHANGE ABOUT THE STRUCTURE OF THE COUNTY SEASON? Put more emphasis on red-ball cricket
BIGGEST INFLUENCE ON YOUR DEVELOPMENT AS A CRICKETER (EXCLUDING PARENTS)? Graham Charlesworth – my coach at Oxford
WHO IS THE BEST BATTER/KEEPER/ALLROUNDER/BOWLER IN COUNTY CRICKET (EXCLUDING TEAMMATES)? David Bedingham/Ben Foakes/Darren Stevens/Darren Stevens
MOST UNDERRATED PLAYER IN COUNTY CRICKET? Tim Murtagh
WHAT WOULD A FLY ON THE WALL HEAR IN YOUR DRESSING ROOM? Terrible trivia answers
MOST BEAUTIFUL THING YOU HAVE EVER SEEN? A well-struck iron shot
HOBBIES? The piano
IF YOU COULD TURN BACK TIME... I'd change everything about my haircuts and fashion sense when I was a kid
WHO WOULD YOU MOST LIKE TO HAVE A NET WITH? Glenn McGrath
MAKE ONE PREDICTION FOR THE FUTURE OF CRICKET: More T20
WHAT GIVES YOU JOY? My dogs
GUILTY PLEASURE? Chess

Batting	Mat	Inns	NO	Runs	HS	Ave	SR	100	50	Ct	St
First-class	7	8	1	122	54*	17.42	31.36	0	1	3	-

Bowling	Mat	Balls	Runs	Wkts	BBI	BBM	Ave	Econ	SR	5w	10
First-class	7	1494	698	33	5/19	8/80	21.15	2.80	45.2	2	0

JOSH PHILIPPE

RHB / WK / R0 / W0

FULL NAME: Joshua Ryan Philippe
BORN: June 1, 1997, Subiaco, Western Australia, Australia
SQUAD NO: TBC
TEAMS: Australia, Sussex, Perth Scorchers, Royal Challengers Bangalore, Sydney Sixers, Western Australia
ROLE: Wicketkeeper/batter
DEBUT: ODI: 2021; T20I: 2021; First-class: 2018; List A: 2018; T20: 2017

BEST BATTING: 129 Western Australia vs Queensland, Brisbane, 2021

NOTES: The Australia wicketkeeper/batter has been signed by Sussex for this summer's County Championship and T20 Blast campaigns. The club had to move fast after learning that keeper Mohammad Rizwan, signed initially to play from April to July, will be around only until June due to unforeseen international commitments. Philippe made his ODI and T20I debuts for Australia last year and has been one of the Big Bash's top performers over the last three seasons. He was Man of the Match in the 2019/20 BBL final, hitting a 29-ball 52 as Sydney Sixers beat Melbourne Stars at the SCG, and was a key part of the side which successfully defended their title the following season. Philippe was in fine form again over the winter, scoring 429 runs in 15 Big Bash fixtures, including a career-best 99 not out against Melbourne Stars

Batting	Mat	Inns	NO	Runs	HS	Ave	SR	100	50	Ct	St
ODIs	3	3	0	65	39	21.66	73.03	0	0	1	-
T20Is	10	10	0	138	45	13.80	109.52	0	0	0	-
First-class	24	46	3	1422	129	33.06	58.59	2	10	45	-
List A	24	24	0	790	137	32.91	100.63	1	5	25	3
T20s	78	77	10	1951	99*	29.11	137.49	0	14	43	13

Bowling	Mat	Balls	Runs	Wkts	BBI	BBM	Ave	Econ	SR	5w	10
ODIs	3	-	-	-	-	-	-	-	-	-	-
T20Is	10	-	-	-	-	-	-	-	-	-	-
First-class	24	-	-	-	-	-	-	-	-	-	-
List A	24	-	-	-	-	-	-	-	-	-	-
T20s	78	-	-	-	-	-	-	-	-	-	-

JACK PLOM   LHB / RFM / R0 / W0

ESSEX

FULL NAME: Jack Henry Plom
BORN: August 27, 1999, Basildon, Essex
SQUAD NO: 77
HEIGHT: 6ft 3in
NICKNAME: Plommy
EDUCATION: Gable Hall School, Corringham;
South Essex College, Southend-on-Sea
TEAMS: Essex, England U19
ROLE: Bowler
DEBUT: First-class: 2018; List A: 2021; T20: 2020

FIRST CRICKET CLUB? Shenfield CC, Brentwood, Essex
MOST EXCITING DAY AS A CRICKETER? My T20 debut in 2020
CHILDHOOD SPORTING HERO? Andrew Flintoff
BIGGEST INFLUENCE ON YOUR DEVELOPMENT AS A CRICKETER (EXCLUDING PARENTS)?
Club cricket – first growing up with it and then learning my trade between the ages of 14 and 18
WHAT WOULD YOU DO IF YOU WERE IN CHARGE OF COUNTY CRICKET? Introduce a "last-man-stands" rule in T20 cricket so that the not-out batter can bat on his own
GUILTY PLEASURE? Chocolate
TWITTER: @JackPlom16

Batting	Mat	Inns	NO	Runs	HS	Ave	SR	100	50	Ct	St
First-class	1	-	-	-	-	-	-	-	-	0	-
List A	5	4	3	11	9*	11.00	78.57	0	0	3	-
T20s	13	9	4	38	12	7.60	100.00	0	0	5	-

Bowling	Mat	Balls	Runs	Wkts	BBI	BBM	Ave	Econ	SR	5w	10
First-class	1	-	-	-	-	-	-	-	-	-	-
List A	5	220	243	6	3/34	3/34	40.50	6.62	36.6	0	0
T20s	13	244	391	16	3/31	3/31	24.43	9.61	15.2	0	0

HARRY PODMORE

RHB / RFM / R0 / W1

FULL NAME: Harry William Podmore
BORN: July 23, 1994, Hammersmith, London
SQUAD NO: 1
HEIGHT: 6ft 3in
NICKNAME: Nu-Nu
EDUCATION: Twyford CE High School, London
TEAMS: Kent, Derbyshire, Glamorgan, Middlesex
ROLE: Bowler
DEBUT: First-class: 2016; List A: 2014; T20: 2014

KENT

BEST BATTING: 66* Derbyshire vs Sussex, Hove, 2017
BEST BOWLING: 6-36 Kent vs Middlesex, Canterbury, 2018
COUNTY CAP: 2019 (Kent)

WHO IS YOUR LOOKALIKE? Gaz from Geordie Shore (reality TV series)
FIRST CRICKET CLUB? Ealing CC, Middlesex
WHO IS THE BEST BATTER/KEEPER/ALLROUNDER/BOWLER IN COUNTY CRICKET
(EXCLUDING TEAMMATES)? Tom Abell/Ben Foakes/Ryan Higgins/Sam Cook
MOST UNDERRATED PLAYER IN COUNTY CRICKET? Stevie Eskinazi
MOST BEAUTIFUL THING YOU HAVE EVER SEEN? Cape Town
WHO WOULD YOU MOST AND LEAST LIKE TO HAVE A NET WITH? Most – Andrew Flintoff,
my cricketing hero. Least – Brian Lara, because we could be there a long time
WHAT MAKES YOU WORRY? Flat pitches
WHAT GIVES YOU JOY? Green tops
SURPRISING FACT ABOUT YOU? I have my family crest tattooed on my chest
GUILTY PLEASURE? Call of Duty (video game)
TWITTER: @harrypod16

Batting	Mat	Inns	NO	Runs	HS	Ave	SR	100	50	Ct	St
First-class	50	71	19	959	66*	18.44	49.17	0	3	12	-
List A	21	11	2	140	40	15.55	91.50	0	0	6	-
T20s	23	10	3	37	9	5.28	57.81	0	0	9	-

Bowling	Mat	Balls	Runs	Wkts	BBI	BBM	Ave	Econ	SR	5w	10
First-class	50	8204	4175	161	6/36	8/110	18.44	25.93	3.05	50.9	4	0
List A	21	958	1030	20	4/57	4/57	51.50	6.45	47.9	0	0
T20s	23	409	619	23	3/13	3/13	26.91	9.08	17.7	0	0

ED POLLOCK
LHB / OB / R0 / W0

FULL NAME: Edward John Pollock
BORN: July 10, 1995, High Wycombe, Buckinghamshire
SQUAD NO: 7
HEIGHT: 5ft 10in
EDUCATION: Royal Grammar School, Worcester; Shrewsbury School; Durham University
TEAMS: Worcestershire, Warwickshire
ROLE: Batter
DEBUT: First-class: 2015; List A: 2018; T20: 2017

BEST BATTING: 52 Durham MCCU vs Gloucestershire, Bristol, 2017

WHO IS YOUR LOOKALIKE? Caoimhín Kelleher (footballer)
FIRST CRICKET CLUB? Barnt Green CC, Worcestershire. Andy and Grant Flower have both played for the club
FAMILY TIES? My dad and brother have both captained Cambridge University
WHO IS THE BEST BATTER/KEEPER/ALLROUNDER/BOWLER IN COUNTY CRICKET (EXCLUDING TEAMMATES)? James Vince/Ben Foakes/Darren Stevens/Chris Rushworth
MOST UNDERRATED PLAYER IN COUNTY CRICKET? Sam Hain
MOST BEAUTIFUL THING YOU HAVE EVER SEEN? Tom Fell's golf swing
WHO WOULD YOU MOST LIKE TO HAVE A NET WITH? Brian Lara
MAKE ONE PREDICTION FOR THE FUTURE OF CRICKET: Bowlers will get fitter and stronger – but will never bowl quick than any of the fastest bowlers of the 1990s
WHAT MAKES YOU WORRY? A narrow fairway
SURPRISING FACT ABOUT YOU? I am a published poet
TWITTER: @EdPollock10

Batting	Mat	Inns	NO	Runs	HS	Ave	SR	100	50	Ct	St
First-class	5	7	1	184	52	30.66	50.13	0	1	1	-
List A	25	23	1	599	103*	27.22	111.33	1	2	6	-
T20s	46	46	1	969	77	21.53	160.96	0	6	12	-

Bowling	Mat	Balls	Runs	Wkts	BBI	BBM	Ave	Econ	SR	5w	10
First-class	5	-	-	-	-	-	-	-	-	-	-
List A	25	-	-	-	-	-	-	-	-	-	-
T20s	46	-	-	-	-	-	-	-	-	-	-

OLLIE POPE

RHB / WK / R2 / W0

FULL NAME: Oliver John Douglas Pope
BORN: January 2, 1998, Chelsea, London
SQUAD NO: 32
HEIGHT: 5ft 10in
NICKNAME: Pope-dog
EDUCATION: Cranleigh School, Surrey
TEAMS: England, Surrey
ROLE: Batter
DEBUT: Test: 2018; First-class: 2017; List A: 2016;
T20: 2017

BEST BATTING: 274 Surrey vs Glamorgan, The Oval, 2021

COUNTY CAP: 2018

WHO IS YOUR LOOKALIKE? Sam Billings (he wishes!)
FIRST CRICKET CLUB? Grayshott CC, Hampshire
MOST UNDERRATED PLAYER IN COUNTY CRICKET? Tom Abell
MOST BEAUTIFUL THING YOU HAVE EVER SEEN? Clapham Common in south London
HOBBIES? I'm learning the guitar
WHO WOULD YOU MOST AND LEAST LIKE TO HAVE A NET WITH? Most – AB de Villiers (just
to watch him). Least – Chris Woakes (too good)
WHAT MAKES YOU WORRY? Darren Stevens
WHAT GIVES YOU JOY? Going for coffee with Reece Topley and Gus Atkinson
TWITTER: @OPope32

Batting	Mat	Inns	NO	Runs	HS	Ave	SR	100	50	Ct	St
Tests	23	40	4	1032	135*	28.66	50.61	1	6	24	-
First-class	63	97	13	4220	274	50.23	62.25	12	13	67	-
List A	31	28	5	767	93*	33.34	79.48	0	5	9	-
T20s	41	39	9	904	60	30.13	135.32	0	2	17	-

Bowling	Mat	Balls	Runs	Wkts	BBI	BBM	Ave	Econ	SR	5w	10
Tests	23	-	-	-	-	-	-	-	-	-	-
First-class	63	-	-	-	-	-	-	-	-	-	-
List A	31	-	-	-	-	-	-	-	-	-	-
T20s	41	-	-	-	-	-	-	-	-	-	-

JAMIE PORTER RHB / RMF / RO / W5

ESSEX

FULL NAME: James Alexander Porter
BORN: May 25, 1993, Leytonstone, Essex
SQUAD NO: 44
HEIGHT: 6ft 1in
NICKNAME: Ports
EDUCATION: Oaks Park High School, Ilford;
Epping Forest College, Essex
TEAMS: Essex, England Lions
ROLE: Bowler
DEBUT: First-class: 2014; List A: 2015; T20: 2017

BEST BATTING: 34 Essex vs Glamorgan, Cardiff, 2015
BEST BOWLING: 7-41 Essex vs Worcestershire, Chelmsford, 2018
COUNTY CAP: 2015

WHO IS YOUR LOOKALIKE? Shane Snater
FIRST CRICKET CLUB? Chingford CC, London
WHAT WOULD YOU CHANGE ABOUT THE STRUCTURE OF THE COUNTY SEASON?
Fewer teams in Division One
WHO IS THE BEST BATTER/KEEPER/BOWLER IN COUNTY CRICKET (EXCLUDING
TEAMMATES)? Joe Clarke/Ben Foakes/Toby Roland-Jones
MOST UNDERRATED PLAYER IN COUNTY CRICKET? Callum Parkinson
MOST BEAUTIFUL THING YOU HAVE EVER SEEN? Manuel Lanzini's last-minute winner for
West Ham against Spurs
IF YOU COULD TURN BACK TIME... I would assassinate a certain bat
MAKE ONE PREDICTION FOR THE FUTURE OF CRICKET: Simon Harmer will be MVP (Most
Valuable Player) in 2022/23/24/25/26
WHAT DO YOU MOST ENJOY LISTENING TO? The Grade Cricketer Podcast
GUILTY PLEASURE? Pie and mash
TWITTER: @jamieporter93

Batting	Mat	Inns	NO	Runs	HS	Ave	SR	100	50	Ct	St
First-class	102	118	45	460	34	6.30	25.41	0	0	28	-
List A	33	12	8	35	7*	8.75	52.23	0	0	7	-
T20s	25	6	5	5	1*	5.00	71.42	0	0	6	-

Bowling	Mat	Balls	Runs	Wkts	BBI	BBM	Ave	Econ	SR	5w	10
First-class	102	17331	9396	390	7/41	12/95	24.09	3.25	44.4	13	2
List A	33	1494	1257	35	4/29	4/29	35.91	5.04	42.6	0	0
T20s	25	421	636	19	4/20	4/20	33.47	9.06	22.1	0	0

FULL NAME: Matthew James Potts
BORN: October 29, 1998, Sunderland, County Durham
SQUAD NO: 35
HEIGHT: 6ft 2in
NICKNAME: Harry
EDUCATION: St Robert of Newminster Catholic School, Sunderland
TEAMS: Durham, England U19
ROLE: Bowler
DEBUT: First-class: 2017; List A: 2018; T20: 2019

DURHAM

BEST BATTING: 81 Durham vs Northamptonshire, Northampton, 2021
BEST BOWLING: 4-32 Durham vs Worcestershire, Worcester, 2021

FIRST CRICKET CLUB? Philadelphia CC, Tyne & Wear
CHILDHOOD SPORTING HERO? Kevin Pietersen
BIGGEST INFLUENCE ON YOUR DEVELOPMENT AS A CRICKETER (EXCLUDING PARENTS)?
Paul Collingwood
WHAT WOULD YOU DO IF YOU WERE IN CHARGE OF COUNTY CRICKET? Establish a
conference league system, set up a charity fund for disabled cricket
GUILTY PLEASURE? Coffee and biscuits
TWITTER: @mattyjpotts

Batting	Mat	Inns	NO	Runs	HS	Ave	SR	100	50	Ct	St
First-class	18	25	6	382	81	20.10	47.39	0	2	5	-
List A	10	4	0	53	30	13.25	70.66	0	0	3	-
T20s	40	15	9	127	40*	21.16	141.11	0	0	14	-

Bowling	Mat	Balls	Runs	Wkts	BBI	BBM	Ave	Econ	SR	5w	10
First-class	18	2859	1422	42	4/32	8/98	33.85	2.98	68.0	0	0
List A	10	384	374	16	4/62	4/62	23.37	5.84	24.0	0	0
T20s	40	789	1101	49	3/8	3/8	22.46	8.37	16.1	0	0

NICK POTTS

RHB / RFM / R0 / W0

DERBYSHIRE

FULL NAME: Nicholas James Potts
BORN: July 17, 2002, Burton-on-Trent, Staffordshire
SQUAD NO: 26
HEIGHT: 6ft 1in
EDUCATION: De Ferrers Academy, Burton-on-Trent
TEAMS: Derbyshire
ROLE: Bowler

FIRST CRICKET CLUB? Tutbury CC, Staffordshire
WHAT WOULD YOU CHANGE ABOUT THE STRUCTURE OF THE COUNTY SEASON? Avoid T20 matches on consecutive days
BIGGEST INFLUENCE ON YOUR DEVELOPMENT AS A CRICKETER (EXCLUDING PARENTS)? Steve Kirby, my former bowling coach at Derbyshire. He helped me to understand my bowling action and showed me what I need to do to be successful at a high level
WHO IS THE BEST BATTER/KEEPER/ALLROUNDER/BOWLER IN COUNTY CRICKET (EXCLUDING TEAMMATES)? Jos Buttler/Jonny Bairstow/Ben Stokes/Jofra Archer
MOST UNDERRATED PLAYER IN COUNTY CRICKET? Ricardo Vasconcelos
HOBBIES? Poker
IF YOU COULD TURN BACK TIME... The whole world would speak the same language
WHO WOULD YOU MOST AND LEAST LIKE TO HAVE A NET WITH? Most – Joe Root. Least – Shaun Tait
MAKE ONE PREDICTION FOR THE FUTURE OF CRICKET: An English bowler will hit 100mph
WHAT MAKES YOU WORRY? Letting someone down
GUILTY PLEASURE? Solving a Rubik's cube
TWITTER: @nickpotts02

OLLIE PRICE RHB / OB / R0 / W0

FULL NAME: Oliver Joseph Price
BORN: June 12, 2001, Oxford
SQUAD NO: 67
EDUCATION: Magdalen College School, Oxford
TEAMS: Gloucestershire
ROLE: Allrounder
DEBUT: First-class: 2021; List A: 2021

BEST BATTING: 33 Gloucestershire vs Middlesex, Cheltenham, 2021

TWITTER: @ollieprice67

NOTES: The 20-year-old allrounder joined his elder brother Tom in signing a first professional contract at Gloucestershire in January 2020. An off-spinner and and right-handed batter, Price was educated at Magdalen College School in Oxford and joined the Gloucestershire Academy in December 2016. He and Tom played for their local side Great & Little Tew, a club which also produced Gloucestershire siblings Jack and Matt Taylor. In 2019 he joined Oxford CC where he opened the batting in the Home Counties Premier League and helped the club gain promotion. Price has captained in all the Oxfordshire age-groups and made his Minor Counties debut aged 17. He featured strongly in Gloucestershire's Second XI 2019 and was given his first-class and List-A debuts last summer, signing a new two-year deal in December

Batting	Mat	Inns	NO	Runs	HS	Ave	SR	100	50	Ct	St
First-class	4	7	0	110	33	15.71	42.63	0	0	4	-
List A	2	2	0	43	24	21.50	52.43	0	0	0	-

Bowling	Mat	Balls	Runs	Wkts	BBI	BBM	Ave	Econ	SR	5w	10
First-class	4	198	100	0	-	-	-	3.03	-	0	0
List A	2	24	30	1	1/9	1/9	30.00	7.50	24.0	0	0

TOM PRICE

RHB / RMF / R0 / W0

GLOUCESTERSHIRE

FULL NAME: Thomas James Price
BORN: January 2, 2000, Oxford
SQUAD NO: 53
EDUCATION: Magdalen College School, Oxford
TEAMS: Gloucestershire
ROLE: Allrounder
DEBUT: First-class: 2020; List A: 2019

BEST BATTING: 71 Gloucestershire vs Glamorgan, Cardiff, 2021
BEST BOWLING: 4-72 Gloucestershire vs Northamptonshire, Bristol, 2021

TWITTER: @_tomprice_
NOTES: An emerging seam-bowling allrounder, Price was handed his first professional contract by Gloucestershire in January 2020, putting pen to paper on a two-year deal. He was given his first-class debut later that year in the Bob Willis Trophy match against Worcestershire at Bristol, claiming the wicket of Daryl Mitchell as the first of his red-ball career. He played in six Championship matches for Gloucestershire last summer, taking 15 wickets at an average of just 24.53 as well as scoring his maiden half-century. The 22-year-old signed a new deal in December that ties him to the club until the end of 2023. "Tom is a player of extremely high potential and he has a calm and ambitious head on his shoulders," said Steve Snell, Gloucestershire's performance director. "He is the type of character that will do whatever role is necessary to help the team get the job done. This attribute is one among many strong characteristics that the players, coaches and our supporters really admire in Tom." His brother is Ollie Price, who is also on the books at Bristol

Batting	Mat	Inns	NO	Runs	HS	Ave	SR	100	50	Ct	St
First-class	7	11	4	177	71	25.28	36.87	0	1	1	-
List A	2	2	0	1	1	0.50	50.00	0	0	0	-

Bowling	Mat	Balls	Runs	Wkts	BBI	BBM	Ave	Econ	SR	5w	10
First-class	7	876	448	16	4/72	7/111	28.00	3.06	54.7	0	0
List A	2	78	91	0	-	-	-	7.00	-	0	0

FULL NAME: Luke Anthony Procter
BORN: June 24, 1988, Oldham, Lancashire
SQUAD NO: 2
HEIGHT: 5ft 11in
NICKNAME: Dickson
EDUCATION: Counthill School, Oldham
TEAMS: Northamptonshire, Lancashire
ROLE: Allrounder
DEBUT: First-class: 2010; List A: 2009; T20: 2011

NORTHAMPTONSHIRE

BEST BATTING: 137 Lancashire vs Hampshire, Old Trafford, 2016
BEST BOWLING: 7-71 Lancashire vs Surrey, Liverpool, 2012
COUNTY CAP: 2020 (Northamptonshire)

FIRST CRICKET CLUB? Oldham CC, Lancashire
WHAT WOULD YOU CHANGE ABOUT THE STRUCTURE OF THE COUNTY SEASON?
Reduce the amount of games
WHO IS THE BEST BATTER/KEEPER/BOWLER IN COUNTY CRICKET (EXCLUDING
TEAMMATES)? Josh Bohannon/Ben Foakes/Sam Cook
SURPRISING FACT ABOUT YOU? I'm a level-two umpire
TWITTER: @vvsprocter

Batting	Mat	Inns	NO	Runs	HS	Ave	SR	100	50	Ct	St
First-class	111	176	19	4905	137	31.24	43.85	4	27	26	-
List A	48	38	13	820	97	32.80	86.49	0	5	8	-
T20s	37	24	7	240	25*	14.11	102.12	0	0	10	-

Bowling	Mat	Balls	Runs	Wkts	BBI	BBM	Ave	Econ	SR	5w	10
First-class	111	7537	4301	121	7/71	8/79	35.54	3.42	62.2	4	0
List A	48	1138	1090	26	3/29	3/29	41.92	5.74	43.7	0	0
T20s	37	296	438	14	3/22	3/22	31.28	8.87	21.1	0	0

CHETESHWAR PUJARA

RHB / LB / R0 / W0

SUSSEX

FULL NAME: Cheteshwar Arvind Pujara
BORN: January 25, 1988, Rajkot, India
SQUAD NO: TBC
TEAMS: India, Sussex, Derbyshire, India Green, Kings XI Punjab, Kolkata Knight Riders, Nottinghamshire, Royal Challengers Bangalore, Saurashtra, Yorkshire
ROLE: Batter
DEBUT: Test: 2010; ODI: 2013; First-class: 2005; List A: 2006; T20: 2007

BEST BATTING: 352 Saurashtra vs Karnataka, Rajkot, 2013
BEST BOWLING: 2-4 Saurashtra vs Rajasthan, Jaipur, 2007
COUNTY CAP: 2017 (Nottinghamshire)

TWITTER: @cheteshwar1
NOTES: Sussex will be Pujara's fourth English county after the club signed the dogged Indian batter to play in the Championship and the One-Day Cup until the end of August. Known for his patient batting style – in contrast to many of his national teammates – Pujara has been a fixture in the top-order of the Indian Test team for over a decade, although he was left out of the side during the recent home series against Sri Lanka. He has found it tough going in county cricket during spells with Derbyshire, Nottinghamshire and Yorkshire, with just three hundreds and three fifties in 21 Championship matches

Batting	Mat	Inns	NO	Runs	HS	Ave	SR	100	50	Ct	St
Tests	95	162	9	6713	206*	43.87	44.25	18	32	64	-
ODIs	5	5	0	51	27	10.20	39.23	0	0	0	-
First-class	226	374	39	16948	352	50.59		50	70	147	-
List A	103	101	19	4445	158*	54.20		11	29	39	-
T20s	64	56	10	1356	100*	29.47	109.35	1	7	32	-

Bowling	Mat	Balls	Runs	Wkts	BBI	BBM	Ave	Econ	SR	5w	10
Tests	95	6	2	0	-	-	-	2.00	-	0	0
ODIs	5	-	-	-	-	-	-	-	-	-	-
First-class	226	251	157	6	2/4	2/4	26.16	3.75	41.8	0	0
List A	103	6	8	0	-	-	-	8.00	-	0	0
T20s	64	-	-	-	-	-	-	-	-	-	-

FULL NAME: Hamidullah Qadri
BORN: December 5, 2000, Kandahar, Afghanistan
SQUAD NO: 75
HEIGHT: 5ft 7in
NICKNAME: Hammy
EDUCATION: Chellaston Academy, Derby; Derby Moor Academy
TEAMS: Kent, Derbyshire, England U19
ROLE: Bowler
DEBUT: First-class: 2017; List A: 2017; T20: 2017

BEST BATTING: 30* Kent vs Sussex, Canterbury, 2021
BEST BOWLING: 5-60 Derbyshire vs Glamorgan, Cardiff, 2017

WHO IS YOUR LOOKALIKE? Colin Cowdrey
FIRST CRICKET CLUB? Alvaston & Boulton CC, Derbyshire
WHAT WOULD YOU CHANGE ABOUT THE STRUCTURE OF THE COUNTY SEASON? Play more games in June and July
BIGGEST INFLUENCE ON YOUR DEVELOPMENT AS A CRICKETER (EXCLUDING PARENTS)? Steve Stubbings at Derbyshire – he was my first-ever coach
WHO IS THE BEST BATTER/KEEPER/ALLROUNDER/BOWLER IN COUNTY CRICKET (EXCLUDING TEAMMATES)? Haseeb Hameed/Ben Foakes/Moeen Ali/Simon Harmer
MOST UNDERRATED PLAYER IN COUNTY CRICKET? Leus du Plooy
HOBBIES? Reading, drawing, football
WHO WOULD YOU MOST LIKE TO HAVE A NET WITH? R Ashwin
WHAT DO YOU MOST ENJOY LISTENING TO? Silence
WHAT GIVES YOU JOY? Bowling
SURPRISING FACT ABOUT YOU? I learnt the art of off-spin by watching YouTube clips
TWITTER: @Hamid_Qadri2000

Batting	Mat	Inns	NO	Runs	HS	Ave	SR	100	50	Ct	St
First-class	15	27	11	126	30*	7.87	33.24	0	0	6	-
List A	8	5	3	107	42*	53.50	83.59	0	0	2	-
T20s	1	-	-	-	-	-	-	-	-	0	-

Bowling	Mat	Balls	Runs	Wkts	BBI	BBM	Ave	Econ	SR	5w	10
First-class	15	1733	974	25	5/60	6/76	38.96	3.37	69.3	1	0
List A	8	205	213	5	3/47	3/47	42.60	6.23	41.0	0	0
T20s	1	6	12	0	-	-	-	12.00	-	0	0

MATT QUINN

RHB / RMF / R0 / W0

KENT

FULL NAME: Matthew Richard Quinn
BORN: February 28, 1993, Auckland, New Zealand
SQUAD NO: 64
HEIGHT: 6ft 4in
NICKNAME: Quinny
EDUCATION: Sacred Heart College, Auckland; Auckland University of Technology
TEAMS: Kent, Auckland, Essex, New Zealand U19
ROLE: Bowler
DEBUT: First-class: 2013; List A: 2013; T20: 2012

BEST BATTING: 50 Auckland vs Canterbury, Auckland, 2013
BEST BOWLING: 7-76 Essex vs Gloucestershire, Cheltenham, 2016

FIRST CRICKET CLUB? Cornwall CC, Auckland – the largest cricket club in New Zealand
FAMILY TIES? My granddad played social cricket in Yorkshire
WHAT WOULD YOU CHANGE ABOUT THE STRUCTURE OF THE COUNTY SEASON? More rest days for fast bowlers
BIGGEST INFLUENCE ON YOUR DEVELOPMENT AS A CRICKETER (EXCLUDING PARENTS)? Rex Smith, PJ Thomas, Tim Wilson and Paresh Vallabh – all from my local club Cornwall CC in Auckland. They taught me a lot to help me move from schoolboy to men's cricket
HOBBIES? Golf
WHO WOULD YOU MOST LIKE TO HAVE A NET WITH? Shane Bond
WHAT DO YOU MOST ENJOY LISTENING TO? Post Malone (American rapper)
SURPRISING FACT ABOUT YOU? I was once attacked by a goose
GUILTY PLEASURE? An early afternoon nap
TWITTER: @quinny_cricket

Batting	Mat	Inns	NO	Runs	HS	Ave	SR	100	50	Ct	St
First-class	42	51	14	392	50	10.59	48.09	0	1	7	-
List A	39	22	13	132	36	14.66	70.96	0	0	7	-
T20s	67	12	10	28	8*	14.00	100.00	0	0	14	-

Bowling	Mat	Balls	Runs	Wkts	BBI	BBM	Ave	Econ	SR	5w	10
First-class	42	7668	4128	141	7/76	11/163	29.27	3.23	54.3	1	1
List A	39	1924	1928	52	4/71	4/71	37.07	6.01	37.0	0	0
T20s	67	1309	1923	72	4/20	4/20	26.70	8.81	18.1	0	0

BEN RAINE

LHB / RMF / R0 / W3 / MVP15

FULL NAME: Benjamin Alexander Raine
BORN: September 14, 1991, Sunderland
SQUAD NO: 44
HEIGHT: 6ft
NICKNAME: Ranger
EDUCATION: St Aidan's Catholic Academy, Sunderland
TEAMS: Durham, Leicestershire, Otago
ROLE: Bowler
DEBUT: First-class: 2011; List A: 2011; T20: 2014

DURHAM

BEST BATTING: 82 Durham vs Northamptonshire, Chester-le-Street, 2019
BEST BOWLING: 6-27 Durham vs Sussex, Hove, 2019
COUNTY CAP: 2018 (Leicestershire)

FIRST CRICKET CLUB? Murton CC, County Durham
MOST EXCITING DAY AS A CRICKETER? Winning in three days at Lord's in 2019
BIGGEST INFLUENCE ON YOUR DEVELOPMENT AS A CRICKETER (EXCLUDING PARENTS)?
Lloyd Tennant at Leicestershire – he encouraged me to take bowling seriously, which shaped my career
BIGGEST CRICKETING REGRET? Taking far too long to realise that it doesn't really matter if I have a bad game
WHAT WOULD YOU DO IF YOU WERE IN CHARGE OF COUNTY CRICKET? Go back to a 40-over competition and play it in March and April
FAVOURITE SMELL? Fear
GUILTY PLEASURE? Call of Duty (video game)
TWITTER: @BenRaine88

Batting	Mat	Inns	NO	Runs	HS	Ave	SR	100	50	Ct	St
First-class	96	151	18	2897	82	21.78	48.82	0	12	19	-
List A	29	21	2	402	83	21.15	104.41	0	1	9	-
T20s	84	65	12	1013	113	19.11	131.21	1	3	19	-

Bowling	Mat	Balls	Runs	Wkts	BBI	BBM	Ave	Econ	SR	5w	10
First-class	96	16931	8247	319	6/27	9/96	25.85	2.92	53.0	10	0
List A	29	1286	1219	30	3/31	3/31	40.63	5.68	42.8	0	0
T20s	84	1308	1949	71	3/7	3/7	27.45	8.94	18.4	0	0

ADIL RASHID

RHB / LB

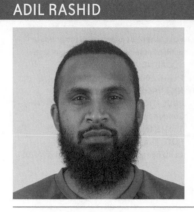

FULL NAME: Adil Usman Rashid
BORN: February 17, 1988, Bradford
SQUAD NO: 3
HEIGHT: 5ft 8in
NICKNAME: Rash
EDUCATION: Heaton School, Bradford;
Bellevue Sixth Form College, Bradford
TEAMS: England, Yorkshire, Adelaide
Strikers, Dhaka Dynamites, Punjab Kings,
South Australia
ROLE: Allrounder
DEBUT: Test: 2015; ODI: 2009; T20I: 2009;
First-class: 2006; List A: 2006; T20: 2008

BEST BATTING: 36* Yorkshire vs Uva Next, Johannesburg, 2012 (T20)
BEST BOWLING: 4-2 England vs West Indies, Dubai, 2021 (T20)
COUNTY CAP: 2008; BENEFIT: 2018

CHILDHOOD SPORTING HERO? Shane Warne
SURPRISING FACT ABOUT YOU? I have a big FIFA (video game) rivalry with Moeen Ali
TWITTER: @AdilRashid03
NOTES: Last September Rashid signed a new two-year deal to play white-ball cricket for
Yorkshire

Batting	Mat	Inns	NO	Runs	HS	Ave	SR	100	50	Ct	St
Tests	19	33	5	540	61	19.28	42.51	0	2	4	-
ODIs	112	50	14	663	69	18.41	101.37	0	1	35	-
T20Is	73	26	14	85	22	7.08	86.73	0	0	17	-
First-class	175	251	41	6822	180	32.48		10	37	79	-
List A	230	133	39	1784	71	18.97	91.53	0	2	74	-
T20s	213	99	39	731	36*	12.18	104.72	0	0	57	-

Bowling	Mat	Balls	Runs	Wkts	BBI	BBM	Ave	Econ	SR	5w	10
Tests	19	3816	2390	60	5/49	7/178	39.83	3.75	63.6	2	0
ODIs	112	5573	5251	159	5/27	5/27	33.02	5.65	35.0	2	0
T20Is	73	1520	1840	81	4/2	4/2	22.71	7.26	18.7	0	0
First-class	175	29901	17949	512	7/107	11/114	35.05	3.60	58.4	20	1
List A	230	10690	9744	305	5/27	5/27	31.94	5.46	35.0	3	0
T20s	213	4406	5420	248	4/2	4/2	21.85	7.38	17.7	0	0

HARIS RAUF

RHB / RFM / R0 / W0

FULL NAME: Haris Rauf
BORN: November 7, 1993, Rawalpindi, Punjab, Pakistan
SQUAD NO: TBC
TEAMS: Pakistan, Yorkshire, Baluchistan, Lahore Qalandars, Melbourne Stars, Northern
ROLE: Bowler
DEBUT: ODI: 2020; T20I: 2020; First-class: 2019; List A: 2019; T20: 2018

BEST BATTING: 9* Northern vs Baluchistan, Rawalpindi, 2019
BEST BOWLING: 6-47 Northern vs Central Punjab, Karachi, 2021

TWITTER: @HarisRauf14

One of the world's fastest bowlers, Rauf is the first beneficiary of Yorkshire's partnership with Lahore Qalandars. Before the summer of 2017 he was an unknown tape-ball tearaway for various village teams across Islamabad. Rauf's searing pace then impressed Qalandars during an open trial and he was brought into the fold. A little over two years later he was playing international cricket and is now considered one of the foremost T20 specialists. Yorkshire's interim managing director of cricket, Darren Gough, hopes that Rauf's impact will be felt beyond the boundary rope: "I have spoken in the past about my passion for developing accessible pathways to cricket – for many people from a background like mine, cricket isn't seen as an option, with the associated costs and access to facilities creating real barriers to entry. This partnership is an opportunity to take the blueprint the Qalandars has developed and work with them to define how that can be used to provide access for potential players from across Yorkshire." It's expected that Rauf will feature for Yorkshire across their T20 campaign

Batting	Mat	Inns	NO	Runs	HS	Ave	SR	100	50	Ct	St
ODIs	8	4	3	2	1*	2.00	16.66	0	0	3	-
T20Is	34	4	2	6	6	3.00	85.71	0	0	11	-
First-class	4	3	2	15	9*	15.00	78.94	0	0	3	-
List A	12	6	3	11	8	3.66	55.00	0	0	5	-
T20s	114	23	8	112	19	7.46	141.77	0	0	36	-

Bowling	Mat	Balls	Runs	Wkts	BBI	BBM	Ave	Econ	SR	5w	10
ODIs	8	408	406	14	4/65	4/65	29.00	5.97	29.1	0	0
T20Is	34	717	1009	41	4/22	4/22	24.60	8.44	17.4	0	0
First-class	4	642	384	16	6/47	9/109	24.00	3.58	40.1	1	0
List A	12	636	617	21	4/65	4/65	29.38	5.82	30.2	0	0
T20s	114	2486	3483	153	5/27	5/27	22.76	8.40	16.2	1	0

DELRAY RAWLINS

LHB / SLA / RO / WO

SUSSEX

FULL NAME: Delray Millard Wendell Rawlins
BORN: September 14, 1997, Bermuda
SQUAD NO: 9
HEIGHT: 6ft 2in
NICKNAME: Del
EDUCATION: St Bede's School, East Sussex
TEAMS: Bermuda, Sussex, England U19
ROLE: Allrounder
DEBUT: T20I: 2019; First-class: 2017; List A: 2017;
T20: 2018

BEST BATTING: 100 Sussex vs Lancashire, Old Trafford, 2019
BEST BOWLING: 3-19 Sussex vs Durham, Hove, 2019

FIRST CRICKET CLUB? Warwick Workmen's Club, Bermuda – playing there helped me grow a love for the sport
BIGGEST INFLUENCE ON YOUR DEVELOPMENT AS A CRICKETER (EXCLUDING PARENTS)?
David Moore (former Australian first-class cricketer and Bermuda coach) – he was one of the first coaches to give me a chance as a young cricketer
WHO IS THE BEST BATTER/KEEPER/ALLROUNDER/BOWLER IN COUNTY CRICKET (EXCLUDING TEAMMATES)? Tom Haines/Ben Foakes/Ed Barnard/Darren Stevens
MOST BEAUTIFUL THING YOU HAVE EVER SEEN? Sunset in Bermuda
HOBBIES? The PlayStation
WHO WOULD YOU MOST AND LEAST LIKE TO HAVE A NET WITH? Most – Brian Lara. Least – Jofra Archer
GUILTY PLEASURE? Eating pineapple slices out of the tin
TWITTER: @Delraw90

Batting	Mat	Inns	NO	Runs	HS	Ave	SR	100	50	Ct	St
T20Is	17	17	1	430	63	26.87	138.26	0	2	15	-
First-class	29	51	1	1127	100	22.54	58.30	1	7	8	-
List A	11	11	0	285	53	25.90	109.61	0	2	7	-
T20s	61	55	7	1158	69	24.12	142.78	0	5	34	-

Bowling	Mat	Balls	Runs	Wkts	BBI	BBM	Ave	Econ	SR	5w	10
T20Is	17	360	421	13	2/18	2/18	32.38	7.01	27.6	0	0
First-class	29	2339	1391	18	3/19	3/52	77.27	3.56	129.9	0	0
List A	11	300	269	3	1/27	1/27	89.66	5.38	100.0	0	0
T20s	61	540	644	23	3/21	3/21	28.00	7.15	23.4	0	0

LUIS REECE

LHB / LMF / RO / W1

FULL NAME: Luis Michael Reece
BORN: August 4, 1990, Taunton
SQUAD NO: 10
HEIGHT: 6ft 2in
NICKNAME: Rexy
EDUCATION: St Michael's School;
Myerscough College; Leeds Metropolitan
University
TEAMS: Derbyshire, Chittagong Vikings,
Dhaka Platoon, Lancashire
ROLE: Allrounder
DEBUT: First-class: 2012; List A: 2011; T20: 2016

DERBYSHIRE

BEST BATTING: 184 Derbyshire vs Sussex, Derby, 2019
BEST BOWLING: 7-20 Derbyshire vs Gloucestershire, Derby, 2018
COUNTY CAP: 2019 (Derbyshire)

FIRST CRICKET CLUB? Vernon Carus CC, Lancashire
WHAT WOULD YOU CHANGE ABOUT THE STRUCTURE OF THE COUNTY SEASON?
White-ball cricket to kick off the season. And possibly use an NFL draft system for the
Championship, allowing the bottom clubs to get first pick on players
WHO IS THE BEST BATTER/KEEPER/ALLROUNDER/BOWLER IN COUNTY CRICKET
(EXCLUDING TEAMMATES)? Alastair Cook/Ben Foakes/Darren Stevens/Simon Harmer
MOST UNDERRATED PLAYER IN COUNTY CRICKET? Ben Slater
WHAT WOULD A FLY ON THE WALL HEAR IN YOUR DRESSING ROOM? George Scrimshaw
panicking because he's padded up too late
MOST BEAUTIFUL THING YOU HAVE EVER SEEN? Christmas dinner
IF YOU COULD TURN BACK TIME... I'd be a spinner (easier on the body)
WHO WOULD YOU MOST LIKE TO HAVE A NET WITH? Brian Lara
SURPRISING FACT ABOUT YOU? As a kid I played chess at national level
GUILTY PLEASURE? An afternoon nap
TWITTER: @lreece17

Batting	Mat	Inns	NO	Runs	HS	Ave	SR	100	50	Ct	St
First-class	76	137	8	4036	184	31.28	48.96	7	23	36	-
List A	40	36	5	908	128	29.29	87.98	1	5	11	-
T20s	65	62	5	1441	97*	25.28	133.17	0	12	25	-

Bowling	Mat	Balls	Runs	Wkts	BBI	BBM	Ave	Econ	SR	5w	10
First-class	76	6250	3167	113	7/20	7/38	28.02	3.04	55.3	4	0
List A	40	938	964	19	4/35	4/35	50.73	6.16	49.3	0	0
T20s	65	605	845	29	3/33	3/33	29.13	8.38	20.8	0	0

NICO REIFER

RHB / RM / R0 / W0

FULL NAME: Nico Reifer
BORN: November 11, 2000, Bridgetown, Barbados
SQUAD NO: 27
HEIGHT: 6ft 4in
NICKNAME: Reif
EDUCATION: Queen's College, Bridgetown; Whitgift School, Croydon
TEAMS: Surrey
ROLE: Allrounder
DEBUT: List A: 2021

FIRST CRICKET CLUB? Wanderers CC, Christ Church, Barbados
MOST EXCITING DAY AS A CRICKETER? Singing the Surrey song for the first time after a win
CHILDHOOD SPORTING HERO? Ricky Ponting
BIGGEST INFLUENCE ON YOUR DEVELOPMENT AS A CRICKETER (EXCLUDING PARENTS)?
Dexter Toppin, former South African cricketer and current Barbados coach – he was the first coach I ever had and still helps me out today
HOBBIES? FIFA (video game)
WHAT DO YOU MOST ENJOY LISTENING TO? Dancehall
FAVOURITE SMELL? Coconut
GUILTY PLEASURE? Ice cream
TWITTER: @reifzzzz

Batting	Mat	Inns	NO	Runs	HS	Ave	SR	100	50	Ct	St
List A	10	5	0	63	28	12.60	91.30	0	0	5	-
Bowling	Mat	Balls	Runs	Wkts	BBI	BBM	Ave	Econ	SR	5w	10
List A	10	-	-	-	-	-	-	-	-	-	-

MATT RENSHAW

LHB / OB / R0 / W0

FULL NAME: Matthew Thomas Renshaw
BORN: March 28, 1996, Middlesbrough, Yorkshire
SQUAD NO: 77
TEAMS: Australia, Somerset, Adelaide Strikers, Brisbane Heat, Kent, Queensland
ROLE: Batter
DEBUT: Test: 2016; First-class: 2015; List A: 2016; T20: 2018

BEST BATTING: 184 Australia vs Pakistan, Sydney, 2017
BEST BOWLING: 2-26 Australia A vs England Lions, Brisbane, 2021

TWITTER: @MattRenshaw449
NOTES: If Matt Renshaw can even partially replicate the impact of his first stint with Somerset in 2018 then the Taunton faithful are in for a treat. His hundred before lunch against Yorkshire – one of three tons in six games that summer – has gone down in legend: he was off the mark with a six, brought up his fifty with a six, and completed the set for his hundred. A willowy left-hander who marries top-order solidity with a wide shot-range, he's yet to fully establish himself in Australia's Test side. Renshaw holds a British passport and was born in Yorkshire, but his family emigrated first to New Zealand and then Australia. He said: "Although I was only there [at Somerset] for a short time, the members and supporters really got behind me and made me feel extremely welcome. I've never forgotten that, and hopefully I can help give them something to cheer about in 2022." He will be available until at least the end of August as an overseas player across both the four-day and 50-over competitions

Batting	Mat	Inns	NO	Runs	HS	Ave	SR	100	50	Ct	St
Tests	11	20	1	636	184	33.47	42.48	1	3	8	-
First-class	78	140	10	4714	184	36.26	48.01	13	13	73	-
List A	42	41	5	1377	156*	38.25	90.71	2	11	20	-
T20s	49	48	6	1062	90*	25.28	126.57	0	6	18	-

Bowling	Mat	Balls	Runs	Wkts	BBI	BBM	Ave	Econ	SR	5w	10
Tests	11	24	13	0	-	-	-	3.25	-	0	0
First-class	78	594	287	5	2/26	2/26	57.40	2.89	118.8	0	0
List A	42	252	223	6	2/17	2/17	37.16	5.30	42.0	0	0
T20s	49	198	270	7	1/2	1/2	38.57	8.18	28.2	0	0

GEORGE RHODES

RHB / OB / R0 / W0

LEICESTERSHIRE

FULL NAME: George Harry Rhodes
BORN: October 26, 1993, Birmingham
SQUAD NO: 34
HEIGHT: 6ft
NICKNAME: Harp splitter
EDUCATION: The Chase School, Malvern;
University of Worcester
TEAMS: Leicestershire, Worcestershire
ROLE: Allrounder
DEBUT: First-class: 2016; List A: 2016; T20: 2016

BEST BATTING: 90 Leicestershire vs Worcestershire, Worcester, 2021
BEST BOWLING: 2-83 Worcestershire vs Kent, Canterbury, 2016

WHO IS YOUR LOOKALIKE? Patrick Dangerfield (Aussie rules player) and Beauden Barrett (rugby player)
FIRST CRICKET CLUB? Rushwick CC, Worcestershire
FAMILY TIES? My father Steve played for England and Worcestershire, and my grandfather William played first-class cricket for Nottinghamshire
BIGGEST INFLUENCE ON YOUR DEVELOPMENT AS A CRICKETER (EXCLUDING PARENTS)?
Damian D'Oliveira, the former Academy director at Worcestershire
IF YOU COULD TURN BACK TIME... I would practise more with my left hand
WHAT DO YOU MOST ENJOY LISTENING TO? The Joe Rogan Experience podcast
WHAT MAKES YOU WORRY? A 4ft putt
TWITTER: @Ghrhodes

Batting	Mat	Inns	NO	Runs	HS	Ave	SR	100	50	Ct	St
First-class	31	56	8	1164	90	24.25	39.61	0	7	16	-
List A	18	14	2	306	106	25.50	86.68	1	1	14	-
T20s	20	15	6	103	30*	11.44	100.00	0	0	8	-

Bowling	Mat	Balls	Runs	Wkts	BBI	BBM	Ave	Econ	SR	5w	10
First-class	31	1061	728	6	2/83	2/83	121.33	4.11	176.8	0	0
List A	18	540	499	12	3/44	3/44	41.58	5.54	45.0	0	0
T20s	20	114	164	10	4/13	4/13	16.40	8.63	11.4	0	0

WILL RHODES   LHB / RMF / R0 / W0 / MVP4

FULL NAME: William Michael Harry Rhodes
BORN: March 2, 1995, Nottingham
SQUAD NO: 35
HEIGHT: 6ft 1in
NICKNAME: Codhead
EDUCATION: Cottingham High School, Hull
TEAMS: Warwickshire, England U19, Essex, Yorkshire
ROLE: Allrounder
DEBUT: First-class: 2015; List A: 2013; T20: 2013

WARWICKSHIRE

BEST BATTING: 207 Warwickshire vs Worcestershire, Worcester, 2020
BEST BOWLING: 5-17 Warwickshire vs Essex, Chelmsford, 2019
COUNTY CAP: 2020 (Warwickshire)

FIRST CRICKET CLUB? Cottingham CC, East Riding of Yorkshire
MOST EXCITING DAY AS A CRICKETER? Winning the 2015 County Championship with Yorkshire and then again with Warwickshire last summer
CHILDHOOD SPORTING HERO? Nick Barmby
BIGGEST INFLUENCE ON YOUR DEVELOPMENT AS A CRICKETER (EXCLUDING PARENTS)?
Richard Damms – my coach when I was in the Yorkshire Academy
WHAT WOULD YOU DO IF YOU WERE IN CHARGE OF COUNTY CRICKET? Forbid play on weekends and bank holidays
FAVOURITE SMELL? An ice-cold beer after a day in the field
GUILTY PLEASURE? Chocolate Hobnobs
TWITTER: @willrhodes_152

Batting	Mat	Inns	NO	Runs	HS	Ave	SR	100	50	Ct	St
First-class	71	116	6	3897	207	35.42	50.00	7	19	46	-
List A	39	35	2	773	69	23.42	77.37	0	3	16	-
T20s	56	51	6	659	79	14.64	122.03	0	1	15	-

Bowling	Mat	Balls	Runs	Wkts	BBI	BBM	Ave	Econ	SR	5w	10
First-class	71	4522	2276	79	5/17	9/55	28.81	3.01	57.2	2	0
List A	39	785	757	21	3/40	3/40	36.04	5.78	37.3	0	0
T20s	56	493	741	36	4/34	4/34	20.58	9.01	13.6	0	0

MOHAMMAD RIZWAN   RHB / WK / R0 / W0

SUSSEX

FULL NAME: Mohammad Rizwan
BORN: June 1, 1992, Peshawar, Khyber
Pakhtunkhwa, Pakistan
SQUAD NO: TBC
TEAMS: Pakistan, Sussex, Karachi Kings,
Khyber Pakhtunkhwa, Lahore Qalandars,
Multan Sultans, Peshawar, Sui Northern Gas
Pipelines Limited, Sylhet Sixers
ROLE: Wicketkeeper/batter
DEBUT: Test: 2016; ODI: 2015; T20I: 2015;
First-class: 2008; List A: 2009; T20: 2009

BEST BATTING: 224 SNGP Limited vs National Bank of Pakistan, Karachi, 2014
BEST BOWLING: 2-10 SNGP Limited vs Federally Administered Tribal Areas, Abbottabad, 2018

TWITTER: @iMRizwanPak
NOTES: Sussex have secured one of the most complete keeper-batters in the game. A
brilliant gloveman, Rizwan has latterly added big runs to his keeping excellence. With Babar
Azam he forms the most formidable T20 opening partnership in international cricket, while
at Test level he has developed into a game-shifting counterpuncher in Pakistan's middle
order. A relatively late developer, he told Wisden Cricket Monthly last year: "If you've had
things very easy throughout your career and your career path has been straightforward,
then perhaps you don't love the sport as much as you do if you've had to really go through
the tough times." He will join up with Sussex in early April and then be available for red-ball
and T20 cricket until the end of May. With Ben Brown's departure, he is expected to take on
keeping duties

Batting	Mat	Inns	NO	Runs	HS	Ave	SR	100	50	Ct	St
Tests	19	28	5	972	115*	42.26	50.12	1	7	52	2
ODIs	41	37	7	864	115	28.80	87.62	2	4	37	1
T20Is	55	44	12	1639	104*	51.21	128.95	1	13	31	7
First-class	99	149	25	5395	224	43.50	52.79	11	28	279	17
List A	140	129	33	4497	141*	46.84	89.24	11	22	130	17
T20s	179	150	40	4611	104*	41.91	125.09	1	36	117	39

Bowling	Mat	Balls	Runs	Wkts	BBI	BBM	Ave	Econ	SR	5w	10
Tests	19	-	-	-	-	-	-	-	-	-	-
ODIs	41	-	-	-	-	-	-	-	-	-	-
T20Is	55	-	-	-	-	-	-	-	-	-	-
First-class	99	225	131	4	2/10	2/10	32.75	3.49	56.2	0	0
List A	140	-	-	-	-	-	-	-	-	-	-
T20s	179	12	22	1	1/22	1/22	22.00	11.00	12.0	0	0

FULL NAME: Kemar Andre Jamal Roach
BORN: June 30, 1988, St Lucy, Barbados
SQUAD NO: 66
TEAMS: West Indies, Surrey, Antigua Hawksbills, Barbados, Brisbane Heat, Deccan Chargers, Jamaica Tallawahs, St Lucia Zouks, Worcestershire
ROLE: Bowler
DEBUT: Test: 2009; ODI: 2008; T20I: 2008; First-class: 2008; List A: 2007; T20: 2008

SURREY

BEST BATTING: 53 Barbados vs Leeward Islands, Basseterre, 2016
BEST BOWLING: 8-40 Surrey vs Hampshire, The Oval, 2021

NOTES: Surrey have re-signed the West Indies fast bowler for the first five Championship games of the season. Roach had a real impact for the club last summer, taking 22 wickets in five matches, including career-best figures of 8-40. The 33-year-old is one of only nine West Indies bowlers to have taken more than 200 Test wickets and continues to be a mainstay of their bowling attack

Batting	Mat	Inns	NO	Runs	HS	Ave	SR	100	50	Ct	St
Tests	68	111	23	1042	41	11.84	39.38	0	0	18	-
ODIs	95	60	36	308	34	12.83	51.85	0	0	22	-
T20Is	11	1	1	3	3*	-	150.00	0	0	1	-
First-class	133	185	38	1951	53	13.27			0	3	39	-
List A	119	74	44	400	34	13.33			0	0	27	-
T20s	46	13	5	59	12	7.37	113.46	0	0	18	-

Bowling	Mat	Balls	Runs	Wkts	BBI	BBM	Ave	Econ	SR	5w	10
Tests	68	12302	6289	231	6/48	10/146	27.22	3.06	53.2	9	1
ODIs	95	4579	3885	125	6/27	6/27	31.08	5.09	36.6	3	0
T20Is	11	234	284	10	2/25	2/25	28.40	7.28	23.4	0	0
First-class	133	20967	11131	432	8/40	10/80	25.76	3.18	48.5	17	2
List A	119	5543	4633	156	6/27	6/27	29.69	5.01	35.5	3	0
T20s	46	912	1229	28	3/18	3/18	43.89	8.08	32.5	0	0

OLLIE ROBINSON

RHB / WK / R0 / W0

KENT

FULL NAME: Oliver Graham Robinson
BORN: December 1, 1998, Sidcup, Kent
SQUAD NO: 21
HEIGHT: 5ft 8in
NICKNAME: Bob
EDUCATION: Hurstmere School, London;
Chislehurst & Sidcup Grammar, London
TEAMS: Kent, England Lions
ROLE: Wicketkeeper/batter
DEBUT: First-class: 2018; List A: 2017; T20: 2019

BEST BATTING: 143 Kent vs Warwickshire, Edgbaston, 2019

WHO IS YOUR LOOKALIKE? Julian Draxler (footballer)
FIRST CRICKET CLUB? Sidcup CC, London
WHAT WOULD YOU CHANGE ABOUT THE STRUCTURE OF THE COUNTY SEASON?
Make more players available to play in the 50-over competition
BIGGEST INFLUENCE ON YOUR DEVELOPMENT AS A CRICKETER (EXCLUDING PARENTS)?
Matt Walker, Kent head coach
WHO IS THE BEST BATTER/KEEPER/ALLROUNDER/BOWLER IN COUNTY CRICKET
(EXCLUDING TEAMMATES)? Ricardo Vasconcelos/Ben Foakes/Tom Abell/Simon Harmer
MOST UNDERRATED PLAYER IN COUNTY CRICKET? David Payne
HOBBIES? Reading
IF YOU COULD TURN BACK TIME... I would have tried to enjoy school more
WHO WOULD YOU MOST AND LEAST LIKE TO HAVE A NET WITH? Most – Ricky Ponting (it'd
be class to see him up close). Least – Mitchell Johnson
WHAT MAKES YOU WORRY? Green pitches and nipping balls
TWITTER: @ollierobinson7

Batting	Mat	Inns	NO	Runs	HS	Ave	SR	100	50	Ct	St
First-class	36	57	3	1708	143	31.62	58.49	4	7	115	1
List A	16	12	0	287	75	23.91	74.73	0	1	8	-
T20s	18	15	2	243	53	18.69	115.71	0	1	11	2
Bowling	Mat	Balls	Runs	Wkts	BBI	BBM	Ave	Econ	SR	5w	10
First-class	36	-	-	-	-	-	-	-	-	-	-
List A	16	-	-	-	-	-	-	-	-	-	-
T20s	18	-	-	-	-	-	-	-	-	-	-

OLLIE ROBINSON RHB / RFM / R0 / W3

FULL NAME: Oliver Edward Robinson
BORN: December 1, 1993, Margate, Kent
SQUAD NO: 25
HEIGHT: 6ft 5in
NICKNAME: The Rig
EDUCATION: King's School, Canterbury
TEAMS: England, Sussex, Hampshire, Yorkshire
ROLE: Bowler
DEBUT: Test: 2021;
First-class: 2015; List A: 2013; T20: 2014

BEST BATTING: 110 Sussex vs Durham, Chester-le-Street, 2015
BEST BOWLING: 9-78 Sussex vs Glamorgan, Cardiff, 2021
COUNTY CAP: 2019 (Sussex)

FIRST CRICKET CLUB? Margate CC, Kent
CHILDHOOD SPORTING HERO? Andrew Flintoff
BIGGEST INFLUENCE ON YOUR DEVELOPMENT AS A CRICKETER (EXCLUDING PARENTS)?
Myself – no one else can do it for you
WHAT WOULD YOU DO IF YOU WERE IN CHARGE OF COUNTY CRICKET? Play five-day matches in the County Championship
GUILTY PLEASURE? My stamp collection
TWITTER: @ollierobinson25

Batting	Mat	Inns	NO	Runs	HS	Ave	SR	100	50	Ct	St
Tests	9	16	2	125	42	8.92	38.94	0	0	4	-
First-class	74	109	19	1813	110	20.14	58.61	1	7	25	-
List A	14	10	3	122	30	17.42	89.70	0	0	6	-
T20s	49	23	10	92	31	7.07	96.84	0	0	20	-

Bowling	Mat	Balls	Runs	Wkts	BBI	BBM	Ave	Econ	SR	5w	10
Tests	9	1888	830	39	5/65	7/81	21.28	2.63	48.4	2	0
First-class	74	13970	6841	323	9/78	14/135	21.17	2.93	43.2	18	5
List A	14	576	568	14	3/31	3/31	40.57	5.91	41.1	0	0
T20s	49	884	1306	45	4/15	4/15	29.02	8.86	19.6	0	0

SAM ROBSON

MIDDLESEX

FULL NAME: Samuel David Robson
BORN: July 1, 1989, Sydney, Australia
SQUAD NO: 12
HEIGHT: 6ft
NICKNAME: Bronco
EDUCATION: Marcellin College, Sydney
TEAMS: England, Middlesex, Australia U19
ROLE: Batter
DEBUT: Test: 2014;
First-class: 2009; List A: 2008; T20: 2011

BEST BATTING: 253 Middlesex vs Sussex, Hove, 2021
BEST BOWLING: 2-0 Middlesex vs Surrey, The Oval, 2020
COUNTY CAP: 2013

WHO IS YOUR LOOKALIKE? Elton John
FIRST CRICKET CLUB? Randwick Junior CC, New South Wales, Australia
WHAT WOULD YOU CHANGE ABOUT THE STRUCTURE OF THE COUNTY SEASON?
More Championship cricket in the middle of summer so that it is played in the best
conditions and allows the best players to flourish
BIGGEST INFLUENCE ON YOUR DEVELOPMENT AS A CRICKETER (EXCLUDING PARENTS)?
WHO IS THE BEST BATTER/KEEPER/ALLROUNDER/BOWLER IN COUNTY CRICKET
(EXCLUDING TEAMMATES)? Gary Ballance/Ben Foakes/Lewis Gregory/Ollie Robinson
MOST UNDERRATED PLAYER IN COUNTY CRICKET? Ben Brown
HOBBIES? Drinking Guinness with friends
WHAT DO YOU MOST ENJOY LISTENING TO? Tim Murtagh reminiscing
WHAT MAKES YOU WORRY? A greentop under floodlights

Batting	Mat	Inns	NO	Runs	HS	Ave	SR	100	50	Ct	St
Tests	7	11	0	336	127	30.54	44.50	1	1	5	-
First-class	176	313	20	11012	253	37.58	51.44	26	42	168	-
List A	24	22	0	772	106	35.09	77.82	1	5	11	-
T20s	7	7	2	128	60	25.60	113.27	0	1	3	-

Bowling	Mat	Balls	Runs	Wkts	BBI	BBM	Ave	Econ	SR	5w	10
Tests	7	-	-	-	-	-	-	-	-	-	-
First-class	176	379	277	8	2/0	2/0	34.62	4.38	47.3	0	0
List A	24	114	136	2	1/26	1/26	68.00	7.15	57.0	0	0
T20s	7	-	-	-	-	-	-	-	-	-	-

GARETH RODERICK

RHB / WK / R0 / W0

FULL NAME: Gareth Hugh Roderick
BORN: August 29, 1991, Durban, South Africa
SQUAD NO: 9
HEIGHT: 6ft
NICKNAME: Roders
EDUCATION: Maritzburg College, South Africa
TEAMS: Worcestershire, Gloucestershire, KwaZulu-Natal
ROLE: Batter/wicketkeeper
DEBUT: First-class: 2011; List A: 2011; T20: 2011

BEST BATTING: 171 Gloucestershire vs Leicestershire, Bristol, 2014

COUNTY CAP: 2013 (Gloucestershire)

FIRST CRICKET CLUB? Northwood Crusaders CC, Durban
WHAT WOULD YOU CHANGE ABOUT THE STRUCTURE OF THE COUNTY SEASON? Go back to each county playing 16 first-class games, make the season run until later in the year
WHO IS THE BEST BATTER/KEEPER/ALLROUNDER/BOWLER IN COUNTY CRICKET (EXCLUDING TEAMMATES)? Alastair Cook/Dane Vilas/Darren Stevens/Chris Rushworth
MOST UNDERRATED PLAYER IN COUNTY CRICKET? Chris Dent
WHAT WOULD A FLY ON THE WALL HEAR IN YOUR DRESSING ROOM? Charlie Morris folding his dirty clothes
IF YOU COULD TURN BACK TIME... I would move to the UK earlier
WHO WOULD YOU MOST AND LEAST LIKE TO HAVE A NET WITH? Most – Chris Rogers. Least – Shane Bond
MAKE ONE PREDICTION FOR THE FUTURE OF CRICKET: The Hundred will rival the IPL
WHAT MAKES YOU WORRY? When I won't be able to do what I love for a living
TWITTER: @Roders369

Batting	Mat	Inns	NO	Runs	HS	Ave	SR	100	50	Ct	St
First-class	107	174	23	5069	171	33.56	50.32	6	32	278	5
List A	58	48	6	1262	104	30.04	81.78	2	8	56	6
T20s	41	24	8	213	32	13.31	119.66	0	0	20	1
Bowling	Mat	Balls	Runs	Wkts	BBI	BBM	Ave	Econ	SR	5w	10
First-class	107	-	-	-	-	-	-	-	-	-	-
List A	58	-	-	-	-	-	-	-	-	-	-
T20s	41	-	-	-	-	-	-	-	-	-	-

TOBY ROLAND-JONES RHB / RFM / R0 / W2

MIDDLESEX

FULL NAME: Tobias Skelton Roland-Jones
BORN: January 29, 1988, Ashford, Middlesex
SQUAD NO: 21
HEIGHT: 6ft 3in
NICKNAME: Rojo
EDUCATION: Hampton School, Greater London; University of Leeds
TEAMS: England, Middlesex
ROLE: Bowler
DEBUT: Test: 2017; ODI: 2017; First-class: 2010; List A: 2010; T20: 2011

BEST BATTING: 103* Middlesex vs Yorkshire, Lord's, 2015
BEST BOWLING: 7-52 Middlesex vs Gloucestershire, Northwood, 2019
COUNTY CAP: 2012

WHO IS YOUR LOOKALIKE? Zlatan Ibrahimovic
FIRST CRICKET CLUB? Sunbury Cricket Club, Surrey
WHAT WOULD YOU CHANGE ABOUT THE STRUCTURE OF THE COUNTY SEASON? The winter is an unexplored opportunity to increase the amount of cricket played in different conditions
BIGGEST INFLUENCE ON YOUR DEVELOPMENT AS A CRICKETER (EXCLUDING PARENTS)? Richard Johnson, my former bowling coach and now head coach at Middlesex
WHO IS THE BEST BATTER/KEEPER/ALLROUNDER/BOWLER IN COUNTY CRICKET (EXCLUDING TEAMMATES)? Ollie Pope/Ben Brown/Lewis Gregory/Craig Overton
MOST UNDERRATED PLAYER IN COUNTY CRICKET? Leus du Plooy
MOST BEAUTIFUL THING YOU HAVE EVER SEEN? The Northern Lights
IF YOU COULD TURN BACK TIME... I'd have stopped the emergence of social media
TWITTER: @tobyrj21

Batting	Mat	Inns	NO	Runs	HS	Ave	SR	100	50	Ct	St
Tests	4	6	2	82	25	20.50	69.49	0	0	0	-
ODIs	1	1	1	37	37*	-	100.00	0	0	0	-
First-class	120	170	32	2962	103*	21.46	57.54	1	11	33	-
List A	79	47	15	684	65	21.37	95.13	0	1	13	-
T20s	54	31	12	317	40	16.68	128.34	0	0	15	-

Bowling	Mat	Balls	Runs	Wkts	BBI	BBM	Ave	Econ	SR	5w	10
Tests	4	536	334	17	5/57	8/129	19.64	3.73	31.5	1	0
ODIs	1	42	34	1	1/34	1/34	34.00	4.85	42.0	0	0
First-class	120	20603	10847	428	7/52	12/105	25.34	3.15	48.1	20	4
List A	79	3671	3181	126	4/10	4/10	25.24	5.19	29.1	0	0
T20s	54	1065	1549	64	5/21	5/21	24.20	8.72	16.6	1	0

BILLY ROOT

LHB / OB / R0 / W0

FULL NAME: William Thomas Root
BORN: August 5, 1992, Sheffield
SQUAD NO: 7
HEIGHT: 5ft 11in
NICKNAME: Ferret
EDUCATION: Worksop College, Nottinghamshire; Leeds Metropolitan University
TEAMS: Glamorgan, Nottinghamshire
ROLE: Batter
DEBUT: First-class: 2015; List A: 2017; T20: 2017

GLAMORGAN

BEST BATTING: 229 Glamorgan vs Northamptonshire, Northampton, 2019
BEST BOWLING: 3-29 Nottinghamshire vs Sussex, Hove, 2017
COUNTY CAP: 2021 (Glamorgan)

WHO IS YOUR LOOKALIKE? Scrat from the Ice Age films
FIRST CRICKET CLUB? Sheffield Collegiate CC
BIGGEST INFLUENCE ON YOUR DEVELOPMENT AS A CRICKETER (EXCLUDING PARENTS)? My brother (Joe)
WHO IS THE BEST BATTER/KEEPER/ALLROUNDER/BOWLER IN COUNTY CRICKET (EXCLUDING TEAMMATES)? Jake Libby/Ben Cox/Lewis Gregory/Luke Fletcher
MOST UNDERRATED PLAYER IN COUNTY CRICKET? Matt Milnes
WHAT WOULD A FLY ON THE WALL HEAR IN YOUR DRESSING ROOM? Marnus Labuschagne
MOST BEAUTIFUL THING YOU HAVE EVER SEEN? Abbeydale Park (home of Sheffield Collegiate)
IF YOU COULD TURN BACK TIME... I wouldn't have gone through a full season batting with my pad!
WHO WOULD YOU MOST AND LEAST LIKE TO HAVE A NET WITH? Most – Brian Lara. Least – Fred Trueman
MAKE ONE PREDICTION FOR THE FUTURE OF CRICKET: A 100-ball World Cup
WHAT MAKES YOU WORRY? Climate change
TWITTER: @Rootdog22

Batting	Mat	Inns	NO	Runs	HS	Ave	SR	100	50	Ct	St
First-class	44	74	5	2193	229	31.78	53.09	6	5	12	-
List A	34	28	4	964	113*	40.16	89.01	2	5	9	-
T20s	38	29	7	460	41*	20.90	106.48	0	0	15	-

Bowling	Mat	Balls	Runs	Wkts	BBI	BBM	Ave	Econ	SR	5w	10
First-class	44	347	240	8	3/29	3/29	30.00	4.14	43.3	0	0
List A	34	292	310	6	2/36	2/36	51.66	6.36	48.6	0	0
T20s	38	18	37	0	-	-	-	12.33	-	0	0

JOE ROOT

RHB / OB / R3 / W0

FULL NAME: Joseph Edward Root
BORN: December 30, 1990, Sheffield
SQUAD NO: 66
HEIGHT: 6ft
NICKNAME: Rootfish
EDUCATION: King Ecgbert School, Sheffield;
Worksop College, Nottinghamshire
TEAMS: England, Yorkshire, Sydney Thunder
ROLE: Batter
DEBUT: Test: 2012; ODI: 2013; T20I: 2012;
First-class: 2010; List A: 2009; T20: 2011

BEST BATTING: 254 England vs Pakistan, Old Trafford, 2016
BEST BOWLING: 5-8 England vs India, Ahmedabad, 2021
COUNTY CAP: 2012

FIRST CRICKET CLUB? Sheffield Collegiate CC
FAMILY TIES? My dad played club cricket and represented Nottinghamshire Second XI and
Colts. My brother Billy has played for Notts and is currently at Glamorgan
CHILDHOOD SPORTING HERO? Michael Vaughan
TWITTER: @root66

Batting	Mat	Inns	NO	Runs	HS	Ave	SR	100	50	Ct	St
Tests	114	210	15	9600	254	49.23	54.76	23	53	148	-
ODIs	152	142	23	6109	133*	51.33	86.84	16	35	77	-
T20Is	32	30	5	893	90*	35.72	126.30	0	5	18	-
First-class	180	315	26	14033	254	48.55	55.57	34	72	191	-
List A	191	180	29	7393	133*	48.96	85.61	17	44	89	-
T20s	83	76	14	1994	92*	32.16	126.76	0	13	36	-

Bowling	Mat	Balls	Runs	Wkts	BBI	BBM	Ave	Econ	SR	5w	10
Tests	114	3719	1977	44	5/8	5/33	44.93	3.18	84.5	1	0
ODIs	152	1552	1491	26	3/52	3/52	57.34	5.76	59.6	0	0
T20Is	32	84	139	6	2/9	2/9	23.16	9.92	14.0	0	0
First-class	180	5898	3092	66	5/8	5/33	46.84	3.14	89.3	1	0
List A	191	2139	1990	40	3/52	3/52	49.75	5.58	53.4	0	0
T20s	83	467	655	21	2/7	2/7	31.19	8.41	22.2	0	0

ADAM ROSSINGTON

RHB / WK / R0 / W0

FULL NAME: Adam Matthew Rossington
BORN: May 5, 1993, Edgware, Middlesex
SQUAD NO: 7
HEIGHT: 6ft
NICKNAME: Rosso
EDUCATION: Belmont Preparatory School, Surrey; Mill Hill School, London
TEAMS: Northamptonshire, England U19, Middlesex
ROLE: Batter/wicketkeeper
DEBUT: First-class: 2010; List A: 2012; T20: 2011

NORTHAMPTONSHIRE

BEST BATTING: 138* Northamptonshire vs Sussex, Arundel, 2016

FIRST CRICKET CLUB? Barnet CC, London
BIGGEST CRICKETING REGRET? That I've never played in the Hong Kong Sixes
WHO IS THE BEST BATTER/KEEPER/ALLROUNDER/BOWLER IN COUNTY CRICKET (EXCLUDING TEAMMATES)? Marnus Labuschagne/Ben Foakes/Darren Stevens/Ollie Robinson
MOST UNDERRATED PLAYER IN COUNTY CRICKET? Chris Rushworth
WHAT WOULD A FLY ON THE WALL HEAR IN YOUR DRESSING ROOM? Commentary on the races
MOST BEAUTIFUL THING YOU HAVE EVER SEEN? Scarborough beach
HOBBIES? Horse-racing
WHO WOULD YOU MOST AND LEAST LIKE TO HAVE A NET WITH? Most – Chris Gayle, to see some range hitting. Least – Mitchell Starc, because broken toes aren't fun
SURPRISING FACT ABOUT YOU? I can't ride a bicycle
TWITTER: @rossington17

Batting	Mat	Inns	NO	Runs	HS	Ave	SR	100	50	Ct	St
First-class	91	145	14	4636	138*	35.38	65.34	7	32	199	13
List A	49	44	7	1381	97	37.32	99.42	0	11	34	5
T20s	98	93	6	1824	85	20.96	140.52	0	10	45	18

Bowling	Mat	Balls	Runs	Wkts	BBI	BBM	Ave	Econ	SR	5w	10
First-class	91	120	86	0	-	-	-	4.30	-	0	0
List A	49	-	-	-	-	-	-	-	-	-	-
T20s	98	-	-	-	-	-	-	-	-	-	-

JASON ROY

RHB / RM / R1 / W0

SURREY

FULL NAME: Jason Jonathan Roy
BORN: July 21, 1990, Durban, South Africa
SQUAD NO: 20
HEIGHT: 6ft
NICKNAME: Roy the Boy
EDUCATION: Whitgift School, Croydon
TEAMS: England, Surrey, Delhi Capitals, Gujarat Lions, Lahore Qalandars, Perth Scorchers, Quetta Gladiators, Sunrisers, Sydney Sixers, Sylhet Sixers
ROLE: Batter
DEBUT: Test: 2019; ODI: 2015; T20I: 2014; First-class: 2010; List A: 2008; T20: 2008

BEST BATTING: 143 Surrey vs Lancashire, The Oval, 2015
BEST BOWLING: 3-9 Surrey vs Gloucestershire, Bristol, 2014
COUNTY CAP: 2014

MOST EXCITING DAY AS A CRICKETER? There's been quite a few of them – winning the Championship with Surrey, making my England T20, ODI and Test debuts, scoring my first century for England in ODI cricket and winning the World Cup in 2019
CHILDHOOD SPORTING HERO? Jacques Kallis
TWITTER: @JasonRoy20

Batting	Mat	Inns	NO	Runs	HS	Ave	SR	100	50	Ct	St
Tests	5	10	0	187	72	18.70	58.80	0	1	1	-
ODIs	98	93	2	3658	180	40.19	107.27	9	20	35	-
T20Is	58	58	1	1446	78	25.36	143.45	0	8	15	-
First-class	87	144	11	4850	143	36.46	80.75	9	23	75	-
List A	194	184	8	6718	180	38.17	107.26	16	36	73	-
T20s	273	267	14	7275	122*	28.75	143.49	5	49	125	-

Bowling	Mat	Balls	Runs	Wkts	BBI	BBM	Ave	Econ	SR	5w	10
Tests	5	-	-	-	-	-	-	-	-	-	-
ODIs	98	-	-	-	-	-	-	-	-	-	-
T20Is	58	-	-	-	-	-	-	-	-	-	-
First-class	87	712	495	14	3/9	4/47	35.35	4.17	50.8	0	0
List A	194	6	12	0	-	-	-	12.00	-	0	0
T20s	273	18	39	1	1/23	1/23	39.00	13.00	18.0	0	0

CHRIS RUSHWORTH   RHB / RFM / R0 / W6 / MVP14

FULL NAME: Christopher Rushworth
BORN: July 11, 1986, Sunderland
SQUAD NO: 22
HEIGHT: 6ft 2in
NICKNAME: Russian
EDUCATION: Castle View Comprehensive School, Sunderland
TEAMS: Durham
ROLE: Bowler
DEBUT: First-class: 2010; List A: 2004; T20: 2011

DURHAM

BEST BATTING: 57 Durham vs Kent, Canterbury, 2017
BEST BOWLING: 9-52 Durham vs Northamptonshire, Chester-le-Street, 2014
BENEFIT: 2019

FIRST CRICKET CLUB? Hylton Colliery CC, Sunderland
MOST EXCITING DAY AS A CRICKETER? The Lord's one-day final in 2014
FAMILY TIES? My brother Lee represented England U19 and my cousin Phil Mustard played for England, Durham and Gloucestershire
BIGGEST CRICKETING REGRET? Trying to sweep Liam Dawson while my partner was on 99 at the other end. I was the last man. Oops
CHILDHOOD SPORTING HERO? Shaun Pollock
BIGGEST INFLUENCE ON YOUR DEVELOPMENT AS A CRICKETER (EXCLUDING PARENTS)? Geoff Cook (former Durham coach) – he coached me when I was a young lad and then was there to hand me a second opportunity to play professional cricket
TWITTER: @ChrisRush22

Batting	Mat	Inns	NO	Runs	HS	Ave	SR	100	50	Ct	St
First-class	144	199	65	1605	57	11.97	61.42	0	1	31	-
List A	80	33	17	188	38*	11.75	87.03	0	0	19	-
T20s	85	15	9	20	5	3.33	50.00	0	0	18	-

Bowling	Mat	Balls	Runs	Wkts	BBI	BBM	Ave	Econ	SR	5w	10
First-class	144	25934	12707	569	9/52	15/95	22.33	2.93	45.5	29	4
List A	80	3569	3093	128	5/31	5/31	24.16	5.19	27.8	2	0
T20s	85	1623	2121	78	3/14	3/14	27.19	7.84	20.8	0	0

JOSH RYMELL

RHB / R0 / W0

ESSEX

FULL NAME: Joshua Sean Rymell
BORN: April 4, 2001, Ipswich, Suffolk
SQUAD NO: 49
EDUCATION: Ipswich School; Colchester Sixth Form College
TEAMS: Essex
ROLE: Batter
DEBUT: First-class: 2021; List A: 2021; T20: 2021

BEST BATTING: 14 Essex vs Gloucestershire, Chelmsford, 2021

TWITTER: @josh_rymell

NOTES: Rymell served notice of his talent in May 2017 when he scored 114 off 107 balls on his debut for Colchester and East Essex in the Essex League Cup. The right-hander has come through the player pathway system at Essex and agreed a new two-year deal with the club last November after strong performances over the summer. As well as making his first-class debut, Rymell impressed during a run in the 50-over side which reached the One-Day Cup semi-finals, scoring his maiden hundred for the club against Yorkshire. Head coach Anthony McGrath said: "I know it was a proud moment for Josh to make his Essex debut and to go on and score a maiden century made it even more memorable. This experience will prove invaluable next season where I hope he can make many more contributions with the bat"

Batting	Mat	Inns	NO	Runs	HS	Ave	SR	100	50	Ct	St
First-class	3	3	0	23	14	7.66	38.98	0	0	2	-
List A	7	6	0	331	121	55.16	71.95	1	1	4	-
T20s	1	1	0	21	21	21.00	123.52	0	0	1	-

Bowling	Mat	Balls	Runs	Wkts	BBI	BBM	Ave	Econ	SR	5w	10
First-class	3	-	-	-	-	-	-	-	-	-	-
List A	7	-	-	-	-	-	-	-	-	-	-
T20s	1	-	-	-	-	-	-	-	-	-	-

ABI SAKANDE

RHB / RFM / R0 / W0

FULL NAME: Abidine Sakande
BORN: September 22, 1994, Chester, Cheshire
SQUAD NO: 20
HEIGHT: 6ft 4in
NICKNAME: Abi
EDUCATION: Ardingly College; St John's College, Oxford University
TEAMS: Leicestershire, England U19, Sussex
ROLE: Bowler
DEBUT: First-class: 2014; List A: 2016

BEST BATTING: 33 Oxford MCCU vs Cambridge MCCU, Cambridge, 2015
BEST BOWLING: 5-43 Sussex vs South Africa A, Arundel, 2017

WHO IS YOUR LOOKALIKE? Will Smith
FIRST CRICKET CLUB? Lindfield CC, Haywards Heath, West Sussex. Home of the infamous ridge where I learnt the basics of the game
BIGGEST CRICKETING REGRET? Not claiming that I was a top-order batter when I was younger
MOST UNDERRATED PLAYER IN COUNTY CRICKET? Anuj Dal
MOST BEAUTIFUL THING YOU HAVE EVER SEEN? Strangers banding together to help one another in a crisis
HOBBIES? Dancing in the kitchen
IF YOU COULD TURN BACK TIME... I'd always act on my beliefs
MAKE ONE PREDICTION FOR THE FUTURE OF CRICKET: More countries will participate in World Cups than ever before, and the audience will keep growing in those new countries
WHAT DO YOU MOST ENJOY LISTENING TO? Afrobeats
WHAT MAKES YOU WORRY? That despite all the hard work of people with good intentions, not much will really change
WHAT GIVES YOU JOY? The rare moments when you see the world giving a fair reward to those who really actually deserve it
TWITTER: @AbiSakande

Batting	Mat	Inns	NO	Runs	HS	Ave	SR	100	50	Ct	St
First-class	21	27	11	174	33	10.87	32.40	0	0	8	-
List A	10	7	3	11	7*	2.75	44.00	0	0	3	-

Bowling	Mat	Balls	Runs	Wkts	BBI	BBM	Ave	Econ	SR	5w	10
First-class	21	2931	1734	47	5/43	6/87	36.89	3.54	62.3	1	0
List A	10	431	499	9	2/53	2/53	55.44	6.94	47.8	0	0

OLLIE SALE

RHB / RFM / R0 / W0

SOMERSET

FULL NAME: Oliver Richard Trethowan Sale
BORN: September 30, 1995, Newcastle-under-Lyme, Staffordshire
SQUAD NO: 82
HEIGHT: 6ft 2in
NICKNAME: Snail
EDUCATION: Sherborne School, Dorset; Newcastle University
TEAMS: Somerset
ROLE: Bowler
DEBUT: T20: 2016

WHO IS YOUR LOOKALIKE? Erling Haaland (footballer). I've got the same right foot too
FIRST CRICKET CLUB? Tavistock CC, Devon
BIGGEST INFLUENCE ON YOUR DEVELOPMENT AS A CRICKETER (EXCLUDING PARENTS)?
My school coach Alan Willows – he not only developed me as a cricketer but also drove me to Somerset Academy sessions
WHO IS THE BEST BATTER/KEEPER/ALLROUNDER/BOWLER IN COUNTY CRICKET (EXCLUDING TEAMMATES)? Darren Stevens all the way through
MOST UNDERRATED PLAYER IN COUNTY CRICKET? Joe Leach
MOST BEAUTIFUL THING YOU HAVE EVER SEEN? Victoria Falls, Zimbabwe
HOBBIES? Learning
WHO WOULD YOU MOST AND LEAST LIKE TO HAVE A NET WITH? Most – Jasprit Bumrah, because he's a bowling guru. Least – Bumrah again (if I'm facing him)
MAKE ONE PREDICTION FOR THE FUTURE OF CRICKET: A format consisting of 21 Super Overs – the first to 11 wins (teams must use four bowlers and six batsmen)
WHAT DO YOU MOST ENJOY LISTENING TO? Podcasts
WHAT MAKES YOU WORRY? Pep Guardiola's starting XI when I'm picking my fantasy football team
TWITTER: @olliesale1

Batting	Mat	Inns	NO	Runs	HS	Ave	SR	100	50	Ct	St
T20s	10	5	3	20	14*	10.00	105.26	0	0	3	-

Bowling	Mat	Balls	Runs	Wkts	BBI	BBM	Ave	Econ	SR	5w	10
T20s	10	196	341	13	3/32	3/32	26.23	10.43	15.0	0	0

JAMES SALES

RHB / RMF / RO / WO

FULL NAME: James John Grimwood Sales
BORN: February 11, 2003, Northampton
SQUAD NO: TBC
NICKNAME: Junior Jumble
EDUCATION: Wellingborough School, Northamptonshire
TEAMS: Northamptonshire, England U19
ROLE: Allrounder
DEBUT: First-class: 2021; List A: 2021

BEST BATTING: 53 Northamptonshire vs Durham, Northampton, 2021
BEST BOWLING: 2-61 Northamptonshire vs Durham, Northampton, 2021

WHO IS YOUR LOOKALIKE? Dumbo
FIRST CRICKET CLUB? Overstone Park CC, Northampton
FAMILY TIES? My dad David also played for Northants
WHO IS THE BEST BATTER/ALLROUNDER/BOWLER IN COUNTY CRICKET (EXCLUDING TEAMMATES)? David Bedingham/Darren Stevens/Mohammad Abbas
MOST UNDERRATED PLAYER IN COUNTY CRICKET? Jamie Smith
WHAT WOULD A FLY ON THE WALL HEAR IN YOUR DRESSING ROOM? Nathan Buck teasing me
MOST BEAUTIFUL THING YOU HAVE EVER SEEN? My dad on the dancefloor
MAKE ONE PREDICTION FOR THE FUTURE OF CRICKET: Test cricket will live on and get stronger
WHAT DO YOU MOST ENJOY LISTENING TO? Party tunes
WHAT MAKES YOU WORRY? My mum
WHAT GIVES YOU JOY? Cricket

Batting	Mat	Inns	NO	Runs	HS	Ave	SR	100	50	Ct	St
First-class	3	6	2	112	53	28.00	43.07	0	1	1	-
List A	3	3	2	47	28	47.00	70.14	0	0	1	-

Bowling	Mat	Balls	Runs	Wkts	BBI	BBM	Ave	Econ	SR	5w	10
First-class	3	240	154	3	2/61	2/61	51.33	3.85	80.0	0	0
List A	3	30	32	0	-	-	-	6.40	-	0	0

MATT SALISBURY

RHB / RMF / R0 / W0

FULL NAME: Matthew Edward Thomas Salisbury
BORN: April 18, 1993, Chelmsford, Essex
SQUAD NO: 32
HEIGHT: 6ft 2in
NICKNAME: Great Wall
EDUCATION: Shenfield High School, Essex; Anglia Ruskin University, Cambridge
TEAMS: Durham, Essex, Hampshire
ROLE: Bowler
DEBUT: First-class: 2012; List A: 2014; T20: 2014

BEST BATTING: 41 Durham vs Essex, Chelmsford, 2021
BEST BOWLING: 6-37 Durham vs Middlesex, Chester-le-Street, 2018

FIRST CRICKET CLUB? Shenfield CC, Essex
TWITTER: @mattsalisbury10
NOTES: The Durham right-arm seamer has had a stop-start career staggered between three counties. Salisbury was first given a chance at Essex and got a run in their first team in 2014, only to be released by the club the following year. He made his Hampshire debut in 2017 but could not nail down a place in the side, before enjoying a breakthrough season in 2018 after being signed by Durham, taking 44 first-class wickets at 24.77 in his first season at the Riverside

Batting	Mat	Inns	NO	Runs	HS	Ave	SR	100	50	Ct	St
First-class	38	61	11	454	41	9.08	32.03	0	0	4	-
List A	17	4	3	10	5*	10.00	35.71	0	0	3	-
T20s	8	2	2	2	1*	-	100.00	0	0	2	-
Bowling	Mat	Balls	Runs	Wkts	BBI	BBM	Ave	Econ	SR	5w	10
First-class	38	5770	3392	111	6/37	7/107	30.55	3.52	51.9	1	0
List A	17	691	652	17	4/55	4/55	38.35	5.66	40.6	0	0
T20s	8	172	256	10	2/19	2/19	25.60	8.93	17.2	0	0

PHIL SALT

RHB / OB / WK / R0 / W0

FULL NAME: Philip Dean Salt
BORN: August 28, 1996, Bodelwyddan, Denbighshire, Wales
SQUAD NO: 7
HEIGHT: 6ft
EDUCATION: Harrison College, Barbados; Reed's School, Surrey
TEAMS: England, Lancashire, Adelaide Strikers, Barbados Tridents, Dambulla Giants, Islamabad United, Sussex
ROLE: Batter
DEBUT: ODI: 2021; T20I: 2022; First-class: 2016; List A: 2015; T20: 2016

LANCASHIRE

BEST BATTING: 148 Sussex vs Derbyshire, Hove, 2018
BEST BOWLING: 1-32 Sussex vs Warwickshire, Hove, 2018

WHO IS YOUR LOOKALIKE? Rob Beckett (TV presenter)
FIRST CRICKET CLUB? St Asaph CC, North Wales
BIGGEST INFLUENCE ON YOUR DEVELOPMENT AS A CRICKETER (EXCLUDING PARENTS)?
Three people in particular: Mike Yardy, Keith Medlycott, and Jason Gillespie
MOST UNDERRATED PLAYER IN COUNTY CRICKET? Jack Carson
WHO WOULD YOU LEAST LIKE TO HAVE A NET WITH? Jofra Archer, because he bombs everyone off 18 yards
WHAT GIVES YOU JOY? Watching Darren Stevens blow shins off
SURPRISING FACT ABOUT YOU? I once picked up Sir Garry Sobers' Indian takeaway by accident
TWITTER: @PhilSalt1

Batting	Mat	Inns	NO	Runs	HS	Ave	SR	100	50	Ct	St
ODIs	3	3	0	104	60	34.66	116.85	0	1	0	-
T20Is	3	3	0	60	57	20.00	193.54	0	1	2	-
First-class	38	66	2	1967	148	30.73	72.50	4	10	33	-
List A	19	19	1	598	137*	33.22	106.59	1	3	5	-
T20s	133	128	9	2889	78*	24.27	150.39	0	21	63	6

Bowling	Mat	Balls	Runs	Wkts	BBI	BBM	Ave	Econ	SR	5w	10
ODIs	3	-	-	-	-	-	-	-	-	-	-
T20Is	3	-	-	-	-	-	-	-	-	-	-
First-class	38	54	32	1	1/32	1/32	32.00	3.55	54.0	0	0
List A	19	-	-	-	-	-	-	-	-	-	-
T20s	133	-	-	-	-	-	-	-	-	-	-

ANDREW SALTER

RHB / OB / R0 / W0

FULL NAME: Andrew Graham Salter
BORN: June 1, 1993, Haverfordwest, Pembrokeshire, Wales
SQUAD NO: 21
HEIGHT: 5ft 9in
NICKNAME: Salts
EDUCATION: Milford Haven School, Pembrokeshire; Cardiff Metropolitan University
TEAMS: Glamorgan, England U19
ROLE: Bowler
DEBUT: First-class: 2012; List A: 2012; T20: 2014

BEST BATTING: 90 Glamorgan vs Durham, Chester-le-Street, 2021
BEST BOWLING: 4-18 Glamorgan vs Northamptonshire, Cardiff, 2021

WHO IS YOUR LOOKALIKE? Jim Levenstein (main character in American Pie)
FIRST CRICKET CLUB? St Ishmaels CC, Pembrokeshire
BIGGEST INFLUENCE ON YOUR DEVELOPMENT AS A CRICKETER (EXCLUDING PARENTS)? Glamorgan legend Alan Jones
MOST BEAUTIFUL THING YOU HAVE EVER SEEN? Kiran Carlson's mullet/mo haircut
HOBBIES? Graphic design
WHO WOULD YOU MOST AND LEAST LIKE TO HAVE A NET WITH? Most – Nathan Lyon, so that I could pick his brains. Least – Dale Steyn, because he's rapid and unbelievably skilful
WHAT DO YOU MOST ENJOY LISTENING TO? The Diary of a CEO (podcast)
SURPRISING FACT ABOUT YOU? I co-manage a motorcycle initiative called Baffle Culture which aims at "seizing the opportunity to bring like-minded riders together"
GUILTY PLEASURE? Toasted banana bread with butter
TWITTER: @AndySalts

Batting	Mat	Inns	NO	Runs	HS	Ave	SR	100	50	Ct	St
First-class	66	98	21	1850	90	24.02	41.50	0	9	31	-
List A	43	31	12	413	51	21.73	91.98	0	1	11	-
T20s	85	50	24	347	39*	13.34	113.02	0	0	22	-

Bowling	Mat	Balls	Runs	Wkts	BBI	BBM	Ave	Econ	SR	5w	10
First-class	66	8490	4817	101	4/18	6/69	47.69	3.40	84.0	0	0
List A	43	1552	1319	26	3/37	3/37	50.73	5.09	59.6	0	0
T20s	85	1278	1761	60	4/12	4/12	29.35	8.26	21.3	0	0

BEN SANDERSON RHB / RMF / RO / W3 / MVP23

FULL NAME: Ben William Sanderson
BORN: January 3, 1989, Sheffield
SQUAD NO: 26
HEIGHT: 6ft
NICKNAME: Sandoooo
EDUCATION: Ecclesfield School, Sheffield;
Sheffield College
TEAMS: Northamptonshire, England U19,
Yorkshire
ROLE: Bowler
DEBUT: First-class: 2008; List A: 2010; T20: 2010

BEST BATTING: 42 Northamptonshire vs Kent, Canterbury, 2015
BEST BOWLING: 8-73 Northamptonshire vs Gloucestershire, Northampton, 2016
COUNTY CAP: 2018 (Northamptonshire)

WHO IS YOUR LOOKALIKE? Sylvester Stallone
FIRST CRICKET CLUB? Whitley Hall CC, Sheffield
WHAT WOULD YOU CHANGE ABOUT THE STRUCTURE OF THE COUNTY SEASON? Have a
three-division Championship with relegation and promotion
BIGGEST INFLUENCE ON YOUR DEVELOPMENT AS A CRICKETER (EXCLUDING PARENTS)?
Steve Oldham – my first bowling coach. And then Kevin Sharp – he played a big part in
getting me back into the professional game
BIGGEST CRICKETING REGRET? Being a bowler
MOST UNDERRATED PLAYER IN COUNTY CRICKET? James Hildreth
MOST BEAUTIFUL THING YOU HAVE EVER SEEN? Table Mountain, Cape Town
WHAT DO YOU MOST ENJOY LISTENING TO? The sound of the ball hitting the stumps
WHAT MAKES YOU WORRY? Tiny boundaries and flat pitches
GUILTY PLEASURE? A cup of tea with a pack of chocolate Hobnobs
TWITTER: @sando567

Batting	Mat	Inns	NO	Runs	HS	Ave	SR	100	50	Ct	St
First-class	75	97	33	516	42	8.06	44.10	0	0	11	-
List A	41	19	6	140	31	10.76	73.68	0	0	10	-
T20s	53	18	12	57	12*	9.50	79.16	0	0	8	-

Bowling	Mat	Balls	Runs	Wkts	BBI	BBM	Ave	Econ	SR	5w	10
First-class	75	13565	5997	287	8/73	10/55	20.89	2.65	47.2	16	3
List A	41	1642	1558	52	3/29	3/29	29.96	5.69	31.5	0	0
T20s	53	998	1481	57	4/21	4/21	25.98	8.90	17.5	0	0

DANE SCHADENDORF

RHB / WK / R0 / W0

NOTTINGHAMSHIRE

FULL NAME: Dane Schadendorf
BORN: July 31, 2002, Harare, Zimbabwe
SQUAD NO: 89
HEIGHT: 5ft 9in
NICKNAME: Shady
EDUCATION: Ruzawi School, Mashonaland East, Zimbabwe; St John's College, Harare
TEAMS: Nottinghamshire, Zimbabwe U19
ROLE: Wicketkeeper/batter
DEBUT: First-class: 2021; List A: 2021

BEST BATTING: 24 Nottinghamshire vs Derbyshire, Trent Bridge, 2021

WHO IS YOUR LOOKALIKE? Ryan Reynolds (actor)
FIRST CRICKET CLUB? Caythorpe CC, Nottingham
BIGGEST INFLUENCE ON YOUR DEVELOPMENT AS A CRICKETER (EXCLUDING PARENTS)?
My brother – I used to watch him play growing up and I always wanted to be up there playing with him. I've always remembered that and it pushes me to keep getting better
WHAT DO YOU MOST ENJOY LISTENING TO? Polo G (rapper)
WHAT MAKES YOU WORRY? Cricket
WHAT GIVES YOU JOY? Cricket
GUILTY PLEASURE? Golf
TWITTER: @DaneSchadendorf

Batting	Mat	Inns	NO	Runs	HS	Ave	SR	100	50	Ct	St
First-class	1	1	0	24	24	24.00	41.37	0	0	4	-
List A	8	6	2	95	44*	23.75	110.46	0	0	6	1

Bowling	Mat	Balls	Runs	Wkts	BBI	BBM	Ave	Econ	SR	5w	10
First-class	1	-	-	-	-	-	-	-	-	-	-
List A	8	-	-	-	-	-	-	-	-	-	-

GEORGE SCOTT

RHB / RM / R0 / W0

FULL NAME: George Frederick Buchan Scott
BORN: November 6, 1995, Hemel Hempstead, Hertfordshire
SQUAD NO: 17
HEIGHT: 6ft 2in
NICKNAME: Scotty
EDUCATION: Beechwood Park School, St Albans; St Albans School; University of Leeds
TEAMS: Gloucestershire, Middlesex
ROLE: Allrounder
DEBUT: First-class: 2015; List A: 2015; T20: 2015

GLOUCESTERSHIRE

BEST BATTING: 55 Middlesex vs Leicestershire, Lord's, 2019
BEST BOWLING: 2-34 Gloucestershire vs Warwickshire, Bristol, 2020

WHO IS YOUR LOOKALIKE? Sean Longstaff (footballer)
FIRST CRICKET CLUB? Potters Bar CC, Hertfordshire
FAMILY TIES? I have three brothers who have all played Minor Counties for Hertfordshire
WHAT WOULD YOU CHANGE ABOUT THE STRUCTURE OF THE COUNTY SEASON? Start and finish the season three weeks later
BIGGEST INFLUENCE ON YOUR DEVELOPMENT AS A CRICKETER (EXCLUDING PARENTS)? Lenny Cooper, my coach at primary school
WHO IS THE BEST BATTER/KEEPER/ALLROUNDER/BOWLER IN COUNTY CRICKET (EXCLUDING TEAMMATES)? Hashim Amla/John Simpson/Liam Dawson/Mohammad Abbas
MOST UNDERRATED PLAYER IN COUNTY CRICKET? Ryan Higgins
MOST BEAUTIFUL THING YOU HAVE EVER SEEN? Finn Russell's pass in rugby's Calcutta Cup in 2018
WHO WOULD YOU MOST LIKE TO HAVE A NET WITH? Jacques Kallis
SURPRISING FACT ABOUT YOU? I was a music scholar at St Albans School, playing the piano and the bassoon
TWITTER: @georgefbscott

Batting	Mat	Inns	NO	Runs	HS	Ave	SR	100	50	Ct	St
First-class	21	31	5	444	55	17.07	36.72	0	1	8	-
List A	19	16	5	432	66*	39.27	98.40	0	3	8	-
T20s	34	26	10	352	38*	22.00	104.45	0	0	16	-

Bowling	Mat	Balls	Runs	Wkts	BBI	BBM	Ave	Econ	SR	5w	10
First-class	21	1002	545	10	2/34	2/49	54.50	3.26	100.2	0	0
List A	19	288	317	1	1/65	1/65	317.00	6.60	288.0	0	0
T20s	34	74	124	3	1/14	1/14	41.33	10.05	24.6	0	0

GEORGE SCRIMSHAW
RHB / RMF / R0 / W0

FULL NAME: George Louis Sheridan Scrimshaw
BORN: February 10, 1998, Burton-on-Trent, Staffordshire
SQUAD NO: 9
HEIGHT: 6ft 7in
NICKNAME: Scrim, Scrimmy, Tank
EDUCATION: Thomas Russel Junior School; John Taylor High School, Burton-on-Trent
TEAMS: Derbyshire, Worcestershire
ROLE: Bowler
DEBUT: First-class: 2021; List A: 2021; T20: 2017

BEST BATTING: 5* Derbyshire vs Nottinghamshire, Derby, 2021
BEST BOWLING: 2-40 Derbyshire vs Nottinghamshire, Derby, 2021

FIRST CRICKET CLUB? Dunstall CC, Burton-upon-Trent, Staffordshire – aka Deer Park, home of the Stags
FAMILY TIES? My dad and grandad both played county age-group cricket
HOBBIES? Coffee, going to the gym, running, travelling the earth
WHO WOULD YOU MOST LIKE TO HAVE A NET WITH? Dale Steyn – I love his aggression. For a fast bowler like myself, he's a role model
WHAT DO YOU MOST ENJOY LISTENING TO? Indie rock (The Stone Roses, The Killers, The Beatles, Blink-182)
WHAT GIVES YOU JOY? Bowling fast
SURPRISING FACT ABOUT YOU? I once hit 16 sixes in a row in Kwik Cricket
TWITTER: @Gscrimshaw98

Batting	Mat	Inns	NO	Runs	HS	Ave	SR	100	50	Ct	St
First-class	3	5	3	5	5*	2.50	19.23	0	0	1	-
List A	3	1	1	13	13*	-	52.00	0	0	0	-
T20s	14	4	3	5	3*	5.00	55.55	0	0	2	-

Bowling	Mat	Balls	Runs	Wkts	BBI	BBM	Ave	Econ	SR	5w	10
First-class	3	210	154	3	2/40	2/65	51.33	4.40	70.0	0	0
List A	3	60	86	3	2/41	2/41	28.66	8.60	20.0	0	0
T20s	14	246	326	17	3/23	3/23	19.17	7.95	14.4	0	0

TOM SCRIVEN

RHB / RMF / RO / WO

FULL NAME: Thomas Antony Rhys Scriven
BORN: November 18, 1998, Oxford
SQUAD NO: 33
HEIGHT: 6ft 1in
NICKNAME: Skippy
EDUCATION: Magdalen College School, Oxford
TEAMS: Hampshire, England U19
ROLE: Allrounder
DEBUT: First-class: 2020; List A: 2021; T20: 2018

LEICESTERSHIRE

BEST BATTING: 68 Hampshire vs Kent, Canterbury, 2020
BEST BOWLING: 2-24 Hampshire vs Kent, Canterbury, 2020

WHO IS YOUR LOOKALIKE? A rooster
FIRST CRICKET CLUB? West Ilsley CC, Berkshire
BIGGEST INFLUENCE ON YOUR DEVELOPMENT AS A CRICKETER (EXCLUDING PARENTS)?
A combination of school and player pathways at Berkshire
WHO IS THE BEST BATTER/KEEPER/ALLROUNDER/BOWLER IN COUNTY CRICKET
(EXCLUDING TEAMMATES)? James Vince/Ben Foakes/Darren Stevens/Chris Rushworth
MOST UNDERRATED PLAYER IN COUNTY CRICKET? Daniel Bell-Drummond
WHAT WOULD A FLY ON THE WALL HEAR IN YOUR DRESSING ROOM? Callum Parkinson
MOST BEAUTIFUL THING YOU HAVE EVER SEEN? Queenstown
WHAT DO YOU MOST ENJOY LISTENING TO? Classical music
GUILTY PLEASURE? Ben and Jerry's ice cream

Batting	Mat	Inns	NO	Runs	HS	Ave	SR	100	50	Ct	St
First-class	2	3	0	84	68	28.00	45.40	0	1	1	-
List A	5	3	1	63	42	31.50	77.77	0	0	0	-
T20s	2	1	0	2	2	2.00	28.57	0	0	0	-

Bowling	Mat	Balls	Runs	Wkts	BBI	BBM	Ave	Econ	SR	5w	10
First-class	2	126	79	3	2/24	2/59	26.33	3.76	42.0	0	0
List A	5	46	46	1	1/6	1/6	46.00	6.00	46.0	0	0
T20s	2	6	8	0	-	-	-	8.00	-	0	0

NASEEM SHAH

RHB / RF / R0 / W0

FULL NAME: Naseem Shah
BORN: February 15, 2003, Lower Dir, North-West Frontier Province, Pakistan
SQUAD NO: TBC
TEAMS: Pakistan, Gloucestershire, Central Punjab, Quetta Gladiators, Southern Punjab, St Kitts & Nevis Patriots, Zarai Taraqiati Bank Limited
ROLE: Bowler
DEBUT: Test: 2019; First-class: 2018; List A: 2018; T20: 2019

BEST BATTING: 31 Pakistan Shaheens vs Sri Lanka A, Pallekele, 2021
BEST BOWLING: 6-59 Zarai Taraqiati Bank Limited vs Pakistan Television, Rawalpindi, 2018

TWITTER: @iNaseemShah
NOTES: Gloucestershire have pulled off a major coup by signing one of the most exciting young quicks in the world. After making his debut for Pakistan at the age of 16, Naseem Shah became the youngest pace bowler to take a five-wicket haul in the history of Test cricket when he claimed 5-31 against Sri Lanka, and then the youngest bowler of any type to take a Test hat-trick, versus Bangladesh at Rawalpindi. He is due to be available for the first half of the Championship season and the group stages of the T20 Blast. "Naseem will bring further depth to our pace-bowling department and provide exciting competition for places in our seam-bowling ranks," said Steve Snell, Gloucestershire's performance director. "I have heard fantastic things about Naseem's attitude and his willingness to stand up in the tough moments in games"

Batting	Mat	Inns	NO	Runs	HS	Ave	SR	100	50	Ct	St
Tests	9	12	5	28	12	4.00	31.81	0	0	1	-
First-class	22	26	8	106	31	5.88	50.71	0	0	2	-
List A	4	1	0	1	1	1.00	20.00	0	0	1	-
T20s	42	16	7	51	11*	5.66	96.22	0	0	6	-

Bowling	Mat	Balls	Runs	Wkts	BBI	BBM	Ave	Econ	SR	5w	10
Tests	9	1348	849	20	5/31	5/87	42.45	3.77	67.4	1	0
First-class	22	3085	1849	70	6/59	9/111	26.41	3.59	44.0	4	0
List A	4	60	26	2	2/26	2/26	13.00	2.60	30.0	0	0
T20s	42	901	1217	39	5/20	5/20	31.20	8.10	23.1	1	0

JOSH SHAW

RHB / RMF / R0 / W0

FULL NAME: Joshua Shaw
BORN: January 3, 1996, Wakefield, Yorkshire
SQUAD NO: 5
HEIGHT: 6ft 1in
EDUCATION: Crofton Academy, West Yorkshire; Skills Exchange College, Wakefield
TEAMS: Gloucestershire, England U19, Yorkshire
ROLE: Bowler
DEBUT: First-class: 2016; List A: 2019; T20: 2015

BEST BATTING: 42 Yorkshire vs Somerset, Headingley, 2018
BEST BOWLING: 5-79 Gloucestershire vs Sussex, Bristol, 2016
COUNTY CAP: 2016 (Gloucestershire)

FIRST CRICKET CLUB? Wakefield Thornes CC, West Yorkshire
FAMILY TIES? My father Chris played for Yorkshire. We lived on the back of Streethouse CC so I was always around cricket from a young age
MOST EXCITING DAY AS A CRICKETER? Taking a hat-trick for Yorkshire Academy in the Yorkshire League Cup final in 2014
CHILDHOOD SPORTING HERO? Andrew Flintoff
SURPRISING FACT ABOUT YOU? I passed my driving test with no minors
TWITTER: @joshuashaw1

Batting	Mat	Inns	NO	Runs	HS	Ave	SR	100	50	Ct	St
First-class	43	58	11	566	42	12.04	41.16	0	0	9	-
List A	7	2	0	2	2	1.00	22.22	0	0	0	-
T20s	21	3	2	2	1*	2.00	66.66	0	0	4	-

Bowling	Mat	Balls	Runs	Wkts	BBI	BBM	Ave	Econ	SR	5w	10
First-class	43	6184	3818	106	5/79	6/102	36.01	3.70	58.3	2	0
List A	7	342	334	8	4/36	4/36	41.75	5.85	42.7	0	0
T20s	21	336	491	17	3/32	3/32	28.88	8.76	19.7	0	0

JACK SHUTT

RHB / OB / R0 / W0

YORKSHIRE

FULL NAME: Jack William Shutt
BORN: June 24, 1997, Barnsley
SQUAD NO: 24
HEIGHT: 6ft 1in
NICKNAME: Sushi
EDUCATION: Kirk Balk School, Barnsley;
Thomas Rotherham College, South
Yorkshire
TEAMS: Yorkshire
ROLE: Bowler
DEBUT: First-class: 2020; List A: 2021; T20: 2019

BEST BATTING: 7* Yorkshire vs Durham, Chester-le-Street, 2020
BEST BOWLING: 2-14 Yorkshire vs Nottinghamshire, Trent Bridge, 2020

MOST EXCITING DAY AS A CRICKETER? Playing in the Roses T20 Blast match at Headingley in 2019 – my first-team debut for Yorkshire
CHILDHOOD SPORTING HERO? Cristiano Ronaldo
BIGGEST INFLUENCE ON YOUR DEVELOPMENT AS A CRICKETER (EXCLUDING PARENTS)?
Ian Swallow (ex-Yorkshire off-spinner) – he taught me how to play the game at Elsecar CC and was the man who got me bowling off-spin
WHAT WOULD YOU DO IF YOU WERE IN CHARGE OF COUNTY CRICKET? Play more Championship games in the summer months when the pitches take turn, try to make the game more accessible to fans who work full-time
GUILTY PLEASURE? A BBQ chicken pizza
TWITTER: @jackshutt_24

Batting	Mat	Inns	NO	Runs	HS	Ave	SR	100	50	Ct	St
First-class	3	4	3	7	7*	7.00	11.86	0	0	2	-
List A	5	2	2	2	1*	-	11.76	0	0	3	-
T20s	11	4	3	0	0*	0.00	0.00	0	0	3	-

Bowling	Mat	Balls	Runs	Wkts	BBI	BBM	Ave	Econ	SR	5w	10
First-class	3	116	104	2	2/14	2/63	52.00	5.37	58.0	0	0
List A	5	66	88	1	1/33	1/33	88.00	8.00	66.0	0	0
T20s	11	216	271	12	5/11	5/11	22.58	7.52	18.0	1	0

DOM SIBLEY

RHB / OB / R1 / W0

FULL NAME: Dominic Peter Sibley
BORN: September 5, 1995, Epsom, Surrey
SQUAD NO: 45
HEIGHT: 6ft 3in
NICKNAME: Frocko
EDUCATION: Whitgift School, Croydon
TEAMS: England, Warwickshire, Surrey
ROLE: Batter
DEBUT: Test: 2019; First-class: 2013; List A: 2013; T20: 2016

BEST BATTING: 244 Warwickshire vs Kent, Canterbury, 2019
BEST BOWLING: 2-103 Surrey vs Hampshire, Southampton, 2016

FIRST CRICKET CLUB? Ashtead CC, Surrey
BEST INNINGS YOU'VE SEEN? Kevin Pietersen's hundred against South Africa in the 2012 Headingley Test
WHAT WOULD YOU DO IF YOU WERE IN CHARGE OF COUNTY CRICKET? Introduce free hits for no-balls in four-day cricket
BIGGEST CRICKETING REGRET? Playing while I did my A-Levels
SURPRISING FACT ABOUT YOU? I am half-French
TWITTER: @DomSibley

Batting	Mat	Inns	NO	Runs	HS	Ave	SR	100	50	Ct	St
Tests	22	39	3	1042	133*	28.94	34.22	2	5	12	-
First-class	100	170	16	5899	244	38.30	40.04	15	30	69	-
List A	22	20	2	416	115	23.11	78.19	1	0	10	-
T20s	35	32	3	859	74*	29.62	121.49	0	7	17	-

Bowling	Mat	Balls	Runs	Wkts	BBI	BBM	Ave	Econ	SR	5w	10
Tests	22	6	7	0	-	-	-	7.00	-	0	0
First-class	100	380	271	4	2/103	2/117	67.75	4.27	95.0	0	0
List A	22	54	62	1	1/20	1/20	62.00	6.88	54.0	0	0
T20s	35	228	338	5	2/33	2/33	67.60	8.89	45.6	0	0

PETER SIDDLE — RHB / RFM / RO / WO

SOMERSET

FULL NAME: Peter Matthew Siddle
BORN: November 25, 1984, Traralgon, Victoria, Australia
SQUAD NO: TBC
HEIGHT: 6ft 2in
NICKNAME: Sid Vicious
TEAMS: Australia, Somerset, Adelaide Strikers, Essex, Lancashire, Melbourne Renegades, Nottinghamshire, Tasmania, Victoria
ROLE: Bowler
DEBUT: Test: 2008; ODI: 2009; T20I: 2009; First-class: 2005; List A: 2005; T20: 2006

BEST BATTING: 103* Australia A vs Scotland, Edinburgh, 2013
BEST BOWLING: 8-54 Victoria vs South Australia, Adelaide, 2015
COUNTY CAP: 2014 (Nottinghamshire); 2021 (Essex)

TWITTER: @petersiddle403
NOTES: The combative Australian seamer has been signed by Somerset to play across all formats until the end of August. Siddle has had previous spells with Lancashire, Nottinghamshire and most recently Essex, for whom he took 91 first-class wickets at 19.53. After 221 wickets in 67 Tests, he retired from international cricket at the end of 2019. In May 2020 Siddle joined Tasmania after 15 years at Victoria, and he continues to be a star performer for Adelaide Strikers in the Big Bash, finishing as the tournament's leading wicket-taker in the 2021/22 season

Batting	Mat	Inns	NO	Runs	HS	Ave	SR	100	50	Ct	St
Tests	67	94	15	1164	51	14.73	47.16	0	2	19	-
ODIs	20	6	3	31	10*	10.33	103.33	0	0	1	-
T20Is	2	1	1	1	1*	-	100.00	0	0	0	-
First-class	196	264	51	3613	103*	16.96	50.92	1	6	59	-
List A	69	35	11	251	62	10.45	95.80	0	1	6	-
T20s	90	26	14	52	11	4.33	72.22	0	0	18	-

Bowling	Mat	Balls	Runs	Wkts	BBI	BBM	Ave	Econ	SR	5w	10
Tests	67	13907	6777	221	6/54	9/104	30.66	2.92	62.9	8	0
ODIs	20	901	743	17	3/55	3/55	43.70	4.94	53.0	0	0
T20Is	2	48	58	3	2/24	2/24	19.33	7.25	16.0	0	0
First-class	196	37787	17908	671	8/54	9/77	26.68	2.84	56.3	26	0
List A	69	3486	2732	90	4/22	4/22	30.35	4.70	38.7	0	0
T20s	90	1868	2344	108	5/16	5/16	21.70	7.52	17.2	2	0

RYAN SIDEBOTTOM

RHB / RMF / R0 / W0

FULL NAME: Ryan Nathan Sidebottom
BORN: August 14, 1989, Shepparton, Victoria, Australia
SQUAD NO: 22
HEIGHT: 6ft 2in
NICKNAME: Siddy
EDUCATION: Wanganui Park Secondary College, Victoria, Australia
TEAMS: Warwickshire, Victoria
ROLE: Bowler
DEBUT: First-class: 2013; List A: 2021; T20: 2021

BEST BATTING: 27* Warwickshire vs Kent, Edgbaston, 2019
BEST BOWLING: 6-35 Warwickshire vs Northamptonshire, Northampton, 2018

FIRST CRICKET CLUB? Northerners CC, Victoria, Australia
CHILDHOOD SPORTING HERO? Glenn McGrath
BIGGEST INFLUENCE ON YOUR DEVELOPMENT AS A CRICKETER (EXCLUDING PARENTS)?
My brothers (see below)
SURPRISING FACT ABOUT YOU? I've got four brothers, one of whom plays Aussie rules for Collingwood. We grew up in Tallygaroopna near Melbourne, but I have a British passport because my mum moved to Devon
TWITTER: @ryansidebottom2

Batting	Mat	Inns	NO	Runs	HS	Ave	SR	100	50	Ct	St
First-class	23	32	16	101	27*	6.31	27.97	0	0	5	-
List A	2	2	2	11	9*	-	68.75	0	0	1	-
T20s	1	1	0	3	3	3.00	50.00	0	0	1	-

Bowling	Mat	Balls	Runs	Wkts	BBI	BBM	Ave	Econ	SR	5w	10
First-class	23	3059	1810	59	6/35	10/96	30.67	3.55	51.8	1	1
List A	2	100	97	2	1/41	1/41	48.50	5.81	50.0	0	0
T20s	1	24	37	1	1/37	1/37	37.00	9.25	24.0	0	0

JOHN SIMPSON **LHB / WK / R0 / W0**

FULL NAME: John Andrew Simpson
BORN: July 13, 1988, Bury, Lancashire
SQUAD NO: 20
HEIGHT: 5ft 11in
NICKNAME: Yon
EDUCATION: St Gabriel's RC High School,
Bury; Holy Cross College, Bury
TEAMS: England, Middlesex
ROLE: Wicketkeeper/batter
DEBUT: ODI: 2021; First-class: 2009; List A:
2009; T20: 2009

BEST BATTING: 167* Middlesex vs Lancashire, Old Trafford, 2019

COUNTY CAP: 2011

WHO IS YOUR LOOKALIKE? Judd Trump
FIRST CRICKET CLUB? Ramsbottom CC, Greater Manchester
BIGGEST INFLUENCE ON YOUR DEVELOPMENT AS A CRICKETER (EXCLUDING PARENTS)?
Grandpa – he supported me hugely in the lead-up to signing my first professional contract
MOST UNDERRATED PLAYER IN COUNTY CRICKET? Callum Parkinson
WHAT WOULD A FLY ON THE WALL HEAR IN YOUR DRESSING ROOM? Robbie White talking
about finances
SURPRISING FACT ABOUT YOU? I don't drink tea or coffee
TWITTER: @johnsimpson_88

Batting	Mat	Inns	NO	Runs	HS	Ave	SR	100	50	Ct	St
ODIs	3	2	0	20	17	10.00	64.51	0	0	9	-
First-class	173	276	41	7465	167*	31.76	47.49	7	42	536	28
List A	96	74	11	1607	82*	25.50	86.39	0	8	90	19
T20s	137	121	23	2342	84*	23.89	131.57	0	9	69	28

Bowling	Mat	Balls	Runs	Wkts	BBI	BBM	Ave	Econ	SR	5w	10
ODIs	3	-	-	-	-	-	-	-	-	-	-
First-class	173	18	23	0	-	-	-	7.66	-	0	0
List A	96	-	-	-	-	-	-	-	-	-	-
T20s	137	-	-	-	-	-	-	-	-	-	-

FATEH SINGH

LHB / SLA / R0 / W0

FULL NAME: Fateh Singh Landa
BORN: April 20, 2004, Nottingham
SQUAD NO: 98
HEIGHT: 6ft
NICKNAME: Fatz
EDUCATION: Trent College, Long Eaton
TEAMS: Nottinghamshire, England U19
ROLE: Bowler
DEBUT: List A: 2021

NOTTINGHAMSHIRE

FIRST CRICKET CLUB? Cavaliers and Carrington CC, Nottingham
MOST UNDERRATED PLAYER IN COUNTY CRICKET? Tom Abell
MOST BEAUTIFUL THING YOU HAVE EVER SEEN? Sunset in Cornwall
WHO WOULD YOU MOST LIKE TO HAVE A NET WITH? Daniel Vettori – he's my favourite bowler of all time
WHAT DO YOU MOST ENJOY LISTENING TO? Melody rap music
WHAT MAKES YOU WORRY? Being late
TWITTER: @fxtz_singh
NOTES: Having initially joined the Nottinghamshire Academy as a seam-bowling allrounder, Singh has developed into a miserly left-arm spinner and accomplished strokemaker. The 17-year-old signed his first professional deal with the club last October after making his first-team debut in the One-Day Cup. Singh made three appearances in the competition and while he failed to take a wicket, he bowled economically and helped steer Notts to victory with the bat in a thrilling two-wicket win over Northants at Grantham. Singh was part of the England squad which reached the 2022 U19 World Cup final in the Caribbean, featuring in the victories over Bangladesh and Canada. He says one of his main ambitions is to play in the IPL. In 2015, he was diagnosed with alopecia universalis, an autoimmune disease that causes loss of body hair. "As I got older, it got harder, but I started to accept me for who I am," he told ESPNcricinfo. "So, regardless of what anyone says, this is me and I am okay with that"

Batting	Mat	Inns	NO	Runs	HS	Ave	SR	100	50	Ct	St
List A	3	2	1	27	21	27.00	117.39	0	0	0	-

Bowling	Mat	Balls	Runs	Wkts	BBI	BBM	Ave	Econ	SR	5w	10
List A	3	78	42	0	-	-	-	3.23	-	0	0

JAS SINGH   RHB / RFM / R0 / W0

FULL NAME: Jaskaran Singh
BORN: September 19, 2002, Denmark Hill, Surrey
SQUAD NO: 19
HEIGHT: 6ft 5in
NICKNAME: Jassy
EDUCATION: Wilmington Academy, Kent
TEAMS: Kent
ROLE: Bowler
DEBUT: First-class: 2021

BEST BATTING: 2 Kent vs Sussex, Canterbury, 2021
BEST BOWLING: 4-51 Kent vs Sussex, Canterbury, 2021

FIRST CRICKET CLUB? Bexley CC, Kent
WHO IS THE BEST BATTER/KEEPER/ALLROUNDER/BOWLER IN COUNTY CRICKET
(EXCLUDING TEAMMATES)? James Vince/Ben Foakes/Matt Critchley/Ollie Robinson
MOST UNDERRATED PLAYER IN COUNTY CRICKET? Rob Yates
HOBBIES? Video games
WHO WOULD YOU MOST AND LEAST LIKE TO HAVE A NET WITH? Most – Andrew Flintoff.
Least – Jofra Archer
WHAT DO YOU MOST ENJOY LISTENING TO? House music
TWITTER: @Jas_Singh19
NOTES: The tall 19-year-old seamer signed his first professional contract with Kent in
October after taking 4-51 on his first-class debut against Sussex at Canterbury last summer.
"Jas is an exciting prospect who has shown that he can perform at Championship level with
his seven wickets so far in two first-class matches for us," said Paul Downton, Kent's director
of cricket. "He has been a consistent wicket-taker in the Kent League for Bexley and is
improving rapidly. Jas is the first seam bowler to have come through the talent pathway for
a few years and it's fantastic to have a young bowler with Jas' potential joining our squad"

Batting	Mat	Inns	NO	Runs	HS	Ave	SR	100	50	Ct	St
First-class	2	2	0	2	2	1.00	28.57	0	0	1	-

Bowling	Mat	Balls	Runs	Wkts	BBI	BBM	Ave	Econ	SR	5w	10
First-class	2	240	140	7	4/51	5/83	20.00	3.50	34.2	0	0

PREM SISODIYA

RHB / SLA / R0 / W0

FULL NAME: Prem Sisodiya
BORN: September 21, 1998, Cardiff
SQUAD NO: 32
HEIGHT: 5ft 11in
NICKNAME: Premo
EDUCATION: Clifton College, Bristol; Cardiff Metropolitan University
TEAMS: Glamorgan, England U19
ROLE: Bowler
DEBUT: First-class: 2018; T20: 2019

BEST BATTING: 38 Glamorgan vs Derbyshire, Swansea, 2018
BEST BOWLING: 4-79 Cardiff MCCU vs Somerset, Taunton, 2019

FIRST CRICKET CLUB? Cardiff CC
MOST EXCITING DAY AS A CRICKETER? Making my first-class debut in 2018
CHILDHOOD SPORTING HERO? Sachin Tendulkar
BIGGEST INFLUENCE ON YOUR DEVELOPMENT AS A CRICKETER (EXCLUDING PARENTS)?
John Derrick, former Glamorgan allrounder and coach
BIGGEST CRICKETING REGRET? Trying to switch-hit when I was on 97
WHAT WOULD YOU DO IF YOU WERE IN CHARGE OF COUNTY CRICKET? Create a new tournament based on football's FA Cup
GUILTY PLEASURE? Nando's
TWITTER: @PremSisodiya

Batting	Mat	Inns	NO	Runs	HS	Ave	SR	100	50	Ct	St
First-class	4	7	1	83	38	13.83	48.82	0	0	2	-
T20s	19	5	4	14	6*	14.00	280.00	0	0	3	-

Bowling	Mat	Balls	Runs	Wkts	BBI	BBM	Ave	Econ	SR	5w	10
First-class	4	731	369	15	4/79	5/73	24.60	3.02	48.7	0	0
T20s	19	450	558	18	3/26	3/26	31.00	7.44	25.0	0	0

BEN SLATER

LHB / OB / R1 / W0 / MVP50

FULL NAME: Benjamin Thomas Slater
BORN: August 26, 1991, Chesterfield, Derbyshire
SQUAD NO: 26
HEIGHT: 5ft 11in
NICKNAME: Slats
EDUCATION: Netherthorpe School, Staveley; Leeds Metropolitan University
TEAMS: Nottinghamshire, Derbyshire, Leicestershire, Southern Rocks
ROLE: Batter
DEBUT: First-class: 2012; List A: 2012; T20: 2012

BEST BATTING: 172 Leicestershire vs Lancashire, Worcester, 2020

COUNTY CAP: 2021 (Nottinghamshire)

FIRST CRICKET CLUB? Chesterfield CC, Derbyshire
BIGGEST CRICKETING REGRET? Getting out for 99 against Middlesex in the first game of 2018
WHO IS THE BEST BATTER/KEEPER/ALLROUNDER/BOWLER IN COUNTY CRICKET (EXCLUDING TEAMMATES)? Alastair Cook/Ben Foakes/Ed Barnard/Chris Rushworth
WHAT WOULD A FLY ON THE WALL HEAR IN YOUR DRESSING ROOM? Dane Paterson talking about how many sixes he's hit in his career
MOST BEAUTIFUL THING YOU HAVE EVER SEEN? Victoria Falls, Zimbabwe
IF YOU COULD TURN BACK TIME... Chesterfield would win the League 1 play-off semi-final in 2015
WHO WOULD YOU MOST AND LEAST LIKE TO HAVE A NET WITH? Most – Brian Lara. Least – Shaun Tait
GUILTY PLEASURE? White-chocolate-chip cookies
TWITTER: @BennySlats

Batting	Mat	Inns	NO	Runs	HS	Ave	SR	100	50	Ct	St
First-class	102	185	10	5866	172	33.52	45.38	9	31	40	-
List A	44	41	5	2006	148*	55.72	87.71	5	13	7	-
T20s	15	14	0	305	57	21.78	109.71	0	1	1	-
Bowling	Mat	Balls	Runs	Wkts	BBI	BBM	Ave	Econ	SR	5w	10
First-class	102	117	121	0	-	-	-	6.20	-	0	0
List A	44	-	-	-	-	-	-	-	-	-	-
T20s	15	-	-	-	-	-	-	-	-	-	-

WILL SMEED

RHB / OB / R0 / W0

FULL NAME: William Conrad Francis Smeed
BORN: October 26, 2001, Cambridge
SQUAD NO: 23
HEIGHT: 6ft
NICKNAME: Smeedy
EDUCATION: King's College, Taunton
TEAMS: Somerset, England U19, Quetta Gladiators
ROLE: Batter
DEBUT: T20: 2020

WHO IS YOUR LOOKALIKE? Philippe Coutinho (footballer)
FIRST CRICKET CLUB? Glastonbury CC, Somerset
WHO IS THE BEST BATTER/KEEPER/ALLROUNDER/BOWLER IN COUNTY CRICKET (EXCLUDING TEAMMATES)? Joe Clarke/Ben Foakes/Darren Stevens/Simon Harmer
MOST UNDERRATED PLAYER IN COUNTY CRICKET? Daniel Bell-Drummond
MOST BEAUTIFUL THING YOU HAVE EVER SEEN? A packed Twickenham
HOBBIES? Reading
IF YOU COULD TURN BACK TIME... I wouldn't get into golf
WHO WOULD YOU MOST LIKE TO HAVE A NET WITH? Chris Gayle – to see how hard he hits it
WHAT MAKES YOU WORRY? Rain
WHAT GIVES YOU JOY? Sunshine
TWITTER: @will_smeed

Batting	Mat	Inns	NO	Runs	HS	Ave	SR	100	50	Ct	St
T20s	31	30	2	885	99	31.60	137.85	0	5	19	-

Bowling	Mat	Balls	Runs	Wkts	BBI	BBM	Ave	Econ	SR	5w	10
T20s	31	-	-	-	-	-	-	-	-	-	-

JAMIE SMITH RHB / WK / R0 / W0

FULL NAME: Jamie Luke Smith
BORN: July 12, 2000, Epsom, Surrey
SQUAD NO: 11
HEIGHT: 6ft 2in
NICKNAME: Smudger
EDUCATION: Whitgift School, Croydon
TEAMS: Surrey, England Lions
ROLE: Batter/wicketkeeper
DEBUT: First-class: 2019; List A: 2019; T20: 2018

BEST BATTING: 138 Surrey vs Glamorgan, The Oval, 2021

WHO IS YOUR LOOKALIKE? Tom Hardy (actor)
FIRST CRICKET CLUB? Sutton CC, Surrey
MOST UNDERRATED PLAYER IN COUNTY CRICKET? Mark Stoneman
HOBBIES? Horse racing
WHAT GIVES YOU JOY? The first day of a new season
TWITTER: @jamiesm148

Batting	Mat	Inns	NO	Runs	HS	Ave	SR	100	50	Ct	St
First-class	26	42	4	1395	138	36.71	50.43	4	4	28	3
List A	15	12	2	425	85	42.50	82.36	0	3	13	2
T20s	25	19	6	393	60	30.23	116.61	0	3	10	-

Bowling	Mat	Balls	Runs	Wkts	BBI	BBM	Ave	Econ	SR	5w	10
First-class	26	-	-	-	-	-	-	-	-	-	-
List A	15	-	-	-	-	-	-	-	-	-	-
T20s	25	-	-	-	-	-	-	-	-	-	-

RUAIDHRI SMITH

RHB / RFM / R0 / W0

FULL NAME: Ruaidhri Alexander James Smith
BORN: August 5, 1994, Glasgow
SQUAD NO: 20
HEIGHT: 6ft 2in
NICKNAME: Trotts
EDUCATION: The Cathedral School, Llandaff; Shrewsbury School; University of Bristol
TEAMS: Scotland, Glamorgan
ROLE: Bowler
DEBUT: ODI: 2016; T20I: 2019; First-class: 2013; List A: 2013; T20: 2014

BEST BATTING: 57* Glamorgan vs Gloucestershire, Bristol, 2014
BEST BOWLING: 5-87 Glamorgan vs Durham, Cardiff, 2018

CHILDHOOD SPORTING HERO? Jonny Wilkinson
BIGGEST INFLUENCE ON YOUR DEVELOPMENT AS A CRICKETER (EXCLUDING PARENTS)?
Phil Makinson, my coach at St Fagans CC (Cardiff)
WHAT WOULD YOU DO IF YOU WERE IN CHARGE OF COUNTY CRICKET? Bring back the 40-over competition, bring back the Lord's one-day final, increase the number of points for draws in the Championship
SURPRISING FACT ABOUT YOU? Born in Scotland, Irish mother, English father, raised in Wales
GUILTY PLEASURE? Doughnuts
TWITTER: @ruaidhrismith

Batting	Mat	Inns	NO	Runs	HS	Ave	SR	100	50	Ct	St
ODIs	2	1	0	10	10	10.00	166.66	0	0	0	-
T20Is	2	1	1	9	9*	-	128.57	0	0	0	-
First-class	31	46	6	693	57*	17.32	60.36	0	2	4	-
List A	18	11	3	71	14	8.87	92.20	0	0	4	-
T20s	30	17	9	91	22*	11.37	113.75	0	0	9	-

Bowling	Mat	Balls	Runs	Wkts	BBI	BBM	Ave	Econ	SR	5w	10
ODIs	2	90	97	1	1/34	1/34	97.00	6.46	90.0	0	0
T20Is	2	41	66	0	-	-	-	9.65	-	0	0
First-class	31	3708	2413	69	5/87	7/148	34.97	3.90	53.7	1	0
List A	18	572	591	18	4/7	4/7	32.83	6.19	31.7	0	0
T20s	30	543	733	24	4/6	4/6	30.54	8.09	22.6	0	0

TOM SMITH

RHB / SLA / R0 / W0

GLOUCESTERSHIRE

FULL NAME: Thomas Michael John Smith
BORN: August 29, 1987, Eastbourne, Sussex
SQUAD NO: 6
HEIGHT: 5ft 9in
NICKNAME: Smudge
EDUCATION: Seaford Head Community College, East Sussex; Sussex Downs College
TEAMS: Gloucestershire, Middlesex, Surrey, Sussex
ROLE: Bowler
DEBUT: First-class: 2007; List A: 2006; T20: 2007

BEST BATTING: 84 Gloucestershire vs Leicestershire, Cheltenham, 2019
BEST BOWLING: 4-35 Gloucestershire vs Kent, Canterbury, 2014
COUNTY CAP: 2013 (Gloucestershire)

FIRST CRICKET CLUB? Eastbourne CC, East Sussex
MOST EXCITING DAY AS A CRICKETER? Beating Surrey in the One-Day Cup final at Lord's in 2015
CHILDHOOD SPORTING HERO? James Kirtley
BIGGEST INFLUENCE ON YOUR DEVELOPMENT AS A CRICKETER (EXCLUDING PARENTS)? I had some great coaches in my early years at Sussex but the most important for my career have been two Gloucestershire coaches: John Bracewell and Richard Dawson
WHAT WOULD YOU DO IF YOU WERE IN CHARGE OF COUNTY CRICKET? Remove the lbw law that says it's not out if it pitches outside leg (if it's hitting, you're out); develop a water-resistant ball (bowling spin with a wet ball is rubbish); establish a more effective procedure than dragging the boundary rope around the outfield to dry it in between rain breaks
FAVOURITE SMELL? Nail-polish remover
GUILTY PLEASURE? Cookie butter

Batting	Mat	Inns	NO	Runs	HS	Ave	SR	100	50	Ct	St
First-class	55	77	14	1422	84	22.57	37.38	0	4	17	-
List A	91	47	23	575	65	23.95	74.19	0	2	39	-
T20s	150	54	37	306	36*	18.00	113.33	0	0	47	-

Bowling	Mat	Balls	Runs	Wkts	BBI	BBM	Ave	Econ	SR	5w	10
First-class	55	7469	4171	82	4/35	6/155	50.86	3.35	91.0	0	0
List A	91	3499	3071	77	4/26	4/26	39.88	5.26	45.4	0	0
T20s	150	2844	3461	147	5/16	5/16	23.54	7.30	19.3	3	0

FULL NAME: Shane Snater
BORN: March 24, 1996, Harare, Zimbabwe
SQUAD NO: 29
EDUCATION: St John's College, Harare
TEAMS: Netherlands, Essex, Kent, Southern Rocks
ROLE: Bowler
DEBUT: ODI: 2018; T20I: 2018; First-class: 2016; List A: 2017; T20: 2018

ESSEX

BEST BATTING: 50* Netherlands vs Namibia, Dubai, 2017
BEST BOWLING: 7-98 Essex vs Nottinghamshire, Trent Bridge, 2021

TWITTER: @ShaneSnater
NOTES: Essex signed the Netherlands seamer following a successful trial period at the club in 2018. Snater played a handful of games during the club's successful T20 campaign in 2019 and again the following season. The 26-year-old signed a new two-year deal last December after a hugely impressive red-ball campaign in which he took 31 wickets at 16.48 after making his first-class debut for the club in April. Snater grew up in Harare and represented Zimbabwe U17 but holds a Dutch passport and made his ODI and T20I debut for Netherlands in 2018

Batting	Mat	Inns	NO	Runs	HS	Ave	SR	100	50	Ct	St
ODIs	2	2	0	12	12	6.00	85.71	0	0	3	-
T20Is	13	6	1	18	10	3.60	112.50	0	0	2	-
First-class	13	13	4	185	50*	20.55	57.27	0	1	2	-
List A	22	13	4	104	23*	11.55	82.53	0	0	11	-
T20s	28	13	6	61	16*	8.71	127.08	0	0	9	-

Bowling	Mat	Balls	Runs	Wkts	BBI	BBM	Ave	Econ	SR	5w	10
ODIs	2	71	63	1	1/41	1/41	63.00	5.32	71.0	0	0
T20Is	13	209	337	13	3/42	3/42	25.92	9.67	16.0	0	0
First-class	13	1725	929	51	7/98	8/94	18.21	3.23	33.8	5	0
List A	22	943	843	27	5/60	5/60	31.22	5.36	34.9	1	0
T20s	28	461	780	24	3/42	3/42	32.50	10.15	19.2	0	0

NATHAN SOWTER

RHB / LB / R0 / W0

MIDDLESEX

FULL NAME: Nathan Adam Sowter
BORN: October 12, 1992, Penrith, New South Wales, Australia
SQUAD NO: 72
HEIGHT: 5ft 11in
NICKNAME: Racing Snake
EDUCATION: Hills Sport High School, New South Wales
TEAMS: Middlesex
ROLE: Bowler
DEBUT: First-class: 2017; List A: 2016; T20: 2015

BEST BATTING: 57* Middlesex vs Glamorgan, Cardiff, 2019
BEST BOWLING: 3-42 Middlesex vs Lancashire, Old Trafford, 2019

WHO IS YOUR LOOKALIKE? Sid from Toy Story
FIRST CRICKET CLUB? Rooty Hill RSL CC – a small club not far from where I grew up in western Sydney
WHAT WOULD YOU CHANGE ABOUT THE STRUCTURE OF THE COUNTY SEASON? Ban red-ball cricket in April
MOST UNDERRATED PLAYER IN COUNTY CRICKET? Callum Parkinson
WHO WOULD YOU MOST AND LEAST LIKE TO HAVE A NET WITH? Most – Mike Gatting, to see if I could knock him over with a similar ball to Warnie's. Least – Ryan Higgins, because it would always end in an argument
MAKE ONE PREDICTION FOR THE FUTURE OF CRICKET: International T20 cricket will be no more
SURPRISING FACT ABOUT YOU? I'm a glazier by trade
GUILTY PLEASURE? Coca-Cola
TWITTER: @nsowter

Batting	Mat	Inns	NO	Runs	HS	Ave	SR	100	50	Ct	St
First-class	13	23	4	292	57*	15.36	65.47	0	2	12	-
List A	19	12	3	134	31	14.88	76.13	0	0	17	-
T20s	76	30	12	184	37*	10.22	114.99	0	0	26	-

Bowling	Mat	Balls	Runs	Wkts	BBI	BBM	Ave	Econ	SR	5w	10
First-class	13	1870	1032	20	3/42	4/100	51.60	3.31	93.5	0	0
List A	19	1008	928	36	6/62	6/62	25.77	5.52	28.0	1	0
T20s	76	1459	1937	73	4/23	4/23	26.53	7.96	19.9	0	0

MITCHELL STANLEY

RHB / RFM / R0 / W0

FULL NAME: Mitchell Terry Stanley
BORN: March 17, 2001, Telford, Shropshire
SQUAD NO: 38
HEIGHT: 6ft 4in
NICKNAME: Lurch
EDUCATION: Idsall School, Shifnal, Shropshire; Shrewsbury Sixth Form College
TEAMS: Worcestershire
ROLE: Bowler

FIRST CRICKET CLUB? Shifnal CC, Shropshire

WHAT WOULD YOU CHANGE ABOUT THE STRUCTURE OF THE COUNTY SEASON? Swap around the order of the competitions so that we have white-ball cricket first and then red-ball cricket played in the middle of the season on good wickets

BIGGEST INFLUENCE ON YOUR DEVELOPMENT AS A CRICKETER (EXCLUDING PARENTS)? Luke Sharples – he has coached me all the way from the beginning and always seems to know what will work for me and what won't work for me

WHO IS THE BEST BATTER/KEEPER/ALLROUNDER/BOWLER IN COUNTY CRICKET (EXCLUDING TEAMMATES)? Rob Yates/Ben Foakes/Tom Abell/Luke Fletcher

WHAT WOULD A FLY ON THE WALL HEAR IN YOUR DRESSING ROOM? Gareth Roderick waffling

HOBBIES? Tinkering with cars

IF YOU COULD TURN BACK TIME... I would try harder at school

WHO WOULD YOU MOST AND LEAST LIKE TO HAVE A NET WITH? Most – Brett Lee (my childhood sporting hero). I would just love to witness him bowling up close. Least – Chris Gayle, because I would be worried about the ball coming straight back at me at pace

WHAT DO YOU MOST ENJOY LISTENING TO? Hip-hop from the 1990s

CAMERON STEEL

RHB / LB / RO / WO

SURREY

FULL NAME: Cameron Tate Steel
BORN: September 13, 1995, Greenbrae, California, USA
SQUAD NO: 14
HEIGHT: 5ft 10in
NICKNAME: Moggy
EDUCATION: Millfield Prep School, Somerset; Scotch College, Perth, Australia; Durham University
TEAMS: Surrey, Durham, Hampshire
ROLE: Batter
DEBUT: First-class: 2014; List A: 2017; T20: 2017

BEST BATTING: 224 Durham vs Leicestershire, Leicester, 2017
BEST BOWLING: 2-7 Durham vs Glamorgan, Cardiff, 2018

WHO IS YOUR LOOKALIKE? Ryan Gosling
FIRST CRICKET CLUB? Glastonbury CC, Somerset
BIGGEST INFLUENCE ON YOUR DEVELOPMENT AS A CRICKETER (EXCLUDING PARENTS)?
David Beale, my first coach at school in Somerset. He convinced me to stop playing chess and start attending cricket practice
WHO IS THE BEST BATTER/KEEPER/ALLROUNDER/BOWLER IN COUNTY CRICKET (EXCLUDING TEAMMATES)? David Bedingham/Lewis McManus/Liam Dawson/Chris Rushworth
MOST UNDERRATED PLAYER IN COUNTY CRICKET? Graham Clark
HOBBIES? Running a silent disco business with my best mate
IF YOU COULD TURN BACK TIME... I'd stop whoever was messing with those bats
WHO WOULD YOU MOST AND LEAST LIKE TO HAVE A NET WITH? Most – Mark Wood. Because it's always a great laugh. Least – Mark Wood. Because it's also scary
MAKE ONE PREDICTION FOR THE FUTURE OF CRICKET: USA and China to play in the T20 World Cup
WHAT MAKES YOU WORRY? My front pad
TWITTER: @CameronSteel2

Batting	Mat	Inns	NO	Runs	HS	Ave	SR	100	50	Ct	St
First-class	43	76	2	2081	224	28.12	40.41	3	11	19	-
List A	16	13	2	186	77	16.90	65.49	0	1	5	-
T20s	6	6	0	93	37	15.50	125.67	0	0	2	-

Bowling	Mat	Balls	Runs	Wkts	BBI	BBM	Ave	Econ	SR	5w	10
First-class	43	1000	758	22	2/7	4/99	34.45	4.54	45.4	0	0
List A	16	300	267	10	4/33	4/33	26.70	5.34	30.0	0	0
T20s	6	48	88	2	2/60	2/60	44.00	11.00	24.0	0	0

SCOTT STEEL

RHB / OB / R0 / W0

FULL NAME: Scott Steel
BORN: April 20, 1999, Durham
SQUAD NO: 55
HEIGHT: 6ft
NICKNAME: Steely
EDUCATION: Belmont Community School, Durham, New College Durham
TEAMS: Leicestershire, Durham
ROLE: Batter
DEBUT: First-class: 2019; List A: 2019; T20: 2019

BEST BATTING: 39 Durham vs Middlesex, Lord's, 2019

FIRST CRICKET CLUB? Durham City CC
WHAT WOULD YOU CHANGE ABOUT THE STRUCTURE OF THE COUNTY SEASON? Set up a T10 competition
WHO IS THE BEST BATTER/KEEPER/ALLROUNDER/BOWLER IN COUNTY CRICKET (EXCLUDING TEAMMATES)? James Vince/Ben Foakes/Darren Stevens/Chris Rushworth
MOST UNDERRATED PLAYER IN COUNTY CRICKET? Joe Clarke
MOST BEAUTIFUL THING YOU HAVE EVER SEEN? Durham Cathedral
HOBBIES? Shopping
WHO WOULD YOU MOST LIKE TO HAVE A NET WITH? Glenn Maxwell
MAKE ONE PREDICTION FOR THE FUTURE OF CRICKET: There will be free hits for a no-ball in red-ball cricket
GUILTY PLEASURE? Takeaways
TWITTER: @scottsteel102

Batting	Mat	Inns	NO	Runs	HS	Ave	SR	100	50	Ct	St
First-class	2	4	0	48	39	12.00	71.64	0	0	1	-
List A	8	7	0	227	68	32.42	80.78	0	2	3	-
T20s	33	29	1	713	70	25.46	121.25	0	4	2	-

Bowling	Mat	Balls	Runs	Wkts	BBI	BBM	Ave	Econ	SR	5w	10
First-class	2	42	16	0	-	-	-	2.28	-	0	0
List A	8	54	53	1	1/38	1/38	53.00	5.88	54.0	0	0
T20s	33	392	441	16	3/20	3/20	27.56	6.75	24.5	0	0

MARK STEKETEE

RHB / RFM / R0 / W0

FULL NAME: Mark Thomas Steketee
BORN: January 17, 1994, Warwick, Queensland, Australia
SQUAD NO: TBC
TEAMS: Essex, Australia U19, Brisbane Heat, Queensland
ROLE: Bowler
DEBUT: First-class: 2015; List A: 2014; T20: 2014

BEST BATTING: 53 Queensland vs New South Wales, Sydney, 2017
BEST BOWLING: 7-44 Queensland vs South Australia, Adelaide, 2021

NOTES: The 28-year-old Queenslander has been signed by Essex for the first six matches of the County Championship and will complement a seam attack led by Jamie Porter and Sam Cook. Steketee earned a call-up to Australia's Test squad for the recent tour of Pakistan after some impressive displays for his state side in the Sheffield Shield. As of March 11 he was the tournament's leading wicket-taker with 32 wickets at less than 18 apiece, including a career-best 7-44 against New South Wales last October. A mainstay of the Queensland bowling attack for several years, in all Steketee has taken 165 wickets in 47 matches for his state. "I've always wanted to get over to England to play some county cricket," he said. "I've got big shoes to fill, as I know how much Peter Siddle enjoyed playing here and the energy he brought to the team"

Batting	Mat	Inns	NO	Runs	HS	Ave	SR	100	50	Ct	St
First-class	52	70	14	822	53	14.67	55.57	0	2	20	-
List A	37	26	11	294	30*	19.60	96.07	0	0	9	-
T20s	61	31	9	169	33	7.68	101.19	0	0	20	-

Bowling	Mat	Balls	Runs	Wkts	BBI	BBM	Ave	Econ	SR	5w	10
First-class	52	9760	4773	185	7/44	10/92	25.80	2.93	52.7	4	1
List A	37	1732	1531	54	4/25	4/25	28.35	5.30	32.0	0	0
T20s	61	1286	1909	78	4/33	4/33	24.47	8.90	16.4	0	0

DARREN STEVENS   RHB / RM / R3 / W4 / MVP5

FULL NAME: Darren Ian Stevens
BORN: April 30, 1976, Leicester
SQUAD NO: 3
HEIGHT: 5ft 11in
NICKNAME: Stevo
EDUCATION: John Cleveland College,
Hinckley; Charles Keene College, Leicester
TEAMS: Kent, Comilla Victorians, Derbyshire,
Dhaka Gladiators, Leicestershire, Mid West
Rhinos, Otago
ROLE: Allrounder
DEBUT: First-class: 1997; List A: 1997; T20: 2003

BEST BATTING: 237 Kent vs Yorkshire, Headingley, 2019
BEST BOWLING: 8-75 Kent vs Leicestershire, Canterbury, 2017
COUNTY CAP: 2002 (Leicestershire); 2005 (Kent); BENEFIT: 2016 (Kent)

FIRST CRICKET CLUB? Swallows Green CC, Hinckley, Leicestershire
MOST EXCITING DAY AS A CRICKETER? T20 Finals Day in 2007 at Edgbaston
CHILDHOOD SPORTING HERO? Michael Jordan
BIGGEST INFLUENCE ON YOUR DEVELOPMENT AS A CRICKETER (EXCLUDING PARENTS)?
My former teammate-turned-coach Neil Burns
WHAT WOULD YOU DO IF YOU WERE IN CHARGE OF COUNTY CRICKET? Make the County
Championship one division, bring back 40-over cricket, scrap the pink ball
FAVOURITE SMELL? A log fire
SURPRISING FACT ABOUT YOU? I am colour blind with browns, reds and greens. I struggled
when I was with Otago in New Zealand because there were no sightscreens!
TWITTER: @Stevo208

Batting	Mat	Inns	NO	Runs	HS	Ave	SR	100	50	Ct	St
First-class	320	500	33	16360	237	35.03		37	81	204	-
List A	321	294	31	7692	147	29.24		7	46	129	-
T20s	225	201	43	4154	90	26.29	136.64	0	17	66	-

Bowling	Mat	Balls	Runs	Wkts	BBI	BBM	Ave	Econ	SR	5w	10
First-class	320	30683	14197	585	8/75		24.26	2.77	52.4	31	2
List A	321	6605	5287	162	6/25	6/25	32.63	4.80	40.7	3	0
T20s	225	2440	3256	125	4/14	4/14	26.04	8.00	19.5	0	0

GRANT STEWART

RHB / RFM / RO / WO

KENT

FULL NAME: Grant Stewart
BORN: February 19, 1994, Kalgoorlie,
Western Australia, Australia
SQUAD NO: 9
HEIGHT: 6ft 3in
NICKNAME: Stewie
EDUCATION: All Saints College, New South
Wales; University of Newcastle, NSW
TEAMS: Italy, Kent
ROLE: Allrounder
DEBUT: T20I: 2021; First-class: 2017; List A:
2018; T20: 2018

BEST BATTING: 103 Kent vs Middlesex, Canterbury, 2018
BEST BOWLING: 6-22 Kent vs Middlesex, Canterbury, 2018

MOST EXCITING DAY AS A CRICKETER? My first-class debut for Kent against Glamorgan at
Canterbury in 2017
CHILDHOOD SPORTING HERO? Steve Waugh
BIGGEST INFLUENCE ON YOUR DEVELOPMENT AS A CRICKETER (EXCLUDING PARENTS)?
My older brothers
SURPRISING FACT ABOUT YOU? I was a wicketkeeper until I was 16
TWITTER: @GStewart195

Batting	Mat	Inns	NO	Runs	HS	Ave	SR	100	50	Ct	St
T20Is	6	5	0	113	51	22.60	139.50	0	1	1	-
First-class	27	41	6	805	103	23.00	62.45	1	4	3	-
List A	12	9	1	104	44	13.00	58.75	0	0	2	-
T20s	31	25	8	234	51	13.76	118.18	0	1	6	-

Bowling	Mat	Balls	Runs	Wkts	BBI	BBM	Ave	Econ	SR	5w	10
T20Is	6	132	110	5	2/17	2/17	22.00	5.00	26.4	0	0
First-class	27	3217	1791	61	6/22	8/58	29.36	3.34	52.7	2	0
List A	12	451	362	11	3/17	3/17	32.90	4.81	41.0	0	0
T20s	31	566	778	23	3/33	3/33	33.82	8.24	24.6	0	0

BEN STOKES

LHB / RFM / RO / WO

FULL NAME: Benjamin Andrew Stokes
BORN: June 4, 1991, Christchurch, New Zealand
SQUAD NO: 38
HEIGHT: 6ft 2in
NICKNAME: Stoker
EDUCATION: Cockermouth School, Cumbria
TEAMS: England, Durham, Melbourne Renegades, Rajasthan Royals, Rising Pune Supergiant
ROLE: Allrounder
DEBUT: Test: 2013; ODI: 2011; T20I: 2011; First-class: 2010; List A: 2009; T20: 2010

DURHAM

BEST BATTING: 258 England vs South Africa, Cape Town, 2016
BEST BOWLING: 7-67 Durham vs Sussex, Chester-le-Street, 2014

FIRST CRICKET CLUB? Cockermouth CC, Cumbria
CHILDHOOD SPORTING HERO? Herschelle Gibbs
SURPRISING FACT ABOUT YOU? My father played one Test match for New Zealand in rugby league. I was a right-handed batsman when I was younger
TWITTER: @benstokes38

Batting	Mat	Inns	NO	Runs	HS	Ave	SR	100	50	Ct	St
Tests	76	140	5	4867	258	36.05	57.07	10	26	84	-
ODIs	101	86	15	2871	102*	40.43	95.35	3	21	47	-
T20Is	34	28	6	442	47*	20.09	136.84	0	0	15	-
First-class	154	263	13	8690	258	34.76		18	45	126	-
List A	172	150	24	4772	164	37.87	97.34	7	28	78	-
T20s	148	135	20	2865	107*	24.91	135.07	2	9	65	-

Bowling	Mat	Balls	Runs	Wkts	BBI	BBM	Ave	Econ	SR	5w	10
Tests	76	9656	5401	167	6/22	8/161	32.34	3.35	57.8	4	0
ODIs	101	3062	3078	74	5/61	5/61	41.59	6.03	41.3	1	0
T20Is	34	490	717	19	3/26	3/26	37.73	8.77	25.7	0	0
First-class	154	17675	10226	344	7/67	10/121	29.72	3.47	51.3	7	1
List A	172	4737	4565	138	5/61	5/61	33.07	5.78	34.3	1	0
T20s	148	1879	2669	86	4/16	4/16	31.03	8.52	21.8	0	0

OLLY STONE

RHB / RF / RO / WO

WARWICKSHIRE

FULL NAME: Oliver Peter Stone
BORN: October 9, 1993, Norwich
SQUAD NO: 6
HEIGHT: 6ft 2in
NICKNAME: Stoney
EDUCATION: Thorpe St Andrew High School, Norwich; Moulton College, Northamptonshire
TEAMS: England, Warwickshire, Northamptonshire
ROLE: Bowler
DEBUT: Test: 2019; ODI: 2018; First-class: 2012; List A: 2012; T20: 2011

BEST BATTING: 60 Northamptonshire vs Kent, Northampton, 2016
BEST BOWLING: 8-80 Warwickshire vs Sussex, Edgbaston, 2018
COUNTY CAP: 2020 (Warwickshire)

FIRST CRICKET CLUB? Vauxhall Mallards CC, Norfolk. Home of the ducks
BEST INNINGS YOU'VE SEEN? David Willey's 27-ball 60 for my former county Northants in the 2013 final of the T20 Blast
WHAT WOULD YOU DO IF YOU WERE IN CHARGE OF COUNTY CRICKET? Allow bowlers to put their feet up after a spell
SURPRISING FACT ABOUT YOU? My great-grandad created the Twix chocolate bar
TWITTER: @ollystone2

Batting	Mat	Inns	NO	Runs	HS	Ave	SR	100	50	Ct	St
Tests	3	6	0	55	20	9.16	38.19	0	0	1	-
ODIs	4	1	1	9	9*	-	128.57	0	0	0	-
First-class	44	58	12	708	60	15.39	46.18	0	1	17	-
List A	30	14	9	122	24*	24.40	70.93	0	0	13	-
T20s	51	16	9	66	22*	9.42	110.00	0	0	14	-

Bowling	Mat	Balls	Runs	Wkts	BBI	BBM	Ave	Econ	SR	5w	10
Tests	3	358	194	10	3/29	4/68	19.40	3.25	35.8	0	0
ODIs	4	96	97	1	1/23	1/23	97.00	6.06	96.0	0	0
First-class	44	6731	3717	150	8/80	11/96	24.78	3.31	44.8	6	1
List A	30	1125	1023	24	4/71	4/71	42.62	5.45	46.8	0	0
T20s	51	948	1405	48	3/22	3/22	29.27	8.89	19.7	0	0

MARK STONEMAN

LHB / OB / R5 / W0

FULL NAME: Mark Daniel Stoneman
BORN: June 26, 1987, Newcastle
SQUAD NO: 11
HEIGHT: 5ft 10in
NICKNAME: Rocky
EDUCATION: Whickham Comprehensive School, Newcastle Upon Tyne
TEAMS: England, Middlesex, Durham, Surrey, Yorkshire
ROLE: Batter
DEBUT: Test: 2017; First-class: 2007; List A: 2008; T20: 2010

BEST BATTING: 197 Surrey vs Sussex, Guildford, 2017

COUNTY CAP: 2018 (Surrey)

WHO IS YOUR LOOKALIKE? Tom Hardy (actor)
FIRST CRICKET CLUB? Burnopfield CC, Newcastle upon Tyne
FAMILY TIES? My grandfather played and umpired locally for many years and my dad played all over the north-east as a local pro
WHAT WOULD YOU CHANGE ABOUT THE STRUCTURE OF THE COUNTY SEASON? Avoid having it changed every season
WHO IS THE BEST BATTER/KEEPER/ALLROUNDER/BOWLER IN COUNTY CRICKET (EXCLUDING TEAMMATES)? Jamie Smith/Ben Foakes/Ed Barnard/Matt Milnes
HOBBIES? Fly fishing
WHO WOULD YOU MOST LIKE TO HAVE A NET WITH? Muttiah Muralitharan – could I pick him?
WHAT MAKES YOU WORRY? Emotionally unstable world leaders
SURPRISING FACT ABOUT YOU? The Lion King makes me cry
TWITTER: @mark23stone

Batting	Mat	Inns	NO	Runs	HS	Ave	SR	100	50	Ct	St
Tests	11	20	1	526	60	27.68	44.27	0	5	1	-
First-class	208	361	8	12113	197	34.31	57.03	26	62	91	-
List A	91	86	7	3092	144*	39.13	91.10	7	18	28	-
T20s	77	71	4	1342	89*	20.02	117.10	0	8	30	-

Bowling	Mat	Balls	Runs	Wkts	BBI	BBM	Ave	Econ	SR	5w	10
Tests	11	-	-	-	-	-	-	-	-	-	-
First-class	208	234	178	0	-	-	-	4.56	-	0	0
List A	91	4	8	1	1/8	1/8	8.00	12.00	4.0	0	0
T20s	77	-	-	-	-	-	-	-	-	-	-

HARRY SWINDELLS

RHB / WK / R0 / W0

FULL NAME: Harry John Swindells
BORN: February 21, 1999, Leicester
SQUAD NO: 28
HEIGHT: 5ft 8in
NICKNAME: Dumbo
EDUCATION: Brockington College,
Leicestershire; Lutterworth College;
Loughborough College
TEAMS: Leicestershire, England U19
ROLE: Wicketkeeper/batter
DEBUT: First-class: 2019; List A: 2018; T20: 2018

BEST BATTING: 171* Leicestershire vs Somerset, Taunton, 2021

FIRST CRICKET CLUB? Narborough & Littlethorpe CC, Leicestershire
CHILDHOOD SPORTING HERO? AB de Villiers
BIGGEST INFLUENCE ON YOUR DEVELOPMENT AS A CRICKETER (EXCLUDING PARENTS)?
Mick Whitmore and Daz Hill – my first coaches in club cricket
WHAT WOULD YOU DO IF YOU WERE IN CHARGE OF COUNTY CRICKET? Increase the
number of four-day games in the middle of the summer
FAVOURITE SMELL? A roast dinner
GUILTY PLEASURE? Ben and Jerry's ice cream
TWITTER: @harryswindells1

Batting	Mat	Inns	NO	Runs	HS	Ave	SR	100	50	Ct	St
First-class	25	36	5	1049	171*	33.83	49.11	2	4	50	2
List A	10	8	1	222	75	31.71	81.61	0	2	10	2
T20s	23	20	2	376	63	20.88	112.57	0	3	6	-

Bowling	Mat	Balls	Runs	Wkts	BBI	BBM	Ave	Econ	SR	5w	10
First-class	25	-	-	-	-	-	-	-	-	-	-
List A	10	-	-	-	-	-	-	-	-	-	-
T20s	23	-	-	-	-	-	-	-	-	-	-

JONATHAN TATTERSALL

RHB / WK / R0 / W0

FULL NAME: Jonathan Andrew Tattersall
BORN: December 15, 1994, Harrogate, Yorkshire
SQUAD NO: 12
HEIGHT: 5ft 8in
NICKNAME: Tatts
EDUCATION: King James's School, Knaresborough
TEAMS: Yorkshire, England U19, Gloucestershire, Surrey
ROLE: Wicketkeeper/batter
DEBUT: First-class: 2018; List A: 2013; T20: 2018

BEST BATTING: 135* Yorkshire vs Leeds/Bradford MCCU, Weetwood, 2019

MOST EXCITING DAY AS A CRICKETER? Beating Surrey at Scarborough in the penultimate over of the 2019 Championship match
CHILDHOOD SPORTING HERO? Michael Vaughan
BIGGEST INFLUENCE ON YOUR DEVELOPMENT AS A CRICKETER (EXCLUDING PARENTS)? Two people: Tim Boon who helped my batting while I was with England U19, and Yorkshire Academy coach Richard Damms who helped me understand the game better
FAVOURITE SMELL? Freshly cut grass – then you know it's the cricket season
GUILTY PLEASURE? Sour sweets
TWITTER: @JonnyTatts

Batting	Mat	Inns	NO	Runs	HS	Ave	SR	100	50	Ct	St
First-class	35	54	6	1540	135*	32.08	40.88	1	10	87	4
List A	24	18	3	528	89	35.20	103.52	0	6	21	3
T20s	35	25	8	382	53*	22.47	124.42	0	1	23	6
Bowling	Mat	Balls	Runs	Wkts	BBI	BBM	Ave	Econ	SR	5w	10
First-class	35	-	-	-	-	-	-	-	-	-	-
List A	24	-	-	-	-	-	-	-	-	-	-
T20s	35	-	-	-	-	-	-	-	-	-	-

GLAMORGAN

CALLUM TAYLOR

RHB / OB / R0 / W0

FULL NAME: Callum Zinzan Taylor
BORN: June 19, 1998, Newport, Monmouthshire
SQUAD NO: 4
HEIGHT: 6ft
EDUCATION: The Southport School, Queensland, Australia
TEAMS: Glamorgan
ROLE: Allrounder
DEBUT: First-class: 2020; List A: 2021; T20: 2019

BEST BATTING: 106 Glamorgan vs Northamptonshire, Northampton, 2020
BEST BOWLING: 2-16 Glamorgan vs Yorkshire, Headingley, 2021

FIRST CRICKET CLUB? Surfers Paradise CC, Queensland, Australia
MOST EXCITING DAY AS A CRICKETER? Scoring a hundred on my first-class debut at Northampton in 2020
CHILDHOOD SPORTING HERO? Michael Clarke
WHAT WOULD YOU DO IF YOU WERE IN CHARGE OF COUNTY CRICKET? Create a knockout competition like the FA Cup to be played in Abu Dhabi and Dubai in the winter
FAVOURITE SMELL? Lavender
GUILTY PLEASURE? Waffles
TWITTER: @CallumZTaylor

Batting	Mat	Inns	NO	Runs	HS	Ave	SR	100	50	Ct	St
First-class	8	12	2	368	106	36.80	47.17	1	2	2	-
List A	3	3	0	53	36	17.66	82.81	0	0	0	-
T20s	16	15	4	138	23	12.54	90.19	0	0	5	-

Bowling	Mat	Balls	Runs	Wkts	BBI	BBM	Ave	Econ	SR	5w	10
First-class	8	1034	565	7	2/16	2/78	80.71	3.27	147.7	0	0
List A	3	108	91	3	1/6	1/6	30.33	5.05	36.0	0	0
T20s	16	66	86	5	2/9	2/9	17.20	7.81	13.2	0	0

RHB / OB / RO / WO

FULL NAME: Jack Martin Robert Taylor
BORN: November 12, 1991, Banbury, Oxfordshire
SQUAD NO: 10
HEIGHT: 6ft
NICKNAME: JT
EDUCATION: Chipping Norton School, Oxfordshire
TEAMS: Gloucestershire
ROLE: Batter
DEBUT: First-class: 2010; List A: 2011; T20: 2011

GLOUCESTERSHIRE

BEST BATTING: 156 Gloucestershire vs Northamptonshire, Cheltenham, 2015
BEST BOWLING: 4-16 Gloucestershire vs Glamorgan, Bristol, 2016
COUNTY CAP: 2010

FIRST CRICKET CLUB? Great & Little Tew CC, Oxfordshire
MOST EXCITING DAY AS A CRICKETER? Beating Surrey in the One-Day Cup final at Lord's in 2015
BIGGEST INFLUENCE ON YOUR DEVELOPMENT AS A CRICKETER (EXCLUDING PARENTS)? John Bracewell, my former coach at Gloucestershire. He gave me an opportunity and supported me through my issues with my bowling action
WHAT WOULD YOU DO IF YOU WERE IN CHARGE OF COUNTY CRICKET? Organise a knockout one-day competition which includes the National Counties
GUILTY PLEASURE? Getting into bed at 7pm
TWITTER: @jacktaylor141

Batting	Mat	Inns	NO	Runs	HS	Ave	SR	100	50	Ct	St
First-class	82	127	9	3433	156	29.09	61.27	7	9	41	-
List A	59	48	10	1357	75	35.71	112.52	0	12	25	-
T20s	103	83	22	1288	80	21.11	138.79	0	2	34	-

Bowling	Mat	Balls	Runs	Wkts	BBI	BBM	Ave	Econ	SR	5w	10
First-class	82	5716	3345	75	4/16	5/140	44.60	3.51	76.2	0	0
List A	59	1205	1049	29	4/38	4/38	36.17	5.22	41.5	0	0
T20s	103	634	862	26	4/16	4/16	33.15	8.15	24.3	0	0

JAMES TAYLOR

RHB / RFM / R0 / W0

SURREY

FULL NAME: James Philip Arthur Taylor
BORN: January 19, 2001, Stoke-on-Trent, Staffordshire
SQUAD NO: 25
HEIGHT: 6ft 3in
NICKNAME: JT
EDUCATION: Trentham High School, Stoke-on-Trent; Newcastle-under-Lyme College, Staffordshire
TEAMS: Surrey, Derbyshire, England U19
ROLE: Bowler
DEBUT: First-class: 2017; List A: 2019; T20: 2020

BEST BATTING: 22 Surrey vs Essex, Chelmsford, 2020
BEST BOWLING: 3-26 Derbyshire vs Leeds/Bradford MCCU, Derby, 2019

FIRST CRICKET CLUB? Barlaston CC, Staffordshire. Always stay on the front foot because the wicket is slow and low at Barlaston
WHAT WOULD YOU CHANGE ABOUT THE STRUCTURE OF THE COUNTY SEASON? Begin the season abroad
WHO IS THE BEST BATTER/KEEPER/ALLROUNDER/BOWLER IN COUNTY CRICKET (EXCLUDING TEAMMATES)? Dan Mousley/Ben Cox/Tom Taylor/Chris Rushworth
HOBBIES? Golf
WHO WOULD YOU MOST AND LEAST LIKE TO HAVE A NET WITH? Most – James Anderson (to learn from him). Least – Mitchell Johnson (danger alert)
WHAT GIVES YOU JOY? Walking my dog
GUILTY PLEASURE? Dairy Milk Oreo
TWITTER: @_Jamestaylor19

Batting	Mat	Inns	NO	Runs	HS	Ave	SR	100	50	Ct	St
First-class	6	8	3	64	22	12.80	25.91	0	0	1	-
List A	2	2	2	6	6*	-	100.00	0	0	1	-
T20s	2	1	0	3	3	3.00	50.00	0	0	0	-

Bowling	Mat	Balls	Runs	Wkts	BBI	BBM	Ave	Econ	SR	5w	10
First-class	6	607	366	13	3/26	6/74	28.15	3.61	46.6	0	0
List A	2	78	93	3	2/66	2/66	31.00	7.15	26.0	0	0
T20s	2	12	34	1	1/6	1/6	34.00	17.00	12.0	0	0

MATT TAYLOR

RHB / LMF / R0 / W1

FULL NAME: Matthew David Taylor
BORN: July 8, 1994, Banbury, Oxfordshire
SQUAD NO: 36
HEIGHT: 6ft 2in
NICKNAME: Bomber
EDUCATION: Chipping Norton Secondary School, Oxfordshire
TEAMS: Gloucestershire
ROLE: Bowler
DEBUT: First-class: 2013; List A: 2011; T20: 2015

BEST BATTING: 56 Gloucestershire vs Somerset, Taunton, 2021
BEST BOWLING: 5-15 Gloucestershire vs Cardiff MCCU, Bristol, 2018
COUNTY CAP: 2013

FIRST CRICKET CLUB? Great & Little Tew CC, Oxfordshire
FAMILY TIES? My older brother Jack also plays for Gloucestershire. My dad and grandad both played Minor Counties for Oxfordshire
CHILDHOOD SPORTING HERO? Darren Gough
BIGGEST INFLUENCE ON YOUR DEVELOPMENT AS A CRICKETER (EXCLUDING PARENTS)? Rupert Evans – he first selected me to play Minor Counties for Oxfordshire when I was very young
GUILTY PLEASURE? Pizza
TWITTER: @matt_taylor94

Batting	Mat	Inns	NO	Runs	HS	Ave	SR	100	50	Ct	St
First-class	66	86	33	723	56	13.64	38.89	0	1	7	-
List A	35	12	7	105	51*	21.00	84.00	0	1	5	-
T20s	42	12	7	34	9*	6.80	77.27	0	0	8	-

Bowling	Mat	Balls	Runs	Wkts	BBI	BBM	Ave	Econ	SR	5w	10
First-class	66	10312	5882	180	5/15	9/59	32.67	3.42	57.2	6	0
List A	35	1551	1405	27	3/39	3/39	52.03	5.43	57.4	0	0
T20s	42	755	1118	36	3/16	3/16	31.05	8.88	20.9	0	0

NORTHAMPTONSHIRE

FULL NAME: Thomas Alexander Ian Taylor
BORN: December 21, 1994, Stoke-on-Trent, Staffordshire
SQUAD NO: 12
HEIGHT: 6ft 3in
NICKNAME: TT
EDUCATION: Trentham High School, Stoke-on-Trent; Newcastle-under-Lyme College; Leeds Metropolitan University
TEAMS: Northamptonshire, Derbyshire, Leicestershire
ROLE: Allrounder
DEBUT: First-class: 2014; List A 2014; T20: 2020

BEST BATTING: 80 Derbyshire vs Kent, Derby, 2016
BEST BOWLING: 6-47 Leicestershire vs Sussex, Hove, 2019

FIRST CRICKET CLUB? Barlaston CC, Stoke-on-Trent, Staffordshire
FAMILY TIES? My father, cousins and uncles all play cricket; other family members used to run my home club. My brother James used to play for Derbyshire and now plays for Surrey
WHAT WOULD YOU CHANGE ABOUT THE STRUCTURE OF THE COUNTY SEASON?
Have a three-division County Championship
WHO IS THE BEST BATTER/KEEPER/ALLROUNDER/BOWLER IN COUNTY CRICKET (EXCLUDING TEAMMATES)? Joe Clarke/Ben Foakes/Darren Stevens/Simon Harmer
MOST UNDERRATED PLAYER IN COUNTY CRICKET? Callum Parkinson
MOST BEAUTIFUL THING YOU HAVE EVER SEEN? Sunset in Mexico
HOBBIES? Badminton
WHAT MAKES YOU WORRY? Being late
GUILTY PLEASURE? Harry Potter
TWITTER: @TomTaylor43

Batting	Mat	Inns	NO	Runs	HS	Ave	SR	100	50	Ct	St
First-class	44	66	10	1137	80	20.30	45.28	0	5	14	-
List A	19	11	4	387	98*	55.28	105.16	0	4	8	-
T20s	19	15	3	173	50*	14.41	121.83	0	1	9	-

Bowling	Mat	Balls	Runs	Wkts	BBI	BBM	Ave	Econ	SR	5w	10
First-class	44	6822	3867	125	6/47	10/122	30.93	3.40	54.5	4	1
List A	19	848	840	22	3/24	3/24	38.18	5.94	38.5	0	0
T20s	19	302	479	15	3/33	3/33	31.93	9.51	20.1	0	0

JORDAN THOMPSON   LHB / RMF / R0 / W0 / MVP10

FULL NAME: Jordan Aaron Thompson
BORN: October 9, 1996, Leeds
SQUAD NO: 44
HEIGHT: 6ft 1in
NICKNAME: Lizard
EDUCATION: Benton Park School, Leeds
TEAMS: Yorkshire, Karachi Kings, Hobart Hurricanes
ROLE: Allrounder
DEBUT: First-class: 2019; List A: 2019; T20: 2018

YORKSHIRE

BEST BATTING: 98 Yorkshire vs Nottinghamshire, Trent Bridge, 2020
BEST BOWLING: 5-31 Yorkshire vs Leicestershire, Headingley, 2020

WHO IS YOUR LOOKALIKE? Jim Levenstein (lead character in American Pie)
FIRST CRICKET CLUB? Guiseley CC, West Yorkshire
BIGGEST INFLUENCE ON YOUR DEVELOPMENT AS A CRICKETER (EXCLUDING PARENTS)?
All my Academy coaches at Yorkshire – over the last 10 years they've helped me develop to the level of the first-team squad
WHO IS THE BEST BATTER/KEEPER/ALLROUNDER/BOWLER IN COUNTY CRICKET (EXCLUDING TEAMMATES)? Hashim Amla/Ben Foakes/Darren Stevens/Ollie Robinson
MOST BEAUTIFUL THING YOU HAVE EVER SEEN? Leeds United being promoted back to the Premier League
HOBBIES? Golf
WHO WOULD YOU MOST AND LEAST LIKE TO HAVE A NET WITH? Most – Andrew Flintoff (my hero as a kid). Least – Morné Morkel
SURPRISING FACT ABOUT YOU? I am a Type 1 diabetic
GUILTY PLEASURE? A McDonald's on the journey back after an away win
TWITTER: @Tommo455

Batting	Mat	Inns	NO	Runs	HS	Ave	SR	100	50	Ct	St
First-class	20	29	1	681	98	24.32	53.36	0	3	6	-
List A	1	-	-	-	-	-	-	-	-	0	-
T20s	54	41	11	505	74	16.83	165.03	0	3	18	-

Bowling	Mat	Balls	Runs	Wkts	BBI	BBM	Ave	Econ	SR	5w	10
First-class	20	2843	1300	66	5/31	7/53	19.69	2.74	43.0	2	0
List A	1	30	43	0	-	-	-	8.60	-	0	0
T20s	54	732	1129	43	4/44	4/44	26.25	9.25	17.0	0	0

ALEX THOMSON   RHB / OB / R0 / W0

FULL NAME: Alexander Thomas Thomson
BORN: October 30, 1993, Stoke-on-Trent, Staffordshire
SQUAD NO: 15
HEIGHT: 6ft 5in
NICKNAME: Sarge
EDUCATION: Denstone College, Uttoxeter, Staffordshire; Cardiff Metropolitan University
TEAMS: Derbyshire, Warwickshire
ROLE: Allrounder
DEBUT: First-class: 2014; List A: 2018; T20: 2018

BEST BATTING: 46 Warwickshire vs Northamptonshire, Edgbaston, 2020
BEST BOWLING: 6-138 Cardiff MCCU vs Hampshire, Southampton, 2017

FIRST CRICKET CLUB? Leek CC, Staffordshire
WHAT WOULD YOU CHANGE ABOUT THE STRUCTURE OF THE COUNTY SEASON? Reshuffle the groups for the T20 Blast
BIGGEST INFLUENCE ON YOUR DEVELOPMENT AS A CRICKETER (EXCLUDING PARENTS)? Former wicketkeeper/batter Tony Frost, now Warwickshire's batting coach. He gives you all the time in the world and only wants the best for you
WHO IS THE BEST BATTER/KEEPER/ALLROUNDER/BOWLER IN COUNTY CRICKET (EXCLUDING TEAMMATES)? Joe Root/Ben Foakes/Liam Dawson/Simon Harmer
MOST UNDERRATED PLAYER IN COUNTY CRICKET? Will Rhodes
WHAT WOULD A FLY ON THE WALL HEAR IN YOUR DRESSING ROOM? Nothing – it'd be squashed in a flash
HOBBIES? Angling
WHO WOULD YOU LEAST LIKE TO HAVE A NET WITH? An angry Tony Frost on the slinger
WHAT MAKES YOU WORRY? Leaving my dogs for too long
TWITTER: @tommo1039

Batting	Mat	Inns	NO	Runs	HS	Ave	SR	100	50	Ct	St
First-class	18	24	0	381	46	15.87	40.44	0	0	6	-
List A	15	11	2	301	68*	33.44	89.85	0	2	3	-
T20s	19	10	4	88	28	14.66	141.93	0	0	5	-

Bowling	Mat	Balls	Runs	Wkts	BBI	BBM	Ave	Econ	SR	5w	10
First-class	18	1581	957	27	6/138	7/176	35.44	3.63	58.5	1	0
List A	15	618	555	18	3/27	3/27	30.83	5.38	34.3	0	0
T20s	19	306	416	14	4/35	4/35	29.71	8.15	21.8	0	0

CHARLIE THURSTON   RHB / RM / RO / WO

FULL NAME: Charlie Oliver Thurston
BORN: August 17, 1996, Cambridge
SQUAD NO: 96
HEIGHT: 6ft
NICKNAME: Chazza
EDUCATION: Bedford School; Loughborough University
TEAMS: Northamptonshire
ROLE: Batter
DEBUT: First-class: 2016; List A: 2018; T20: 2018

BEST BATTING: 126 Loughborough MCCU vs Northamptonshire, Northampton, 2017

WHO IS YOUR LOOKALIKE? Ryan Gosling (actor)
FIRST CRICKET CLUB? Shenley Village CC, Hertfordshire. I can just about remember meeting Brian Lara when West Indies and Pakistan once played a warm-up there
WHO IS THE BEST BATTER/KEEPER/ALLROUNDER/BOWLER IN COUNTY CRICKET (EXCLUDING TEAMMATES)? Jake Libby/James Bracey/Darren Stevens/Luke Fletcher
MOST UNDERRATED PLAYER IN COUNTY CRICKET? Sam Cook
MOST BEAUTIFUL THING YOU HAVE EVER SEEN? Martinborough Vineyard, New Zealand
IF YOU COULD TURN BACK TIME... I'd change Frank Lampard's disallowed goal against Germany in the 2010 World Cup
WHO WOULD YOU MOST AND LEAST LIKE TO HAVE A NET WITH? Most – Ricky Ponting. Least – Muttiah Muralitharan
WHAT DO YOU MOST ENJOY LISTENING TO? That Peter Crouch Podcast
GUILTY PLEASURE? Listening to Stephen A Smith and Skip Bayless debating US sports
TWITTER: @ThurstonCharlie

Batting	Mat	Inns	NO	Runs	HS	Ave	SR	100	50	Ct	St
First-class	19	28	0	735	126	26.25	59.75	2	2	7	-
List A	8	6	1	153	53	30.60	84.06	0	1	3	-
T20s	12	9	0	109	41	12.11	99.09	0	0	6	-

Bowling	Mat	Balls	Runs	Wkts	BBI	BBM	Ave	Econ	SR	5w	10
First-class	19	18	16	0	-	-	-	5.33	-	0	0
List A	8	-	-	-	-	-	-	-	-	-	-
T20s	12	-	-	-	-	-	-	-	-	-	-

JOSH TONGUE   RHB / RFM / R0 / W0

WORCESTERSHIRE

FULL NAME: Joshua Charles Tongue
BORN: November 15, 1997, Redditch, Worcestershire
SQUAD NO: 24
HEIGHT: 6ft 4in
NICKNAME: Tonguey
EDUCATION: King's School, Worcester; Christopher Whitehead Language College, Worcester
TEAMS: Worcestershire, England U19
ROLE: Bowler
DEBUT: First-class: 2016; List A: 2017; T20: 2017

BEST BATTING: 41 Worcestershire vs Glamorgan, Worcester, 2017
BEST BOWLING: 6-97 Worcestershire vs Glamorgan, Worcester, 2017

WHO IS YOUR LOOKALIKE? Mickey Mouse
FIRST CRICKET CLUB? Redditch CC, Worcestershire
BIGGEST INFLUENCE ON YOUR DEVELOPMENT AS A CRICKETER (EXCLUDING PARENTS)?
Former Worcestershire allrounder Gavin Haynes – he was my first coach at the club's Academy and he's happy to help out even now
WHO IS THE BEST BATTER/BOWLER IN COUNTY CRICKET (EXCLUDING TEAMMATES)?
Joe Clarke/Luke Fletcher
WHAT MAKES YOU WORRY? Leaving the front door unlocked
GUILTY PLEASURE? A bar of Galaxy from the freezer
TWITTER: @JoshTongue

Batting	Mat	Inns	NO	Runs	HS	Ave	SR	100	50	Ct	St
First-class	39	52	10	459	41	10.92	44.78	0	0	4	-
List A	13	7	3	76	34	19.00	95.00	0	0	2	-
T20s	7	2	2	3	2*	-	150.00	0	0	3	-

Bowling	Mat	Balls	Runs	Wkts	BBI	BBM	Ave	Econ	SR	5w	10
First-class	39	6203	3395	138	6/97	9/98	24.60	3.28	44.9	6	0
List A	13	529	600	14	2/35	2/35	42.85	6.80	37.7	0	0
T20s	7	114	163	4	2/32	2/32	40.75	8.57	28.5	0	0

REECE TOPLEY

RHB / LFM / R0 / W0

FULL NAME: Reece James William Topley
BORN: February 21, 1994, Ipswich
SQUAD NO: 24
HEIGHT: 6ft 7in
NICKNAME: Toppers
EDUCATION: Royal Hospital School, Suffolk
TEAMS: England, Surrey, Essex, Hampshire, Melbourne Renegades, Sussex
ROLE: Bowler
DEBUT: ODI: 2015; T20I: 2015; First-class: 2011; List A: 2011; T20: 2012

BEST BATTING: 16 Hampshire vs Yorkshire, Southampton, 2017
BEST BOWLING: 6-29 Essex vs Worcestershire, Chelmsford, 2013
COUNTY CAP: 2013 (Essex)

FAMILY TIES? My father Don played for Essex and Surrey and also coached Zimbabwe. My uncle Peter played for Kent
MOST EXCITING DAY AS A CRICKETER? Taking 4-50 for England in an ODI against South Africa in Port Elizabeth
CHILDHOOD SPORTING HERO? Kobe Bryant
BIGGEST INFLUENCE ON YOUR DEVELOPMENT AS A CRICKETER (EXCLUDING PARENTS)? Chris Silverwood, my bowling coach when I was at Essex
SURPRISING FACT ABOUT YOU? I speak Spanish
TWITTER: @reece_topley
NOTES: Topley signed a white-ball contract with Surrey in October 2019 but last year agreed a new deal with the club to play across all formats

Batting	Mat	Inns	NO	Runs	HS	Ave	SR	100	50	Ct	St
ODIs	13	6	5	8	6	8.00	19.51	0	0	4	-
T20Is	10	3	3	3	2*	-	75.00	0	0	1	-
First-class	43	52	22	131	16	4.36	20.69	0	0	8	-
List A	58	18	12	55	19	9.16	48.24	0	0	15	-
T20s	104	22	17	57	14*	11.40	82.60	0	0	20	-

Bowling	Mat	Balls	Runs	Wkts	BBI	BBM	Ave	Econ	SR	5w	10
ODIs	13	621	557	20	4/50	4/50	27.85	5.38	31.0	0	0
T20Is	10	199	285	8	3/24	3/24	35.62	8.59	24.8	0	0
First-class	43	7298	4098	154	6/29	11/85	26.61	3.36	47.3	8	2
List A	58	2716	2513	97	4/16	4/16	25.90	5.55	28.0	0	0
T20s	104	2121	2904	131	4/20	4/20	22.16	8.21	16.1	0	0

LIAM TREVASKIS

RHB / SLA / RO / WO

DURHAM

FULL NAME: Liam Trevaskis
BORN: April 18, 1999, Carlisle, Cumberland
SQUAD NO: 80
HEIGHT: 5ft 10in
NICKNAME: T-rev
EDUCATION: Queen Elizabeth Grammar School, Penrith, Cumbria
TEAMS: Durham, England U19
ROLE: Bowler
DEBUT: First-class: 2017; List A: 2019; T20: 2017

BEST BATTING: 77* Durham vs Northamptonshire, Northampton, 2021
BEST BOWLING: 5-78 Durham vs Gloucestershire, Bristol, 2021

FIRST CRICKET CLUB? Penrith CC, Cumbria
WHAT WOULD YOU CHANGE ABOUT THE STRUCTURE OF THE COUNTY SEASON?
No Championship cricket in the middle of the T20 block
BIGGEST INFLUENCE ON YOUR DEVELOPMENT AS A CRICKETER (EXCLUDING PARENTS)?
My brother – no one has thrown more balls at me
WHO IS THE BEST BATTER/KEEPER/ALLROUNDER/BOWLER IN COUNTY CRICKET
(EXCLUDING TEAMMATES)? Joe Clarke/Ben Foakes/Darren Stevens/Simon Harmer
MOST UNDERRATED PLAYER IN COUNTY CRICKET? Sam Cook
WHO WOULD YOU MOST AND LEAST LIKE TO HAVE A NET WITH? Most – Shane Warne.
Least – Curtly Ambrose
MAKE ONE PREDICTION FOR THE FUTURE OF CRICKET: More people will bowl with both arms
TWITTER: @LiamTrevaskis

Batting	Mat	Inns	NO	Runs	HS	Ave	SR	100	50	Ct	St
First-class	14	23	3	541	77*	27.05	40.37	0	4	4	-
List A	17	11	2	95	23	10.55	89.62	0	0	3	-
T20s	41	27	11	229	31*	14.31	119.27	0	0	24	-

Bowling	Mat	Balls	Runs	Wkts	BBI	BBM	Ave	Econ	SR	5w	10
First-class	14	1543	712	16	5/78	6/101	44.50	2.76	96.4	1	0
List A	17	708	588	14	3/38	3/38	42.00	4.98	50.5	0	0
T20s	41	739	902	34	4/16	4/16	26.52	7.32	21.7	0	0

MUJEEB UR RAHMAN RHB / OB

FULL NAME: Mujeeb Ur Rahman
BORN: March 28, 2001, Khost, Afghanistan
SQUAD NO: 88
TEAMS: Afghanistan, Middlesex, Boost
Defenders, Brisbane Heat, Comilla Victorians,
Fortune Barisal, Hampshire, Jamaica
Tallawahs, Kings XI Punjab, Nangarhar
Leopards, Peshawar Zalmi, Sunrisers
ROLE: Bowler
DEBUT: Test: 2018; ODI: 2017; T20I: 2018;
First-class: 2018; List A: 2017; T20: 2017

MIDDLESEX

BEST BATTING: 27 Brisbane Heat vs Adelaide Strikers, Brisbane, 2018 (T20)
BEST BOWLING: 5-15 Brisbane Heat vs Hobart Hurricanes, 2020 (T20)

TWITTER: @MujeebR99
NOTES: The Afghan mystery spinner returns for his fourth T20 Blast campaign with
Middlesex after taking 10 wickets for the county in 2021 at the healthy economy rate of
6.91 runs per over. The 21-year-old previously played for Hampshire in 2018 and has
also impressed in the IPL and Big Bash League for Kings XI Punjab and Brisbane Heat
respectively. An off-spinner with a leg-break and googly in his locker, Mujeeb burst onto the
scene at the 2018 U19 World Cup and has since been a regular at senior level. In February
2018 he became the youngest player to take an ODI five-wicket haul and later that year
played in Afghanistan's inaugural Test match – to date his only first-class appearance

Batting	Mat	Inns	NO	Runs	HS	Ave	SR	100	50	Ct	St
Tests	1	2	0	18	15	9.00	105.88	0	0	0	-
ODIs	49	25	12	96	18*	7.38	76.80	0	0	8	-
T20Is	23	5	4	12	8*	12.00	92.30	0	0	5	-
First-class	1	2	0	18	15	9.00	105.88	0	0	0	-
List A	56	27	14	100	18*	7.69	78.74	0	0	9	-
T20s	173	56	26	212	27	7.06	99.06	0	0	36	-

Bowling	Mat	Balls	Runs	Wkts	BBI	BBM	Ave	Econ	SR	5w	10
Tests	1	90	75	1	1/75	1/75	75.00	5.00	90.0	0	0
ODIs	49	2661	1761	78	5/50	5/50	22.57	3.97	34.1	1	0
T20Is	23	522	532	32	5/20	5/20	16.62	6.11	16.3	1	0
First-class	1	90	75	1	1/75	1/75	75.00	5.00	90.0	0	0
List A	56	3045	2008	86	5/50	5/50	23.34	3.95	35.4	1	0
T20s	173	3934	4360	190	5/15	5/15	22.94	6.64	20.7	2	0

GRAEME VAN BUUREN

RHB / SLA / RO / WO

GLOUCESTERSHIRE

FULL NAME: Graeme Lourens van Buuren
BORN: August 22, 1990, Pretoria, South Africa
SQUAD NO: 12
HEIGHT: 5ft 7in
NICKNAME: GV
EDUCATION: Pretoria Boys High School, South Africa
TEAMS: Gloucestershire, Northerns, Titans, South Africa U19
ROLE: Allrounder
DEBUT: First-class: 2010; List A: 2010; T20: 2011

BEST BATTING: 235 Northerns vs Eastern Province, Centurion, 2015
BEST BOWLING: 4-12 Northerns vs South Western Districts, Oudtshoorn, 2013
COUNTY CAP: 2016

FIRST CRICKET CLUB? Tuks CC, Pretoria, South Africa
MOST EXCITING DAY AS A CRICKETER? Winning promotion with Gloucestershire in 2019
CHILDHOOD SPORTING HERO? AB de Villiers
WHAT WOULD YOU DO IF YOU WERE IN CHARGE OF COUNTY CRICKET? Keep with this year's Championship structure, look at staging tournaments in Dubai
GUILTY PLEASURE? Biltong
TWITTER: @GraemeGVB

Batting	Mat	Inns	NO	Runs	HS	Ave	SR	100	50	Ct	St
First-class	96	149	23	5309	235	42.13	61.68	11	34	52	-
List A	78	70	14	1656	119*	29.57	81.33	1	8	20	-
T20s	71	51	17	780	64	22.94	120.93	0	4	29	-

Bowling	Mat	Balls	Runs	Wkts	BBI	BBM	Ave	Econ	SR	5w	10
First-class	96	6303	2991	95	4/12	6/87	31.48	2.84	66.3	0	0
List A	78	2610	2063	63	5/35	5/35	32.74	4.74	41.4	1	0
T20s	71	1003	1169	47	5/8	5/8	24.87	6.99	21.3	1	0

TIMM VAN DER GUGTEN   RHB / RFM / R0 / W1

FULL NAME: Timm van der Gugten
BORN: February 25, 1991, Sydney, Australia
SQUAD NO: 64
HEIGHT: 6ft 2in
NICKNAME: Vander, Sock
EDUCATION: St Pius X College, Sydney;
Swinburne University, Melbourne
TEAMS: Netherlands, Glamorgan, Hobart
Hurricanes, New South Wales, Northern
Districts, Tasmania
ROLE: Bowler
DEBUT: ODI: 2012; T20I: 2012; First-class: 2011;
List A: 2011; T20: 2012

BEST BATTING: 85* Glamorgan vs Yorkshire, Headingley, 2021
BEST BOWLING: 7-42 Glamorgan vs Kent, Cardiff, 2018
COUNTY CAP: 2018

WHO IS YOUR LOOKALIKE? Ellen DeGeneres (actress/writer)
FIRST CRICKET CLUB? Normanhurst-Warrawee CC, New South Wales, Australia
WHO IS THE BEST BATTER/KEEPER/ALLROUNDER/BOWLER IN COUNTY CRICKET
(EXCLUDING TEAMMATES)? Sam Robson/Ben Cox/Darren Stevens/Sam Cook
MOST UNDERRATED PLAYER IN COUNTY CRICKET? Jake Libby
HOBBIES? Sudoku
IF YOU COULD TURN BACK TIME... I would have travelled to the UK earlier in my life
MAKE ONE PREDICTION FOR THE FUTURE OF CRICKET: USA will break into the top 10 teams
in the world within the next decade
WHAT DO YOU MOST ENJOY LISTENING TO? Country
WHAT MAKES YOU WORRY? Darren Stevens on a green seamer
GUILTY PLEASURE? Disney films

Batting	Mat	Inns	NO	Runs	HS	Ave	SR	100	50	Ct	St
ODIs	8	4	0	54	49	13.50	80.59	0	0	0	-
T20Is	40	11	4	109	40*	15.57	134.56	0	0	9	-
First-class	58	82	23	944	85*	16.00	49.68	0	4	16	-
List A	62	35	12	400	49	17.39	90.70	0	0	8	-
T20s	109	41	17	294	40*	12.25	125.10	0	0	28	-

Bowling	Mat	Balls	Runs	Wkts	BBI	BBM	Ave	Econ	SR	5w	10
ODIs	8	324	195	12	5/24	5/24	16.25	3.61	27.0	1	0
T20Is	40	731	879	41	3/9	3/9	21.43	7.21	17.8	0	0
First-class	58	9886	5289	192	7/42	10/121	27.54	3.20	51.4	10	1
List A	62	2764	2491	72	5/24	5/24	34.59	5.40	38.3	1	0
T20s	109	1978	2665	123	5/21	5/21	21.66	8.08	16.0	1	0

ROELOF VAN DER MERWE RHB / SLA / RO / WO

FULL NAME: Roelof Erasmus van der Merwe
BORN: December 31, 1984, Johannesburg, SA
SQUAD NO: 52
HEIGHT: 5ft 8in
NICKNAME: Bulldog
EDUCATION: Pretoria High School, South Africa; University of Hertfordshire
TEAMS: Netherlands, South Africa, Somerset, Brisbane Heat, Delhi Daredevils, Northerns, RC Bangalore, Titans, Tshwane Spartans
ROLE: Allrounder
DEBUT: ODIs: 2009; T20I: 2009; First-class: 2006; List A: 2006; T20: 2008

BEST BATTING: 205* Titans vs Warriors, Benoni, 2014
BEST BOWLING: 4-22 Somerset vs Middlesex, Taunton, 2017
COUNTY CAP: 2018

FIRST CRICKET CLUB? Pretoria CC, South Africa
BIGGEST INFLUENCE ON YOUR DEVELOPMENT AS A CRICKETER (EXCLUDING PARENTS)?
Jonty Rhodes – as a kid I would watch him play for South Africa and replicate everything he did in our backyard cricket games
WHO IS THE BEST BATTER/KEEPER/ALLROUNDER/BOWLER IN COUNTY CRICKET (EXCLUDING TEAMMATES)? Joe Denly/Adam Rossington/Darren Stevens/James Anderson
MOST UNDERRATED PLAYER IN COUNTY CRICKET? Chris Dent
WHO WOULD YOU MOST LIKE TO HAVE A NET WITH? Ben Green, because he's my bunny
MAKE ONE PREDICTION FOR THE FUTURE OF CRICKET: Bowlers hitting 170kmph
WHAT MAKES YOU WORRY? The pitches in April
TWITTER: @Roela52

Batting	Mat	Inns	NO	Runs	HS	Ave	SR	100	50	Ct	St
ODIs	16	8	3	96	57	19.20	101.05	0	1	6	-
T20Is	46	32	12	460	75*	23.00	130.31	0	2	20	-
First-class	77	122	16	3483	205*	32.85	70.01	6	21	61	-
List A	188	152	44	2901	165*	26.86	98.94	1	11	81	-
T20s	259	189	66	2699	89*	21.94	131.72	0	10	106	-

Bowling	Mat	Balls	Runs	Wkts	BBI	BBM	Ave	Econ	SR	5w	10
ODIs	16	825	685	19	3/27	3/27	36.05	4.98	43.4	0	0
T20Is	46	931	995	54	4/35	4/35	18.42	6.41	17.2	0	0
First-class	77	9752	4768	142	4/22	8/104	33.57	2.93	68.6	0	0
List A	188	8227	6681	250	5/26	5/26	26.72	4.87	32.9	4	0
T20s	259	5044	6050	242	5/32	5/32	25.00	7.19	20.8	1	0

PAUL VAN MEEKEREN

RHB / RFM / R0 / W0

FULL NAME: Paul Adriaan van Meekeren
BORN: January 15, 1993, Amsterdam, Netherlands
SQUAD NO: TBC
HEIGHT: 6ft 4in
NICKNAME: Meerkat, Smacky, Meeks
TEAMS: Netherlands, Gloucestershire, Durham, Somerset, St Kitts & Nevis Patriots
ROLE: Bowler
DEBUT: ODI: 2013; T20I: 2013; First-class: 2013; List A: 2013; T20: 2013

BEST BATTING: 34 Netherlands vs Papua New Guinea, Amstelveen, 2015
BEST BOWLING: 4-60 Somerset vs Essex, Chelmsford, 2017

WHO IS YOUR LOOKALIKE? Marv from Home Alone
FIRST CRICKET CLUB? Rood & Wit CC, Haarlem, Netherlands
WHAT WOULD YOU CHANGE ABOUT THE STRUCTURE OF THE COUNTY SEASON? Go to a franchise system
WHO IS THE BEST BATTER/KEEPER/ALLROUNDER/BOWLER IN COUNTY CRICKET (EXCLUDING TEAMMATES)? Joe Root/Steven Davies/Darren Stevens/Simon Harmer
MOST UNDERRATED PLAYER IN COUNTY CRICKET? Graham Clark
MOST BEAUTIFUL THING YOU HAVE EVER SEEN? Amsterdam
HOBBIES? I'm passionate about finding the best coffee, pizza and hamburger joints in the area
IF YOU COULD TURN BACK TIME... I love where I am today so wouldn't risk going back in time
TWITTER: @paulvanmeekeren

Batting	Mat	Inns	NO	Runs	HS	Ave	SR	100	50	Ct	St
ODIs	7	5	4	36	15*	36.00	67.92	0	0	1	-
T20Is	46	12	2	44	18	4.40	93.61	0	0	15	-
First-class	8	14	3	106	34	9.63	34.98	0	0	2	-
List A	56	31	16	129	15*	8.60	58.10	0	0	17	-
T20s	72	23	7	77	18	4.81	91.66	0	0	24	-

Bowling	Mat	Balls	Runs	Wkts	BBI	BBM	Ave	Econ	SR	5w	10
ODIs	7	294	218	7	2/28	2/28	31.14	4.44	42.0	0	0
T20Is	46	901	1081	48	4/11	4/11	22.52	7.19	18.7	0	0
First-class	8	1346	785	21	4/60	5/75	37.38	3.49	64.0	0	0
List A	56	2097	1700	63	3/21	3/21	26.98	4.86	33.2	0	0
T20s	72	1371	1772	65	4/11	4/11	27.26	7.75	21.0	0	0

RICARDO VASCONCELOS   LHB / WK / R0 / W0 / MVP21

FULL NAME: Ricardo Surrador Vasconcelos
BORN: October 27, 1997, Johannesburg, South Africa
SQUAD NO: 27
HEIGHT: 5ft 5in
NICKNAME: Vasco
EDUCATION: St Stithians College, Johannesburg; Stellenbosch University, Western Cape
TEAMS: Northamptonshire, Boland, South Africa U19
ROLE: Batter/wicketkeeper
DEBUT: First-class: 2016; List A: 2016; T20: 2017

BEST BATTING: 185* Northamptonshire vs Glamorgan, Northampton, 2021

COUNTY CAP: 2021

WHO IS YOUR LOOKALIKE? Gabriel Iglesias (comedian)
FIRST CRICKET CLUB? Old Edwardians CC, Johannesburg
WHAT WOULD YOU CHANGE ABOUT THE STRUCTURE OF THE COUNTY SEASON? Play each competition in one block
BIGGEST INFLUENCE ON YOUR DEVELOPMENT AS A CRICKETER (EXCLUDING PARENTS)? Bongani Ndaba – my coach since I was 12
WHO IS THE BEST BATTER/KEEPER/ALLROUNDER/BOWLER IN COUNTY CRICKET (EXCLUDING TEAMMATES)? David Bedingham/Ben Cox/Darren Stevens/Ollie Robinson
MOST UNDERRATED PLAYER IN COUNTY CRICKET? Ollie Robinson (Kent)
HOBBIES? Fishing
WHO WOULD YOU MOST LIKE TO HAVE A NET WITH? Kumar Sangakkara
WHAT DO YOU MOST ENJOY LISTENING TO? That Peter Crouch Podcast
WHAT GIVES YOU JOY? Doing absolutely nothing
TWITTER: @RicardoVasco27

Batting	Mat	Inns	NO	Runs	HS	Ave	SR	100	50	Ct	St
First-class	52	93	7	3124	185*	36.32	56.80	7	15	89	6
List A	34	33	2	931	112	30.03	81.02	1	6	27	3
T20s	25	24	4	557	78*	27.85	117.75	0	2	13	2
Bowling	Mat	Balls	Runs	Wkts	BBI	BBM	Ave	Econ	SR	5w	10
First-class	52	9	9	0	-	-	-	6.00	-	0	0
List A	34	-	-	-	-	-	-	-	-	-	-
T20s	25	-	-	-	-	-	-	-	-	-	-

DANE VILAS

RHB / WK / R1 / W0

FULL NAME: Dane James Vilas
BORN: June 10, 1985, Johannesburg, SA
SQUAD NO: 33
HEIGHT: 6ft
NICKNAME: Vili
EDUCATION: King Edward VII School, Johannesburg
TEAMS: South Africa, Lancashire, Dolphins, Gauteng, Lahore Qalandars, Lions, Western Province
ROLE: Batter/wicketkeeper
DEBUT: Test: 2015; T20I: 2012; First-class: 2006; List A: 2006; T20: 2009

BEST BATTING: 266 Lancashire vs Glamorgan, Colwyn Bay, 2019

COUNTY CAP: 2018

FIRST CRICKET CLUB? Old Edwardians CC, Johannesburg
WHO IS THE BEST BATTER/KEEPER/BOWLER IN COUNTY CRICKET (EXCLUDING TEAMMATES)? James Vince/Ben Cox/Darren Stevens
WHAT WOULD A FLY ON THE WALL HEAR IN YOUR DRESSING ROOM? Tall stories
WHO WOULD YOU MOST LIKE TO HAVE A NET WITH? AB de Villiers
MAKE ONE PREDICTION FOR THE FUTURE OF CRICKET: Batters and bowlers using both hands/arms
WHAT MAKES YOU WORRY? Time away from my kids
TWITTER: @DaneVilas

Batting	Mat	Inns	NO	Runs	HS	Ave	SR	100	50	Ct	St
Tests	6	9	0	94	26	10.44	44.76	0	0	13	-
T20Is	1	-	-	-	-	-	-	-	-	0	-
First-class	176	264	30	9703	266	41.46	65.82	22	44	454	20
List A	173	158	25	4919	166	36.98	98.89	9	24	174	30
T20s	193	163	39	3512	75*	28.32	126.83	0	13	105	30

Bowling	Mat	Balls	Runs	Wkts	BBI	BBM	Ave	Econ	SR	5w	10
Tests	6	-	-	-	-	-	-	-	-	-	-
T20Is	1	-	-	-	-	-	-	-	-	-	-
First-class	176	12	9	0	-	-	-	4.50	-	0	0
List A	173	-	-	-	-	-	-	-	-	-	-
T20s	193	-	-	-	-	-	-	-	-	-	-

JAMES VINCE

RHB / RM / R2 / W0 / MVP28

HAMPSHIRE

FULL NAME: James Michael Vince
BORN: March 14, 1991, Cuckfield, Sussex
SQUAD NO: 14
HEIGHT: 6ft 2in
NICKNAME: JV
EDUCATION: Warminster School, Wiltshire
TEAMS: England, Hampshire, Auckland, Karachi Kings, Multan Sultans, Paarl Rocks, Quetta Gladiators, Sydney Sixers, Sydney Thunder
ROLE: Batter
DEBUT: Test: 2016; ODI: 2015; T20I: 2015; First-class: 2009; List A: 2009; T20: 2010

BEST BATTING: 240 Hampshire vs Essex, Southampton, 2014
BEST BOWLING: 5-41 Hampshire vs Loughborough MCCU, Southampton, 2013
COUNTY CAP: 2013

FIRST CRICKET CLUB? Erlestoke CC, Wiltshire
CHILDHOOD SPORTING HERO? Alan Shearer
WHAT WOULD YOU DO IF YOU WERE IN CHARGE OF COUNTY CRICKET? Play each format in a set block, don't punish clubs who prepare result pitches, reduce ticket prices
FAVOURITE SMELL? A Sunday roast
TWITTER: @vincey14

Batting	Mat	Inns	NO	Runs	HS	Ave	SR	100	50	Ct	St
Tests	13	22	0	548	83	24.90	49.81	0	3	8	-
ODIs	19	16	0	480	102	30.00	93.93	1	2	7	-
T20Is	17	17	0	463	59	27.23	128.25	0	2	7	-
First-class	175	289	20	10508	240	39.06	61.92	26	40	150	-
List A	142	132	7	5063	190	40.50	98.19	10	24	54	-
T20s	287	278	26	7525	107*	29.86	133.04	2	45	144	-

Bowling	Mat	Balls	Runs	Wkts	BBI	BBM	Ave	Econ	SR	5w	10
Tests	13	24	13	0	-	-	-	3.25	-	0	0
ODIs	19	42	38	1	1/18	1/18	38.00	5.42	42.0	0	0
T20Is	17	-	-	-	-	-	-	-	-	-	-
First-class	175	1747	1116	23	5/41	6/56	48.52	3.83	75.9	1	0
List A	142	174	162	3	1/18	1/18	54.00	5.58	58.0	0	0
T20s	287	78	87	3	1/5	1/5	29.00	6.69	26.0	0	0

FULL NAME: Guramar Singh Virdi
BORN: July 19, 1998, Chiswick, London
SQUAD NO: 19
HEIGHT: 5ft 10in
NICKNAME: Virds
EDUCATION: Guru Nanak Sikh Academy,
Hayes, London
TEAMS: Surrey, England Lions
ROLE: Bowler
DEBUT: First-class: 2017

SURREY

BEST BATTING: 47 Surrey vs Northamptonshire, Northampton, 2021
BEST BOWLING: 8-61 Surrey vs Nottinghamshire, Trent Bridge, 2019

WHO IS YOUR LOOKALIKE? Simba from The Lion King
FIRST CRICKET CLUB? Indian Gymkhana CC, London. It's the oldest South Asian cricket club in the UK
WHAT WOULD YOU CHANGE ABOUT THE STRUCTURE OF THE COUNTY SEASON? Play more red-ball games in the middle of the summer
BIGGEST CRICKETING REGRET? Dropping a catch in a club cricket final
WHO IS THE BEST BATTER/KEEPER/BOWLER IN COUNTY CRICKET (EXCLUDING TEAMMATES)? Dan Lawrence/Adam Wheater/Simon Harmer
MOST UNDERRATED PLAYER IN COUNTY CRICKET? Max Holden
MOST BEAUTIFUL THING YOU HAVE EVER SEEN? Cape Town
HOBBIES? Table-tennis
WHO WOULD YOU MOST LIKE TO HAVE A NET WITH? Kumar Sangakkara or my childhood sporting hero Saqlain Mushtaq
MAKE ONE PREDICTION FOR THE FUTURE OF CRICKET: A revival of Test cricket
WHAT GIVES YOU JOY? Sunshine
TWITTER: @amarsinghvirdi

Batting	Mat	Inns	NO	Runs	HS	Ave	SR	100	50	Ct	St
First-class	39	48	24	210	47	8.75	42.42	0	0	7	-

Bowling	Mat	Balls	Runs	Wkts	BBI	BBM	Ave	Econ	SR	5w	10
First-class	39	6541	3517	119	8/61	14/139	29.55	3.22	54.9	5	1

MATTHEW WAITE — RHB / RMF / R0 / W0

YORKSHIRE

FULL NAME: Matthew James Waite
BORN: December 24, 1995, Leeds
SQUAD NO: 6
NICKNAME: Pingu
EDUCATION: Brigshaw High School, West Yorkshire
TEAMS: Yorkshire
ROLE: Allrounder
DEBUT: First-class: 2017; List A: 2014; T20: 2015

BEST BATTING: 42 Yorkshire vs Nottinghamshire, Trent Bridge, 2018
BEST BOWLING: 5-16 Yorkshire vs Leeds/Bradford MCCU, Weetwood, 2019

TWITTER: @mat_waite
NOTES: A seam-bowling allrounder, Waite signed a junior professional contract with Yorkshire at the end of 2015 but is yet to have an extended run in the first team. He made his Championship debut against Somerset at Taunton in 2017 but his career has been hampered by a recurring ankle injury. He impressed in 2018 with eight wickets at an average of 27.62 in a handful of four-day matches but was rooted in the Second XI the following summer. In 2020 he was ruled out for the season just a day before Yorkshire's red-ball campaign got underway. But the club showed faith by offering him a two-year contract in October 2020. Last summer he played white-ball cricket only, taking 21 wickets across both shorter formats

Batting	Mat	Inns	NO	Runs	HS	Ave	SR	100	50	Ct	St
First-class	8	11	1	160	42	16.00	52.45	0	0	1	-
List A	22	16	4	437	71	36.41	98.42	0	1	0	-
T20s	17	9	5	52	19*	13.00	120.93	0	0	3	-

Bowling	Mat	Balls	Runs	Wkts	BBI	BBM	Ave	Econ	SR	5w	10
First-class	8	966	583	23	5/16	6/57	25.34	3.62	42.0	1	0
List A	22	792	842	28	5/59	5/59	30.07	6.37	28.2	1	0
T20s	17	231	345	11	2/17	2/17	31.36	8.96	21.0	0	0

THILAN WALALLAWITA
LHB / SLA / R0 / W0

FULL NAME: Thilan Nipuna Walallawita
BORN: June 23, 1998, Colombo, Sri Lanka
SQUAD NO: 32
HEIGHT: 5ft 11in
NICKNAME: Thils
EDUCATION: Mount Grace School, Potters Bar; Hertfordshire University
TEAMS: Middlesex
ROLE: Bowler
DEBUT: First-class: 2020; List A: 2021; T20: 2020

MIDDLESEX

BEST BATTING: 20* Middlesex vs Derbyshire, Lord's, 2021
BEST BOWLING: 3-28 Middlesex vs Hampshire, Radlett, 2020

FIRST CRICKET CLUB? Potters Bar CC, Hertfordshire
WHAT WOULD YOU CHANGE ABOUT THE STRUCTURE OF THE COUNTY SEASON? Play four-day cricket in June and July
BIGGEST INFLUENCE ON YOUR DEVELOPMENT AS A CRICKETER (EXCLUDING PARENTS)?
All my mates – they've been keeping me on my toes through thick and thin
MOST UNDERRATED PLAYER IN COUNTY CRICKET? Tom Haines
WHAT WOULD A FLY ON THE WALL HEAR IN YOUR DRESSING ROOM? Stories about our social lives
MOST BEAUTIFUL THING YOU HAVE EVER SEEN? My missus
HOBBIES? Swimming
WHO WOULD YOU MOST LIKE TO HAVE A NET WITH? Kumar Sangakkara (my hero)
MAKE ONE PREDICTION FOR THE FUTURE OF CRICKET: A 100-ball World Cup
TWITTER: @walallawita

Batting	Mat	Inns	NO	Runs	HS	Ave	SR	100	50	Ct	St
First-class	9	12	5	76	20*	10.85	69.09	0	0	2	-
List A	6	5	0	69	29	13.80	140.81	0	0	1	-
T20s	1	1	0	0	0	0.00	0.00	0	0	0	-

Bowling	Mat	Balls	Runs	Wkts	BBI	BBM	Ave	Econ	SR	5w	10
First-class	9	1144	571	9	3/28	4/51	63.44	2.99	127.1	0	0
List A	6	330	287	4	2/54	2/54	71.75	5.21	82.5	0	0
T20s	1	24	19	3	3/19	3/19	6.33	4.75	8.0	0	0

ROMAN WALKER — RHB / RFM / R0 / W0

FULL NAME: Roman Isaac Walker
BORN: August 6, 2000, Wrexham, Clwyd, Wales
SQUAD NO: TBC
HEIGHT: 6ft 3in
NICKNAME: Stroller
EDUCATION: Ysgol Bryn Alyn, Wrexham
TEAMS: Leicestershire, England U19, Glamorgan
ROLE: Bowler
DEBUT: List A: 2019; T20: 2019

WHO IS YOUR LOOKALIKE? Mitchell Marsh
FIRST CRICKET CLUB? Bersham CC, Wrexham
WHAT WOULD YOU CHANGE ABOUT THE STRUCTURE OF THE COUNTY SEASON? Play more Championship cricket in the middle of the summer
WHO IS THE BEST BATTER/KEEPER/ALLROUNDER/BOWLER IN COUNTY CRICKET (EXCLUDING TEAMMATES)? David Bedingham/Chris Cooke/Darren Stevens/Darren Stevens
MOST UNDERRATED PLAYER IN COUNTY CRICKET? Joe Clarke
MOST BEAUTIFUL THING YOU HAVE EVER SEEN? Lake Wakatipu, Queenstown, New Zealand
IF YOU COULD TURN BACK TIME... I'd stop KP from sending that message...
WHO WOULD YOU MOST AND LEAST LIKE TO HAVE A NET WITH? Most – Kevin Pietersen. I adore the way he batted and would love to learn a few things from him. Least – Mitchell Jonson. I'd like to keep my rib cage intact
MAKE ONE PREDICTION FOR THE FUTURE OF CRICKET: T10 replaces the 50-over format
WHAT DO YOU MOST ENJOY LISTENING TO? The Ricky Gervais podcast
WHAT GIVES YOU JOY? Spending time with people while doing an activity
TWITTER: @RomanWalker17

Batting	Mat	Inns	NO	Runs	HS	Ave	SR	100	50	Ct	St
List A	2	2	2	22	15*	-	88.00	0	0	1	-
T20s	9	4	1	3	2	1.00	33.33	0	0	1	-

Bowling	Mat	Balls	Runs	Wkts	BBI	BBM	Ave	Econ	SR	5w	10
List A	2	80	74	1	1/53	1/53	74.00	5.55	80.0	0	0
T20s	9	179	247	13	3/15	3/15	19.00	8.27	13.7	0	0

MAX WALLER RHB / LB

FULL NAME: Maximilian Thomas Charles Waller
BORN: March 3, 1988, Salisbury, Wiltshire
SQUAD NO: 10
HEIGHT: 6ft
NICKNAME: Goose
EDUCATION: Millfield School, Somerset; Bournemouth University
TEAMS: Somerset
ROLE: Bowler
DEBUT: First-class: 2009; List A: 2009; T20: 2009

SOMERSET

BEST BATTING: 17 Somerset vs Gloucestershire, Bristol, 2017 (T20)
BEST BOWLING: 4-16 Somerset vs Warwickshire, Taunton, 2012 (T20)
COUNTY CAP: 2021

WHO IS YOUR LOOKALIKE? Brendan Cole (Strictly Come Dancing) and Bastian Schweinsteiger (ex-footballer)
FIRST CRICKET CLUB? Bashley Rydal CC, New Forest, Hampshire
BIGGEST INFLUENCE ON YOUR DEVELOPMENT AS A CRICKETER (EXCLUDING PARENTS)? Terry Jenner, the former Australia Test cricketer and spin-bowling coach. I loved working with him on my bowling. Also Justin Langer – he gave me an opportunity and backed me, which is just what you need as a young player
BIGGEST CRICKETING REGRET? Not yet winning a T20 final for Somerset
WHO IS THE BEST BATTER/KEEPER/ALLROUNDER/BOWLER IN COUNTY CRICKET (EXCLUDING TEAMMATES)? Hashim Amla/Ben Foakes/Craig Overton/Simon Harmer
MOST UNDERRATED PLAYER IN COUNTY CRICKET? Jake Libby
WHO WOULD YOU MOST LIKE TO HAVE A NET WITH? Shane Warne
TWITTER: @MaxTCWaller
NOTES: Waller signed a two-year contract to play T20 cricket in October 2020

Batting	Mat	Inns	NO	Runs	HS	Ave	SR	100	50	Ct	St
First-class	9	10	1	91	28	10.11	42.32	0	0	5	-
List A	58	22	15	109	25*	15.57	70.77	0	0	32	-
T20s	143	36	21	106	17	7.06	77.94	0	0	86	-

Bowling	Mat	Balls	Runs	Wkts	BBI	BBM	Ave	Econ	SR	5w	10
First-class	9	840	493	10	3/33	3/57	49.30	3.52	84.0	0	0
List A	58	1801	1696	45	3/37	3/37	37.68	5.65	40.0	0	0
T20s	143	2756	3383	137	4/16	4/16	24.69	7.36	20.1	0	0

PAUL WALTER
LHB / LMF / R0 / W0

ESSEX

FULL NAME: Paul Ian Walter
BORN: May 28, 1994, Basildon, Essex
SQUAD NO: 22
HEIGHT: 6ft 7in
EDUCATION: Billericay School, Essex
TEAMS: Essex
ROLE: Allrounder
DEBUT: First-class: 2016; List A: 2017; T20: 2016

BEST BATTING: 96 Essex vs Gloucestershire, Chelmsford, 2021
BEST BOWLING: 3-44 Essex vs Derbyshire, Derby, 2016

TWITTER: @PWalter_22

NOTES: Walter signed a professional contract with his hometown club midway through the 2016 season and has become an increasingly influential contributor. The 6ft 7in batting allrounder played in all 10 of Essex's T20 matches in 2020 impressing with seven wickets at the frugal economy rate of 6.64 and smashing a 45-ball 76 against Sussex at Chelmsford. He also lined up for five of Essex's seven matches in the Bob Willis Trophy, including the final, playing primarily as a middle-order batter. He was a mainstay of the Championship and T20 sides last summer, playing primarily as a batter, and signed a new two-year deal in December. Essex head coach Anthony McGrath said: "Paul has developed into an impressive county cricketer following his step-up from Essex League cricket during my first year at the club. He has an important role to play for us over the next two years, especially following the departure of Ryan ten Doeschate. I believe he can stake a real claim in our middle order if he continues to work hard and apply his skills like I know he can"

Batting	Mat	Inns	NO	Runs	HS	Ave	SR	100	50	Ct	St
First-class	28	35	6	1050	96	36.20	46.43	0	5	7	-
List A	16	13	3	253	50	25.30	95.47	0	1	7	-
T20s	61	44	13	581	76	18.74	132.04	0	1	25	-

Bowling	Mat	Balls	Runs	Wkts	BBI	BBM	Ave	Econ	SR	5w	10
First-class	28	1218	713	15	3/44	4/68	47.53	3.51	81.2	0	0
List A	16	368	434	14	4/37	4/37	31.00	7.07	26.2	0	0
T20s	61	606	922	29	3/24	3/24	31.79	9.12	20.8	0	0

HARRISON WARD

LHB / OB / R0 / W0

FULL NAME: Harrison David Ward
BORN: October 25, 1999, Oxford
SQUAD NO: 35
HEIGHT: 6ft 2in
NICKNAME: Indy
EDUCATION: St Edward's School, Oxford; Cardiff Metropolitan University
TEAMS: Sussex, England U19
ROLE: Batter
DEBUT: First-class: 2021; List A: 2021; T20: 2021

BEST BATTING: 19 Sussex vs Derbyshire, Hove, 2021

WHO IS YOUR LOOKALIKE? Rob Beckett (comedian)
FIRST CRICKET CLUB? Abingdon Vale CC, Oxfordshire
WHAT WOULD YOU CHANGE ABOUT THE STRUCTURE OF THE COUNTY SEASON? Create a knockout competition which involves the National (Minor) Counties
WHO IS THE BEST BATTER/KEEPER/ALLROUNDER/BOWLER IN COUNTY CRICKET (EXCLUDING TEAMMATES)? Joe Clarke/Ben Foakes/Darren Stevens/Simon Harmer
MOST UNDERRATED PLAYER IN COUNTY CRICKET? Kiran Carlson
MOST BEAUTIFUL THING YOU HAVE EVER SEEN? A Guinness
WHAT DO YOU MOST ENJOY LISTENING TO? 1980s music
WHAT MAKES YOU WORRY? A dark-red Dukes ball
WHAT GIVES YOU JOY? A 300-yard drive down the middle of a fairway
TWITTER: @HarrisonWard35

Batting	Mat	Inns	NO	Runs	HS	Ave	SR	100	50	Ct	St
First-class	3	6	0	30	19	5.00	23.80	0	0	2	-
List A	2	2	0	24	20	12.00	82.75	0	0	0	-
T20s	6	6	1	73	22	14.60	114.06	0	0	2	-

Bowling	Mat	Balls	Runs	Wkts	BBI	BBM	Ave	Econ	SR	5w	10
First-class	3	6	2	0	-	-	-	2.00	-	0	0
List A	2	-	-	-	-	-	-	-	-	-	-
T20s	6	-	-	-	-	-	-	-	-	-	-

JARED WARNER

RHB / RFM / RO / WO

GLOUCESTERSHIRE

FULL NAME: Jared David Warner
BORN: November 14, 1996, Wakefield, Yorkshire
SQUAD NO: 4
HEIGHT: 6ft 1in
NICKNAME: Jazz
EDUCATION: Silcoates School, West Yorkshire; Kettlethorpe High School, Wakefield
TEAMS: Gloucestershire, England U19, Sussex, Yorkshire
ROLE: Bowler
DEBUT: First-class: 2019; List A: 2019

BEST BATTING: 13* Sussex vs Middlesex, Hove, 2019
BEST BOWLING: 3-35 Sussex vs Glamorgan, Hove, 2019

FIRST CRICKET CLUB? Wakefield Thornes CC, West Yorkshire
MOST EXCITING DAY AS A CRICKETER? Taking 9-19 from 10.2 overs for Yorkshire Academy against Castleford in a Yorkshire Premier League North match in 2016
CHILDHOOD SPORTING HERO? Andrew Flintoff – my first memories of watching cricket are of him winning the Ashes in 2005
SURPRISING FACT ABOUT YOU? I'm a big Sheffield United fan
TWITTER: @JaredWarner96

Batting	Mat	Inns	NO	Runs	HS	Ave	SR	100	50	Ct	St
First-class	5	5	3	38	13*	19.00	19.89	0	0	1	-
List A	7	1	0	0	0	0.00	0.00	0	0	2	-

Bowling	Mat	Balls	Runs	Wkts	BBI	BBM	Ave	Econ	SR	5w	10
First-class	5	461	282	9	3/35	3/78	31.33	3.67	51.2	0	0
List A	7	306	278	6	3/42	3/42	46.33	5.45	51.0	0	0

MARK WATT

LHB / SLA

FULL NAME: Mark Robert James Watt
BORN: July 29, 1996, Edinburgh, Scotland
SQUAD NO: TBC
TEAMS: Scotland, Derbyshire, Lancashire
ROLE: Bowler
DEBUT: ODI: 2016; T20I: 2015; First-class: 2016; List A: 2015; T20: 2015

BEST BATTING: 22 Scotland vs Bangladesh, Al Amerat, 2021 (T20)
BEST BOWLING: 5-27 Scotland vs Netherlands, Dubai, 2016 (T20)

TWITTER: @markwatt123
NOTES: The Scotland left-armer spinner has been re-signed by Derbyshire for the whole of this summer's T20 Blast campaign. Watt played five T20 games for the club in 2019, the year the Falcons reached Finals Day, and has also turned out for Lancashire. He was part of the Scotland side which upset England at Edinburgh in 2018, taking 3-55 as the home side beat their opponents for the first time. The 25-year-old was an impressive performer at last year's T20 World Cup, taking seven wickets and boasting an economy rate of a shade over six runs an over. "We have been looking for a left-arm spinner to mix up our bowling in T20 and Mark ticks all of the boxes for us," said Mickey Arthur, Derbyshire's new head coach. "Mark showed at the World Cup he has the ability to take the game to any opposition"

Batting	Mat	Inns	NO	Runs	HS	Ave	SR	100	50	Ct	St
ODIs	33	19	8	175	31*	15.90	72.01	0	0	7	-
T20Is	47	19	7	104	22	8.66	116.85	0	0	8	-
First-class	4	3	1	128	81*	64.00	52.24	0	1	2	-
List A	49	26	8	235	36	13.05	76.29	0	0	10	-
T20s	58	23	8	122	22	8.13	107.96	0	0	13	-

Bowling	Mat	Balls	Runs	Wkts	BBI	BBM	Ave	Econ	SR	5w	10
ODIs	33	1719	1182	38	4/42	4/42	31.10	4.12	45.2	0	0
T20Is	47	1002	1164	56	5/27	5/27	20.78	6.97	17.8	1	0
First-class	4	726	322	8	3/60	5/97	40.25	2.66	90.7	0	0
List A	49	2425	1744	52	4/42	4/42	33.53	4.31	46.6	0	0
T20s	58	1205	1464	65	5/27	5/27	22.52	7.28	18.5	1	0

JOE WEATHERLEY

RHB / OB / R0 / W0

FULL NAME: Joe James Weatherley
BORN: January 19, 1997, Winchester, Hampshire
SQUAD NO: 5
HEIGHT: 6ft 2in
NICKNAME: Lord
EDUCATION: King Edward VI School, Southampton; The Open University, Milton Keynes
TEAMS: Hampshire, England U19, Kent
ROLE: Batter
DEBUT: First-class: 2016; List A: 2016; T20: 2016

BEST BATTING: 126* Hampshire vs Lancashire, Old Trafford, 2018
BEST BOWLING: 1-2 Hampshire vs Nottinghamshire, Southampton, 2018

WHO IS YOUR LOOKALIKE? Chris Martin?
FIRST CRICKET CLUB? St Cross Symondians CC, Winchester, Hampshire
BIGGEST INFLUENCE ON YOUR DEVELOPMENT AS A CRICKETER (EXCLUDING PARENTS)? Tony Middleton, my batting coach at Hampshire
WHO IS THE BEST BATTER/KEEPER/ALLROUNDER/BOWLER IN COUNTY CRICKET (EXCLUDING TEAMMATES)? Joe Clarke/Ben Foakes/Simon Harmer/Ollie Robinson
MOST UNDERRATED PLAYER IN COUNTY CRICKET? Luke Fletcher
WHAT WOULD A FLY ON THE WALL HEAR IN YOUR DRESSING ROOM? How to improve your golf off the tee
MOST BEAUTIFUL THING YOU HAVE EVER SEEN? The west coast of the Scottish Highlands
WHAT DO YOU MOST ENJOY LISTENING TO? Noel Gallagher
WHAT MAKES YOU WORRY? Needles
SURPRISING FACT ABOUT YOU? My dad played at Wimbledon in the 1972 Championships
TWITTER: @Joe_Weatherley

Batting	Mat	Inns	NO	Runs	HS	Ave	SR	100	50	Ct	St
First-class	50	81	4	1827	126*	23.72	40.89	1	8	37	-
List A	27	27	4	664	105*	28.86	71.24	1	4	10	-
T20s	33	31	2	712	71	24.55	130.64	0	3	8	-

Bowling	Mat	Balls	Runs	Wkts	BBI	BBM	Ave	Econ	SR	5w	10
First-class	50	354	250	5	1/2	1/2	50.00	4.23	70.8	0	0
List A	27	327	221	8	4/25	4/25	27.62	4.05	40.8	0	0
T20s	33	6	9	0	-	-	-	9.00	-	0	0

JAMES WEIGHELL
LHB / RMF / R0 / W0

FULL NAME: William James Weighell
BORN: January 28, 1994, Middlesbrough, Yorkshire
SQUAD NO: 29
HEIGHT: 6ft 4in
NICKNAME: Weighelly
EDUCATION: Stokesley School, North Yorkshire
TEAMS: Glamorgan, Durham
ROLE: Bowler
DEBUT: First-class: 2015; List A: 2017; T20: 2017

BEST BATTING: 84 Durham vs Kent, Chester-le-Street, 2018
BEST BOWLING: 7-32 Durham vs Leicestershire, Chester-le-Street, 2018

WHO IS YOUR LOOKALIKE? Jason Statham (actor)
WHAT WAS YOUR FIRST CRICKET CLUB? Stokesley CC, North Yorkshire
CHILDHOOD SPORTING HERO? Andrew Flintoff
TWITTER: @jamesweighell
NOTES: The former Durham and Leicestershire seamer signed a two-year contract with Glamorgan in April 2021, with director of cricket Mark Wallace saying: "It's great news to bring in someone of the calibre of James to the club. He's a very versatile cricketer with pedigree across all formats [and] will add depth to our squad and bolster our seam-bowling options." Weighell, who is also a handy lower-order batter, played a handful of red-ball matches last summer but was more effective in the shorter formats, part of the XI which won the One-Day Cup final at Trent Bridge against his former club Durham

Batting	Mat	Inns	NO	Runs	HS	Ave	SR	100	50	Ct	St
First-class	20	31	4	581	84	21.51	69.08	0	3	6	-
List A	17	9	1	64	23	8.00	80.00	0	0	6	-
T20s	34	23	9	197	51	14.07	133.10	0	1	18	-

Bowling	Mat	Balls	Runs	Wkts	BBI	BBM	Ave	Econ	SR	5w	10
First-class	20	3084	1860	59	7/32	9/130	31.52	3.61	52.2	2	0
List A	17	793	801	30	5/57	5/57	26.70	6.06	26.4	1	0
T20s	34	555	902	25	3/28	3/28	36.08	9.75	22.2	0	0

NICK WELCH RHB / LB / RO / WO

FULL NAME: Nicholas Roy Welch
BORN: February 5, 1998, Harare, Zimbabwe
SQUAD NO: 67
HEIGHT: 5ft 11in
NICKNAME: Welchie
EDUCATION: St John's College, Harare; Whitgift School, Croydon; Loughborough University
TEAMS: Leicestershire, Mashonaland Eagles
ROLE: Batter
DEBUT: First-class: 2014; List A: 2014; T20: 2020

BEST BATTING: 83 Mashonaland Eagles vs Southern Rocks, Harare, 2014

WHO IS YOUR LOOKALIKE? Patrick Swayze
FIRST CRICKET CLUB? Country Club, Harare, Zimbabwe
WHAT WOULD YOU CHANGE ABOUT THE STRUCTURE OF THE COUNTY SEASON? Not split the Championship with a phase at the beginning and a phase at the end
WHO IS THE BEST BATTER/KEEPER/ALLROUNDER/BOWLER IN COUNTY CRICKET (EXCLUDING TEAMMATES)? Joe Root/Ben Foakes/Darren Stevens/Ollie Robinson
MOST UNDERRATED PLAYER IN COUNTY CRICKET? Jamie Smith
WHAT WOULD A FLY ON THE WALL HEAR IN YOUR DRESSING ROOM? Callum Parkinson trying to make someone laugh
MOST BEAUTIFUL THING YOU HAVE EVER SEEN? Victoria Falls, Zimbabwe
IF YOU COULD TURN BACK TIME... I wouldn't lose that fish when I was 11 years old
WHO WOULD YOU LEAST LIKE TO HAVE A NET WITH? Pat Cummins
WHAT DO YOU MOST ENJOY LISTENING TO? Country music
WHAT MAKES YOU WORRY? Missing the fairway
WHAT GIVES YOU JOY? Leather on willow
TWITTER: @nickwelchie

Batting	Mat	Inns	NO	Runs	HS	Ave	SR	100	50	Ct	St
First-class	5	7	0	179	83	25.57	51.43	0	1	1	-
List A	6	6	0	134	52	22.33	75.28	0	1	3	-
T20s	5	5	0	101	43	20.20	103.06	0	0	1	-

Bowling	Mat	Balls	Runs	Wkts	BBI	BBM	Ave	Econ	SR	5w	10
First-class	5	-	-	-	-	-	-	-	-	-	-
List A	6	-	-	-	-	-	-	-	-	-	-
T20s	5	-	-	-	-	-	-	-	-	-	-

BEN WELLS

RHB / WK / R0 / W0

FULL NAME: Ben Joseph James Wells
BORN: July 30, 2000, Bath, Somerset
SQUAD NO: 72
EDUCATION: Monkton Combe School, Bath
TEAMS: Gloucestershire
ROLE: Wicketkeeper
DEBUT: First-class: 2021; List A: 2021

BEST BATTING: 40 Gloucestershire vs Glamorgan, Cardiff, 2021

NOTES: The 21-year-old wicketkeeper/batter made his first-class and List-A debuts for Gloucestershire last summer after leaving the Somerset Academy to sign a two-year contract at Bristol in July. "I'm really happy to be here and very excited to get going with Gloucestershire," said Wells after putting pen to paper. "My goal at the club is to break into the first team and then to try and dominate at the county level and see where that can take me." He scored 40 against Glamorgan at Cardiff, his only first-class innings to date and also featured in four One-Day Cup matches last summer. Before signing his first professional contract, Wells had impressed by making 139 off 86 for his local club Bath CC in a 40-over match and then an unbeaten 111 off 61 balls in a T20 for Somerset Second XI against Northants

Batting	Mat	Inns	NO	Runs	HS	Ave	SR	100	50	Ct	St
First-class	1	1	0	40	40	40.00	42.55	0	0	2	-
List A	4	2	0	9	7	4.50	25.71	0	0	2	-
Bowling	Mat	Balls	Runs	Wkts	BBI	BBM	Ave	Econ	SR	5w	10
First-class	1	-	-	-	-	-	-	-	-	-	-
List A	4	-	-	-	-	-	-	-	-	-	-

LUKE WELLS

LHB / OB / R2 / W0

FULL NAME: Luke William Peter Wells
BORN: December 29, 1990, Eastbourne, Sussex
SQUAD NO: 3
HEIGHT: 6ft 4in
NICKNAME: Dave
EDUCATION: St Bede's, Hailsham, East Sussex; Loughborough University
TEAMS: Lancashire, Colombo, England U19, Sussex
ROLE: Batter
DEBUT: First-class: 2010; List A: 2010; T20: 2011

BEST BATTING: 258 Sussex vs Durham, Hove, 2017
BEST BOWLING: 5-63 Sussex vs Glamorgan, Hove, 2019
COUNTY CAP: 2016 (Sussex)

FIRST CRICKET CLUB? Glynde & Beddingham CC, Sussex
BIGGEST INFLUENCE ON YOUR DEVELOPMENT AS A CRICKETER (EXCLUDING PARENTS)?
The legendary Les Lenham – former Sussex batsman who became a master batting coach, especially on the fundamentals of technique
WHO IS THE BEST BATTER/KEEPER/ALLROUNDER/BOWLER IN COUNTY CRICKET (EXCLUDING TEAMMATES)? Joe Clarke/Alex Davies/Darren Stevens/Simon Harmer
MOST UNDERRATED PLAYER IN COUNTY CRICKET? Ben Brown
MOST BEAUTIFUL THING YOU HAVE EVER SEEN? Sunset over Port Phillip Bay in Melbourne with my family on a balcony
HOBBIES? Cooking
IF YOU COULD TURN BACK TIME... I'd change the Brexit referendum
MAKE ONE PREDICTION FOR THE FUTURE OF CRICKET: America will become a cricketing powerhouse
WHAT MAKES YOU WORRY? The future of the kids
WHAT GIVES YOU JOY? Watching my son playing and laughing
TWITTER: @luke_wells07

Batting	Mat	Inns	NO	Runs	HS	Ave	SR	100	50	Ct	St
First-class	154	255	18	8392	258	35.40	46.42	19	36	81	-
List A	33	26	1	390	66*	15.60	68.18	0	2	8	-
T20s	12	10	1	66	30	7.33	84.61	0	0	5	-

Bowling	Mat	Balls	Runs	Wkts	BBI	BBM	Ave	Econ	SR	5w	10
First-class	154	5806	3358	78	5/63	5/63	43.05	3.47	74.4	1	0
List A	33	587	516	14	3/19	3/19	36.85	5.27	41.9	0	0
T20s	12	97	122	3	1/15	1/15	40.66	7.54	32.3	0	0

W

ESSEX

FULL NAME: Thomas Westley
BORN: March 13, 1989, Cambridge
SQUAD NO: 21
HEIGHT: 6ft 2in
NICKNAME: Westie
EDUCATION: Linton Valley College, South Cambridgeshire; Hills Road College, Cambridge; Durham University
TEAMS: England, Essex, Bloomfield Cricket & Athletic Club
ROLE: Batter
DEBUT: Test: 2017; First-class: 2007; List A: 2006; T20: 2010

BEST BATTING: 254 Essex vs Worcestershire, Chelmsford, 2016
BEST BOWLING: 4-55 Durham MCCU vs Durham, Durham University, 2010
COUNTY CAP: 2013

FAMILY TIES? My dad, uncle and brother all play for Weston Colville CC. My dad also harbours ambitions to play for England over-50s
CHILDHOOD SPORTING HERO? Jacques Kallis
SURPRISING FACT ABOUT YOU? I was one of the first students to study Harry Potter academically
TWITTER: @Westley21

Batting	Mat	Inns	NO	Runs	HS	Ave	SR	100	50	Ct	St
Tests	5	9	1	193	59	24.12	42.60	0	1	1	-
First-class	199	328	23	10849	254	35.57	51.09	24	49	123	-
List A	98	92	6	3268	134	38.00	88.27	5	26	23	-
T20s	93	86	8	2341	109*	30.01	129.91	2	8	34	-

Bowling	Mat	Balls	Runs	Wkts	BBI	BBM	Ave	Econ	SR	5w	10
Tests	5	24	12	0	-	-	-	3.00	-	0	0
First-class	199	5143	2705	59	4/55	5/122	45.84	3.15	87.1	0	0
List A	98	1312	1065	29	4/60	4/60	36.72	4.87	45.2	0	0
T20s	93	234	296	7	2/27	2/27	42.28	7.58	33.4	0	0

BRAD WHEAL

RHB / RFM / R0 / W0

FULL NAME: Bradley Thomas James Wheal
BORN: August 28, 1996, Durban, South Africa
SQUAD NO: 58
HEIGHT: 5ft 11in
NICKNAME: Whealy
EDUCATION: Clifton School, Durban
TEAMS: Scotland, Hampshire
ROLE: Bowler
DEBUT: ODI: 2016; T20I: 2016; First-class: 2015;
List A: 2016; T20: 2016

BEST BATTING: 46* Hampshire vs Warwickshire, Edgbaston, 2021
BEST BOWLING: 6-51 Hampshire vs Nottinghamshire, Trent Bridge, 2016

FIRST CRICKET CLUB? Berea Rovers CC, Durban, South Africa
WHO IS THE BEST BATTER/KEEPER/ALLROUNDER/BOWLER IN COUNTY CRICKET
(EXCLUDING TEAMMATES)? Harry Brook/Ben Foakes/Colin de Grandhomme/Luke Fletcher
MOST BEAUTIFUL THING YOU HAVE EVER SEEN? Colin de Grandhomme's mullet
HOBBIES? Cooking
WHO WOULD YOU LEAST LIKE TO HAVE A NET WITH? Brett Lee
TWITTER: @Brad_wheal

Batting	Mat	Inns	NO	Runs	HS	Ave	SR	100	50	Ct	St
ODIs	13	7	3	16	14	4.00	51.61	0	0	3	-
T20Is	14	5	4	5	2*	5.00	62.50	0	0	5	-
First-class	41	48	16	362	46*	11.31	26.15	0	0	13	-
List A	28	16	7	63	18*	7.00	66.31	0	0	6	-
T20s	37	11	7	30	16	7.50	90.90	0	0	11	-

Bowling	Mat	Balls	Runs	Wkts	BBI	BBM	Ave	Econ	SR	5w	10
ODIs	13	687	508	23	3/34	3/34	22.08	4.43	29.8	0	0
T20Is	14	284	404	13	3/20	3/20	31.07	8.53	21.8	0	0
First-class	41	5511	3165	95	6/51	7/71	33.31	3.44	58.0	1	0
List A	28	1319	1154	45	4/38	4/38	25.64	5.24	29.3	0	0
T20s	37	732	1002	45	4/17	4/17	22.26	8.21	16.2	0	0

ADAM WHEATER   RHB / WK / R0 / W0

FULL NAME: Adam Jack Aubrey Wheater
BORN: February 13, 1990, Whipps Cross Hospital, London
SQUAD NO: 31
EDUCATION: Millfield School, Somerset; Anglia Ruskin University
TEAMS: Essex, Badureliya Sports Club, England U19, Hampshire, Matabeleland Tuskers
ROLE: Batter/wicketkeeper
DEBUT: First-class: 2008; List A: 2010; T20: 2009

BEST BATTING: 204* Hampshire vs Warwickshire, Edgbaston, 2016
BEST BOWLING: 1-86 Essex vs Leicestershire, Leicester, 2012
COUNTY CAP: 2016 (Hampshire); 2020 (Essex)

NOTES: The hard-hitting wicketkeeper signed a new deal last December, keeping him at Essex until the end of next season. Wheater was part of the side which won the County Championship in 2017 and again in 2019, having re-joined his old club after a spell at Hampshire. Behind Alastair Cook, the 31-year-old was Essex's most consistent run-scorer in the club's successful red-ball campaign in 2020, with 291 runs at an average of 58.20. He remains the first-choice keeper at Chelmsford, despite the the encouraging progress shown by his understudy, Will Buttleman

Batting	Mat	Inns	NO	Runs	HS	Ave	SR	100	50	Ct	St
First-class	158	227	28	7098	204*	35.66	63.67	12	39	277	21
List A	89	72	5	1924	135	28.71	99.43	2	11	51	14
T20s	129	106	16	1736	78	19.28	124.17	0	4	51	29
Bowling	Mat	Balls	Runs	Wkts	BBI	BBM	Ave	Econ	SR	5w	10
First-class	158	24	86	1	1/86	1/86	86.00	21.50	24.0	0	0
List A	89	-	-	-	-	-	-	-	-	-	-
T20s	129	-	-	-	-	-	-	-	-	-	-

GRAEME WHITE — RHB / SLA / R0 / W0

FULL NAME: Graeme Geoffrey White
BORN: April 18, 1987, Milton Keynes, Buckinghamshire
SQUAD NO: 87
HEIGHT: 5ft 11in
NICKNAME: G
EDUCATION: Royal Latin School, Buckinghamshire; Stowe School
TEAMS: Northamptonshire, England Lions, Nottinghamshire
ROLE: Bowler
DEBUT: First-class: 2006; List A: 2007; T20: 2007

BEST BATTING: 37* Northamptonshire vs Warwickshire, Edgbaston, 2020 (T20)
BEST BOWLING: 5-22 Nottinghamshire vs Lancashire, Trent Bridge, 2013 (T20)

FIRST CRICKET CLUB? Milton Keynes CC, Buckinghamshire
WHAT WOULD YOU CHANGE ABOUT THE STRUCTURE OF THE COUNTY SEASON? Introduce a mid-season break so that I could go on a summer holiday for the first time
BIGGEST INFLUENCE ON YOUR DEVELOPMENT AS A CRICKETER (EXCLUDING PARENTS)? David Ripley – he's coached me ever since I joined the Northants Academy
WHO IS THE BEST BATTER/KEEPER/ALLROUNDER/BOWLER IN COUNTY CRICKET (EXCLUDING TEAMMATES)? Wayne Madsen/Ben Cox/Darren Stevens/Chris Rushworth
MOST UNDERRATED PLAYER IN COUNTY CRICKET? Jake Libby
WHO WOULD YOU MOST AND LEAST LIKE TO HAVE A NET WITH? Most – Alex Hales, to get my confidence back. Least – Andre Adams, because he's a wizard
WHAT MAKES YOU WORRY? My son becoming a Liverpool fan
WHAT GIVES YOU JOY? When Manchester United win
SURPRISING FACT ABOUT YOU? I have 35 tattoos
NOTES: The Northants spinner signed a new contract to play white-ball cricket this summer and double up as head coach of the Second XI. He is also the club's fielding and spin-bowling coach

Batting	Mat	Inns	NO	Runs	HS	Ave	SR	100	50	Ct	St
First-class	39	55	5	659	65	13.18	48.85	0	2	12	-
List A	89	53	16	558	41*	15.08	85.97	0	0	29	-
T20s	131	58	27	449	37*	14.48	135.24	0	0	46	-

Bowling	Mat	Balls	Runs	Wkts	BBI	BBM	Ave	Econ	SR	5w	10
First-class	39	4776	2730	65	6/44	7/89	42.00	3.42	73.4	1	0
List A	89	3360	2804	94	6/37	6/37	29.82	5.00	35.7	2	0
T20s	131	2147	2899	107	5/22	5/22	27.09	8.10	20.0	1	0

JACK WHITE

LHB / RFM / R0 / W0

FULL NAME: Curtley-Jack White
BORN: February 19, 1992, Kendal, Cumberland
SQUAD NO: 9
HEIGHT: 6ft 2in
EDUCATION: Ullswater Community College, Penrith, Cumbria; Queen Elizabeth Grammar School, Penrith
TEAMS: Northamptonshire
ROLE: Bowler
DEBUT: First-class: 2020; List A: 2021

BEST BATTING: 15* Northamptonshire vs Gloucestershire, Bristol, 2021
BEST BOWLING: 4-35 Northamptonshire vs Glamorgan, Northampton, 2020

FIRST CRICKET CLUB? Penrith CC, Cumbria
WHAT WOULD YOU CHANGE ABOUT THE STRUCTURE OF THE COUNTY SEASON?
Fewer games so that players are fresher
MOST UNDERRATED PLAYER IN COUNTY CRICKET? Brooke Guest
WHAT WOULD A FLY ON THE WALL HEAR IN YOUR DRESSING ROOM? A Nathan Buck joke
MOST BEAUTIFUL THING YOU HAVE EVER SEEN? Diamond dust
HOBBIES? Skiing, mountain biking, Land Rovers
IF YOU COULD TURN BACK TIME... I would have stopped the invention of the average-speed check
WHAT DO YOU MOST ENJOY LISTENING TO? A V12 engine
WHAT MAKES YOU WORRY? The erosion of free speech
WHAT GIVES YOU JOY? The mountains
GUILTY PLEASURE? Nutella
TWITTER: @CJackWhite9

Batting	Mat	Inns	NO	Runs	HS	Ave	SR	100	50	Ct	St
First-class	8	11	7	38	15*	9.50	46.91	0	0	0	-
List A	7	3	1	20	10*	10.00	90.90	0	0	2	-

Bowling	Mat	Balls	Runs	Wkts	BBI	BBM	Ave	Econ	SR	5w	10
First-class	8	1092	579	18	4/35	8/83	32.16	3.18	60.6	0	0
List A	7	258	220	10	4/20	4/20	22.00	5.11	25.8	0	0

ROBBIE WHITE RHB / WK / R0 / W0

FULL NAME: Robert George White
BORN: September 15, 1995, Ealing, London
SQUAD NO: 14
HEIGHT: 5ft 10in
NICKNAME: Chalky
EDUCATION: Harrow School, London;
Loughborough University
TEAMS: Middlesex, Essex
ROLE: Batter/wicketkeeper
DEBUT: First-class: 2015; List A: 2018; T20: 2018

BEST BATTING: 120 Middlesex vs Derbyshire, Lord's, 2021

WHO IS YOUR LOOKALIKE? Jordan Spieth
FIRST CRICKET CLUB? Ealing CC, London
WHAT WOULD YOU CHANGE ABOUT THE STRUCTURE OF THE COUNTY SEASON?
More Championship cricket in the middle of the summer
BIGGEST CRICKETING REGRET? Leaving my first Championship ball at Lord's…
MOST UNDERRATED PLAYER IN COUNTY CRICKET? Matt Milnes
WHAT WOULD A FLY ON THE WALL HEAR IN YOUR DRESSING ROOM? Attempts to solve the Times crossword
MOST BEAUTIFUL THING YOU HAVE EVER SEEN? Tom Helm's golf swing
IF YOU COULD TURN BACK TIME... I would have learnt the guitar
WHO WOULD YOU MOST AND LEAST LIKE TO HAVE A NET WITH? Most – Tim Murtagh.
Least – Blake Cullen
MAKE ONE PREDICTION FOR THE FUTURE OF CRICKET: Big hits will be worth more than six runs
WHAT MAKES YOU WORRY? Martin Andersson's golf swing
WHAT GIVES YOU JOY? A roast lamb at Lord's
TWITTER: @rwhitey15

Batting	Mat	Inns	NO	Runs	HS	Ave	SR	100	50	Ct	St
First-class	33	54	5	1215	120	24.79	42.73	2	6	44	2
List A	15	14	4	239	55	23.90	79.40	0	1	19	3
T20s	3	2	1	11	11*	11.00	100.00	0	0	1	-

Bowling	Mat	Balls	Runs	Wkts	BBI	BBM	Ave	Econ	SR	5w	10
First-class	33	-	-	-	-	-	-	-	-	-	-
List A	15	-	-	-	-	-	-	-	-	-	-
T20s	3	-	-	-	-	-	-	-	-	-	-

ROSS WHITELEY

LHB / LM / R0 / W0

FULL NAME: Ross Andrew Whiteley
BORN: September 13, 1988, Sheffield
SQUAD NO: 4
HEIGHT: 6ft 2in
NICKNAME: Rossco
EDUCATION: Repton School, Derbyshire; Leeds Metropolitan University
TEAMS: Hampshire, Derbyshire, England Lions, Multan Sultans, Sylhet Sixers, Worcestershire
ROLE: Batter
DEBUT: First-class: 2008; List A: 2008; T20: 2011

BEST BATTING: 130* Derbyshire vs Kent, Derby, 2011
BEST BOWLING: 2-6 Derbyshire vs Hampshire, Derby, 2012
COUNTY CAP: 2013 (Worcestershire)

FIRST CRICKET CLUB? Eckington CC, South Yorkshire
WHO IS THE BEST BATTER/KEEPER/ALLROUNDER/BOWLER IN COUNTY CRICKET (EXCLUDING TEAMMATES)? Jake Libby/Ben Cox/Moeen Ali/Brydon Carse
HOBBIES? I'm a part-time builder
IF YOU COULD TURN BACK TIME... I'd have chosen black instead of red that time at the casino
MAKE ONE PREDICTION FOR THE FUTURE OF CRICKET: Players will be able to bat with both hands and bowl with both arms
WHAT DO YOU MOST ENJOY LISTENING TO? Oasis
WHAT MAKES YOU WORRY? Whether my dog is happy or not
SURPRISING FACT ABOUT YOU? I once had each squad number of the 2012 Derbyshire side which won Division Two shaved onto 11 sheep
GUILTY PLEASURE? White chocolate
TWITTER: @RossWhiteley44

Batting	Mat	Inns	NO	Runs	HS	Ave	SR	100	50	Ct	St
First-class	89	145	13	3577	130*	27.09	49.29	3	19	60	-
List A	81	71	11	1660	131	27.66	99.81	1	10	23	-
T20s	153	137	36	2585	91*	25.59	141.87	0	5	60	-

Bowling	Mat	Balls	Runs	Wkts	BBI	BBM	Ave	Econ	SR	5w	10
First-class	89	3013	2097	41	2/6	4/43	51.14	4.17	73.4	0	0
List A	81	507	563	14	4/58	4/58	40.21	6.66	36.2	0	0
T20s	153	102	181	4	1/10	1/10	45.25	10.64	25.5	0	0

YORKSHIRE

FULL NAME: David Jonathan Willey
BORN: February 28, 1990, Northampton
SQUAD NO: 15
HEIGHT: 6ft 1in
NICKNAME: Will Mildman
EDUCATION: Northampton School for Boys
TEAMS: England, Yorkshire, Chennai Super Kings, Multan Sultans, Northamptonshire, Perth Scorchers, Royal Challengers Bangalore
ROLE: Allrounder
DEBUT: ODI: 2015; T20I: 2015; First-class: 2009; List A: 2009; T20: 2009

BEST BATTING: 104* Northamptonshire vs Gloucestershire, Northampton, 2015
BEST BOWLING: 5-29 Northamptonshire vs Gloucestershire, Northampton, 2011
COUNTY CAP: 2013 (Northamptonshire); 2016 (Yorkshire)

FIRST CRICKET CLUB? Old Northamptonians CC, Northampton
FAMILY TIES? My dad Peter played for England, Northamptonshire and Leicestershire
MOST EXCITING DAY AS A CRICKETER? Making my England debut in 2015
SURPRISING FACT ABOUT YOU? My wife Carolyn is a country singer and was a two-time X Factor contestant
TWITTER: @david_willey

Batting	Mat	Inns	NO	Runs	HS	Ave	SR	100	50	Ct	St
ODIs	52	29	13	377	51	23.56	88.29	0	2	23	-
T20Is	32	21	8	182	29*	14.00	132.84	0	0	15	-
First-class	77	108	16	2515	104*	27.33	63.75	2	14	18	-
List A	135	94	21	1859	167	25.46	95.62	3	7	49	-
T20s	211	157	32	2971	118	23.76	140.20	2	12	87	-

Bowling	Mat	Balls	Runs	Wkts	BBI	BBM	Ave	Econ	SR	5w	10
ODIs	52	2305	2181	69	5/30	5/30	31.60	5.67	33.4	1	0
T20Is	32	641	854	38	4/7	4/7	22.47	7.99	16.8	0	0
First-class	77	10745	5895	198	5/29	10/75	29.77	3.29	54.2	6	1
List A	135	5096	4823	157	5/30	5/30	30.71	5.67	32.4	2	0
T20s	211	3593	4742	209	4/7	4/7	22.68	7.91	17.1	0	0

CHRIS WOAKES

RHB / RFM / R0 / W3

FULL NAME: Christopher Roger Woakes
BORN: March 2, 1989, Birmingham
SQUAD NO: 19
HEIGHT: 6ft 1in
NICKNAME: Wiz
EDUCATION: Barr Beacon Language College, Walsall
TEAMS: England, Warwickshire, Delhi Capitals, Kolkata Knight Riders, RC Bangalore, Sydney Thunder, Wellington
ROLE: Allrounder
DEBUT: Test: 2013; ODI: 2011; T20I: 2011; First-class: 2006; List A: 2007; T20: 2008

BEST BATTING: 152* Warwickshire vs Derbyshire, Derby, 2013
BEST BOWLING: 9-36 Warwickshire vs Durham, Edgbaston, 2016
COUNTY CAP: 2009

FAMILY TIES? My brothers played Birmingham League cricket
CHILDHOOD SPORTING HERO? Jacques Kallis
SURPRISING FACT ABOUT YOU? I won a keep-uppy competition when I was 10 (70 keepy-ups)
TWITTER: @chriswoakes

Batting	Mat	Inns	NO	Runs	HS	Ave	SR	100	50	Ct	St
Tests	42	68	12	1535	137*	27.41	52.08	1	6	18	-
ODIs	106	72	21	1315	95*	25.78	90.87	0	5	46	-
T20Is	16	8	4	98	37	24.50	148.48	0	0	5	-
First-class	159	236	51	6211	152*	33.57		10	25	66	-
List A	188	125	37	2056	95*	23.36	90.69	0	6	63	-
T20s	125	73	38	852	57*	24.34	136.97	0	2	47	-

Bowling	Mat	Balls	Runs	Wkts	BBI	BBM	Ave	Econ	SR	5w	10
Tests	42	7326	3752	125	6/17	11/102	30.01	3.07	58.6	4	1
ODIs	106	5016	4567	155	6/45	6/45	29.46	5.46	32.3	3	0
T20Is	16	327	427	15	2/23	2/23	28.46	7.83	21.8	0	0
First-class	159	26962	13824	540	9/36	11/97	25.60	3.07	49.9	21	4
List A	188	8284	7543	233	6/45	6/45	32.37	5.46	35.5	3	0
T20s	125	2472	3393	137	4/21	4/21	24.76	8.23	18.0	0	0

CHRIS WOOD
RHB / LMF / R0 / W0

FULL NAME: Christopher Philip Wood
BORN: June 27, 1990, Basingstoke, Hampshire
SQUAD NO: 25
HEIGHT: 6ft 3in
NICKNAME: Nuts
EDUCATION: St Lawrence CE Primary School; Amery Hill School; Alton College, Hampshire
TEAMS: Hampshire, England U19
ROLE: Bowler
DEBUT: First-class: 2010; List A: 2010; T20: 2010

BEST BATTING: 27 Hampshire vs Surrey, The Oval, 2014 (T20)
BEST BOWLING: 5-32 Hampshire vs Somerset, Taunton, 2018 (T20)
COUNTY CAP: 2018

WHO IS YOUR LOOKALIKE? No one is lucky enough
FIRST CRICKET CLUB? Liphook & Ripsley CC, West Sussex
WHAT WOULD YOU CHANGE ABOUT THE STRUCTURE OF THE COUNTY SEASON? Play fewer Championship games
WHO IS THE BEST BATTER/KEEPER/ALLROUNDER/BOWLER IN COUNTY CRICKET (EXCLUDING TEAMMATES)? Ollie Pope/Ben Foakes/Darren Stevens/Sam Cook
WHAT WOULD A FLY ON THE WALL HEAR IN YOUR DRESSING ROOM? Mason Crane saying "What I would say…" about a million times a day
MOST BEAUTIFUL THING YOU HAVE EVER SEEN? Machu Picchu, Peru
IF YOU COULD TURN BACK TIME… I'd change my body so that I could play Championship cricket
MAKE ONE PREDICTION FOR THE FUTURE OF CRICKET: The whole game franchised
TWITTER: @CWoody27
NOTES: The left-armer announced his retirement from four-day cricket in March 2020 and signed a white-ball contract with Hampshire

Batting	Mat	Inns	NO	Runs	HS	Ave	SR	100	50	Ct	St
First-class	43	62	6	1326	105*	23.67	64.65	1	6	14	-
List A	79	45	14	400	41	12.90	96.85	0	0	24	-
T20s	146	58	21	397	27	10.72	107.88	0	0	41	-

Bowling	Mat	Balls	Runs	Wkts	BBI	BBM	Ave	Econ	SR	5w	10
First-class	43	6169	3174	105	5/39	7/49	30.22	3.08	58.7	3	0
List A	79	3304	2964	105	5/22	5/22	28.22	5.38	31.4	2	0
T20s	146	2964	4070	152	5/32	5/32	26.77	8.23	19.5	1	0

LUKE WOOD

LHB / LFM / R0 / W0

FULL NAME: Luke Wood
BORN: August 2, 1995, Sheffield
SQUAD NO: 14
HEIGHT: 5ft 9in
NICKNAME: Biscuit
EDUCATION: Portland Comprehensive School, Worksop; Outwood Post 16 Centre Worksop
TEAMS: Lancashire, England U19, Quetta Gladiators, Nottinghamshire, Worcestershire
ROLE: Bowler
DEBUT: First-class: 2014; List A: 2016; T20: 2016

BEST BATTING: 100 Nottinghamshire vs Sussex, Trent Bridge, 2015
BEST BOWLING: 5-40 Nottinghamshire vs Cambridge MCCU, Cambridge, 2016

MOST EXCITING DAY AS A CRICKETER? Winning the T20 Blast for the second year running with Nottinghamshire in 2018
CHILDHOOD SPORTING HERO? Ryan Sidebottom
BIGGEST INFLUENCE ON YOUR DEVELOPMENT AS A CRICKETER (EXCLUDING PARENTS)? Chris Tolley, the former Notts bowler. He was my first coach at the Notts Academy and it really helped that he was also a left-arm swing bowler
FIRST CRICKET CLUB? Cuckney CC, Nottinghamshire
IF YOU COULD TAKE ONE COUNTY CRICKETER'S BEST SHOT AND ADD IT TO YOUR OWN GAME? Alastair Cook's pull
GUILTY PLEASURE? Biscuits
TWITTER: @lwood_95

Batting	Mat	Inns	NO	Runs	HS	Ave	SR	100	50	Ct	St
First-class	52	78	16	1694	119	27.32	61.15	2	6	17	-
List A	4	3	2	73	52	73.00	119.67	0	1	0	-
T20s	57	19	7	94	33*	7.83	100.00	0	0	22	-

Bowling	Mat	Balls	Runs	Wkts	BBI	BBM	Ave	Econ	SR	5w	10
First-class	52	6791	3986	117	5/40	8/83	34.06	3.52	58.0	3	0
List A	4	126	125	5	2/36	2/36	25.00	5.95	25.2	0	0
T20s	57	946	1313	47	4/20	4/20	27.93	8.32	20.1	0	0

DURHAM

FULL NAME: Mark Andrew Wood
BORN: January 11, 1990, Ashington, Northumberland
SQUAD NO: 33
HEIGHT: 6ft
EDUCATION: Ashington High School; Newcastle College
TEAMS: England, Durham, Chennai Super Kings, Lucknow Super Giants
ROLE: Bowler
DEBUT: Test: 2015; ODI: 2015; T20I: 2015; First-class: 2011; List A: 2011; T20: 2013

BEST BATTING: 72* Durham vs Kent, Chester-le-Street, 2017
BEST BOWLING: 6-37 England vs Australia, Hobart, 2022

FAMILY TIES? My dad Derek and uncle Neil played for Ashington CC and Minor Counties for Northumberland
CHILDHOOD SPORTING HERO? Steve Harmison
SURPRISING FACT ABOUT YOU? I was in the Newcastle United FC Academy
TWITTER: @MAWood33

Batting	Mat	Inns	NO	Runs	HS	Ave	SR	100	50	Ct	St
Tests	25	43	7	563	52	15.63	65.23	0	1	8	-
ODIs	57	19	11	72	14	9.00	79.12	0	0	12	-
T20Is	19	3	3	11	5*	-	84.61	0	0	0	-
First-class	67	107	19	1729	72*	19.64	57.44	0	5	17	-
List A	91	35	16	134	24	7.05	77.01	0	0	22	-
T20s	40	14	8	107	27*	17.83	102.88	0	0	4	-

Bowling	Mat	Balls	Runs	Wkts	BBI	BBM	Ave	Econ	SR	5w	10
Tests	25	4632	2572	81	6/37	9/100	31.75	3.33	57.1	3	0
ODIs	57	2903	2642	69	4/33	4/33	38.28	5.46	42.0	0	0
T20Is	19	429	621	26	3/9	3/9	23.88	8.68	16.5	0	0
First-class	67	10804	5913	217	6/37	9/100	27.24	3.28	49.7	11	0
List A	91	4282	3782	115	4/33	4/33	32.88	5.29	37.2	0	0
T20s	40	849	1168	46	4/25	4/25	25.39	8.25	18.4	0	0

TOM WOOD

RHB / RM / RO / WO

FULL NAME: Thomas Anthony Wood
BORN: May 11, 1994, Derby
SQUAD NO: 24
HEIGHT: 6ft
NICKNAME: Woody
EDUCATION: Heanor Gate Science College, Derbyshire
TEAMS: Derbyshire
ROLE: Batter
DEBUT: First-class: 2016; List A: 2016; T20: 2017

DERBYSHIRE

BEST BATTING: 31 Derbyshire vs Nottinghamshire, Derby, 2021

WHO IS YOUR LOOKALIKE? Brad Pitt
FIRST CRICKET CLUB? Stainsby Hall CC, Derbyshire
WHAT WOULD YOU CHANGE ABOUT THE STRUCTURE OF THE COUNTY SEASON?
That matches only take place when it is a minimum of 10 degrees
BIGGEST INFLUENCE ON YOUR DEVELOPMENT AS A CRICKETER (EXCLUDING PARENTS)?
Tony Borrington, the former Derbyshire batter
WHO IS THE BEST BATTER/KEEPER/ALLROUNDER/BOWLER IN COUNTY CRICKET
(EXCLUDING TEAMMATES)? Alastair Cook/Ben Foakes/Darren Stevens/Simon Harmer
MOST UNDERRATED PLAYER IN COUNTY CRICKET? Matt Critchley
HOBBIES? Dog-training
WHO WOULD YOU MOST AND LEAST LIKE TO HAVE A NET WITH? Most – Sachin Tendulkar.
Least – Shaun Tait
MAKE ONE PREDICTION FOR THE FUTURE OF CRICKET: The Hundred will take over the game!
WHAT MAKES YOU WORRY? Away-swinging nip-backers
TWITTER: @tom_wood

Batting	Mat	Inns	NO	Runs	HS	Ave	SR	100	50	Ct	St
First-class	11	19	0	202	31	10.63	38.62	0	0	9	-
List A	9	7	0	235	109	33.57	113.52	1	0	0	-
T20s	8	7	1	242	67	40.33	126.04	0	2	4	-
Bowling	Mat	Balls	Runs	Wkts	BBI	BBM	Ave	Econ	SR	5w	10
First-class	11	-	-	-	-	-	-	-	-	-	-
List A	9	102	93	3	1/13	1/13	31.00	5.47	34.0	0	0
T20s	8	-	-	-	-	-	-	-	-	-	-

SURREY

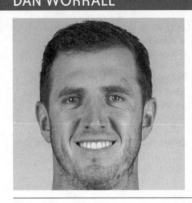

FULL NAME: Daniel James Worrall
BORN: July 10, 1991, Melbourne, Australia
SQUAD NO: 40
TEAMS: Australia, Surrey, Adelaide Strikers, Gloucestershire, Melbourne Stars, South Australia
ROLE: Bowler
DEBUT: ODI: 2016; First-class: 2012; List A: 2012; T20: 2014

BEST BATTING: 50 Gloucestershire vs Glamorgan, Bristol, 2018
BEST BOWLING: 7-64 South Australia vs Western Australia, Adelaide, 2018
COUNTY CAP: 2018 (Gloucestershire)

NOTES: The 30-year-old Australian pace bowler has been signed by Surrey on a three-year contract to play across all formats. Worrall holds a British passport and has renounced his status as a local player in his home country, meaning he will not be classed as overseas during his time at The Oval. He has featured intermittently for Gloucestershire since 2018, injuries restricting him to just 12 Championship appearances in which he has taken an impressive 43 wickets at an average of 22.53. Worrall made his first-class debut in 2012 and appeared in three ODIs for Australia in 2016 but hasn't played international cricket since, largely due to persistent injury. "Dan is a high-quality bowler with a wealth of experience in Sheffield Shield, Big Bash and county cricket to draw on," said Alec Stewart, Surrey's director of cricket. "With no Rikki Clarke or Jade Dernbach with us this year, the need to add to our pool of fast-bowling options to play for the club over the course of our punishing six-month season was crucial and Dan will add significant experience and expertise to the group we already have in place"

Batting	Mat	Inns	NO	Runs	HS	Ave	SR	100	50	Ct	St
ODIs	3	1	1	6	6*	-	150.00	0	0	1	-
First-class	63	97	36	767	50	12.57	47.17	0	1	17	-
List A	43	23	11	128	31*	10.66	80.50	0	0	15	-
T20s	57	24	13	155	62*	14.09	120.15	0	1	14	-

Bowling	Mat	Balls	Runs	Wkts	BBI	BBM	Ave	Econ	SR	5w	10
ODIs	3	158	171	1	1/43	1/43	171.00	6.49	158.0	0	0
First-class	63	13158	6519	234	7/64	10/148	27.85	2.97	56.2	9	1
List A	43	2161	1944	50	5/62	5/62	38.88	5.39	43.2	1	0
T20s	57	1166	1575	45	4/23	4/23	35.00	8.10	25.9	0	0

CHRIS WRIGHT

RHB / RMF / R0 / W2

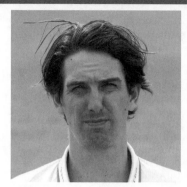

FULL NAME: Christopher Julian Clement Wright
BORN: July 14, 1985, Chipping Norton, Oxfordshire
SQUAD NO: 31
HEIGHT: 6ft 3in
NICKNAME: Dog
EDUCATION: Eggars Grammar School, Alton
TEAMS: Leicestershire, England Lions, Essex, Middlesex, Tamil Union, Warwickshire
ROLE: Bowler
DEBUT: First-class: 2004; List A: 2004; T20: 2004

BEST BATTING: 87 Leicestershire vs Derbyshire, Derby, 2021
BEST BOWLING: 7-53 Leicestershire vs Gloucestershire, Bristol, 2021
COUNTY CAP: 2013 (Warwickshire)

WHO IS YOUR LOOKALIKE? Paolo Maldini, Hugh Grant, Unai Emery, Fernando Alonso and the butler from Mr Deeds
FIRST CRICKET CLUB? Liphook and Ripsley CC, Hampshire
WHAT WOULD YOU CHANGE ABOUT THE STRUCTURE OF THE COUNTY SEASON? Reduce the amount of white-ball games so that better wickets could be produced across all formats
MOST UNDERRATED PLAYER IN COUNTY CRICKET? Keith Barker
WHAT WOULD A FLY ON THE WALL HEAR IN YOUR DRESSING ROOM? The question is WHO. To which the answer is Callum Parkinson and Paul Nixon
MOST BEAUTIFUL THING YOU HAVE EVER SEEN? Aside from my family (obvious but true), my dog when asleep or running across a field
IF YOU COULD TURN BACK TIME... I'd learn to dance and sing properly
WHAT DO YOU MOST ENJOY LISTENING TO? The Property Podcast
WHAT MAKES YOU WORRY? The state of the earth (climate and politics) – it's so divided
WHAT GIVES YOU JOY? My family, Arsenal, being a geek about stuff (details matter)
TWITTER: @chriswright1985

Batting	Mat	Inns	NO	Runs	HS	Ave	SR	100	50	Ct	St
First-class	176	227	48	3288	87	18.36	48.76	0	13	31	-
List A	107	45	21	271	42	11.29	73.44	0	0	17	-
T20s	62	16	9	30	6*	4.28	90.90	0	0	13	-

Bowling	Mat	Balls	Runs	Wkts	BBI	BBM	Ave	Econ	SR	5w	10
First-class	176	28422	16410	513	7/53		31.98	3.46	55.4	17	0
List A	107	4199	3973	104	4/20	4/20	38.20	5.67	40.3	0	0
T20s	62	1222	1834	53	4/24	4/24	34.60	9.00	23.0	0	0

LUKE WRIGHT

RHB / RM

SUSSEX

FULL NAME: Luke James Wright
BORN: March 7, 1985, Grantham, Lincolnshire
SQUAD NO: 10
HEIGHT: 5ft 10in
NICKNAME: Bam Bam
EDUCATION: Loughborough University; Manchester Metropolitan University
TEAMS: England, Sussex, Leicestershire, Melbourne Stars, Pune Warriors
ROLE: Batter
DEBUT: ODI: 2007; T20I: 2007; First-class: 2003; List A 2002; T20: 2004

BEST BATTING: 153* Sussex vs Essex, Chelmsford, 2014 (T20)
BEST BOWLING: 3-17 Sussex vs Surrey, The Oval, 2006 (T20)
COUNTY CAP: 2007 (Sussex); BENEFIT: 2017 (Sussex)

WHO IS YOUR LOOKALIKE? Shane Watson
FIRST CRICKET CLUB? Bottesford CC, Leicestershire
WHAT WOULD YOU CHANGE ABOUT THE STRUCTURE OF THE COUNTY SEASON?
Allow three overseas players in the XI
BIGGEST INFLUENCE ON YOUR DEVELOPMENT AS A CRICKETER (EXCLUDING PARENTS)?
My brother Ashley Wright – the best batting coach I ever had
MOST UNDERRATED PLAYER IN COUNTY CRICKET? Ben Brown
HOBBIES? Wine
MAKE ONE PREDICTION FOR THE FUTURE OF CRICKET: Some counties will not play four-day cricket
WHAT MAKES YOU WORRY? Sussex CCC
TWITTER: @lukewright204
NOTES: Wright signed a three-year white-ball contract with Sussex in October 2020

Batting	Mat	Inns	NO	Runs	HS	Ave	SR	100	50	Ct	St
ODIs	50	39	4	707	52	20.20	86.21	0	2	18	-
T20Is	51	45	5	759	99*	18.97	137.00	0	4	14	-
First-class	144	223	23	7622	226*	38.11	65.54	17	38	58	-
List A	211	176	21	5126	166	33.07		11	19	66	-
T20s	336	312	28	8368	153*	29.46	143.09	7	46	102	-

Bowling	Mat	Balls	Runs	Wkts	BBI	BBM	Ave	Econ	SR	5w	10
ODIs	50	1038	884	15	2/34	2/34	58.93	5.10	69.2	0	0
T20Is	51	330	465	18	2/24	2/24	25.83	8.45	18.3	0	0
First-class	144	8264	4862	120	5/65		40.51	3.53	68.8	3	0
List A	211	4752	4231	111	4/12	4/12	38.11	5.34	42.8	0	0
T20s	336	1799	2563	79	3/17	3/17	32.44	8.54	22.7	0	0

ROB YATES

LHB / OB / R0 / W0 / MVP26

FULL NAME: Robert Michael Yates
BORN: September 19, 1999, Solihull, Warwickshire
SQUAD NO: 17
HEIGHT: 6ft 2in
NICKNAME: Robot
EDUCATION: Warwick School; University of Birmingham
TEAMS: Warwickshire, England Lions
ROLE: Batter
DEBUT: First-class: 2019; List A: 2019; T20: 2020

WARWICKSHIRE

BEST BATTING: 141 Warwickshire vs Somerset, Edgbaston, 2019
BEST BOWLING: 2-54 Warwickshire vs Worcestershire, Worcester, 2021

WHO IS YOUR LOOKALIKE? Nemo from Finding Nemo
FIRST CRICKET CLUB? Moseley CC, Solihull, West Midlands
BIGGEST CRICKETING REGRET? Dropping someone on 10 who went on to make 190. The match would have been over a day earlier if I'd taken that catch
WHO IS THE BEST BATTER/KEEPER/ALLROUNDER/BOWLER IN COUNTY CRICKET (EXCLUDING TEAMMATES)? Alastair Cook/Ben Foakes/Tom Abell/Sam Cook
MOST UNDERRATED PLAYER IN COUNTY CRICKET? Lyndon James
MOST BEAUTIFUL THING YOU HAVE EVER SEEN? Steak and kidney pudding with chips and gravy
HOBBIES? Tennis
MAKE ONE PREDICTION FOR THE FUTURE OF CRICKET: Cricket will be played in the UK during the winter indoors
TWITTER: @robert_yates99

Batting	Mat	Inns	NO	Runs	HS	Ave	SR	100	50	Ct	St
First-class	33	55	3	1656	141	31.84	42.06	6	5	35	-
List A	8	8	0	348	103	43.50	92.06	1	3	4	-
T20s	9	9	0	144	37	16.00	122.03	0	0	1	-

Bowling	Mat	Balls	Runs	Wkts	BBI	BBM	Ave	Econ	SR	5w	10
First-class	33	480	217	4	2/54	2/54	54.25	2.71	120.0	0	0
List A	8	142	121	2	1/27	1/27	60.50	5.11	71.0	0	0
T20s	9	48	66	1	1/13	1/13	66.00	8.25	48.0	0	0

WILL YOUNG

RHB / OB / R0 / W0

FULL NAME: William Alexander Young
BORN: November 22, 1992, New Plymouth, New Zealand
SQUAD NO: TBC
HEIGHT: 5ft 10in
NICKNAME: Chorizo
EDUCATION: New Plymouth Boys' High School; University of Canterbury, Christchurch
TEAMS: New Zealand, Northamptonshire, Central Districts, Durham
ROLE: Batter
DEBUT: Test: 2020; ODI: 2021; T20I: 2021; First-class: 2012; List A: 2013; T20: 2012

BEST BATTING: 162 Central Districts vs Auckland, Auckland, 2018

WHO IS YOUR LOOKALIKE? I've been told it's Flume (Australian musician)
FIRST CRICKET CLUB? New Plymouth Old Boys CC, New Zealand
MOST BEAUTIFUL THING YOU HAVE EVER SEEN? Sunset over New Zealand's Southern Alps on a calm winter evening
WHO WOULD YOU MOST AND LEAST LIKE TO HAVE A NET WITH? Most – Ajaz Patel (we always have a good battle). Least – Kieran Noema-Barnett bowling off spin (only one winner there)
NOTES: Northamptonshire have signed the Kiwi opener as an overseas player for the County Championship and One-Day Cup, although his availability is likely to be restricted due to New Zealand's Test tour of England. This will be Young's second stint in county cricket following a short spell at Durham last year which included two four-day centuries

Batting	Mat	Inns	NO	Runs	HS	Ave	SR	100	50	Ct	St
Tests	9	14	0	439	89	31.35	41.18	0	5	6	-
ODIs	2	2	1	12	11*	12.00	92.30	0	0	1	-
T20Is	8	7	0	166	53	23.71	102.46	0	1	2	-
First-class	92	152	13	5807	162	41.77	48.09	12	34	50	-
List A	65	65	5	2257	136	37.61	86.40	6	12	24	-
T20s	81	75	4	1892	101	26.64	133.61	1	10	35	-

Bowling	Mat	Balls	Runs	Wkts	BBI	BBM	Ave	Econ	SR	5w	10
Tests	9	-	-	-	-	-	-	-	-	-	-
ODIs	2	-	-	-	-	-	-	-	-	-	-
T20Is	8	-	-	-	-	-	-	-	-	-	-
First-class	92	18	8	0	-	-	-	2.66	-	0	0
List A	65	-	-	-	-	-	-	-	-	-	-
T20s	81	-	-	-	-	-	-	-	-	-	-

SAIF ZAIB

LHB / SLA / RO / WO

FULL NAME: Saif Ali Zaib
BORN: May 22, 1998, High Wycombe, Buckinghamshire
SQUAD NO: 5
HEIGHT: 5ft 8in
NICKNAME: Danger
EDUCATION: Royal Grammar School, High Wycombe
TEAMS: Northamptonshire
ROLE: Allrounder
DEBUT: First-class: 2015; List A: 2014; T20: 2017

NORTHAMPTONSHIRE

BEST BATTING: 135 Northamptonshire vs Sussex, Northampton, 2021
BEST BOWLING: 6-115 Northamptonshire vs Loughborough MCCU, Northampton, 2017

WHO IS YOUR LOOKALIKE? Novak Djokovic
FIRST CRICKET CLUB? High Wycombe CC, Buckinghamshire
WHAT WOULD YOU CHANGE ABOUT THE STRUCTURE OF THE COUNTY SEASON? More T20!
BIGGEST INFLUENCE ON YOUR DEVELOPMENT AS A CRICKETER (EXCLUDING PARENTS)?
My grandad – he showed me how hard work gets rewarded
WHO IS THE BEST BATTER/KEEPER/ALLROUNDER/BOWLER IN COUNTY CRICKET
(EXCLUDING TEAMMATES)? Harry Brook/Ben Foakes/Lewis Gregory/Sam Cook
MOST UNDERRATED PLAYER IN COUNTY CRICKET? Jamie Smith
MOST BEAUTIFUL THING YOU HAVE EVER SEEN? A broken Wattbike
HOBBIES? Shopping
IF YOU COULD TURN BACK TIME... I'd know about Bitcoin
WHO WOULD YOU MOST LIKE TO HAVE A NET WITH? Kumar Sangakkara
GUILTY PLEASURE? Cinnamon swirls
TWITTER: @zaib_05

Batting	Mat	Inns	NO	Runs	HS	Ave	SR	100	50	Ct	St
First-class	33	51	4	1106	135	23.53	45.42	1	6	9	-
List A	18	12	0	205	43	17.08	84.36	0	0	2	-
T20s	25	19	4	257	36	17.13	129.79	0	0	11	-

Bowling	Mat	Balls	Runs	Wkts	BBI	BBM	Ave	Econ	SR	5w	10
First-class	33	1088	636	20	6/115	6/115	31.80	3.50	54.4	2	0
List A	18	306	294	8	3/37	3/37	36.75	5.76	38.2	0	0
T20s	25	108	150	2	1/20	1/20	75.00	8.33	54.0	0	0

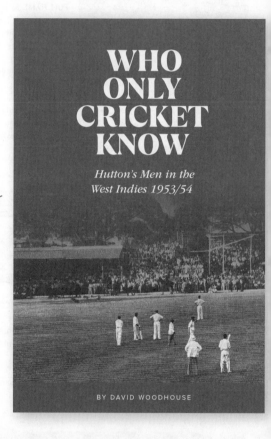

Women's Players

FIXTURES

CAPTAIN: Heather Knight
COACH: Lisa Keightley

2022 SUMMER FIXTURES

June 27-30
England vs South Africa
Only Test, Taunton

July 11
England vs South Africa
1st ODI, Northampton

July 15
England vs South Africa
2nd ODI, Bristol

July 18
England vs South Africa
3rd ODI, Leicester

July 21
England vs South Africa
1st T20I, Chelmsford

July 23
England vs South Africa
2nd T20I, Worcester

July 25
England vs South Africa
3rd T20I, Derby

July 30
England vs Sri Lanka
Commonwealth Games
Group B
T20I, Edgbaston

August 2
England vs South Africa
Commonwealth Games
Group B
T20I, Edgbaston

August 4
England vs New Zealand
Commonwealth Games
Group B
T20I, Edgbaston

September 10
England vs India
1st T20I, Chester-le-Street

September 13
England vs India
2nd T20I, Derby

September 15
England vs India
3rd T20I, Bristol

September 18
England vs India
1st ODI, Hove

September 21
England vs India
2nd ODI, Beckenham

September 24
England vs India
3rd ODI, Lord's

2022 – KEY DOMESTIC DATES

May 14-June 4	Charlotte Edwards Cup (T20) group phase
June 11	Charlotte Edwards Cup Finals Day, Northampton
July 2-23	First phase of Rachael Heyhoe Flint Trophy (50-over)
August 11-September 3	The Hundred (final at Lord's on September 3)
September 9-21	Second phase of Rachael Heyhoe Flint Trophy
September 25	Rachael Heyhoe Flint Trophy final, Lord's

GEORGIA ADAMS   RHB / OB / MVP6

FULL NAME: Georgia Louise Adams
BORN: October 4, 1993, Chesterfield, Derbyshire
SQUAD NO: 1
HEIGHT: 5ft 9in
NICKNAME: Gadz
EDUCATION: Brighton College; Loughborough University
TEAMS: England A, Southern Vipers, Sussex, Loughborough Lightning
ROLE: Batter
DEBUT: List A: 2009; T20: 2009

SOUTHERN VIPERS

BEST BATTING: 154* Southern Vipers vs Western Storm, Southampton, 2020
BEST BOWLING: 4-35 Southern Vipers vs Northern Diamonds, Northampton, 2021

FIRST CRICKET CLUB? Henfield CC, West Sussex
WHAT WOULD YOU CHANGE ABOUT THE STRUCTURE OF THE DOMESTIC SEASON?
Introduce some red-ball cricket
BIGGEST INFLUENCE ON YOUR DEVELOPMENT AS A CRICKETER (EXCLUDING PARENTS)?
Salliann Briggs – former England player and Loughborough Lightning head coach. She
taught me to how to take myself out of my comfort zone
WHO IS THE BEST BATTER/KEEPER/ALLROUNDER/BOWLER IN DOMESTIC CRICKET
(EXCLUDING TEAMMATES)? Evelyn Jones/Ellie Threlkeld/Alice Capsey/Issy Wong
MOST UNDERRATED PLAYER IN DOMESTIC CRICKET? Jo Gardner
MOST BEAUTIFUL THING YOU HAVE EVER SEEN? My two bulldogs
HOBBIES? Walking my bulldogs
WHO WOULD YOU MOST AND LEAST LIKE TO HAVE A NET WITH? Most – AB de Villiers.
Least – Jofra Archer
MAKE ONE PREDICTION FOR THE FUTURE OF CRICKET: Charlotte Edwards to coach England
to a World Cup win
WHAT MAKES YOU WORRY? Being late
WHAT GIVES YOU JOY? Being in the nets
TWITTER: @GeorgiaAdams01

Batting	Mat	Inns	NO	Runs	HS	Ave	SR	100	50	Ct	St
List A	70	67	6	1954	154*	32.03	67.96	3	11	44	-
T20s	106	96	15	1907	88*	23.54	99.63	0	12	42	-

Bowling	Mat	Balls	Mdns	Runs	Wkts	BB	Ave	4wI	5wI	SR	Econ
List A	70	1146	19	759	30	4-35	25.30	1	0	38.20	3.97
T20s	106	210	0	236	10	3-9	23.60	0	0	21.00	6.74

EMILY ARLOTT

RHB / RMF / MVP16

CENTRAL SPARKS

FULL NAME: Emily Louise Arlott
BORN: February 23, 1998, King's Lynn, Norfolk
SQUAD NO: 14
HEIGHT: 6ft
NICKNAME: Arlo
EDUCATION: John Masefield High School, Ledbury, Herefordshire
TEAMS: England A, Central Sparks, Worcestershire
ROLE: Bowler
DEBUT: List A: 2013; T20: 2013

BEST BATTING: 33 Worcestershire vs Ireland, Kidderminster, 2015
BEST BOWLING: 5-29 Central Sparks vs Southern Vipers, Hove, 2021

FIRST CRICKET CLUB? Eastnor CC, Ledbury, Herefordshire
WHAT WOULD YOU CHANGE ABOUT THE STRUCTURE OF THE DOMESTIC SEASON?
Introduce a two-day format
BIGGEST INFLUENCE ON YOUR DEVELOPMENT AS A CRICKETER (EXCLUDING PARENTS)?
Elliot Wilson – Academy coach at Worcestershire. He helped me progress as a cricketer from the age of 13 to where I am now. He's always been there to support me on and off the field and has been a very good friend during some tough times in my life
WHO IS THE BEST BATTER/KEEPER/ALLROUNDER/BOWLER IN DOMESTIC CRICKET (EXCLUDING TEAMMATES)? Alice Capsey/Ellie Threlkeld/Alice Capsey/Alice Davidson-Richards
MOST UNDERRATED PLAYER IN DOMESTIC CRICKET? Bryony Smith
MOST BEAUTIFUL THING YOU HAVE EVER SEEN? A sunset in Adelaide
HOBBIES? Golf
WHO WOULD YOU LEAST LIKE TO HAVE A NET WITH? Mitchell Starc
WHAT DO YOU MOST ENJOY LISTENING TO? Imagine Dragons
WHAT MAKES YOU WORRY? Not doing enough
WHAT GIVES YOU JOY? Cricket
GUILTY PLEASURE? Nando's
TWITTER: @EmArlott

Batting	Mat	Inns	NO	Runs	HS	Ave	SR	100	50	Ct	St
List A	52	42	6	376	33	10.44	-	0	0	26	-
T20s	54	42	12	440	54	14.66	-	0	1	14	-

Bowling	Mat	Balls	Mdns	Runs	Wkts	BB	Ave	4wI	5wI	SR	Econ
List A	52	1907	32	1424	49	5-29	29.06	1	1	38.91	4.48
T20s	54	862	1	876	35	3-21	25.02	0	0	24.62	6.09

HOLLIE ARMITAGE   RHB / LB / MVP30

FULL NAME: Hollie Jade Armitage
BORN: June 14, 1997, Huddersfield
SQUAD NO: 57
HEIGHT: 5ft 9in
NICKNAME: Armo
EDUCATION: Honley High School, West Yorkshire; Loughborough College
TEAMS: Northern Diamonds, Yorkshire, Sydney Sixers, Tasmania, Yorkshire Diamonds
ROLE: Allrounder
DEBUT: List A: 2013; T20: 2013

BEST BATTING: 70 Yorkshire vs Staffordshire, Hanley, 2016
BEST BOWLING: 4-17 Yorkshire vs Berkshire, Finchampstead, 2016

WHO IS YOUR LOOKALIKE? Lissy Macleod
FIRST CRICKET CLUB? Meltham CC, Kirklees, West Yorkshire
WHAT WOULD YOU CHANGE ABOUT THE STRUCTURE OF THE DOMESTIC SEASON? Have 15 fully contracted pros for each regional team
WHO IS THE BEST BATTER/KEEPER/ALLROUNDER/BOWLER IN DOMESTIC CRICKET (EXCLUDING TEAMMATES)? Nat Sciver/Ellie Threlkeld/Nat Sciver/Beth Langston
MOST UNDERRATED PLAYER IN DOMESTIC CRICKET? Alice Davidson-Richards
WHAT WOULD A FLY ON THE WALL HEAR IN YOUR DRESSING ROOM? The theme from RuPaul's Drag Race (reality TV series)
MOST BEAUTIFUL THING YOU HAVE EVER SEEN? Koopa Troopa
HOBBIES? Golf
WHO WOULD YOU LEAST LIKE TO HAVE A NET WITH? Phoebe Graham – because she thinks everything is out!
MAKE ONE PREDICTION FOR THE FUTURE OF CRICKET: The women's IPL
WHAT DO YOU MOST ENJOY LISTENING TO? Miguel
WHAT MAKES YOU WORRY? Arriving less than 30 minutes early
GUILTY PLEASURE? Putting hot sauce on pretty much every meal
TWITTER: @HollieArmo

Batting	Mat	Inns	NO	Runs	HS	Ave	SR	100	50	Ct	St
List A	57	55	5	1217	70	24.34	59.92	0	9	19	-
T20s	63	60	7	944	71*	17.81	105.82	0	4	23	-

Bowling	Mat	Balls	Mdns	Runs	Wkts	BB	Ave	4wI	5wI	SR	Econ
List A	57	982	8	795	35	4-17	22.71	1	0	28.05	4.85
T20s	63	409	2	377	19	3-7	19.84	0	0	21.52	5.53

TAMMY BEAUMONT RHB / WK

FULL NAME: Tamsin Tilley Beaumont
BORN: March 11, 1991, Dover, Kent
SQUAD NO: 12
HEIGHT: 5ft 2in
NICKNAME: Tambo
EDUCATION: Sir Roger Manwood's School, Kent; Loughborough University
TEAMS: England, Lightning, Kent, Adelaide Strikers, Melbourne Renegades, Southern Vipers, Surrey Stars, Sydney Thunder
ROLE: Batter
DEBUT: Test: 2013; ODI: 2009; T20I: 2009; List A: 2007; T20: 2008

BEST ODI BATTING: 168* England vs Pakistan, Taunton, 2016

WHO IS YOUR LOOKALIKE? Nicole Bolton (Australia allrounder)
FIRST CRICKET CLUB? Sandwich Town CC, Kent
WHAT WOULD YOU CHANGE ABOUT THE STRUCTURE OF THE DOMESTIC SEASON?
More games!
BIGGEST INFLUENCE ON YOUR DEVELOPMENT AS A CRICKETER (EXCLUDING PARENTS)?
Carl Crowe – he was our England assistant coach on some of my first tours and has since been a close friend and mentor
WHO IS THE BEST BATTER/KEEPER/ALLROUNDER/BOWLER IN DOMESTIC CRICKET
(EXCLUDING TEAMMATES)? Heather Knight/Amy Jones/Nat Sciver/Katherine Brunt
MOST BEAUTIFUL THING YOU HAVE EVER SEEN? Baby turtles released into the sea at midnight in Barbados
HOBBIES? Getting out into the countryside or on the coast
WHO WOULD YOU MOST AND LEAST LIKE TO HAVE A NET WITH? Most – Brendon McCullum. I'd be massively fan-girling him! Least – Jofra Archer. That bouncer looks vicious!
WHAT DO YOU MOST ENJOY LISTENING TO? Musicals
WHAT GIVES YOU JOY? My dog doing something stupid every day
TWITTER: @Tammy_Beaumont

Batting	Mat	Inns	NO	Runs	HS	Ave	SR	100	50	Ct	St
Tests	6	9	0	239	70	26.55	43.77	0	2	5	-
ODIs	85	77	9	2949	168*	43.36	73.03	8	14	22	4
T20Is	99	83	11	1721	116	23.90	108.37	1	10	14	4

Bowling	Mat	Balls	Runs	Wkts	BBI	BBM	Ave	Econ	SR	5w	10
Tests	6	-	-	-	-	-	-	-	-	-	-
ODIs	85	-	-	-	-	-	-	-	-	-	-
T20Is	99	-	-	-	-	-	-	-	-	-	-

LAUREN BELL

RHB / RFM / MVP15

FULL NAME: Lauren Katie Bell
BORN: January 2, 2001, Swindon, Wiltshire
SQUAD NO: 14
HEIGHT: 6ft 1in
NICKNAME: Belly
EDUCATION: Bradfield College;
Loughborough University
TEAMS: England A, Southern Vipers,
Middlesex, Berkshire
ROLE: Bowler
DEBUT: List A: 2015; T20: 2015

SOUTHERN VIPERS

BEST BATTING: 36 Berkshire vs Surrey, Maidenhead, 2018
BEST BOWLING: 4-17 Berkshire vs Devon, Maidenhead, 2018

FIRST CRICKET CLUB? Hungerford CC, Berkshire
WHAT WOULD YOU CHANGE ABOUT THE STRUCTURE OF THE DOMESTIC SEASON?
Schedule the 50-over competition before The Hundred
WHO IS THE BEST BATTER/KEEPER/BOWLER IN DOMESTIC CRICKET (EXCLUDING
TEAMMATES)? Emma Lamb/Ellie Threlkeld/Kirstie Gordon
WHAT WOULD A FLY ON THE WALL HEAR IN YOUR DRESSING ROOM? "We are the
Southern Viperssssss"
HOBBIES? Online shopping
WHO WOULD YOU MOST AND LEAST LIKE TO HAVE A NET WITH? Most – Andrew Flintoff,
because he's funny. Least – Charlotte Edwards, because she'd send it
WHAT DO YOU MOST ENJOY LISTENING TO? The 1975
WHAT MAKES YOU WORRY? Being in busy, crowded places
WHAT GIVES YOU JOY? My boyfriend, family and friends
TWITTER: @_laurenbell2

Batting	Mat	Inns	NO	Runs	HS	Ave	SR	100	50	Ct	St
List A	39	26	6	194	36	9.70	-	0	0	6	-
T20s	56	23	6	164	35	9.64	71.30	0	0	13	-

Bowling	Mat	Balls	Mdns	Runs	Wkts	BB	Ave	4wl	5wl	SR	Econ
List A	39	1659	23	1151	57	4-17	20.19	2	0	29.10	4.16
T20s	56	907	4	943	41	3-22	23.00	0	0	22.12	6.23

MAIA BOUCHIER

RHB / RM / MVP33

SOUTHERN VIPERS

FULL NAME: Maia Emily Bouchier
BORN: December 5, 1998, Kensington, London
SQUAD NO: 16
HEIGHT: 5ft 9in
NICKNAME: The Mighty Bouch
EDUCATION: Rugby School, Warwickshire; Oxford Brookes University
TEAMS: England, Southern Vipers, Hampshire, Auckland, Melbourne Stars, Middlesex
ROLE: Allrounder
DEBUT: T20I: 2021; List A: 2014; T20: 2014

BEST T20I BATTING: 25 England vs New Zealand, Hove, 2021

WHO IS YOUR LOOKALIKE? Mila Kunis
FIRST CRICKET CLUB? Primrose Hill CC, London
BIGGEST INFLUENCE ON YOUR DEVELOPMENT AS A CRICKETER (EXCLUDING PARENTS)?
Tim Roberts and Michael Powell, my old coaches at Rugby School. They helped build my confidence against quick bowlers at school, where I was playing boys' First XI cricket
WHO IS THE BEST BATTER/KEEPER/ALLROUNDER/BOWLER IN DOMESTIC CRICKET (EXCLUDING TEAMMATES)? Emma Lamb/Ellie Threlkeld/Kelly Castle/Emily Arlott
MOST UNDERRATED PLAYER IN DOMESTIC CRICKET? Sarah Bryce
WHO WOULD YOU MOST AND LEAST LIKE TO HAVE A NET WITH? Most – Brian Lara. Least – Brett Lee
MAKE ONE PREDICTION FOR THE FUTURE OF CRICKET: Women's cricket will be more entertaining than the men's game
WHAT MAKES YOU WORRY? Environmental issues and the advances in technology
WHAT GIVES YOU JOY? Family, friends and nature
GUILTY PLEASURE? Marmite
TWITTER: @maiabouchier

Batting	Mat	Inns	NO	Runs	HS	Ave	SR	100	50	Ct	St
T20Is	3	2	0	26	25	13.00	100.00	0	0	0	-
Bowling	Mat	Balls	Runs	Wkts	BBI	BBM	Ave	Econ	SR	5w	10
T20Is	3	-	-	-	-	-	-	-	-	-	-

GEORGIE BOYCE RHB / RM

FULL NAME: Georgie Eva Burton Boyce
BORN: October 4, 1998, Nottingham
SQUAD NO: 8
HEIGHT: 5ft 6in
EDUCATION: The Holgate Academy, Hucknall, Nottinghamshire; Loughborough University
TEAMS: Thunder, Lancashire, Lancashire Thunder, Nottinghamshire
ROLE: Batter
DEBUT: List A: 2014; T20: 2013

BEST BATTING: 91 Thunder vs Sunrisers, Chester, 2021
BEST BOWLING: 2-20 Lancashire vs Yorkshire, Harrogate, 2019

FIRST CRICKET CLUB? Notts & Arnold CC, Nottingham
WHAT WOULD YOU CHANGE ABOUT THE STRUCTURE OF THE DOMESTIC SEASON?
Introduce some multi-day games
BIGGEST INFLUENCE ON YOUR DEVELOPMENT AS A CRICKETER (EXCLUDING PARENTS)?
Sue Day, my primary-school PE teacher. She introduced me to cricket and took me to see some women's matches
WHO IS THE BEST BATTER/KEEPER/ALLROUNDER/BOWLER IN DOMESTIC CRICKET (EXCLUDING TEAMMATES)? Alice Capsey/Sarah Bryce/Dani Gibson/Lauren Bell
MOST UNDERRATED PLAYER IN DOMESTIC CRICKET? Hollie Armitage
MOST BEAUTIFUL THING YOU HAVE EVER SEEN? My brother getting married
HOBBIES? Hiking
WHO WOULD YOU MOST LIKE TO HAVE A NET WITH? Enid Bakewell – legend of the game
WHAT DO YOU MOST ENJOY LISTENING TO? Radio 1
GUILTY PLEASURE? Watching Neighbours
TWITTER: @GeorgieBoyce

Batting	Mat	Inns	NO	Runs	HS	Ave	SR	100	50	Ct	St
List A	48	48	1	1117	91	23.76	-	0	6	8	-
T20s	72	66	4	1240	96*	20.00	-	0	7	10	-

Bowling	Mat	Balls	Mdns	Runs	Wkts	BB	Ave	4wl	5wl	SR	Econ
List A	48	438	6	298	6	2-20	49.66	0	0	73.00	4.08
T20s	72	222	0	227	6	2-15	37.83	0	0	37.00	6.13

KATHERINE BRUNT

RHB / RFM

FULL NAME: Katherine Helen Brunt
BORN: July 2, 1985, Barnsley
SQUAD NO: 26
HEIGHT: 5ft 5in
NICKNAME: Baby Rhino
EDUCATION: Penistone Grammar School, South Yorkshire
TEAMS: England, Northern Diamonds, Yorkshire, Melbourne Stars, Perth Scorchers, Yorkshire Diamonds
ROLE: Allrounder
DEBUT: Test: 2004; ODI: 2005; T20I: 2005; List A: 2004; T20: 2004

BEST ODI BATTING: 72* England vs South Africa, Worcester, 2018
BEST ODI BOWLING: 5-18 England vs Australia, Wormsley, 2011

FIRST CRICKET CLUB? Barnsley CC, South Yorkshire
WHAT WOULD YOU CHANGE ABOUT THE STRUCTURE OF THE DOMESTIC SEASON? Ensure that England players can play in all of the domestic 50-over and T20 matches
WHO IS THE BEST BATTER/KEEPER/ALLROUNDER/BOWLER IN DOMESTIC CRICKET (EXCLUDING TEAMMATES)? Georgia Adams/Ellie Threlkeld/Bryony Smith/Katie Levick
MOST BEAUTIFUL THING YOU HAVE EVER SEEN? Natalie Sciver
HOBBIES? Property renovation
IF YOU COULD TURN BACK TIME.... I'd have been a leggie
WHO WOULD YOU MOST AND LEAST LIKE TO HAVE A NET WITH? Most – my brother Daniel. Least – Jenny Gunn with the slinger
MAKE ONE PREDICTION FOR THE FUTURE OF CRICKET: I'll be England Women head coach in six-and-a-half years
WHAT DO YOU MOST ENJOY LISTENING TO? The sound of someone nicking off
WHAT MAKES YOU WORRY? Childbirth, and the prospect of Natty (Sciver) going on tour without me
TWITTER: @KBrunt26

Batting	Mat	Inns	NO	Runs	HS	Ave	SR	100	50	Ct	St
Tests	14	18	4	184	52	13.14	28.93	0	1	5	-
ODIs	131	74	21	1007	72*	19.00	74.92	0	2	38	-
T20Is	96	58	26	504	42*	15.75	112.50	0	0	27	-

Bowling	Mat	Balls	Runs	Wkts	BBI	BBM	Ave	Econ	SR	5w	10
Tests	14	2611	1098	51	6/69	9/111	21.52	2.52	51.1	3	0
ODIs	131	6410	3759	163	5/18	5/18	23.06	3.51	39.3	5	0
T20Is	96	2045	1888	98	3/6	3/6	19.26	5.53	20.8	0	0

KATHRYN BRYCE

RHB / RM / MVP13

FULL NAME: Kathryn Emma Bryce
BORN: November 17, 1997, Edinburgh
SQUAD NO: 17
HEIGHT: 5ft 4in
NICKNAME: Brycie
EDUCATION: Loughborough University
TEAMS: Scotland, Lightning, Warwickshire, Loughborough Lightning
ROLE: Allrounder
DEBUT: T20I: 2018; List A: 2017; T20: 2017

LIGHTNING

BEST T20I BATTING: 73* Scotland vs Netherlands, Arbroath, 2019
BEST T20I BOWLING: 2-5 Scotland vs Germany, La Manga, 2021

FIRST CRICKET CLUB? Watsonian CC, Edinburgh
MOST EXCITING DAY AS A CRICKETER? Playing in my first global qualifying tournament for Scotland in Thailand in 2015
WHO IS THE BEST BATTER/KEEPER/ALLROUNDER/BOWLER IN DOMESTIC CRICKET (EXCLUDING TEAMMATES)? Eve Jones/Ellie Threlkeld/Jenny Gunn/Tara Norris
MOST UNDERRATED PLAYER IN DOMESTIC CRICKET? Laura Jackson
WHAT WOULD A FLY ON THE WALL HEAR IN YOUR DRESSING ROOM? Musicals
MOST BEAUTIFUL THING YOU HAVE EVER SEEN? Elephants in the flesh
HOBBIES? Hockey and golf
WHO WOULD YOU MOST LIKE TO HAVE A NET WITH? Andrew Flintoff
MAKE ONE PREDICTION FOR THE FUTURE OF CRICKET: There will be a women's domestic multi-day competition
WHAT GIVES YOU JOY? Going for coffee with friends
GUILTY PLEASURE? Grey's Anatomy
TWITTER: @Kathryn_Bryce

Batting	Mat	Inns	NO	Runs	HS	Ave	SR	100	50	Ct	St
T20Is	26	24	8	647	73*	40.43	98.47	0	4	15	-

Bowling	Mat	Balls	Runs	Wkts	BBI	BBM	Ave	Econ	SR	5w	10
T20Is	26	527	339	25	2/5	2/5	13.56	3.85	21.0	0	0

SARAH BRYCE

RHB / WK

FULL NAME: Sarah Jennifer Bryce
BORN: January 8, 2000, Edinburgh
SQUAD NO: 8
HEIGHT: 5ft 7in
NICKNAME: Sazzle
EDUCATION: Loughborough University
TEAMS: Scotland, Lightning, Kent, Nottinghamshire
ROLE: Wicketkeeper/batter
DEBUT: T20I: 2018; List A: 2019; T20: 2018

BEST T20I BATTING: 65 Scotland vs Netherlands, Arbroath, 2019

FIRST CRICKET CLUB? Watsonian CC, Edinburgh
WHAT WOULD YOU CHANGE ABOUT THE STRUCTURE OF THE DOMESTIC SEASON? Bring in some multi-day cricket
MOST EXCITING DAY AS A CRICKETER? Being part of the Scotland team which beat Ireland during the T20I quadrangular series in the Netherlands in 2019
WHO IS THE BEST BATTER/KEEPER/ALLROUNDER/BOWLER IN DOMESTIC CRICKET (EXCLUDING TEAMMATES)? Emma Lamb/Ellie Threlkeld/Jenny Gunn/Lauren Bell
MOST UNDERRATED PLAYER IN DOMESTIC CRICKET? Sophie Luff
HOBBIES? The piano
MAKE ONE PREDICTION FOR THE FUTURE OF CRICKET: There will be more women's Test matches
WHAT DO YOU MOST ENJOY LISTENING TO? Musicals
GUILTY PLEASURE? The Vicar of Dibley
TWITTER: @Sarah_Bryce08

Batting	Mat	Inns	NO	Runs	HS	Ave	SR	100	50	Ct	St
T20Is	32	32	8	706	65	29.41	105.53	0	2	19	23

Bowling	Mat	Balls	Runs	Wkts	BBI	BBM	Ave	Econ	SR	5w	10
T20Is	32	-	-	-	-	-	-	-	-	-	-

AMI CAMPBELL   LHB / RM

FULL NAME: Ami Campbell
BORN: June 6, 1991, Newcastle upon Tyne, Northumberland
SQUAD NO: TBC
HEIGHT: 5ft 7in
NICKNAME: AC
EDUCATION: Leeds Metropolitan Unversity
TEAMS: Central Sparks, Durham, Northern Diamonds, Northumberland, Yorkshire
ROLE: Batter
DEBUT: List A: 2008; T20: 2010

BEST BATTING: 135 Northumberland vs Cumbria, Stocksfield, 2016
BEST BOWLING: 5-31 Northumberland vs Shropshire, Stocksfield, 2010

WHO IS YOUR LOOKALIKE? Ducky from The Land Before Time
FIRST CRICKET CLUB? South Northumberland CC, Newcastle upon Tyne
WHO IS THE BEST BATTER/KEEPER/ALLROUNDER/BOWLER IN DOMESTIC CRICKET (EXCLUDING TEAMMATES)? Tammy Beaumont/Abbey Freeborn/Nat Sciver/Sophie Ecclestone
MOST BEAUTIFUL THING YOU HAVE EVER SEEN? Sunrise from the top of Mount Batur volcano in Bali, Indonesia
HOBBIES? Stroking dogs, scenic walks
IF YOU COULD TURN BACK TIME... I'd change nothing – it's all experience
WHO WOULD YOU LEAST LIKE TO HAVE A NET WITH? Sterre Kalis – she hogs all the batting time! (Love her though)
MAKE ONE PREDICTION FOR THE FUTURE OF CRICKET: Pro women's domestic players will be on a minimum salary of £30,000 within the next 10 years
WHAT DO YOU MOST ENJOY LISTENING TO? James Morrison
WHAT MAKES YOU WORRY? Underperforming
WHAT GIVES YOU JOY? Structure, love, family, healthy friends
TWITTER: @ACfit_wellbeing

Batting	Mat	Inns	NO	Runs	HS	Ave	SR	100	50	Ct	St
List A	50	47	2	1131	135	25.13	-		1	5	22	-
T20s	33	32	2	683	81	22.76	-	0	5	12	-

Bowling	Mat	Balls	Mdns	Runs	Wkts	BB	Ave	4wl	5wl	SR	Econ
List A	50	344	11	198	11	5-31	18.00	0	1	31.27	3.45
T20s	33	72	0	66	1	1-22	66.00	0	0	72.00	5.50

ALICE CAPSEY

RHB / OB / MVP3

FULL NAME: Alice Rose Capsey
BORN: August 11, 2004, Surrey
SQUAD NO: 26
HEIGHT: 5ft 4in
NICKNAME: Caps
EDUCATION: Bede's Senior School, Hailsham, East Sussex; Lancing College, West Sussex
TEAMS: England A, South East Stars, Surrey
ROLE: Allrounder
DEBUT: List A: 2019; T20: 2019

BEST BATTING: 78 South East Stars vs Lightning, Beckenham, 2021
BEST BOWLING: 3-65 Surrey vs Hampshire, Totton, 2019

FIRST CRICKET CLUB? Capel CC, Surrey
WHAT WOULD YOU CHANGE ABOUT THE STRUCTURE OF THE DOMESTIC SEASON?
Schedule more games!
WHO IS THE BEST BATTER/KEEPER/ALLROUNDER/BOWLER IN DOMESTIC CRICKET
(EXCLUDING TEAMMATES)? Emma Lamb/Ellie Threlkeld/Hollie Armitage/Lauren Bell
MOST UNDERRATED PLAYER IN DOMESTIC CRICKET? Bess Heath
WHAT WOULD A FLY ON THE WALL HEAR IN YOUR DRESSING ROOM? People having fun
MOST BEAUTIFUL THING YOU HAVE EVER SEEN? A sunset in Corfu
HOBBIES? Tennis and squash
IF YOU COULD TURN BACK TIME... I'd be more open to change sooner
WHO WOULD YOU MOST AND LEAST LIKE TO HAVE A NET WITH? Most – Sarah Taylor. Least
– Nat Sciver
MAKE ONE PREDICTION FOR THE FUTURE OF CRICKET: More women's players will be on
professional contracts and salaries will grow
WHAT MAKES YOU WORRY? Bad performances
TWITTER: @AliceCapsey

Batting	Mat	Inns	NO	Runs	HS	Ave	SR	100	50	Ct	St
List A	14	14	1	284	78	21.84	71.35	0	2	4	-
T20s	29	21	2	487	61	25.63	125.19	0	3	10	-

Bowling	Mat	Balls	Mdns	Runs	Wkts	BB	Ave	4wl	5wl	SR	Econ
List A	14	468	2	372	10	3-65	37.20	0	0	46.80	4.76
T20s	29	495	1	489	32	3-13	15.28	0	0	15.46	5.92

AMARA CARR

RHB / WK

FULL NAME: Amara Danielle Carr
BORN: April 17, 1994, Plymouth, Devon
SQUAD NO: 17
HEIGHT: 5ft 2in
NICKNAME: Mars
EDUCATION: University of Essex
TEAMS: Sunrisers, Devon, Middlesex, Somerset
ROLE: Wicketkeeper/batter
DEBUT: List A: 2008; T20: 2009

BEST BATTING: 105 Devon vs Middlesex, Eastcote, 2019

FIRST CRICKET CLUB? Mount Wise CC, Plymouth, Devon
BIGGEST INFLUENCE ON YOUR DEVELOPMENT AS A CRICKETER (EXCLUDING PARENTS)? My older brother. He's coached me at various times since I started playing cricket in Devon and has spent much of his free time throwing balls at me
WHO IS THE BEST BATTER/KEEPER/ALLROUNDER/BOWLER IN DOMESTIC CRICKET (EXCLUDING TEAMMATES)? Bryony Smith/Ellie Threlkeld/Alice Capsey/Lauren Bell
MOST UNDERRATED PLAYER IN DOMESTIC CRICKET? Linsey Smith
MOST BEAUTIFUL THING YOU HAVE EVER SEEN? Sunrise from the top of Lion's Head in Cape Town
WHO WOULD YOU MOST AND LEAST LIKE TO HAVE A NET WITH? Most – Eoin Morgan (to pick his brains). Least – Malcolm Marshall (bouncers!)
WHAT GIVES YOU JOY? The sea
TWITTER: @Amara_Carr

Batting	Mat	Inns	NO	Runs	HS	Ave	SR	100	50	Ct	St
List A	96	90	6	1640	105	19.52	-	1	7	47	34
T20s	61	49	11	751	52	19.76	-	0	2	12	24

KELLY CASTLE

RHB / RMF / MVP39

SUNRISERS

FULL NAME: Kelly Shannon Castle
BORN: September 4, 1997, Southend-on-Sea, Essex
SQUAD NO: 7
HEIGHT: 5ft 8in
NICKNAME: KC
EDUCATION: The King Edmund School, Rochford, Essex; Anglia Ruskin University
TEAMS: Sunrisers, Essex
ROLE: Allrounder
DEBUT: List A: 2012; T20: 2011

BEST BATTING: 52 Sunrisers vs Lightning, Loughborough, 2021
BEST BOWLING: 5-18 Essex vs Scotland, Billericay, 2015

WHO IS YOUR LOOKALIKE? Rapunzel from the film Tangled (because of the long blonde hair)
FIRST CRICKET CLUB? Rayleigh CC, Wickford, Essex
WHAT WOULD YOU CHANGE ABOUT THE STRUCTURE OF THE DOMESTIC SEASON? More games!
BIGGEST INFLUENCE ON YOUR DEVELOPMENT AS A CRICKETER (EXCLUDING PARENTS)? My primary-school teacher Mr G. He's the reason I started playing and he always told me to follow my dreams
WHO IS THE BEST BATTER/BOWLER IN DOMESTIC CRICKET (EXCLUDING TEAMMATES)? Sophie Luff/Beth Langston
MOST UNDERRATED PLAYER IN DOMESTIC CRICKET? Tash Farrant
WHAT WOULD A FLY ON THE WALL HEAR IN YOUR DRESSING ROOM? Grace Scrivens talking absolute waffle and playing the same music every single day
HOBBIES? Tap dancing
MAKE ONE PREDICTION FOR THE FUTURE OF CRICKET: Katherine Brunt will play until she's 50 while still taking five-fors for fun
WHAT GIVES YOU JOY? Summer
GUILTY PLEASURE? EastEnders
TWITTER: @KellyyShannon

Batting	Mat	Inns	NO	Runs	HS	Ave	SR	100	50	Ct	St
List A	54	51	5	560	52	12.17	-	0	1	8	-
T20s	56	49	12	493	48	13.32	76.19	0	0	10	-

Bowling	Mat	Balls	Mdns	Runs	Wkts	BB	Ave	4wI	5wI	SR	Econ
List A	54	1384	26	876	37	5-18	23.67	0	1	37.40	3.79
T20s	56	830	4	705	36	3-6	19.58	0	0	23.05	5.09

AYLISH CRANSTONE

LHB / LM

FULL NAME: Aylish Cranstone
BORN: August 28, 1994, Guildford, Surrey
SQUAD NO: 28
HEIGHT: 5ft 2in
EDUCATION: University of Exeter
TEAMS: South East Stars, Surrey, Devon, Hampshire, Surrey Stars
ROLE: Allrounder
DEBUT: List A: 2008; T20: 2010

SOUTH EAST STARS

BEST BATTING: 134* Devon vs Essex, Dunmow, 2016
BEST BOWLING: 5-5 Devon vs Leicestershire, Bolham, 2016

FIRST CRICKET CLUB? Rowledge CC, Surrey
WHAT WOULD YOU CHANGE ABOUT THE STRUCTURE OF THE DOMESTIC SEASON? Introduce home and away fixtures for the 50-over competition and add in some four-day matches
MOST BEAUTIFUL THING YOU HAVE EVER SEEN? A school of manta rays I swam with in the Maldives
HOBBIES? Cooking. I like to dip into bread-making every now and again
WHO WOULD YOU MOST AND LEAST LIKE TO HAVE A NET WITH? Most – Tash Farrant, my teammate and fellow leftie. She's great company and very challenging to bat against so we always have a great battle. Least – Mitchell Johnson
MAKE ONE PREDICTION FOR THE FUTURE OF CRICKET: A cricket ball that glows
WHAT DO YOU MOST ENJOY LISTENING TO? Relaxing music in high-quality headphones
WHAT GIVES YOU JOY? The sunshine
GUILTY PLEASURE? One Direction
TWITTER: @AylishCranstone

Batting	Mat	Inns	NO	Runs	HS	Ave	SR	100	50	Ct	St
List A	86	84	11	2124	134*	29.09	-	1	13	22	-
T20s	68	51	11	787	78*	19.67	105.35	0	3	13	-

Bowling	Mat	Balls	Mdns	Runs	Wkts	BB	Ave	4wl	5wl	SR	Econ
List A	86	883	16	662	23	5-5	28.78	0	1	38.39	4.49
T20s	68	153	1	120	8	3-17	15.00	0	0	19.12	4.70

KATE CROSS — RHB / RMF / MVP11

ENGLAND WOMEN

FULL NAME: Kathryn Laura Cross
BORN: October 3, 1991, Manchester
SQUAD NO: 16
HEIGHT: 5ft 7in
NICKNAME: Crossy, Sunny
EDUCATION: Bury Grammar School;
University of Leeds
TEAMS: England, Thunder, Lancashire,
Brisbane Heat, Lancashire Thunder, Perth
Scorchers, Western Australia
ROLE: Bowler
DEBUT: Test: 2014; ODI: 2013; T20I: 2013;
List A: 2005; T20: 2008

BEST ODI BATTING: 29 England vs New Zealand, Leicester, 2021
BEST ODI BOWLING: 5-24 England vs New Zealand, Lincoln, 2015

WHO IS YOUR LOOKALIKE? Harmanpreet Kaur
FIRST CRICKET CLUB? Heywood CC, Greater Manchester
WHAT WOULD YOU CHANGE ABOUT THE STRUCTURE OF THE DOMESTIC SEASON? Play
everyone home and away in T20 and 50-over cricket, plus introduce some multi-day games
WHO IS THE BEST BATTER/KEEPER/ALLROUNDER/BOWLER IN DOMESTIC CRICKET
(EXCLUDING TEAMMATES)? Eve Jones/Ellie Threlkeld (sorry, she is a teammate, but she's the
best!)/Alice Davidson-Richards/Alice Capsey
HOBBIES? Podcasting
WHO WOULD YOU MOST AND LEAST LIKE TO HAVE A NET WITH? Most – Glenn McGrath, to
talk all things bowling. Least – Cathryn Fitzpatrick, because she was rapid!
MAKE ONE PREDICTION FOR THE FUTURE OF CRICKET: Women will play more Tests than
one a year
WHAT DO YOU MOST ENJOY LISTENING TO? Anya Shrubsole rapping Eminem
WHAT MAKES YOU WORRY? Checking my phone after a night out
WHAT GIVES YOU JOY? Seeing so many young girls in the crowds during The Hundred
TWITTER: @katecross16

Batting	Mat	Inns	NO	Runs	HS	Ave	SR	100	50	Ct	St
Tests	5	8	4	27	11	6.75	28.12	0	0	0	-
ODIs	37	16	7	90	29	10.00	56.96	0	0	7	-
T20Is	13	1	1	0	0*	-	0.00	0	0	3	-

Bowling	Mat	Balls	Runs	Wkts	BBI	BBM	Ave	Econ	SR	5w	10
Tests	5	872	397	15	3/29	6/70	26.46	2.73	58.1	0	0
ODIs	37	1665	1191	55	5/24	5/24	21.65	4.29	30.2	2	0
T20Is	13	264	296	11	2/18	2/18	26.90	6.72	24.0	0	0

NAOMI DATTANI

LHB / LMF / MVP42

FULL NAME: Naomi Dilip Dattani
BORN: April 28, 1994, Ealing, London
SQUAD NO: 23
HEIGHT: 5ft 4in
NICKNAME: Nomes
EDUCATION: Greenford High School, Ealing; Loughborough University
TEAMS: Sunrisers, Middlesex, Surrey Stars, Western Storm
ROLE: Allrounder
DEBUT: List A: 2008; T20: 2009

SUNRISERS

BEST BATTING: 71 Middlesex vs Sussex, Billingshurst, 2016
BEST BOWLING: 4-23 Middlesex vs Worcestershire, Worcester, 2010

FIRST CRICKET CLUB? Perivale Phonecians CC, London
WHAT WOULD YOU CHANGE ABOUT THE STRUCTURE OF THE DOMESTIC SEASON? Have some two-day games
WHO IS THE BEST BATTER/KEEPER/ALLROUNDER/BOWLER IN DOMESTIC CRICKET (EXCLUDING TEAMMATES)? Georgia Adams/Carla Rudd/Dani Gibson/Beth Langston
MOST BEAUTIFUL THING YOU HAVE EVER SEEN? Lion Rock, Auckland – the black-sand beach and being at the top of the rock at sunset
HOBBIES? Preparing for a life after cricket!
IF YOU COULD TURN BACK TIME... I'd put a greater emphasis on teaching sport at school going back hundreds of years in order to create more healthy, resilient and confident people
WHO WOULD YOU MOST AND LEAST LIKE TO HAVE A NET WITH? Most – Katherine Brunt. I'd love to get into that battle! Least – Sophie Devine, because she'd take my head off!
WHAT MAKES YOU WORRY? Not achieving my full potential
WHAT GIVES YOU JOY? Winning! And creating memories across the world
GUILTY PLEASURE? French music
TWITTER: @NaomiDattani

Batting	Mat	Inns	NO	Runs	HS	Ave	SR	100	50	Ct	St
List A	78	61	1	877	71	14.61	-	0	3	30	-
T20s	93	69	6	914	62	14.50	85.42	0	2	26	-

Bowling	Mat	Balls	Mdns	Runs	Wkts	BB	Ave	4wI	5wI	SR	Econ
List A	78	2236	18	1907	50	4-23	38.14	2	0	44.72	5.11
T20s	93	950	3	1155	37	3-35	31.21	0	0	25.67	7.29

ALICE DAVIDSON-RICHARDS   RHB / RFM / MVP12

FULL NAME: Alice Natica Davidson-Richards
BORN: May 29, 1994, Tunbridge Wells, Kent
SQUAD NO: 24
HEIGHT: 5ft 9in
NICKNAME: ADR
EDUCATION: Epsom College, Surrey;
University of Leeds
TEAMS: England, South East Stars, Kent,
Otago, Yorkshire Diamonds
ROLE: Allrounder
DEBUT: ODI: 2018; T20I: 2018; List A: 2010;
T20: 2010

BEST ODI BATTING: 9 England vs India, Nagpur, 2018

FIRST CRICKET CLUB? Tunbridge Wells CC, Kent
BIGGEST INFLUENCE ON YOUR DEVELOPMENT AS A CRICKETER (EXCLUDING PARENTS)?
Mark Dekker, former head coach of Kent Women. He was the person with whom I started
talking about cricket, rather than just hitting or bowling balls
WHO IS THE BEST BATTER/KEEPER/BOWLER IN DOMESTIC CRICKET (EXCLUDING
TEAMMATES)? Sophie Luff/Ellie Threlkeld/Beth Langston
MOST BEAUTIFUL THING YOU HAVE EVER SEEN? A perfect cup of tea
HOBBIES? Finding adventures
IF YOU COULD TURN BACK TIME... I'd change the price of tea at cafes
WHO WOULD YOU MOST AND LEAST LIKE TO HAVE A NET WITH? Most – Darren Stevens, to
see if I could survive without getting snicked off. Least – Bryony Smith, because she'll smash
me everywhere
WHAT DO YOU MOST ENJOY LISTENING TO? Old stuff – Elton John, Whitney Houston
WHAT MAKES YOU WORRY? If the ground has tea-making facilities or not
WHAT GIVES YOU JOY? The little things
GUILTY PLEASURE? Loose-leaf tea
TWITTER: @alicedr24

Batting	Mat	Inns	NO	Runs	HS	Ave	SR	100	50	Ct	St
ODIs	1	1	0	9	9	9.00	28.12	0	0	0	-
T20Is	5	3	0	28	24	9.33	82.35	0	0	2	-

Bowling	Mat	Balls	Runs	Wkts	BBI	BBM	Ave	Econ	SR	5w	10
ODIs	1	-	-	-	-	-	-	-	-	-	-
T20Is	5	24	44	0	-	-	-	11.00	-	0	0

FREYA DAVIES · RHB / RFM

FULL NAME: Freya Ruth Davies
BORN: October 27, 1995, Chichester, Sussex
SQUAD NO: 61
HEIGHT: 5ft 9in
NICKNAME: Frey-Frey
EDUCATION: Brighton College; University of Exeter
TEAMS: England, South East Stars, Sussex, Western Storm
ROLE: Bowler
DEBUT: ODI: 2019; T20I: 2019; List A: 2012; T20: 2010

ENGLAND WOMEN

BEST ODI BATTING: 2 England vs New Zealand, Dunedin, 2021
BEST ODI BOWLING: 2-46 England vs New Zealand, Derby, 2021

FIRST CRICKET CLUB? Singleton CC, West Sussex
WHAT WOULD YOU CHANGE ABOUT THE STRUCTURE OF THE DOMESTIC SEASON? Make sure that the regional competitions are arranged so that the England centrally-contracted players are available for more games to improve the standard
BIGGEST INFLUENCE ON YOUR DEVELOPMENT AS A CRICKETER (EXCLUDING PARENTS)? My older brother – I got bored watching him play so started playing myself
WHO IS THE BEST BATTER/KEEPER/ALLROUNDER/BOWLER IN DOMESTIC CRICKET (EXCLUDING TEAMMATES)? Eve Jones/Ellie Threlkeld/Bryony Smith/Lauren Bell
MOST UNDERRATED PLAYER IN DOMESTIC CRICKET? Dani Gibson
WHAT WOULD A FLY ON THE WALL HEAR IN YOUR DRESSING ROOM? Katherine Brunt
MOST BEAUTIFUL THING YOU HAVE EVER SEEN? An untouched piste in the Alps
MAKE ONE PREDICTION FOR THE FUTURE OF CRICKET: The women's IPL
WHAT DO YOU MOST ENJOY LISTENING TO? Acoustic music
GUILTY PLEASURE? TikTok
TWITTER: @FreyaRuth

Batting	Mat	Inns	NO	Runs	HS	Ave	SR	100	50	Ct	St
ODIs	6	3	1	3	2	1.50	30.00	0	0	2	-
T20Is	17	1	1	1	1*	-	100.00	0	0	4	-

Bowling	Mat	Balls	Runs	Wkts	BBI	BBM	Ave	Econ	SR	5w	10
ODIs	6	282	214	6	2/46	2/46	35.66	4.55	47.0	0	0
T20Is	17	288	315	15	4/23	4/23	21.00	6.56	19.2	0	0

GWENAN DAVIES LHB / RMF / WK

FULL NAME: Gwenan Mai Davies
BORN: May 12, 1994, Neath, Glamorgan
SQUAD NO: 79
HEIGHT: 5ft 2in
NICKNAME: G
EDUCATION: Loughborough University
TEAMS: Central Sparks, Warwickshire, Somerset, Surrey Stars, Wales, Worcestershire, Yorkshire Diamonds
ROLE: Wicketkeeper/batter
DEBUT: List A: 2008; T20: 2010

BEST BATTING: 96 Somerset vs Durham, Midsomer Norton, 2015
BEST BOWLING: 2-7 Wales vs Leicestershire, Wolvey, 2008

FIRST CRICKET CLUB? Clydach CC, Swansea
WHAT WOULD YOU CHANGE ABOUT THE STRUCTURE OF THE DOMESTIC SEASON? Bring in the red ball
WHO IS THE BEST BATTER/KEEPER/ALLROUNDER/BOWLER IN DOMESTIC CRICKET (EXCLUDING TEAMMATES)? Bryony Smith/Ellie Threlkeld/Charlie Dean/Beth Langston
WHAT WOULD A FLY ON THE WALL HEAR IN YOUR DRESSING ROOM? Eve Jones blasting out Sweet Caroline
MOST BEAUTIFUL THING YOU HAVE EVER SEEN? The background of Table Mountain seen from grounds across Cape Town
HOBBIES? Learning the guitar
WHO WOULD YOU MOST AND LEAST LIKE TO HAVE A NET WITH? Most – Eve Jones (for the funny one-liners). Least – Paul Pridgeon (you never know when he's going to put a ball in the machine when you're not looking)
WHAT DO YOU MOST ENJOY LISTENING TO? Dominic Ostler's stories from his Warwickshire days
TWITTER: @gmdavies79

Batting	Mat	Inns	NO	Runs	HS	Ave	SR	100	50	Ct	St
List A	89	87	2	1498	96	17.62	-	0	8	37	8
T20s	85	73	6	1295	66*	19.32	-	0	3	25	29

Bowling	Mat	Balls	Mdns	Runs	Wkts	BB	Ave	4wl	5wl	SR	Econ
List A	89	945	11	735	23	2-7	31.95	0	0	41.08	4.66
T20s	85	245	0	328	10	2-18	32.80	0	0	24.50	8.03

CHARLIE DEAN　　　　　RHB / OB / MVP18

FULL NAME: Charlotte Ellen Dean
BORN: December 22, 2000, Burton-upon-Trent, Staffordshire
SQUAD NO: 22
HEIGHT: 5ft 6in
NICKNAME: Deano
EDUCATION: Portsmouth Grammar School; University of Southampton
TEAMS: England, Southern Vipers, Hampshire
ROLE: Bowler
DEBUT: Test: 2022; ODI: 2021; T20I: 2022; List A: 2016; T20: 2016

BEST ODI BATTING: 18* England vs Australia, Melbourne (St Kilda), 2022
BEST ODI BOWLING: 4-36 England vs New Zealand, Worcester, 2021

FIRST CRICKET CLUB? Havant CC, Hampshire
WHAT WOULD YOU CHANGE ABOUT THE STRUCTURE OF THE DOMESTIC SEASON? Have the whole of the T20 tournament at the beginning of the season and the whole of the 50-over competition at the end, rather than splitting the two over the whole summer and having The Hundred in between
WHO IS THE BEST BATTER/KEEPER/ALLROUNDER/BOWLER IN DOMESTIC CRICKET (EXCLUDING TEAMMATES)? Eve Jones/Nat Wraith/Emma Lamb/Beth Langston
MOST UNDERRATED PLAYER IN DOMESTIC CRICKET? Grace Scrivens
WHAT WOULD A FLY ON THE WALL HEAR IN YOUR DRESSING ROOM? A lot of off-pitch singing
MOST BEAUTIFUL THING YOU HAVE EVER SEEN? A south-coast sunset
HOBBIES? The guitar
MAKE ONE PREDICTION FOR THE FUTURE OF CRICKET: Women's cricket will have a big television audience
WHAT DO YOU MOST ENJOY LISTENING TO? Sleep podcasts
WHAT MAKES YOU WORRY? The existence of sea urchins
WHAT GIVES YOU JOY? Having a job I truly love

Batting	Mat	Inns	NO	Runs	HS	Ave	SR	100	50	Ct	St
Tests	1	2	0	12	9	6.00	26.66	0	0	0	-
ODIs	7	5	1	37	18*	9.25	52.85	0	0	1	-
T20Is	1	-	-	-	-	-	-	-	-	0	-

Bowling	Mat	Balls	Runs	Wkts	BBI	BBM	Ave	Econ	SR	5w	10
Tests	1	114	69	2	2/24	2/69	34.50	3.63	57.0	0	0
ODIs	7	292	233	10	4/36	4/36	23.30	4.78	29.2	0	0
T20Is	1	-	-	-	-	-	-	-	-	-	-

SOPHIA DUNKLEY

RHB / LB / MVP38

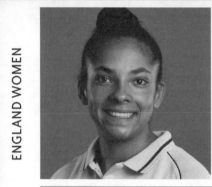

FULL NAME: Sophia Ivy Dunkley
BORN: July 16, 1998, Lambeth, Surrey
SQUAD NO: 47
HEIGHT: 5ft 6in
NICKNAME: Dunks
EDUCATION: Mill Hill School, London;
Loughborough University
TEAMS: England, South East Stars,
Middlesex, Lancashire Thunder, Surrey
Stars
ROLE: Batter
DEBUT: Test: 2021; ODI: 2021; T20I: 2018;
List A: 2013; T20: 2012

BEST ODI BATTING: 73* England vs India, Taunton, 2021

FIRST CRICKET CLUB? Finchley CC, London
WHAT WOULD YOU CHANGE ABOUT THE STRUCTURE OF THE DOMESTIC SEASON?
Introduce a red-ball competition
BIGGEST INFLUENCE ON YOUR DEVELOPMENT AS A CRICKETER (EXCLUDING PARENTS)?
I always looked up to Beth Morgan, the former England player, when she was my coach
WHO IS THE BEST BATTER/KEEPER/ALLROUNDER/BOWLER IN DOMESTIC CRICKET
(EXCLUDING TEAMMATES)? Eve Jones/Ellie Threlkeld/Kathryn Bryce/Lauren Bell
MOST UNDERRATED PLAYER IN DOMESTIC CRICKET? Kalea Moore
HOBBIES? Puzzle books
IF YOU COULD TURN BACK TIME... I'd have gone to more concerts
WHAT DO YOU MOST ENJOY LISTENING TO? Justin Bieber
WHAT MAKES YOU WORRY? Not having butter on my toast in the morning
WHAT GIVES YOU JOY? A good brekkie
GUILTY PLEASURE? Coronation Street
TWITTER: @dunkleysophia

Batting	Mat	Inns	NO	Runs	HS	Ave	SR	100	50	Ct	St
Tests	2	3	1	134	74*	67.00	69.43	0	1	0	-
ODIs	10	9	2	163	73*	23.28	74.42	0	1	1	-
T20Is	23	13	6	159	35	22.71	104.60	0	0	7	-

Bowling	Mat	Balls	Runs	Wkts	BBI	BBM	Ave	Econ	SR	5w	10
Tests	2	6	9	0	-	-	-	9.00	-	0	0
ODIs	10	-	-	-	-	-	-	-	-	-	-
T20Is	23	24	13	1	1/6	1/6	13.00	3.25	24.0	0	0

SOPHIE ECCLESTONE

RHB / SLA

FULL NAME: Sophie Ecclestone
BORN: May 6, 1999, Chester, Cheshire
SQUAD NO: 71
HEIGHT: 5ft 10in
NICKNAME: Eccles
EDUCATION: Helsby High School, Cheshire
TEAMS: England, Thunder, Lancashire, Cheshire, Lancashire Thunder
ROLE: Bowler
DEBUT: Test: 2017; ODI: 2016; T20I: 2016; List A: 2013; T20: 2014

BEST ODI BATTING: 32* England vs Australia, Melbourne (St Kilda), 2022
BEST ODI BOWLING: 4-14 England vs India, Nagpur, 2018

FIRST CRICKET CLUB? Alvanley CC, Cheshire
WHO IS THE BEST BATTER/KEEPER/ALLROUNDER/BOWLER IN DOMESTIC CRICKET (EXCLUDING TEAMMATES)? Eve Jones/Ellie Threlkeld/Alice Capsey/Linsey Smith
MOST UNDERRATED PLAYER IN DOMESTIC CRICKET? Sophie Luff
MOST BEAUTIFUL THING YOU HAVE EVER SEEN? Milford Sound in Queenstown, New Zealand
HOBBIES? Everton FC
WHO WOULD YOU MOST AND LEAST LIKE TO HAVE A NET WITH? Most – Joe Root. Least – Jimmy Anderson
MAKE ONE PREDICTION FOR THE FUTURE OF CRICKET: Women's Test matches will be played over five days rather than four
WHAT DO YOU MOST ENJOY LISTENING TO? Justin Bieber
WHAT MAKES YOU WORRY? Upsetting people
WHAT GIVES YOU JOY? Enjoying cricket with my teammates
TWITTER: @Sophecc19

Batting	Mat	Inns	NO	Runs	HS	Ave	SR	100	50	Ct	St
Tests	4	5	3	68	34	34.00	32.07	0	0	2	-
ODIs	38	25	7	142	32*	7.88	57.02	0	0	11	-
T20Is	50	16	9	93	17*	13.28	109.41	0	0	14	-

Bowling	Mat	Balls	Runs	Wkts	BBI	BBM	Ave	Econ	SR	5w	10
Tests	4	1172	582	15	4/88	8/206	38.80	2.97	78.1	0	0
ODIs	38	2071	1273	55	4/14	4/14	23.14	3.68	37.6	0	0
T20Is	50	1094	1084	68	4/18	4/18	15.94	5.94	16.0	0	0

BETHAN ELLIS   RHB / RMF

FULL NAME: Bethan Louisa Ellis
BORN: July 7, 1999, Leamington Spa, Warwickshire
SQUAD NO: 14
HEIGHT: 5ft 6in
NICKNAME: Bellis
EDUCATION: University of Birmingham; Loughborough University
TEAMS: Lightning, Derbyshire, Shropshire, Warwickshire, Worcestershire
ROLE: Allrounder
DEBUT: List A: 2015; T20: 2016

BEST BATTING: 74 Warwickshire vs Kent, Beckenham, 2019
BEST BOWLING: 4-20 Worcestershire vs Wales, Griffithstown, 2017

WHO IS YOUR LOOKALIKE? My twin (but the boy version)
FIRST CRICKET CLUB? Leamington CC, Warwickshire
WHAT WOULD YOU CHANGE ABOUT THE STRUCTURE OF THE DOMESTIC SEASON? Play all the 50-over matches in one block
BIGGEST INFLUENCE ON YOUR DEVELOPMENT AS A CRICKETER (EXCLUDING PARENTS)? Dominic Ostler at Warwickshire – he gave me confidence in my own game from a young age
WHO IS THE BEST BATTER/KEEPER/ALLROUNDER/BOWLER IN DOMESTIC CRICKET (EXCLUDING TEAMMATES)? Eve Jones/Ellie Threlkeld/Alice Capsey/Lauren Bell
MOST UNDERRATED PLAYER IN DOMESTIC CRICKET? Emma Lamb
WHAT WOULD A FLY ON THE WALL HEAR IN YOUR DRESSING ROOM? The Bryces (Sarah and Kathryn) dancing a Ceilidh
MOST BEAUTIFUL THING YOU HAVE EVER SEEN? Cape Town from the top of Table Mountain
HOBBIES? Hockey
WHO WOULD YOU MOST LIKE TO HAVE A NET WITH? Andrew Flintoff
MAKE ONE PREDICTION FOR THE FUTURE OF CRICKET: There will be more women's Test matches
WHAT DO YOU MOST ENJOY LISTENING TO? The Tailenders podcast
TWITTER: @BethanEllis7

Batting	Mat	Inns	NO	Runs	HS	Ave	SR	100	50	Ct	St
List A	29	23	4	423	74	22.26	51.58	0	4	10	-
T20s	32	23	9	308	55*	22.00	-	0	1	7	-

Bowling	Mat	Balls	Mdns	Runs	Wkts	BB	Ave	4wI	5wI	SR	Econ
List A	29	823	21	493	22	4-20	22.40	1	0	37.40	3.59
T20s	32	469	1	431	28	4-21	15.39	1	0	16.75	5.51

GEORGIA ELWISS — RHB / RM / MVP7

FULL NAME: Georgia Amanda Elwiss
BORN: May 31, 1991, Wolverhampton
SQUAD NO: 34
HEIGHT: 5ft 7in
NICKNAME: Gelwiss
EDUCATION: Wolverhampton Girls' High School; Loughborough University
TEAMS: England, Southern Vipers, Sussex, Loughborough Lightning, Melbourne Stars, Staffordshire
ROLE: Allrounder
DEBUT: Test: 2015; ODI: 2011; T20I: 2011; List A: 2004; T20: 2005

BEST ODI BATTING: 77 England vs Pakistan, Taunton, 2016
BEST ODI BOWLING: 3-17 England vs India, Wormsley, 2012

FIRST CRICKET CLUB? Wolverhampton CC, West Midlands
WHAT WOULD YOU CHANGE ABOUT THE STRUCTURE OF THE DOMESTIC SEASON? Play more two- or three-day cricket
WHO IS THE BEST BATTER/KEEPER/ALLROUNDER/BOWLER IN DOMESTIC CRICKET (EXCLUDING TEAMMATES)? Heather Knight/Amy Jones/Nat Sciver/Katherine Brunt
MOST UNDERRATED PLAYER IN DOMESTIC CRICKET? Kathryn Bryce
MOST BEAUTIFUL THING YOU HAVE EVER SEEN? The Phi Phi Islands, Thailand
HOBBIES? Making speciality coffee
WHO WOULD YOU MOST LIKE TO HAVE A NET WITH? AB de Villiers
MAKE ONE PREDICTION FOR THE FUTURE OF CRICKET: All women's international series will feature all three formats
WHAT MAKES YOU WORRY? When I can't see or hear my dog
TWITTER: @gelwiss

Batting	Mat	Inns	NO	Runs	HS	Ave	SR	100	50	Ct	St
Tests	4	6	1	145	46	29.00	28.54	0	0	1	-
ODIs	36	24	5	388	77	20.42	73.20	0	2	11	-
T20Is	14	5	2	29	18	9.66	96.66	0	0	3	-

Bowling	Mat	Balls	Runs	Wkts	BBI	BBM	Ave	Econ	SR	5w	10
Tests	4	174	91	1	1/40	1/40	91.00	3.13	174.0	0	0
ODIs	36	1097	679	26	3/17	3/17	26.11	3.71	42.1	0	0
T20Is	14	163	161	8	2/9	2/9	20.12	5.92	20.3	0	0

TASH FARRANT

LHB / LMF / MVP35

ENGLAND WOMEN

FULL NAME: Natasha Eleni Farrant
BORN: May 29, 1996, Athens, Greece
SQUAD NO: 53
HEIGHT: 5ft 5in
NICKNAME: Faz
EDUCATION: Sevenoaks School;
Loughborough University
TEAMS: England, South East Stars, Kent,
Southern Vipers, Western Australia
ROLE: Bowler
DEBUT: ODI: 2013; T20I: 2013; List A: 2012;
T20: 2012

BEST ODI BATTING: 22 England vs New Zealand, Worcester, 2021
BEST ODI BOWLING: 2-31 England vs New Zealand, Christchurch, 2021

FIRST CRICKET CLUB? Holmesdale CC, Sevenoaks, Kent
WHAT WOULD YOU CHANGE ABOUT THE STRUCTURE OF THE DOMESTIC SEASON? Begin
the season earlier so that England players can play more regional matches. It would also
allow teams to play each other home and away. And I'd bring in some four-day cricket
MOST UNDERRATED PLAYER IN DOMESTIC CRICKET? Grace Scrivens
WHAT WOULD A FLY ON THE WALL HEAR IN YOUR DRESSING ROOM? The laughter of Alice
Davidson-Richards
MOST BEAUTIFUL THING YOU HAVE EVER SEEN? Sunset in Dharamshala, India
HOBBIES? Fashion
WHO WOULD YOU MOST AND LEAST LIKE TO HAVE A NET WITH? Most – Wasim Akram, the
best left-armer ever. Least – Geoffrey Boycott, don't think he'd like my reverse-sweeps
WHAT DO YOU MOST ENJOY LISTENING TO? Happy Place Podcast
WHAT MAKES YOU WORRY? Leg-side wides
WHAT GIVES YOU JOY? My niece and nephew
TWITTER: @tashfarrant

Batting	Mat	Inns	NO	Runs	HS	Ave	SR	100	50	Ct	St
ODIs	6	4	1	42	22	14.00	61.76	0	0	1	-
T20Is	18	4	3	7	3*	7.00	43.75	0	0	4	-
Bowling	Mat	Balls	Runs	Wkts	BBI	BBM	Ave	Econ	SR	5w	10
ODIs	6	253	190	5	2/31	2/31	38.00	4.50	50.6	0	0
T20Is	18	388	405	15	2/15	2/15	27.00	6.26	25.8	0	0

ABBEY FREEBORN — RHB / WK / MVP26

FULL NAME: Abigail Johanna Freeborn
BORN: November 12, 1996, Eastbourne, Sussex
SQUAD NO: TBC
HEIGHT: 5ft 7in
NICKNAME: Freebs
EDUCATION: Loughborough University
TEAMS: Central Sparks, Loughborough Lightning, Lightning, Sussex, Yorkshire
ROLE: Wicketkeeper/batter
DEBUT: List A: 2013; T20: 2013

CENTRAL SPARKS

BEST BATTING: 58 Yorkshire vs Sussex, Cobham, 2019

FIRST CRICKET CLUB? Hastings & St Leonards Priory CC, East Sussex
WHAT WOULD YOU CHANGE ABOUT THE STRUCTURE OF THE DOMESTIC SEASON? More T20
WHO IS THE BEST BATTER/KEEPER/ALLROUNDER/BOWLER IN DOMESTIC CRICKET (EXCLUDING TEAMMATES)? Nat Sciver/Ellie Threlkeld/Katherine Brunt/Katherine Brunt
MOST UNDERRATED PLAYER IN DOMESTIC CRICKET? Sonia Odedra
MOST BEAUTIFUL THING YOU HAVE EVER SEEN? The Alps
WHO WOULD YOU MOST AND LEAST LIKE TO HAVE A NET WITH? Most – Tammy Beaumont. I could learn loads from the way she bats. Least – Sophie Ecclestone. She gets me out far too often
MAKE ONE PREDICTION FOR THE FUTURE OF CRICKET: The Hundred will be the biggest competition in world cricket
WHAT DO YOU MOST ENJOY LISTENING TO? James Bay
WHAT MAKES YOU WORRY? Not having a plan
WHAT GIVES YOU JOY? Travelling in the campervan
GUILTY PLEASURE? Re-watching Grace and Frankie
TWITTER: @abbey_freeborn

Batting	Mat	Inns	NO	Runs	HS	Ave	SR	100	50	Ct	St
List A	52	42	8	732	58	21.52	59.12	0	1	38	12
T20s	55	37	11	500	61	19.23	86.80	0	1	16	25

JO GARDNER   RHB / OB

SUNRISERS

FULL NAME: Jo-Anne Lynda Gardner
BORN: March 25, 1997, Newport, Isle of Wight
SQUAD NO: 14
HEIGHT: 5ft 6in
NICKNAME: Joey G
EDUCATION: Loughborough University
TEAMS: Sunrisers, Warwickshire,
Loughborough Lightning, Northamptonshire
ROLE: Allrounder
DEBUT: List A: 2011; T20: 2011

BEST BATTING: 86 Northamptonshire vs Cheshire, Horton, 2016
BEST BOWLING: 6-21 Northamptonshire vs Oxfordshire, Chesterton, 2013

FIRST CRICKET CLUB? Great Houghton CC, Northampton
WHAT WOULD YOU CHANGE ABOUT THE STRUCTURE OF THE DOMESTIC SEASON? More
fixtures, introduce a multi-day format, create a North v South competition
WHO IS THE BEST BATTER/KEEPER/ALLROUNDER/BOWLER IN DOMESTIC CRICKET
(EXCLUDING TEAMMATES)? Georgia Adams/Ellie Threlkeld/Kathryn Bryce/Kirstie Gordon
MOST UNDERRATED PLAYER IN DOMESTIC CRICKET? Dani Gibson
WHAT WOULD A FLY ON THE WALL HEAR IN YOUR DRESSING ROOM? Rogue singing
MOST BEAUTIFUL THING YOU HAVE EVER SEEN? Bajan beaches
HOBBIES? Making (and drinking) coffee, baking, hacking my way around a golf course
MAKE ONE PREDICTION FOR THE FUTURE OF CRICKET: A fully professional women's
domestic set-up
WHAT DO YOU MOST ENJOY LISTENING TO? Any dance pop
GUILTY PLEASURE? Eating Nutella from the jar
TWITTER: @JoLGardner

Batting	Mat	Inns	NO	Runs	HS	Ave	SR	100	50	Ct	St
List A	66	58	11	882	86	18.76	-	0	5	18	-
T20s	67	50	13	505	55*	13.64	-	0	2	18	-

Bowling	Mat	Balls	Mdns	Runs	Wkts	BB	Ave	4wI	5wI	SR	Econ
List A	66	1866	35	1234	59	6-21	20.91	0	3	31.62	3.96
T20s	67	735	6	724	21	3-25	34.47	0	0	35.00	5.91

KATIE GEORGE

RHB / LFM

FULL NAME: Katie Louise George
BORN: April 7, 1999, Haywards Heath, Sussex
SQUAD NO: 46
HEIGHT: 5ft 5in
EDUCATION: The Mountbatten School, Hampshire; Richard Taunton Sixth Form, Southampton
TEAMS: England, Western Storm, Hampshire, Southern Vipers, Yorkshire Diamonds
ROLE: Bowler
DEBUT: ODI: 2018; T20I: 2018; List A: 2013; T20: 2015

BEST ODI BATTING: 9 England vs New Zealand, Derby, 2018
BEST ODI BOWLING: 3-36 England vs New Zealand, Derby, 2018

FIRST CRICKET CLUB? Poole Town CC, Dorset
WHAT WOULD YOU CHANGE ABOUT THE STRUCTURE OF THE DOMESTIC SEASON? Play some long-format cricket
BIGGEST INFLUENCE ON YOUR DEVELOPMENT AS A CRICKETER (EXCLUDING PARENTS)? The late Rick Kellaway, my former club coach and mentor at Old Tauntonians & Romsey CC. He was the first person who helped me slow down and think about the game
WHO IS THE BEST BATTER/KEEPER/ALLROUNDER/BOWLER IN DOMESTIC CRICKET (EXCLUDING TEAMMATES)? Alice Capsey/Carla Rudd/Dani Gibson/Kirstie Gordon
MOST UNDERRATED PLAYER IN DOMESTIC CRICKET? Sophie Luff
MOST BEAUTIFUL THING YOU HAVE EVER SEEN? Sunset seen from a volcano
WHO WOULD YOU MOST LIKE TO HAVE A NET WITH? Jimmy Anderson – probably wouldn't get a bat on one but I'm sure I would learn a lot
MAKE ONE PREDICTION FOR THE FUTURE OF CRICKET: Red-ball cricket will be the norm in the women's game
GUILTY PLEASURE? Jazz
TWITTER: @KaTie_George46

Batting	Mat	Inns	NO	Runs	HS	Ave	SR	100	50	Ct	St
ODIs	2	1	0	9	9	9.00	47.36	0	0	1	-
T20Is	5	1	0	0	0	0.00	0.00	0	0	0	-

Bowling	Mat	Balls	Runs	Wkts	BBI	BBM	Ave	Econ	SR	5w	10
ODIs	2	75	70	4	3/36	3/36	17.50	5.60	18.7	0	0
T20Is	5	78	117	2	1/22	1/22	58.50	9.00	39.0	0	0

DANI GIBSON

RHB / RMF / MVP9

FULL NAME: Danielle Rose Gibson
BORN: April 30, 2001, Cheltenham, Gloucestershire
SQUAD NO: 28
HEIGHT: 5ft 6in
NICKNAME: Gibbo
EDUCATION: Hartpury College, Gloucestershire
TEAMS: Western Storm, Wales, Gloucestershire
ROLE: Bowler
DEBUT: List A: 2015; T20: 2014

BEST BATTING: 73 Gloucestershire vs Buckinghamshire, Moreton-in-Marsh, 2015
BEST BOWLING: 5-17 Gloucestershire vs Cornwall, Falmouth, 2017

FIRST CRICKET CLUB? Dumbleton CC, Evesham, Worcestershire
WHAT WOULD YOU CHANGE ABOUT THE STRUCTURE OF THE DOMESTIC SEASON? Put the T20 competition before The Hundred rather than the 50-over comp
WHO IS THE BEST BATTER/BOWLER IN DOMESTIC CRICKET (EXCLUDING TEAMMATES)? Emma Lamb/Lauren Bell
MOST UNDERRATED PLAYER IN DOMESTIC CRICKET? Charlie Dean
HOBBIES? Golf
IF YOU COULD TURN BACK TIME... I would spend more time with my family while growing up
MAKE ONE PREDICTION FOR THE FUTURE OF CRICKET: All women players will be professionals
WHAT MAKES YOU WORRY? Family
WHAT GIVES YOU JOY? Sport
GUILTY PLEASURE? Having a massage
TWITTER: @Dani_Gibson01

Batting	Mat	Inns	NO	Runs	HS	Ave	SR	100	50	Ct	St
List A	33	30	4	520	73	20.00	-	0	3	12	-
T20s	55	41	12	488	36	16.82	122.00	0	0	30	-

Bowling	Mat	Balls	Mdns	Runs	Wkts	BB	Ave	4wI	5wI	SR	Econ
List A	33	924	9	689	37	5-17	18.62	2	1	24.97	4.47
T20s	55	753	4	736	40	3-9	18.40	0	0	18.82	5.86

SARAH GLENN

RHB / LB

FULL NAME: Sarah Glenn
BORN: August 27, 1999, Derby
SQUAD NO: 3
HEIGHT: 5ft 10in
EDUCATION: Trent College, Long Eaton; The Open University, Milton Keynes
TEAMS: England, Central Sparks, Worcestershire, Derbyshire, Loughborough Lightning, Perth Scorchers
ROLE: Bowler
DEBUT: ODI: 2019; T20I: 2019; List A: 2013; T20: 2013

BEST ODI BATTING: 11 England vs New Zealand, Dunedin, 2021
BEST ODI BOWLING: 4-18 England vs Pakistan, Kuala Lumpur, 2019

WHO IS YOUR LOOKALIKE? Mrs Potato Head
FIRST CRICKET CLUB? Denby CC, Ripley, Derbyshire
WHAT WOULD YOU CHANGE ABOUT THE STRUCTURE OF THE DOMESTIC SEASON? Add a three-day format
WHO IS THE BEST BATTER/KEEPER/ALLROUNDER/BOWLER IN DOMESTIC CRICKET (EXCLUDING TEAMMATES)? Eve Jones/Ellie Threlkeld/Alice Capsey/Kathryn Bryce
MOST UNDERRATED PLAYER IN DOMESTIC CRICKET? Dani Gibson
WHAT WOULD A FLY ON THE WALL HEAR IN YOUR DRESSING ROOM? Anything from field plans to dinner plans
HOBBIES? Walking the dog
IF YOU COULD TURN BACK TIME... I'd change my clothing style when I was a kid
WHO WOULD YOU MOST AND LEAST LIKE TO HAVE A NET WITH? Most – my mum. Least – my dad
WHAT MAKES YOU WORRY? That I'll never beat my dad's stats by the time I retire
WHAT GIVES YOU JOY? Seeing my family at my games supporting me
TWITTER: @Lg3Sarah

Batting	Mat	Inns	NO	Runs	HS	Ave	SR	100	50	Ct	St
ODIs	9	2	0	17	11	8.50	100.00	0	0	3	-
T20Is	26	8	4	62	26	15.50	112.72	0	0	3	-

Bowling	Mat	Balls	Runs	Wkts	BBI	BBM	Ave	Econ	SR	5w	10
ODIs	9	401	277	12	4/18	4/18	23.08	4.14	33.4	0	0
T20Is	26	496	503	33	3/15	3/15	15.24	6.08	15.0	0	0

KIRSTIE GORDON　　　　　　　　RHB / SLA / MVP8

FULL NAME: Kirstie Louise Gordon
BORN: October 20, 1997, Huntly, Aberdeenshire, Scotland
SQUAD NO: 24
HEIGHT: 5ft 5in
NICKNAME: Gordo
EDUCATION: Loughborough University
TEAMS: England, Lightning, Kent, Loughborough Lightning, Nottinghamshire, Scotland
ROLE: Bowler
DEBUT: Test: 2019; T20I: 2018

BEST T20I BATTING: 1* England vs Australia, North Sound, Antigua, 2018
BEST T20I BOWLING: 3-16 England vs Bangladesh, Gros Islet, St Lucia, 2018

FIRST CRICKET CLUB? Huntly CC, Aberdeenshire
BIGGEST INFLUENCE ON YOUR DEVELOPMENT AS A CRICKETER (EXCLUDING PARENTS)?
Salliann Briggs – she invested a lot of time with me at Loughborough and played a huge part in helping me bridge the gap to international cricket
WHO IS THE BEST BATTER/KEEPER/ALLROUNDER/BOWLER IN DOMESTIC CRICKET
(EXCLUDING TEAMMATES)? Eve Jones/Ellie Threlkeld/Alice Capsey/Lauren Bell
MOST UNDERRATED PLAYER IN DOMESTIC CRICKET? Grace Scrivens
MOST BEAUTIFUL THING YOU HAVE EVER SEEN? The views from Table Mountain in Cape Town
HOBBIES? Manchester United
WHO WOULD YOU LEAST LIKE TO HAVE A NET WITH? Ellyse Perry – too hard to get out
MAKE ONE PREDICTION FOR THE FUTURE OF CRICKET: T10 franchise cricket around the world
WHAT MAKES YOU WORRY? Man United during the transfer window
GUILTY PLEASURE? Cleaning the bathroom
TWITTER: @kirstiegordon97

Batting	Mat	Inns	NO	Runs	HS	Ave	SR	100	50	Ct	St
Tests	1	-	-	-	-	-	-	-	-	0	-
T20Is	5	1	1	1	1*	-	100.00	0	0	0	-
Bowling	Mat	Balls	Runs	Wkts	BBI	BBM	Ave	Econ	SR	5w	10
Tests	1	220	119	3	2/50	3/119	39.66	3.24	73.3	0	0
T20Is	5	114	98	8	3/16	3/16	12.25	5.15	14.2	0	0

PHOEBE GRAHAM

RHB / RMF

FULL NAME: Phoebe Claire Graham
BORN: October 23, 1991, Steeton, Yorkshire
SQUAD NO: TBC
HEIGHT: 5ft 11in
NICKNAME: PG
EDUCATION: University of Exeter
TEAMS: Thunder, Berkshire, Devon, Northern Diamonds, Nottinghamshire, Yorkshire
ROLE: Bowler
DEBUT: List A: 2010; T20: 2010

THUNDER

BEST BATTING: 29* Northern Diamonds vs Thunder, Liverpool, 2020
BEST BOWLING: 3-14 Berkshire vs Worcestershire, Maidenhead, 2019

WHO IS YOUR LOOKALIKE? Margot Robbie (I'm claiming it!)
FIRST CRICKET CLUB? Pool CC, Otley, West Yorkshire
WHO IS THE BEST BATTER/KEEPER/ALLROUNDER/BOWLER IN DOMESTIC CRICKET (EXCLUDING TEAMMATES)? Sophie Luff/Bess Heath/Jenny Gunn/Tash Farrant
MOST UNDERRATED PLAYER IN DOMESTIC CRICKET? Jenny Gunn MBE – she is worth her weight in gold
MOST BEAUTIFUL THING YOU HAVE EVER SEEN? Lake Como, Italy
HOBBIES? Cycling
IF YOU COULD TURN BACK TIME... I've got no regrets – live life to the full!
WHO WOULD YOU LEAST LIKE TO HAVE A NET WITH? A fired-up Katherine Brunt. Scary
MAKE ONE PREDICTION FOR THE FUTURE OF CRICKET: The schedules for men's and women's domestic cricket mirror each other
WHAT DO YOU MOST ENJOY LISTENING TO? Discover Weekly on Spotify
WHAT GIVES YOU JOY? The sea
TWITTER: @phoebeg23

Batting	Mat	Inns	NO	Runs	HS	Ave	SR	100	50	Ct	St
List A	49	30	8	175	29*	7.95	54.17	0	0	5	-
T20s	36	15	4	120	26*	10.90	93.02	0	0	8	-

Bowling	Mat	Balls	Mdns	Runs	Wkts	BB	Ave	4wI	5wI	SR	Econ
List A	49	1514	18	1139	33	3-14	34.51	0	0	45.87	4.51
T20s	36	662	3	649	26	3-26	24.96	0	0	25.46	5.88

DANIELLE GREGORY

RHB / LB

FULL NAME: Danielle Lucy Gregory
BORN: December 4, 1998, Surrey
SQUAD NO: 19
HEIGHT: 5ft 6in
NICKNAME: Greggo
EDUCATION: Weydon School, Farnham, Surrey; Alton College, Hampshire; University of Chichester, Sussex
TEAMS: South East Stars, Surrey
ROLE: Bowler
DEBUT: List A: 2019; T20: 2018

BEST BATTING: 1* South East Stars vs Thunder, Beckenham, 2021
BEST BOWLING: 3-44 South East Stars vs Southern Vipers, The Oval, 2020

WHO IS YOUR LOOKALIKE? Rapunzel
FIRST CRICKET CLUB? Rowledge CC, Surrey
WHAT WOULD YOU CHANGE ABOUT THE STRUCTURE OF THE DOMESTIC SEASON?
Introduce a red-ball competition similar to the men's County Championship
WHO IS THE BEST BATTER/KEEPER/ALLROUNDER/BOWLER IN DOMESTIC CRICKET
(EXCLUDING TEAMMATES)? Eve Jones/Ellie Threlkeld/Charlie Dean/Lauren Bell
WHAT WOULD A FLY ON THE WALL HEAR IN YOUR DRESSING ROOM? Laughter
MOST BEAUTIFUL THING YOU HAVE EVER SEEN? The Greek island of Thassos
HOBBIES? Sports performance analysis – I'm currently undertaking a Masters Degree in the subject. I'm enjoying learning how to code and present information back to players and coaches across a range of sports including football, rugby and basketball
WHO WOULD YOU MOST LIKE TO HAVE A NET WITH? Ben Foakes, for his passion for the game despite his setbacks with injuries and being overlooked by England
MAKE ONE PREDICTION FOR THE FUTURE OF CRICKET: Women's cricket to be fully professional
WHAT DO YOU MOST ENJOY LISTENING TO? Chart music
WHAT MAKES YOU WORRY? University assignments
TWITTER: @DaniGregs

Batting	Mat	Inns	NO	Runs	HS	Ave	SR	100	50	Ct	St
List A	16	7	3	3	1*	0.75	10.00	0	0	1	-
T20s	36	5	2	3	2	1.00	15.00	0	0	6	-

Bowling	Mat	Balls	Mdns	Runs	Wkts	BB	Ave	4wI	5wI	SR	Econ
List A	16	630	2	450	13	3-44	34.61	0	0	48.46	4.28
T20s	36	574	1	633	27	4-7	23.44	2	0	21.25	6.61

CORDELIA GRIFFITH   RHB / RM / MVP45

FULL NAME: Cordelia Lauren Griffith
BORN: September 19, 1995, Islington, London
SQUAD NO: 6
HEIGHT: 5ft 5in
NICKNAME: Cords
EDUCATION: Chigwell School, Essex; Durham University
TEAMS: Sunrisers, Middlesex, Essex, Surrey Stars, Yorkshire Diamonds
ROLE: Batter
DEBUT: List A: 2010; T20: 2010

BEST BATTING: 155* Essex vs Suffolk, Long Melford, 2018
BEST BOWLING: 1-6 Essex vs Berkshire, Sindlesham, 2013

FIRST CRICKET CLUB? Loughton CC, Essex
WHAT WOULD YOU CHANGE ABOUT THE STRUCTURE OF THE DOMESTIC SEASON?
Introduce the multi-day format
MOST BEAUTIFUL THING YOU HAVE EVER SEEN? Sunrise at Þingvellir National Park in Iceland
HOBBIES? Baking
MAKE ONE PREDICTION FOR THE FUTURE OF CRICKET: More women's Test cricket
WHAT DO YOU MOST ENJOY LISTENING TO? Podcasts
WHAT GIVES YOU JOY? Family, friends and good food
GUILTY PLEASURE? Gemma Collins: Diva Forever and Ever (reality tv show)
TWITTER: @cordeliagriff

Batting	Mat	Inns	NO	Runs	HS	Ave	SR	100	50	Ct	St
List A	47	46	3	1308	155*	30.41	-		3	6	14	-
T20s	67	56	6	927	73	18.54	92.14	0	5	14	-

Bowling	Mat	Balls	Mdns	Runs	Wkts	BB	Ave	4wI	5wI	SR	Econ
List A	47	271	3	192	7	1-6	27.42	0	0	38.71	4.25
T20s	67	150	0	167	2	1-12	83.50	0	0	75.00	6.68

ALEX GRIFFITHS RHB / RMF

FULL NAME: Alexandra Clare Griffiths
BORN: June 12, 2002, Swansea
SQUAD NO: 25
HEIGHT: 5ft 7in
NICKNAME: Ali G
EDUCATION: Dyffryn Comprehensive School, Port Talbot, Wales; Cardiff Metropolitan University
TEAMS: Western Storm, Wales
ROLE: Allrounder
DEBUT: List A: 2016; T20: 2016

BEST BATTING: 80 Western Storm vs Sunrisers, Bristol, 2020
BEST BOWLING: 2-2 Wales vs Essex, Griffithstown, 2019

WHO IS YOUR LOOKALIKE? Nessa (American TV host)
FIRST CRICKET CLUB? Port Talbot CC, Swansea
BIGGEST INFLUENCE ON YOUR DEVELOPMENT AS A CRICKETER (EXCLUDING PARENTS)? My coaches in Wales: Alan Jones, John Derrick and Aimee Rees. They coached me from a young age and have stuck by me all the way
WHAT WOULD A FLY ON THE WALL HEAR IN YOUR DRESSING ROOM? Anything but cricket
MOST BEAUTIFUL THING YOU HAVE EVER SEEN? My nephew
HOBBIES? Mario Kart
IF YOU COULD TURN BACK TIME... I'd prevent Ned Stark from dying in Game of Thrones
WHO WOULD YOU MOST LIKE TO HAVE A NET WITH? Viv Richards
MAKE ONE PREDICTION FOR THE FUTURE OF CRICKET: England will win back the Ashes
WHAT DO YOU MOST ENJOY LISTENING TO? Funk and house
WHAT MAKES YOU WORRY? If dinner will be on the table when I get home
TWITTER: @alex_griff7

Batting	Mat	Inns	NO	Runs	HS	Ave	SR	100	50	Ct	St
List A	30	28	1	584	80	21.62	63.89	0	3	10	-
T20s	37	24	1	129	24	5.60	64.50	0	0	6	-

Bowling	Mat	Balls	Mdns	Runs	Wkts	BB	Ave	4wI	5wI	SR	Econ
List A	30	489	8	363	7	2-2	51.85	0	0	69.85	4.45
T20s	37	214	1	265	14	3-12	18.92	0	0	15.28	7.42

JENNY GUNN

RHB / RMF / MVP10

FULL NAME: Jennifer Louise Gunn
BORN: May 9, 1986, Nottingham
SQUAD NO: 24
HEIGHT: 5ft 10in
NICKNAME: Chuckie
EDUCATION: South Nottingham College
TEAMS: England, Northern Diamonds, Nottinghamshire, Loughborough Lightning, South Australia, Warwickshire, Western Australia, Yorkshire
ROLE: Allrounder
DEBUT: Test: 2004; ODI: 2004; T20I: 2004; List A: 2001; T20: 2004

NORTHERN DIAMONDS

BEST ODI BATTING: 73 England vs New Zealand, Taunton, 2007
BEST ODI BOWLING: 5-22 England vs Pakistan, Louth, 2013

FIRST CRICKET CLUB? Lady Bay Boots CC, Nottingham. I loved playing alongside my dad and brother and it's always fun getting men out
FAMILY TIES? Dad was a professional footballer. And no, I'm not related to the Gunns that played for Notts many years ago
WHAT WOULD A FLY ON THE WALL HEAR IN YOUR DRESSING ROOM? Some dreadful singing
HOBBIES? Dog-walking, cooking
IF YOU COULD TURN BACK TIME... I wouldn't be a seam bowler
WHAT DO YOU MOST ENJOY LISTENING TO? Motown
WHAT MAKES YOU WORRY? Thunderstorms
WHAT GIVES YOU JOY? Spending time with family and friends
TWITTER: @GunnJenny

Batting	Mat	Inns	NO	Runs	HS	Ave	SR	100	50	Ct	St
Tests	11	19	2	391	62*	23.00	30.38	0	1	6	-
ODIs	144	111	28	1629	73	19.62	57.19	0	5	49	-
T20Is	104	67	18	682	69	13.91	100.44	0	1	58	-

Bowling	Mat	Balls	Runs	Wkts	BBI	BBM	Ave	Econ	SR	5w	10
Tests	11	2189	645	29	5/19	5/59	22.24	1.76	75.4	1	0
ODIs	144	5906	3822	136	5/22	5/22	28.10	3.88	43.4	2	0
T20Is	104	1385	1487	75	5/18	5/18	19.82	6.44	18.4	1	0

ALEX HARTLEY   RHB / SLA / MVP31

FULL NAME: Alexandra Hartley
BORN: September 26, 1993, Blackburn, Lancashire
SQUAD NO: 65
HEIGHT: 5ft 4in
EDUCATION: Ribblesdale High School, Clitheroe; Loughborough College
TEAMS: England, Thunder, Lancashire, Hobart Hurricanes, Lancashire Thunder, Middlesex, Surrey Stars, Tasmania
ROLE: Bowler
DEBUT: ODI: 2016; T20I: 2016; List A: 2008; T20: 2010

BEST ODI BATTING: 3* England vs India, Nagpur, 2018
BEST ODI BOWLING: 4-24 England vs West Indies, Kingston, 2016

FIRST CRICKET CLUB? Read CC, Burnley, Lancashire
WHO IS THE BEST BATTER/KEEPER/ALLROUNDER/BOWLER IN DOMESTIC CRICKET (EXCLUDING TEAMMATES)? Eve Jones/Carla Rudd/Alice Capsey/Lauren Bell
MOST UNDERRATED PLAYER IN DOMESTIC CRICKET? Sophie Luff
MOST BEAUTIFUL THING YOU HAVE EVER SEEN? Anything by open water
HOBBIES? Podcasting
IF YOU COULD TURN BACK TIME... I'd change absolutely nothing
WHO WOULD YOU MOST AND LEAST LIKE TO HAVE A NET WITH? Most – Shane Warne, then we can chat cricket over a beer afterwards. Least – Jos Buttler, because it could be very painful if he hits the ball straight back at me
MAKE ONE PREDICTION FOR THE FUTURE OF CRICKET: An England team will win the Ashes in Australia
WHAT MAKES YOU WORRY? My future career
WHAT GIVES YOU JOY? Commentating
TWITTER: @AlexHartley93

Batting	Mat	Inns	NO	Runs	HS	Ave	SR	100	50	Ct	St
ODIs	28	12	11	10	3*	10.00	19.60	0	0	4	-
T20Is	4	1	1	2	2*	-	100.00	0	0	0	-

Bowling	Mat	Balls	Runs	Wkts	BBI	BBM	Ave	Econ	SR	5w	10
ODIs	28	1390	950	39	4/24	4/24	24.35	4.10	35.6	0	0
T20Is	4	70	79	3	2/19	2/19	26.33	6.77	23.3	0	0

BESS HEATH   RHB / WK

FULL NAME: Bess Alice May Heath
BORN: August 20, 2001, Chesterfield, Derbyshire
SQUAD NO: 25
HEIGHT: 5ft 6in
NICKNAME: Bam Bam
TEAMS: Northern Diamonds, Yorkshire, Derbyshire, Yorkshire Diamonds
ROLE: Wicketkeeper/batter
DEBUT: List A: 2015; T20: 2014

BEST BATTING: 114 Derbyshire vs Norfolk, Spondon, 2016

FIRST CRICKET CLUB? Baslow CC, Derbyshire
WHAT WOULD YOU CHANGE ABOUT THE STRUCTURE OF THE DOMESTIC SEASON? Create space for the longer version of the game
WHAT WOULD A FLY ON THE WALL HEAR IN YOUR DRESSING ROOM? Bad singing
MOST BEAUTIFUL THING YOU HAVE EVER SEEN? My doggies Poppy and Coco
HOBBIES? Doing up Land Rovers
IF YOU COULD TURN BACK TIME... I'd reverse all my injuries
MAKE ONE PREDICTION FOR THE FUTURE OF CRICKET: Women's and men's cricket will be on an equal footing
WHAT MAKES YOU WORRY? The prospect of my Land Rover breaking down
WHAT GIVES YOU JOY? The countryside
SURPRISING FACT ABOUT YOU? I used to be a tree surgeon

Batting	Mat	Inns	NO	Runs	HS	Ave	SR	100	50	Ct	St
List A	38	33	6	769	114	28.48	92.76	2	4	29	4
T20s	61	55	16	793	58*	20.33	-	0	4	14	4

GEORGIA HENNESSY   RHB / RFM / MVP14

WESTERN STORM

FULL NAME: Georgia May Hennessy
BORN: November 4, 1996, Worcester
SQUAD NO: 64
HEIGHT: 5ft 6in
NICKNAME: Tracy Beaker
EDUCATION: University of Worcester
TEAMS: Western Storm, Somerset, Devon, Warwickshire, Worcestershire
ROLE: Allrounder
DEBUT: List A: 2010; T20: 2013

BEST BATTING: 105 Western Storm vs Sunrisers, Bristol, 2020
BEST BOWLING: 5-38 Warwickshire vs Surrey, Cobham, 2014

WHO IS YOUR LOOKALIKE? Ryan Sidebottom
FIRST CRICKET CLUB? Barnards Green CC, Malvern, Worcestershire
WHAT WOULD YOU CHANGE ABOUT THE STRUCTURE OF THE DOMESTIC SEASON? Create Second XI and Academy competitions
BIGGEST INFLUENCE ON YOUR DEVELOPMENT AS A CRICKETER (EXCLUDING PARENTS)? Gavin Haynes, who was my coach at Worcestershire Academy for a few years. My teammates have also been very important in helping me to fall back in love with the game after a couple of years out of it
WHO IS THE BEST BATTER/KEEPER/ALLROUNDER/BOWLER IN DOMESTIC CRICKET (EXCLUDING TEAMMATES)? Cordelia Griffith/Amara Carr/Hollie Armitage/Lauren Bell
MOST UNDERRATED PLAYER IN DOMESTIC CRICKET? Liz Russell
MOST BEAUTIFUL THING YOU HAVE EVER SEEN? A sunset in Sri Lanka
HOBBIES? Golf
WHAT DO YOU MOST ENJOY LISTENING TO? Post Malone
WHAT GIVES YOU JOY? Food
GUILTY PLEASURE? Call of Duty (video game)
TWITTER: @GeorgiaHennessy

Batting	Mat	Inns	NO	Runs	HS	Ave	SR	100	50	Ct	St
List A	75	74	12	1599	105	25.79	-	1	7	31	-
T20s	76	69	19	1698	97*	33.96	-	0	9	22	-

Bowling	Mat	Balls	Mdns	Runs	Wkts	BB	Ave	4wI	5wI	SR	Econ
List A	75	2165	22	1504	64	5-38	23.50	2	2	33.82	4.16
T20s	76	931	4	934	40	3-14	23.35	0	0	23.27	6.01

LUCY HIGHAM

RHB / OB

FULL NAME: Lucy Florence Higham
BORN: October 17, 1997, Leicester
SQUAD NO: 7
HEIGHT: 5ft 3in
EDUCATION: Leicester Grammar School;
Loughborough University
TEAMS: Lightning, Nottinghamshire,
Leicestershire, Loughborough Lightning
ROLE: Bowler
DEBUT: List A: 2013; T20: 2013

LIGHTNING

BEST BATTING: 74 Leicestershire vs Northamptonshire, Northampton, 2015
BEST BOWLING: 4-46 Leicestershire vs Derbyshire, Ticknall, 2014

FIRST CRICKET CLUB? Houghton & Thurnby CC, Leicester
WHAT WOULD YOU CHANGE ABOUT THE STRUCTURE OF THE DOMESTIC SEASON? I
would have said put the T20 comp before the 50-over stuff – but they've already done that
for this season!
WHO IS THE BEST BATTER/KEEPER/ALLROUNDER/BOWLER IN DOMESTIC CRICKET
(EXCLUDING TEAMMATES)? Eve Jones/Ellie Threlkeld/Emma Lamb/Lauren Bell
MOST UNDERRATED PLAYER IN DOMESTIC CRICKET? Sophie Luff
MOST BEAUTIFUL THING YOU HAVE EVER SEEN? A sunset from the top of the Empire State
Building in New York
HOBBIES? Trying to reduce my golf handicap
WHO WOULD YOU MOST AND LEAST LIKE TO HAVE A NET WITH? Most – Jos Buttler. Least
– Jofra Archer
WHAT DO YOU MOST ENJOY LISTENING TO? Indie folk
TWITTER: @lucy_higham

Batting	Mat	Inns	NO	Runs	HS	Ave	SR	100	50	Ct	St
List A	63	55	6	724	74	14.77	45.73	0	2	24	-
T20s	74	48	9	586	43*	15.02	-	0	0	18	-

Bowling	Mat	Balls	Mdns	Runs	Wkts	BB	Ave	4wl	5wl	SR	Econ
List A	63	2566	35	1584	74	4-46	21.40	1	0	34.67	3.70
T20s	74	981	5	870	46	4-16	18.91	1	0	21.32	5.32

LAURA JACKSON

RHB / RM

THUNDER

FULL NAME: Laura Elizabeth Jackson
BORN: December 27, 1997
SQUAD NO: 22
HEIGHT: 5ft 7in
NICKNAME: Jacko
EDUCATION: Ormskirk High School, Lancashire
TEAMS: Thunder, Lancashire, Cheshire, Cumbria
ROLE: Bowler
DEBUT: List A: 2015; T20: 2015

BEST BATTING: 30 Thunder vs Central Sparks, Worcester, 2021
BEST BOWLING: 7-9 Cumbria vs Scotland A, Kirkby Stephen, 2019

WHO IS YOUR LOOKALIKE? A pineapple
FIRST CRICKET CLUB? Halsall West End CC, Ormskirk, Lancashire
WHO IS THE BEST BATTER/KEEPER/ALLROUNDER/BOWLER IN DOMESTIC CRICKET
(EXCLUDING TEAMMATES)? Eve Jones/Ellie Threlkeld/Alice Capsey/Beth Langston
MOST UNDERRATED PLAYER IN DOMESTIC CRICKET? Cordelia Griffith
WHAT WOULD A FLY ON THE WALL HEAR IN YOUR DRESSING ROOM? "Turn that music off!"
MOST BEAUTIFUL THING YOU HAVE EVER SEEN? The view from the top of Mount Vesuvius
HOBBIES? I have a season ticket for Liverpool FC
IF YOU COULD TURN BACK TIME... I'd appeal for and celebrate wickets better
WHO WOULD YOU MOST AND LEAST LIKE TO HAVE A NET WITH? Most – Andrew Flintoff,
because he's a legend and hilarious. Least – Sheldon Cottrell, because his celebrations
would get under my skin!
MAKE ONE PREDICTION FOR THE FUTURE OF CRICKET: Women will play long-format cricket
WHAT MAKES YOU WORRY? Breaking a nail in the field!
WHAT GIVES YOU JOY? A sausage butty
TWITTER: @laurajacko22

Batting	Mat	Inns	NO	Runs	HS	Ave	SR	100	50	Ct	St
List A	26	20	4	154	30	9.62	34.52	0	0	7	-
T20s	36	16	8	107	24	13.37	52.19	0	0	7	-

Bowling	Mat	Balls	Mdns	Runs	Wkts	BB	Ave	4wI	5wI	SR	Econ
List A	26	871	21	500	26	7-9	19.23	0	1	33.50	3.44
T20s	36	460	4	445	24	3-9	18.54	0	0	19.16	5.80

AMY JONES

RHB / WK / MVP23

FULL NAME: Amy Ellen Jones
BORN: June 13, 1993, Solihull, Warwickshire
SQUAD NO: 40
HEIGHT: 5ft 9in
EDUCATION: John Willmott School;
Loughborough College
TEAMS: England, Central Sparks,
Warwickshire, Loughborough Lightning,
Perth Scorchers, Sydney Sixers, Western
Australia
ROLE: Wicketkeeper/batter
DEBUT: Test: 2019; ODI: 2013; T20I: 2013; List
A: 2008; T20: 2010

ENGLAND WOMEN

BEST ODI BATTING: 94 England vs India, Nagpur, 2018

WHO IS YOUR LOOKALIKE? Dora the Explorer (cartoon)
FIRST CRICKET CLUB? Walmley CC, West Midlands
WHAT WOULD YOU CHANGE ABOUT THE STRUCTURE OF THE DOMESTIC SEASON? Nothing
– I think they nailed it last year
WHO IS THE BEST BATTER/KEEPER/ALLROUNDER/BOWLER IN DOMESTIC CRICKET
(EXCLUDING TEAMMATES)? Georgia Adams/Ellie Threlkeld/Alice Capsey/Beth Langston
MOST BEAUTIFUL THING YOU HAVE EVER SEEN? Queenstown, New Zealand
IF YOU COULD TURN BACK TIME... I'd start to play golf much earlier
WHO WOULD YOU MOST AND LEAST LIKE TO HAVE A NET WITH? Most – Ben Foakes, to
have a good wicket-keeping net. Least – Cathryn Fitzpatrick (I hear she had a very fast
bouncer!)
MAKE ONE PREDICTION FOR THE FUTURE OF CRICKET: The Hundred will be an Olympic sport
WHAT DO YOU MOST ENJOY LISTENING TO? I Drink Wine by Adele
WHAT MAKES YOU WORRY? Climate change

Batting	Mat	Inns	NO	Runs	HS	Ave	SR	100	50	Ct	St
Tests	3	4	0	82	64	20.50	45.30	0	1	11	-
ODIs	58	49	3	1234	94	26.82	80.65	0	9	38	10
T20Is	65	53	7	931	89	20.23	119.66	0	5	26	24

Bowling	Mat	Balls	Runs	Wkts	BBI	BBM	Ave	Econ	SR	5w	10
Tests	3	-	-	-	-	-	-	-	-	-	-
ODIs	58	-	-	-	-	-	-	-	-	-	-
T20Is	65	-	-	-	-	-	-	-	-	-	-

EVE JONES LHB / SLA / MVP1

CENTRAL SPARKS

FULL NAME: Evelyn Jones
BORN: August 8, 1992, Shrewsbury, Shropshire
SQUAD NO: 11
HEIGHT: 5ft 8in
EDUCATION: Oxford Brookes University
TEAMS: Central Sparks, Warwickshire, Canterbury, Lancashire, Lancashire Thunder, Loughborough Lightning, Melbourne Renegades, Shropshire, Staffordshire
ROLE: Batter
DEBUT: List A: 2008; T20: 2010

BEST BATTING: 115* Staffordshire vs Durham, Durham, 2015
BEST BOWLING: 6-29 Shropshire vs Northumberland, Madeley, 2011

FIRST CRICKET CLUB? Whitchurch CC, Shropshire
WHAT WOULD YOU CHANGE ABOUT THE STRUCTURE OF THE DOMESTIC SEASON? Throw in a few longer-format games
BIGGEST INFLUENCE ON YOUR DEVELOPMENT AS A CRICKETER (EXCLUDING PARENTS)? Lisa Keightley (current England Women head coach). She first selected me for the England Academy
WHO IS THE BEST BATTER/KEEPER/ALLROUNDER/BOWLER IN DOMESTIC CRICKET (EXCLUDING TEAMMATES)? Sophie Luff/Ellie Threlkeld/Alice Capsey/Lauren Bell
WHAT WOULD A FLY ON THE WALL HEAR IN YOUR DRESSING ROOM? Gwen Davies misbehaving
MOST BEAUTIFUL THING YOU HAVE EVER SEEN? My baby niece
IF YOU COULD TURN BACK TIME... I'd have made women's cricket turn professional five years earlier
WHO WOULD YOU MOST AND LEAST LIKE TO HAVE A NET WITH? Most – Charlotte Edwards, an all-time great. Least – Cathryn Fitzpatrick. She was a bit scary!
WHAT MAKES YOU WORRY? The amount of time spent away from my family
GUILTY PLEASURE? Ozan's BBQ Pizza (my local takeaway)
TWITTER: @eve_jones11

Batting	Mat	Inns	NO	Runs	HS	Ave	SR	100	50	Ct	St
List A	90	87	12	2595	115*	34.60	-	5	14	31	-
T20s	112	106	13	2401	76	25.81	96.15	0	12	22	-

Bowling	Mat	Balls	Mdns	Runs	Wkts	BB	Ave	4wI	5wI	SR	Econ
List A	90	1121	26	750	25	6-29	30.00	1	1	44.84	4.01
T20s	112	395	0	421	17	3-14	24.76	0	0	23.23	6.39

HANNAH JONES
LHB / SLA / MVP34

FULL NAME: Hannah Emily Jones
BORN: February 10, 1999
SQUAD NO: 7
HEIGHT: 5ft 5in
EDUCATION: St Thomas More RC College, Manchester; Myerscough College, Lancashire
TEAMS: Thunder, Lancashire
ROLE: Bowler
DEBUT: List A: 2014; T20: 2014

THUNDER

BEST BATTING: 9 Thunder vs South East Stars, Beckenham, 2021
BEST BOWLING: 5-33 Thunder vs South East Stars, Beckenham, 2021

WHO IS YOUR LOOKALIKE? No one looks like me with my red hair
FIRST CRICKET CLUB? Denton St Lawrence CC, Manchester
WHAT WOULD YOU CHANGE ABOUT THE STRUCTURE OF THE DOMESTIC SEASON? Play on Saturday rather than Sunday – most women's club-level games are on a Sunday so those who are involved can't come to watch us play
WHO IS THE BEST BATTER/KEEPER/ALLROUNDER/BOWLER IN DOMESTIC CRICKET (EXCLUDING TEAMMATES)? Eve Jones/Bess Heath/Naomi Dattani/Lauren Bell
MOST BEAUTIFUL THING YOU HAVE EVER SEEN? The moment I was asked to be a bridesmaid at my best friend's wedding
WHO WOULD YOU MOST AND LEAST LIKE TO HAVE A NET WITH? Most – Laura Jackson, because we have played together since we were young and laugh a lot together. Least – Sammy-Jo Johnson, she has a great range of shots and a lot of power
WHAT DO YOU MOST ENJOY LISTENING TO? Ed Sheeran
WHAT MAKES YOU WORRY? I don't worry too much – just enjoy the ride
WHAT GIVES YOU JOY? Playing cricket

Batting	Mat	Inns	NO	Runs	HS	Ave	SR	100	50	Ct	St
List A	33	18	10	41	9	5.12	30.37	0	0	5	-
T20s	31	5	5	3	2*	-	37.50	0	0	4	-

Bowling	Mat	Balls	Mdns	Runs	Wkts	BB	Ave	4wI	5wI	SR	Econ
List A	33	1422	29	828	31	5-33	26.70	0	1	45.87	3.49
T20s	31	610	3	468	29	3-17	16.13	0	0	21.03	4.60

MARIE KELLY

RHB / RM / MVP46

LIGHTNING

FULL NAME: Marie Kelly
BORN: February 9, 1996, Birmingham
SQUAD NO: TBC
HEIGHT: 5ft 7in
NICKNAME: MK
EDUCATION: Loughborough University
TEAMS: Lightning, Warwickshire, Central Sparks, Loughborough Lightning, Southern Vipers
ROLE: Batter
DEBUT: List A: 2011; T20: 2012

BEST BATTING: 64 Warwickshire vs Lancashire, Newton-le-Willows, 2018
BEST BOWLING: 4-13 Warwickshire vs Surrey, Wellesbourne, 2013

WHO IS YOUR LOOKALIKE? My twin sister
FIRST CRICKET CLUB? Earlswood CC, Solihull, Warwickshire
WHAT WOULD YOU CHANGE ABOUT THE STRUCTURE OF THE DOMESTIC SEASON? Play each tournament in single blocks: first the 50-over, then T20, then The Hundred
MOST UNDERRATED PLAYER IN DOMESTIC CRICKET? Katie Levick
MOST BEAUTIFUL THING YOU HAVE EVER SEEN? The turtles I went swimming with
HOBBIES? Drawing
IF YOU COULD TURN BACK TIME... I would put less energy and time into my degree
WHO WOULD YOU MOST AND LEAST LIKE TO HAVE A NET WITH? Most – Rachael Heyhoe Flint. Least – Jhulan Goswami
MAKE ONE PREDICTION FOR THE FUTURE OF CRICKET: Closed-roof stadiums
WHAT DO YOU MOST ENJOY LISTENING TO? The Joe Rogan Experience podcast
WHAT MAKES YOU WORRY? The public perception of women's cricket
WHAT GIVES YOU JOY? Seeing women perform well in sport
TWITTER: @MarieKelly96

Batting	Mat	Inns	NO	Runs	HS	Ave	SR	100	50	Ct	St
List A	71	67	6	1393	64	22.83	-	0	8	22	-
T20s	60	54	11	1072	100*	24.93	-	1	5	22	-

Bowling	Mat	Balls	Mdns	Runs	Wkts	BB	Ave	4wI	5wI	SR	Econ
List A	71	926	13	607	26	4-13	23.34	1	0	35.61	3.93
T20s	60	361	3	298	22	3-9	13.54	0	0	16.40	4.95

HEATHER KNIGHT   RHB / OB / MVP24

FULL NAME: Heather Clare Knight
BORN: December 26, 1990, Plymouth
SQUAD NO: 5
HEIGHT: 5ft 7in
NICKNAME: Trev
EDUCATION: Plymstock School, Plymouth;
Cardiff University
TEAMS: England, Western Storm, Berkshire,
Devon, Hobart Hurricanes, Sydney Thunder,
Tasmania, Western Storm
ROLE: Batter
DEBUT: Test: 2011; ODI: 2010; T20I: 2010;
List A: 2008; T20: 2009

ENGLAND WOMEN

BEST ODI BATTING: 106 England vs Pakistan, Leicester, 2017
BEST ODI BOWLING: 5-26 England vs Pakistan, Leicester, 2016

FIRST CRICKET CLUB? Plymstock CC, Plymouth
WHAT WOULD YOU CHANGE ABOUT THE STRUCTURE OF THE DOMESTIC SEASON?
Schedule more games
MOST UNDERRATED PLAYER IN DOMESTIC CRICKET? Sophie Luff
MOST BEAUTIFUL THING YOU HAVE EVER SEEN? Sunset at Lake Bled in Slovenia
HOBBIES? Road biking
WHO WOULD YOU MOST AND LEAST LIKE TO HAVE A NET WITH? Most – Clare Connor. I
reckon I could take down her in-drifters! Least – Cathryn Fitzpatrick. She was rapid!
MAKE ONE PREDICTION FOR THE FUTURE OF CRICKET: In T20 cricket, the lbw rule about
pitching outside leg stump will be scrapped
WHAT DO YOU MOST ENJOY LISTENING TO? Indie rock
WHAT MAKES YOU WORRY? Climate change
WHAT GIVES YOU JOY? Food and wine
GUILTY PLEASURE? Bacon
TWITTER: @heatherknight55

Batting	Mat	Inns	NO	Runs	HS	Ave	SR	100	50	Ct	St
Tests	9	16	2	697	168*	49.78	47.96	2	3	10	-
ODIs	115	110	23	3250	106	37.35	71.80	2	22	38	-
T20Is	87	76	16	1389	108*	23.15	118.11	1	4	26	-

Bowling	Mat	Balls	Runs	Wkts	BBI	BBM	Ave	Econ	SR	5w	10
Tests	9	383	153	7	2/7	3/48	21.85	2.39	54.7	0	0
ODIs	115	1773	1304	53	5/26	5/26	24.60	4.41	33.4	1	0
T20Is	87	531	517	20	3/9	3/9	25.85	5.84	26.5	0	0

EMMA LAMB RHB / RM / MVP2

THUNDER

FULL NAME: Emma Louise Lamb
BORN: December 16, 1997, Preston, Lancashire
SQUAD NO: 6
HEIGHT: 5ft 7in
EDUCATION: Cardinal Newman College, Preston; Edge Hill University, Ormskirk, Lancashire
TEAMS: England, Thunder, Lancashire, Lancashire Thunder
ROLE: Allrounder
DEBUT: ODI: 2022; T20I: 2021; List A: 2012; T20: 2012

WHO IS YOUR LOOKALIKE? Ellie Goulding (so I'm told, but I don't see it myself)
FIRST CRICKET CLUB? Chorley CC, Lancashire
WHAT WOULD YOU CHANGE ABOUT THE STRUCTURE OF THE DOMESTIC SEASON? Have all 50-over cricket at the beginning of the season and all T20 cricket at the end
WHO IS THE BEST BATTER/ALLROUNDER/BOWLER IN DOMESTIC CRICKET (EXCLUDING TEAMMATES)? Eve Jones/Dani Gibson/Lauren Bell
MOST BEAUTIFUL THING YOU HAVE EVER SEEN? An Aussie brunch
HOBBIES? Drawing
IF YOU COULD TURN BACK TIME... I'd stress less about the small stuff
WHO WOULD YOU MOST AND LEAST LIKE TO HAVE A NET WITH? Most – Ellie Threlkeld. Least – Virat Kohli
WHAT DO YOU MOST ENJOY LISTENING TO? Podcasts (Katherine Ryan) and music (Chris Brown)
WHAT MAKES YOU WORRY? Global warming
WHAT GIVES YOU JOY? My house
GUILTY PLEASURE? Banana bread
TWITTER: @EmmaLamb236

Batting	Mat	Inns	NO	Runs	HS	Ave	SR	100	50	Ct	St
ODIs	1	1	0	0	0	0.00	0.00	0	0	1	-
T20Is	1	1	1	0	0*	-	-	0	0	0	-

Bowling	Mat	Balls	Runs	Wkts	BBI	BBM	Ave	Econ	SR	5w	10
ODIs	1	-	-	-	-	-	-	-	-	-	-
T20Is	1	-	-	-	-	-	-	-	-	-	-

FULL NAME: Bethany Alicia Langston
BORN: September 6, 1992, Harold Wood, Essex
SQUAD NO: 42
HEIGHT: 5ft 7in
NICKNAME: Bev
EDUCATION: Loughborough University
TEAMS: England, Northern Diamonds, Yorkshire, Essex, Loughborough Lightning, Otago, Yorkshire Diamonds
ROLE: Bowler
DEBUT: ODI: 2016; T20I: 2013; List A: 2009; T20: 2009

NORTHERN DIAMONDS

BEST ODI BATTING: 21 England vs Sri Lanka, Colombo, 2016
BEST ODI BOWLING: 1-23 England vs Sri Lanka, Colombo, 2016

FIRST CRICKET CLUB? Upminster CC, London
WHAT WOULD YOU CHANGE ABOUT THE STRUCTURE OF THE DOMESTIC SEASON? Play at least one red-ball game
WHO IS THE BEST BATTER/KEEPER/ALLROUNDER/BOWLER IN DOMESTIC CRICKET (EXCLUDING TEAMMATES)? Bryony Smith/Ellie Threlkeld/Alice Davidson-Richards/Lauren Bell
MOST BEAUTIFUL THING YOU HAVE EVER SEEN? A Roger Federer one-handed backhand
HOBBIES? Finding nice coffee spots and reading
IF YOU COULD TURN BACK TIME... I'd reverse climate change
WHO WOULD YOU MOST AND LEAST LIKE TO HAVE A NET WITH? All my Northern Diamonds teammates – we're a hoot!
MAKE ONE PREDICTION FOR THE FUTURE OF CRICKET: The Hundred will take off all over the world and there will be a Hundred Champions League featuring each country's winners
WHAT DO YOU MOST ENJOY LISTENING TO? Harry Potter-themed podcasts
WHAT MAKES YOU WORRY? Composing an Instagram post
TWITTER: @B_Langers92

Batting	Mat	Inns	NO	Runs	HS	Ave	SR	100	50	Ct	St
ODIs	4	2	1	21	21	21.00	100.00	0	0	2	-
T20Is	2	-	-	-	-	-	-	-	-	1	-

Bowling	Mat	Balls	Runs	Wkts	BBI	BBM	Ave	Econ	SR	5w	10
ODIs	4	186	94	2	1/23	1/23	47.00	3.03	93.0	0	0
T20Is	2	48	44	1	1/16	1/16	44.00	5.50	48.0	0	0

KATIE LEVICK   RHB / LB / MVP22

FULL NAME: Katie Ann Levick
BORN: July 17, 1991, Sheffield
SQUAD NO: 23
HEIGHT: 5ft 7in
NICKNAME: Lev
EDUCATION: Ecclesfield School, Sheffield;
Thomas Rotherham College, South
Yorkshire; Sheffield Hallam University
TEAMS: Northern Diamonds, Yorkshire,
Yorkshire Diamonds
ROLE: Bowler
DEBUT: List A: 2008; T20: 2010

BEST BATTING: 30* Yorkshire vs Berkshire, Harrogate, 2017
BEST BOWLING: 6-25 Yorkshire vs Lancashire, Harrogate, 2015

WHO IS YOUR LOOKALIKE? Katy Perry (I'm backing myself)
FIRST CRICKET CLUB? Upper Haugh CC, Rotherham, South Yorkshire
WHAT WOULD YOU CHANGE ABOUT THE STRUCTURE OF THE DOMESTIC SEASON? I'd love
the domestic girls to get a taste of red-ball cricket. It's the format I grew up loving to watch.
Plus there are two breaks in the day for food
WHO IS THE BEST BATTER/KEEPER/ALLROUNDER/BOWLER IN DOMESTIC CRICKET
(EXCLUDING TEAMMATES)? Sophie Luff/Ellie Threlkeld/Emma Lamb/Lauren Bell
WHAT WOULD A FLY ON THE WALL HEAR IN YOUR DRESSING ROOM? Old-school bangers
coming from my retro iPod classic, the official soundtrack of our dressing room
MOST BEAUTIFUL THING YOU HAVE EVER SEEN? The love my parents have for each other.
And Harry Styles in a leather suit at the 2021 Grammys
HOBBIES? Live music. I'm also trying to take up golf because that seems to be what every pro
cricketer does in their spare time and I suffer from FOMO
WHO WOULD YOU MOST AND LEAST LIKE TO HAVE A NET WITH? Most – Shane Warne.
Least – my brother Adam
WHAT DO YOU MOST ENJOY LISTENING TO? David Bowie, Arctic Monkeys
WHAT MAKES YOU WORRY? Watching Sheffield Wednesday
WHAT GIVES YOU JOY? RuPaul's Drag Race (reality TV series)
TWITTER: @Katie_Lev

Batting	Mat	Inns	NO	Runs	HS	Ave	SR	100	50	Ct	St
List A	97	50	23	186	30*	6.88	40.61	0	0	19	-
T20s	101	34	12	92	13	4.18	-	0	0	8	-

Bowling	Mat	Balls	Mdns	Runs	Wkts	BB	Ave	4wl	5wl	SR	Econ
List A	97	4591	110	2473	147	6-25	16.82	5	3	31.23	3.23
T20s	101	2043	9	1942	114	5-16	17.03	1	1	17.92	5.70

SOPHIE LUFF   RHB / RM / MVP17

FULL NAME: Sophie Natasha Luff
BORN: December 6, 1993, Taunton, Somerset
SQUAD NO: 63
HEIGHT: 5ft 2in
NICKNAME: Queen of Somerset, Miss Logical
EDUCATION: Cardiff Metropolitan University
TEAMS: England A, Western Storm, Somerset
ROLE: Batter
DEBUT: List A: 2009; T20: 2010

WESTERN STORM

BEST BATTING: 157* Western Storm vs Sunrisers, Bristol, 2021
BEST BOWLING: 1-27 Western Storm vs Sunrisers, Bristol, 2020

WHO IS YOUR LOOKALIKE? Rory Burns
FIRST CRICKET CLUB? Western-super-Mare CC, Somerset
WHAT WOULD YOU CHANGE ABOUT THE STRUCTURE OF THE DOMESTIC SEASON?
Introduce two-day cricket, perhaps initially North v South
WHO IS THE BEST BATTER/KEEPER/ALLROUNDER/BOWLER IN DOMESTIC CRICKET
(EXCLUDING TEAMMATES)? Eve Jones/Carla Rudd/Kathryn Bryce/Charlie Dean
MOST UNDERRATED PLAYER IN DOMESTIC CRICKET? Cordelia Griffith
WHAT WOULD A FLY ON THE WALL HEAR IN YOUR DRESSING ROOM? The song The
Combine Harvester by The Wurzels
HOBBIES? Baking (you can find me @luffybakes on Instagram)
WHO WOULD YOU MOST AND LEAST LIKE TO HAVE A NET WITH? Most – Kane Williamson.
Least – Joel Garner
MAKE ONE PREDICTION FOR THE FUTURE OF CRICKET: Batters can bat right- or left-handed,
choosing to do so based on the bowler and the field dimensions
WHAT DO YOU MOST ENJOY LISTENING TO? The High Performance Podcast
WHAT GIVES YOU JOY? Food
GUILTY PLEASURE? Drumstick Squashies
TWITTER: @LuffSophie

Batting	Mat	Inns	NO	Runs	HS	Ave	SR	100	50	Ct	St
List A	94	93	24	3147	157*	45.60	-	0	6	19	30	-
T20s	117	98	30	1942	60*	28.55	-	0	7	34	-

Bowling	Mat	Balls	Mdns	Runs	Wkts	BB	Ave	4wI	5wI	SR	Econ
List A	94	296	1	261	2	1-27	130.50	0	0	148.00	5.29
T20s	117	191	0	221	8	2-12	27.62	0	0	23.87	6.94

FI MORRIS

RHB / OB / MVP25

WESTERN STORM

FULL NAME: Fritha Mary Kie Morris
BORN: January 31, 1994, Reading, Berkshire
SQUAD NO: 88
HEIGHT: 5ft 6in
NICKNAME: Princess Fiona
EDUCATION: University of Exeter
TEAMS: Western Storm, Hampshire, Berkshire, Gloucestershire, Oxfordshire, Southern Vipers
ROLE: Allrounder
DEBUT: List A: 2008; T20: 2009

BEST BATTING: 127 Gloucestershire vs Oxfordshire, Charlbury, 2011
BEST BOWLING: 5-26 Western Storm vs Sunrisers, Chelmsford, 2020

FIRST CRICKET CLUB? Charlbury CC, Chipping Norton, Oxfordshire
WHAT WOULD YOU CHANGE ABOUT THE STRUCTURE OF THE DOMESTIC SEASON?
Schedule more matches
BIGGEST INFLUENCE ON YOUR DEVELOPMENT AS A CRICKETER (EXCLUDING PARENTS)? My brother Digs – he bowled off-spin and I copied his action and everything he did
WHO IS THE BEST BATTER/KEEPER/ALLROUNDER/BOWLER IN DOMESTIC CRICKET (EXCLUDING TEAMMATES)? Emma Lamb/Ellie Threlkeld/Bryony Smith/Katie Levick
MOST UNDERRATED PLAYER IN DOMESTIC CRICKET? Ami Campbell
MOST BEAUTIFUL THING YOU HAVE EVER SEEN? A giraffe
WHO WOULD YOU MOST AND LEAST LIKE TO HAVE A NET WITH? Most – Shane Warne, to teach me leggies. Least – Amanda-Jade Wellington, she always gets me out
MAKE ONE PREDICTION FOR THE FUTURE OF CRICKET: Equal pay for men and women in The Hundred
WHAT MAKES YOU WORRY? Dropping a catch on TV
GUILTY PLEASURE? Crumpets
TWITTER: @FiMorris8

Batting	Mat	Inns	NO	Runs	HS	Ave	SR	100	50	Ct	St
List A	73	68	9	1399	127	23.71	-	1	4	21	-
T20s	92	65	11	760	47*	14.07	-	0	0	18	-

Bowling	Mat	Balls	Mdns	Runs	Wkts	BB	Ave	4wl	5wl	SR	Econ
List A	73	3279	67	1906	107	5-26	17.81	8	1	30.64	3.48
T20s	92	1761	13	1654	96	4-22	17.22	2	0	18.34	5.63

TARA NORRIS — LHB / LFM / MVP19

FULL NAME: Tara Gabriella Norris
BORN: June 4, 1998, Philadelphia, USA
SQUAD NO: 24
HEIGHT: 5ft 7in
NICKNAME: Tino
EDUCATION: Portslade Aldridge Community Academy, Brighton; Loughborough University
TEAMS: USA, Southern Vipers, Sussex, Loughborough Lightning
ROLE: Bowler
DEBUT: T20I: 2021; List A: 2014; T20: 2014

BEST T20I BATTING: 13 USA vs Brazil, Naucalpan, 2021
BEST T20I BOWLING: 2-4 USA vs Brazil, Naucalpan, 2021

FIRST CRICKET CLUB? Horsham CC, East Sussex
WHAT WOULD YOU CHANGE ABOUT THE STRUCTURE OF THE DOMESTIC SEASON? Have all the players on full contracts
BIGGEST INFLUENCE ON YOUR DEVELOPMENT AS A CRICKETER (EXCLUDING PARENTS)? Being part of the MCCU programme at Loughborough University
WHO IS THE BEST BATTER/KEEPER/ALLROUNDER/BOWLER IN DOMESTIC CRICKET (EXCLUDING TEAMMATES)? Eve Jones/Ellie Threlkeld/Linsey Smith/Beth Langston
MOST UNDERRATED PLAYER IN DOMESTIC CRICKET? Fi Morris
MOST BEAUTIFUL THING YOU HAVE EVER SEEN? A sunset looking over Half Dome at Yosemite National Park in California
HOBBIES? Any racket sport, open-water swimming, cooking, reading
WHO WOULD YOU MOST LIKE TO HAVE A NET WITH? Stuart Broad
MAKE ONE PREDICTION FOR THE FUTURE OF CRICKET: Women's regional cricket will have a four-day format
WHAT MAKES YOU WORRY? Being late
GUILTY PLEASURE? One Direction
TWITTER: @Tara_norris98

Batting	Mat	Inns	NO	Runs	HS	Ave	SR	100	50	Ct	St
T20Is	5	3	1	15	13	7.50	65.21	0	0	0	-

Bowling	Mat	Balls	Runs	Wkts	BBI	BBM	Ave	Econ	SR	5w	10
T20Is	5	108	31	4	2/4	2/4	7.75	1.72	27.0	0	0

PAIGE SCHOLFIELD   RHB / RFM

SOUTHERN VIPERS

FULL NAME: Paige Jamie Scholfield
BORN: December 19, 1995, Durban, South Africa
SQUAD NO: 7
HEIGHT: 5ft 7in
EDUCATION: Beacon Academy, East Sussex; Loughborough College
TEAMS: Southern Vipers, Sussex, Loughborough Lightning
ROLE: Allrounder
DEBUT: List A: 2012; T20: 2013

BEST BATTING: 48 Sussex vs Middlesex, Ditchling, 2013
BEST BOWLING: 3-16 Southern Vipers vs Thunder, Sale, 2021

FIRST CRICKET CLUB? Bells Yew Green CC, Tunbridge Wells, Kent
WHAT WOULD YOU CHANGE ABOUT THE STRUCTURE OF THE DOMESTIC SEASON? Bring in the longer format of the game
BIGGEST INFLUENCE ON YOUR DEVELOPMENT AS A CRICKETER (EXCLUDING PARENTS)? Charlotte Edwards, the former England captain and now my coach at Southern Vipers
WHO IS THE BEST BATTER/KEEPER/ALLROUNDER/BOWLER IN DOMESTIC CRICKET (EXCLUDING TEAMMATES)? Eve Jones/Ellie Threlkeld/Georgia Hennessy/Tash Farrant
MOST UNDERRATED PLAYER IN DOMESTIC CRICKET? Sophie Luff
WHAT WOULD A FLY ON THE WALL HEAR IN YOUR DRESSING ROOM? R&B classics
MOST BEAUTIFUL THING YOU HAVE EVER SEEN? Table Mountain, Cape Town
HOBBIES? The gym
WHO WOULD YOU LEAST LIKE TO HAVE A NET WITH? Katherine Brunt – either because of getting pinned or else the death stare
MAKE ONE PREDICTION FOR THE FUTURE OF CRICKET: The Hundred will overtake the Big Bash
WHAT MAKES YOU WORRY? The media
GUILTY PLEASURE? Taylor Swift
TWITTER: @PaigeSchol

Batting	Mat	Inns	NO	Runs	HS	Ave	SR	100	50	Ct	St
List A	58	45	10	658	48	18.80	67.76	0	0	23	-
T20s	76	66	13	731	63*	13.79	97.59	0	1	23	1

Bowling	Mat	Balls	Mdns	Runs	Wkts	BB	Ave	4wl	5wl	SR	Econ
List A	58	1167	11	805	32	3-16	25.15	0	0	36.46	4.13
T20s	76	512	1	541	22	3-12	24.59	0	0	23.27	6.33

NAT SCIVER

RHB / RMF / MVP37

FULL NAME: Natalie Ruth Sciver
BORN: August 20, 1992, Tokyo, Japan
SQUAD NO: 39
HEIGHT: 5ft 10in
NICKNAME: Sciv
EDUCATION: Epsom College, Surrey;
Loughborough University
TEAMS: England, Northern Diamonds,
Surrey, Melbourne Stars, Perth Scorchers,
Surrey Stars
ROLE: Allrounder
DEBUT: Test: 2014; ODI: 2013; T20I: 2013;
List A: 2010; T20: 2010

BEST ODI BATTING: 137 England vs Pakistan, Leicester, 2017
BEST ODI BOWLING: 3-3 England vs West Indies, Bristol, 2017

WHO IS YOUR LOOKALIKE? Olivia Wilde (actress)
FIRST CRICKET CLUB? Stoke d'Abernon CC, Surrey
WHAT WOULD YOU CHANGE ABOUT THE STRUCTURE OF THE DOMESTIC SEASON? Make sure there are more matches where all players are available
WHO IS THE BEST BATTER/KEEPER/ALLROUNDER/BOWLER IN DOMESTIC CRICKET (EXCLUDING TEAMMATES)? Georgia Adams/Ellie Threlkeld/Alice Capsey/Issy Wong
MOST BEAUTIFUL THING YOU HAVE EVER SEEN? The snow-capped French Alps
HOBBIES? DIY
IF YOU COULD TURN BACK TIME... I'd be left-handed
WHO WOULD YOU MOST AND LEAST LIKE TO HAVE A NET WITH? Most – Katherine Brunt. She'd give me some nice half-volleys! Least – Enid Bakewell (ex-England allrounder). She'd get me out the whole time!
MAKE ONE PREDICTION FOR THE FUTURE OF CRICKET: There'll be women's Test matches played between all nations
WHAT MAKES YOU WORRY? The world
WHAT GIVES YOU JOY? My dog Bella
TWITTER: @natsciver

Batting	Mat	Inns	NO	Runs	HS	Ave	SR	100	50	Ct	St
Tests	7	11	0	343	88	31.18	42.29	0	2	5	-
ODIs	80	71	12	2275	137	38.55	92.74	3	15	32	-
T20Is	91	87	18	1720	82	24.92	113.30	0	10	45	-

Bowling	Mat	Balls	Runs	Wkts	BBI	BBM	Ave	Econ	SR	5w	10
Tests	7	645	287	9	3/41	4/70	31.88	2.66	71.6	0	0
ODIs	80	2175	1571	55	3/3	3/3	28.56	4.33	39.5	0	0
T20Is	91	1338	1435	72	4/15	4/15	19.93	6.43	18.5	0	0

GRACE SCRIVENS   LB / OB / MVP32

SUNRISERS

FULL NAME: Grace Elizabeth Scrivens
BORN: November 13, 2003, Kent
SQUAD NO: 29
HEIGHT: 5ft 9in
NICKNAME: Scriv
EDUCATION: Sutton Valence School,
Maidstone, Kent
TEAMS: Sunrisers, Kent
ROLE: Allrounder
DEBUT: List A: 2019; T20: 2018

BEST BATTING: 72 Sunrisers vs Western Storm, Bristol, 2020
BEST BOWLING: 1-27 Sunrisers vs Western Storm, Chelmsford, 2020

FIRST CRICKET CLUB? Hollingbourne CC, Kent
WHO IS THE BEST BATTER/KEEPER/ALLROUNDER/BOWLER IN DOMESTIC CRICKET
(EXCLUDING TEAMMATES)? Emma Lamb/Ellie Threlkeld/Alice Davidson-Richards/Kirstie
Gordon
MOST UNDERRATED PLAYER IN DOMESTIC CRICKET? Sophie Luff
WHAT WOULD A FLY ON THE WALL HEAR IN YOUR DRESSING ROOM? Encouragement
MOST BEAUTIFUL THING YOU HAVE EVER SEEN? The beaches in the Caribbean
HOBBIES? Walking the dog, going for brunch with friends, badminton
WHO WOULD YOU MOST LIKE TO HAVE A NET WITH? Eoin Morgan – a left-handed batter
like me, and he has a wealth of knowledge about the game
MAKE ONE PREDICTION FOR THE FUTURE OF CRICKET: All women's domestic players will
get paid to train and play so that there is more opportunity to practise together as one team
all year round
WHAT DO YOU MOST ENJOY LISTENING TO? The latest pop music
WHAT MAKES YOU WORRY? Sometimes new things that I haven't experienced before
WHAT GIVES YOU JOY? Winning as a team

Batting	Mat	Inns	NO	Runs	HS	Ave	SR	100	50	Ct	St
List A	15	15	0	324	72	21.60	58.16	0	1	3	-
T20s	23	21	8	341	94*	26.23	92.66	0	1	4	-

Bowling	Mat	Balls	Mdns	Runs	Wkts	BB	Ave	4wI	5wI	SR	Econ
List A	15	434	3	383	7	1-27	54.71	0	0	62.00	5.29
T20s	23	198	0	152	9	2-10	16.88	0	0	22.00	4.60

ANYA SHRUBSOLE

RHB / RMF / MVP44

FULL NAME: Anya Shrubsole
BORN: December 7, 1991, Bath
SQUAD NO: 41
HEIGHT: 5ft 10in
NICKNAME: Hoof
EDUCATION: Hayesfield School, Bath;
Loughborough University
TEAMS: England, Western Storm, Berkshire,
Perth Scorchers, Somerset
ROLE: Bowler
DEBUT: Test: 2013; ODI: 2008; T20I: 2008;
List A: 2004; T20: 2005

BEST ODI BATTING: 32* England vs West Indies, Worcester, 2019
BEST ODI BOWLING: 6-46 England vs India, Lord's, 2017

FIRST CRICKET CLUB? Bath CC, Somerset
WHAT WOULD YOU CHANGE ABOUT THE STRUCTURE OF THE DOMESTIC SEASON? Add
some multi-day cricket (if there's time to fit it in)
BIGGEST INFLUENCE ON YOUR DEVELOPMENT AS A CRICKETER (EXCLUDING PARENTS)?
Tom Baker – my first coach at Bath CC
WHO IS THE BEST BATTER/KEEPER/ALLROUNDER/BOWLER IN DOMESTIC CRICKET
(EXCLUDING TEAMMATES)? Bryony Smith/Nat Wraith/Alice Capsey/Lauren Bell
MOST BEAUTIFUL THING YOU HAVE EVER SEEN? My dog Niko
HOBBIES? Portsmouth FC
MAKE ONE PREDICTION FOR THE FUTURE OF CRICKET: Women's cricket will go through the
roof
WHAT DO YOU MOST ENJOY LISTENING TO? Musicals
WHAT GIVES YOU JOY? Watching my dog throw himself into water
TWITTER: @anya_shrubsole

Batting	Mat	Inns	NO	Runs	HS	Ave	SR	100	50	Ct	St
Tests	8	12	0	118	47	9.83	37.10	0	0	4	-
ODIs	78	36	11	275	32*	11.00	82.08	0	0	19	-
T20Is	79	19	10	104	29	11.55	105.05	0	0	20	-

Bowling	Mat	Balls	Runs	Wkts	BBI	BBM	Ave	Econ	SR	5w	10
Tests	8	1556	635	19	4/51	7/99	33.42	2.44	81.8	0	0
ODIs	78	3660	2546	97	6/46	6/46	26.24	4.17	37.7	2	0
T20Is	79	1598	1587	102	5/11	5/11	15.55	5.95	15.6	1	0

RACHEL SLATER

RHB / LM

FULL NAME: Rachel Elizabeth Slater
BORN: November 20, 2001, Glens Falls, New York, USA
SQUAD NO: 72
HEIGHT: 5ft 7in
NICKNAME: Slats
EDUCATION: Boston Spa School, Wetherby, West Yorkshire
TEAMS: Scotland, Northern Diamonds, Yorkshire
ROLE: Bowler
DEBUT: T20I: 2022; List A: 2019; T20: 2019

BEST T20I BATTING: 6* Scotland vs Malaysia, Kuala Lumpur, 2022

FIRST CRICKET CLUB? Collingham & Linton CC, West Yorkshire
WHAT WOULD YOU CHANGE ABOUT THE STRUCTURE OF THE DOMESTIC SEASON?
Schedule more games!
WHO IS THE BEST BATTER/KEEPER/ALLROUNDER/BOWLER IN DOMESTIC CRICKET
(EXCLUDING TEAMMATES)? Eve Jones/Ellie Threlkeld/Bryony Smith/Lauren Bell
MOST UNDERRATED PLAYER IN DOMESTIC CRICKET? Sophie Luff
WHAT WOULD A FLY ON THE WALL HEAR IN YOUR DRESSING ROOM? Lots of music and
laughter
HOBBIES? Going out for coffee
IF YOU COULD TURN BACK TIME... I'd change nothing
MAKE ONE PREDICTION FOR THE FUTURE OF CRICKET: They'll be more women's Test cricket
WHAT DO YOU MOST ENJOY LISTENING TO? House music
WHAT GIVES YOU JOY? Friends
TWITTER: @rachelslater72

Batting	Mat	Inns	NO	Runs	HS	Ave	SR	100	50	Ct	St
T20Is	4	4	2	12	6*	6.00	52.17	0	0	0	-

Bowling	Mat	Balls	Runs	Wkts	BBI	BBM	Ave	Econ	SR	5w	10
T20Is	4	54	81	0	-	-	-	9.00	-	0	0

BRYONY SMITH　　　　　　　RHB / OB / MVP4

FULL NAME: Bryony Frances Smith
BORN: December 12, 1997, Sutton, Surrey
SQUAD NO: 4
HEIGHT: 5ft 6in
NICKNAME: Bry
EDUCATION: St Andrews High School, London; Archbishop Tenison's Sixth Form
TEAMS: England, South East Stars, Surrey, Surrey Stars
ROLE: Allrounder
DEBUT: ODI: 2019; T20I: 2018; List A: 2014; T20: 2014

BEST ODI BOWLING: 1-20 England vs West Indies, Chelmsford, 2019

FIRST CRICKET CLUB? Wallington CC, London
WHAT WOULD YOU CHANGE ABOUT THE STRUCTURE OF THE DOMESTIC SEASON?
Schedule more games!
BIGGEST INFLUENCE ON YOUR DEVELOPMENT AS A CRICKETER (EXCLUDING PARENTS)?
Richard Bedbrook – as full-time women's coach at Surrey he spent lots of time working with me and planning how I would take my game to the next level
WHO IS THE BEST BATTER/KEEPER/ALLROUNDER/BOWLER IN DOMESTIC CRICKET (EXCLUDING TEAMMATES)? Eve Jones/Ellie Threlkeld/Emma Lamb/Lauren Bell
MOST UNDERRATED PLAYER IN DOMESTIC CRICKET? Sophie Luff
IF YOU COULD TURN BACK TIME... I wouldn't be so shy when I was younger
WHO WOULD YOU MOST AND LEAST LIKE TO HAVE A NET WITH? Most – Kevin Pietersen. Least – Shane Warne
MAKE ONE PREDICTION FOR THE FUTURE OF CRICKET: Cricket will become an Olympic sport
WHAT DO YOU MOST ENJOY LISTENING TO? Comedy podcasts and cheesy music
WHAT MAKES YOU WORRY? Forgetting my equipment
WHAT GIVES YOU JOY? Freshly toasted bread
TWITTER: @BrySmith97

Batting	Mat	Inns	NO	Runs	HS	Ave	SR	100	50	Ct	St
ODIs	1	-	-	-	-	-	-	-	-	0	-
T20Is	3	3	0	16	15	5.33	100.00	0	0	0	-

Bowling	Mat	Balls	Runs	Wkts	BBI	BBM	Ave	Econ	SR	5w	10
ODIs	1	48	20	1	1/20	1/20	20.00	2.50	48.0	0	0
T20Is	3	-	-	-	-	-	-	-	-	-	-

LINSEY SMITH — LHB / SLA / MVP5

NORTHERN DIAMONDS

FULL NAME: Linsey Claire Neale Smith
BORN: March 10, 1995, Hillingdon, Middlesex
SQUAD NO: 50
HEIGHT: 5ft 2in
NICKNAME: Neal
EDUCATION: Loughborough University
TEAMS: England, Northern Diamonds, Sussex, Berkshire, Loughborough Lightning, Melbourne Stars, Southern Vipers, Yorkshire Diamonds
ROLE: Bowler
DEBUT: T20I: 2018; List A: 2011; T20: 2011

BEST T20I BOWLING: 3-18 England vs Sri Lanka, Colombo, 2019

FIRST CRICKET CLUB? Aston Rowant CC, Oxfordshire
BIGGEST INFLUENCE ON YOUR DEVELOPMENT AS A CRICKETER (EXCLUDING PARENTS)?
John Stanworth, my coach at the England Academy. He sorted my attitude out and focused my mind on getting into the England team
WHO IS THE BEST BATTER/KEEPER/ALLROUNDER/BOWLER IN DOMESTIC CRICKET (EXCLUDING TEAMMATES)? Georgia Adams/Ellie Threlkeld/Alice Davidson-Richards/Lauren Bell
MOST UNDERRATED PLAYER IN DOMESTIC CRICKET? Kalea Moore
WHAT WOULD A FLY ON THE WALL HEAR IN YOUR DRESSING ROOM? Plans for the pub
MOST BEAUTIFUL THING YOU HAVE EVER SEEN? My niece when I met her for the first time
HOBBIES? Coffee, brunching, football
IF YOU COULD TURN BACK TIME... I'd work harder at school
WHO WOULD YOU MOST AND LEAST LIKE TO HAVE A NET WITH? Most – Ravindra Jadeja, just because I like the way he plays. Least – Sophie Devine, because she hits the ball so hard
MAKE ONE PREDICTION FOR THE FUTURE OF CRICKET: Robots for umpires
WHAT DO YOU MOST ENJOY LISTENING TO? Elton John
WHAT MAKES YOU WORRY? The unknown
TWITTER: @LinseySmith95

Batting	Mat	Inns	NO	Runs	HS	Ave	SR	100	50	Ct	St
T20Is	9	-	-	-	-	-	-	-	-	0	-

Bowling	Mat	Balls	Runs	Wkts	BBI	BBM	Ave	Econ	SR	5w	10
T20Is	9	186	188	13	3/18	3/18	14.46	6.06	14.3	0	0

ELLIE THRELKELD   RHB / WK / MVP49

FULL NAME: Eleanor Threlkeld
BORN: November 16, 1998, Knowsley, Lancashire
SQUAD NO: 21
HEIGHT: 5ft 6in
NICKNAME: Threlks
EDUCATION: Winstanley College, Wigan; Loughborough University
TEAMS: England A, Thunder, Lancashire, Lancashire Thunder
ROLE: Wicketkeeper/batter
DEBUT: List A: 2014; T20: 2013

THUNDER

BEST BATTING: 72 Lancashire vs Nottinghamshire, Carnforth, 2019

FIRST CRICKET CLUB? Rainford CC, St Helens, Merseyside
WHAT WOULD YOU CHANGE ABOUT THE STRUCTURE OF THE DOMESTIC SEASON? Play each competition in one block rather than jump between formats
BIGGEST INFLUENCE ON YOUR DEVELOPMENT AS A CRICKETER (EXCLUDING PARENTS)? My older brother – he got me into the sport and I always wanted to be like him
WHO IS THE BEST BATTER/KEEPER/ALLROUNDER/BOWLER IN DOMESTIC CRICKET (EXCLUDING TEAMMATES)? Eve Jones/Nat Wraith/Alice Capsey/Lauren Bell
HOBBIES? Studying for my masters
IF YOU COULD TURN BACK TIME... I'd get a dog earlier in my life
WHAT DO YOU MOST ENJOY LISTENING TO? Audiobooks
WHAT MAKES YOU WORRY? Covid rules
WHAT GIVES YOU JOY? My dog
GUILTY PLEASURE? Playing the ukulele
TWITTER: @EllieThrelkeld

Batting	Mat	Inns	NO	Runs	HS	Ave	SR	100	50	Ct	St
List A	55	52	4	732	72	15.25	50.06	0	3	28	24
T20s	88	73	17	947	56*	16.91	-	0	4	25	55

MADY VILLIERS   RHB / OB / MVP47

ENGLAND WOMEN

FULL NAME: Mady Kate Villiers
BORN: August 26, 1998, Havering, Essex
SQUAD NO: 22
HEIGHT: 5ft 5in
NICKNAME: AB, Mandy
EDUCATION: Shenfield High School, Brentwood, Essex
TEAMS: England, Sunrisers, Essex, Surrey Stars
ROLE: Bowler
DEBUT: T20I: 2019; List A: 2013; T20: 2013

BEST T20I BATTING: 9* England vs New Zealand, Hove, 2021
BEST T20I BOWLING: 3-10 England vs New Zealand, Wellington, 2021

FIRST CRICKET CLUB? Bentley CC, Brentford, Essex
WHO IS THE BEST BATSMAN/KEEPER/ALLROUNDER/BOWLER IN DOMESTIC CRICKET (EXCLUDING TEAMMATES)? Alice Capsey/Ellie Threlkeld/Alice Davidson-Richards/Lauren Bell
MOST UNDERRATED PLAYER IN COUNTY CRICKET? Amara Carr
WHAT WOULD A FLY ON THE WALL HEAR IN YOUR DRESSING ROOM? Katherine Brunt screaming or singing
MOST BEAUTIFUL THING YOU HAVE EVER SEEN? Milford Sound on the South Island of New Zealand
WHO WOULD YOU MOST AND LEAST LIKE TO HAVE A NET WITH? Most – AB de Villiers. Least – Jofra Archer
MAKE ONE PREDICTION FOR THE FUTURE OF CRICKET: The Hundred will have leagues all over the world
WHAT DO YOU MOST ENJOY LISTENING TO? The rain
WHAT MAKES YOU WORRY? Being away from my family
WHAT GIVES YOU JOY? Golf
TWITTER: @VilliersMady

Batting	Mat	Inns	NO	Runs	HS	Ave	SR	100	50	Ct	St
T20Is	17	4	2	13	9*	6.50	108.33	0	0	9	-

Bowling	Mat	Balls	Runs	Wkts	BBI	BBM	Ave	Econ	SR	5w	10
T20Is	17	216	242	14	3/10	3/10	17.28	6.72	15.4	0	0

FRAN WILSON

RHB / OB

FULL NAME: Frances Claire Wilson
BORN: November 7, 1991, Farnham, Surrey
SQUAD NO: 35
HEIGHT: 5ft 4in
NICKNAME: Franki
EDUCATION: University of Bath; Loughborough University
TEAMS: England, Western Storm, Kent, Hobart Hurricanes, Middlesex, Somerset, Sunrisers, Sydney Thunder, Wellington
ROLE: Batter
DEBUT: Test: 2017; ODI: 2010; T20I: 2010; List A: 2006; T20: 2010

WESTERN STORM

BEST ODI BATTING: 85* England vs Pakistan, Kuala Lumpur, 2019

WHO IS YOUR LOOKALIKE? A quokka
FIRST CRICKET CLUB? Bath CC, Somerset
WHAT WOULD YOU CHANGE ABOUT THE STRUCTURE OF THE DOMESTIC SEASON? Introduce two-day fixtures
WHO IS THE BEST BATTER/KEEPER/ALLROUNDER/BOWLER IN DOMESTIC CRICKET (EXCLUDING TEAMMATES)? Heather Knight/Amy Jones/Nat Sciver/Sophie Ecclestone
WHAT WOULD A FLY ON THE WALL HEAR IN YOUR DRESSING ROOM? The Wurzels
MOST BEAUTIFUL THING YOU HAVE EVER SEEN? Trees and clouds
HOBBIES? Long hikes
IF YOU COULD TURN BACK TIME... I would not copy my friend's work in year six Maths
WHO WOULD YOU MOST AND LEAST LIKE TO HAVE A NET WITH? Most – KP, to see him smash it. Least – Murali, because I wouldn't hit anything
WHAT MAKES YOU WORRY? The internet
WHAT GIVES YOU JOY? The countryside
TWITTER: @fwilson07

Batting	Mat	Inns	NO	Runs	HS	Ave	SR	100	50	Ct	St
Tests	1	1	0	13	13	13.00	24.52	0	0	0	-
ODIs	33	23	2	468	85*	22.28	87.96	0	2	14	-
T20Is	30	26	10	356	43*	22.25	99.16	0	0	7	-

Bowling	Mat	Balls	Runs	Wkts	BBI	BBM	Ave	Econ	SR	5w	10
Tests	1	-	-	-	-	-	-	-	-	-	-
ODIs	33	-	-	-	-	-	-	-	-	-	-
T20Is	30	-	-	-	-	-	-	-	-	-	-

LAUREN WINFIELD-HILL   RHB / WK / MVP43

FULL NAME: Lauren Winfield-Hill
BORN: August 16, 1990, York
SQUAD NO: 58
HEIGHT: 5ft 8in
NICKNAME: Loz
EDUCATION: Loughborough University
TEAMS: England, Northern Diamonds, Yorkshire, Adelaide Strikers, Brisbane Heat, Hobart Hurricanes, Yorkshire Diamonds
ROLE: Batter
DEBUT: Test: 2014; ODI: 2013; T20I: 2013; List A: 2007; T20: 2010

BEST ODI BATTING: 123 England vs Pakistan, Worcester, 2016

FIRST CRICKET CLUB? Stamford Bridge CC, Yorkshire
BIGGEST INFLUENCE ON YOUR DEVELOPMENT AS A CRICKETER (EXCLUDING PARENTS)? Graham Dilley, the former England cricketer who was head coach of the Academy at Loughborough
WHO IS THE BEST BATTER/KEEPER/ALLROUNDER/BOWLER IN DOMESTIC CRICKET (EXCLUDING TEAMMATES)? Bryony Smith/Ellie Threlkeld/Alice Capsey/Beth Langston
MOST UNDERRATED PLAYER IN DOMESTIC CRICKET? Linsey Smith
HOBBIES? Golf
WHO WOULD YOU LEAST LIKE TO HAVE A NET WITH? Brett Lee
MAKE ONE PREDICTION FOR THE FUTURE OF CRICKET: Substitutes
WHAT DO YOU MOST ENJOY LISTENING TO? Sting
WHAT MAKES YOU WORRY? Getting old
GUILTY PLEASURE? Music of the 1970s

Batting	Mat	Inns	NO	Runs	HS	Ave	SR	100	50	Ct	St
Tests	5	9	0	166	35	18.44	32.54	0	0	1	-
ODIs	53	53	4	1174	123	23.95	66.78	1	3	19	-
T20Is	40	31	6	552	74	22.08	111.29	0	3	16	-

Bowling	Mat	Balls	Runs	Wkts	BBI	BBM	Ave	Econ	SR	5w	10
Tests	5	-	-	-	-	-	-	-	-	-	-
ODIs	53	-	-	-	-	-	-	-	-	-	-
T20Is	40	-	-	-	-	-	-	-	-	-	-

ISSY WONG   RHB / RF / MVP20

FULL NAME: Isabelle Eleanor Chih Ming Wong
BORN: May 15, 2002, Chelsea, London
SQUAD NO: 95
HEIGHT: 5ft 7in
NICKNAME: Wongi
EDUCATION: Shrewsbury School
TEAMS: England A, Central Sparks, Warwickshire, Southern Vipers, Sydney Thunder, Worcestershire
ROLE: Bowler
DEBUT: List A: 2018; T20: 2018

BEST BATTING: 49 Worcestershire vs Shropshire, Kidderminster, 2018
BEST BOWLING: 5-49 Central Sparks vs Northern Diamonds, Headingley, 2021

WHO IS YOUR LOOKALIKE? Slim Shady (Eminem)
FIRST CRICKET CLUB? Knowle & Dorridge CC, Solihull, Warwickshire
WHAT WOULD YOU CHANGE ABOUT THE STRUCTURE OF THE DOMESTIC SEASON? Add in some red-ball cricket
WHO IS THE BEST BATTER/KEEPER/ALLROUNDER/BOWLER IN DOMESTIC CRICKET (EXCLUDING TEAMMATES)? Emma Lamb/Ellie Threlkeld/Alice Capsey/Beth Langston
MOST BEAUTIFUL THING YOU HAVE EVER SEEN? Cape Hillsborough beach in Queensland, Australia
HOBBIES? Rubik's cube – I have at least 10 of them in different designs and sizes
WHO WOULD YOU MOST AND LEAST LIKE TO HAVE A NET WITH? Brett Lee – both most and least. I'd love to chat about bowling with him but I wouldn't fancy facing him
MAKE ONE PREDICTION FOR THE FUTURE OF CRICKET: A women's IPL in the next five years
WHAT MAKES YOU WORRY? Being late – I'm always ridiculously early to training because I stress about not being on time
WHAT GIVES YOU JOY? Playing NBA 2K on the PlayStation, especially when I'm against my brother
TWITTER: @Wongi95

Batting	Mat	Inns	NO	Runs	HS	Ave	SR	100	50	Ct	St
List A	23	19	5	155	49	11.07	72.09	0	0	6	-
T20s	45	29	4	202	43	8.08	122.42	0	0	8	-

Bowling	Mat	Balls	Mdns	Runs	Wkts	BB	Ave	4wI	5wI	SR	Econ
List A	23	908	21	661	34	5-49	19.44	3	1	26.70	4.36
T20s	45	749	2	922	31	3-21	29.74	0	0	24.16	7.38

NAT WRAITH RHB / WK

WESTERN STORM

FULL NAME: Natasha Agnes Jessica Wraith
BORN: October 3, 2001, Bristol
SQUAD NO: 37
HEIGHT: 5ft 6in
NICKNAME: Aggy
EDUCATION: SGS College, Gloucestershire;
Cardiff Metropolitan University
TEAMS: Western Storm, Somerset,
Gloucestershire
ROLE: Wicketkeeper
DEBUT: List A: 2016; T20: 2016

BEST BATTING: 68 Western Storm vs Southern Vipers, Southampton, 2020

WHO IS YOUR LOOKALIKE? Kerry Mucklowe (from the sitcom This Country)
FIRST CRICKET CLUB? Frenchay CC, Bristol
WHO IS THE BEST BATTER/KEEPER/ALLROUNDER/BOWLER IN DOMESTIC CRICKET
(EXCLUDING TEAMMATES)? Ella McCaughan/Ellie Threlkeld/Charlie Dean/Linsey Smith
MOST UNDERRATED PLAYER IN DOMESTIC CRICKET? Ella McCaughan
WHAT WOULD A FLY ON THE WALL HEAR IN YOUR DRESSING ROOM? What we're all having
for tea
MOST BEAUTIFUL THING YOU HAVE EVER SEEN? A perfectly cooked poached egg
HOBBIES? Spotify
IF YOU COULD TURN BACK TIME... I would have got into wicketkeeping earlier
WHO WOULD YOU MOST AND LEAST LIKE TO HAVE A NET WITH? Most – Quinton de Kock
(I'm obsessed). Least – Marizanne Kapp (she seems scary)
WHAT DO YOU MOST ENJOY LISTENING TO? Liquid drum and bass
WHAT MAKES YOU WORRY? Bean bags
WHAT GIVES YOU JOY? When I get back from training to discover my housemates have
made dinner
GUILTY PLEASURE? The Crown
TWITTER: @NatWraith

Batting	Mat	Inns	NO	Runs	HS	Ave	SR	100	50	Ct	St
List A	33	29	3	480	68	18.46	-	0	2	21	16
T20s	37	32	10	362	42*	16.45	90.72	0	0	9	19

DANNI WYATT

RHB / OB / MVP27

FULL NAME: Danielle Nicole Wyatt
BORN: April 22, 1991, Stoke-on-Trent, Staffordshire
SQUAD NO: 28
HEIGHT: 5ft 4in
EDUCATION: St Peter's High School; Stoke-On-Trent Sixth Form College
TEAMS: England, Southern Vipers, Sussex, Lancashire Thunder, Melbourne Renegades, Nottinghamshire, Staffordshire, Victoria
ROLE: Batter
DEBUT: ODI: 2010; T20I: 2010; List A: 2005; T20: 2006

ENGLAND WOMEN

BEST ODI BATTING: 110 England vs Pakistan, Kuala Lumpur, 2019
BEST ODI BOWLING: 3-7 England vs South Africa, Cuttack, 2013

FIRST CRICKET CLUB? Whitmore CC, Staffordshire
WHAT WOULD YOU CHANGE ABOUT THE STRUCTURE OF THE DOMESTIC SEASON? Make sure that England players are available for most of the Rachael Heyhoe Flint Trophy and at least three county games
WHO IS THE BEST BATTER/KEEPER/ALLROUNDER/BOWLER IN DOMESTIC CRICKET? Georgia Adams/Carla Rudd/Sonia Odedra/Charlotte Taylor
MOST UNDERRATED PLAYER IN DOMESTIC CRICKET? Sophie Luff
MOST BEAUTIFUL THING YOU HAVE EVER SEEN? My grandparents dancing
HOBBIES? Fantasy Premier League. We have a league between the England girls
IF YOU COULD TURN BACK TIME... I'd listen more to myself and do what works for me earlier in my career
WHO WOULD YOU MOST AND LEAST LIKE TO HAVE A NET WITH? Most – Rashid Khan, to see if I could pick his googlies. Least – Shoaib Akhtar (I'd be in the side net)
MAKE ONE PREDICTION FOR THE FUTURE OF CRICKET: A first women's IPL in 2023 and it will be huge!
WHAT MAKES YOU WORRY? My loved ones getting old
GUILTY PLEASURE? Dairy Milk Buttons dipped in a cup of tea
TWITTER: @Danni_Wyatt

Batting	Mat	Inns	NO	Runs	HS	Ave	SR	100	50	Ct	St
ODIs	84	70	10	1218	110	20.30	81.20	1	2	18	-
T20Is	124	103	11	1966	124	21.36	124.19	2	9	27	-

Bowling	Mat	Balls	Runs	Wkts	BBI	BBM	Ave	Econ	SR	5w	10
ODIs	84	918	770	27	3/7	3/7	28.51	5.03	34.0	0	0
T20Is	124	759	715	46	4/11	4/11	15.54	5.65	16.5	0	0

fairfield books

Scyld Berry has been covering England cricket tours since 1977. In that time he has seen more England Tests than anyone else, nearly 500. Here, he takes us deep into the heart of each of the nine Test-playing nations he has visited, recounting tales of tours gone by, as well as his own non-cricketing encounters off the beaten track.

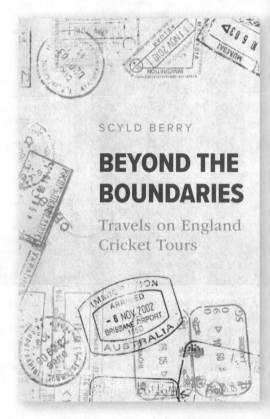

SCYLD BERRY

BEYOND THE BOUNDARIES

Travels on England Cricket Tours

Roll of
Honour

ROLL OF HONOUR

Group 1

Team	Mat	Won	Lost	Tied	Draw	Aban	Pts
Nottinghamshire	10	4	2	0	4	0	151
Warwickshire	10	4	1	0	5	0	145
Durham	10	3	2	0	5	0	132
Essex	10	3	2	0	5	0	129
Worcestershire	10	1	3	0	6	0	109
Derbyshire	10	0	5	0	5	0	72

Group 2

Team	Mat	Won	Lost	Tied	Draw	Aban	Pts
Somerset	10	4	1	0	5	0	148
Hampshire	10	4	2	0	4	0	145
Gloucestershire	10	5	3	0	2	0	131
Surrey	10	2	2	0	6	0	123
Leicestershire	10	2	4	0	4	0	111
Middlesex	10	2	7	0	1	0	84

Group 3

Team	Mat	Won	Lost	Tied	Draw	Aban	Pts
Lancashire	10	4	1	0	5	0	150
Yorkshire	10	5	1	0	4	0	149
Glamorgan	10	2	2	0	6	0	127
Northamptonshire	10	3	3	0	4	0	123
Kent	10	0	3	0	7	0	97
Sussex	10	1	5	0	4	0	94

Division One

Team	Mat	Won	Lost	Tied	Draw	Aban	Pts
Warwickshire	4	2	1	0	1	0	77
Lancashire	4	2	1	0	1	0	73.5
Nottinghamshire	4	3	1	0	0	0	73
Hampshire	4	2	1	0	1	0	61.5
Yorkshire	4	1	2	0	1	0	44.5
Somerset	4	0	4	0	0	0	32.5

Division Two

Team	Mat	Won	Lost	Tied	Draw	Aban	Pts
Essex	4	3	0	0	1	0	96
Gloucestershire	4	3	1	0	0	0	76
Durham	3	1	1	0	1	0	44
Northamptonshire	4	1	2	0	1	0	54
Surrey	3	0	1	0	2	0	40
Glamorgan	4	0	3	0	1	0	34.5

Division Three

Team	Mat	Won	Lost	Tied	Draw	Aban	Pts
Kent	4	4	0	0	0	0	94
Middlesex	4	3	1	0	0	0	80
Worcestershire	4	2	2	0	0	0	67.5
Leicestershire	4	1	2	0	1	0	54.5
Derbyshire	4	1	2	0	1	0	51.5
Sussex	4	0	4	0	0	0	30

BOB WILLIS TROPHY FINAL

Warwickshire v Lancashire at Lord's
September 28-October 1 – Warwickshire won by an innings and 199 runs
Lancashire 78 & 241; Warwickshire 518

ROYAL LONDON ONE-DAY CUP

Group A							
Team	Mat	Won	Lost	Tied	N/R	Pts	Net RR
Durham	8	6	1	0	1	13	0.921
Essex	8	5	2	1	0	11	0.238
Gloucestershire	7	4	3	0	0	8	0.094
Lancashire	8	3	2	1	2	9	0.014
Worcestershire	8	3	4	0	1	7	0.256
Hampshire	8	3	4	0	1	7	0.161
Sussex	8	2	4	0	2	6	-0.689
Middlesex	7	2	4	0	1	5	-0.286
Kent	8	1	5	0	2	4	-1.258

Group B							
Team	Mat	Won	Lost	Tied	N/R	Pts	Net RR
Glamorgan	8	4	2	0	2	10	0.818
Surrey	8	4	2	0	2	10	0.409
Yorkshire	8	4	2	0	2	10	-0.024
Leicestershire	8	4	3	0	1	9	-0.428
Warwickshire	8	4	4	0	0	8	-0.025
Nottinghamshire	8	3	3	0	2	8	0.686
Somerset	8	3	3	0	2	8	-0.412
Northamptonshire	8	2	4	0	2	6	-0.412
Derbyshire	8	1	6	0	1	3	-0.558

QUARTER-FINALS

Essex v Yorkshire at Chelmsford
August 14 – Essex won by 129 runs
Essex 317-7 (50/50 ov); Yorkshire 188 (38.4/50 ov)

Surrey v Gloucestershire at The Oval
August 15 – Surrey won by 5 wickets
Gloucestershire 242-7 (50/50 ov); Surrey 246-5 (42.4/50 ov)

The two group winners progressed straight into the semi-finals; the second- and third-placed teams played two 'quarter-finals'

SEMI-FINALS

Glamorgan v Essex at Cardiff
August 16 – Glamorgan won by 5 wickets
Essex 289 (49.4/50 ov); Glamorgan 293-5 (48/50 ov)

Durham v Surrey at Chester-le-Street
August 17 – Durham won by 5 wickets
Surrey 280-8 (50/50 ov); Durham 281-5 (47.3/50 ov)

FINAL

Glamorgan v Durham at Trent Bridge
August 19 – Glamorgan won by 58 runs
Glamorgan 296-9 (50/50 ov); Durham 238 (45.1/50 ov)

ROLL OF HONOUR

North Group

Team	Mat	Won	Lost	Tied	N/R	Pts	Net RR
Nottinghamshire	14	9	2	3	0	21	1.503
Yorkshire	13	7	5	0	1	15	0.305
Lancashire	14	7	5	1	1	16	0.205
Birmingham Bears	14	7	6	0	1	15	0.006
Worcestershire	14	6	6	1	1	14	-0.629
Leicestershire	14	6	8	0	0	12	-0.019
Durham	14	5	8	0	1	11	-0.228
Derbyshire	12	4	7	1	0	9	-0.326
Northamptonshire	13	4	8	0	1	9	-0.871

South Group

Team	Mat	Won	Lost	Tied	N/R	Pts	Net RR
Kent	14	9	4	0	1	19	0.657
Somerset	14	8	4	0	2	18	0.371
Sussex	14	6	3	0	5	17	0.479
Hampshire	14	6	5	0	3	15	0.388
Surrey	14	6	5	0	3	15	0.332
Gloucestershire	14	6	6	0	2	14	0.201
Essex	14	5	8	0	1	11	-0.468
Middlesex	14	4	9	0	1	9	-0.389
Glamorgan	14	3	9	0	2	8	-1.371

QUARTER-FINALS

Yorkshire v Sussex at Chester-le-Street
August 24 – Sussex won by 5 wickets
Yorkshire 177-7 (20/20 ov); Sussex 178-5 (19.4/20 ov)

Nottinghamshire v Hampshire at Trent Bridge
August 25 – Hampshire won by 2 runs
Hampshire 125-9 (20/20 ov); Nottinghamshire 123 (19.4/20 ov)

Somerset v Lancashire at Taunton
August 26 – Somerset won by 7 wickets
Lancashire 184-9 (20/20 ov); Somerset 185-3 (18.1/20 ov)

Kent v Birmingham Bears at Canterbury
August 27 – Kent won by 21 runs
Kent 162-7 (20/20 ov); Birmingham Bears 141 (20/20 ov)

SEMI-FINALS

Hampshire v Somerset at Edgbaston
September 18 – Somerset won by 2 wickets
Hampshire 150 (20/20 ov); Somerset 153-8 (19.4/20 ov)

Kent v Sussex at Edgbaston
September 18 – Kent won by 21 runs
Kent 168-8 (20/20 ov); Sussex 147 (19.1/20 ov)

FINAL

Kent v Somerset at Edgbaston
September 18 – Kent won by 25 runs
Kent 167-7 (20/20 ov); Somerset 142-9 (20/20 ov)

Table							
Team	Mat	Won	Lost	Tied	N/R	Pts	Net RR
Southern Vipers	7	6	1	0	0	27	0.417
Northern Diamonds	7	5	2	0	0	23	1.182
Central Sparks	7	5	2	0	0	22	0.822
Lightning	7	3	4	0	0	13	0.274
South East Stars	7	3	4	0	0	13	-0.226
Western Storm	7	3	4	0	0	13	-0.462
Thunder	7	3	4	0	0	13	-0.62
Sunrisers	7	0	7	0	0	0	-1.598

SEMI-FINAL ELIMINATOR

Central Sparks v Northern Diamonds at Scarborough
September 22 – Northern Diamonds won by 6 wickets
Central Sparks 175-7 (50/50 ov); Northern Diamonds 176-4 (32.5/50 ov)

FINAL

Southern Vipers v Northern Diamonds at Northampton
September 25 – Southern Vipers won by 3 wickets
Northern Diamonds 183 (49.2/50 ov); Southern Vipers 187-7 (49.4/50 ov)

Lauren Bell of Southern Vipers
photographed by Tony Marshall

Group A							
Team	Mat	Won	Lost	Tied	N/R	Pts	Net RR
South East Stars	6	5	1	0	0	21	1.05
Southern Vipers	6	4	2	0	0	19	0.875
Central Sparks	6	3	3	0	0	12	-0.669
Lightning	6	0	6	0	0	0	-1.139

Group B							
Team	Mat	Won	Lost	Tied	N/R	Pts	Net RR
Northern Diamonds	6	4	2	0	0	17	0.655
Western Storm	6	4	2	0	0	17	0.182
Thunder	6	2	3	1	0	11	0.029
Sunrisers	6	1	4	1	0	6	-0.871

The best of the two group winners progressed straight into the final; the other group winner played against the best second-placed team in the 'semi-final'

SEMI-FINAL

Northern Diamonds v Southern Vipers at Southampton
September 5 – Northern Diamonds won by 18 runs
Northern Diamonds 135-6 (20/20 ov); Southern Vipers 117 (20/20 ov)

FINAL

Northern Diamonds v South East Stars at Southampton
September 5 – South East Stars won by 5 wickets
Northern Diamonds 138-4 (20/20 ov); South East Stars 139-5 (18/20 ov)

ROLL OF HONOUR

Name	Mat	Inns	NO	Runs	HS	Ave	BF	SR	100	50	0	4s	6s
TJ Haines	13	25	0	1176	156	47.04	2231	52.71	3	6	2	143	1
JD Libby	14	23	4	1075	180*	56.57	2209	48.66	4	4	1	120	5
SD Robson	14	27	1	1047	253	40.26	1985	52.74	3	2	1	139	1
DG Bedingham	13	20	3	1029	257	60.52	1718	59.89	3	3	2	124	8
MJJ Critchley	14	26	3	1000	109	43.47	1752	57.07	1	8	1	124	7
HM Amla	13	20	3	994	215*	58.47	2248	44.21	3	2	4	105	1
BC Brown	12	21	2	976	157	51.36	1636	59.65	4	2	3	115	2
LJ Hill	14	22	1	944	145	44.95	1587	59.48	3	5	1	117	5
KS Carlson	14	23	4	928	170*	48.84	1396	66.47	3	5	2	120	0
OJ Pope	9	13	2	861	274	78.27	1121	76.80	3	0	2	108	5
JJ Bohannon	14	18	2	853	170	53.31	1790	47.65	2	5	0	101	7
R Vasconcelos	14	24	1	845	185*	36.73	1384	61.05	2	2	1	114	3
BT Slater	14	24	3	837	114*	39.85	1892	44.23	2	5	1	114	2
DL Lloyd	14	25	1	828	121	34.50	1302	63.59	1	5	2	116	3
MD Stoneman	14	22	0	827	174	37.59	1608	51.43	3	4	4	120	2
SR Hain	14	25	2	826	118	35.91	2004	41.21	1	6	2	92	1
A Lyth	14	22	1	819	153	39.00	1581	51.80	3	3	4	117	4
JM Vince	13	20	0	816	231	40.80	1386	58.87	1	4	2	126	5
CB Cooke	14	21	7	816	205*	58.28	1506	54.18	4	1	3	75	6
HC Brook	14	22	1	797	118	37.95	1286	61.97	2	5	2	110	4
RM Yates	13	23	2	793	132*	37.76	1776	44.65	4	2	4	93	3
NRT Gubbins	14	26	2	769	137*	32.04	1476	52.10	2	5	3	95	4
IG Holland	14	24	1	766	146*	33.30	1537	49.83	2	4	3	106	1
RI Keogh	14	24	2	766	126	34.81	1363	56.19	2	4	0	100	0
RG White	14	26	4	765	120	34.77	1775	43.09	2	4	2	87	0
JM Clarke	13	22	1	760	109	36.19	1329	57.18	1	7	3	103	7
EG Barnard	13	18	3	746	128	49.73	1458	51.16	2	3	0	90	0
JA Leaning	13	21	5	745	127*	46.56	1777	41.92	1	6	3	81	1
OG Robinson	13	21	1	725	120	36.25	1241	58.42	2	3	1	93	5
JR Bracey	11	21	2	715	118	37.63	1434	49.86	1	6	1	89	2
TB Abell	12	20	2	711	132*	39.50	1477	48.13	1	4	3	97	0
BM Duckett	13	21	2	705	177*	37.10	1023	68.91	1	4	1	99	0
HJ Swindells	13	19	3	693	171*	43.31	1268	54.65	2	3	1	89	3
H Hameed	11	19	1	679	114*	37.72	1564	43.41	2	4	2	84	1
WL Madsen	11	20	0	675	111	33.75	1279	52.77	1	4	1	78	4
SJ Mullaney	14	22	0	657	117	29.86	1185	55.44	1	3	0	94	13
JL Smith	12	17	2	656	138	43.73	1228	53.42	3	1	3	85	7
MS Harris	8	13	1	655	185	54.58	1214	53.95	3	1	0	85	1
AL Davies	13	19	2	652	84	38.35	1112	58.63	0	6	2	82	5
DI Stevens	12	18	3	650	190	43.33	804	80.84	3	2	4	75	25
DW Lawrence	10	13	1	640	152*	53.33	1067	59.98	1	4	0	76	8
Z Crawley	12	21	2	637	90	33.52	1148	55.48	0	6	2	93	0
SM Davies	13	22	2	634	87	31.70	1173	54.04	0	5	2	88	2
WMH Rhodes	14	26	2	633	91	26.37	1329	47.62	0	5	2	77	6
T Westley	13	18	1	631	213	37.11	1408	44.81	3	1	1	90	2
AZ Lees	11	17	1	625	129	39.06	1450	43.10	1	5	4	72	2
RJ Burns	9	14	1	617	104*	47.46	1220	50.57	1	7	1	83	2
AN Cook	14	19	0	611	165	32.15	1204	50.74	2	2	1	87	1

Name	Mat	Overs	Mdns	Runs	Wkts	BBI	BBM	Ave	Econ	SR	5	10
LJ Fletcher	13	420.5	135	984	66	7/37	10/57	14.90	2.33	38.2	4	1
C Rushworth	13	435.3	125	1073	59	6/49	9/108	18.18	2.46	44.2	3	0
SJ Cook	13	382.2	128	837	58	5/20	10/41	14.43	2.18	39.5	3	1
TJ Murtagh	12	402.4	113	1079	58	5/64	7/85	18.60	2.67	41.6	1	0
D Paterson	12	352.5	98	971	54	5/90	7/88	17.98	2.75	39.2	1	0
SR Harmer	14	558.4	182	1233	53	9/80	12/202	23.26	2.20	63.2	3	2
ER Bamber	12	407	111	1084	52	5/41	7/80	20.84	2.66	46.9	1	0
RF Higgins	13	443	118	1143	51	5/46	7/87	22.41	2.58	52.1	2	0
TE Bailey	12	340	108	843	50	7/37	9/61	16.86	2.47	40.8	1	0
CF Parkinson	13	479.4	122	1452	50	5/45	10/108	29.04	3.02	57.5	3	1
LC Norwell	12	346.4	97	895	49	6/57	7/65	18.26	2.58	42.4	2	0
CJC Wright	12	351	74	1116	49	7/53	7/117	22.77	3.17	42.9	4	0
JA Thompson	13	329.5	91	949	46	5/52	7/53	20.63	2.87	43.0	1	0
KJ Abbott	11	329.3	87	996	46	6/44	11/85	21.65	3.02	42.9	3	1
BA Raine	13	406.1	128	968	43	5/9	9/109	22.51	2.38	56.6	2	0
BW Sanderson	13	435.2	117	1155	43	5/28	10/99	26.86	2.65	60.7	3	1
C Overton	8	270.3	93	650	42	5/25	8/64	15.47	2.40	38.6	4	0
Mohammad Abbas	10	309.5	113	650	41	6/11	9/39	15.87	2.10	45.3	3	0
KHD Barker	10	310	88	755	41	7/46	7/33	18.41	2.43	45.3	3	0
DI Stevens	12	284	93	725	39	5/53	7/115	18.58	2.55	43.6	2	0
J Leach	13	428	108	1141	38	5/68	9/136	30.02	2.66	67.5	1	0
CN Miles	11	277.4	62	807	37	5/30	6/55	21.81	2.90	45.0	2	0
JJ Carson	14	449.4	65	1336	37	5/85	7/96	36.10	2.97	72.9	1	0
MW Parkinson	11	321.2	87	740	36	7/126	9/164	20.55	2.30	53.5	1	0
BO Coad	10	287.1	79	766	35	4/48	7/112	21.88	2.66	49.2	0	0
JH Davey	12	292.2	84	781	35	5/30	7/62	22.31	2.67	50.1	2	0
DA Payne	10	258.2	59	719	34	6/56	11/87	21.14	2.78	45.5	2	1
BA Carse	8	203.2	26	724	34	5/49	8/119	21.29	3.56	35.8	2	0
BW Aitchison	13	275.4	50	792	34	6/28	6/28	23.29	2.87	48.6	1	0
JA Porter	12	299.4	73	842	34	4/31	7/58	24.76	2.80	52.8	0	0
MG Hogan	13	332.5	78	874	34	5/28	7/61	25.70	2.62	58.7	1	0
BTJ Wheal	13	298.5	62	882	34	4/59	4/63	25.94	2.95	52.7	0	0
OE Robinson	6	207	49	547	33	9/78	13/128	16.57	2.64	37.6	2	1
ME Milnes	8	205.3	42	687	32	6/53	9/77	21.46	3.34	38.5	2	0
SA Patterson	13	364	111	815	32	4/26	6/61	25.46	2.23	68.2	0	0
J Clark	12	276	36	904	32	6/21	6/54	28.25	3.27	51.7	2	0
MJJ Critchley	14	343.3	42	1230	32	5/67	8/143	38.43	3.58	64.4	1	0
S Snater	9	168.5	42	511	31	7/98	7/56	16.48	3.02	32.6	2	0
NN Gilchrist	9	160.1	26	620	30	5/38	8/74	20.66	3.87	32.0	1	0
DR Briggs	12	290	81	664	30	4/36	6/89	22.13	2.28	58.0	0	0
BA Hutton	8	254	75	679	29	5/62	7/148	23.41	2.67	52.5	2	0
SC Kerrigan	11	298.5	57	766	29	5/39	7/75	26.41	2.56	61.8	2	0
TAI Taylor	11	263.2	63	783	29	5/41	7/95	27.00	2.97	54.4	1	0
DY Pennington	10	282.4	57	898	29	5/32	9/76	30.96	3.17	58.4	1	0
MK Andersson	13	250.1	41	916	29	4/27	5/130	31.58	3.66	51.7	0	0
S Mahmood	8	233.1	52	669	28	5/47	6/96	23.89	2.86	49.9	1	0
DM Bess	14	405.4	122	912	28	7/43	9/102	32.57	2.24	86.9	2	0
A Virdi	11	299.4	48	961	28	6/171	7/142	34.32	3.20	64.2	1	0

ROLL OF HONOUR

Name	Mat	Inns	Dis	Ct	St	Max Dis Inns	Dis/Inn
TJ Moores	12	22	54	52	2	5 (5ct 0st)	2.45
JA Simpson	13	24	48	45	3	5 (5ct 0st)	2.00
MGK Burgess	14	22	44	40	4	5 (5ct 0st)	2.00
OB Cox	14	25	44	42	2	5 (5ct 0st)	1.76
CB Cooke	14	23	41	40	1	4 (4ct 0st)	1.78
OG Robinson	13	19	39	38	1	5 (5ct 0st)	2.05
SM Davies	13	22	38	37	1	4 (4ct 0st)	1.73
JR Bracey	11	19	33	33	0	4 (4ct 0st)	1.74
HG Duke	9	16	31	31	0	6 (6ct 0st)	1.94
LD McManus	11	21	29	28	1	3 (3ct 0st)	1.38
EJH Eckersley	13	13	28	27	1	5 (5ct 0st)	2.15
HJ Swindells	13	19	27	26	1	5 (5ct 0st)	1.42
AJA Wheater	14	25	27	23	4	4 (3ct 1st)	1.08
BD Guest	12	11	26	23	3	4 (3ct 1st)	2.36
BC Brown	12	15	26	23	3	4 (4ct 0st)	1.73
AM Rossington	11	17	26	24	2	4 (4ct 0st)	1.53
JA Tattersall	8	12	23	23	0	5 (5ct 0st)	1.92
SW Poynter	6	11	22	22	0	5 (5ct 0st)	2.00
AL Davies	13	10	18	15	3	4 (4ct 0st)	1.80
BT Foakes	8	12	18	16	2	5 (5ct 0st)	1.50
R Vasconcelos	14	5	16	15	1	3 (3ct 0st)	3.20
DJ Vilas	14	9	16	16	0	5 (5ct 0st)	1.78
JL Smith	12	7	13	12	1	4 (4ct 0st)	1.86
TP Alsop	14	6	12	12	0	5 (5ct 0st)	2.00
OJ Carter	6	8	12	12	0	4 (4ct 0st)	1.50
RG White	14	4	11	11	0	4 (4ct 0st)	2.75
HR Hosein	8	11	11	11	0	4 (4ct 0st)	1.00
SW Billings	4	2	6	6	0	4 (4ct 0st)	3.00
GID Lavelle	2	4	5	5	0	3 (3ct 0st)	1.25
BM Duckett	13	2	4	4	0	4 (4ct 0st)	2.00
JP Inglis	2	2	4	4	0	3 (3ct 0st)	2.00
D Schadendorf	1	0	3	3	0	3 (3ct 0st)	-
SD Bates	1	2	3	2	1	3 (2ct 1st)	1.50
HF Houillon	1	2	3	3	0	3 (3ct 0st)	1.50
JM Clarke	13	2	2	2	0	1 (1ct 0st)	1.00
BJJ Wells	1	2	2	2	0	2 (2ct 0st)	1.00
TC Lace	14	0	1	1	0	1 (1ct 0st)	-
T Banton	8	1	1	1	0	1 (1ct 0st)	1.00

'Inns' refers to innings in which the player was the designated wicketkeeper

Name	Mat	Inns	Ct	Max	Ct/Inn
A Lyth	14	25	25	3	1.00
T Kohler-Cadmore	11	20	21	3	1.05
RM Yates	13	20	21	3	1.05
JJ Weatherley	13	25	21	3	0.84
CN Ackermann	10	15	20	3	1.33
WL Madsen	11	18	20	4	1.11
SR Hain	14	22	18	3	0.82
R Vasconcelos	14	18	17	3	0.94
LA Dawson	12	23	17	4	0.74
HC Brook	14	25	17	2	0.68
AD Thomason	9	15	16	3	1.07
TT Bresnan	10	17	16	6	0.94
LWP Wells	12	19	16	2	0.84
AN Cook	14	25	16	3	0.64
SD Robson	14	28	16	2	0.57
JC Hildreth	13	21	14	2	0.67
SG Borthwick	13	24	14	3	0.58
SR Harmer	14	25	14	3	0.56
R Clarke	11	16	13	3	0.81
WMH Rhodes	14	22	13	2	0.59
DKH Mitchell	14	25	13	2	0.52
JM Vince	13	25	13	2	0.52
BW Aitchison	13	21	12	2	0.57
EG Barnard	13	24	12	3	0.50
MAH Hammond	9	14	11	3	0.79
RP Jones	8	14	11	2	0.79
TB Abell	12	20	11	3	0.55
H Hameed	11	21	11	2	0.52
JA Leaning	13	21	11	4	0.52
BM Duckett	13	22	11	2	0.50
DG Bedingham	13	24	11	2	0.46
JM Cox	13	21	10	2	0.48
C Overton	8	14	9	2	0.64
RN ten Doeschate	10	17	9	3	0.53
Z Crawley	12	19	9	2	0.47
TC Fell	12	21	9	2	0.43
BA Hutton	8	15	8	2	0.53
KK Jennings	10	15	8	1	0.53
SJ Croft	10	16	8	3	0.50
JA Haynes	9	16	8	3	0.50
SS Eskinazi	9	18	8	2	0.44
DW Lawrence	10	18	8	2	0.44
MJJ Critchley	14	22	8	3	0.36
TC Lace	14	23	8	2	0.35
RG White	14	24	8	2	0.33
BT Slater	14	26	8	1	0.31
IG Holland	14	27	8	2	0.30

ROLL OF HONOUR

ROLL OF HONOUR

#	Name	County	Batting	Bowling	Field	Win	Cap.	MVP	Total	Mat	Avg.
1	Simon Harmer	Essex	93.07	423.89	55.6	16.4	5	5.8	599.76	37	16.21
2	Matt Critchley	Derbyshire	226.32	227.16	43	5	2	5	508.48	31	16.4
3	Luke Fletcher	Nottinghamshire	26.91	419.85	7	16	0	6	475.76	34	13.99
4	Will Rhodes	Warwickshire	186.89	180.08	54	17	17	5	459.97	35	13.14
5	Darren Stevens	Kent	175.06	256.83	12	13	0	3	459.88	32	14.37
6	Craig Overton	Somerset	46.8	319.7	44	13	3	3	429.51	22	19.52
7	Callum Parkinson	Leicestershire	50.95	346.17	15	9	1	2	424.12	29	14.62
8	Sam Cook	Essex	21.73	374.55	8	10.4	0	3.8	418.48	30	13.95
9	Harry Brook	Yorkshire	306.23	34.85	60	13	0	1	415.08	32	12.97
10	Jordan Thompson	Yorkshire	119.76	241.6	22	12	0	2	397.36	28	14.19
11	Tom Bailey	Lancashire	56.34	315.47	6	11	2	3	393.81	24	16.41
12	Scott Borthwick	Durham	148.03	154.05	59.2	15.8	10.8	2	389.88	34	11.47
13	Brett D'Oliveira	Worcestershire	193.27	145.72	28	11	0	4	382	33	11.58
14	Chris Rushworth	Durham	11.98	348.15	7.2	9.8	0	1	378.13	21	18.01
15	Ben Raine	Durham	57.03	294.69	14	8.8	0	3	377.52	31	12.18
16	Ed Barnard	Worcestershire	148.85	170.35	45	12	0	1	377.2	33	11.43
17	Ryan Higgins	Gloucestershire	84.47	267.2	10	12.4	0	2	376.07	25	15.04
18	David Bedingham	Durham	314.74	0	34.2	15.8	0	2	366.74	35	10.48
19	Matt Milnes	Kent	49.92	273.99	20	14	0	2	359.9	30	12
20	Fynn Hudson-Prentice	Derbyshire	114.77	212.65	22	5	0	2	356.41	31	11.5
21	Ricardo Vasconcelos	Northamptonshire	259.12	0	81	9.8	2	1	352.92	34	10.38
22	Steven Mullaney	Nottinghamshire	157.72	111.31	48	16	16	0	349.03	35	9.97
23	Ben Sanderson	Northamptonshire	16.29	305.39	12	7.8	0	2	343.48	29	11.84
24	Danny Briggs	Warwickshire	66.47	252.56	12	12	0	0	343.03	30	11.43
25	Jake Libby	Worcestershire	303.16	8.7	18	12	0	1	342.85	34	10.08
26	Rob Yates	Warwickshire	235.62	36.23	53	11	0	3	338.85	25	13.55
27	Jack Leaning	Kent	208.93	58.79	50	16	1	4	338.72	31	10.93
28	James Vince	Hampshire	254.86	2.75	56	11	11	2	337.62	35	9.65
29	Dom Bess	Yorkshire	64.18	242.28	14	13	1	2	336.46	27	12.46
30	Marchant de Lange	Somerset	79.37	225.93	19	11	0	0	335.29	34	9.86
31	Joe Leach	Worcestershire	82.9	218.91	12	6	6	2	327.81	20	16.39
32	Ben Duckett	Nottinghamshire	265.09	-0.57	49	14	0	0	327.53	34	9.63
33	Colin Ackermann	Leicestershire	135.37	117.15	59	8	5	3	327.52	29	11.29
34	Dane Paterson	Nottinghamshire	14.14	283.54	16	12	0	0	325.69	26	12.53
35	Danny Lamb	Lancashire	85.7	196.19	27	14	0	2	324.89	30	10.83
36	Samit Patel	Nottinghamshire	107.04	183.79	18	9	0	5	322.82	24	13.45
37	Ethan Bamber	Middlesex	31.28	271.99	8	7	0	0	318.27	23	13.84
38	Josh Davey	Somerset	52.63	247.58	8	10	0	0	318.21	25	12.73
39	David Lloyd	Glamorgan	199.13	93.85	16.8	5	1	1	316.78	28	11.31
40	Tom Westley	Essex	233.1	41.13	18	11.6	9.6	3	316.43	30	10.55
41	Kyle Abbott	Hampshire	26.57	267.72	8	7	4	2	315.3	19	16.59
42	Adam Lyth	Yorkshire	187.96	28.47	80	13	2	3	314.43	32	9.83
43	Liam Dawson	Hampshire	83.68	180.66	36	10	0	2	312.34	25	12.49
44	Craig Miles	Warwickshire	30.45	239.14	26	13	0	2	310.59	27	11.5
45	Tom Taylor	Northamptonshire	84.02	177.28	38.6	8.8	0	1	309.71	30	10.32
46	Tim Murtagh	Middlesex	14.27	275.4	6	5	4	1	305.67	16	19.1
47	Brydon Carse	Durham	67.93	215.5	14	8	0	0	305.43	25	12.22
48	Sam Hain	Warwickshire	230.85	0	58	13	0	3	304.95	29	10.52
49	Tom Abell	Somerset	193.58	63.24	32	7	4	2	301.82	19	15.89
50	Ben Slater	Nottinghamshire	259.17	-0.4	28	13	0	2	301.77	26	11.61

Simon Harmer of Essex
photographed by Jacques Feeney

ROLL OF HONOUR

#	Name	County	Batting	Bowling	Field	Win	Cap.	MVP	Total	Mat	Avg.
1	Eve Jones	Central Sparks	227.78	48.73	16	8	8	6	314.51	23	13.67
2	Emma Lamb	Thunder	166.88	80.81	17	4	0	3	271.69	17	15.98
3	Alice Capsey	South East Stars	126.96	96.48	18	8	0	1	250.44	23	10.89
4	Bryony Smith	South East Stars	102.47	111.59	16	9	6	2	247.07	21	11.77
5	Linsey Smith	Northern Diamonds	43.28	170.66	14	10	0	0	237.94	23	10.35
6	Georgia Adams	Southern Vipers	147.05	34.85	30	11	11	1	234.9	25	9.4
7	Georgia Elwiss	Southern Vipers	83.81	94.22	10	10	0	3	201.02	22	9.14
8	Kirstie Gordon	Lightning	38.55	133.21	25	3	0	1	200.76	22	9.13
9	Dani Gibson	Western Storm	63.3	82.33	37	7	0	1	190.63	21	9.08
10	Jenny Gunn	Northern Diamonds	65.71	100.18	10	9	0	3	187.89	14	13.42
11	Kate Cross	Thunder	45.28	126.21	8	2	1	2	184.4	15	12.29
12	Alice Davidson-Richards	South East Stars	79.75	63.2	32	8	0	1	183.95	20	9.2
13	Kathryn Bryce	Lightning	76.9	78.19	20	3	3	2	183.09	18	10.17
14	Georgia Hennessy	Western Storm	62.15	97.3	14	7	0	1	181.45	21	8.64
15	Lauren Bell	Southern Vipers	3.23	156.17	8	10	0	0	177.41	21	8.45
16	Emily Arlott	Central Sparks	48.02	93.47	23	7	0	1	172.49	20	8.62
17	Sophie Luff	Western Storm	139.67	1.5	12	7	7	4	171.17	21	8.15
18	Charlie Dean	Southern Vipers	35.59	103.45	25	6	0	1	171.03	16	10.69
19	Tara Norris	Southern Vipers	21.97	111.94	18	11	0	1	163.91	21	7.81
20	Issy Wong	Central Sparks	35.4	103.98	14	8	0	0	161.38	22	7.34
21	Nicole Harvey	Western Storm	9.9	127.23	13	7	0	1	158.12	20	7.91
22	Katie Levick	Northern Diamonds	9.21	137.42	0	11	0	0	157.63	23	6.85
23	Amy Jones	Central Sparks	121.16	0	30	3	0	1	155.16	12	12.93
24	Heather Knight	Western Storm	112.63	27.9	10	1	0	0	151.54	11	13.78
25	Fi Morris	Western Storm	58.51	66.97	8	7	0	0	140.48	22	6.39
26	Abigail Freeborn	Lightning	95.19	0	39	3	0	1	138.19	21	6.58
27	Danni Wyatt	Southern Vipers	106.38	12.32	12	5	0	2	137.69	15	9.18
28	Grace Gibbs	South East Stars	51.81	48.52	30	7	0	0	137.33	21	6.54
29	Beth Langston	Northern Diamonds	45.61	79.5	4	7	0	1	137.11	13	10.55
30	Hollie Armitage	Northern Diamonds	73.82	21.61	18	11	11	0	135.43	20	6.77
31	Alex Hartley	Thunder	12.94	96.62	16	5	4	0	134.55	20	6.73
32	Grace Scrivens	Sunrisers	52.7	76.65	4	1	0	0	134.35	15	8.96
33	Maia Bouchier	Southern Vipers	98.4	2.57	22	9	0	0	131.96	20	6.6
34	Hannah Jones	Thunder	8.8	107.63	10	5	0	0	131.44	17	7.73
35	Tash Farrant	South East Stars	16.73	97.34	10	3	3	0	130.07	14	9.29
36	Dané van Niekerk	Oval Invincibles	82.86	36.33	10	0	0	0	129.19	10	12.92
37	Nat Sciver	Northern Diamonds	89.9	19.46	13	2	0	0	124.36	11	11.31
38	Sophia Dunkley	South East Stars	110.27	0	11	2	0	1	124.27	12	10.36
39	Kelly Castle	Sunrisers	27.44	88.39	2	1	1	1	120.83	13	9.29
40	Charlotte Taylor	Southern Vipers	0.79	102.91	5	11	0	0	120.7	18	6.71
41	Sterre Kalis	Northern Diamonds	98.61	1.24	8	11	0	0	118.85	18	6.6
42	Naomi Dattani	Sunrisers	52.24	44.05	21	1	0	0	118.29	20	5.91
43	Lauren Winfield-Hill	Northern Diamonds	88.48	0	23	5	0	1	117.48	14	8.39
44	Anya Shrubsole	Western Storm	36.25	76.6	3	1	0	0	116.84	12	9.74
45	Cordelia Griffith	Sunrisers	100.42	0.07	14	0	0	1	115.49	18	6.42
46	Marie Kelly	Central Sparks	90.02	3.74	10	8	0	1	112.76	14	8.05
47	Mady Villiers	Sunrisers	37.27	68.06	6	1	0	0	112.33	16	7.02
48	Sophie Munro	Lightning	30.24	70.9	8	2	0	0	111.14	17	6.54
49	Ellie Threlkeld	Thunder	67.12	0	35	5	0	1	108.12	20	5.41
50	Erin Burns	Birmingham Phoenix	61.28	44.53	2	0	0	0	107.81	9	11.98